ENCYCLOPEDIA OF SPORTING FIREARMS

ENCYCLOPEDIA OF SPORTING FIREARMS

DAVID E. PETZAL

CONSULTANT EDITORS

John T. Amber
Bob Brister
Pete Brown
Jim Carmichel
Phil Johnston
Layne Simpson
Skeeter Skelton
Ken Waters
John Wootters
Don Zutz

Facts On File
New York • Oxford

ENCYCLOPEDIA OF SPORTING FIREARMS

Facts On File, Inc.   Facts On File Limited
460 Park Avenue South   Collins Street
New York NY 10016   Oxford OX4 1XJ
USA   United Kingdom

Library of Congress Cataloging-in-Publication Data

Petzal, David E.
   Encyclopedia of sporting firearms / by David Petzal.
      p.   cm.
   Includes bibliographical references (p.   ) and index.
   ISBN 0-8160-2305-0 (alk. paper)
   1. Firearms—Dictionaries.   I. Title.
TS532.15.P47   1991
683.4′003—dc20   90-3919

A British CIP catalogue record for this book is available from the British Library.

Facts On File books are available at special discounts when purchased in bulk quantities for businesses, associations, institutions or sales promotions. Please call our Special Sales Department in New York at 212/683-2244 (dial 800/322-8755 except in NY, AK or HI) or in Oxford at 865/728399.

Text design by Ron Monteleone
Jacket design by Levavi & Levavi
Composition by the Maple-Vail Manufacturing Group
Manufactured by the Maple-Vail Manufacturing Group
Printed in the United States of America

10 9 8 7 6 5 4 3 2 1

This book is printed on acid-free paper.

This book is dedicated to the memory of Mel Bookstein, whose idea it was, and who did so much to make it a reality.

CONTENTS

ACKNOWLEDGMENTS

My special thanks to writers Creighton Audette, Bob Hagel, Dan Flores, Rick Jamison, and Larry S. Sterett, who wrote more than their share.

To Steve Torborg of the Armonk Gun Shop and Bill Ward of Griffin & Howe for allowing me to photograph their guns.

To Bill Garry, for copyediting this monster.

To my wife, Arlene, for her proofreader's eye, good handwriting, unfailing sense of order, and many, many hours of work.

And to my sister-in-law, friend, and agent Victoria Pryor, who in the course of her labors performs the occasional miracle.

CONSULTANT EDITORS

DAVID E. PETZAL has been a competitive small-bore rifle and trapshooter and is an NRA-certified rifle instructor. He has hunted throughout the United States and in Canada, Europe, and Africa. He is the executive editor of *Field & Stream* magazine and is the author of *The .22 Rifle*.

JOHN T. AMBER was the editor of *Gun Digest*. A hunter and arms collector of note, Amber was a leading authority on antique arms.

ROBERT M. BRISTER is the shooting editor of *Field & Stream* magazine. He has hunted extensively in North America and Africa and was a world class live bird competitor. He is the author of *Shotgunning: The Art and the Science*.

EDWARDS "PETE" BROWN was the shooting editor of *Sports Afield*. A noted ballistician and authority on shooting optics, Brown was also a hunter of wide experience as well as an arms designer.

JAMES CARMICHEL is the shooting editor of *Outdoor Life* magazine. Carmichel is noted as a big-game hunter, gunsmith, competitive high power rifle shooter and raconteur. He is the author of *Jim Carmichel's Book of the Rifle*.

PHILIP JOHNSTON is a free-lance writer on handgunning who has taken trophies throughout North America. He is a member of the board of directors of the National Rifle Association and the author of *Successful Handgun Hunting*.

LAYNE SIMPSON is a contributing editor to *Rifle* and *Shooting Times* magazines and to *Gun Digest*. Simpson is noted as a benchrest shooter, experimental handloader, and big-game hunter. He has taken trophies in the United States, Canada, and Africa.

CHARLES "SKEETER" SKELTON was a regular contributor to *Shooting Times* magazine. He was a career law enforcement officer and a handgun hunter and target shooter of note.

KENNETH WATERS is a longtime contributor to *Rifle* and *Handloader* magazines. He is a hunter, target shooter, and ballistic experimenter of note and is a leading authority on black-powder and transition-period arms.

JOHN H. WOOTTERS JR. is a prolific writer on firearms and hunting and is the executive editor of *Petersen's Hunting* magazine. He has taken trophies on both American continents and in Africa. Wootters is the author of *The Complete Book of Practical Handloading* and *Hunting Trophy Deer*.

DONALD ZUTZ writes on all aspects of shotgun shooting, both competition and hunting. He is a regular contributor to several gun magazines and a columnist for *Trap & Field*. Zutz is the author of *The Double Shotgun*.

CONTRIBUTING WRITERS

CREIGHTON AUDETTE is a gunsmith, arms designer, and champion big bore rifle competitor.

JAMES BRADY was a Treasury agent and the author of many articles on all phases of shooting.

DONALD L. DAVIS is a collector and user of black-powder arms and a contributing editor of *The American Rifleman*.

WILLIAM C. DAVIS JR. is a professional engineer in the firearms field. He is a contributing editor of *The American Rifleman*.

ROY F. DUNLAP has for many years been a gunsmith specializing in target rifles. He has also written widely on all phases of firearms.

ROBERT ELMAN specializes in the history of arms and shooting. He is the author of many books and articles in this area.

SAM FADALA has written widely on both firearms and hunting. He is a specialist in black-powder shooting.

DAN L. FLORES is a college professor who is also an expert on rifles and their uses in varmint and big-game hunting.

GEORGE H. HAAS is an all-around hunter and was a senior editor of *Outdoor Life* magazine.

ROBERT HAGEL is a former big-game guide and an expert on rifles and was a regular columnist for *Rifle* and *Handloader* magazines.

KEN HOWELL is a hunter and shooter of long experience and the former editor of *Rifle* and *Handloader* magazines.

RICK JAMISON is an expert on rifle and black-powder shooting and a contributing editor of *Shooting Times* magazine.

E. B. MANN has been writing on firearms for nearly 50 years. He specializes in their history and in arms legislation.

ROBERT MILEK is a shooter and hunter of wide experience who specializes in handguns and rifles.

NORM NELSON has been an outdoor writer for many years, specializing in big-game and waterfowl hunting.

DOUG PAINTER is an employee of the National Shooting Sports Foundation and specializes in arms legislation.

LARRY S. STERETT is an all-around firearms authority and consultant and has written widely on the subject.

OTHER EDITORIAL CONTRIBUTORS

Linda Caricabarou, Debbie Ford, Patricia Mulvihill, Lois Wilde.

INTRODUCTION

Few machines have changed man's destiny or captured his imagination as profoundly as the firearm. It has been with us for something like half a millennium, which is scarcely a heartbeat in terms of our history as a species, but it has shaped the world no less than other creations of *Homo sapiens*.

Inescapably, the gun is a weapon, but this book does not deal with that aspect of its use. This volume deals with sporting firearms; those interested in militaria will have to look elsewhere. Its purpose is to provide a single source in which any reasonable question on sporting arms and ammunition can be answered. There are several other firearms encyclopedias extant, and useful though some of them are, none of them matches the size or scope of this one.

One of the things you learn very quickly if you try to become knowledgeable about guns is that no one can know it all—or even come close. There are people who collect Parker shotguns, or who hunt big game, or who compete in benchrest matches, or who dote on bowling-pin shoots with handguns. Each of these individuals has a highly specialized fund of knowledge that he or she has built up over the years by reading, by experimentation, and by talking to others with a similar interest.

They are all firearms enthusiasts, but their interests make them as different as Bulgars and Zulus, or Aleuts and Gypsies. And what none of them had until now was a single place they could go and get their questions on the *other* aspects of shooting answered.

When this book was in the planning stages, more than 15 years ago, it was decided that since no one knew it all, it would take a large number of people with specialized knowledge to write the *Encyclopedia* as a joint effort. And that is what we did. All told, there are more than 20 experts who have contributed to a greater or lesser degree.

Here is how you can use what they've done: Let's say that you come across a Parker shotgun and that it sells for $1,000, because it is, after all, a *Parker*, which carries great cachet among lovers of fine scatterguns. If you look up the entry **Parker Brothers Company** in the *Encyclopedia*, you will learn that this line of guns was made in many grades, ranging from the Trojan, which was quite common and which has no collector's value, to the A-1 Special, which was made in very limited numbers, and today is selling for fabulous prices. Is the Parker in question worth $1,000? If it's one of the better grades, the answer is yes.

Or let's say that you want a custom stock built, and that the gunsmith offers you a choice of American walnut (*Juglans niger*) or French walnut (*Juglans regia*). French, he says, is much more expensive than American. *Why?* you wonder. So you look under **stock woods** and find that French walnut is lighter, stronger, and carves better than American walnut, and that it is in shorter supply, and you have your answer.

On a different note, let's say that you hear a high-power-rifle competitor refer to **"Maggie's drawers."** Is this fetishism? you wonder. So you look up that entry and discover that it means a complete miss, where the bullet failed to hit the target at all, and that the expression stems from the old military custom of waving a red flag from the target pits when a shooter did something completely wrong.

We have, in compiling this book, cross-referenced many entries so that the pursuit of one subject will lead to another of direct interest. For example, if your binoculars are not working right, you look up **aberration** and discover that there are several kinds of illness that can beset an optical instrument, each different from the other, and each described under its own heading.

Which leads to another point: You can use this book as a reference, or you can simply sit down and read it from **aberration** to **Zulu Shotgun** (which was a trade name, and not a shotgun used by Zulus). That is fine with me, and you will learn a lot in the process.

Firearms are an endless fascination. They are also fine investments (if you know what you're doing), sporting implements, the basis for lifelong friendships, and much more. I hope this book adds to your enjoyment of them.

David E. Petzal
Bedford, New York

Abbe, Ernst See ZEISS, CARL, INC.

Aberdeen chronograph See CHRONOGRAPH.

aberration Failure of an optical device's lens system to produce an exact point-to-point correspondence between an object and its image. Aberration is due to the failure of light rays to pass through a single point in the lens or lenses after refraction. Six forms of aberration are recognized: chromatic, spherical, coma, astigmatic, curvature of field, and distortion. The two most commonly found in telescopic sights are curvature of field and distortion. (See BINOCULARS; COMPOUND LENS; MONOCULAR; SPOTTING SCOPE; TELESCOPIC SIGHTS.)

abutment Any part of a firearm, either action or stock, that acts as a stop to hold another part in a fixed position. The term is most often applied to the portion of a gun stock that fits against the recoil lug to prevent rearward movement of the action upon recoil. (See RECOIL BOLT; RECOIL LUG.)

accelerator This term originally designated a part of the mechanism of certain kinds of automatic weapons that acted as a catalyst to speed up the

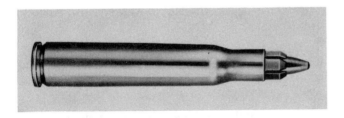

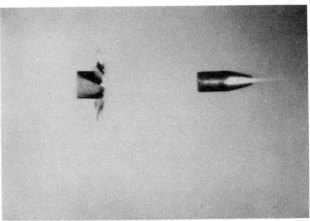

The idea behind the accelerator is allowing the owner of a big-game rifle to use bullets of a lesser caliber in the gun for varmint hunting. The Remington .30/06 Accelerator round utilizes a .22-caliber varmint bullet seated in a plastic sabot, loaded in a .30/06 shell. As the projectile clears the muzzle (at a velocity of 4,080 feet per second), the sabot falls away. By the time the bullet is 18 inches from the muzzle, the sabot is completely clear of it.

extraction/ejection/chambering process, hence, an "accelerator."

In 1976, Remington Arms introduced the Accelerator cartridge for .30/06 rifles. It features a fully charged .30/06 case behind a .22-caliber 55-grain bullet encased in a plastic .30-caliber sabot, which falls away when the bullet clears the muzzle. Intended for target and varmint shooting, this cartridge has a muzzle velocity of 4,080 feet per second (fps). Accuracy in some rifles is under two minutes of angle, and recoil is light.

Remington followed with a .30/30 Accelerator in 1979; it uses a 55-grain .224 bullet listed as having a muzzle velocity, of 3,400 fps. It was joined in 1980 by a .308 Accelerator using an identical bullet at a claimed muzzle velocity of 3,770 fps. The .308 version has generally superior accuracy, and may be the best of the series. (See SABOT.)

accuracy block A spacer designed to improve accuracy on the Remington Model 740 autoloading rifle. In the original design, tightening the fore-end retaining screw tended to thrust the rear of the fore-end against the front of the receiver. In repeated firing, heating of the barrel caused the fore-end to expand, changing the pressure of the fore-end against the receiver and altering the point of impact from shot to shot. The steel accuracy block was installed between the fore-end and the gas cylinder block on the barrel, eliminating contact between the back of the fore-end and the receiver and obviating this problem.

accurize The term used for the process of hand-tuning a firearm to improve both its grouping ability and its capability for shooting to a consistent point of impact. Many firearms, of course, are quite accurate as they come from the factory, but the shooter who wishes to realize his firearm's full potential should be aware that proper tuning can greatly enhance accuracy.

Among handguns, the Browning-designed Colt .45-caliber semiautomatic Model 1911 is one piece for which accurizing techniques have been widely employed. The tolerances of the standard arm do not allow for maximum accuracy, and a brisk business exists in converting these to match-quality guns. To accurize a Model 1911, the first step is the substitution of adjustable sights for the factory-installed fixed rear sight. The receiver's inside cuts are polished and smoothed, and the trigger mechanism is carefully worked over to make the pull lighter and more positive. The real secret of accurizing a Model 1911, however, is in getting the barrel tight in the slide and frame. This is sometimes accomplished by welding tiny bits of metal to strategic spots, or by installing a barrel with a "bulge" near the muzzle that fits tightly against the slide.

The Model 1911 is not the only handgun that responds to accurizing. Although the problems vary somewhat from model to model, virtually any handgun can be considerably improved by honing the action parts to ensure smooth flats with square edges, reworking the trigger, substituting grips fitted to the individual hand, and polishing the interior of the barrel.

A crisp, fairly light trigger pull that will let off shots without disturbing the shooter's hold is important with rifles also, but of even greater importance with rifles is bedding fit. The action must fit evenly and flatly with no irregular pressure points. A master stockman can produce such a fit in wood, but any gunsmith can perform it just as well by using a glass-bedding compound. Regardless of who performs the work, it is especially important that the recoil lug bear solidly and evenly against its mortise. Fore-ends are more difficult to bed, and in many rifles—including most single shots and some lever actions—the forearm is best set up to avoid touching the barrel at all. With one-piece stocks, one of two forearm bedding methods will usually result in tighter groups and a consistent zero. Rifles with light barrels generally shoot best with some upward pressure at the fore-end tip to tame "whip." A small pad of glass bedding, or a piece of plastic such as a sliver of a credit card, inserted between barrel and stock can sometimes improve accuracy greatly. Any other high spots should be sanded down. With other rifles, particularly heavy barrels, peak accuracy is obtained by eliminating all contact between barrel and stock back to within a couple of inches of the receiver. Some manufacturers employ these "free-floating" barrels as a matter of course, and such rifles generally shoot very well.

For consistent accuracy, care should also be taken to degrease all stock and sight mount screws on any gun and to tighten them securely with a fitted screwdriver.

Shotguns are not discussed here because the accurizing procedure does not apply to them. (See BEDDING; CUSTOM GUNS; GLASS BEDDING; METALLIC SIGHTS.)

achromatic lens A lens that is color corrected, i.e., free from chromatic (color) aberration. An achromatic lens is made of two lenses ground from different kinds of glass (usually crown and flint) with different refractive indices and cemented together. The lens made of crown glass is convex on both sides; the one made of flint glass is concave on one side, to match the convex surface of the crown glass lens, and may be either flat or slightly convex on the other side. Used singly, the achromatic lens is placed with the crown element facing the object viewed. Used in pairs, two achromats are placed crown to crown, as in an erector lens system. Achromatic lenses are used in all high-quality optical instruments. (See CHROMATIC ABERRATION; REFRACTION.)

achromatized Ramsden eyepiece See KELLNER EYEPIECE.

Ackley wildcats Ackley wildcat cartridges, composed of cartridges of from .17 to .475 caliber, are perhaps the most complete line of wildcats ever developed. They are based on cases that range in size from the .218 Bee to the .375 H&H Magnum. In general the case bodies are expanded for minimum taper and to increase shoulder angle—both for greater powder capacity. This, in turn, gives greater velocity than is possible with the parent case.

The most well-known Ackley wildcat cartridges are those referred to as the "Ackley Improved." In these versions case-head-to-shoulder length remains the same as in the factory cartridge; a standard factory cartridge is fired in an Improved chamber to reform the body and shoulder for greater powder capacity. (See K-SERIES WILDCATS; WILDCAT CARTRIDGE.)

ACP The common abbreviation for Automatic Colt Pistol (cartridge). ACP is, in fact, a misnomer, which through years of use has become standard. The cartridge should actually be identified as the .45 Semi-automatic Pistol. It achieved its greatest notoriety in the Colt Model 1911 Automatic Pistol and became firmly associated in the public mind with that arm. The mislabeling extends to the .25 Automatic and the .32 Automatic, which are sometimes suffixed with ACP.

action The basis of every gun, it consists of the receiver, breechblock, and loading and firing mechanism. The breech mechanism enables a firearm to function. The barrel, stock, sights, etc. are attached to the action. (See AUTOLOADING ACTION; BOLT ACTION; DOUBLE ACTION; LEVER ACTION; PUMP ACTION; SIDE-BY-SIDE GUN; SINGLE ACTION; SINGLE-SHOT ACTION.)

action bar A forward projection of the action body of a single-barrel or side-by-side double-barrel shotgun. The action bar, which extends forward of the action's face, is cut out to contain the locking lugs of the barrels, the hinge pin, and, in some cases, the gun's locking mechanism. Some action bars also contain components of the gun's ejection system.

The term is also used to describe the operating rod or rods that connect the slide and bolt of a pump-action gun or the gas piston and bolt of a semiautomatic arm.

action bar flat The upper surface of the action bar. When the action of a single-barrel or side-by-side shotgun is closed in the firing position, the barrel flat (on the bottom of the breech end of the barrel or barrels) comes to rest on the action bar flat.

action bedding See BEDDING.

adapter An insert chambered to fire a smaller cartridge or shot shell than a gun was originally chambered for. The outer surface of the adapter must fit into the chamber of the gun and the firing mechanism of the gun must be mechanically capable of firing the smaller ammunition. Adapters are used in big-caliber handguns (the .45 is made into a .22), rifles (the .30/06 is made into a .32 ACP), and shotguns (the 12 gauge is made into a 20 gauge). Adapters provide a means of shooting a bigger gun less expensively than would otherwise be the case. Recoil is also substantially lessened, but the use of adapters considerably diminish a firearm's inherent accuracy.

(See AUXILIARY CARTRIDGE; BARREL ADAPTER; GAUGE ADAPTER.)

adjustable choke A muzzle device to make a single-barrel shotgun produce different patterns at varying ranges under different hunting conditions. Typically, they are designed to give any degree of constriction from practically no choke (slug or cylinder bore), suitable for close range gunning, to ultratight chokes (extra full) that produce tighter patterns for long-range shooting.

Basically, adjustable chokes fall into two categories: (1) changeable choke tubes that screw into the end of a chokeless barrel; and (2) collet-type choke devices that can be opened up or tightened down in degree of choking by adjusting the device much in the manner that a garden hose nozzle is adjusted for width of spray pattern. The Cutts Compensator and Pachmayr interchangeable tube chokes are typical examples of the former type, while the Poly-Choke colleted device is the best known example of the latter. In addition, collet-type chokes designed to tighten up automatically with successive shots have been developed and put on the market at times. In Europe, choke devices for double-barrel shotguns have been marketed. Several American interchangeable chokes of both various-tube and collet types have been made with integral muzzle brake systems to reduce recoil.

Theoretically, an adjustable choke device makes a shotgun into an all-purpose smoothbore, suitable for any hunting from close-range quail and rabbit shooting to long-range pass shooting on waterfowl.

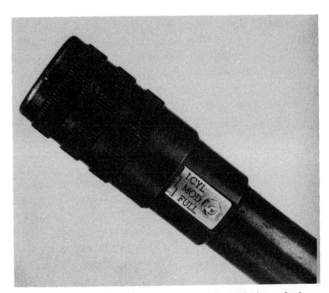

An adjustable choke offers owners of single-barrel shotguns a selection of constrictions. This one can be set for improved cylinder, modified, or full by turning it to the proper setting.

In practice, the usefulness of such a device can be limited by improper installation; many such chokes are not concentrically installed on their barrels and hence center their shot patterns off the shooter's points of aim. Another limitation of most such chokes is that their bulk tends to raise the front line of sight, causing a shooter to shoot low.

Further, shot fired through an adjustable choke may not pattern as uniformly as that fired through an integrally choked barrel. This can be corrected by either expert bending of the barrel to a slight degree or by raising the comb of the shotgun's stock to correct for the increased bead height caused by the choke device.

Installation of an adjustable choke is one way to restore to usefulness a shotgun barrel whose muzzle has been damaged by firing when plugged with snow or mud. (See CUTTS COMPENSATOR.)

adjustable trigger A trigger provided with adjustments for engagement, weight of pull, and overtravel. Some triggers used in free rifles have two-stage pulls and also have an adjustment for the preliminary pull, or takeup, prior to the actual release pull.

The adjustment for engagement controls the amount of trigger movement required to release the hammer or firing pin from its cocked position in order to fire the cartridge. The weight of pull adjustment controls the force required on the finger piece, and the overtravel adjustment controls the amount of movement of the trigger after the hammer or firing pin is released. Excessive engagement is called "creep." It generally results in a jerky or irregular pull because the relative position of the parts changes during movement. Excessive overtravel is called "slap" or "backlash," and because of the uncontrolled movement of the trigger finger after firing pin release it tends to disturb the aim of the firearm prior to bullet exit.

The quality of the trigger pull and the weight of pull attainable is controlled to a large degree by the design of the trigger, the geometry of its engaging parts relative to pivot points, and the hardness, fits and finishes of rotating and sliding surfaces. Without proper design and workmanship, it may not be possible to obtain a crisp and positive trigger pull, even in an adjustable trigger.

Many triggers are advertised as "adjustable" when they actually have only weight of pull and overtravel adjustments. Because the amount of engagement is a vital factor in the quality of the trigger pull and because it also affects the weight of pull, it is often difficult or impossible to obtain a crisp pull from these triggers without grinding or stoning parts to provide tight and smooth engagement. (See DOUBLE-STAGE TRIGGER; FREE PISTOL; FREE RIFLE; SINGLE SET TRIGGER.)

aerodynamic performance The flight characteristics of bodies as a result of the motion of the bodies in air. Consideration of such performance is necessary in the design of aircraft and projectiles. Many of the present-day problems associated with ammunition and high speed aircraft are the same. Consequently engineers working in this field are sometimes referred to as aeroballisticians. (See BALLISTIC COEFFICIENT; EXTERIOR BALLISTICS.)

Afghan stock A kind of rifle stock, indigenous to Afghanistan and nearby areas, that is characterized by sharply curved lines of comb and belly, and a narrow butt. Afghan stocks are often embellished with brass tacks in primitive decorative patterns. As an aid to marksmanship, the stock shape has no application and, consequently, its design features are not found on firearms manufactured in the Western world.

African dangerous game, guns and loads for The African big-game species traditionally classified as "dangerous" are lion, leopard, rhinoceros, elephant, and Cape buffalo. Of these, the rhinoceros is mentioned only incidentally, as its scarcity and the very high license fees that the species commands when it is available for hunting make it less of a practical consideration for sportsmen than the others mentioned.

Before the invention of smokeless powder, the customary rifles for these species were doubles (side-by-side) or single shots chambered for extremely large black-powder cartridges, which were commonly measured in gauge rather than caliber and which propelled unjacketed lead bullets at low velocities. With the development of smokeless powder toward the end of the 19th century, bullet diameters diminished and velocities increased, but the double, or side-by-side, rifle had established a strong tradition of use.

In the heyday of African hunting—from the turn of the century until the late 1950s—the most highly regarded double rifles were built in limited numbers by the best London gunmakers such as Westley Richards, Holland & Holland, Jeffrey, Purdey, and Rigby. Although double rifles were made in many different calibers, the most popular cartridges for African dangerous game were the .500, .450, .465, .470, .470 No. 2, .577, and .600. These cartridges, using cordite as a propellant, drove jacketed bullets (ranging from 480 grains for the .450 to 900 for the .600) at low velocities, generally between 1,800 and 2,200 feet per second (fps). The bullets were either

Of the so-called big-five dangerous species, the rhino has largely been eliminated. Shrinking habitat and merciless pressure from poachers who seek its horns have drastically reduced the rhinos' numbers. Leopard, lion, and buffalo remain plentiful. Elephants have been killed in huge numbers by poachers and game-control officers alike, and while they remain in shootable numbers, trophies are very scarce.

soft-nosed expanding or full-jacketed nonexpanding "solids."

However, some hunters either could not afford a double rifle or considered its two-shot capacity a handicap. As an alternative, various British gunmakers developed less expensive bolt action rifles with magazine capacities of three to five rounds. Built on commercial Mauser actions, those guns were chambered for large rimless cartridges, whereas the case extraction design of most double rifles required rimmed cartridges. The various British rimless cartridges such as the .416 Rigby, .404 Jeffrey, .425 Westley Richards, and .505 Gibbs are loaded with 400- to 500-grain bullets at 2,200 to 2,400 fps.

In 1956, Winchester introduced its .458 Magnum for use on dangerous game, a cartridge that went on to become the number one choice of African professional hunters for backup work. With its 500-grain softnose and 510-grain solid bullets at a velocity of 2,040 fps, the "Four-Five-Eight," as it is commonly called, duplicates the performance of a number of older British-designed cartridges, but it does so with a case small enough to work in most standard-size bolt actions. No small part of its popularity is due to the fact that the .458 was introduced in the excellent Winchester Model 70, a bolt-action rifle that sold (and still sells) for a fraction of the cost of British bolt actions.

In 1958, the Calfornia firm of Weatherby followed Winchester's lead with its .460 Magnum. Despite its name, the Weatherby cartridge uses bullets of the same diameter as the .458, but its larger case pushes the same weights about 600 fps faster. The .460 Magnum is available only in the Weatherby Mark V rifle. The effectiveness of the .460 Weatherby Magnum on large and dangerous game is a sight to behold, but its fearsome recoil is quite difficult for all but the most experienced shooters to manage.

Introduced in 1989 in the Model 700 rifle, the .416 Remington Magnum may be the best dangerous game cartridge for the average hunter. In pushing a 400-grain bullet along at 2,400 fps, it virtually duplicates the performance of the much larger .416 Rigby. The Remington cartridge also generates a bit less recoil than Winchester's .458 Magnum, and it shoots much flatter. This latter characteristic makes the .416 somewhat more flexible and therefore more suitable for those hunters who prefer to take one rifle to Africa and use it on all game from the smallest antelope to the largest dangerous game.

Within a few months after Remington introduced its new dangerous game cartridge, Weatherby followed suit with its .416 Magnum. Like the .378 and .460 Magnums, the .416 Weatherby is basically the .416 Rigby case with a belt and Weatherby's rounded shoulder. The .416 Weatherby Magnum generates

2,700 fps with the 400-grain bullet, and, although recoil is less than with the .460 Magnum, only seasoned shooters are able to fire it without flinching.

The shooting of African game is often done from the offhand position, but if time and place allow, a tree, an anthill, or other solid object should be used for a rest. Most professional hunters insist that their clients use a shooting stick (a homemade bipod carried by a native tracker) when attempting a shot offhand. When trailing game across hot dusty country, a carrying sling for the rifle is a necessity, but when a shot is imminent, or when entering thick brush, the sling should be detached and stowed in a pocket.

A suitable rifle for the hunting of dangerous African game must be mechanically reliable, powerful, and fast handling. Its user should also be able to aim, fire, and operate the rifle quickly and surely.

African plains game, guns and loads for   As it is commonly used, the term "plains game" encompasses the various African antelope, zebra, and other nondangerous species, even though their habitat may range from dense brush to tropical rain forest. In size, these animals range from a Thompson gazelle, which will usually weigh well under 100 pounds, to the Lord Derby, or giant, eland, which often weighs as much as a ton. Some species, such as the bongo, which inhabits dense swamps and mountain rain forests, may be taken at ranges as close as 25 yards, while others—plains dwellers— may present shots at the very limit of a long-range cartridge's capability.

The variety and the size of African plains game is enormously varied. A Thompson's gazelle will scale 90 to 100 pounds; a zebra will weigh 700; and an eland can weigh close to a ton.

The majority of American and European sportsmen who pursue plains game bring two rifles, a light and a medium. The light rifle is used exclusively on the smaller and medium-sized nondangerous species, while the medium will be employed against the largest antelope and some species of dangerous game, such as lion and leopard. It should be noted, however, that the terms "light" and "medium" are somewhat imprecise. For example, a .300 Magnum could be viewed either as a light or a medium rifle, since it is powerful enough to be used on large nondangerous or dangerous game.

The most popular action type for both classes of rifle is the bolt. It is universally selected because of its accuracy and reliability. The most common chamberings for a light rifle are .270, .30/06, 7mm Magnum, and .300 Magnum. European hunters use such cartridges as the 7×64mm, 7×57mm, .303, and .318. As a general rule any cartridge that can propel a bullet of at least 150 grains at no less than 2,700 feet per second (fps) will be satisfactory as a light rifle. A bullet of lower weight will lack sufficient penetration, while less velocity will prove a handicap if a long shot must be taken.

Without question, the most common cartridge for the medium classification is the .375 H&H Magnum. It combines ample bullet weight and relatively high velocity with manageable recoil, and is generally regarded as the most useful of all African cartridges. Other loads that are selected for medium rifles include the .338, .340 Weatherby, 8×68S, .333 Nitro Express, and 9.3×62mm.

A satisfactory medium rifle cartridge can fire a bullet of at least 200 grains at a velocity of no less than 2,500 fps. The .375 H&H employs a 270-grain bullet that it fires at a velocity of 2,700 fps, or a 300-grain projectile at 2,500 fps.

Regardless of the caliber chosen, in either classification, the hunter must select bullets that are strongly constructed and that will give maximum penetration. Quick-expanding projectiles are unsatisfactory for all but the smallest species. It is not unusual for hunters to use solids (full-jacketed ammunition) for the larger antelope species such as eland.

Telescopic sights are universally preferred for light rifles and are used almost without exception for medium rifles. A light rifle is well equipped with a 4X scope, or a variable of 2X–7X or 3X–9X. Advocates of the fixed-power sight claim that it is lighter and mechanically simpler, therefore less likely to malfunction. Those who prefer the variable believe that it is better adapted to extreme close-range and long-range shooting. Medium rifles are best equipped with scopes of somewhat lower magnification. A fixed-power sight of 2.5X or 3X is suitable, or a variable of 1X–4X. The reason for this is that the medium rifle is used against larger species and, in the case of dangerous game, must be able to be employed quickly at close range.

It should be stressed that a strong scope mount is essential. Any safari will involve much air travel, and most African hunting is done over rough ground in four-wheel-drive vehicles. The combination of constant vibration from these sources and less-than-careful handling will render useless any scope that is improperly mounted. All screws must be securely in place before the safari is begun and should be checked at frequent intervals while it is in progress. Some experienced hunters take an extra scope in case of accident.

On a safari of three weeks' duration, a hunter can expect to fire a minimum of 20 shots from his light rifle, unless the hunt is restricted as to species. The total for the medium rifle will be somewhat less. It is considered prudent to bring 60 rounds of ammunition for a light rifle and 40 for a medium.

Both rifles must be strongly cased; aluminum cases, which lock with padlocks, are preferred. It is also recommended that the hunter bring a complete cleaning kit and, if he is knowledgeable enough to install them, a selection of spare parts (such as firing pin, extractor, screws, sling swivels, etc.) for each rifle. It is also imperative that each rifle have a sling, since it is not common to have a gunbearer, and the hunter will frequently be walking long distances.

Before departure, all firearms must be registered with customs, and most African countries require that all firearms be declared and registered upon entry. In addition, some require a statement as to the amount of ammunition the hunter brings in and takes out. (It is suggested that ammunition be packed in plastic boxes designed for that purpose, not in the original cardboard boxes.)

A pair of high-quality binoculars is invaluable for hunting African plains game. Most foreign hunters are not nearly so adept at spotting game as are professional hunters and native trackers, so binoculars are a necessity. The minimum magnification should be 7X; the maximum, 10X.

It is likely that nearly all plains game is killed (or lost) by shooting from the offhand position. Because of the knee-high level of plant growth, prone, sitting, and kneeling positions are usually impossible. The prudent shooter should look for trees, anthills or other support to aid in a steady hold. Indeed, it is quite possible that skillful shooting from the offhand position can do more to ensure the success of a safari than the most intelligently chosen light and medium rifles.

Aguirre y Aranzabal (company)   See SPANISH GUN-MAKERS.

air gauge   See BORE GAUGE.

air gun   A rifle-like or pistol-like gun that utilizes compressed air or gas to propel its projectile. The air or gas may be stored as liquid in a cylinder, compressed by a pump and stored before firing, or it may be compressed at the instant of firing by a spring-driven piston.

Combination air and ignitible fuel guns use highly volatile gases pumped into the compression chamber. There they form an ignitible mixture with air that is exploded by compression.

The earliest existing air guns date from the late 16th century and are of the spring-driven piston type. Stored air or pneumatic guns appeared in the early 17th century.

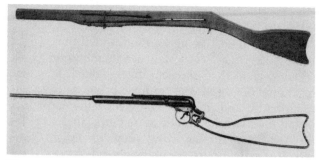

These are two early American air rifles. The upper one is the all-wood Chicago Model produced in 1886 by the Markham Air Rifle Company. Below it is the first all-metal Daisy air rifle, marketed in 1888.

Air guns offer varying degrees of sophistication. This one, intended for casual use, is of the break-open type and relies on a spring powered plunger.

Early air guns were of large caliber, often .50 or more, and were used by the Austrian Army (as weapons) from 1780 to about 1800, as well as for hunting deer-sized game. One, the Girardoni, a .50-caliber Italian gun, required 2,000 pump strokes for full charging. It was supposed to have fired a lead ball at nearly 1,000 feet per second. (See BB GUN; CO_2 GUN.)

air resistance   The force exerted on the point of a bullet or shot pellet by air, which acts to retard the projectile's velocity. Dense air sets up greater resistance than thin air, and the higher the velocity at which the bullet travels, the greater the air resistance will be. (See BALLISTIC COEFFICIENT; BALLISTICS; BERNOULLI EFFECT; EXTERIOR BALLISTICS.)

airspace   In a loaded metallic cartridge, the space inside the case left unoccupied by the powder charge and bullet. It is unavoidable in some cartridges and in reduced loads, but best accuracy with full loads is generally obtained with a powder that leaves little or no airspace; this condition promotes uniform ignition and burning of the powder. (See LOADING DENSITY.)

air spiral   The turbulence created by an unbalanced bullet in flight. The imbalance is most frequently the result of the bullet's center of gravity not being coincident with its center of form. Bullet "wobble" or "tipping" describe imperfect bullet flight.

alignment   The act or state of being properly positioned in a form or line, or concentrically. The word refers to a number of relationships pertaining to firearms and shooting, for example, lining up the front and rear sights of a gun. Having all of the components in alignment—bullet/bore, cartridge/bore, bolt/bore, etc.—is said to be a key to accuracy.

All-America Skeet and Trap Teams   Each year, officials of the Amateur Trapshooting Association and National Skeet Shooting Association select honorary teams of outstanding shooters, based on the year's cumulative records. Teams are selected for each of six categories: Open, Ladies, Seniors, Juniors, Industry, and Military/International. In skeet, the selections are based on four-gauge averages; in trap, they are based on 16-yard, handicap, and doubles scores. (See SKEET SHOOTING; TRAPSHOOTING.)

Allen & Wheelock revolver   See LIPFIRE CARTRIDGE.

All-Gauge   Skeet competitions sanctioned by the National Skeet Shooting Association are fired with four gauges: 12, 20, 28, and .410. All-Gauge is a registered skeet event in which the competitor can use any legitimate skeet gun or load in any of these four gauges.

altered bolt   The use of telescopic sights led to the practice of bolt alteration. Since bolt handles of most military rifles are too high for low-mounted scopes, these bolts are ground down or have their handles welded on at a lower angle. Some bolt handles are altered to improve appearance, the handsome slant of the pre-1964 Winchester Model 70 bolt often serving as a model. (See SPORTERIZING.)

altitude effect   The effect of altitude on projectiles in flight has long been a cause of puzzlement and speculation among shooters. Since air provides resistance to a speeding projectile, and since air density (and thus resistance) lessens in going from sea level to higher altitudes, it seemed obvious to early ballisticians that high altitude should produce a perceptible flattening of trajectory. Nineteenth-century British sportsmen blamed the altitude difference between London and the Serengeti Plain (as much as 9,000 feet) for their misses on East African big game, while early mountain hunters, not realizing that a bullet drops according to horizontal (and not slant) distance, similarly were convinced that altitude was the reason for their consistent overshooting. Actually, the difference in air density does not significantly affect rifle shooting at ranges of up to 400–500 yards until about four miles above sea level—considerably higher than any hunting altitude. (See AIR RESISTANCE; DOWNHILL SHOOTING; EXTERIOR BALLISTICS; UPHILL SHOOTING.)

Amateur Trapshooting Association (ATA) Trapshooting in the United States originated with the use of pigeons released from cages; the live birds were to be shot for score. Between 1870 and 1880, a new version of the sport evolved, with the pigeons replaced by various kinds of inanimate targets, hurled by spring-operated catapults that came to be called traps.

As the targets and traps were perfected, the sport gained in popularity until, in 1895, the Interstate Association was formed as the governing body of trapshooting. In 1908, registered tournaments were begun, with the scores forwarded to association headquarters and recorded.

In 1918, the Interstate Association changed its name to the one it now bears. Headquartered in Vandalia, Ohio since 1923, the ATA administers all registered shoots—including the annual Grand American in Vandalia—and compiles and records all shooting statistics of ATA competitors. Membership of the ATA is approximately 50,000. (See TRAPSHOOTING.)

Amber, John T. (1903–1986) From 1949 until 1979, John T. Amber was editor—and later editor-in-chief—of *Gun Digest* and its companion publications. Since his childhood in northern Illinois, he was a shooter as well as a collector of early firearms and of firearms books. He hunted throughout the world—Africa, Europe (from Scotland and England east to Yugoslavia and Russia), and over much of North America.

Amber was born in Freeport, Illinois and educated at Lewis Institute. He held a wide variety of jobs through the 1920s and 1930s and served in the Navy during World War II.

In 1979 he became editor emeritus of *Gun Digest*. (See GUN DIGEST.)

American choke See TAPER CHOKE.

American Rifleman, The The National Rifle Association of America (NRA) was founded in 1871 to create a system of rifle training among National Guard units. To a large extent, the founders were men who had been in service in the Civil War or who were members of military organizations. News of NRA activities and accounts of matches were published in *The Army & Navy Journal,* which was edited by one of the founders of the NRA. (In addition, shooting was a sport that attracted much more public interest in those times than it does today, and news accounts were carried frequently in newspapers and magazines.)

In 1885, A. C. Gould launched a monthly magazine titled *The Rifle,* devoted entirely to rifles and rifle shooting. Publisher Gould was a strong advocate of the NRA, and the magazine was, to some degree, an unofficial publication of the organization. Three years later, the magazine's name was changed to *Shooting and Fishing,* and it was issued as a weekly that reported on hunting, fishing, and all types of target shooting.

After Gould's death in 1906, management of *Shooting and Fishing* was taken over by General James A. Drain, a director and life member of the NRA and a member of the National Board for the Promotion of Rifle Practice; the magazine's name was changed to *Arms and The Man.* For another decade it continued as an unofficial NRA journal while covering rifle and pistol competitions and publishing some hunting stories and articles of general interest; it took on a heavy emphasis on military matters and supported the military viewpoint, particularly in editorial policy, during Drain's stewardship. On July 1, 1916, for the price of $1.00, Drain transferred ownership of *Arms and The Man* to the NRA with the understanding that it would become the official NRA publication.

From December 1919 to May 1923, *Arms and The Man* was issued as a biweekly. Magazine content became less military in viewpoint and more oriented toward the technical side of the shooting sports. In June 1923, its name was once again changed to *The American Rifleman;* the publication was expanded in length and scope, and experts in the shooting field were enlisted to contribute articles and columns on a regular basis. It remained a biweekly until January 1927, when it was changed to a monthly, a frequency it has retained to the present.

Perhaps the best description of the stated purpose of *The American Rifleman* and its predecessors is the following quotation. It is from the December 1952 issue and it commemorated the publication of 100 volumes of a shooters' magazine that began with *The Rifle* in May 1885. "For one hundred volumes, over a 67-year period, this magazine has promoted and reported the growth of shooting in America. It has kept its readers abreast of developments and changes in military, sporting, and target arms, and has been an intelligent leader of thought and discussion on firearms and their use in war and peace." (See NATIONAL BOARD FOR THE PROMOTION OF RIFLE PRACTICE [NBPRP]; NATIONAL RIFLE ASSOCIATION [NRA].)

ametropic This term refers to an abnormal condition of the eye in which images fail to focus on the retina caused by faulty refraction. Faults in optical equipment are sometimes blamed for problems that are, in reality, the result of an ametropic condition in the shooter.

anastigmat A compound lens corrected for astigmatism. An anastigmat lens is one that forms an accurate image of a pointed object. Anastigmatic correction is one of the features to look for in any quality optical instrument. (See ASTIGMATISM.)

Anderson, Gary (1939–   ) At the peak of his shooting career, Gary Anderson dominated International-type and position rifle shooting for nearly a decade and must be classed as one of the great rifle shooters of all time. He was born in Holdreg, Nebraska, and his introduction to rifle shooting came at the age of 10, when he started to hunt. He began competitive rifle shooting in 1957 and was a member of the University of Nebraska rifle team in 1957–58. Joining the U.S. Army in 1958, he was detailed to the Army Advanced Marksmanship Unit (AAMU) at Fort Benning, Georgia, in 1959 and remained there through 1962. He also belonged to the National Guards of both Nebraska and California and was commissioned through Officer Candidate School.

The following is a chronology of the major events of his shooting career:

1959: First International competition at the Pan American Games. Won a silver medal in 300-meter standing and a bronze in the 50-meter three-position.

1960: Alternate member of the U.S. team to the Olympic Games in Rome.

1961: Won a gold medal in the CISM (International Military Sports Council) Championships in Rio de Janeiro. Won his first U.S. National Championship, the 50-meter three-position event.

1962: Won four gold medals in the World Shooting Championships in Cairo and established new world records in 50-meter three-position, 50-meter standing, and 300-meter prone events.

1963: Won gold medals in the Pan American Games in Brazil in 50-meter three-position and 300-meter free rifle.

1964: Won gold medal in the Olympics in Tokyo in 300-meter free rifle and set new world record.

1966: Won three gold medals, two silver medals and a bronze medal in the World Shooting Championships in Germany. Set new world record in 300-meter free rifle.

1967: Won bronze medal at the Pan American Games in Winnepeg in 50-meter free rifle.

1968: Won gold medal in 300-meter free rifle and

This Nebraskan (shown here in a recent photograph and during his days as a competitor) is one of the greatest rifle marksmen America has produced.

set new world record at the Olympic Games in Mexico City.

1969: In his last International match, in Barcelona, he won the 50-meter three-position event, shooting 1182 × 1200, the highest score fired in International competition until 1985. He retired from active International competition after that match.

His successes in shooting in America are numerous; specific mention should be made of his winning the National High Power Championship at Camp Perry, Ohio in 1975 and again in 1976.

Anderson is largely self-taught as a rifle shooter. His membership in the AAMU at Fort Benning came before its coaches reached their peak of excellence. He credits some of his skill to the opportunity to watch world-class shooters at International matches, particularly the Russians, who were the first to make scientific studies of the psychology and physiology of shooting.

Gary Anderson graduated from Hastings College, Hastings, Nebraska in 1965, and from San Francisco Theological Seminary in 1968. He was elected to the Nebraska State Senate in 1972 and served there from 1973 to 1976. In October 1976, he became executive director of the Southwest Nebraska Council of Governments and held this position until he was appointed executive director for general operations of the National Rifle Association in August 1977. He is married and has a son and a daughter. (See ARMY MARKSMANSHIP UNIT; OLYMPIC GAMES SHOOTING EVENTS; PAN AMERICAN GAMES SHOOTING EVENTS; WORLD SHOOTING CHAMPIONSHIPS.)

anemometer An instrument for measuring wind speed, and sometimes direction. The totalizing anemometer has cup-shaped vanes and a gauge recorder mounted on its main stem. An anemometer's findings may be transferred to a recording instrument called an anemograph. Useful for artillery op-erations, anemometers are usually not allowed in formal target shooting, where mechanical wind testing devices may be prohibited.

angle of departure The angle at which a bullet leaves the gun barrel in relation to a straight line from muzzle to target. (See EXTERIOR BALLISTICS.)

angle of elevation The vertical angle of the bore, expressed in minutes of angle, in relation to a straight line to the target from the muzzle. Also, the angle that is required to compensate for bullet drop from line of sight. (See EXTERIOR BALLISTICS.)

annealing A process used to soften metal and make it easier to work with—such as in engraving steel or resizing metallic cartridge cases—generally by heating to a moderate temperature and then cooling slowly. Brass case necks become brittle with use (work hardening) but then may be annealed to allow further sizing and working (in the reloading process) without cracking. (See ENGRAVING; HANDLOAD; WORK HARDENING.)

annular rim A circular rim such as the rim on the head of a cartridge case. Some metallic cartridges and all shotgun shells seat on the rim when fully chambered. In a rimfire cartridge, an annular rim, formed by a fold in the metal at the head, contains the primer mix. The rim also provides a purchase point for a gun's extractor.

Anschütz (company) The J. G. Anschütz Germania-Waffenwerk (J. G. Anschütz-Germania Arms Works), Zella-Mehlis, Germany, was well established before World War I. The company is now located in Ulm/

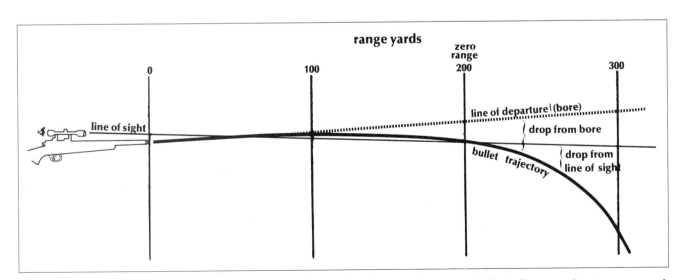

In order to extend the useful trajectory of a bullet, the angle or line of departure of the bullet must lie in an upward direction relative to the line of sight.

Donau, Germany. Aside from military production, this company makes fine small game rifles, target rifles and pistols, some especially designed for Olympic and International Shooting Union events. Rimfire .22 rifles by Anschütz are currently imported into America by Precision Sales. (See INTERNATIONAL SHOOTING UNION; OLYMPIC GAMES SHOOTING EVENTS; PAN AMERICAN GAMES SHOOTING EVENTS.)

Anson and Deeley action A hammerless boxlock design of shotgun action that was introduced in 1875. The patent was granted to Messrs. William Anson and John Deeley, employees of Westley Richards of London. The design, in many variations, has continued in wide use, and it remains the most common type of break-action for side-by-side shotguns. (See BOXLOCK; WESTLEY RICHARDS.)

antimony A metallic element used in a wide variety of alloys, antimony is frequently added to lead bullet cores and cast bullets in amounts from 3 percent to 10 percent to increase hardness. (See BULLET MOLD; CHILLED SHOT; DROPPED SHOT.)

anvil That part of a cartridge against which the explosive composition of the primer is crushed by the blow of the firing pin. In Boxer primers, the anvil is part of the primer assembly, placed in the primer cup after the explosive pellet and held there by a friction fit inside the cup. Cases that use Berdan primers contain an integral anvil—a central projection in the center of the bottom of the primer pocket. (See BERDAN PRIMER; BOXER PRIMER.)

aperture The opening through a kind of metallic front or rear sight, that is used on rifles. The front sight is visually centered in the aperture to effect aiming of the firearm. (See APERTURE SIGHT; METALLIC SIGHTS; SIGHT PICTURE.)

aperture sight Except for the front sights on some target rifles, the aperture sight is almost always a rear sight. The vast majority of aperture sights are employed on rifles, although a few are installed on shotguns intended for slug use. Aperture sights have also been adapted for handguns used in silhouette shooting. Rear aperture sights are also called peep sights. (See METALLIC SIGHTS.)

aplanatic objective An objective lens of an optical instrument that is free of both chromatic and spherical aberration. (See CHROMATIC ABERRATION, SPHERICAL ABERRATION.)

armory See ARSENAL.

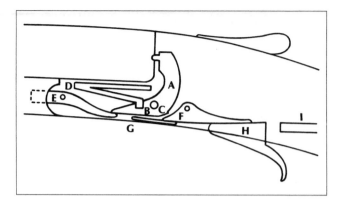

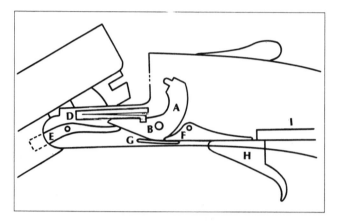

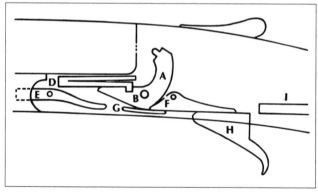

One of the most popular boxlock shotgun actions is the Anson and Deeley, which was patented in 1875. It is shown here, from top: closed and fired, open, and closed and cocked. The parts are as follows: a) tumbler, or hammer, b) tumbler pin, c) bent, d) mainspring, e) cocking lever, f) sear, g) sear spring, h) trigger, and i) safety.

Army Marksmanship Unit In 1955, President Dwight D. Eisenhower, disturbed by reports of poor shooting performance by American soldiers in combat, both in World War II and Korea, as well as by poor performance of service class marksmen in U.S., Olympic, and World-level competitions, ordered the formation of a marksmanship training unit. Established in March 1956 and stationed at Fort Benning, Georgia, it was originally titled the U.S. Army Advanced Marksmanship Unit, then the U.S. Army Marksmanship Training Unit, and finally was given its present designation of U.S. Army Marksmanship Unit (USAMU).

Backed by funds from the U.S. government and with assistance from American and foreign manufacturers of both military and target arms, the USAMU has achieved notable results in marksmanship training and in the performance of military and competitive small arms and ammunition. These include the following:

Development of marksmanship training methods based on a sound understanding of human physiology and psychology;

Publication of numerous instruction manuals on various aspects of marksmanship training, coaching, firearms, and gunsmithing methods;

Development of marksmanship training methods for the armed services, both general and specialized (such as sniper units);

Development of new weapons systems, such as the M-21 sniper rifle; the basic configuration of the Army rifle, used in the Army rifle competitions in International, Olympic, and Pan American Games competitions; and modifications to improve accuracy in service weapons, such as the M-14 rifle and .45 service pistol.

USAMU competitive shooters have largely dominated competitive military shooting in the armed services and in NRA regional and national matches, both individual and team; and in International, Olympic, and Pan American Games matches, so far as placing shooters on the U.S. squad. Of the American medal winners in International, Olympic, and Pan American Games shooting events, the great majority come out of the USAMU or have been trained by the USAMU or by methods developed by USAMU. The foregoing is true for all of the types of shooting competitions: rifle, shotgun (skeet and trap), pistol, and running target.

Since 1964, the Small Arms Firing School at the National Matches has been the responsibility of the USAMU.

Among USAMU manuals available to the public are: *Basic Smallbore Guide; International Rifle Marksmanship Guide; The Service Rifle Marksmanship Guide; Accurized National Match M-14 Rifle; Service Rifle Instructors and Coaches Guide; Rifle Instructors and Coaches Guide; International Running Target Guide; International Skeet & Trap Guide; Basic Pistol Marksmanship Guide; Accurized National Match Cal. .45 Pistol and Cal. .38 Spec. Wadcutter Pistol; Pistol Marksmanship Guide; The Marksmanship Instructors and Coaches Guide;* and *Profile of a Champion.*

They are available from the Office of the Director of Civilian Marksmanship, Room 1E053, West Forrestal Bldg., Washington, D.C. 20314.

arquebus   The weapon known as the arquebus enjoys the distinction of being the first firearm that could be hand held and fired from the shoulder by an individual acting alone. The innovation that made this possible was the advance in ignition called the matchlock. The arquebus was provided with a trigger that when depressed caused an S-shaped lock clasping the burning fuse, or match, to drop into the priming pan. This freed the shooter's hands so that he could hold and aim the gun while ignition took place.

Exactly when and by whom the arquebus was invented is open to conjecture. At least a half-dozen European countries claim to be the place of origin of the design. Variants of arquebus (*hak-buchse, hacquebut, hagbutt*) appear in several languages, which has not helped to clear up matters. There is even confusion over the word itself. Although it is generally agreed that arquebus and its variants mean "hook gun," some historians believe the hook refers to the curved jaws of the match holder, while others point to the projection below the barrel of larger specimens, a device clearly intended to hook over a rest, or perhaps a wall, to absorb recoil. Certainly arquebus-type weapons were in widespread use all over Europe by the early 1500s, when they revolutionized warfare, abruptly ending the heyday of the pikeman.

The arquebus is important in New World history also, for it was this weapon with which Cortes and Pizarro and their tiny bands of *conquistadores* destroyed the Aztec and Inca empires. (See MATCHLOCK.)

arsenal   A facility for the manufacture and/or storage of military small arms and ammunition. In the United States, the first federal arsenal to manufacture weapons was established in Springfield, Massachusetts, in 1777, and in 1795 the second national arsenal was established in Harpers Ferry, Virginia. The term "arsenal" is used today more or less interchangeably with "armory."

Asian game, guns and loads for   Today, hunting in Asia is of primary concern to sportsmen who have set their sights on collecting a "world slam" of sheep. Asia is the major home of game sheep and such sheep-related species as Iran's Armenian, Urial, red, and Alburz species. In Mongolia one finds the *argali* and in Afghanistan the magnificent Marco Polo.

The smaller of these species, such as the ibex, can be taken with ease by any standard cartridge such as the .270, .280, or .30/06. Bolt-action rifles are the universal choice because of their reliability and accuracy, and scopes are also standard equipment. The Duplex style of reticle is excellent, and magnification should be no less than 4X.

Sheep such as the Marco Polo grow to large size (400 pounds), and most hunters who pursue them prefer rifles with somewhat more power—the 7mm or .300 Magnum. In addition to their size, these animals are not infrequently taken at long ranges—sometimes 400 yards and more—and flat trajectory is needed, along with considerable bullet energy.

Asia is also home to a wide variety of plains and forest game. These range from the Iranian gazelle through the *moral*, or Persian, stag and the *hangul* of northern India (both large, elklike deer), through a variety of lesser deer, boar, and bear. The *guar*, a wild ox that ranges the high rain forests from India to Indochina, is a stupendous game animal seldom hunted because of its difficult environment. To hunt this giant (a big bull weighs well over a ton), one should use at least a .458 Winchester Magnum.

The most glamorous of all Asian hunting—the tiger hunt—is a thing of the past. The great estates of the maharajahs that supported the beasts were dissolved at the end of British rule, and since then human encroachment on wild land has drastically reduced the numbers of all of India's large predators. Today, tiger hunting is forbidden in India, and the tiger is an endangered species.

It is possible to be optimistic about future Asian hunting opportunities. The Soviet Union is allowing American sportsmen to pursue its game in increasing numbers, and a hunter who is able to afford the very substantial cost is able to take such species as boar, bear, *tur* (a large wild goat), and upland game on extremely well-run (if closely supervised) hunts.

Moreover, improved relations with China have resulted in the opening of that land to sport hunting, and those who are privileged to travel there have taken some desirable trophies.

astigmatic aberration   A refractive defect of a lens or lens system that prevents it from being sharply focused. To detect astigmatism, view a set of parallel lines placed vertically, and then place the set horizontally or at angles. Through an optical instrument characterized by astigmatism, the lines may be sharply defined at one angle, but it may be impossible to get sharp focus when they are rotated to another. (See ABERRATION.)

astigmatism   Astigmatism is an aberration of the eyeball wherein there is no exact focus because of irregularity in the curvature of the refracting surfaces (the cornea or lens) of the eye. There are many causes, ranging from genetic ones to scars from accidents or surgery to the strain of 20th-century living. Often astigmatism is found in conjunction with other vision impairments, such as near- or farsightedness.

Because of the nature of the shooting sports, eyesight must be as nearly perfect as possible for success. Regardless of how minor, astigmatism must be corrected. Cylindrical eyeglasses or hard contact lenses will clear the image. Soft contact lenses have been developed that are effective in treating astigmatism, as well.

Astra handguns   See SPANISH GUNMAKERS.

autoloading action   Also termed a semiautomatic or self-loading action; erroneously called an automatic action or auto action. It is the method of operation of a repeating firearm (rifle, shotgun, pistol) in which the arm is loaded and then cocked manually by the shooter for the first shot. Thereafter, the firearm automatically loads a new cartridge from the magazine into the firing chamber and cocks itself for the next shot. The trigger must be pulled for each shot. Strictly speaking, only a machine gun or submachine gun is "automatic" since it continues to fire as long as the trigger remains depressed until the magazine is empty. When a clear distinction is desired, the terms semiautomatic and full automatic are often used, though some military arms can fire in either mode by means of a selector mechanism operated by the shooter.

Basically there are two kinds of autoloading actions—recoil operated and gas operated. In a recoil-operated firearm, the energy of recoil is used to cycle the action. In a gas-operated firearm, expanding powder gas is tapped from the barrel through a small port and is used to operate the action, often by means of a piston attached to an operating rod. Except for .22 autoloaders, self-loading pistols and some military arms, all modern autoloaders operate by means of the more effective gas-activated method.

Recoil-operated arms can be divided into three types:

The simple blowback action is used mostly for pistols; in these low-powered arms, it is enough to have the breechblock or breechbolt recoil away from the fixed barrel to open the action and extract the spent cartridge before reloading a fresh one from the magazine. With more powerful arms where the powder gas pressures are higher, this method is dangerous, and to overcome the problem the barrel and the breechblock or breechbolt are locked together and recoil together for some distance before they separate—the fixed-bolt action. This allows gas pressure to drop to safe levels before the breech is unsealed.

The third type is the hesitation, or delayed blowback action. The breechblock and barrel are not locked together mechanically, but their separation is delayed after a shot. A rough or fluted firing chamber wall, for instance, grips the expanded cartridge case long enough to allow gas pressure to drop to safe levels. The case contracts when gas pressure falls, and the breechblock then moves to the rear, operating the action.

Recently, double-action semiautomatic pistols have become popular. With these arms, the shooter loads magazine and chamber, but the action is not cocked. To fire the first shot, the shooter merely pulls the trigger through a long travel. This cocks the action, drops the hammer or striker, and fires the cartridge in the chamber. Thereafter the arm functions in normal semiautomatic fashion with a much shorter trigger pull. A double-action pistol permits the shooter to get off a quick first shot without first loading the chamber and cocking the action, which requires the use of two hands with most autoloaders.

These descriptions may seem simple, but there are many variations and subtypes. For instance, the English Fosbery *revolver* is recoil operated. The cylinder is loaded and the hammer cocked for the first shot. Thereafter, recoil energy is used to recock the hammer and rotate the cylinder for the next shot. The whole top of the revolver, including cylinder and barrel, is a recoil-operated slide. The most common type of recoil operated pistol is the simple blow-back, but there is also a *blow-forward* Mannlicher action in which the barrel recoils or bounces forward from a standing breech. No design problem has produced as many variations as the desire for rapid loading from the magazine. (See GAS OPERATION; LONG RECOIL PRINCIPLE; SHORT RECOIL SHOTGUN.)

Auto Mag In late January 1970, the first public announcement of the new stainless steel Auto Mag pistol was made. Conceived by Harry W. Sanford, then owner of the Pasadena (California) Gun Shop, the original pistol was to have been a double-action, stainless steel hunting handgun chambered in a choice of special .30, 9mm, or .44-caliber cartridges. During development the two smaller calibers were dropped, and work continued on the .44, which would eventually turn out to be the successor to the "world's most powerful pistol"—the Gabbitt–Fairfax "Mars" of some seven decades before.

The Auto Mag Corporation of Pasadena, formed to manufacture the pistol, failed because of lack of operating capital after only a few pistols were produced. A new firm—T.D.E. Corporation—located in North Hollywood, built pistols in .357 AMP and the original .44 AMP chamberings. Later, when the firm was based in El Monte, additional pistols were produced, including a third caliber—the .41 JMP, designed by Lee Jurras, who took over exclusive distribution rights to the Auto Mag in 1974.

The Auto Mag, as finally produced, was a locked-breech, rotary bolt, short recoil, single-action autoloading design with an outside hammer and twin recoil springs, or mainsprings, located on each side of the frame. The finish was a brush (matte) gray, and the standard barrel length was 6½ inches. Standing 6½ inches high and measuring 11⅝ inches in overall length with the standard barrel length, the .44 Auto Mag weighed 60 ounces empty. The detachable box magazine had a capacity of seven rounds. The rear sight on the Auto Mag was adjustable, and additional barrel lengths, including 8½ and 10 inches, became available, making the pistol popular with silhouette handgun shooters and hunters, for whom its great power is a decided asset.

When the pistol was originally manufactured, all cartridges had to be hand produced from shortened and reamed .308 Winchester brass, although one lot of .44 AMP cartridges was manufactured in Mexico by a subsidiary of Remington. In 1978, Norma introduced both loaded .44 AMP ammunition and unprimed brass to the market. None of the major ammunition manufacturers has produced brass or loaded AMP ammunition for the Auto Mag.

The size, weight, and production costs of the Auto Mag, plus the difficulty in obtaining ammunition, prevented the gun from achieving widespread popularity.

Although the original Auto Mag is not presently produced, it may have inspired the creation of a gun very similar in concept: the Wildey automatic, a gas operated pistol of large size and power that is designed specifically for silhouette shooting and hunting. In addition, Harry Sanford and Larry Grossman, who offered the first Auto Mag, currently manage Irwindale Arms (Irwindale, California). Irwindale Arms manufactures the Auto Mag II, chambered for the .22 WMR round, and the Auto Mag III, chambered for the .30 Carbine. (See SILHOUETTE SHOOTING [*SILUETAS METALICAS*].)

automatic pistol A pistol having one chamber, integral with the barrel, fed with cartridges from a magazine, and so designed that the recoil or gas pressure from firing the cartridge in the chamber automatically accomplishes the sequence of extraction and ejection of the fired case, stripping a fresh cartridge from the magazine and feeding it into the chamber, and cocking the mechanism in preparation for the next shot.

Two kinds of semiautomatic pistol designs are currently employed: single-action designs, most no-

The most successful automatic pistol design of all time is the Colt Model 1911, which was adopted by the U.S. Army in that year and remains in service to this day. Designed to provide great power and reliability, it has proven capable of high accuracy as well and is made in target versions such as this Gold Cup National Match Model.

tably the Colt Model 1911 Government, and the double-action designs associated with the Walther P-38 and Smith & Wesson Model 39. Either design requires the shooter to manually cycle the slide to chamber the first round and cock the hammer. Subsequent operation is semiautomatic in nature. To maintain a single action ready for immediate use, the user must leave the hammer in the cocked position with the safety in the desired position.

Double-action semiautomatics are designed so the user can safely drop the hammer after chambering the first round, and subsequently fire the first round with the "long" trigger pull that cocks the hammer again before firing the first shot. As with the single-action semiautomatic, all subsequent operation is semiautomatic.

In a strict sense, the adjective "automatic" is a misnomer, since the word is also used in contradistinction to "semiautomatic" or "autoloading." "Automatic" implies that an arm continues to fire repeatedly for as long as the trigger is depressed, until the ammunition supply is exhausted, whereas "semiautomatic" or "autoloading" implies that the arm fires only once for each separate trigger pull, so that the "automatic" aspect of its operation involves reloading. In that strict sense, practically all "automatic" pistols are actually semiautomatic, though long usage has established that "automatic pistols" may include both semiautomatic and full-automatic types. Full-automatic pistols are uncommon, being restricted to a few types employed as military weap-

ons, mostly before the use of modern submachine guns. Automatic pistols, as the term is commonly applied, came into use during the late 19th century, about 50 years after the invention of the revolver. (See AUTOLOADING ACTION.)

automatic revolver A revolver that fires in the manner of an automatic pistol. In an automatic revolver, the rotation of the cylinder and the cocking of the hammer are accomplished by recoil produced upon firing the cartridge, rather than manually by manipulation of the trigger or hammer as in a more typical revolver. Automatic revolvers' mechanisms are relatively complicated, with many of the disadvantages of both revolvers and automatic pistols, and have never achieved great popularity. The only fairly common example is the Webley-Fosbery automatic revolver, made in England. (See AUTOMATIC PISTOL; DOUBLE-ACTION REVOLVER; SINGLE ACTION.)

automatic safety The automatic safety is a mechanical toggle often incorporated into .22 rifles and other firearms used by young shooters. It ensures that the safety is engaged each time the piece is cocked. The feature is most commonly found on bolt actions and single shots, but also on some models of double-barrel shotguns.

automatic selective ejector In some double- and single-barrel shotguns the ejector is linked to the firing pin. When the gun is opened, if the firing pin remains cocked—indicating that the chambered round has not been fired—the ejector rod will not activate the ejector. Thus the ejector is automatic and selective, selecting only fired cases for ejection. (See DOUBLE-BARREL SHOTGUN; EXTRACTOR; OVER/UNDER GUN; SIDE-BY-SIDE GUN.)

Auto-Rim (AR) During World War I, both Colt and Smith & Wesson produced the Model 1917 double-action service revolver, chambered for the .45 ACP cartridge. Because this cartridge was rimless (it was originally designed for the Model 1911 Colt Automatic Pistol), it could not conveniently be used in a revolver cylinder unless first inserted in a special half-moon clip that was loaded with three cartridges. Without the half-moon clips, extraction was difficult.

After the war, because of the large number of Model 1917 revolvers in use, the Peters Cartridge Company made a special version of the .45 ACP— the Auto-Rim—which was equipped with a rim, eliminating the need for the half-moon clip. Some of these cartridges saw use in World War II. (See ACP.)

auxiliary cartridge A dummy cartridge case that fits the chamber of a rifle or handgun and that holds a rimfire or centerfire cartridge of smaller size and less power than the standard cartridge while using bullets of the same diameter as the original cartridge. Auxiliary cartridges are used for practice shooting to avoid needless noise, recoil, and expense. (See ADAPTER.)

average pressure The average pressure in pounds per square inch or copper units of pressure generated in the chamber by any cartridge when it is fired. Also, the average of the highest and lowest pressures for a given number of cartridges fired in testing. (See CHAMBER PRESSURE; C.U.P. [COPPER UNITS OF PRESSURE]; PRESSURE ESTIMATION; PSI [POUNDS PER SQUARE INCH].)

axis of bore An imaginary line that follows the exact longitudinal center of the bore in a rifle or handgun barrel and around which the bullet revolves as it travels through the bore.

axis of lens A straight line through the geometrical center of the lens and perpendicular to the two faces at the points of intersection.

axis pin The axis of an object is the imaginary line about which that object turns. In the case of firearms, such an object might be a trigger or a hammer, and the pin used for a pivot would be called an axis pin.

Aydt action A kind of single-shot rifle action, of German origin, in which the breechblock is pivoted in the receiver and is swung in an arc by movement of a finger lever at the bottom of the trigger guard. It was made chiefly by Haenel, of Suhl, Germany from 1870 to 1935, and was used for low-pressure target cartridges such as the 8.15 × 46R, which resembles the American .32/40 cartridge. The Aydt action is simple and reliable, features a fast lock time, and was highly regarded among German Schuetzen riflemen. Unlike many high-quality single-shot actions, it is not particularly strong and is therefore suited only to cartridges developing low or moderate chamber pressure. (See CHAMBER PRESSURE; LOCK TIME; SCHUETZEN RIFLE.)

azimuth In artillery fire, the measure of an angle of horizontal distance from a fixed position, usually true north, to the aiming point. The angles are measured with a graduated dial called an azimuth circle. In small arms shooting, azimuths are employed to measure the lateral deviation of a bullet from the line of sight.

back-action sidelock A sidelock mechanism in which the main spring, generally a V-spring, rests behind the tumbler and action body and has its apex pointed backward. It is the opposite of the bar action, in which the V-spring is situated along the action bar, its apex pointed forward.

backing See TARGET BACKING.

backlash The slight reverse movement of the reticle in a telescopic sight after the adjustment screw has been moved the desired amount. Also, the excessive movement of the trigger after the sear has been released. (See ADJUSTABLE TRIGGER; RETICLE.)

back lock See BACK-ACTION SIDELOCK.

backsight The word used in the British Commonwealth for the rear sight of a gun. It is an uncommon usage in the United States.

backstop See TARGET BACKSTOP.

backstrap The part of the frame of a handgun that forms the rear of the grip and onto which the stocks are affixed.

Bakelite Trademark for a group of thermosetting plastics invented by Leo H. Baekeland. Bakelite is widely used in the manufacture of pistol grips and shoulder arm buttplates.

Baker shotguns Produced in Batavia, New York, from 1903 to 1933 by the Baker Gun Co., this series of double-barrel shotguns was offered in a wide range of grades and prices. A sidelock design, the Bakers ranged from the Batavia Special model, the least expensive, through eight higher grades. These were, in ascending order: Leader, Black Beauty Special, Batavia Ejector, Grade S, Grade R, Paragon, Expert, and Deluxe. A single-barrel trap gun was also produced.

Bakers were made with both Damascus and fluid steel barrels, and in 12, 16, or 20 gauge. In the higher grades, a wide variety of options was available, including extra fancy wood, single trigger, special checkering and engraving patterns, and automatic ejectors.

Fluid-steel-barrel Bakers are collectors' items to-day; when in excellent condition the highest grades sell for more than $3,000. (See DAMASCUS BARREL; FLUID STEEL BARREL; SIDELOCK.)

balance A device or apparatus, such as a powder scale, designed to measure the weight of an object or substance. Typical versions consist of a beam or lever supported by a fulcrum at the midpoint to form two arms of equal length. Such models have a pan or tray suspended from each arm, one to hold an object of known weight and the other to hold the material to be weighed. The weight of this latter material would be registered by the deflection of a pointer fastened to the beam and swinging before a scale.

Most modern powder and bullet scales consist of a beam or lever supported by a fulcrum but with unequal arms. The material to be weighed is suspended from the shorter arm, while a counterpoise is moved along the graduated scale that forms the other arm to produce equilibrium and indicate the material's weight.

Also, balance is stability produced by even distribution of weight on each side of a vertical axis, for example, the physical balance or distribution of weight in a firearm. Good balance is especially important in a hunting gun.

balk The failure of a side-by-side or over/under shotgun to fire when the trigger is pulled is called a balk. The most common form of balking occurs when single-trigger mechanisms fail to cock the trigger for the second shot. (See MALFUNCTIONS, DOUBLE-BARREL SHOTGUNS.)

ball A single bullet. The word has been carried over from times when projectiles were spherical.

Also, ammunition loaded with full-metal-jacketed bullets, usually military.

Also, the trade name applied by Winchester-Western to spherical-grained powder manufactured by that company. The word is sometimes used to describe any gunpowder with spherical grains or grains shaped like flattened spheres.

Ballard action A single-shot action patented by C. H. Ballard in 1861 and manufactured by various companies until 1891. It is distinctive for a breechblock that is split longitudinally along the centerline, fitting together like the halves of a clamshell, and housing most of the mechanism inside. The Ballard's breechblock pivots at the rear; it is actuated by a finger lever underneath the trigger.

The Ballard rifle was well thought of as a target rifle among Schuetzen marksmen in the United States and was chambered for a great variety of black-powder cartridges. Its popularity was attributable, at least in part, to the excellent quality of Ballard barrels, and to its tight breeching, light hammer, and short hammer fall, but the action was also well suited to black-powder target cartridges. The action is not particularly strong and should not be rebarreled for high-pressure, smokeless powder cartridges. Many high-quality smallbore match rifles were custom built on Ballard actions during the 1930s and 1940s. Ballard rifles are now sought after by collectors. (See CHAMBER PRESSURE; SCHUETZEN RIFLE.)

ballistic coefficient   A relative value assigned to a bullet that represents the ability to overcome the retardation of velocity caused by air resistance. Given as a three-digit figure, the ballistic coefficient (BC) expresses a relationship among a bullet's weight, diameter, and shape, and provides a means of comparing the downrange performance of one bullet with that of another.

A pointed, or spitzer bullet is less affected by air resistance in flight than is one of roundnose design. Spitzer bullets will therefore have a higher ballistic coefficient than will semispitzer or roundnose bullets of the same caliber and weight. The heavier of two bullets with the same diameter will usually (but not always) have a higher ballistic coefficient. The shape of the bullet also must be considered. For example, a 160-grain Speer 7mm (.284) spitzer has a BC of .502, while a 175-grain Speer 7mm has a BC of .385.

Although ballistic coefficients are assigned to handgun bullets, they are much more important in regard to rifle bullets, since pistols are employed at close range where velocity retention is not a crucial factor. Ballistic coefficients for rifle bullets range from 100 to over 500. (See BULLET DRAG; BULLET VELOCITY; EXTERIOR BALLISTICS; RIFLE CARTRIDGES, TARGET.)

ballistic gelatin   See IMPACT BEHAVIOR BALLISTICS.

ballistic pendulum   See PENDULUM CHRONOGRAPH.

ballistics   Defined as the "science of a projectile in motion," ballistics is broken down into two separate entities: interior or internal ballistics, and exterior or external ballistics. Or, what happens before the bullet emerges from the barrel, and what takes place between the time it leaves the muzzle and the time it ends its flight.

Interior ballistics begins the instant the firearm's sear is released, freeing the hammer to contact the cartridge's primer. This interval is known as lock time. The second interval in the sequence is ignition time; it occurs when the striker hits the primer, detonating it. This in turn ignites the powder charge, which creates expanding gas and sufficient pressure to push the bullet from the cartridge case. The third and last stage of interior ballistics is barrel time, the interval from the time the bullet leaves the case neck until it emerges from the muzzle.

Many factors affect the movement and acceleration of the bullet between the time the hammer falls and the time the projectile exits the muzzle: the detonating speed of the various brands and kinds of primers affect the ignition of the powder charge; the position of the powder charge within the case also influences how it ignites if loading density is much less than 100 percent; the burning rate of the powder greatly affects the acceleration rate of the bullet as it moves up the bore, as does the velocity/pressure ratio, the variable of when the pressure reaches its peak, and the position of the bullet in the barrel when peak pressure is reached; the temperature of the powder at the time of firing also has great effect on velocity.

The configuration of the bullet and the alloy and/or hardness of its jacket and core also influence the pressure required to obtain the desired velocity. The influence of a bullet's configuration on pressure and velocity is related to the shape of its base, its diameter in relation to the diameter of the bore, and the length of its bearing surface. The thickness and hardness of the jacket material also affect pressure, as does the hardness of the core.

The chamber dimensions, length of throat and angle of leade, condition of the bore, its diameter, type of rifling and twist—all these affect internal ballistics. The foregoing are the major factors that are generally recognized as influencing interior ballistics; there are, in addition, many minor factors that are not thoroughly understood.

Exterior ballistics begins when the bullet exits the muzzle and continues until it comes to a halt. This may take place after the pull of gravity and the force of air resistance have ended its flight, or after the projectile has completed its penetration of the target, such as some game animal. Basically, anything that influences the bullet's flight after it leaves the barrel is a part of external ballistics. The major factors are: rate of twist of the rifling and its effect on bullet stabilization; bullet shape and its influence on retained velocity and energy; trajectory; wind deflection; and bullet performance after it reaches the target, particularly when the target is an animal.

Because of what a shotgun is intended to do and because the structure of a shotshell is so different from a rifle or handgun cartridge, shotgun ballistics must be considered separately.

Unlike rifle or pistol ammunition, there is little variation in velocity among shotgun cartridges, regardless of the weight of the shot charge they carry; moreover, the range at which a shotgun can be effectively used is limited. The single most important objective in shotgun shooting is to attain the even distribution of the shot charge within a circle, or pattern, at a given distance, and shotgun ballistics are directed to this end.

Interior ballistics are perhaps the most important determinant of the behavior of shot pellets because of the ballistic inferiority of the sphere to the conoid projectile. Factors influencing the behavior of a shot charge include the size and burning speed of the powder charge, the kind of wads used, the wad pressure, and the kind of crimp employed. When it enters the barrel, the charge is influenced by the length and steepness of the forcing cone and by the degree and kind of choke.

Once it emerges from the barrel, a shot pellet cannot duplicate the flight of a bullet. Unlike the bullet, it is self-stabilizing (that is, it will not tumble during flight because it does not need a directional force—spin—imparted by rifling), but its range, resistance to wind, and retention of velocity are all severely limited. (See EXTERIOR BALLISTICS; INTERIOR BALLISTICS; RIFLING.)

Ballistite A trademark for an early smokeless gunpowder made of nitrocellulose dissolved in nitroglycerin. It was invented in 1887 by Swedish chemist Alfred B. Nobel, the tamer of nitroglycerin. Ballistite was one of the first double-base gunpowders and was used extensively in mortar ammunition and in small arms cartridges. (See DOUBLE-BASE POWDER; SMOKELESS POWDER.)

balloonhead case A metallic cartridge case intermediate (1865–1875) in development between the folded-head and solid-head cases. Unlike the folded head, the balloonhead case utilized a solid rim and its base was slightly thicker than its predecessor's. However, the balloonhead did not have the additional strength of the thick web surrounding the primer, as did the later solid-head case.

ball powder See BALL.

bar-action sidelock Employed originally in percussion guns, this kind of lock is fitted to a bar extending forward from the breech end of the barrel. It permits an efficient stock shape at the grip and a superior linkage of the stirrup, mainspring, and hammer.

In a modern double-barrel shotgun a bar-action sidelock (commonly called a bar lock) is one in which a part of the mechanism extends to the front and is set into the side of the action bar.

American usage also defines a bar lock as a mechanism that locks the bolt of a pump-action shotgun in the forward position. (See ACTION BAR.)

barleycorn sight A front rifle sight that forms a fine edge at the top similar to an inverted V. This sight was designed for use with open rear sights on the theory that its pointed blade covered less of the aiming point on the target, thereby making possible a more accurate hold. (See METALLIC SIGHTS; SIGHT PICTURE.)

bar lock See BAR-ACTION SIDELOCK.

barrel, chopper lump See CHOPPER LUMP.

barrel, handgun The rifled tube through which a bullet passes, propelled by the expanding powder gases, thus acquiring its forward velocity and stabilizing spin. In single-shot and autoloading pistols, the barrel contains the cartridge chamber. In revolvers, the barrel is fixed in the frame ahead of the cylinder containing the chambers, in such position that the chamber to be fired is aligned with the barrel by cylinder rotation prior to firing. Handgun barrels are usually between 2 and 10 inches long.

Many autoloading pistols feature interchangeable barrels that can be replaced by the user without individual fitting. This is a particular advantage in military arms; weapons having unserviceable barrels can be easily and cheaply restored to serviceability by barrel replacement.

A few sporting pistols, the single-shot Thompson/Center Contender, for instance, feature a system of interchangeable barrels in a wide variety of calibers, all for attachment by the user to one common frame.

Revolver barrels are usually screwed into the frame and are replaceable only by a skilled gunsmith or the manufacturer, though the Dan Wesson Arms revolver features a system of interchangeable barrels of various lengths (in the same caliber) that can be installed by the user with simple tools provided by the company. (See BARREL MAKING.)

barrel, monobloc A kind of barrel construction—used chiefly for over/under and side-by-side shotguns—in which the barrels pass through and are joined at the breech by brazing to a block of steel that incorporates the lumps. The monobloc is a strong method of attachment, and less costly in manufacture than the chopper-lump-tube system favored in best grade English double-barrel guns.

The monobloc method permits the use of round tubes for the barrels, rather than steel blanks having integral projections from which the lumps are subsequently formed. The alternatives to monobloc or chopper-lump construction are various systems of joining the barrels by brazing them externally to the piece that incorporates the lumps, but these systems are considered inferior in strength to monobloc or chopper lump construction. (See CHOPPER LUMP; CHOPPER LUMP TUBE; DOUBLE-BARREL SHOTGUN.)

barrel, rifle One of the three main components of a rifled shoulder arm; the others are the stock and the action. A rifle barrel is a steel tube that is affixed to the action with an interior that is scored with spiral grooves to impart spin to the bullet. Rifle barrels vary in length from 16 to 26 inches (in common modern use) and have a wide range of weights and tapers, depending on the kind of rifle for which they are intended.

Rifle barrels are made of one of two types of steel: chrome-molybdenum or stainless alloy. The latter is easier to manufacture because its machining characteristics are somewhat better than chrome-moly. The latter is also used in benchrest and target rifles that are subject to repeated firing, and where barrel life is of paramount importance. Because of the problems inherent in bluing them (bluing is a rusting process, and stainless steel is resistant to rust), these barrels are made only on a custom basis.

Barrel manufacture begins with a steel tube that is drilled longitudinally by a deep-hole drilling machine to the land diameter of the bore. The rifling is then cut or cold-formed with a twist, or rate of spin, that is appropriate to the cartridge for which the barrel is intended. The chamber is cut at the rear, and the barrel is then turned to its final profile (some swaging processes perform this step at the same time the rifling is cold-formed) and stress-relieved by heating. Finally, it is threaded at the chamber end and screwed, clamped, or epoxy-glued to the receiver.

The final phase in the manufacturing operation is bluing, although a few custom rifles are made with chrome-plated barrels (and some with chrome-plated bores). On most big-game rifles, rear and front sights are then screwed or sweated to the barrel. On rifles of very heavy recoil, such as a .458 or .416, a band is sweated to the barrel ahead of the fore-end with a flat projection from its bottom through which a hole is drilled; this acts as a forward-sling-swivel stud.

Most barrels for modern sporting rifles are 22 inches long in standard calibers and 23½ or 24 inches long for magnums. Carbine barrels are from 16 to 20 inches long. Varmint or target rifles employ barrels of 26 inches. Barrel taper varies greatly, but a typical lightweight sporter barrel will measure .560-inch at the muzzle, while a bull barrel may span a full inch.

The number of rifling grooves can vary from as few as two (found in some World War I Springfield Model 1903 rifles) to as many as eight. Most barrels have four or six grooves.

Rifle barrels produced in the second half of this century have been of a far higher quality than previously attainable. Improved methods of mass production—notably, button rifling and swaging—have resulted in smoother, more uniform bores. This advance, combined with equally significant strides in the manufacture of bullets, has provided mass-produced rifles with an inherent degree of accuracy that was unreachable even with custom arms 20 years ago. (See BARREL, RIFLED; BLUING.)

barrel, rifled A tube through which a bullet is driven by the expanding powder gases and that has raised surfaces or ridges formed in a helix on its internal surface. The raised surfaces are called lands and the surfaces between them grooves. The total pattern of lands and grooves is called rifling, from the French *rifler*—to file or scrape—because the first rifling was undoubtedly cut with small filelike tools that were attached to a rod, passed through the bore on a helix, and fed outward with shims on successive cuts.

The rifling grips the outside of the bullet as it travels through the barrel, causing it to rotate on its axis and to maintain stable, point-forward flight, resulting in an accuracy of bullet flight unattainable with smoothbore barrels. The distance in which the helix of the rifling makes one turn is the pitch, or twist rate, and this must be adapted to the shape and length of the bullet to be fired and to its velocity. Round balls require the slowest twist, i.e., the longest pitch; long, pointed boattail bullets the fastest; and low velocities a faster twist than high velocities.

The date of origin and the inventor of rifling are unknown. Probably, like many other important inventions, it was developed by several people in different countries at about the same time. There are a number of references in arms literature attributing the invention of rifling to Kaspar (or Gaspard) Kollner of Vienna in the 1490s or to August (or Augustus) Kotter of Nuremberg about 1520, though there are extant rifled arms that were made before the second decade of the 16th century. No documentary evidence in support of these claims is available. There is evidence to support this period and the area of Austria, Germany, Switzerland as the time and location of invention. An article in the March 1953, *American Rifleman* shows a photograph of a bronze barreled, snap-matchlock "hand-gun" with faint traces of rifling in the muzzle. The stock bears a single-headed eagle design, known to have been used by Emperor Maximilian I between 1493 and 1508. Celebrated for his fondness for the chase, Maximilian would have had the very latest in sporting firearms. There are several rifled-barrel firearms in museums in Copenhagen and Zurich that can be dated to the early 1500s.

Early rifle barrels were made by forge-welding strips of iron around a mandrel, either spirally or with one longitudinal weld (the technology for deep hole drilling was about 300 years in the future). The resulting rough hole was rough bored to a cylinder, then smooth bored with a square reamer, backed by wood packing and shims to adjust it to size. Rifling was cut with a single cutter having several teeth, fixed in a supporting head in the end of a rod passing through the bore. During passage, the rod was made to revolve by a guide, which had the helix of the rifling cut into it, and forced to rotate by a fixed pin or shoe in the helix as the assembly was moved longitudinally. The guide, rod, and cutter were indexed to produce the desired number of lands and grooves. Because of the lack of uniformity of welded barrels, the cut rifling was rather rough and barrels were finished in most cases by casting a lead lap on the end of a rod inside the barrel. This was charged with abrasive and oil and pushed back and forth in the barrel to provide uniform size and smoothness. The lap was upset, or recast, as it wore, and several castings of the lap were sometimes needed to finish one barrel. It is interesting that today, almost 500 years after the invention of rifling, the very best rifle barrels are still finished by a similar lapping operation.

Many forms of rifling have been tried. The most common is that formed by bore and grooves that are basically cylindrical, with the sides of the lands radial or at an angle resulting in the land being narrower at the minor diameter. Star shapes (seen in cross section), polygons, oval, ratchet, and almost every possible groove shape have been tried. A rifle in the Tower Arms Museum in London has a bore shaped like a heart, with the outside of the barrel also heart shaped and formed on the helix of the rifling! Made as a presentation piece, it has probably never been fired. Numbers of lands and grooves have been tried from as low as two to as high as 32. Experiment indicates that the number or shape of the lands and grooves has little to do with accuracy so long as the cross-sectional area of the lands is

sufficient to grip the bullet without having excessive clearance around the bullet, and so long as the bullet is not unbalanced by being forced through too small a bore.

Land and groove shapes and dimensions do have an appreciable effect on barrel life, however, and the dimensions and weight of a rifle barrel have a significant effect on accuracy. The effect is attributable to the vibrations set up in the barrel by the fall of the firing pin, the explosion of the primer, the burning of the powder, and the process of engraving the rifling into the bullet—all of which cause the muzzle end of the barrel, at the time of bullet exit, to assume slightly different positions and angles relative to the line of sight.

A hunting rifle, which must be carried for extended periods, will have a rather light barrel usually about 22 to 24 inches long with a muzzle diameter of just over ½ inch, to have an acceptable weight and balance. Such a rifle will deliver a lower standard of accuracy than an unrestricted class benchrest rifle, which may have a barrel 1½ inches in diameter. The larger diameter barrel is stiffer and less affected by vibrations. Where a weight limitation is in effect on rifles in hunter or varmint class benchrest shooting, optimum accuracy is attained by using barrels as short as 18 or 20 inches and utilizing a barrel diameter as large as possible that still meets the weight restriction.

In modern manufacture, the single cutter indexing system of rifling, which started out as a hand powered operation and graduated, over the centuries, into an automatic, power driven one using a single toothed cutter, has been superseded by faster methods of manufacture except in a very few small gun shops. The next great advance in rifling methods was broaching, in which a long cutter with many rows of teeth, set in a helical pattern matching the pitch of the rifling, with each succeeding row just a little larger in diameter than the preceding, was pushed or pulled through the bore of the barrel, controlled by a helical guide, to produce the complete rifling in one operation. About the time of World War II, two other methods were developed, and these are the methods used in quantity production today. One method is called "button rifling." In it the barrel blank is drilled and reamed slightly smaller than its finished internal dimensions. Then a tungsten carbide tool, of a length perhaps two or three times its diameter and having the rifling formed on it in reverse, is pushed or pulled through the undersized bore. The tough, heat-treated barrel steel, having a tensile strength of 120,000 pounds per square inch or more, is forced to assume the shape of the button, taking a permanent set and producing the rifling in one pass. Some manufacturers guide the button to produce the required helix or pitch of rifling; others depend on the carbide button to guide itself from the helix formed into it. Since the steel of the barrel has elasticity, the finished bore will be smaller than the button passed through it, and allowance for the spring-back must be made in designing the button.

In the rotary swaging method, the barrel blank is shorter in length than it will be when finished, larger in outside diameter, and it is drilled and reamed to a larger diameter than the finished bore. This blank is placed in a rotary swaging machine equipped with radially reciprocating forming dies to reduce the outside diameter of the barrel by striking hundreds of blows of the dies per minute. A carbide mandrel having the reverse shape of the rifling is positioned inside the barrel blank, axially located and held in place at the location of the forming dies on the outside. As the dies are reciprocated, producing total forces of as much as 500 tons, the barrel blank is fed longitudinally, the outside diameter is reduced, the inside diameter is swaged to the shape and size of the mandrel, and the blank increases in length. By incorporating a chamber forming section on the mandrel and by relative movements of blank, mandrel, and dies, barrels have been produced that are completely finished inside—complete with chamber, throat, and rifling. In some manufacturing plants, this method of rifling is done with the barrel blank at room temperature; it is called cold formed swaging. In others, the blank is heated to 700–800 degrees Fahrenheit for the swaging or forging operation—called warm swaging. This temperature is below that at which a scalelike crust will form on the steel, but high enough so that the tensile strength of the blank is lowered, making it easier to forge. The steel recovers its full strength when it returns to room temperature, as it has not been heated above the critical point at which it will soften permanently. By controlling die movement, it is possible to produce taper or a contour on the outside of the barrel.

Many advertising claims have been made for the "advantages" of button rifled and cold formed or warm swaged barrels. (These last two are also sometimes referred to as "hammered" barrels.) The fact is that these processes are used largely because of economics. All three methods produce good barrels, but regardless, the very best barrels are produced by final lapping of the rifling to size and finish with a lead lap cast or formed in the barrel. Barrels of equal quality can be made by the older methods of cutting the rifling, then finishing with a lap. (See BARREL LIFE; BARREL MAKING; BUTTON RIFLING.)

barrel, setting back of the   When the chamber, throat, or thread of a rifle barrel is worn or damaged, the barrel may be shortened at the breech end, rethreaded, rechambered, and set back into the action, thereby restoring accuracy and/or the firearm's ability to operate. This is a comparatively simple and inexpensive operation that can be performed by any competent gunsmith.

barrel, shotgun   The barrel of a shotgun is possibly the most important single feature of this kind of firearm, and in most cases the gun's most delicate component. Modern shotgun barrels are of one-piece seamless steel construction. By contrast, barrels used in the black-powder era were built of strips of flat metal or wire, formed around a mandrel, and then somewhat crudely welded together by forging after the metal strips were heated enough to be ductile. These so-called Damascus barrels, made well into the 20th century, are not strong enough for the sharply higher pressures that are normal with modern smokeless powder ammunition.

Because of their relatively thin walled construction (required to keep weight within practical limits), shotgun barrels are relatively fragile. They can be easily bent or dented and are highly vulnerable to bursting when fired with almost any degree of obstruction in the bore. Various forms of inner barrel finishing, including fine polishing or plating, have been attempted with the goal of producing more consistent shot patterns. nsteel barrel materials have been used by some gunmakers, including composite fiberglass/steel-lined tubes, but high quality steel remains the most desirable shotgun barrel material.

The average shotgun barrel in America is 28 inches long. Upland and skeet guns typically have 26-inch barrels to promote faster handling; guns for waterfowl or trap most often have 30- or 32-inch barrels. Longer barrels offer the advantage of a more precise sighting plane, but there is no significant difference in velocities obtained with any of the standard barrels so long as factory loads are used.

In shotguns with more than one barrel, the tubes are typically joined by some form of soldering or brazing, although some high-quality double guns use mechanical interlocks to mate barrels. Double guns are often furnished optionally with more than one set of barrels for different kinds of shooting. This is also possible with many of today's single-barreled repeating shotguns, although in some cases special factory fitting is necessary to assure that a spare barrel will be properly headspaced.

Smoothbores were used for many generations before the advent of choking (the constriction of the muzzle to reduce and control the dispersal of the shot charge, thus making tighter patterns possible at longer ranges). A few shotguns—the British Paradox is an example—have been made with short segments of rifling near the muzzle in an attempt to make the gun suitable for use with either a typical shot charge or a single ball projectile on animals larger than birds and small game. Other barrel modifications include installation of a solid or skeletonized (so-called ventilated) rib to improve the shooter's gun-pointing or the installation of interchangeable choke tubes. (See ADJUSTABLE CHOKE; BARREL MAKING; CHOKE; DOUBLE-BARREL SHOTGUN; OVER/UNDER GUN; RIB; SIDE-BY-SIDE GUN.)

barrel adapter A tube that is inserted into the barrel of a rifle, shotgun, or pistol, and that is chambered for subcaliber ammunition. These are also often called barrel inserts. Recoil is, of course, less than with the standard cartridge for which the gun is chambered, which makes the adapted barrel ideal for practice shooting. (See ADAPTER.)

barrel band A metal band that fits around the barrel of a rifle and holds some other part of the gun in place. Front or rear sights are examples, some models' forearms are tied to the barrel by bands, as are tubular magazines of some rifles. A sling swivel is frequently attached to a barrel band.

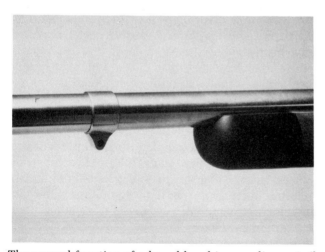

The normal function of a barrel band is as a sling swivel on heavy recoiling rifles. It can also pass down through the fore-end and act as an additional anchor for the barrel.

barrel blank A piece of barrel steel of the correct diameter for the class or weight of a finished rifle. It has been bored, reamed, and rifled and is usually 28 inches in length. These blanks are usually furnished in one of two forms: straight blanks that are the same full diameter for the entire length, and ones pre-turned to approximately the contour the finished barrel will have. These barrel blanks are not threaded for the action to be used, nor are they chambered. They are produced by barrelmakers especially for the gunsmithing trade.

barrel channel A groove in the forearm in which the barrel of a firearm lies. The depth of the barrel channel should be one-half the barrel diameter.

barrel erosion The wearing away of the bore, especially the rifling lands, of a rifled barrel. It may occur at any point in the bore or over its entire length, but is normally more evident in the throat area, where it starts and continues to work forward. Such erosion may have a number of causes, but the two most prominent are the passage of hot gunpowder gas and the friction generated by the bullet traveling through the bore at high velocity.

The combination of great friction and high temperature at the same time causes the barrel steel to be worn and burned away simultaneously. Once this process starts, the area becomes rough and the eroding action is accentuated. (It follows that corrosion of the bore will then start and hasten the erosion process.)

Barrel erosion, particularly in the throat area of a rifle, frequently comes about from rapid and repeated firing without allowing the barrel to cool; the surface of the bore actually reaches its melting point in these circumstances. (See BARREL, RIFLED; BARREL LIFE; THROAT.)

barrel extension A piece of steel extending backward from the breech end of a shotgun barrel to assist in bolting the gun, as in a double-barrel arm, or to establish alignment with the receiver, as in a repeater.

The blank is the first step in the manufacture of a barrel. This one (intended for a rifle barrel) is, typically, a thick tube of steel drilled with a hole the diameter of the caliber intended.

barrel flats On side-by-side shotguns, the flat surfaces on the underside of the barrels at the breech end are called barrel flats. When the action is closed, they abut the action flats, or water table. Choke markings are often stamped on the barrel flats. (See CHOKE MARKING; SIDE-BY-SIDE GUN.)

barrel flip The vibration a rifle barrel undergoes at the instant of firing, occurring as a result of the shock wave of the powder burn and the rotational torque of the bullet's travel. Degree and direction of flip depends upon length and thickness of the barrel, rigidity of the barreled action, and bedding tension. It is compensated for in sighting in. (See SIGHTING IN.)

barrel hanger See FORE-END HANGER.

barrel insert See BARREL ADAPTER.

barrel length—effect on accuracy The effect that a barrel's length has on the accuracy of a firearm depends largely on whether that arm, rifle or handgun, is used with iron sights or optical sights. If iron sights are used, a longer barrel leads to greater accuracy, not because of anything inherent in the barrel but because the longer barrel creates a greater distance between the front and rear sight (the sight radius), which lessens the effect of misalignment of the sights when the gun is aimed. Thus, a revolver with a 6-inch barrel is considerably more accurate than one with a 2-inch barrel because of the increased sight radius (and, in this instance, because the added weight of the longer barrel permits steadier holding).

In rifles that employ telescopic sights, where the sight radius is not a factor, the greatest degree of accuracy can be obtained with a relatively short barrel. When a rifle is fired, the force of the expanding powder gas and the blow of the firing pin cause the barrel to vibrate. The less vibration, the greater the shot-to-shot consistency of the gun, and the shorter the barrel, the more rigid it is, hence, less vibration. Benchrest rifles frequently use barrels of 20 inches to obtain greater accuracy, while sporting rifles have barrels of 2 to 6 inches longer.

Unlike rifles and handguns, where barrel length can be a determining factor in a gun's accuracy, barrel length has no effect on the accuracy of a shotgun. A shotgun barrel is required to deliver uniformly dispersed patterns and to deliver them to a proper point of impact, the latter being a function of stock fit rather than barrel length. (See SHOTGUN BALLISTICS; SIGHT PICTURE; SIGHT RADIUS.)

barrel length—effect on velocity The distance traveled within the barrel has an effect on the muzzle velocity of all projectiles and shot charges fired from rifle, pistol, or shotgun. However, many elements of interior ballistics are involved that influence the amount of velocity loss or gain even within a given barrel length.

Most sources fail to agree (because of the many variables involved) on the loss in feet per second (fps) per inch from a barrel length of 26 inches on a test rifle to the shorter barrels found on sporting rifles. The loss per inch of barrel length has been listed as being anywhere from 25 fps to as much as 50 fps. The fact is that the powder capacity of the cartridge case, the burning rate of the powder used, the diameter of the bore, and the weight of the bullet in relation to its diameter (roughly sectional density), all influence the loss or gain in fps in relation to the distance it travels within the bore.

As an example, a .22-caliber bullet from a standard .22 rimfire cartridge reaches its maximum velocity in 17 to 18 inches of barrel travel. A longer barrel adds nothing to the muzzle velocity. The smaller capacity centerfire rifle cases that use powders with fast to medium burning rates show very little velocity loss between the normal sporter length barrels of 24 and 22 inches. Large capacity and magnum cases that use the slowest burning powders lose much more velocity per inch of barrel reduction.

The effect of barrel length on velocity places rather severe limitations upon rifle and handgun design. Target rifles, which have no restrictions except for weight, can utilize longer barrels for maximum velocity. Rifle barrels for hunting arms, however, cannot be shorter than 22 inches (in most cases) or longer than 26. Too short, and too much velocity is lost; too long, and they become unwieldy.

In handguns, the same rule applies; for a revolver, the maximum length that can conveniently be carried is 6 to 7 inches; the minimum, for standard loads to be fully utilized, is 2 inches.

Shotgun barrel length is predicated largely on the firearm's handling qualities. Shotguns (with the exception of slug and riot guns, which must be compact) employ 26-inch barrels as the minimum length. Trap guns and waterfowl guns utilize barrels of 30 to 34 inches. (See INTERIOR BALLISTICS; SECTIONAL DENSITY.)

barrel life A term used to denote the number of rounds that can be fired through a rifle or pistol barrel before accuracy falls below a level acceptable for the purpose for which the firearm is used. As an example, a varmint rifle barrel will give big-game hunting accuracy for many hundreds or thousands of rounds after acceptable varmint shooting accuracy is gone. And a benchrest rifle will prove deadly for varmint shooting after its accuracy is no longer competitive at a bench match.

A rifle barrel usually starts to lose its initial, optimum accuracy because of erosion of the throat—that section of the bore just forward of the chamber. The erosion process is caused primarily by the intense heat generated by the expanding powder gas. Large capacity cases that burn large powder charges in small bores create more heat and speed up the erosion process. Higher pressures also produce greater heat and erosion. The burning of the rifling lands in the throat is more intense when large powder charges are used in small bores.

The greater heat caused by higher pressure is the main reason why the .220 Swift has lower barrel life expectancy than the .458 Winchester, even though the .458 burns much more powder.

Many barrels are burned out with comparatively little ammunition because the shooter fired too many rounds without letting the barrel cool.

Barrels made from stainless steel, which tends to resist extreme heat, have a much longer life expectancy than those made of other barrel steels.

barrel liner A barrel of small outside diameter used to replace the bore in a worn or damaged barrel. After reaming out the original bore to a size permitting proper wall thickness and strength, the liner is secured in place by soldering, with epoxy or mechanically, then chambered, headspaced and extractor slots cut. The liner may be the same caliber as the original or it may be larger or smaller. The process is also used to restore the bores on old guns of obsolete types without destroying the original barrel or the original appearance.

barrel loop See BARREL TENON.

barrel lug A metal projection on the underside of the barrel of many big bore rifles of .375 or larger caliber. Its purpose is to provide a second point of contact (in addition to the recoil lug) to prevent stock splitting from heavy recoil. For best accuracy, such lugs should be integral with the barrel. (See ABUTMENT; RECOIL LUG.)

barrel making The barrels of the earliest firearms, which are called hand cannons today, were simple forged and welded iron tubes. Some of these early 15th century barrels may have been cast of bronze. All were of short length, perhaps a foot or so. As the development of firearms proceeded, the increased accuracy of longer barrels became apparent and barrels were made by forge welding strips of iron around a mandrel, either spirally or with one longitudinal weld (the technology for deep-hole drilling was about 300 years in the future). The resulting rough hole was bored to a cylinder, then smooth-bored with a square reamer, backed by a wood packing and shims. Shotgun barrels continued to be made by this process into the late 1800s.

Early rifle barrels were rifled with a single cutter having several teeth, similar to a narrow file, with the teeth spaced at increasing intervals along the length of the cutter. (The name "rifling" comes from the French word *rifler*—to file or scrape.) The cutter was fixed in a slot in a supporting head attached to a rod and was fed outward on successive cuts with shims. During passage through the bore, the rod was made to revolve by a guide, having the helix of the rifling cut into it, and forced to rotate by a pin or a shoe in the helix as the assembly moved longitudinally. The required number of grooves was cut by indexing the guide and rod. Because of the lack of uniformity of the forged and welded metal, the cut rifling was rather rough, and barrels were finished in most cases by casting a lead lap on the end of a rod inside the barrel. This was charged with abrasive and oil and pushed back and forth inside the barrel to provide uniform size and a smooth surface. The lap was upset or recast as it wore and several castings were sometimes needed to finish one barrel. It is interesting that today, 500 years after the invention of rifling, the very best rifle barrels are still finished by a lapping process.

In modern methods of manufacture, the single cutter indexing system, which started out as a hand-powered operation and evolved, over the centuries, into an automatic, power driven operation using a single-toothed cutter, has been superseded by faster methods of manufacture, except in a very few small gun shops. In these shops, the barrels are prepared for rifling by deep-hole drilling and reaming. The deep-hole drill has a single cutting edge and is brazed to the end of a long piece of tubing. The drill is started into the blank through a centering bushing and, once into the cut, pilots itself on its outside diameter in the section of the hole that it has drilled. The tubing has a V-groove formed on one side for its full length and has a corresponding groove in the drill that forms one side of the cutting edge. A cutting fluid is pumped at high pressure through the tube and through a small hole in the body of the drill to lubricate and cool the cutting edge. Chips from the drilling operation are propelled from the cutting area, down the V-groove, and out of the drilled bore. The barrel blank is rotated at high speed while the drill is fed forward very slowly. Reaming is done at slower speeds on machines of similar construction and operation, using a reamer mounted

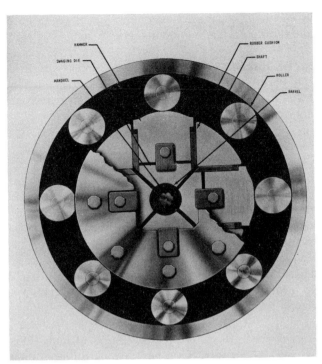

This schematic of a swaging head shows the hammers in closed position.

on a tube, and again using a flow of oil to lubricate, cool, and wash away chips.

The next great advance in rifling methods was broaching, in which a long cutter with many rows of teeth, set in a helical pattern to match the rifling, with each succeeding row just a little larger in diameter than the preceding, was pushed or pulled through the bore of the barrel, controlled by a helical guide, to produce the rifling in one pass of the broach. This method is still used to rifle short barrels for pistols and submachine guns.

About the time of World War II, two other methods were developed, and these are the methods most used in quantity production today. One method is called "button rifling." Here the blank is drilled and reamed slightly smaller than its finished internal dimensions. Then a tungsten carbide tool, of a length perhaps two or three times its diameter and having the rifling formed on it in reverse, is pushed or pulled through the undersize bore. The tough, heat-treated barrel steel, having a tensile strength of 120,000 or more pounds per square inch, is forced to assume the shape of the button, taking a permanent set and producing the rifling in one pass. Some manufacturers guide the button to produce the required helix, or pitch of rifling, some depend on the carbide button to guide itself from the helix formed into it. Since the steel of the barrel has elasticity, the finished bore will be smaller than the button passed through it, and allowance for the springback must be made in designing the button.

In the other of today's rifling methods, the barrel blank is shorter in length than it will be when finished, larger in outside diameter, and it is drilled and reamed to a larger diameter than the finished bore. This blank is placed in a rotary swaging machine equipped with radially reciprocating forming dies to reduce the outside diameter of the barrel by striking hundreds of blows per minute. A carbide mandrel having the reverse shape of the rifling is positioned inside the barrel blank, axially located and held in place at the location of the forming dies on the outside. As the dies reciprocate, producing total forces of as much as 500 tons, the barrel blank is fed longitudinally while the dies rotate around it, the outside diameter is reduced, the inside diameter is swaged to the size and shape of the mandrel and the blank increases in length. By incorporating a chamber forming section on the mandrel and by relative movements of blank, mandrel and dies, barrels have been produced completely finished inside—that is, complete with chamber, throat and rifling. In some plants, this operation is done at room temperature and is called "cold forming." In others, the blank is heated to 700–800 degrees Fahrenheit for the swaging operation. This temperature is below that at which the steel will scale, or form oxide on the exposed surfaces, but it is high enough so that the tensile strength of the steel is lowered, making it easier to swage. The steel recovers its full strength when it returns to room temperature, as it hasn't been heated above the critical point at which it will soften permanently. By controlling die movement, it is possible to produce a taper or contour on the outside of the barrel.

Many shotgun barrels are produced today by the swaging process. In such thin-walled tubes, it is possible to produce the outside dimensions and the bore dimensions, including choke, to an accuracy where only a minimum of finishing to remove tool marks is needed. The chambers and forcing cones may also be swaged during the process. Some manufacturers find it easier to finish the bore of the shotgun barrel cylindrically, and then produce the choke by swaging the outside of the barrel on a taper at the muzzle, using a simple rotary swaging machine. The availability of high-quality seamless drawn steel tubing having a wall thickness very near the required finish dimensions has prompted other manufacturers to use it for shotgun barrels, reaming and honing the inside and turning or grinding the outside to finished contour.

barrel pin A pin that attaches a barrel to its stock in Pennsylvania and Plains rifles and similar arms of the 1750–1860 period.

Barrel pins are made of brass, German silver, or

iron. They fit into the escutcheon. (See ESCUTCHEON; PLAINS RIFLE; PENNSYLVANIA RIFLE.)

barrel porting A modification for shotguns, rifles and handguns, porting involves the cutting of holes through the upper surface of the barrel to permit the upward escape of powder gases. Porting dampens muzzle jump, thus holding the gun level during recoil. The upward surge of powder gases push down on the barrel to stabilize it. This practice was first popularized by the Mag-Na-Port Company, the shotgun division of which is known as Pro-Port.

barrel relining The process of renewing the life of a worn or damaged barrel by boring it out and installing a liner. It is generally used on old or obsolete rifles and pistols that have value as antiques and whose owners wish to continue shooting them without destroying the original barrel. (See BARREL LINER.)

barrel shank The portion of a gun barrel that fits inside the frame of a handgun or receiver of a shoulder arm and secures it in place. Generally, the shank is threaded and positioned against the receiver, but it may be pressed in place, clamped, or held by a transverse screw or pin.

barrel striking In early methods of barrel manufacture, prior to the development of machines capable of accurate contour turning or grinding, the barrel was rough forged to shape, the basic outside contour established by turning a number of short sections to nearly finished diameter, and then the metal between the sections ground and filed off to the desired diameters. In order to establish a smooth, unbroken, longitudinal curve, the barrel was then "struck" by filing in the longitudinal plane. Part of this operation was often done by "draw filing," in which a flat, single-cut file was held at nearly right angles to the axis of the barrel and the file pushed or drawn so that the angle of the teeth had a shearing effect in removing metal.

Technically, striking was a finishing operation done with a special kind of file (a striker) that was radiused on the short axis; the file was made with widely spaced, curving teeth, single cut. It was equipped with an offset handle and pushed longitudinally along the barrel. (See BARREL MAKING.)

barrel tenon In common usage, the same thing as a barrel shank. The term is more properly applied to an unthreaded shank, held in place with a pin, clamp or screw. Also known as a barrel loop, for underpinning the barrel or other parts to the stock, by means of a wedge, key, or pin. Common in muzzleloading arms. (See BARREL PIN; BARREL SHANK.)

barrel threads The threads at the rear portion of the barrel that screw into female threads in the forward portion of the receiver to attach barrel and action.

barrel throat See THROAT.

barrel time The elapsed time between ignition of the primer and emergence of the bullet from the muzzle. Optimum accuracy is possible only when velocities—hence barrel times—are consistent. (See INTERIOR BALLISTICS.)

barrel turning Reducing the diameter of a barrel in a lathe by cutting away excess steel is known as barrel turning.

barrel vent In muzzleloading arms of matchlock, wheel lock, or flintlock type, the small hole through the wall of the barrel, at the breech, provided for the ignition of the main powder charge in the bore.

A few caplock guns were made with a vent, based on the theory that a hole leading from the powder chamber to the outside atmosphere provided for better ignition of the powder charge by the hot gases of the cap, driving through the nipple.

The term is also applied to the holes or slots of an integral muzzle brake. (See CAPLOCK; FLINTLOCK; MATCHLOCK; PERCUSSION IGNITION; WHEEL LOCK.)

barrel vibration Barrel vibration or movement in rifles is generated by the firing process when the bullet contacts the rifling and continues until it leaves the bore. The amount of vibration is influenced to some extent by the amount of powder being burned and the velocity of the bullet, but the diameter of the bore in relation to the outside diameter of the barrel, as well as the contour of the barrel, affect it more.

A heavy, large diameter barrel vibrates less than a light barrel that tapers to a small diameter muzzle, and the less the vibration the greater the accuracy, everything else being equal.

The vibration of the barrel is approximately circular as the bullet passes through it, and this affects accuracy in one or both of two ways: either in enlarged shot groups if vibration is excessive, and/or in an off-center point of impact of the group when bullets of different weights are used.

The more consistently the barrel vibrates as each bullet passes through it, the better the firearm's accuracy will be. If the muzzle is in exactly the same position when each bullet emerges, accuracy will obviously be increased. The difference in point of impact between light and heavy bullets used in the same cartridge case when the rifle is sighted in at the same range with one weight is governed mostly by where the muzzle is pointed on its vibration cycle when the bullet leaves the muzzle. The heavy bullet, even though traveling at lower velocity, will strike higher on the target if it leaves the muzzle when the barrel is at the top of the vibration cycle.

base wad   The bottom wad found inside all paper and some plastic shotshells. Its primary function is to support the thin walled metal case head and primer pocket. It also regulates the capacity of the case. A high base wad is typical in shotshells designed for lighter loadings of both powder and shot. Compressed paper, fiber materials, and plastic have all been used as base wad material. (See SHOTGUN CARTRIDGES, TARGET.)

battery cup primer   Because the base of a shotshell does not offer adequate support for a primer, shotshells use a two-piece assembly consisting of a cup containing the primer proper and, seated in an outer, supporting, cup (the battery cup), the anvil.

Bausch & Lomb (company)   This leading manufacturer of optical equipment for sportsmen was founded in Rochester in 1853 by John Jacob Bausch and Henry Lomb. At the outset of their partnership, Bausch and Lomb operated a retail store, but they later began to manufacture their own eyeglasses, telescopes, and microscopes.

Bausch & Lomb came into its greatest prominence for shooters in the 1930s, as its line of Porro-prism binoculars came to be recognized as among the world's best. In the 1950s, Bausch & Lomb marketed a successful line of externally adjusted variable and fixed-power riflescopes, which included the unique 6X-24X Balvar-24 target scope. This last was exceptionally powerful for an instrument of its kind. Bausch & Lomb shooting glasses and spotting scopes also gained great success during this period.

In 1971, the firm acquired the David P. Bushnell Company, which continues to operate under its own name, producing the Bushnell riflescopes, handgun scopes, and spotting scopes. Bausch & Lomb presently produces spotting scopes, shooting glasses, binoculars, riflescopes, and handgun scopes.

BB   When referring to air guns, it is a copper-plated steel ball measuring .175-inch; in lead shot it is a pellet of .181-inch diameter.

BB cap   The tiny BB cap was the first successful self-contained cartridge. It was developed by Frenchman Louis Flobert around 1845 and exhibited at the Paris Exposition in 1851. It was little more than a percussion cap with a rim added and a round .22-caliber ball set in its mouth. Originally, there was no powder charge, the projectile instead being propelled only by the priming compound in the rim, for use in indoor target shooting. "BB" in the designation stands for "bullet breech," to imply a superior method of loading. Later BB caps fired 18–20-grain roundnose bullets at about 780 feet per second. The round was once widely used as an indoor target and gallery cartridge, but its chief importance is that it led to the creation of the .22 Short.

BB gun   A kind of air gun. It is the generic term for all types of spring and air-operated guns, usually smoothbore, that discharge a projectile of lead or copper-coated shot .175-inch in diameter (BB).

Because compressed air or gas propels the projectile, rather than any form of combustion, a BB gun is not by definition a firearm. The air or gas may be compressed by a pump and stored before firing, or it may be compressed at the instant of firing by a spring driven piston. The effective range is about 15 yards.

The BB gun was developed in America in the early 1900s. Millions are sold each year, and many youngsters receive their initial training in the use of firearms with the BB gun. Daisy, the largest manufacturer of BB guns, sponsors an annual world target shooting championship for young shooters, which attracts hundreds of entrants from all over the world. (See DAISY.)

bead (cheekpiece)   It is customary on high-quality rifles for the edge of the cheekpiece to be scalloped at the point where it runs along the lower edge of the stock. This edge is called the bead, and if properly shaped and finished it will be sharp along its entire length, with no accumulated finish at its base.

bead (sight)   The round aiming point of some front sights that, when aligned with a rear notch of a handgun or a rear sight or aperture of a rifle, or the top of the receiver of a shotgun, causes a firearm to be accurately aimed.

beads, fine and coarse   The terms "fine bead" and "coarse bead" apply to open sight rifle or handgun shooting with a firearm equipped with a U- or V-notch rear sight and a bead or blade front sight. Shooters with good eyesight sometimes prefer a "fine bead" alignment, wherein the bead or blade is drawn down to the bottom of the rear notch in aiming. (Hence the term, "Draw a bead on.") Shooters with less acute eyesight (and practically all iron sight users firing in dim light) often aim with a "coarse bead" and align the front bead/blade so that it projects above the notch and is more visible. In fact, vertical dispersion with iron sights is best controlled by aligning the sights so that the top of the front sight is on a level with the top of the rear notch. Aligned high, a fine bead will cause the gun to shoot low, a coarse bead high, something to be remembered in long-distance shooting. (See DISPERSION; METALLIC SIGHTS; SIGHT PICTURE.)

beanfield rifle This term is used to describe a rifle that is used for hunting from a treestand in southern states where beanfields are common. (In many areas of the South, the only practical way to hunt whitetail deer is from an elevated stand that overlooks an open field.) These rifles are bolt actions, chambered for high-velocity cartridges using light bullets, and most are exceedingly accurate, since they are designed for shooting at very long ranges. Telescopic sights are used exclusively, and many of the guns are equipped with "twilight scopes," which have heavy reticles and larger-than-standard lenses for added light-gathering ability.

bearing surface The cylindrical section of a bullet body having a diameter corresponding to that of the grooves of the barrel's rifling.

bears, guns and loads for There is a vast difference in the performance required of those cartridges and loads for killing black bears surely and quickly, and those that will efficiently perform the same task on the larger bears—the mountain grizzly, the Alaskan brown bear, and the polar bear.

The majority of black bears are no larger than a big buck deer and are killed at moderate ranges, mostly by hunters hunting deer. Fortunately, the same cartridges used for hunting deer are suitable for black bears. The main point the black bear hunter should consider is that while black bears average about the same weight as deer, they are much more compact, have heavier bones and muscle, thicker hides with longer fur, and hold more tenaciously to life. The thick layer of fat they normally carry, combined with the long hair, serves to plug entrance and exit holes so that there is often no blood trail to follow.

For these reasons it is best to use a bullet that will penetrate deeply, preferably making exit, and to place it in the shoulder area to disable the bear so it will not get into heavy cover where it will be very difficult to follow. The heavier bullets in deer cartridges are the best choice—those of at least 140 grains.

Bears of the grizzly family, found in the Rocky Mountains, western Canada and Alaska, are an entirely different matter. Grizzlies, and particularly the big Alaskan brown bears, are large animals. They are not only compact in build, but have heavy bone enclosed in a thick layer of tough, bullet stopping muscle. Grizzlies not only have the ability to keep going after bullets have been placed in a vital area, but they also often fight back as long as life remains. It is highly important that the first bullet be placed in the right spot and that it have energy enough to convey a great deal of shock, but it is even more critical that it perform correctly after it lands.

To be quickly effective and either kill instantly or immobilize the bear so it will not run off or charge

The sizes of bears vary greatly. This Idaho black bear scaled about 300 pounds (big for its species) and was killed with a .25 wildcat deer rifle. This grizzly is not huge—a big boar will weigh 600 pounds or so—but is formidable and must be hunted with a powerful rifle, such as the .300 Winchester that took this one. The two largest species are the Alaska brown and the polar. Big males of both kinds can weigh 1,200 pounds, and may go as large as 1,600. The brown bear was shot with a .340 Weatherby; the polar bear with a .300 Weatherby. Cartridges for the dangerous bear species should fire heavy bullets capable of breaking large bones. Here is the recommended lineup (from left): 7mm Remington Magnum, .300 Winchester, .300 Weatherby, .338, .340, .358 Norma, and .375 H&H.

the hunter, the bullet should be placed to break up as much bone as possible. Breaking the spine is very effective, but the spine is difficult to hit solidly. Shoulder shots are the best. If both shoulders are broken, the bear will be permanently disabled; a bullet that is angled from either front or rear to break one shoulder while penetrating the lungs will disable the bear and kill quickly.

To accomplish this on the big bears, the bullet must be of fairly large caliber, from 7mm up, of heavy weight and, most important, of controlled expansion design so that it will smash big bones and penetrate heavy muscle while expanding enough to ensure a quick kill. High velocity should be combined with the heavy bullet weight to deliver great shocking power.

For the big Alaskan brown bears, 200- and 220-grain bullets in the .300 Magnums are the minimum, and the various .338, .35, and .375 Magnum cartridges with 250- to 300-grain bullets are among the best choices, as is the .416 Remington Magnum with 350- to 400-grain bullets.

A bolt-action rifle is the preferred arm, equipped with a scope of low magnification. A 1X-4X is about ideal.

While brown and grizzly bears should be shot from fairly close range (100 to 200 yards) to ensure a solid hit, they are spotted from a considerable distance. Binoculars and a spotting scope are invaluable to the hunter who either scouts the shoreline from a boat or stalks on foot.

The hunter of the coastal brown bears should take care that the wood stock of his rifle is sealed against penetration by water, since rain, or at least high humidity, is usually present. Synthetic stocks and rust-resistant metal finishes are invaluable for this wet-weather hunting, and quick-detachable lens caps for a telescopic sight are absolutely required. Another invaluable piece of equipment is hip boots that fit tightly at the instep; these are used constantly in walking the tidal flats and inland bogs.

beavertail fore-end   An enlarged fore-end that gets its name from the broad tail of a beaver. It provides a hand-filling grip, and can also be used (because it weighs more than a conventional splinter fore-end) to establish a desired balance in a shotgun.

bedding   Bedding is the fitting of the action and barrel of a rifle into its stock. More specifically, it is not only the fitting of the metal to the wood, but fitting it correctly so that there are no points of strain on the action that will set up stress in the wrong places when the rifle is fired. Some barrels require pressure at certain points to dampen the vibration generated by the bullet passing through the bore.

While some stockmakers feel that the action should be bedded so that all parts fit as tightly as possible to the wood, most believe that this method causes change of point of bullet impact from day to day attributable to changes in atmospheric conditions. Such changes tend to warp and move the wood, which may then exert pressure at the wrong points of the action. It is generally agreed that the action should be bedded so that the recoil lug/receiver ring and tang area make perfect contact, with contact relieved between those points. If done correctly, there will be no movement of barrel or action when the guard screws are loosened and tightened. On rifles that have a center guard screw, contact should be made at that point also to avoid action strain with the screw kept only moderately tight.

Some barrels shoot best when there is no contact between metal and stock from a point an inch or so forward of the receiver ring; these are called free-floating barrels. Others require slight upward pressure near the forearm tip to damp barrel vibration.

Bedding can be done directly in the wood by inletting or with bedding compounds such as fiberglass that are made for the purpose. (See ACCURIZE; BARREL VIBRATION; GLASS BEDDING; INLETTING.)

bedding (pillar)   A type of bedding whereby two holes are drilled down through a rifle stock, one beneath the receiver ring of the action, the other beneath the tang. The two holes are then filled with an epoxy-type compound or aluminum rods with smaller holes through their centers for passage of the action screws. With the bottom of the action resting against the tops of the pillars and the trigger guard/floorplate assembly resting against their bottom ends, the pillars act as rigid and noncompressible bedding areas when the action bolts or screws are tightened. This bedding method was first developed for use in benchrest rifles, but is now far more popular in hunting rifles. Pillar bedding is used in stocks made of wood or the various synthetic materials.

bedding block   A system for the precise bedding of target and benchrest rifles developed in the mid-1950s, the use of bedding blocks involves a set of two steel or aluminum blocks lapped to and fitted around a heavy barrel. The blocks are held together by socket-head screws, and the whole is fitted into, or onto, the stock by connecting bolts through a plate set in the bottom of the stock. The purpose of bedding blocks is to bed the barreled action firmly and rigidly while allowing both barrel and action to vibrate freely forward of and behind the bedding point. Frequently a scope-supporting bar is added so that a telescopic sight can be mounted without touching the barrel. The bedding block method has evolved into the present sleeved action in current use on benchrest rifles. (See SLEEVED ACTION.)

bedding device A spring loaded device installed in the forearm of a target rifle stock, 1 to 2 inches from the fore-end tip, with the intent of providing an adjustable and precise way to control bedding tension. Several designs exist, most featuring a pair of spring loaded plungers that provide the sole bedding contact in the fore-end, the rest of the barrel channel being routed out so that a gap exists between wood and barrel. These plungers are externally adjustable by means of screws set into the stock, so that the barreled action need not be removed from the stock in order to experiment with bedding tension. Some types also have an attached battery powered unit with a light that goes on when both plungers make contact with the barrel. The shooter can match up screw turns from that point to achieve even pressure.

bedding tension This term, expressed in pounds, refers to the tension or pressure between the fore-end of a stock and the barrel of a rifle. Because the delicate suspension of the steel barrel in the wooden fore-end is so critical in governing barrel vibration and in the maintenance of a consistent point of bullet impact, correct bedding tension is of enormous importance to accurate shooting. Poor accuracy or sudden loss of accuracy many times can be traced to irregular forearm tension or to forearm warpage.

Generally, rifle barrels are bedded with either one or two suspension points. Bedding with tension only under the chamber and without contact elsewhere in the fore-end is called free-float bedding. Light sporter barrels usually shoot better with a second tension point at the tip of the fore-end, but the pressure here should never be more than 15 pounds and the suspension surface must be even, with no high spots. (See BARREL VIBRATION.)

bell See MUZZLE BELL.

belly gun Any short-barreled, easily concealable handgun carried in a holster in the waistband of the trousers.

belted case Originated by Holland & Holland, the famous British gunmakers, in 1905, in the .400/375 H & H as a means of controlling headspace without resorting to a rim in bolt-action rifles, and designed for certain high-pressure, high-powered centerfire rifles, the belted cartridge case features a thick external band around its base. The extra strength this design gives to the case head makes it one of the strongest of all modern case designs. Cartridges of this type are called magnum cartridges—although not all magnums have belts. Since the introduction of .300 and .375 Holland & Holland Magnums, belted cases have also been characterized by a larger case diameter than most standard rimless cartridges. In America, the most popular belted cartridges have been Winchester-Western's line of "short magnums" (of .30/06 length), including the .264, .300, .338, and .458 caliber. The 7mm Remington Magnum actually belongs to the .264/.338 family. Weatherby also offers belted magnum calibers in three different case diameters.

benchrest A table or other platform that forms a supporting base for a rifle and that allows the shooter to be seated while firing. Benchrests are portable or nonportable and may vary from a discarded ironing board to a concrete and steel table weighing many hundreds of pounds and whose legs are embedded in earth.

A good benchrest is absolutely stable and allows the shooter to fire from a comfortable position. Some rests, such as the discarded ironing board mentioned above, are little better than useless because the slightest movement by the shooter or from other external forces is transferred to the rifle and, consequently, shot placement suffers.

The best rests are nonportable because of their weight and permanent placement. However, a barely portable rest can be constructed of concrete and heavy lumber so as to perform as well as the permanent kinds.

The benchrest is used primarily by riflemen for sighting in or accuracy testing, and it is used for competition shooting. Nothing short of a machine rest is better for obtaining maximum accuracy from a rifle or for determining its inherent degree of accuracy. The benchrest is not a cure-all, however. It does not eliminate human error in shooting; it only decreases its effect. (See BENCHREST COMPETITION SHOOTING; MACHINE REST.)

benchrest competition shooting Two recognized organizations in America sanction rifle matches based entirely upon shooting from a benchrest, and their names are derived from the shooting table: the National Bench Rest Shooter's Association (NBRSA), and the International Benchrest Shooters (IBS). Benchrest matches are also held in Canada, Australia, Italy, and other countries, but there is no single world championship match.

The sport consists of shooting five- or 10-shot groups, the latter in two sequences of five. Generally, the average measurement of groups fired at 100 and 200 yards constitute an overall aggregate that determines the winner in each class; the kind of rifle used determines the class. The NBRSA and IBS keep world records at 300 yards, and sometimes 200- or 300-yard matches are held instead of the 100 and 200, but this is the exception.

Although many rules govern the rifles used in benchrest shooting competition, there are almost none regarding the construction of the benchrests themselves. For instance, according to the revised edition No. 21 of the NBRSA rule book, "A bench shall be a rigidly constructed table of a height to permit a shooter of more or less than average height to sit comfortably thereat by merely increasing or decreasing the height of the stool on which he sits. It shall preferably be constructed to permit firing by either a right- or left-handed shooter."

Prior to a match, a drawing is held to determine which benchrest each shooter shall fire the first group from. After each record match (five- or 10-shot groups), the shooter rotates a predetermined number of benches to the right. This allows all shooters an equal chance by firing from many points along the firing line.

During all officially sanctioned matches, both moving and stationary target backers are utilized. The moving backer is nothing more than a continually running motor-driven strip of paper that moves very slowly immediately behind the target. Its purpose is to detect and verify the number of separate bullets that strike the target. The stationary backer is placed 36 inches behind the 100-yard target, and its purpose is to certify that all shots come from the proper benchrests. If someone crossfires (fires on another competitor's target), it can not only be detected, but it can also be determined from which benchrest the foul shot or shots originated, and the appropriate shooter is then penalized. The reason for the use of the backers is that a five-shot group size is smaller than the individual diameter of five nonoverlapping bullet holes. (See BENCHREST RIFLE; BENCHREST TARGET; INTERNATIONAL BENCHREST SHOOTERS; NATIONAL BENCH REST SHOOTER'S ASSOCIATION.)

benchrest rifle A rifle designed and used specifically for shooting from a benchrest. A competition benchrest rifle is designed, within the regulations that govern the sport, to be as mechanically accurate as possible. Benchrest rifles, with few exceptions, are custom built based on a manufactured bolt action, or a custom-made action designed especially for the sport.

National Bench Rest Shooter's Association (NBRSA) regulations divide benchrest rifles into five major classes: unlimited, heavy varmint, light varmint, sporter, and hunter. Limitations for each class of

Benchrest rifles are divided into classes depending on weight. These are guns in the Heavy Varmint class.

rifle are specifically spelled out in the NBRSA rulebook.

In brief, the basic limitations are as follows.

Unlimited rifle: "Any rifle having a barrel 18 or more inches long, measured from the face of the bolt to the muzzle, and having a safely operated firing mechanism." In other words, nearly any rifle or cartridge-firing device is allowed—any weight, size, or caliber. Rests for an unlimited rifle may incorporate a guiding means to return the rifle to original point of aim, including sight elevation and windage adjustments.

Heavy varmint rifle: has a weight limitation of 13½ pounds inclusive of sight. The stock forearm cannot exceed 3 inches in width. The underside of the buttstock must form an angle within specified limitations and the barrel contour is regulated. Also, "the barrel may be attached to the receiver, bedding blocks, sleeve or combination thereof for a distance of no more than four inches, measured from the face of the bolt. The overall length of the receiver, bedding blocks or sleeve or combination thereof not to exceed fourteen inches. (Maximum dimensions shall not include normal scope blocks and sight bases.)"

Light varmint rifle: "Any rifle of not more than 10½ pounds in weight inclusive of sights and otherwise meeting the requirements of the heavy varmint rifle."

Sporter rifle: any rifle otherwise meeting the requirements of the light varmint rifle but not less than .23 caliber.

Hunter rifle: stock cannot be more than 2¼ inches wide; the rifle must have a working safety and a workable magazine that holds at least two cartridges. It must weigh no more than 10 pounds with scope, must be at least 6mm, and cannot have a scope of over 6X. Hunter class competition is fired at targets

This shooter, although using a hunting rifle, is employing the technique used by benchrest competitors. Note that the body and arms are firmly set, and that the grip on the rifle is very light. This is to eliminate any tremor resulting from the tension of a tight grip.

with six bull's-eyes (one sighter and five for record). Points are awarded not for group size, but for hits on the 10-ring.

Because precise aiming is of utmost importance, benchrest scopes are of high magnification—usually 20X to 50X—and utilize fine crosshairs. (See BENCHREST COMPETITION SHOOTING; BULL BARREL.)

benchrest target The specially designed target sanctioned for benchrest shooting. The National Bench Rest Shooter's Association 100-yard target consists of five concentric rings spaced ¼-inch apart with a ⅜-inch center circle diameter. An aiming square composed of a box measuring 1 inch on each side printed within a ¼-inch-thick line is incorporated onto the rings. Proportionally larger targets are used for 200- and 300-yard matches.

The official record match target actually consists of two separate targets printed on one piece of paper. The lower one is used for testing wind shift or other shooting conditions and is called the sighter. The top target is used for firing the official group and is called the record target.

Benchrest scores are based on the size of the group, measured center-to-center, of the bullet holes at the widest point on the group. Therefore, it doesn't matter where shots are placed on the target as long as they are within the 4¾ X 3½-inch border (on the 100-yard target). A shooter is penalized one minute of angle for each shot outside the borderline.

There is no limit on the number of shots that may be fired on the sighter, although a 7-minute limit is enforced for record firing for Varmint and Sporter classes, and a 12-minute limit for Heavy Varmint. (See BENCHREST COMPETITION SHOOTING.)

bend The bend of a shotgun stock is the perpendicular distance between the comb and heel of the

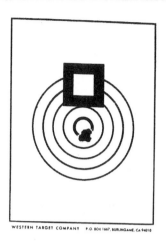

WESTERN TARGET COMPANY   P.O. BOX 1667, BURLINGAME, CA 94010

OFFICIAL 100 YD.
BENCH REST TARGET

BENCH................DATE............
COMP.................GROUP...........
RELAY................SCORE...........
MATCH No...........

WESTERN TARGET COMPANY   P.O. BOX 1667, BURLINGAME CA 94010

A benchrest target consists of a square aiming point and a bull's eye. There are no points affixed to the rings; the size of the group is all that counts.

butt and the continuation of the line extending from the top rib. This term is British in origin and is seldom used in America.

Benet primer   Invented in 1866 by Colonel S. V. Benet, commandant of Frankford Arsenal, the original Benet primer comprised a cup with anvil that was inserted into a pocket formed integrally with a folded-head case.

It was preceded by an experimental folded-head case, *not* of Colonel Benet's design but developed at Frankford Arsenal. This case lacked an anvil, the priming compound being inserted through the mouth of the case and held in place by a compressed powder charge. When that experiment proved both too fragile and too sensitive, Colonel Benet developed his case the same year (1866) for the .50/70 government rifle.

In March, 1868, Colonel Benet introduced his improved cup anvil case in which a tinned sheet-iron cup anvil spanned the entire base of the case and was held in place by crimping or indenting the walls of the copper case at the forward edge of the priming cup. This crimping produced some difficulties with extraction.

In August 1870, copper was substituted for sheet iron in forming the priming cup, greatly improving its resistance to deterioration from oxidation.

Because its complicated design was not suited for reloading, the Benet case and primer were phased out by the U.S. Army in the early 1870s and the Berdan primer adopted in its place.

Benjamin Air Rifle (company)   Founded in St. Louis in 1885 by designer Walter Benjamin, this firm has specialized in the manufacture of pump-operated air rifles. The first Benjamin designs were simple, reliable guns that sold at modest prices, and subsequent models have retained these characteristics. Today, Benjamin produces a variety of rifles and pistols that operate with air power.

Benner, Huelet L. (1917–)   "Joe" Benner was born in Jonesboro, Arkansas, on November 1, 1917. In 1935 he enlisted in the Army, where his interest in pistol shooting was fostered and recognized, resulting in his assignment to the gunnery department of the Armored Force School at Fort Knox, Kentucky. National recognition of his shooting abilities came after World War II.

Benner won the National Pistol Championship in 1947, 1949, 1951, 1955, 1956, and 1959, as well as many area and regional championships. Probably the most outstanding of his accomplishments was winning seven prestigious Mid-Winter Pistol Matches in a decade. Between 1948 and 1957, he won each year but 1949, 1950, and 1955.

Equally proficient with revolver, automatic, or free pistol, Benner represented America on nine International teams from 1948 through 1958, competing in both rapid- and slow-fire events, winning four World Championships and placing in seven of the nine International Championships in which he competed.

In 1959, Benner was assigned as pistol coach of the Cadet Pistol Team, West Point. He retired from active duty as a sergeant major in 1964.

bent In an Anson and Deeley shotgun action, the bent is a notch in the lower edge of the tumbler that engages the end of the sear. Its function is to prevent the tumbler, which compresses the mainspring, from returning to its original position when pressure exerted by the cocking lever is removed. (See ANSON AND DEELEY ACTION.)

Berdan primer An external primer in which the priming cup contains only the priming composition, the anvil being formed integrally with the web of the primer pocket. Small holes, generally two in number, in the case web around the base of the anvil allow ignition of the powder charge.

In fact, Colonel Hiram Berdan of the U.S. Army did not invent a primer, though it is generally assumed that he did. His patent of 1866 covered an externally primed cartridge case in which a separate primer pocket was pressed into the base of the case and held there by a retaining flange. The anvil was punched up from the bottom of the primer pocket, at first not in the center, but at one side, later changing to the center. The cup containing the priming compound was inserted into the pocket.

Berdan's patent of 1868 covered a drawn metal, folded-head cartridge case with a reinforcing cup inside the head of the case; an anvil, integral to the case and swaged from the center of the primer pocket; and two small holes punched beside the anvil.

The manufacture of externally primed centerfire ammunition under these patents was begun in 1868 by the Union Metallic Cartridge Co. (UMC) of Bridgeport, Connecticut. The "Berdan primer" (compound or pellet, as distinguished from "primer" used to designate the assembly) was patented by A. C. Hobbs of UMC in 1869 and was essentially an adaptation of the percussion cap. Hobbs's patent basically covered the shape and location of the pellet in the cup.

Within a few decades, Berdan primers were largely superseded in America by the Boxer type because of the greater ease of reloading with the latter. Berdan primers are still used in many other parts of the world in rifle ammunition. (See BOXER PRIMER; PRIMER.)

Berenger pellet An early ignition system, patented in 1824, it was probably the first pellet percussion system. A pellet of explosive chemicals was struck by the gun's hammer. The resulting flame was directed through a touch hole into the main powder charge inside the muzzleloading gun's barrel. It is similar to the Forsyth percussion system developed in Scotland in 1807 by the Reverend Alexander J. Forsyth, but the Forsyth system used loose percussion powder, not pellets. A pellet enclosed in a copper cap was central to the percussion system of ignition until the invention of self-contained metallic cartridges in the mid-19th century.

Beretta (company) One of the world's oldest manufacturers of sporting firearms, Armi P. Beretta, S.p.A., is located in Gardonne in Brescia, Italy, and has been in operation since 1680. The company specializes in shotguns and handguns and produces a wide variety of each, ranging from economy models to custom shotguns costing many thousands of dollars. Among the company's more notable offerings are the Model 76 .22 automatic pistol, a highly sophisticated target arm, and the SO3-EELL, an elaborately engraved sidelock over/under shotgun with gold plated internal mechanism.

Berlin–Wannsee pattern The original Berlin–Wannsee procedure for patterning shotguns was developed by the German Experimental Station for Small Arms in Berlin–Wannsee and put into use in 1893. The pattern used was divided by rings and radial lines into 100 sections called fields. It gave a precise method of measurement for shotgun patterns. In fact, it was too precise for practical applications, and it was modified in 1937 to the patterning target now in use.

The present Berlin–Wannsee patterning target is used at 35 meters (38.3 yards) range and has two concentric circles: the outer is 75 centimeters (29.5 inches) in diameter and the inner is 37.5 centimeters in diameter. The inner circle is divided into four equal sections by radial lines and the outer similarly divided into 12 equal sections. Thus, all the fields are of equal size. The sizes were chosen to provide a measurement of the performance of shotguns on game. One-third of a field is equal to the vital area of a partridge, two-thirds to the vital area of a pheasant or duck, and two full adjoining fields to the vital area of a hare.

This patterning target does an excellent job of measuring all the necessary characteristics of a shotgun pattern: *percentage* (the fraction of the total number of pellets striking the 75-centimeter ring from the total number of pellets in the charge); *coverage* (the fields receiving the required number of hits for sure killing of any particular game); *evenness* (the uniformity of hits among the fields); and *thickening* (the number of hits in the inner ring compared with the number in the outer ring).

The percentage of hits in the overall target area, although it is a figure much used by American shotgunners, is not a good indicator of shotgun performance. A high proportion does not take into account what may be uneven and patchy distribution of shot holes, which in turn leads to unreliable performance on game or clay targets. Consideration must also be given to coverage and evenness of the pattern.

Shotguns put a disproportionately large percentage of shot into a central cone, from about 20 yards out to about 45 or 50 yards (with standard 12-gauge loads in a full-choked gun). The inner circle of the Berlin–Wannsee target contains one-fourth of the total area and it is thus one-third the area of the outer ring. Counting hits in the inner, multiplying by three and comparing with total hits in the outer ring gives a measure of thickening.

Tables developed from extensive 35-meter testing at Berlin–Wannsee are used to assess shotgun pattern performance at other ranges.

American shooters should be aware that the Berlin–Wannsee method of pattern evaluation does not greatly differ from the standards U.S. gunners apply. The Berlin–Wannsee range of 38.3 yards compares to our 40 yards, and the target size of 29.5 inches is just over 98 percent of our 30-inch circle—in all, essentially a 2 percent scaledown of the American procedure. (See PATTERN BOARD.)

Bernardelli (company) The Vincenzo Bernardelli firm is noted in America for its high-grade side-by-side shotguns, which are closely patterned on British shotguns. Five models are currently imported, most on a to-order basis, in a wide variety of gauges, barrel lengths, choke combinations, and with many optional features. Bernardelli also produces service-type and target automatic pistols.

Its base of operations, since its founding in 1865, has been in Gardonne, Brescia, Italy.

Bernoulli effect Bernoulli's principle refers to fluid flow in pipes of an incompressible fluid under steady-state conditions, and states that where the velocity is high, the pressure is low, and where the velocity is low, the pressure is high. The same principle applies to objects moving through stationary fluid, as in the case of a shotgun pellet moving through air.

When a round ball is fired from a smoothbore gun, the ball bounces erratically down the bore, and these contacts cause the ball to spin on axes transverse to the line of flight and variable from shot to shot in a random fashion. As will be explained, this causes the path of the ball through the air to be curved, and the direction of the curve will vary with the axis of spin, thus increasing the dispersion of a series of shots.

In the accompanying diagram, the ball is spinning counterclockwise, dragging a layer of air around with it, as represented by the dashed arrows. In

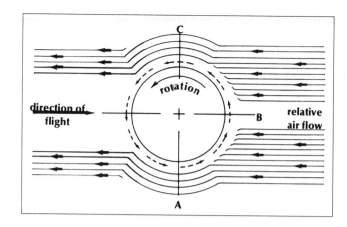

section A–B, since the rotary air movement opposes the relative air movement in the direction of flight, the velocity of the air (fluid) is low and the pressure is high. The opposite occurs in section B–C: the velocity is high and the pressure low. These forces causes the ball to fly in a curved path in the direction shown—the Bernoulli effect.

Sometimes called "magnus force," this effect causes the curved flight of sliced or hooked golf balls, pitched or hit baseballs, etc. It should not be confused with the drift and precession caused by gyroscopic effect on spin-stabilized, elongated projectiles—rifle or pistol bullets. (See EXTERIOR BALLISTICS.)

best grade A term traditionally employed by the London gunmakers (Purdey, Holland & Holland, Westley Richards, etc.), and gunmakers associated with their high quality work, to describe a top-of-the-line gun. It can also be used to describe an available feature: "best" engraving, for example, means the most ornate grade available.

bifurcated lump In constructing an over/under shotgun, a shallow receiver is regarded as desirable. To achieve this end, divided, or bifurcated, lumps are employed instead of a full knuckle pin, usually on either side of the lower barrel. (See CHOPPER LUMP; OVER/UNDER GUN.)

big bore The term big bore has two meanings. When applied to rifle or pistol target shooting, it differentiates between the .22 rimfire matches and the centerfire matches. As applied to hunting rifle cartridges the term probably originated in England, where anything of over .450 caliber was once considered a big-bore arm. Americans usually consider everything over .375 caliber big bore. In pistol cartridges, any bullet diameter of .357 (.38) or over is considered big bore.

BIMOCO match pellets BIMOCO is the trade name of Bildstein, Mommer & Co., KG., of Gressenich, Germany. The company manufactures a variety of air rifle pellets in .177, .22, and .25 calibers. The BIMOCO match pellets are skirted, flat nose match pellets suitable for the most demanding requirements of competitive air gun shooting.

binoculars Binoculars are magnifying optical devices designed to be used by both eyes at the same time. Their major purpose is to facilitate the observation of objects some distance away from the user, and as such they are among the most important items of outdoor gear for all shooters, especially hunters. Selection of a binocular should be undertaken with as much care and forethought as goes into the choice of a gun or a telescopic sight because, as an instrument for locating and judging game animals, it will be used extensively in the field. Additionally, binocular use is a considerable deterrent to hunting accidents.

The binocular market is a highly competitive one, and many models and designs are available. Germany, Japan, and the United States produce the very best binoculars. Companies such as Leitz, Zeiss, Nikon, Bushnell, Pentax and Bausch & Lomb produce a myriad of designs of generally high quality.

Binoculars are made in various sizes, a wide range of magnifications, and differing light gathering capabilities. Several manufacturers produce compact lines by utilizing unusual prism arrangements or roof prisms in small H-shaped models. These compacts weigh only half as much as standard size binoculars and are far handier. However, they do sacrifice some image quality and brightness to models with larger objective lenses, comparing coated lenses of similar quality. Full lens coating is a must for optimum light transmission, as well as for glare prevention.

In addition to various sizes, binoculars are also

These are three common kinds of binoculars. They are, from left: 10×40 roof prism, 8×25 roof prism compacts, and 15×50 Porro prism. The last are too powerful to be hand-held; they must be used with a tripod or placed on a rest.

made with such special features as wide-angle lenses, which can increase field of view as much as 40 percent, and variable power, wherein magnification can be changed over a range of powers, say from 7X to 12X.

Binoculars range in power from 5X to as much as 30X in huge military field glasses. The most commonly used range of powers is 6X to 10X. The lower the power, the smaller and lighter the binocular and the greater its field of view. The higher powers require large front, or objective, lenses to gather light. The most used power is 7X, and in fixed magnification models 10X is considered the limit for hand-held field use. More powerful models are difficult to hold steady enough for comfortable viewing; tripod mounting is required to use them effectively.

Most binoculars have a numerical designation in addition to the power, such as 7x35, 8x40, 10x50, etc. The first number is the magnification, the second refers to the size, in millimeters, of the front, or objective, lens. The larger this second figure, the greater the relative brightness of the binocular's image. A 7x50, for example, would gather more light under dim conditions than a 7x35.

The relationship between magnification and the size of the front objective is expressed by the term exit pupil, which refers to the diameter of the light circle conducted to the eye. The human pupil can dilate to as large as 5mm in poor light, and about 7mm in total darkness, so for a binocular to provide the eye with all the light it can use it must have an exit pupil of roughly that diameter. The size of a binocular's exit pupils are determined by dividing the size of the objective lenses by the power (for example, $35 \div 7 = 5$). Therefore a 35mm objective in 7X is required to provide the eye with as much brightness as it can utilize for most hunting conditions.

A good binocular should possess a device that allows it to be focused for both eyes simultaneously. Smooth and rapid operation of focus mechanisms is a mandatory requirement. Quick-focus models are available for users who find instantaneous focusing desirable. Better binoculars commonly feature a dioptic focus ring on one eyepiece to adjust the lenses to match eyeglass prescriptions so that the binocular can be used with or without glasses.

Ultimately, the selection of a binocular should be based on need in much the same manner that a telescopic sight is chosen. Two factors to consider are the environment in which the binocular will be employed and its intended use. Binoculars for woodland use should be of lower power and have a wider field and greater brightness than is necessary for an instrument to be looked through in plains or mountain habitat. If a binocular is to be carried for long periods around the neck or in a pack, weight should be a major criterion. Generally, a standard 7x35 glass of high quality is probably the best overall choice, although a 10x50 is better for Western trophy judging and varmint hunting.

The truly excellent models are quite expensive, but they are invariably far better, optically and mechanically, than less expensive ones.

In buying a used instrument, it is advisable before purchase to have it checked by a dealer who is franchised by the binocular's manufacturer. If there are defects, they can be corrected by trained repairmen with the proper equipment.

A top quality binocular is invariably a superior investment to a moderately priced one. It will outperform the cheaper glass, and, with proper care, will last a lifetime. (See ABERRATION; BRIGHTNESS; MAGNIFICATION.)

bipod   A two-legged rest that supports a rifle. The rifle's forearm rests in a padded cradle. Some bipods are semipermanently attached to the rifle by a rubber band or strap, while others are separate. Bipods are especially useful for varmint shooting from the prone position.

bird's head grip   From the middle 19th century through the early 20th, a number of companies, most notably Colt, produced a series of double-action revolvers and derringers that employed a so-called bird's head grip. This grip, which was sharply curved, terminated in a sharp point at the forward bottom edge of the grip strap, and somewhat resembled the shape of a bird's beak. The grip screw, located in the middle of the grip, gave the appearance of an eye and added to the overall resemblance to a bird's head.

The bird's head is an obsolete kind of handgun grip. Here, it is seen on a British Webley service revolver.

Birmingham Small Arms (company)   This English firm has, since 1956, exported a variety of sporting and target rifles and air guns to America. The best known BSA imports are bolt-action centerfire hunting rifles—sold either under the BSA trademark or marketed under the name of the American company. The most notable BSA import is the Martini International Match rifle. This single-shot falling block .22 Long Rifle arm, designed for target competition, is imported by Freeland's of Rock Island, Illinois.

bites   This term refers to the cuts or slots in a break-open shotgun's lumps into which the locking bolt fits when the action is closed. (See HINGED FRAME.)

Bitterroot bullet   Made by the Bitterroot Bullet Co. of Lewiston, Idaho, the Bitterroot bullet is designed and built to give high-level performance on large game animals. Of the expanding type, it depends on a relatively large, deep cavity in its point to start expansion of the jacket. It is of pointed form and has a high ballistic coefficient for all rifle calibers for which it is made.

The jacket is made from pure copper tubing that is quite soft and malleable and is thicker than that of any other expanding bullet, which makes the projectile longer than typical for a given weight.

The unique feature of the Bitterroot bullet is that its lead core is bonded to the jacket by a process its maker, Bill Steigers, will not divulge. When the jacket expands the core adheres solidly to it, which acts in two ways to attain outstanding performance on animal tissue and bone:

First, the core does not leave the jacket regardless of the amount of expansion, which causes a high retention of the original weight and provides for deep, bone smashing penetration. Second, the fact that the lead core stays with the thick copper jacket creates a large frontal mass of classic mushroom form, which delivers great shock and high tissue destructivity. (See BALLISTIC COEFFICIENT; EXTERIOR BALLISTICS; IMPACT BEHAVIOR BALLISTICS.)

black powder   Although the invention of black powder had a profound effect on the history of civilization, the exact date of its invention and its inventor will probably never be known.

The first mention of gunpowder in Western history occurs in the writings of an English scholar, Roger Bacon (1214?–1294) in a work entitled *De Mirabili Potestate Artis et Naturae (On the Marvelous Power of Art and Nature)* written in 1242. While Bacon has been named the inventor, nothing in this work supports the claim.

Incendiary compounds such as Greek Fire had

been in use for many years when the treatise was written, and it is possible that gunpowder was an Oriental invention. The formula (used through the 18th century) that Bacon gave was: 41.2 percent saltpeter (potassium nitrate), 29.4 percent sulphur, and 29.4 percent charcoal. The mixture was ground into a fine powder, and the three elements contributed as follows: charcoal provided fuel in the form of carbon; saltpeter supplied oxygen for combustion, and sulphur reduced the temperature of ignition while increasing the heat of the explosion.

In addition to being highly unstable, this early gunpowder suffered from another major defect, in that when stored or transported the three elements tended to separate. By 1600, this fault was eliminated by "corning" the powder—mixing the ingredients into a cake after wetting, and then breaking up the cake into grains. Moreover, the formula had been rendered more efficient by altering it to consist of 75 percent saltpeter, 15 percent charcoal, and 10 percent sulphur. Modern black powder is screened through a sieve to obtain grains of a uniform size and burning rate, and the grains are then coated with graphite and polished, making them less susceptible to damage from humidity.

The granulation sizes of black powder and the recommended uses are as follows:

GRANULATION	PASSES OPENING	NOT PASS
F (1F)	.0689	.0582
FF (2F)	.0582	.0376
FFF (3F)	.0376	.0170
FFFF (4F)	.0170	.0111

Curtis & Harvey black powder comes in four grades: Priming Powder (very fine), Pistol Powder (3½F), Rifle Powder (2½F) and Musket Powder.

F (1F) is used mainly for cannons. FF is used in rifles of .50 caliber or larger and also for shotguns. FFF is for rifles of less than .50 caliber. FFFF is priming powder and should never be used as a primary load.

Curtis & Harvey powder is for use as follows: Musket Powder for cannons; Pistol Powder for pistols and calibers up to and including .36; Rifle Powder, for .40 caliber on up. Priming powder is used to ignite all types of black-powder arms.

It cannot be too heavily stressed that, while smokeless powder is a propellant that burns progressively and is safe to handle and transport, black powder is an explosive, and extreme care must always be used in its storage, handling, and transportation. Black powder must be shielded from dampness, shock, sparks or extreme heat. Quite often, state and local regulations govern its purchase and storage. Quantities of 50 pounds or more must be stored in a government-approved fireproof locker a specified distance from the nearest dwelling.

Because it is not as efficient as smokeless powder, black powder cannot produce the high velocities that the former does; nevertheless, effective performance can be had from a black-powder gun. The following are typical ballistics of conservative loads, using balls rather than conical projectiles:

CHARGE (grains)	VELOCITY (feet per second)	PRESSURE (lead [or copper] units of pressure)	MUZZLE ENERGY (foot-pounds)	ENERGY (100 yards)
.32 cal. 25 grains	1,550	3,200	300	90
.36 cal. 35 grains	1,579	7,800	393	100
.40 cal. 40 grains	1,455	4,610	432	(NA)
.45 cal. 60 grains	1,585	7,500	822	260
.50 cal. 70 grains	1,663	9,500	1,104	389
.54 cal. 80 grains	1,453	7,060	1,030	436
.58 cal. 90 grains	1,153	4,710	766	406
.75 cal. 100 grains	1,047	(NA)	1,223	860

In the early 1970s, muzzleloader shooters were introduced to a black-powder substitute called Pyrodex. The invention of Dan Pawlak, Pyrodex is a modified black powder that burns without the heavy fouling of its predecessor. Since it ignites at 600 degrees Fahrenheit rather than the 350 of black powder, it is far safer to ship and store, and is classed as a propellant rather than an explosive by the Interstate Trade Commission. (Unfortunately, Pyrodex is highly unstable and very dangerous in manufacture. In 1977, Pawlak was killed when his Pyrodex factory exploded.) Because of its high ignition point, Pyrodex does not work well in flintlocks, and in percussion ignition guns special "hot" caps and nipples are needed. Pyrodex is presently sold by the B. E. Hodgdon Co.

black-powder shooting This is the fastest growing form of sport shooting in America, at least in part due to the fact that many states now have muzzle-loading deer seasons, which can greatly lengthen a typical hunting season. But hunting with old-style guns is not the sport's only appeal. Competition shooting is sponsored and regulated by such groups as the National Muzzle Loading Rifle Association (NMLRA), the largest of a number of similar organizations. At the NMLRA spring and fall championship matches, more than 2,500 shooters compete. In all, the best estimates put the number of black-powder shooters in the United States at some 5,000,000.

From the names of other black-powder shooting organizations, one can see the interests of their members and the range of activities available to them: Brigade of the American Revolution; Civil War Skirmish Association, Crown & Continental Line; National Association of Primitive Riflemen; National Rifle Association; North-South Skirmish Association; U.S. International Muzzleloading Committee.

Many muzzleloader enthusiasts are attracted by the history of the old guns and the time during which the guns were in use. For instance, in the North-South Skirmish Association, obviously oriented to the Civil War, uniforms of the period are

When shooting a black-powder firearm, glasses are necessary, since the eyes are only inches away from the source of ignition.

This black-powder shooter is more casual than most; his patching material is simply stuffed, uncut, into his pockets.

required. The Primitives, to take another example, wear buckskins and headgear of the 1790–1830 period. No modern equipment is allowed. The members make their own "skins," accessories, and tepees and most make their own guns, or have them specially made—there are very few "production" guns in this organization.

In competition, the Primitives throw the tomahawk, throw knives, build a fire from tinder, flint, and steel, and shoot at difficult targets. Most of the matches are for flintlock rifles, although percussion matches are on the programs of many chapters of the organization.

The addresses of the various organizations and of local chapters may be had by writing to the National Muzzle Loading Rifle Association, Box 67, Friendship, Indiana 47021, or to the National Association of Primitive Riflemen, Big Timber, Montana 59011. (See BLACK POWDER; MUZZLELOADER.)

blade sight A type of iron front sight usually found on older rifles and service handguns. A typical blade front sight is a thin, upward-projecting element integral with the gun barrel. The blade on the Colt Model 1873 Army single-action revolver—the Peacemaker—is a typical example. Blade front sights have fallen into disuse because sighting with them is imprecise. (See METALLIC SIGHTS.)

blank cartridge Commonly known as a "blank," this kind of cartridge is designed to produce noise and smoke, but operates without a projectile. The most commonly used blanks are those employed in starters' pistols. They are copper .22 cases, loaded with priming compound and a small charge of powder, and crimped shut. Larger blanks are loaded with standard primers and powder, and are sealed with wax or with a cardboard wad.

Despite the fact that they do not fire a projectile, blanks are dangerous if misused.

Blankenship, William B., Jr. (1929–) Noted American pistol marksman. Although he hunted with a shotgun as a youngster, Blankenship, who was born in Richlands, Virginia, in 1929, did not come into contact with competitive target shooting until he joined the Army. He was stationed in Hawaii, a musician in the 264th Army Band, when his wife purchased a Colt .45 auto for him for Christmas, 1952. His first attempt to shoot it on the range resulted in only four hits on the target. He accepted an offer of help from Lieutenant Colonel Elgin Radcliff and Radcliff coached him for the next year and a half.

Blankenship soon began to win matches. In 1957 he was transferred to the Army's Advanced Marksmanship Unit at Fort Benning, Georgia, as an instructor. In 1958 he was a member of the U.S. team that competed in the World Championships in Moscow. In 1959 he won the National Indoor Pistol Championship. He won the National Pistol Championship at Camp Perry, Ohio, six times, 1960 through 1964 and again in 1967. He won the National Trophy Individual Pistol Match, shot with the service pistol, in 1964, 1965, and 1966. He set a number of national records, the most outstanding performance being that of breaking the record for the three-gun, 2,700 aggregate, three times in the summer of 1960.

In International, Olympic and Pan American Games competitions, Blankenship was a member of the U.S. team in 1958, 1960, 1962, 1963, and 1967, winning four gold, four silver, and one bronze medal.

Blankenship spent most of the late years of his Army career as a marksmanship instructor at the AAMU at Fort Benning; he retired from active duty in 1970, having attained the rank of Master Sergeant. His last competitive pistol shooting was in 1972. Known primarily as a pistol shooter, with Distinguished status, he was also Distinguished with the service rifle (1955). (See ARMY MARKSMANSHIP UNIT.)

blind A structure or natural growth used to conceal the stationary hunter while he lies in wait for game. Simplest is the natural "hide" in which the hunter merely conceals himself in thick vegetation, a natural ground formation, or even a depression in the snow. Most complex is the elaborate waterfowl blind constructed on a solid and permanent wooden framework. The variations are unlimited.

Blinds fall into two general categories—permanent and portable. Portable blinds can either be picked up and carried to any desirable location or they are floating, or anchored, and camouflaged watercraft; permanent blinds are fixed in place.

In almost all blinds, local vegetation—leafy twigs, reeds, evergreen branches, etc.—is used to make the blind blend with its surroundings. A variation in portable blinds is a set of large mirrors. The hunter conceals himself behind the mirrors, which reflect the natural landscape back to the game. This method is effective so long as the sun does not reflect brightly from the glass. A more common artificial material is camouflage pattern cloth screening. Portable blinds also include leaves or reeds or even ice and snow placed across the bow of a boat to conceal the hunter.

In deer hunting, one form of blind is the elevated tree stand (called *Hochsitz* in central Europe, *Machan* by the jungle big game hunter). Since deer and many other game animals seldom look upward, elevating the hunter as little as 10 feet effectively hides him. Concealing vegetation is not necessary; height is sufficient. Elevated blinds are also shooting boxes on stilts, lightly camouflaged, used by waterfowl hunters in tidewater areas.

Some permanent waterfowl blinds are replete with a boat dock, a heating system, a gas refrigerator and even a telephone.

blind (box) magazine A nonremovable box magazine completely concealed within the stock of a rifle (or, rarely, a shotgun). The top of the magazine is exposed for loading by pulling the bolt fully to the rear. This kind of magazine lacks a hinged floorplate.

Blish principle A design (circa 1920) for bolt locking incorporated into the two bolt locking lugs of submachine guns. It operates by means of helical grooves that were intended to act by lock adhesion during the time of peak pressure. However, the design was found to be a hesitation system of questionable value and is no longer in use.

blitz action A German-made type of break-action, falling block, single-shot rifle design made in the late 19th century. Though "break-action" and "falling block" appear to be a contradiction, when the action was broken, a breechblock fell into a receiver mortise, exposing the chamber. The exposed hammer, which appeared something like a sliding safety, had to be manually cocked after the action was broken and then locked.

The action was quite complex and considerable care was required to hand inlet it into its two-piece stock. One example featured false sideplates and an unusual ejector system. After firing, the shooter had the option of ejecting the case completely free of the chamber or, if a small button were pushed near the top of the receiver tang, the case would be ejected only far enough to be grasped with the fingers.

Blondeau shotgun slug A shotgun slug of French origin, shaped similarly to a "wasp-waisted" air rifle pellet, having two bore-riding bands of lead, one at the front and another at the rear. The body of the slug may be of metal harder than the soft bore-riding bands. Stabilization is achieved by drag rather than rotation, which is the same principle by which stabilization of rifled shotgun slugs is achieved, notwithstanding the helical grooves or rifling around the circumference of rifled slugs. Called the *balle Blondeau* in France, where it is quite widely used, this slug has not become popular elsewhere and is seldom seen in the United States. (See SHOTGUN SLUG.)

blooper A slang expression for an underpowered rifle or pistol bullet or shotshell load. The reason for the lack of power is most frequently insufficient or contaminated propellant, or in shotshells a cocked wad that doesn't seal properly or a weak crimp that yields too rapidly.

blowback action A blowback action is a kind of recoil operation in which conventional locking lugs are not used. Instead, the action is held shut during firing by the inertia of the bolt and bolt spring, and the bullet is launched into flight before the rearward thrust of the expanding powder gases opens the bolt and puts the action through the ejecting, cocking, and reloading cycles. This kind of action, which is also called a retarded blowback action, is employed on automatic and semiautomatic rifles and handguns. (See SEMIAUTOMATIC.)

blow-forward action With this type of rifle action, the barrel, restrained by spring pressure, is designed to move forward a given distance relative to the breech face, which remains in a fixed position in the gun. When the gun has been fired, the empty cartridge case is held to the rear as gas pressure forces the barrel forward. This brings about extraction and ejection of the empty case. The compressed action spring then returns the barrel to battery as a live round is chambered.

blown pattern A blown pattern, also known as a "doughnut" pattern, is one that leaves the center of the pattern extremely weak while forcing the pellets outward and into the fringe areas very quickly after muzzle exit; hence, the "doughnut" outline, which finds few pellets in the core of the pattern.

It is popularly believed that blown patterns were caused by the presence of the top, or over-shot, wad of old-style shotshells used in tandem with a rolled crimp. However, it is more likely that doughnut patterns are caused by the trailing stack of card/filler wads that ram into the emerging shot charge at the muzzle, thus upsetting the development of a uniform pattern. When the powder gases are strong at the muzzle, they can push the trailing card/filler wad column into the through-the-shot charge, forcing the pellets to the outside of the pattern as a cigar smoker forces air through the center of a smoke cloud to blow a smoke ring.

The blown pattern has been eliminated from modern shotgunning not so much by the folded crimp *without* an overshot wad, but rather by the plastic shotcup wad, which is slowed rapidly upon muzzle exit when its elements open upon encountering air resistance and act as brakes to keep the wad from slamming into the shot mass. It is still theorized that even in the older days the full choke suffered less from blown patterns than did the more open bores because the tight full-choke constriction pinched down on the trailing wad column to retard it and permit the shot charge to exit without being jostled from behind by the wad column. (See PATTERN BOARD; SHOTSHELL CRIMPS.)

blown primer A primer is said to be "blown" when high pressures cause the primer pocket to expand sufficiently upon firing to loosen or rupture the primer and allow gas to escape. (See CHAMBER PRESSURE; PRESSURE ESTIMATION.)

blue pill load The term is applied to proof loads used by the military to test rifles under high internal pressure conditions. These cartridges generate about 40 percent more pressure than standard loads, and they are tin plated to give them a bluish color and thereby distinguish them from standard cartridges.

American commercial proof loads are marked with red and are normally loaded to produce 25 percent more pressure than standard factory ammunition.

In proofing any gun, the use of one blue pill load is followed by firing several standard pressure loads

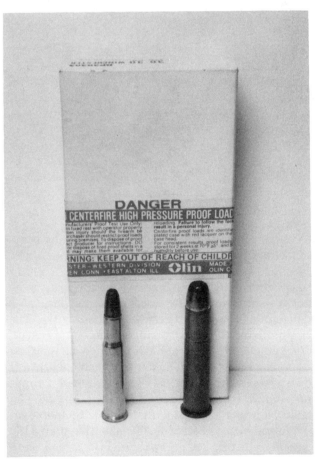

These are "blue pill," or proof loads in .30/30 (left) and .45/70. The cases are steel rather than brass, to withstand higher pressures, and the bullets are lacquered purple to keep them from being confused with conventional ammunition. Note the warning on the box.

to test the functioning of the rifle and to determine if any damage has been done by the excessive pressure created by the proof load. (See PROOF; PROOF HOUSE.)

bluing Artificially inducing the chemical process of oxidation in gun steel to produce a blue-black or black finish. The finish is applied to enhance appearance, to reduce secondary rusting, and in some instances, to reduce surface glare. There are many methods and formulas for applying bluing.

Bluing is more than merely coloring the metal's surface. It is etching *into* the surface of the metal by the rusting process. A variety of appearances can result from the process, depending on the finish of the metal surface prior to the induced oxidation and the formula and method of applying it.

The three basic kinds of bluing are the traditional rust blue, which derives from the old browning process and is applied in a similar manner; the hot caustic blue, the most commonly used process today; and the cold blue, generally used for touch-up work, which can be applied by the hobbyist.

Many shooters prefer the traditional rust blue, but this process takes considerable time because repeated applications of the bluing solution and carding away of rust is required until a satisfactory finish is achieved. Depending upon the air and solution temperatures, humidity, the solution's content, and metal conditions, this may require many applications over a period of several weeks.

The caustic hot blue has the advantage of being fast. Only one application is required, and the process is completed in a few hours. The steel part to be blued is first submerged in a boiling degreasing solution, then a boiling clear water rinse, and, finally, a boiling acid solution that imparts the color to the metal. Chromium and nickel steels tend to resist coloring by this method, and it cannot be employed where tin solder has been used in the construction of the firearm. The boiling acid solution tends to melt the solder, destroying the joint. The process may be used on silver soldering, however.

Cold bluing touch-up formulas have been used with varying degrees of success. The composition of the metal, the condition of the metal surface, and the application technique all have bearing on the quality of finish that will result. (See BROWNING [PROCESS].)

blunderbuss An unrifled firearm, flared or belled at the muzzle and often having a gradually expanding bore. Most blunderbusses were carbines or pistols, but large versions were used as naval swivel guns. The name is probably derived from the German *Dunder* and *Buchse*, meaning "thunder gun."

Bluing involves repeated immersion of the barreled action in a corrosive bath. It is actually a process of controlled rusting.

Though wheel lock and percussion specimens are known, this was an arm of the flintlock period, developed in Europe during the early 17th century. Its purpose was to scatter shot pellets widely at short range. It protected homes, businesses and coaches against bandits and was also used as a ship-boarding weapon. During the 18th century, folding bayonets and corrosion resistant brass barrels were fashionable.

The early design reflected the existing fallacy that muzzle flare spread the shot. Some pieces had horizontal oval-shaped flares intended to disperse pellets horizontally. Eventually, the spread was increased by a large, short, slowly expanding bore and the flare was replaced by a decorative, muzzle-thickening bell.

Contrary to legend, customary loads were not stones, nails, broken glass or scrap iron—which would have patterned unpredictably and ruined the bore—but heavy charges of lead pistol balls or buckshot.

boar, guns and loads for Wild European swine, now established in most southeastern states, can be dangerous because of their large, sharp tusks. They are hunted with hounds, and the shooting is usually done at 50 yards or less. Most hunters use their deer rifles but employ heavier bullets than they use for deer. For instance, in .30/06, the 180-grain round-nose bullet is favored over the 150-grain load. Generally, a heavy, slow moving bullet with an expanding round nose is better for this shooting than a high velocity spitzer, and .30 caliber is regarded as the minimum. About 1,800 foot-pounds of energy at the muzzle are required.

Because of the short range, pinpoint accuracy is not required, and iron sighted semiautomatics, lever

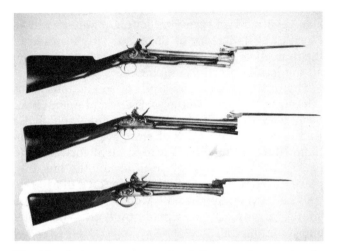

The blunderbuss was a gun for defense and came in pistol or carbine form. (The three English-made carbines are thoughtfully equipped with folding bayonets.) Despite the popular belief, the belling of the muzzle had no effect on the patterning of the gun.

A boattail bullet derives its name from the taper at its base, not unlike the stern of a small boat. Its streamlined shape produces lowered air resistance and flatter trajectory.

actions or pump rifles work well because quick second or third shots may be needed. Some competent hunters and guides prefer a .41 Magnum or .44 Magnum revolver because it is easy to carry when following the hounds, but in these cases the hunter must be willing to approach the boar very closely and he must be an excellent shot. The object is to kill the boar outright with one shot so that the animal cannot maim or kill a hound. In Europe, where wild boars are often shot from elevated stands, big-bore rifles and slow, easily expanded bullets are favored. The same hunting method is also employed in some southeastern states, but hunters there seem to prefer flat-shooting rifles in calibers from .25 to .30.

boattail bullet A bullet on which the base is tapered to reduce air drag. The reduction in air drag results in higher ballistic coefficient of the bullet, which in turn results in less bullet drop, lower trajectory, and greater retained velocity and energy

at extended ranges. The boattail was originally a military development and was first used in military ammunition in 1919 in full-metal-jacket form. It was adapted to civilian use almost immediately thereafter.

This design is in wide use today for both target and hunting rifle bullets. For match shooting, the boattail bullet usually has a very small cavity in its point and is sometimes of full-metal-jacket structure. It is made with larger cavities in the point for varmint and big game hunting use. Many soft point bullets are also made in boattail design in various calibers and weights. (See BALLISTIC COEFFICIENT; EXTERIOR BALLISTICS.)

bobber A bobbing rifle or handgun target, usually a silhouette, that is briefly exposed to the view of the shooter and then disappears, either by being pulled into the target pit or rotated on its vertical axis so that only its thin edge is exposed to the shooter's view.

body That part of a metallic cartridge case situated between the neck (or the shoulder of a bottlenecked case) and the base or head of the cartridge at the opposite end. Also, that part of a bullet situated behind the nose or ogive.

In British usage, the part of a gun that is called the receiver in America.

Bogardus, Adam H. Adam Bogardus was one of a considerable coterie of match and exhibition shooters who, in the late 1800s, competed with each other for purses and/or side bets sometimes amounting to thousands of dollars. The rivalries were keen and often controversial. Notable among these shooters were Bogardus, Ira Paine, and Doc W. F. Carver.

Each proclaimed himself "Champion of the World," backing these claims with victories in head-to-head competitions or records scored in matches in America and abroad. All except Carver were basically shotgunners, and most of their shooting was at aerial targets, ranging from live birds to cubical wooden blocks to glass balls (invented by Bogardus), all thrown by hand or from traps.

Typical scores were 241 out of 300 trap-thrown glass balls (by Bogardus); 5,000 out of 5,156 trap-thrown glass balls (also by Bogardus, although this record was challenged as fraudulent and was generally discredited). Doc Carver registered similar or better scores shooting heavy rifles at identical targets under identical conditions.

For detailed (if not entirely unbiased) data regarding these shooters and their records, see the book, *Doc W. F. Carver, Spirit Gun of the West,* by Raymond W. Thorpe, published in 1957 by The Arthur H. Clark Company, Glendale, California. (See CARVER, DOC WILLIAM FRANK.)

bolster In muzzleloading guns, an iron or a steel drum, or similar device, located near the breech end of the barrel and containing the nipple. (See NIPPLE.)

bolsters The protruding lumps of metal, integral with the frame of a double-barrel shotgun, that support the outer portion of the shell heads in the chambers when the gun is fired. (See DOUBLE-BARREL SHOTGUN.)

bolt The sliding part in any breechloader's action that guides a round into the chamber and rotates to tightly lock the mechanism and prevent it from opening upon firing. The bolt houses the firing pin and cartridge case extractor, and through its locking lugs resists the backward pressure of the discharge. (See BOLT ACTION.)

bolt action The modern bolt-action design, used primarily in rifles, evolved from the single-shot bolt action invented and developed by Johann N. von Dreyse in 1837 and adopted by the Prussian military in 1841. A few decades later, Peter Paul Mauser refined the Dreyse action, primarily by altering it to cock on the uplift of the bolt. Mauser continued to work on a bolt-action design of his own but was unable to interest the Prussian or Austrian military

authorities in his rifle. However, the Austrian ambassador was impressed with Mauser's results to the point of arranging a meeting between Peter and his brother Wilhelm and an American representative of the Remington Arms Company, Samuel Norris, who agreed to finance manufacture of the rifles in Belgium and secured the first Mauser patent—not in Germany but in the United States—on June 2, 1868.

When Norris was unable to raise the money to carry out the Belgian manufacture, he tried to interest the Prussian government; and when that attempt failed, his contract became void. His efforts did pay off for the brothers Mauser when in 1872, the Prussian government began production of Mauser Model 71 rifles at its factory in Spandau. This resulted in the immediate success of the Mauser action on which all modern bolt actions are based.

There have been many kinds of bolt actions since the time of Dreyse and the Mausers, and not all have been true turn-bolt design. Some, like the Swiss Rubin bolt action, were of straight-pull design; in them, the bolt handle moved straight forward and back while a rotating bolt head locked the lugs into place in the receiver ring to, in turn, lock the action. The Lee Navy straight-pull Model 1895 action is a similar example; it was made by both Winchester and Remington.

The locking lugs of the bolt system have also varied greatly in design from the earliest models to those of the present, and there is even a wide difference among the locking lug systems used in today's bolt actions. Some of the early bolt systems for big-bore rifles were locked only by the bolt handle fitting against the forward edge of the receiver bridge. (Most .22 rimfire bolt actions use that design even today.) There were also bolt actions that employed only a single locking lug at the front of the bolt body, which was turned into a recess in the lower receiver ring when the bolt handle was turned down. The Krag-Jorgensen rifle of both Norwegian and American manufacture is an example.

A number of bolt actions have utilized locking lugs placed on the rear of the bolt; the lugs lock into the receiver bridge. This system has not been overly successful in rifles chambered for cartridges that have acute shoulder angles, large head diameter and that develop high working pressures. The long bolt body between the cartridge head and the locking lugs compresses slightly under high pressures, and the receiver is inclined to stretch somewhat. This allows the case to stretch and, in the worst instances, leads to case head separations on repeated resizing and firing of the same case in reloading.

Perhaps the most unusual bolt-action system is the rear-lockup design; the Colt Sauer rifle's bolt body has three retractable locking lugs—actually struts—that lock into the receiver bridge. They retract into the bolt body under cam action when the bolt handle is lifted.

The conventional Mauser bolt design has two lugs at the forward end of the bolt, necessitating a 90 degree bolt handle lift to withdraw the bolt, but many of today's actions have three-lug systems that cut bolt lift to 60 degrees. Some of these have three single lugs, while others—like the Weatherby Mark V—have multiple lugs within each bank of three, which normally add up to a total of nine. This latter design is sometimes called the interrupted thread system because the bolt body is machined with a series of grooves to form the multiple lugs, and then cut lengthwise to form the three banks and allow the lugs to lock into place in the receiver when the bolt handle is turned down. According to some sources, this design is stronger than the two- or three-lug system, but that claim is more a matter of opinion than of fact.

There is no doubt that any design that places the lugs on the front of the bolt immediately behind the cartridge head, whether employing two heavy lugs as found in the true Mauser system or three lugs in single or multiple form, is the strongest and most reliable of all bolt-action designs. (See DREYSE, JOHANN NIKOLAUS VON; MAUSER, PETER PAUL.)

bolt body   That part of the action that contains the striker (hammer) mechanism, extractor assembly, and the locking system. Generally, the locking system is integral with the bolt body, and it is designed to withstand the backward thrust that results from firing. (See BOLT ACTION.)

bolt cylinder   In a one-piece bolt the cylinder is the entire bolt body, including the extractor on the bolt head, the locking lugs, and the striker mechanism. (See BOLT ACTION.)

bolt face   The forward part of the bolt that engages the cartridge head and from which the firing pin emerges when the trigger is pulled.

The Weatherby Mark V bolt body employs relieving flutes along its length to lessen friction.

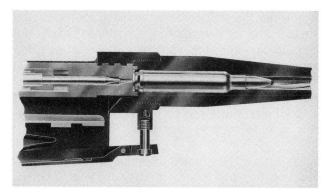

A recessed bolt face, as employed on this Weatherby Mark V bolt, allows the case head to be completely enclosed.

bolt guide   A small metal projection milled into the side of a bolt to guide it in its raceway. Some modern actions utilize their locking lugs as guides. (See BOLT RACEWAY; LOCKING LUG.)

bolt handle   On a bolt-action rifle or shotgun, the external lever of the bolt that is pulled back by the shooter to open the action and pushed forward to chamber a round and close the action. (See BOLT KNOB; BUTTERKNIFE BOLT HANDLE.)

bolt knob   On most bolt actions the bolt handle has a round or pear-shaped end called a bolt knob. It is gripped by the shooter when working the bolt. (See BOLT HANDLE; BUTTERKNIFE BOLT HANDLE.)

bolt lift   The amount of vertical movement required for the shooter to raise the bolt handle sufficiently to unlock the action and (in most bolt-action rifles and shotguns) cock the mechanism. (See BOLT ACTION.)

bolt lugs   Projections on the breechbolt that lock into corresponding cuts in the receiver to secure the breechbolt against backward thrust caused by the pressure of cartridge ignition. These projections are cammed into the receiver in a variety of ways, depending upon the design of the action. They are of various sizes and number and are located at different points along the bolt, depending upon the action type. The most common arrangement consists of two large lugs located near the forward portion of the bolt. (See BOLT ACTION; LOCKING LUG.)

bolt raceway   The parallel tracks or rails in the sidewalls of a receiver that serve to guide the bolt in its back-and-forth motion through the action.

bolt release   The bolt release is the device on a bolt-action rifle or shotgun that negates the bolt stop, permitting the bolt to be removed from the action for cleaning or boresighting. In actions where the sear acts as bolt stop, the bolt release is activated merely by depressing the trigger completely. Most Mauser-derived bolt actions feature an independent bolt release located on the left side of the receiver; it is either swung out or depressed to release the bolt. (See BOLT STOP; BORESIGHT.)

bolt sleeve The shield, over the rear of the bolt, that encases the cocking mechanism and to which the safety is occasionally fitted. It sometimes acts as a gas deflector.

bolt stop The metal projection in a bolt-action firearm that stops the rearward travel of the bolt when it is fully pulled back. (See BOLT RELEASE.)

bolt travel The distance between the bolt face and the rear of the chamber when the bolt is in its rearmost position. The distance is variable, depending upon action length.

Boone and Crockett Club In 1932, the Boone and Crockett Club was founded to provide formal recognition of the collecting of outstanding North American big-game trophies and to keep systematic records of these trophies.

Located in Pittsburgh, Pennsylvania, the club sponsored the first edition of *Records of North American Big Game*, of which 500 copies were printed by Derrydale Press in the Club's first year. In that year also, Prentiss N. Gray, who compiled the book, sought to develop a more satisfactory trophy evaluating, or scoring, system than was in use, and placed the project in the hands of Dr. James L. Clark of the American Museum of Natural History. Dr. Clark devised such a system and, in 1935, ran a competition based on it.

In 1939, Boone and Crockett published an expanded edition of the 1932 record book, entitled *North American Big Game*. In order to correct shortcomings in Dr. Clark's rating method, the club turned to Grancel Fitz, a noted big-game hunter.

World War II brought a halt to most big-game hunting, but in 1949, under the direction of Samuel B. Webb, a third scoring system, this one highly sophisticated, came into being. It first appeared in the club's 1952 book (its first postwar publication) and used the title of the 1932 book. Since 1952, only a few minor modifications have been made in this system, and the book's title reverted to *North American Big Game*.

Boone and Crockett trophies are scored by a complex measuring system that, in the case of horned and/or antlered game, takes into account the spread, length, symmetry, number of tines, and thickness of the horns or antlers. Bears and cats are scored on the dimensions of the skull. Trophies can be measured for official entry in the records only by a specially trained official scorer, and the measurements can take place only after a 60-day "drying" period that permits the trophy to shrink to its permanent dimensions.

In 1973, Boone and Crockett entered into an agreement with the National Rifle Association, whereby the B and C Awards Programs would be cosponsored by the NRA's Hunter Services Division. The Awards Programs provide recognition of outstanding trophies; each competition is based on a three-year period.

Trophies that meet the minimum Boone and Crockett point score are entered in the records book. Especially outstanding heads that were taken with an unusual degree of difficulty are eligible for a special Awards Program. Boone and Crockett medals and certificates of merit are presented to the winners.

Hunters who desire to enter a head in the competition should contact Boone and Crockett for the address of the nearest official scorer.

Nine editions of *North American Big Game* were published by Boone and Crockett through 1971. (The book is now issued approximately every seven years.) The 1988 edition contains listings of 6,000 trophies in 31 categories. It is priced at $30, and is available from Boone and Crockett.

In 1973, the Boone and Crockett Club moved its offices from Pittsburgh to 424 North Washington St., Alexandria, Virginia 22314. (See NATIONAL RIFLE ASSOCIATION [NRA].)

boot See SCABBARD.

Borchardt pistol See LUGER (PARABELLUM) PISTOL.

bore The interior of a firearm's barrel. In Great Britain, the word is used as Americans use the word "gauge"; a 12-gauge shotgun being referred to as a 12-bore, for example.

bore cast Bore and chamber casting are accomplished in the same way and for the same purpose. That is, similar material is used to learn the diameter and shape of the bore and chamber in a firearm.

The material used to make the cast has changed down through the years, but all have had in common low melting temperatures and a minimum of shrinkage upon cooling and hardening. Plain sulphur makes a good cast, but powdered lamp black and spirits of camphor should be added to minimize shrinkage during cooling.

A commercial compound called Cerrosafe, available from gunsmith supply houses, makes a better cast. It shrinks slightly on cooling for easy removal, but expands to exact bore dimensions one hour later. It melts at 158–190 degrees Fahrenheit and can be reused many times.

bore diameter Bore diameter is measured in a rifled barrel from the face of the lands on opposite sides of the bore. It is the true diameter of the original bored hole in the barrel blank after it has been reamed to uniform diameter. Bore diameter should not be confused with groove diameter, which is the distance across the bore from the bottom of one groove to that on the opposite side, as the grooves are cut or otherwise formed into the sides of the bore after it is reamed to true bore diameter.

Bore diameter in shotguns is generally referred to in terms of gauge. (See BARREL, RIFLED; SHOTGUN GAUGES.)

bore gauge In the manufacture of a rifle barrel, extreme care must be taken to assure the dimensional uniformity of the bore, since this factor strongly affects the barrel's accuracy. The first bore gauges were typified by the so-called star gauge used at the Springfield Armory in the manufacture of the Model 1903 Springfield rifle. Star gauges utilized metal "fingers," which rode in the barrel grooves and measured their uniformity.

The star gauge has been superseded by the air gauge, which is considerably more accurate. Air gauges employ a constant stream of air blown through a barrel. The air must force its way past a plug that is drawn through the barrel, and the amount of air passing between the plug and the wall of the bore causes a ball in a glass tube to rise or fall. If the plug passes a loose spot in the bore, more air escapes past it, and the ball rises; a tight spot causes the ball to drop. The air gauge is so accurate that variances of .00005 inch can be detected.

bore plating The application of a coating of dissimilar material to the bore of a rifle, pistol, or shotgun barrel. This plating, is normally of hard chrome and is usually from .001 to .0005 of an inch in thickness.

Chrome plating a bore affords a number of advantages. When applied correctly, the surface is made extremely smooth and friction is reduced when the bullet or shot charge passes through. Being very hard, it is less subject to erosion by hot powder gas and so wears less than bare barrel steel. But perhaps the greatest advantage that chrome bore plating offers is that it is corrosion-proof. It is therefore especially valuable where there is high humidity, particularly if the area is near salt water. (See BARREL EROSION.)

boresight To boresight a rifle is to roughly sight it in by adjusting the sights, either metallic or optical, to align with the bore.

With a bolt-action rifle, remove the bolt (or with a single shot that has a falling breechblock, open the action) and place the rifle on a rest so that it is solidly in place. Visually align the bore on a distant object, preferably 100 yards from the muzzle, making certain that the object is centered in the outline of the bore and that your eye is on a line with the true axis of the bore as you look through it from the rear. Without moving the rifle, adjust the metallic sights or the telescope reticle to correspond precisely with what is seen through the bore. When this is done, recheck to make sure that the sight and bore are on the same zero point, and readjust as necessary.

Several companies offer optical boresights, or collimators, which may be used for rifles with actions lacking detachable bolts or other means that allow looking through the bore from the rear. A rod, or spud, on the bottom of the instrument fits into the bore and is aligned with a screen grid in the optical window. The screen may have on it a plain cross to be used as an aiming point, an X, or a grid that has a center cross and lines forming squares that usually subtend 4 inches at 100 yards.

Shotguns are not boresighted since they are not aimed, except when used with rifled slugs. In this case, they are zeroed in at close range—25 to 50 yards, the distance at which they will most likely be used. No collimator spuds are made in shotgun sizes.

Handguns, like shotguns, are used at extremely short ranges, where problems of trajectory and sight alignment are minimal. Therefore, they are not boresighted. (See BENCHREST; COLLIMATOR; SIGHTING IN.)

bore slugging The purpose of bore slugging is to measure the diameter of a rifled bore to the bottom of the grooves and/or the true bore diameter on the face of opposite lands. Measurements should be taken with a micrometer caliper that reads in ten-thousandths of an inch (.0001), as measurements less precise than this will not be helpful in judging the bore's consistency.

Bore slugging is accomplished by the use of a bullet cast or swaged of pure lead, or a piece of lead wire. If the lead object is large enough to fill the bore fully to the bottom of the lands, it is simply pushed through with a stiff rod. However, a slug or lead wire of slightly smaller diameter than the bore may be used by inserting it into the bore and bringing a rod of almost bore diameter up against it, then expanding the lead object to fully fill the bore by placing a second rod against it from the opposite side and tapping with a hammer. The expanded lead is then pushed through the bore with one of the rods.

Boss (company) In the middle years of the 19th century, the shooting of trapped live pigeons was a prime sport among the wealthier gentry in London. During much of that period three gunmakers attended the shoots regularly—Thomas Boss, Stephen Grant, and James Purdey. These men were on hand to help their customers in whatever way they could, including lending them the benefit of the gun lore they had absorbed over many years.

At this time it was said of Thomas Boss that he was and had been for many years a "London maker in every sense of the word," for he supplied guns "built entirely in London, of the best materials and at the best price."

Thomas Boss's father had worked for Joseph Manton, as had the first James Purdey. An apprentice under his father at Manton's, Boss also worked for a few years—1817 to 1821—for the original James Purdey. Boss went into business for himself in 1830 at 3 Grosvenor Street, London.

He died in 1858. His widow kept up the business, taking Stephen Grant as a partner in 1860. Grant left Boss and Co. in 1867 to open his own business. A nephew of Thomas Boss carried on the business thereafter, until in 1891 he took as a partner John Robertson, a gifted designer.

Robertson had worked under Joseph Purdey for 10 years and was a thorough master of his craft in all respects. He patented an intercepting safety sear, copatented with Henry Holland several designs for hammerless guns and ejectors and, in addition, a reliable single trigger.

In 1909, Boss and Co. introduced its over/under, a development of John Robertson. This was the first over/under to be made with a low breech profile, its barrel locking system lying alongside the bottom barrel rather than underneath the lower barrel.

In 1930 the firm moved to Albemarle Street, London, with the three sons of John Robertson acting as directors. In 1961 Boss and Co. moved to 13–14 Cork Street, London.

Although the firm remains in business, it is not producing guns at the present, and those Boss shotguns that are available at the Boss shop or elsewhere command extremely high prices.

bottleneck case Any metallic cartridge case whose diameter changes sharply enough to form a distinct shoulder is referred to as a bottleneck case. For example, the .458 case tapers almost imperceptibly from base to mouth, but when this same case is swaged to form the .338, it tapers quite sharply at the shoulder and is therefore called a bottleneck. (See CASE TAPER.)

bottom plate The plate set into the bottom of some types of hinged-barrel shotgun actions that encloses the gun's operating mechanism. Triggers are frequently attached to the bottom plate, in which case it is sometimes called a trigger plate. (See HINGED FRAME; TRIGGER-PLATE ACTION.)

Boulengé chronograph See CHRONOGRAPH.

Boxer primer The Boxer primer, one of the outstanding breakthroughs in ammunition development, was invented in 1867 by British Colonel Edward M. Boxer of the Royal Laboratory at Woolwich. It differed from earlier rudimentary centerfire priming mechanisms by having its anvil self-contained within the primer; the flash was transmitted to the powder charge by means of a single central hole in the base of the cartridge case.

The Boxer design has become the primer type used in American centerfire rifle and pistol ammunition. It consists of a metal cup within which is the priming compound and the anvil, the latter two separated by a protective disc. The gun's firing pin crushes the compound against the anvil to detonate the primer. The Boxer primer's easy removal and replacement have greatly stimulated modern handloading. (See PRIMER.)

box lock A term used to describe a kind of shotgun action in which the locks are fitted into the action body rather than on separate and detachable sideplates.

box magazine One of three kinds of magazines used in most modern repeating shoulder arms, the

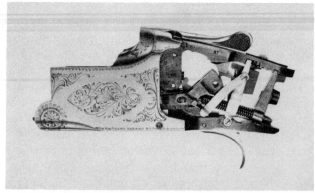

One of the most successful boxlock designs was the action for the Browning Superposed shotgun.

box magazine was patented by James Paris Lee in 1879. It is a boxlike receptacle placed underneath the gun's action, and it holds cartridges in a staggered position. Cartridge feeding is effected by the pressure of a spring from below. Box magazines made the safe use of spitzer bullets possible in repeating rifles, since the box magazine removed the hazard of accidental detonation created if spitzers are used in tubular magazines, which align them bullet-point-to-primer. (See CLIP; ROTARY MAGAZINE; SPITZER BULLET.)

box pigeon shooting The American name for European live bird shooting competition in which birds are released from "boxes" (also called traps).

There are usually five, but may be as many as nine, boxes lined up in the center of a scoring circle that is surrounded by a low wire fence. The shooter takes his position at his assigned shooting yardage (usually 27 meters in a major international competition), loads his shotgun, and asks if the "trapper" (releaser of the birds who is stationed in a small scoring house behind the shooter) is ready. When the affirmative answer is given, the shooter shoulders his gun and not knowing from which of the boxes a bird will appear, calls "pull." The box from which the bird is released has been predetermined by a "selector" (a mechanical device much like a miniature roulette wheel) or by drawing box numbers at random from a leather cup that has been shaken, like a dice cup, to ensure a fair draw.

When a bird appears, the shooter must fire very quickly; the bird needs to fly only 17½ yards to clear the scoring fence, and if it does, dead or alive, it is declared a "lost bird." Two shots are permitted at each bird and are very often necessary. Even when well hit, hard driving pigeons may fly out of the ring unless anchored by a quick second shot.

Most shooters use double or over/under guns, and the most common choke borings are full-and-full or modified-and-full. The typical gun in this sport is stocked to shoot high (trap stocks are common) because the birds are almost invariably rising and it is an advantage to have the built-in lead provided by high shot placement. Although it looks easy, runs of even 25 straight are sufficiently uncommon to be worth a great deal of money at a major shoot. This is an expensive game, with high entrance fees and the shooter charged for each bird released for him. Prizes are also large.

The area around London seems to have been the birthplace of box pigeon shooting in the middle of the 18th century, and one of the earliest pigeon shooting clubs was called "Old Hats," a name derived from the practice of placing pigeons in holes in the ground and covering them with old tophats

until release. The sport's most glamorous period was around 1900 and shortly thereafter when European nobility competed for great sums of money in live pigeon shoots in Monte Carlo.

Box pigeon shooting led to the design of the raised comb Monte Carlo stock; when the gentry realized they could hit the fast-rising pigeons better with a higher comb, they began adding build-up devices to their gunstocks to raise their eye position. The Monte Carlo stock, of course, remains popular for both shotguns and rifles.

Princess Grace of Monaco halted live bird shooting at Monte Carlo, but the sport remains well organized worldwide and world championships are staged each year, usually in Italy, Spain, Portugal, Argentina, or Mexico. Pigeon shooting is illegal in England, and although not specifically illegal in America, the relatively few private shoots staged here are not publicized because of the broad nature of animal anticruelty laws. Its proponents claim, however, that pigeon shooting is no less humane than field trial shooting of birds or, for that matter, hunting, and actually serves a worthwhile purpose. Birds used are raised specially overseas or are trapped by professional trappers, who often operate under contract with municipalities where the birds pose health hazards as well as do damage to statues and buildings. (See LIVE PIGEON SHOOTING; MONTE CARLO COMB.)

box rib This term is sometimes used in reference to the solid, or nonventilated, rib used on some shotgun barrels. (See RIB.)

Bradley sight Popular front sight used on many shotguns. It features an ivory or white plastic bead—a half-sphere mounted on a small steel ramp—and is designed to offer an eyecatching point of reference for quick pointing at game or targets. (See BEAD SIGHT.)

brass (in cartridge cases) Cartridge brass is a distinct alloy consisting of approximately 70 percent copper and 30 percent zinc; it is further characterized by an unusual degree of freedom from impurities.

Because cartridge cases are frequently subjected to exceedingly high stress at the rear, or head, where the case is not supported during firing by the chamber or the breechblock, the brass must be extremely strong (and correspondingly hard) in this area. Because, too, the case neck must be sufficiently ductile to readily expand and seal the chamber at the instant of firing and to hold the bullet securely for many years without cracking under the continual hoop stress, the case must be softer and more ductile in the front region.

The characteristic of differential hardness and physical properties from end to end of a cartridge case is achieved by an elaborately controlled process of manufacture in which the hardness is imparted by controlled cold-working of the metal and modified by a series of heat treatments to impart the different physical properties required in the various portions of the case.

The composition of cartridge brass has evolved from more than 100 years of experience in producing and testing various alloys for the manufacture of cases and is now virtually standardized throughout the world. (See ANNEALING; HANDLOAD; WORK HARDENING.)

brass shotshell Until a few decades ago, all-brass shotshells were popular with wildfowl hunters because they were almost impervious to moisture and were simple to reload. Wad column height was not important in these cartridges because no crimp was required; an overshot wad was used. All gauges of brass shells are 2½ inches in length except for the .410, which is 2 inches long. With the advent of the plastic shotshell case, the advantages of the all-brass shells diminished and they are no longer popular.

brazing A method of joining metal parts with copper alloy (usually brass, a copper-zinc alloy). The assembly is heated so that the alloy flows and fills the joint. Brazing is used to attach ribs and lugs to barrels of double-barrel firearms and in repair work.

break-action A firearm with a hinged frame is a break-action gun. This kind of construction is most commonly employed in double-barrel and over/under shotguns, but some rifles and handguns utilize it as well. (See HINGED FRAME.)

break-open See HINGED FRAME.

Breda (company) Located in Brescia, Italy, Breda Meccanica Bresciana manufactures lightweight semiautomatic 12- and 20-gauge shotguns in a wide variety of grades. Breda guns were imported by Stoeger Arms from the mid-1950s to the late 1970s, but at present are not brought into the United States by any commercial agent.

breech The rear portion of a rifle, repeating shotgun or automatic handgun barrel, usually the rear opening of the chamber into the barrel. The face of the breech abuts with the face of the bolt, and sometimes a portion of the breech is cut away to accommodate a claw extractor.

breechblock That part of a rifle that closes the chamber at the rear and supports the head of the cartridge case during firing. The word is often used to imply a member that moves transversely in the action and/or is locked by some means other than rotation about a longitudinal axis through the center of the bore. In this sense, it is used in contradistinction to "breechbolt." Falling blocks, tilting blocks, and hinged blocks are some common kinds of breechblocks.

breechbolt A particular kind of breechblock, usually circular in cross section, having projecting lugs that are engaged by rotation into corresponding abutments in the receiver or in an extension that is rigidly attached to rifle, shotgun, or handgun barrel. The word bolt is often used alone to indicate the breechbolt of a gun. The terms breechbolt and breechblock are sometimes used interchangeably, even when the member described does not have all of the characteristics that usually distinguish one from the other.

breechloader Any gun that is loaded from the breech, usually with a cartridge, as distinguished from a muzzleloader.

breechplug A plug threaded into the breech of the barrel of a muzzleloading gun, the purpose of which is to seal the breech against the rearward escape of propellant gases when the gun is fired. (See MUZZLELOADER.)

breech-seated A bullet introduced into a rifled barrel from the rear and engaged with the rifling, prior to insertion of the propellant, is said to be breech-seated.

Brenneke shotgun slug Brenneke is the brand name of a rifled slug, designed for big-game hunting with a shotgun, made in Germany but widely marketed around the world. In construction it differs from other slugs by featuring a conical point combined with a hard paper wadding that is firmly attached to the lead plug. The manufacturer states that these features produce a projectile of superior ballistic performance that can be used in any shotgun regardless of its choke. (See SHOTGUN SLUG.)

Brevex action The French-made Brevex Magnum Mauser rifle action was imported into America by Tradewinds, Inc., of Tacoma, Washington beginning in 1955. Patterned after the original Magnum Mauser action, the Brevex is designed to handle long, large diameter cartridges of magnum classification. It has been made in two models, the Model 300 for standard belted cartridges like the .300 and .375 H&H, and the Model 400 for the .416 Rigby. The 400 is also suitable for .378-.460 Weatherby cases.

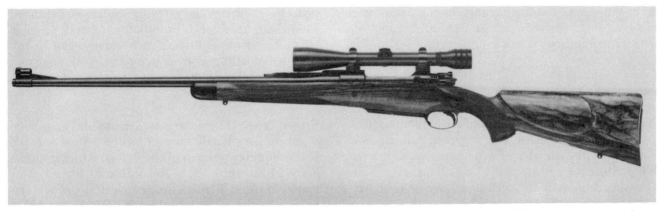

The Brevex action was manufactured in Paris and was designed to provide an action that could contain four extra-large cartridges such as the .416 Rigby and .505 Gibbs. To accomplish this, the Brevex employed a very deep magazine well, which can be seen on this Brevex-based rifle by Griffin & Howe.

The configuration of the Brevex action very closely resembles the standard Model 98 Mauser action, but it has a bolt and safety designed for lower scope mounting and a decided "belly" at the bottom of its magazine. With a magazine length of 3.925 inches, it is ideal for all the longer magnum cartridges. No longer produced, the Brevex is still in considerable demand on the used gun market.

bridge Also known as the receiver bridge, it is the top side of a rifle action.

bridge mount A bridge mount for a telescopic sight spans the opening in the top of a bolt-action rifle's receiver with a single piece of steel to which the front and rear rings of the scope mount are attached. Both of the tapped holes in the receiver ring are utilized by a bridge mount's base, but normally only one of the holes in the receiver bridge is used. A bridge mount base is considered to be more rigid and stronger than a two-piece scope mounting base system. (See SCOPE MOUNTS.)

The bridge mount is a one-piece scope base. It is strong and enjoys great popularity in the United States.

bridging of shot See SHOT, BRIDGING OF.

bridle The plate inside a percussion or flintlock firearm that retains the tumbler and guides it as the hammer and tumbler rotate during cocking and firing. It is commonly attached with three screws, one of which may also act as a pin for the sear. (See TUMBLER.)

brightness A subjective term sometimes used to describe the brilliance of the image seen in a telescope, telescopic sight, or similar optical instrument such as binoculars.

When modified by the word "relative" (relative brightness), it is specifically defined as the square of the ratio of the unobstructed diameter of the objective lens in millimeters to the magnification of the instrument. Thus, a 10X telescope having a 40mm objective lens has a relative brightness of $(\frac{40}{10})^2$, or 16.

The relative brightness is not necessarily a quantitative index of the brilliance of the image as perceived by the eye, however, because that perception is also affected by the diameter of the exit pupil and the ratio of the light transmitted to that reflected or absorbed within the optical system of the instrument. (See BINOCULARS; RELATIVE BRIGHTNESS; SPOTTING SCOPE; TELESCOPIC SIGHTS.)

Brinell hardness scale A numerical scale for assigning relative hardness to metals. A hardened ball is forced against the surface of the metal being tested. The depth of penetration of the ball is then measured and related to an arbitrary measure of hardness known as a Rockwell scale. For example, a receiver for a modern bolt-action rifle that measured 45 on the Rockwell scale would be hard; one that measured 35 would be very soft.

brisance The shattering or crushing effect of an explosive. The amount of brisance is dependent upon the rate of detonation and the relative power of demolition. The term is often used in conjunction with primers. (See PRIMER.)

Brister, Bob (1930–) This native Texan is an internationally recognized authority on shooting and hunting. He has been the shooting editor of *Field & Stream* magazine since 1972, and the outdoors editor for the *Houston Chronicle* for 36 years. Although he is a hunter and shooter of wide experience, Brister is best known for his expertise with the shotgun. He has won numerous national and international trophies in several shotgun sports and is the author of *Shotgunning: the Art and the Science*, which is America's best-selling modern work on the scattergun.

He has been particularly influential in the public acceptance of steel shot and in popularizing sporting clays. Brister has won prizes both for writing and photography, including a Pulitzer Prize nomination for his coverage of Hurricane Carla in 1961.

Shooting editor for Field & Stream.

broach A broach is a rifling cutter—a hardened steel shaft on which is mounted a series of progressively larger teeth. Broach cutters can make a complete set of rifling grooves in a barrel with one pass, each tooth taking a deeper bite than its predecessor. (See BARREL, RIFLED.)

Brown Bess One of the most famous and long-lived of all military small arms, the Brown Bess was the chief shoulder weapon of the British Army from the early 1700s until 1815. According to British arms expert Howard Blackmore, the earliest printed reference to the nickname Brown Bess appeared in 1785. In current usage the name is applied to British military flintlock muskets in service from the 1720s to the 1830s, not precisely the same arms contemporaneously known as Brown Besses.

The original designation for the 46-inch barrel version was Long Land Musket, while a 42-inch barrel model was known as the Short Land Musket. There was a light infantry model and a marine or militia model, which also had 42-inch barrels.

The origin of the term Brown Bess is uncertain. Some historians feel that "Bess" is a corruption of the German word *Buchse* (gun), while others think it is merely a term of affection. "Brown" probably referred to the color of the barrel. Early models of the Brown Bess had black, painted stocks, but the later models utilized walnut stained a reddish-brown, and the barrels were browned, a rust-inhibiting process used in the Brown Bess's day.

All Brown Besses were made in .75 caliber and were smoothbore, to facilitate rapid loading. Military tactics of the time stressed rapid volleys of fire (a recruit was considered unskilled until he could get off four shots in a minute) rather than accuracy; a British officer estimated that an aimed shot from a Brown Bess would probably strike an adversary at 80 yards, might possibly strike at 100, and was essentially inaccurate at longer range.

The Long Land Musket weighed 14 pounds—nearly twice the weight of a modern service rifle. This was necessary because British tactics stressed the use of the bayonet, and the musket's weight aided thrusting movements with the arm, as well as making it useful as a club.

Brown Bess muskets were fitted with brass mountings, and the lockplates were marked with the letters GR (for *Georgius Rex*) and the British Broad Arrow, signifying that the gun was government property. The date of manufacture and the name of the maker were stamped behind the cock. Those Brown Besses not made under civilian contract were manufactured at the Tower of London or at Dublin Castle.

During its extraordinarily long life, the Brown Bess proved itself a highly reliable and effective arm that saw action all over the world, and many of the guns saw use long after percussion ignition had rendered them obsolete. (See BROWNING [PROCESS]; FLINTLOCK.)

Browning (company) Formerly Browning Arms Co., now known simply as Browning, this firm distributes a variety of outdoor products, including firearms. Founded at Ogden, Utah Territory, in 1879, by John M. Browning, the firm was originally known as Browning Bros. and specialized in the manufacture of the founder's Model 1879 Single-Shot rifle.

In 1883, a Winchester representative took note of the Model 1879, and Winchester vice-president T. G. Bennett arranged for the New Haven firm to acquire manufacturing rights. This arrangement—Browning designs turned out by Winchester—was to last for 19 years. Browning and Winchester ended their association when they disagreed about the rights to the Browning automatic shotgun and, in 1902, Browning arranged for Fabrique Nationale of Belgium to manufacture the gun.

In the ensuing years, F. N.-made guns of Browning design imported under the Browning name brought the Utah firm to prominence. The Browning Automatic-5 shotgun, Superposed over/under shotgun, and Hi-Power automatic pistol are especially noteworthy and have sold in large numbers.

During the late 1960s, Browning began a program of diversification and now sells—in addition to firearms of Belgian, Japanese, and American manufacture—outdoor clothing, fishing tackle, archery equipment, and cutlery. The firm's repair and warehouse facilities are located in St. Louis, Missouri and the headquarters are in Morgan, Utah. (See BROWNING, JOHN M.)

browning (process) A chemically induced oxidation process used to finish gun barrels and other ferrous parts in a brown color. A repeated treatment of sulphuric acid and water produces a fine rust, which is then removed, and the metal is oiled and waxed or varnished. Employed primarily in the 18th and 19th centuries, this process was the forerunner of the modern bluing process.

Proper temperature and humidity controls were necessary for the best browning results in olden days. A damp box—one in which a combination of low temperature and high humidity could be maintained—was sometimes used. Browning solutions are sold today by gunsmithing supply houses, but any solution that produces adequate rusting will result in a brown surface. (See BLUING.)

Browning, John M. (1854–1926) John M. Browning was born in Ogden, Utah, the son of Jonathan

Browning, a gunsmith. He held patents for 50 rifles, shotguns, pistols and machine guns, not to mention labor-saving and precision machines for the manufacture of such weapons, more than any other man in the history of firearms. He was decorated by almost every civilized country in the world, and Browning guns have been manufactured by nearly every major nation. Browning, born a Mormon, retained throughout his life an abiding loyalty to that church and to his native state.

In 1879, Browning sold to the Winchester company a single-shot breechloading rifle he invented and patented, the first of many such arrangements he made with that company and today it can be said that most of the Winchester guns are derived from Browning patents. The same can be said of many of the Remington line, and of all of the Colt autoloading centerfire pistols.

Browning's first semiautomatic pistol was manufactured beginning in 1899 by Fabrique Nationale d'Arms de Guerre in Liège, Belgium. This was the little .32-caliber pistol later manufactured by Colt in .32 and .380 calibers. Millions of Browning guns (rifles, shotguns, and pistols) have been made by FN and by American manufacturers and sold in the United States and abroad. The Browning Colt .45 ACP, official sidearm of U.S. troops since 1911, was manufactured by the millions during World War I and since. Many companies, some not ordinarily involved in gun making, have manufactured them to meet wartime needs. Since about 1910, all sporting guns bearing the Browning name have been manufactured originally in Liège but recently in Japan and distributed in America by the Browning company, with headquarters currently in Morgan, Utah.

John Browning was not only an inventor who could design guns on paper, he was a gunsmith who could make guns, and he was a shooter. He enjoyed hunting, and at the age of 70 he broke 98 out of 100 birds at the traps. At the time of his death he was perfecting the now-famous Browning over/under shotgun, which appeared on the American market a few years later and which became the favorite of countless shooters here and abroad. As a contemporary biographer wrote years ago, "While the United States can claim John Browning as its outstanding inventor of firearms, the world pays similar tribute. John Browning was an international figure, and his memory will last as long as guns are built." (See BROWNING [COMPANY].)

buck fever Buck fever, a condition of nervous excitement, is responsible, in all likelihood, for a majority of missed shots at game animals. The term is an old one, of frontier origin, and is hunters' vernacular for what could be called "game excitement." Almost every hunter experiences buck fever, whether he goes after squirrels, ducks, whitetails or a bull elk in the Rockies. The more desirable the animal, however, the harder buck fever is liable to strike.

The causes of buck fever are three: the sheer thrill of seeing animals in the wild; overeagerness to down a trophy; and (perhaps subconsciously) a lack of confidence in one's shooting ability. A mild case of buck fever adds spice to a hunt; any hunter who does not experience a bit of it surely does not have much fun. But in extreme cases buck fever can cause a hunter to lose control, to shoot without aiming and miss wildly, or sometimes to be incapable of shooting at all.

Hunting being what it is, the total elimination of excitement at seeing game is hardly desirable. Buck fever can be controlled, however. Experience is the best arresting agent, but lacking that buck fever can still be mastered if the hunter has confidence in his gun and in himself. If he or she has personally sighted-in the gun, has practiced enough with it to feel proficient, doesn't rush unduly while preparing to shoot, quells shaking limbs by shooting from a rest so that the sight picture is steady and confidence inspiring—then buck fever can be relegated to its proper position as savored and controlled excitement rather than an ungovernable disaster.

buckhorn sight The buckhorn is a type of open rifle sight that features a deep V along with "ears" (the buckhorns), which turn in to nearly meet above the V. It was developed in an attempt to create a sight that could be readily picked up by the shooter's eye. Actually, the overhanging ears block out light and make this sight a poor choice.

Buckhorn sights were so named because of their fancied resemblance to a deer's antlers. (See METAL-LIC SIGHTS; SEMIBUCKHORN SIGHT.)

This kind of sight (a semi-buckhorn is shown here) takes its name from the fact that its outline is similar to the curve of a deer's antlers. It is an inefficient sight and is found mostly on older rifles.

Buckingham, Nash (1880–1971) Nash Buckingham is considered one of our finest writers on the outdoors.

Born in Memphis and educated at Harvard and the University of Tennessee Law School, he was an outstanding athlete, winning letters in boxing, track, baseball, and football. He was also known as one of the best wingshots of his generation.

Buckingham began his writing career as a sports columnist for the Memphis *Commercial Appeal*. In 1927 he helped to found the Outdoor Writers Association of America. For years he was an associate editor of *Field & Stream*, one of the magazines for which he wrote articles and poetry. He produced nine books as well as numerous articles and contributions to anthologies. His first book, a 1934 collection of stories entitled *De Shootinest Gent'man*, was lauded by *The New York Times* as "refreshingly different" and unmarred by artificiality. *Mark Right!*, a companion volume published in 1936, received comparable praise. Among his other works, *Ole Miss'* (1937) and *Tattered Coat* (1944) may be best remembered.

A notable authority on bird dogs, Buckingham served as a judge at national field trials from 1934 to 1951. In 1964 he was elected to the Field Trial Hall of Fame.

Buckingham welcomed the end of the market-shooting era and helped establish America's conservation movement. In 1925 he became director of game restoration for the Western Cartridge Company. In 1928 he went to Washington, D. C., as executive secretary of American Wildfowlers, which later became Ducks Unlimited. He remained in Washington until 1936, working for the Wildlife Institute and promoting conservation legislation. In 1947 he was the first individual ever awarded the *Field & Stream* Trophy for Outstanding Service to Conservation. (See FIELD & STREAM.)

buckshot Relatively large diameter round lead shot used in 12-gauge shotshells. Buckshot sizes run 00, 0, 1, 3, and 4. Smaller shot, beginning with BB, .181-inch in diameter, is not considered buckshot. 00 buckshot is .33-inch in diameter, No. 4 is .24 inch.

Buckshot is generally used in hunting larger animals such as deer, hence its name. It is also used by police and the military.

Some heavily populated states require hunters to use buckshot or rifled slugs because they don't carry as far as centerfire rifle bullets and are therefore thought to be safer. Other states prohibit buckshot or slugs on game such as deer because their authorities feel that these projectiles aren't lethal and encourage the wounding of animals. (See SHOTGUN SLUG.)

Nash Buckingham (center) was a leading writer on hunting and the outdoors for more than a half-century.

A load of 12-gauge 00 buckshot consists of nine lead pellets of about .32 caliber (shown here with a dime for comparison).

buffalo rifle See PLAINS RIFLE.

bugged primer See PRIMER PROTRUSION.

buggy rifles Any of a variety of short muzzleloading rifles much in vogue during the 1800s. Their barrels averaged about 20 inches in length, and they were typically of small caliber.

These rifles got their name from the fact that they could fit into a buggy, where a longer rifle would be awkward. While they were sometimes used for target shooting, their accuracy was not exceptional because of their light weight and short sighting radius.

bulk powder The term bulk powder came into use in the late 19th century when black powder was superseded by smokeless powder. It was soon discovered that smokeless powder was less dense, so that although the bulk size of the two kinds of powder was similar, there was a difference when they were measured by weight. "Bulk" became applied to smokeless powders that, through the artificial regulation of their densities with inert fillers, could be correctly loaded into cartridges with standardized black-powder measures. With the transition of sporting ammunition to smokeless powder, the need for this interchangeability by volume was no longer a factor, and bulk powder was replaced by the more efficient dense powder. (See DENSE POWDER; SMOKELESS POWDER.)

bull barrel A type of heavyweight barrel developed for precision shooting with target rifles. Bull barrels mimimize barrel vibration, hence promote maximum accuracy. Originally used for 1,000-yard big-bore target shooting, they are now also popular on smallbore target rifles and pistols and on benchrest rifles—particularly the latter, where sacrifices are sometimes made in sights, stock material and design in order to get as much weight as possible into the barrel. A decade or more ago, bull rifle barrels were 26 to 28 inches long, and that length is still favored for big bore 1,000-yard guns because of ballistic advantage, but in benchrest rifles the recent trend has been toward shorter, stiffer barrels of 20 to 22 inches. Regardless of length, bull barrels have little or no taper, with muzzle diameter rarely under .875 inch, and more commonly 1.00 inch or larger.

bullet An elongated conoidal projectile designed to be fired from a rifled barrel. While the form of a bullet is aerodynamically efficient, it is not self-stabilizing and depends on the spin imparted by the rifling to achieve stability in flight.

bullet bag Made to carry round lead balls for muzzleloading guns, most bullet bags are made of leather, with a leather drawstring at the top. Their size depends on the caliber of ball used; for a .32-caliber ball, for instance, a small 2½ × 3-inch bag is indicated. Larger bullets of course require a larger bag.

Buckskin and cowhide are the most used of the leathers. Some bullet bags have a wooden neck that will accommodate a ball up to .54 caliber or so, and

Bull barrels are used on target, varmint, and benchrest rifles where weight is an asset rather than a handicap. This is a Winchester Model 52 .22 target rifle.

a wooden stopper. They are worn on a thong around the body and are the fastest styles to use.

bullet casting See BULLET MOLD; CAST BULLET.

bullet casting (for muzzleloaders) Pure, virgin lead should be heated in a lead-melting pot or, preferably, in an electric furnace made expressly for this purpose. The lead should be heated for 20 to 30 minutes, or until it reaches a molten state with a temperature of 800 degrees Fahrenheit or slightly higher. (A guide to temperature can be had from the finished balls: If they are wrinkled and have air holes, the lead is not hot enough; if they are frosted, the lead is too hot.) Skim the lead frequently to remove dross.

The mold should be degreased, smoked with the flame of a paper match, and any soot from the match removed with cotton. While the lead is melting, the mold should be heated to 180 degrees.

When both the lead and mold are at the proper temperature, fill the lead dipper with lead and rapidly pour it into the mold, in sufficient quantity so that there is some slight overflow. This latter, when cooled, is known as the sprue.

Knock the sprue off with a fiber hammer and drop the bullet on a very soft, fireproof surface. While the balls are still hot, roll them on a lightly oiled surface and, after they have cooled, sort out any with holes, dimples or wrinkles.

If the balls are to be used in match shooting, or where high accuracy is important, they should be weighed, and only those that are within ³⁄₁₀-grain of each other should be used.

The mold should be stored with the last ball in it, sprue intact, to prevent rust. (See SPRUE CUTTER.)

bullet deflection Deflection is lateral deviation from the line of aim by a projectile in flight. It is caused by wind movement, and is thus differentiated from ballistic drift imparted by the rifling spin. Deflection is proportional to the difference in retardation between the bullet in the atmosphere and in a vacuum.

Deflection can be explained in part by the same physical laws that govern the crossing of a stream by a swimmer. The current carries the swimmer downstream, the actual distance dependent on the speed of the current, the swimmer's strength, and the length of time the swimmer is in the current. Wind deflection of a speeding bullet is governed by similar factors, but is complicated by the aerodynamic properties of the bullet—similar to the strength and time factors that affect the swimmer.

Every bullet is deflected to a certain extent by any angling wind, but heavier bullets and those with high ballistic coefficients are deflected much less than light or blunt projectiles, which shed velocity rapidly. Deflection is compensated for by windage allowance in aiming. (See BALLISTIC COEFFICIENT; BULLET SPIN; EXTERIOR BALLISTICS.)

bullet drag Drag is the slowing effect produced by air resistance on a bullet in flight. In a vacuum, drag would be totally eliminated. Its effect is dependent upon atmospheric density, the bullet's velocity, its length and weight in relation to its diameter, and its aerodynamic qualities. (See BALLISTIC COEFFICIENT; BOATTAIL BULLET; EXTERIOR BALLISTICS.)

bullet drift See DRIFT.

bullet drop From the moment a bullet emerges from the muzzle of a rifle or handgun, it is affected by gravity and is drawn toward the ground. This downward motion is known as bullet drop and usually refers to the distance a projectile falls below the line of sight. (See TRAJECTORY.)

bullet energy The capacity to do work possessed by a bullet in flight. Stated in foot-pounds, bullet energy is calculated by squaring the velocity of the bullet; dividing the result by 7,000; dividing the quotient by 64.32, twice the rate of acceleration of gravity; and multiplying the quotient by the bullet weight.

For example, to obtain the muzzle energy of a 180-grain .30/06 bullet that has a muzzle velocity of 2,700 feet per second, you would first square 2,700 (7,290,000); divide by 7,000 (1,041.43); divide 1,041.43 by 64.32 (16.19); and multiply 16.19 by 180 (2,914). The energy of this bullet, therefore, is 2,914 foot-pounds.

Bullet energy may be calculated at any point along a bullet's flight. It is proportional to the bullet's velocity and therefore is greater near the muzzle and less downrange. Two kinds of energy are commonly considered, muzzle and terminal. As the name implies, muzzle energy is the energy of the bullet at the firearm's muzzle, excluding the forces of muzzle pressure. Terminal energy is the energy of the projectile upon striking.

Laws in some states define the requirements for a legal hunting gun and load in terms of bullet energy. For example, Colorado requires that at least 1,000 foot-pounds of energy remain at 100 yards with any cartridge used for deer hunting. (See IMPACT BEHAVIOR BALLISTICS.)

bullet engraving Engraving is the impression left by the lands of the rifling on the surface of a bullet after it has been fired. Minor but often detectable differences may exist in the rifling marks engraved on bullets by individual firearms, allowing ballistics experts to trace bullets to individual guns. (See LAND.)

bullet jacket The jacket is the metal envelope or covering of a lead bullet intended for use in moderate-to-high-velocity rifles and handguns.

Prior to the advent of smokeless powders and the dramatic velocity jump that accompanied their use, bullets could be constructed of pure lead. Higher velocities and greater powder pressures created enough heat to melt the bases of lead bullets, however, so brass cups—called gas checks—were fitted onto bullet bases. As velocities went still higher, to 2,200 feet per second and more, bullet stripping became a problem even with gas checks. Consequently, in early smokeless powder cartridges such as the .30/30, bullets were almost completely enclosed in metal, with only the lead tip left exposed for game hunting.

Today many kinds of metal jackets are used, from copper and brass to nickel and steel, but gilding metal—an alloy of copper and zinc—is most widespread because of its nonfouling properties. (See BULLET STRIPPING; GILDING METAL.)

bullet jump The distance traversed by a bullet from its release from the cartridge case mouth to the point where it engages the rifling of the barrel. Some jump to allow even gas pressure buildup is advantageous but excessive jump will ruin accuracy, since the bullet can enter the rifling at an angle and deform itself.

bullet lubricant Any of various solid lubricants, usually consisting of mineral or animal waxes and/or greases, applied to lead alloy bullets to lubricate their passage through the bore.

Dry lubricants such as graphite or molybdenum disulfide are occasionally used, either alone or in combination with waxes or greases, or in an adhesive matrix that causes the particles of dry lubricant to adhere to the bullets.

A lubricant widely favored by cast bullet shooters consists of equal parts beeswax and Alox 2138F, a petroleum-base proprietary lubricant with a variety of industrial applications. Its use on bullets was originated by Colonel E. H. Harrison of the National Rifle Association, and it is commonly called "NRA Formula."

A waxlike lubricant often used on commercial handgun bullets is calcium stearate, sometimes in combination with a dry-particle lubricant. Many other materials have been used, however, especially by cast-bullet shooters who mold and lubricate their own bullets and sometimes concoct their own lubricants. (See CAKE CUTTER; LUBRICATOR-SIZER.)

bullet mold   A mold in which bullets are cast, usually from lead or an alloy of lead with antimony and/or tin.

Bullet mold blocks are in two parts, each containing half of the mold cavity, which is split through its center in an axial plane. The blocks are attached to handles that are hinged together so that the mold can be conveniently opened and closed. A sprue plate is pivoted to one of the block halves, with a hole through which the molten metal is poured. After the metal has solidified, an extension on the sprue plate is struck lightly to shear the sprue away from the bullet.

Mold blocks are most commonly made of iron or steel, but aluminum and bronze are also used. The cavities may be formed by a bullet-shaped cutter called a "cherry" or bored in a lathe. (See BULLET CASTING [FOR MUZZLELOADERS]; HANDLOAD; SPRUE; SPRUE CUTTER.)

bullet placement   See SHOT PLACEMENT.

bullet pull   The force necessary to propel a bullet from a loaded cartridge case. The amount of bullet pull, caused by its tightness in the case neck, is dependent upon such factors as case neck hardness, neck elasticity, bullet and case neck dimensions, presence of bullet lubricant, neck thickness, surface area in contact with the bullet, and crimp.

The amount of bullet pull slightly influences chamber pressure and bullet velocity; a heavier bullet pull will induce powder burning, increasing internal gas pressure and velocity—the pressures will have more time to build and they will be greater by the time they propel a bullet down the barrel.

Increasing bullet pull by crimping or neck sizing is sometimes necessary to prevent bullets from moving in their cases during recoil when they are in magazine-housed cartridges. (See HANDLOAD; NECK RESIZING.)

bullet puller   A device for mechanically removing a bullet from its case, ideally without damaging either element. There are two kinds of bullet pullers, inertia and collet.

The inertia puller is a hollow-headed hammer that does not require the use of a loading press, and with a full set of case rim clips one puller can be used for a variety of cartridges. A rim clip holds the cartridge firmly, and with the bullet pointing downward it can be removed by striking the puller several times on a hard surface until momentum causes the bullet to drop out of the cartridge. Crimped-in or

Inertia-type bullet pullers are used like a hammer. The loaded cartridge is held in place inside the head by means of a collet and screw cap, and the puller is struck smartly on a hard surface. The bullet is jerked free of the case neck, and it and the powder charge drop into the bottom of the puller's "head."

very lightweight bullets are difficult to remove by this method, however.

Collet pullers require attachment to a loading press, and a different collet (which grasps the bullet) for each caliber. (See HANDLOAD.)

bullet recovery   It is possible, by various means, to recover a bullet in the same condition in which it leaves the muzzle of a gun. The object of this is to learn what happens to the bullet during its passage through the bore—to check for signs of upsetting, gas cutting, distinctive marks on the bullet for purposes of identification, etc. A medium that will not alter the bullet—water, for instance—is fired into though in the interest of safety this is not a practice that should be indulged in by the amateur.

A bullet may also be recovered after it has been fired into a test medium to determine the performance of the bullet—mushrooming, weight loss, penetration capability, etc. A gelatinous compound is used here, though the same cautions apply as those expressed above.

Bullets are often recovered from the bodies of game animals that have been shot. A bullet will frequently be found under an animal's hide, on the side opposite the point of entry.

bullet recovery box   A box containing a medium for stopping bullets so that they can be recovered for evaluation of penetration and expansion qualities. Some of the expansion mediums used consist of either wet sawdust, silt, gelatin or clay. The penetration box is designed to measure depth of penetration and bullet expansion only. It does not always provide a cavity for evaluation of destruction.

As yet, no expansion medium has been devised

that will reproduce the complex structure of a live animal.

bullet sizing   Truing up and, if necessary, reducing or expanding the outside diameter of a bullet, generally after casting. Usually, lead bullets are cast slightly oversize and are then run through a die to smooth them and reduce their outside dimensions to slightly more than groove diameter of the rifled barrel they will be fired in.

For revolver bullets, some studies have shown that sizing to cylinder mouth diameter produces the best accuracy. Others disagree, stressing barrel groove diameter as paramount. An undersized bullet contributes to leading and excessive bullet deformation upon firing, which results in reduced accuracy.

A number of factors determine the extent to which a cast bullet must be sized: the alloy composition, dimensions of the mold and sizing die, and temperature at which the alloy was cast.

The final stage in forming jacketed bullets is also referred to as sizing. (See HANDLOAD.)

bullet slippage   When a bullet drives through a barrel's rifling, only partially engaging the lands. Slippage sometimes occurs when a soft-jacketed or lead-cast bullet is shot at a high velocity. (See BULLET STRIPPING.)

bullet spin   Spin is the rotational movement imparted to a bullet as it passes through a rifled bore. This rotation serves to stabilize the bullet in flight, and thereby aids accuracy.

Bullet velocity and the rate of rifling twist govern the rate of spin. A bullet fired at high velocity through a bore whose rifling has a rapid, or steep twist may spin 100,000 times per second in flight. This extremely high rate of rotation is one of the factors that contributes to the explosive striking power of high-velocity bullets, as powerful centrifugal forces in the spinning projectile are released upon impact.

Spin also imparts a lateral ballistic drift, in the direction of the rifling twist, to a bullet in flight. This comes about as a result of the precessional rotation of the bullet's nose around the curve of the trajectory, as well as a frictional tendency for the bullet to "roll" on the air in the direction in which it is spinning. (See DRIFT; EXTERIOR BALLISTICS; INTERIOR BALLISTICS; RIFLING.)

bullet spinner   A device used to determine the presence of bullet shape eccentricity or the absence of it. The spinner allows the bullet to be manually rotated on its longitudinal axis while the base and tip are supported. During rotation, a dial indicator sensor is brought into contact with the bullet and identifies the extent of imperfections.

The spinner is used primarily by benchrest and other competition shooters where the highest degree of accuracy is of the utmost importance. Bullets not meeting certain criteria are usually set aside for other uses.

Considerable disagreement exists among benchrest shooters regarding the importance of bullet spinning. Some say that it is necessary; others maintain that the "culls" shoot just as well as the bullets that test well.

bullet splash   A bullet, when instantly stopped by an impenetrable material, will disintegrate and most of the particles will "splash" at high velocity parallel to the resisting surface.

bullet stabilization   A bullet that is fully stabilized in flight is spinning around its true longitudinal axis, or centerline. If it is not so stabilized, accuracy will suffer. A bullet that is not concentric will not fully stabilize; uneven jacket thickness, or a void in the core, will throw it out of balance so that it will not revolve around its true axis.

To fully stabilize in flight, a bullet must be spun by the rifling at the correct rate for its specific diameter, weight, length, and the velocity at which it is started. (See EXTERIOR BALLISTICS; HANDLOAD.)

bullet starter   See STARTER.

bullet stripping   Stripping refers to the effect that occurs when a soft bullet fails to follow the pitch of the rifling and skids through the barrel with its bearing surfaces stripped away rather than being engraved by the rifling.

Stripping is most frequent with sharp rifling twists and with cast lead projectiles driven at velocities in excess of 2,200 to 2,500 feet per second. Bullet stripping became a consideration when smokeless powder (and higher velocities) replaced black powder; the problem was obviated by covering the lead bullet with a jacket of harder metal. (See BULLET JACKET; GILDING METAL.)

bullet swaging   The process of cold-forming bullets by forcing them into dies under heavy pressure. In this process, a lead core, which has been cut to the proper length, is forced into a die that contains a gilding metal jacket. The die forms the jacket to the proper shape around the lead core, resulting in a finished bullet. This technique is also used for unjacketed projectiles such as wadcutter bullets and buckshot. In these instances, the lead is simply molded, or swaged, to shape in the die; there is no jacketing operation. (See LOADING DIE; LOADING PRESS.)

bullet tipping A bullet in flight is said to tip when it fails to fly with its point straight on and instead wobbles like a poorly thrown football. Bullet tipping may occur when a bullet with an imperfect base allows gunpowder gases to escape past it as it travels through the bore, thus tipping the bullet to one side as it leaves the muzzle. More commonly, tipping comes from lack of stabilization in flight. If long, heavy bullets are fired through a rifling twist that is too gradual or slow, tipping and poor accuracy result. (See AIR SPIRAL.)

bullet trap A device for safely absorbing the energy of a fired bullet and bringing it to a stop in a designated location. Indoor ranges at which small caliber guns are fired often employ steel bullet traps with angled sides and tops that serve to divert the bullet downward to a pit or reservoir. Homemade traps can be designed around wooden boxes filled with such bullet-stopping materials as lime or sawdust.

To preserve a bullet in an undamaged state for examination after firing in order to study its engraving or identify the firearm it came from, a nonabrasive material (such as cotton) should be employed.

bullet tumble See TUMBLING.

bullet upset Because of pressures generated in the gun barrel by the expanding powder gases, coupled with the bullet's own inertia, the base section of the bullet actually moves forward slightly faster than the front section. This causes the bullet to expand, or upset, in the bore of the gun.

While this phenomenon holds true with jacketed

Commercial bullet traps are available, but not always necessary. This one is a dirt-filled hole in a concrete wall. A gunsmith uses it to test the functioning of the arms on which he works.

bullets, it is the prime principle behind the pure lead conical projectiles used in black-powder arms: The upset from the gas pressure shortens and expands the lead bullet to fill the bore and engage the rifling for proper contact and accuracy.

bullet velocity Bullet velocity is governed by both internal and exterior, or external, ballistics. Peak velocity, reached when the bullet exits the bore, is generated by the expanding gunpowder gas that results from the burning of the propellant charge. From that point on, velocity is continuously reduced by air resistance.

The velocity attained by the bullet within the bore depends on a number of factors: the amount and kind of powder used in the cartridge case; the diameter of the bullet; and its weight in relation to its diameter. For highest velocity in a small or medium caliber, a fast-burning powder that creates sufficient gas to push a light bullet to its velocity peak quickly before it exits the bore is necessary, but a slower-burning powder is required for high velocity with a heavy bullet in these same calibers in order to obtain the steadily rising pressure that the gas generates until the bullet exits. Faster powders are also required for maximum velocity of heavy bullets of large diameter because the expansion ratio (the space in which the gas has room to expand) is greater, and gas must be generated faster so that the top allowable pressure peak is reached before the bullet exits.

The shape of the bullet is the main factor in velocity retention. The more streamlined the bullet, the less air resistance it creates and the higher the downrange retained velocity. Atmospheric conditions also affect bullet velocity; dense or cold air causes more resistance than hot or thin air. (See EXPANSION RATIO; EXTERIOR BALLISTICS; INTERIOR BALLISTICS.)

bullet wobble See AIR SPIRAL.

bullet yaw Bullet yaw takes place when a bullet does not rotate perfectly around its longitudinal axis in flight and assumes an angular position as it moves forward, swerving slightly back and forth in flight. The typical cause of bullet yaw is imperfect stabilization.

Bullets that are long in comparison to their diameter often do not fully stabilize over the first few hundred feet of flight, with the result that accuracy may be better, in terms of minutes of angle, at longer ranges than at close range. (See BULLET STABILIZATION; INTERIOR BALLISTICS; MINUTE OF ANGLE.)

bull gun Any rifle with a very heavy barrel may be referred to as a bull gun. However, while some rifles made for benchrest shooting have extremely heavy barrels, attributable to stocking and other special features, they are not considered bull guns.

The term is normally applied to rifles used for target shooting, especially those designed and stocked for shooting from the prone position in competitions such as the 1,000-yard Wimbledon Match. It is also used in reference to heavy-barrel varmint rifles.

A bull gun offers many advantages where nth-degree accuracy is demanded. The heavy barrel, being stiffer and vibrating less than a lighter barrel, delivers consistently higher accuracy when shot continually. The heavy barrel heats less rapidly than lighter barrels, thereby better retaining its point of impact.

The heavy bull gun also transmits less recoil to the shooter, making it possible to concentrate on accurate shooting rather than thinking about recoil, especially with cartridges suitable for 1,000-yard matches. In addition, the heavy weight also makes the rifle easier to hold steadily. (See BARREL VIBRATION.)

bull pup rifle A kind of bolt-action rifle, whose development is credited to the late J. R. Buhmiller, in which the action is located near the buttplate and the stock is so shaped that the shooter's face rests at or forward of the receiver-barrel junction. The trigger is set forward of the action and operates the sear by means of a connecting rod extending rearward inside the stock.

The bull pup design offered the advantage of extreme compactness, even with a relatively long barrel. Made in standard centerline calibers, it enjoyed a measure of popularity from 1936 to 1955. Bull pup rifles were suited for shooting from cars, which was legal in some states in the design's early years, and were tested by the military. They were made only by a limited number of custom gunsmiths.

Offsetting its compactness were a high sight line,

The bull pup design offers extreme compactness as its main advantage but has never enjoyed wide acceptance, possibly because it places the action alongside the shooter's face.

an unconventional and unattractive appearance, and the fact that the shooter's face was located next to the action, which could be highly dangerous in the event of a cartridge case rupture.

bullseye (powder) Bullseye is the trade name of a high-energy, quick-burning double-base smokeless gunpowder made by Hercules Incorporated and designed for handloaded pistol and revolver ammunition. It is much favored for match and target shooting in everything from the .38 Special through and including the .44s and .45s, although it really burns too quickly for the big-bore magnums. Bullseye is nearly twice as expensive as most other canistered powders, but very small charges are usually used. (See DOUBLE-BASE POWDER.)

bull's-eye (target) On a target that consists of a series of concentric rings, the area encompassed by the smallest, center, ring is considered the bull's-eye.

Also, a shot that strikes the center of the target is referred to as a bull's-eye.

bump The edge between the comb and the heel of the buttstock of a shoulder arm. (See RIFLE STOCK.)

burning rate The relative speed or rapidity with which a given gunpowder burns, which is of critical importance to reloaders. Burning rate is determined by the size and shape of powder granules, their perforation, and the amount and nature of the powder's deterrent coating. Relative burning rates are established by means of pressure-bomb tests in which powders are ignited and their ignition is measured under uniform conditions.

Burning rates vary as conditions vary. Case capacity, bore diameter, bullet weight, etc., may alter burning rate. For instance, in one cartridge H-4831 powder may be faster burning than H-205. In a second cartridge with greater capacity but with the same diameter and weight bullet, H-205 may be the faster of the two powders.

In general, powders with faster burning rates are used in conjunction with lighter bullets in rifles and handguns, lighter-shot charges in shotguns, smaller-capacity cartridges, or straight-walled cases. But there are many other variables that affect burning rate, including the age of the propellant and the pressure at which it is burned. Because of these variables, the handloader should never make any assumptions regarding burning rate when developing a load. (See HANDLOAD.)

Burrard, Major Sir Gerald This many-faceted Englishman wrote several books, but his 1930–1931 three-volume set, *The Gun, The Gun and the Cartridge,* and *The Cartridge,* quickly became and remains the most important work in the field. Burrard spent great amounts of money and years of time in its preparation. It is an exhaustive and authoritative effort, full of costly and extensive experiments not likely to be ever repeated.

Major Burrard was one of the earliest forensic ballisticians, publishing in 1934 his *The Identification of Firearms and Forensic Ballistics* (issued in revised and enlarged form in 1951). He also wrote *In the Gunroom* (1930), and two books on rifles and rifle hunting—*Big Game Hunting in Himalaya and Tibet* (1925) and *Notes on Sporting Rifles* (1920 and later issues).

burr hammer   See HAMMER BURR.

Burton, James H.   See MINIÉ BALL.

bushed firing pins.   A mechanical method that makes it easy to replace firing pins (strikers) in break-action shotguns. The face of the standing breech is drilled and tapped to receive a circular bushing that is drilled for firing pin fit. If firing pin breakage occurs, the bushing can readily be removed by a tool (generally a three-pronged tool) and the firing pin can be gotten to without necessitating the complete disassembly of the gun's action from the rear.

bushing   A bushing is a tightening ring or band often used in firearms to give two adjoining parts a tighter fit or increased bearing surface. A common example of a bushing is the ring used on the barrel and slide of the Colt Model 1911 .45 ACP pistol.

Bushnell (company)   In the 1930s, David Bushnell, an American sportsman, took a trip around the world that convinced him that the Japanese optical industry could be competitive in the manufacture of American rifle sights and optical goods. By 1950, he had established D. P. Bushnell & Co., Inc., in Pasadena, California, to operate in the sports optics field.

In 1971, the optical firm of Bausch & Lomb acquired the assets of the Bushnell company.

Bushnell manufactures and markets several lines of binoculars, telescopic sights, telescopes, and other hunting and general consumer optical goods. (See BAUSCH & LOMB [COMPANY].)

Butler, Frank   See OAKLEY, ANNIE.

butterknife bolt handle   The butterknife is a distinctive design given to the bolt handles of some European rifles, notably Austrian Mannlicher-Schoenauer rifles. In place of the conventional knob

The butterknife bolt handle is a distinguishing feature of the classic Mannlicher rifle. It is compact, but some shooters claim it does not give as firm a grip as a knobbed bolt handle.

at the end of the bolt handle, the butterknife is flat; the end that is grasped by the shooter, when he works the action, is thicker than the end that is joined to the bolt. A butterknife bolt handle rests closer to the stock than the standard bolt handle.

button rifling   The button method is one of several modern methods used to rifle barrels. Its development in the 1950s is considered to be responsible for much of the advance of modern rifle accuracy, and most custom and target grade barrels from major manufacturers are button rifled.

In the button technique a single pearl, or "button," of an extremely hard metal—usually tungsten carbide—is shaped to the desired rifling pattern on a diamond grinding wheel. The button is then inserted into one end of the drilled barrel blank and either pushed or pulled through to the opposite end using a heavy hydraulic press. The button technique produces a very smooth interior surface, slightly work hardened, with a high level of probability that the interior dimensions will be extremely uniform. (See BARREL, RIFLED.)

buttplate   Any protective covering of metal, rubber, plastic, horn or other material attached to the rear end of a gunstock. The buttplate protects the exposed end grain (on wood stocks) from splintering or splitting.

Steel or other metal was generally used in buttplates on early sporting guns and military weapons. Then rubber came into vogue. In recent years, however, plastics have replaced steel and rubber on sporting guns.

Custom gun makers sometimes fashion elaborate buttplates of horn, ivory, or form a variety of wood that contrasts with the kind used for the rest of the stock. Buttplates are of many different designs, depending partially upon the gun's intended use, the era in which the rifle was made, and the personal taste of the maker or owner.

buttstock   That portion of a long gun's stock that extends rearward from the receiver area to the point that contacts the shoulder when the gun is held in firing position. With a two-piece stock, the buttstock is usually considered the entire rear section.

The shape and proportions of the buttstock are of primary importance in determining the fit of a gun to the shooter. Its dimensions also partially determine the amount of recoil felt by the shooter when he fires the gun. (See GUN FIT.)

cake cutter A tubular device used for separating cast bullets from the lubricant that has been allowed to harden around the projectiles, thus filling the grease grooves molded into the circumference of the projectiles to hold the lubricant. (See CAST BULLET.)

calculated recoil A formula for calculating the free recoil of a firearm in foot-pounds of kinetic energy. In calculating recoil, a number of factors are considered: the weight of the gun; weight of the ejecta (which includes the bullet or shot charge and powder charge; gravitational constant; and the muzzle velocity of the bullet or shot and powder gases). The formula is:

$$\frac{\text{(Wt. of bullet in grains} \times \text{M.V.)} + \text{(Powder wt. in grains} \times 4700)^2}{7000 \times \text{rifle weight in lbs.}}$$

$$\times \frac{\text{Rifle wt. lbs.}}{64.4} = \text{ft. lbs.}$$

Using this formula, the recoil for a 7-pound rifle firing a 100-grain bullet at a muzzle velocity of 2,000 feet per second by means of a 50-grain powder charge would be calculated thus:

$$\frac{(100 \times 2000) + (50 \times 4700)^2}{7000 \times 7} \times \frac{7}{64.4}$$

$$\frac{435,000}{49,000} = 8.87751^2 = 78.8109 \times 0.1086956 = 8.566$$

RE = 8.566 foot-pounds of recoil.

(See RECOIL.)

caliber The interior diameter of a barrel, sometimes listed as its bore diameter, as in .30 caliber or .300 magnum, but often denoting the barrel's groove diameter, as in .308 or .458 Winchester. The dimension may be expressed as a decimal part of an inch, or in millimeters, as with European cartridges.

caliber designation To understand caliber designation it is first necessary to correctly define "caliber", which may refer to either the bore diameter or the groove diameter of a rifled bore.

One caliber subtends 1/100-inch (.01), thus a .25-caliber bullet is roughly .25- or ¼-inch. We say roughly, because .25-inch is the land-to-land diameter of the rifling in the bore, but the bullet, in order to be stabilized when it leaves the gun, must be equal to the groove-to-groove diameter of the bore—.257-inch in this case. So a .25-caliber bullet actually has a diameter of .257-inch, not an even .250.

Caliber designation is often confused with cartridge designation. The .340 Weatherby, for example, actually uses a .338-inch-diameter bullet. The .340 designation is used to distinguish it from another cartridge, the .338 Winchester Magnum.

In Europe, and in some instances in America, the designation of a caliber is made by the metric system—where .010-inch equals 0.2540-millimeter (or 1 millimeter equals .03937-inch). Accordingly, the 7mm designation, which translates to .276-inch bore diameter, has a groove-to-groove (and bullet) diameter of .284-inch, or 7.2136 millimeters. (See CARTRIDGE DESIGNATION.)

California stock A stock design best exemplified in production rifles by those marketed by Weatherby, Inc. Many sources credit Roy Weatherby and his company with creating the California stock. However, the California stock is not of one specific configuration. The term is applied to any of a number of modernistic stocks tending toward flashy appearance.

A roll-over Monte Carlo comb is probably the single feature that distinguishes the California style from the traditional stock. On a California stock the Monte Carlo is very pronounced, rising rather high about 3½ inches forward of the butt, then sloping sharply down to the pistol grip. The idea behind the severe forward-sloping angle on the California stock's Monte Carlo is that it positions the shooter's eye comfortably for the use of scope sights, yet in recoil the stock moves away from the shooter's face.

But the Monte Carlo is not the sole feature of a California stock. A teardrop shaped pistol grip, streamlined fore-end cap, fancy cheekpiece, multicolored inlays, and carving are all common features of the California style, which reaches its highest form in custom stocks. (See MONTE CARLO COMB; WEATHERBY [COMPANY].)

calling the shot The act of predicting where the shot will strike the target based upon the sight picture at the instant of firing. Perhaps the sights were aligned horizontally but slightly high at the instant of firing. In this case, without looking at the target, the shooter would say "out at twelve o'clock," indicating that he thought the shot struck high.

Expert rifle and handgun shooters have highly developed mental concentration and can usually call their shots. By so doing, it is possible to detect such problems as flinch or improper hold. (See SIGHT PICTURE.)

cam In firearms, a cam is an eccentrically pivoting and sloping gun part that, upon sliding into contact with another part, imparts either a locking action or motion to the second part. Cam surfaces are most frequently found in action mechanisms, as in the pivot cams of a lever action or the camming surfaces that lock a bolt mechanism.

The word is also used as a verb to express the actions described above.

camlock The designation of a firearm action-locking mechanism and the official name of the single-shot Model 1873 Springfield .45/70 breechloader used by the U.S. Army during the Plains and Mountain Indian wars. It was so named because its hinged breechblock was locked closed by a pivoted cam at the right rear of the action.

canister powders Smokeless gunpowders designed for use by handloaders. They are so called because they are generally packed by the manufacturer in metal cans that contain one-half or one pound. Canistered powders are carefully standardized for consistency and to give specified velocities, though slight variations between lots do exist.

cannelure A circumferential groove in the external surface of a bullet or cartridge case. A case mouth is sometimes crimped into a bullet cannelure to prevent the projectile from moving under recoil or from spring pressure in a tubular magazine while a cannelured case prevents rearward movement of the bullet during recoil. A lead bullet cannelure also provides a receptacle for lubricant. These are usually referred to as "grease grooves" rather than cannelures.

cannon lock The simplest means of igniting a propellant charge of gunpowder. It is accomplished by applying a flame to the charge through a touch hole at the breech end of the barrel. It was used on matchlock guns, where pulling the trigger touched a burning fuse to a powder charge next to the touch hole. Matchlocks were employed from the 15th through the 17th centuries. (See MATCHLOCK.)

cant In aiming, the canting of a firearm to an angle off the horizontal. Many champion target shooters currently cant the arm. (See SIGHT PICTURE.)

cap See PERCUSSION CAP.

cap and ball revolver This is a generic term for a kind of handgun that enjoyed great popularity from 1835, when Samuel Colt patented his Paterson model revolver, until after the Civil War, when the development of fixed ammunition made the percussion cap obsolete.

The term is derived from the fact that this class of firearms utilized round balls rather than conical bullets (in the earliest models); and these round bullets were ignited by percussion caps affixed to nipples at the rear of the chambers in the cylinder.

Although the principle of the revolver mechanism was not new, the Colt Paterson was the first handgun to combine compactness, reliable ignition, adequate accuracy, and reasonable power. Made in .31 and .40 calibers, these arms had cylinders, capable of holding six shots, that rotated on a heavy shaft attached to the frame. The cylinder was rotated by a "hand," and cocking the hammer caused the cylinder to rotate and readied the gun for firing.

Colt revolvers, which were regarded as the finest of the cap and ball type, underwent rapid evolution. The Walker model, which followed the Paterson, was a heavy, cumbersome .44 caliber that was as effective as many shoulder arms of the day. It evolved into the No. 1 Dragoon, which was nearly as powerful but considerably more compact. These .44s fired either round or conical bullets.

Cap and ball revolvers achieved their highest point of development in three models: the Colt .36 Model 1851 Navy and .44 Model 1860 Army, and the Remington Model 1860 .44 Army. These (and a host of imitations) were the standard sidearms of the Civil War and are, even by modern standards, effective arms at moderate ranges.

cap box A box or container of brass or German silver inletted into the right side of the buttstock of a percussion rifle. Cap boxes were either round or oval in shape and occasionally had engraved covers.

Although they nominally were intended to carry percussion caps, more often than not they were filled with lubricated patches, and many antique cap boxes still contain traces of sperm oil or tallow. (See PERCUSSION IGNITION.)

cap flash   The flame resulting when a percussion cap is detonated by the blow of the hammer. (See PERCUSSION IGNITION.)

caplock   A synonym for percussion lock, used during the time percussion ignition was in common use. It refers to any type of ignition using a percussion cap. (See PERCUSSION IGNITION.)

capper   A device, usually made of brass, for storing and placing percussion caps on the nipple of a black-powder gun. In its most common form, the capper consists of a brass rail, along which 20 to 25 percussion caps are held. At one end is a stopper that forces the caps to the other end, where they are held, one at a time, by spring clamps.

In use, the shooter pushes the stopper until a cap is forced into the clamp, then simply pushes the cap onto the nipple and pulls the capper away, which causes the clamp to release the cap. Cappers are especially handy in cold weather, when handling percussion caps is difficult. (See PERCUSSION IGNITION.)

carbide die   See TUNGSTEN-CARBIDE DIE.

carbide lamp   A kind of lamp that gives off a hot, bright flame and produces a thick smoke composed of carbon particles. Carbide lamps are used by target shooters to blacken iron sights, giving a nonreflective finish to the metal. The soot rubs off easily and must be renewed frequently.

carbine   Carbine refers to any short, light rifle or musket; the word was originally applied to shoulder arms intended for use from horseback. In early times, carbines were considered to be transition arms between handguns and full-size rifle/muskets.

The origin of the word and the concept is somewhat clouded. France is often given credit both for developing and naming the carbine, but recent scholarship indicates that the French likely were recipients of both term and gun type when, in the 17th century, France incorporated into its army as skirmishers a Spanish light cavalry of "wild carabineers" armed with "carabines." Some researchers have speculated that these were Moors from Granada, and they point out that the Arabs were renowned for horses and horsemanship and that the Arabic word for weapon is "carib."

In contemporary usage, a carbine is usually a lightweight hunting rifle with a barrel of 20 inches or less, frequently featuring a full-length Mannlicher-style stock.

carbon dioxide   A chemical compound, gaseous at normal temperature and pressure, of which the molecule contains one atom of carbon and two of oxygen (CO_2). It is one of the products of combustion of practically all propellants, including smokeless powder and black powder.

It can be liquified by compression at normal ambient temperature, and in that form is stored in small tanks or capsules for use as the propellant in pneumatic guns that fire lead pellets or air-rifle shot. (See AIR GUN.)

card wad   Before the advent of plastic shotshells, card wads were employed in paper shotshells. They were placed directly over the powder to seal gases and to give the expanding powder gases a hard surface to push against. They were also used to keep the wax on filler wads from contaminating the powder. (See SPACER WAD.)

caribou, guns and loads for   While the caribou is not an especially large or tough animal (a big bull will weigh 450 pounds or so), it is one that is frequently taken at long range. The majority of the animals are bagged at modest yardages, but there are numerous occasions when the relatively open country of the northernmost reaches of North America that they inhabit will force a shot at more than 400 yards.

In addition, caribou are often pursued on hunts for them as well as other species: moose, grizzly, and sheep. For this reason, it is prudent to use a bolt-action rifle that is on the powerful side. The minimum advisable is a .270 firing 130-grain bullets. Other cartridges, on the light side but suitable, are the 7×57, .280, and .30/06. A hunter might be better advised to used a 7mm or .300 Magnum with 160- or 180-grain bullets.

A scope is a necessity, and one of at least 4X, or a 2X-7X variable, is ideal when equipped with a Duplex-type reticle.

Since caribou hunting is often conducted in rain or snow, the rifle should be thoroughly sealed against moisture, and the action and safety should not be sensitive to freezing. Caps for the scope lenses are a must.

Because the country is so open and the ground vegetation usually low, the rifleman can often shoot from the prone position, or from sitting or kneeling. In light of this, a Whelen sling, or other sling with an arm loop, can be helpful.

A binocular of at least 7X, a spotting scope of at least 20X, and a sturdy saddle scabbard are also essential.

Caribou, while not as tough and heavy-boned as elk, are nevertheless large animals and must often be taken at long range. A rifle such as this 7mm Mashburn Super Magnum is ideal.

Carmichel, Jim (1936–   ) Born in Arkansas and educated in Tennessee, Jim Carmichel holds degrees in engineering, English, history, and philosophy from East Tennessee State University. Interested in guns from childhood, Carmichel began his competitive shooting career as a member of the All-Army rifle team in the late 1950s and has competed in all forms of rifle, handgun, and shotgun events since then.

He began his career with the Tennessee Game and Fish Department and also began writing for various firearms magazines. In 1971, he was named shooting editor of *Outdoor Life* magazine, a position he has held ever since. During his years at that publication, Carmichel has made 24 African safaris and has hunted in 30 countries. He serves on the board of directors of the National Rifle Association.

Carmichel's books include *The Women's Guide to*

Handguns (The Bobbs-Merrill Company, New York, 1982); *The Modern Rifle* (Winchester Press, New York, 1975); and *The Book of the Rifle* (Outdoor Life Books, New York, 1985).

carrying strap   See SLING.

cartridge   This term is used to describe fixed, or self-contained, small arms ammunition, i.e., a unit consisting of case, primer, propellant, and projectile. In the United States, "cartridge" is almost invariably applied to metallic ammunition, while in Great Britain it refers to shotshells as well.

cartridge belt   A belt with loops or other receptacles designed to carry cartridges on the person. Also, the cartridge feed belt used with automatic military weapons is sometimes referred to as a cartridge belt.

cartridge block A block of wood or other material with receptacles drilled in it to hold metallic cartridges for loading convenience, particularly while target shooting.

cartridge carrier The part in a repeating-firearm mechanism that moves the cartridge from the magazine to a position directly in line with the chamber.

cartridge designation Cartridge designation is highly confusing, especially where American decimal-system-designated cartridges are concerned. An example of this is the fact that the .220 Swift, .222, .223, .22/250, and .222 Magnum all use bullets of .224-inch. The metric system is much simpler and to the point. Example: For the 7×57 Mauser, the 7 indicates the bullet is of 7mm diameter and the 57 is the length of the case in millimeters. Mauser is simply the name of the designer and may or may not be attached to the cartridge designation. An "R" after the designation means the case is rimmed; a "J" shows it is a military round, and an "S" means the cartridge uses a spitzer bullet.

American black-powder cartridge designation was generally simpler than that used for modern rounds. The first figure showed the caliber, while the second meant the grains of black powder loaded in the cartridge. Thus, the .45/70 was of .45 caliber and loaded with 70 grains of black powder. Some of the old cartridges also gave the bullet weight in grains after the powder charge or the case length.

Cartridges that appeared during the time of transition from black to smokeless powder during the late 19th century retained the caliber/powder charge designation, the .30/30 and .30/40 being examples. But the true confusion began with cartridges like the .35 Remington and .405 Winchester that used the caliber and designer name, a practice used today with the 7mm Remington Magnum and .300 Winchester Magnum being examples. Then came cartridges such as the .220 Swift, whose name implied high velocity. Savage also leaned that way in naming the .250/3000, the first number referring to caliber, the second approximating the muzzle velocity of its 87-grain bullet.

The term "magnum" refers to large capacity cases, usually but not always belted. And wildcats often use the caliber before the designation of the parent case—.25/284 for the .284 Winchester necked down for .25-caliber bullets.

cartridge indicator A cartridge indicator may be either a device that indicates whether a rifle or pistol chamber contains a cartridge, or a visible counter that specifies the number of rounds in a rotary magazine. The latter operates by means of numbers, engraved on the magazine spool, that are displayed through a cutout in the receiver wall. Cartridge indicators are rarely seen on today's guns.

cartridge length See OVERALL CARTRIDGE LENGTH.

cartridge spinner One of the determining factors in the accuracy of rifle ammunition is the concentricity and uniformity of its cases. Benchrest shooters, whose requirement for case precision is extreme, use dial-readout gauges to determine the thickness of case necks, and the alignment of the bullet within the case neck. The term "spinner" is used because the cases or loaded rounds are rotated while a "feeler" takes its reading and transfers its information to a micrometer dial. (See BENCHREST COMPETITION SHOOTING.)

cartridge trap A recess cut into the buttstock of a rifle. It is closed by a hinged cover and intended for the storage and convenient carrying of three or four cartridges. Cartridge traps are almost invariably found on custom rifles of European make.

Carver, Doc William Frank A match and exhibition shooter, contemporary with Adam Bogardus and Ira Paine. Carver was not a medical doctor, a dentist, or holder of a doctoral degree. As a child, he was nicknamed "Little Doc" because of his efforts to save the lives of wounded birds and animals.

Carver preferred rifles to shotguns, even when shooting aerial targets. He proclaimed himself

This device enables a shooter to determine if the bullet is seated perfectly concentric with the cartridge case. Any deviation shows on the readout dial.

Champion of the World in the early 1880s after defeating Paine, Bogardus and many others in highly publicized matches in America and Europe, using heavy big bore rifles against their shotguns on hand-thrown or trap-thrown aerial targets. In December 1888, Carver, firing six .38-caliber Winchester rifles, established an incredible endurance-accuracy record by breaking 60,000 out of 60,674 1¼-inch wooden cubes that were thrown 30 to 35 feet in the air from a point 30 feet from the shooter. This use of heavy, hard-kicking rifles sets Carver's record apart from later marks by Adolf Topperwein and Tom Frye, both of whom used .22-caliber rifles.

Carver used shotguns upon occasion and was also a remarkable shot with handguns. Overall, he was probably the top marksman of his era, and one of the greatest of all time.

Doc W. F. Carver, Spirit Gun of the West, by Raymond W. Thorpe (published in 1957 by The Arthur H. Clarke Company of Glendale, California) tells the story of the exhibition shooters around the turn of the century. It must be noted, however, that the book's point of view is not as objective as one might like it to be. (See BOGARDUS, ADAM H.; TOPPERWEIN, ADOLF.)

case capacity Case capacity is generally considered to be the amount of gunpowder a metallic cartridge case will hold when filled to the top of its neck. The true capacity of a case is, however, subject to variable factors. While all cases of a given designation have the same outside dimensions, inside dimensions will vary from brand to brand and even from lot to lot in the same brand, with thicker cases having smaller capacity than thinner ones.

Bullet seating depth also alters the effective case capacity, as the farther the bullet intrudes into the powder space, the more the powder capacity is reduced.

Water is the best medium for measuring case capacity, but fine-grained spherical gunpowder works well if it is sifted slowly through a long-necked funnel. (See POWDER MEASURE.)

case extraction groove In metallic cartridges, a circumferential groove immediately forward of the case rim. It is designed to allow ample purchase for the gun's extracting mechanism to withdraw the case from the chamber. On "rimless" cases, the extraction groove forms what is referred to as the case rim. (See RIMLESS CASE; RIMMED CASE.)

case extractor A case extractor is a device for removing stuck headless metallic cartridge cases from a firearm's chamber. Case extractors are made for specific cartridges or families of cartridges. Most

designs feature four expanding plugs or hooks at the forward end; when the device is inserted into the chamber and turned or partially withdrawn to get a bite, the plugs adhere to the case. Complete withdrawal of the extractor then removes the headless case.

Another kind of case extractor, resembling the claws of a hammer, has been used to remove shotshell cases whose heads were intact but that resisted extraction.

Both kinds are rarely used today because case weakness, which leads to separation, is readily recognizable to handloaders; the problem that would necessitate use of an extractor is thus easily avoided. (See CASE SEPARATION.)

case forming Whenever the outside dimensions of a rifle cartridge case are changed, it is considered to be case forming, even though altering only neck diameter is not so labeled. Case forming is done to obtain a nonstandard (in size, shape, or both) cartridge case that offers a particular advantage to a shooter, such as increased capacity. It is accomplished with form and sizing dies, by fire forming or by hydraulic forming. Very often the use of a form die and fire forming are combined in the process.

A form die is used when the object is to shorten case size from that of the original, typically when the original shoulder is set back to form a shorter body and/or a longer neck. If at the same time the shorter body is to be expanded to allow added powder capacity, the case is then fire formed to fill the rifle chamber. If the case is to be widened while other dimensions remain the same, only fire forming is used.

Making the .30/06 Ackley Improved from .30/06 brass is an example of the use of fire forming, as is firing a standard cartridge in an "Improved" chamber that had been re-reamed to accommodate a case with less taper and a sharper shoulder angle. During the 1940s and 1950s, before the wide selection of factory cartridges now available, there was considerable interest among rifle enthusiasts in obtaining superior performance by modifying factory cartridges, and by firing a standard .30/06 factory load in a re-reamed chamber, the brass expanded to conform to the chamber's dimensions. This resulted in a case with greater powder capacity than it previously had and, it was thought, superior performance at minimum expense, since neither a new barrel nor altered bolt face was required.

However, in many instances, fire forming and "improving" standard cases not only led to a lack of improvement, but actually resulted in somewhat inferior performance.

Another kind of case forming, the so-called hydraulic method, involves placing the original case inside a form die, filling the case with water, and inserting a plunger into the neck so that the water pressure expands the case to fit the die.

Today, case forming is seldom used except by a few experimental shooters, since factory ammunition offers high performance and easy availability as well as lower expense. (See ACKLEY WILDCATS; FIRE FORMING; HANDLOAD.)

case gauge A gauge for checking the length of metallic cartridge cases that are to be reloaded so that they may be trimmed back to correct dimension if they have stretched. The gauge has a shelf rest that the case head is placed against and notches marked with the cartridge designation (.270, for example) for the case mouth to slip under.

Case length gauges are scarce since most of today's handloaders prefer to use one of the inexpensive dial calipers available from firms such as RCBS, Lee Precision, and Lyman. Maximum length and trim-to-length dimensions for cartridge cases are listed in most handloading manuals. (See CASE TRIMMING.)

case harden Case hardening is a method of hardening steel and iron while giving it an attractive surface design of brown, violet, and gray swirls. Case-hardened metal has a very hard carbon-steel skin, or "case," formed on its surface to a depth of .005-inch to .007-inch. This comes from heating the metal to 800–900 degrees centigrade in a fire commonly fueled by animal charcoal—bone dust or charred horn or leather—and then plunging the piece into a quenching bath of cold water that is agitated to form bubbles, which produce the mottled coloring effect.

Case hardening is useful on guns subject to surface wear, but its primary function is aesthetic.

case head expansion Expansion of a metallic cartridge case head is caused by internal pressure built up by the powder charge. Case head expansion should not be confused with pressure ring expansion, which occurs forward of the head.

For the most accurate reading, measurements to determine amount of expansion should be taken with a micrometer caliper. Rimmed cases are "miked" on the rim; belted cases on the case belt; and rimless cases on the solid portion of the case head (web) between the start of the case body and the extractor groove or rim. Any expansion over the original diameter indicates the effect of high pressure, but the exact amount of expansion that shows excessive pressure varies according to the original diameter of the case and the hardness of the brass.

Handloaders should check for case head expan-

sion as a precaution against excessive loads. (See HANDLOAD.)

case head forms The term refers in a collective sense to the various case head designs that have been developed for brass cartridge cases.

When self-contained metallic cartridges were first produced in the mid-19th century, they were of the so-called balloonhead or folded-head type. Their cases were made of soft copper, which necessarily meant that powder pressures had to be held to low levels. Hiram Berdan, the American gunsmith and Civil War sharpshooter, was at the forefront of ammunition development in the postwar period, and one of his outstanding contributions was the drawn, solid-head brass case.

Modern case heads are made by punching a round disc out of a strip of brass, then stamping the disc into a cup, and shaping and annealing that into the final case head form—rimmed, semirimmed, rimless, rebated-rimless, or belted. (See ANNEALING; BALLOONHEAD CASE.)

case head rupture This phenomenon, in which the case of a cartridge is burst at its head by expanding powder gas, can vary both in cause and seriousness. Case head ruptures can occur in rifles, shotguns, and handguns and can result from excessive pressure, improper headspace, or brittleness of the case head itself. At the least, a case head rupture ruins the shell for further use. A rupture can also result in a stoppage of the gun or can damage or destroy the gun and injure the shooter as well. (See WAVE THEORY.)

caseless cartridge A kind of ammunition that does not employ a conventional case or primer. It dates back to the early days of World War II, when German ammunition makers tried to develop a cartridge that didn't require the use of the relatively expensive brass case.

In manufacture, the propellant is molded around the rear of the projectile. A consumable primer is inserted into the propellant and is detonated by means of percussion or battery generated electric current. Cartridges of this kind have been developed to withstand handling and feeding abuse. The firearm utilizing such ammunition must be specially designed with an integral gas seal to prevent propellant gases from leaking into the action.

Upon firing, the propellant in the caseless cartridge burns in the conventional manner, but it also consumes the primer.

The advantages of such a cartridge include reduction in weight and cost of components. Caseless cartridges, in turn, eliminate the need for an extrac-

This is a 9mm caseless cartridge developed by Smith & Wesson in the late 1960s. The propellant is molded to the rear of the bullet, and the priming compound, which is electrically ignited, can be seen on its base. A standard 9mm round is shown for comparison.

tion and ejecting mechanism in the firearm—all are military advantages.

In 1969, the Daisy/Heddon company introduced the caseless cartridge to civilian shooters with the V-L system developed by Jules Van Langenhoven of Belgium. The V-L did not utilize a primer; the propellant was ignited by a jet of compressed air. The system was not a commercial success.

In the late 1960s, Smith & Wesson briefly experimented with a 9mm caseless cartridge designed for pistol and submachine gun use. This ammunition utilized an electrically ignited consumable primer. The S&W M76 submachine gun was converted to function with the ammunition, but the gun reached only the test stage. No production guns have been distributed.

case life Case life is measured by the number of times an individual cartridge case can be reloaded safely, not by the age of the case.

The quality of the brass, especially its hardness but also its grain structure, is a vital determinant of case life. Cases whose head areas are too soft will not stand high-pressure loads, and cases that are too hard often crack, especially in the neck. New cases that have excessive headspace for the average cham-

ber will stretch during firing, causing head separations.

During shooting, high pressures can expand the case head and cause the primer pocket to leak gas. In reloading, resizing dies that are too small and therefore overwork the brass will soon cause splits in the case body or neck. Pushing the shoulder back too far during the resizing operation will lead to excessive headspace and head separation.

Paper shotshells have comparatively short reloading lives, but plastic shells can be reloaded up to a dozen times. The point of failure in these shells occurs most often at the juncture of the brass head and the case body.

As a rule, as chamber pressure increases, case life decreases. (See HEADSPACE.)

case resizing Resizing of cartridge cases is done for two reasons: to reduce any shell to its prefered diameter so that it will chamber easily; and, with metallic ammunition, to reduce the case neck to prefered size so that it will hold a bullet securely.

During the reloading process, brass cases can be neck-sized, a technique used only for rifle ammunition where ease of chambering is not of great importance, such as in benchrest and varmint rifles. Here, only the neck is resized to hold a bullet; the rest of the case is untouched, leaving it contoured to the chamber in which it was fired. Or, if the cartridge is to be used in a hunting rifle or target rifle where reliability and ease of feeding are important, the case must be full-length-sized, reduced to the dimensions of an unfired factory case.

Care must be taken when resizing rifle ammunition that the case not be compressed too far. Reducing its base-to-shoulder length can result in excessive headspace. This, in turn, can lead to lengthwise expansion that will strain the brass beyond its limits, which can destroy a rifle and severely injure a shooter. (See HEADSPACE; LOADING DIE.)

case separation Case separation takes place in shotgun and rifle cartridges when the load is fired and the head section splits away from the rest of the case. If separation is complete, only the head section will be extracted from the chamber during the firearm's operating cycle.

Separation normally occurs just in front of the solid head of the case (in shotshells, it can occur just ahead of the brass base, or in the base itself), though it occasionally takes place farther forward. It is caused by excessive headspace—that is, when the case is shorter between the head face and shoulder than the chamber is between bolt face and shoulder. The material from which the case is made— brass or plastic—becomes work-hardened and brittle

The case at left has split around its axis upon firing, because of the repeated stretching and compressing of the brass. The compression takes place in the resizing die; the stretching in the rifle chamber. This condition can damage the rifle and can be hazardous to the shooter as well.

from repeated expansion and contraction, and loses its elasticity, resulting in a break.

Separation is easily avoided by checking to see that guns do not have excessive headspace; by properly adjusting loading dies so that cases are not unduly shortened; and by discarding cases when the sign of excess stretching—a band of unusual brightness just ahead of the rim—begins to appear. (See CASE HEAD EXPANSION; HEADSPACE; INCIPIENT SEPARATION.)

case shoulder The conical surface of a bottleneck metallic cartridge case, tapering much more sharply than the body, that joins the body and the neck. In modern cartridges, the angle between the shoulder cone and the central axis of the case is usually between 17 and 35 degrees. It is rather widely believed that relatively small changes in the angle of the shoulder cone have an important effect on the interior ballistic performance of the cartridge, but there is little scientific evidence to support this contention. (See BOTTLENECK CASE.)

case taper Taper is the amount of slope, measured in degrees, from the case head to the start of the

case shoulder in bottleneck metallic cartridges. Early brass cartridge cases featured considerable taper, which facilitated chambering and extraction, but more modern designs show far less taper, indicative of a trend toward increased powder capacity. (See BOTTLENECK CASE.)

case trimming A practice regularly employed by handloaders, case trimming is the reduction of an overly long metallic cartridge case neck. It is necessary not only for cases that have been fired and repeatedly passed through a sizing expander plug, but is sometimes required when making cases for one cartridge out of those of a different type.

Where more than ⅛ inch of brass must be removed, a hacksaw or file is called for, but for ordinary stretched necks a rotary tool called a case trimmer will do a neater, more uniform job. Correct case length is determined by using a case length gauge (one gauge works for most popular rounds). Trimmed cases should also be chamfered. Case necks that are not trimmed will eventually jam into a gun's barrel throat and cause increased chamber pressure. (See CASE GAUGE; CHAMFER.)

cast (stock) In order to better accommodate a gun to a shooter's anatomy, the stock can be bent to either side. A stock that is bent in this manner is said to have cast off (if it is bent to the right for a right-handed shooter) or cast on (if it is bent to the left for the left-handed shooter). In addition, the stock can be cast to different measurements at heel and toe.

Giving a stock cast is of value only to shotguns, where the gun is pointed rather than aimed and instant and precise alignment with the eye is necessary. The degree of cast is measured in fractions of an inch and is determined by means of a try gun, which is adjusted until it fits an individual shooter precisely.

At present, most American shotgun manufacturers either do not cast their stocks, or else incorporate a very small degree of cast off. The practice is common only among manufacturers of high-grade shotguns, where the shooter's measurements are taken as a matter of course. Some custom rifles are given cast at a customer's request, but this is rare. (See SHOTGUN STOCK; TRY GUN.)

cast at heel The degree of cast off or cast on of a rifle or shotgun stock measured at the heel of the stock. (See CAST [STOCK].)

cast at toe The degree of cast off or cast on of a rifle or shotgun stock measured at the toe of the stock. (See CAST [STOCK].)

cast bullet   Early in the development of firearms it was discovered that lead, because of its ballistic properties, made ideal material for projectiles and that, because of its low melting point, projectiles of a uniform size and weight could be readily manufactured by casting, or allowing liquid lead to harden in molds.

Until the advent of smokeless powder, the lead bullet was the standard projectile for rifles and handguns alike. However, the higher velocities created by the new propellant created stresses that made unjacketed lead bullets unsuitable, and so jacketed projectiles superseded them in high-velocity rifle and handgun loads.

Nevertheless, cast bullets continue to occupy a place of great usefulness. They are still standard for muzzleloading arms that utilize black powder and are often fired at moderate velocities in handguns as practice or target loads. Centerfire rifles also employ cast bullets in reduced velocity practice loads that are powered by small charges of fast-burning powder.

Cast bullets are composed of lead or lead alloy that is melted in a special pot and poured into an iron mold to cool. If the bullets are for a modern handgun or rifle, where velocities are relatively high and greased patches are not used (as they are in muzzleloaders), grooves are cast around their circumference, and these are filled with lubricant (usually beeswax) that helps prevent leading the barrel. (See BULLET CASTING [FOR MUZZLELOADERS]; BULLET LUBRICANT; BULLET MOLD.)

CB cap   The CB (conical bullet) cap was a transition cartridge between the BB cap and the .22 Short. Introduced during the late 1850s, it differed from the BB cap in that it used a small powder charge (rather than just the primer) to propel a heavier (29-grain) conical bullet. The BB cap used an 18–20-grain round projectile. Because it had a heavier projectile, the CB cap offered no velocity improvement over the BB cap, but even at only 780 feet per second at the muzzle, the conical CB was far more accurate than the round BB.

Through the 1950s the CB cap was used because of its low noise and good accuracy for indoor gallery shooting and by exhibition and trick shooters; now, it is mostly used for pest control and informal shooting.

cementing lenses   The correction of chromatic aberration in optical instruments is accomplished by means of a two-lens system made of two kinds of glass or by one lens made of two kinds of glass that are cemented together. For years, the cement commonly employed was Canada balsam, which proved satisfactory for ordinary use but would not withstand test extremes of cements formulated during World War II. Synthetic thermal-setting plastics have proved greatly superior to Canada balsam. The newer materials are free from crystallization, separation, or discoloration, caused by age. (See CHROMATIC ABERRATION.)

centerfire   The designation for a system of metallic cartridge ignition wherein the primer is located in a pocket in the center of the case head. A hole in the center of the pocket transmits the explosive force of the primary (primer) compound into the powder charge.

Centerfire ignition, a tremendous firearms design breakthrough, was developed in America in the 1860s and 1870s. Most of the experimental work was done at the Frankford Arsenal by Colonel S. V. Benet, although Hiram Berdan, the New York gunsmith, ammunition designer, and Civil War sharpshooter, was also a significant contributor.

A centerfire cartridge's primer is not an integral part of the case (and is therefore discardable). This attribute led to several related advantages: much stronger cartridge cases could be made economically because they could easily be reloaded for future use, and the increased strength of the brass resulted in the design of much more powerful cartridges. (See BERDAN PRIMER.)

center of dispersion   See CENTER OF IMPACT.

center of impact   This term refers to the center point of a group of shots made on a target by firing from a rest and using the same aiming point and brand and kind of ammunition for every shot. It is also called center of dispersion. Determining the center of impact is essential to zeroing a rifle or handgun, for which purpose three to five shots are usually fired in the manner indicated so as to get a true picture of the actual center of the dispersion. (See SIGHTING IN.)

chamber (noun)   The rearmost section of a rifle, shotgun, or autoloading or single-shot handgun barrel. It is designed to accept a cartridge for firing.

chamber (verb)   The act of inserting or directing a cartridge into the breech of a firearm. Chambering is accomplished either manually or (with a repeater) by closing the breechbolt.

chamber cast   See BORE CAST.

chamberless gun   In conventional shotgun barrels, shot is funneled through a forcing cone after it leaves the chamber, the forcing cone being a graduated constriction of the barrel that leads into the true bore diameter area. A chamberless shotgun has a bore diameter basically the same size as the chamber to eliminate the need for a forcing cone. It is believed by some gunsmiths that eliminating the forcing cone reduces pellet deformation.

chamber pressure Chamber pressure is that pressure generated within a firearm by the expanding gas created by a burning gunpowder charge. The two basic methods of determining chamber pressure give similar results but express the pressure value in different terms. In order to understand a pressure figure, it is therefore mandatory to know which measuring procedure was used.

The method used by nearly all of the ammunition and rifle manufacturers is known as the "crusher system." A hole is drilled into the chamber of a special pressure barrel and a housing containing a cylinder and piston is positioned over the hole. The round to be pressure tested is chambered, a skirt seal resembling a primer cup effectively seals off gas leakage around the piston, and a copper cylindrical slug of known hardness and length—the crusher—is inserted between the piston and a stop. When the round is fired, the cartridge case wall ruptures and the gas pressure forces the piston against the copper crusher, compressing it lengthwise. The crusher is then removed and measured, and the amount of compression is referred to a table that gives the amount of pressure expressed in pounds per square inch (psi). The reading is given in Copper Units of Pressure (C.U.P.) for rifles and in Lead Units of Pressure (L.U.P.) for shotguns, where a lead crusher is used instead of copper because of the much lower chamber pressures developed by shotshells. Measurements in psi and C.U.P. are approximately the same; both denote the pressure per square inch exerted on the chamber walls.

The other pressure-measuring system, coming into increased use, is the electronic transducer system. With it, a strain gauge is attached to the outside of the barrel, over the chamber, and vibration created by the pressure inside the chamber is transmitted to the recording instruments. The pressure-curve line is shown on the screen of a cathode-ray oscilloscope. Transducer system pressures are recorded regardless of the location within the barrel where they are reached; they are expressed in pounds of pressure per square inch absolute (psia), and may be several thousand pounds higher than psi or C.U.P. readings. The resulting difference between psi and psia figures is not only confusing but also causes a load recorded with the transducer system to appear to generate excessive, unsafe pressure, when it actually is well within safe limits.

The main point to remember when considering chamber pressure is that the weak link in the pressure/firearm relationship is not the action—if it is of strong modern design—but the cartridge case. Whenever indications of excessive pressure—such as case head expansion—occur, reduce the powder charge until they are no longer present. (See CASE HEAD EXPANSION; CRUSHER GAUGE.)

chamber reamer A device used to cut the chamber in a rifle barrel. Reamers are usually used in a set of two: one designed to cut the chamber to shape, but slightly under specifications, sometimes called a "rougher"; and the other to complete the job and apply a very smooth finish to the metal surface, called a "finisher."

Reamers are designed with straight or spiral flutes and must be checked for wear periodically to be certain that they will cut the finished chamber to proper dimensional specifications. Prior to chamber reaming, the firearm's barrel is bored, and step drills are used to remove the bulk of the metal for the chamber.

chamfer In handloading, the practice of beveling and deburring a case mouth to permit easy entry of the bullet is called chamfering. A chamfer tool, made

After the barrel has been rifled, a chamber reamer is used to cut the recess for the cartridge case.

of hard steel, is used to so treat both the inside and outside of a case mouth. (See HANDLOAD.)

Champlin (company) This company, founded in 1967 by Douglas Champlin and Jerry Haskins, had, as its original purpose, the manufacture of high-quality sporting rifles. The firm's bolt action, based on a design by Haskins, employs three large locking lugs and three guide ribs to extend the length of the bolt and gain a low bolt lift and smooth withdrawal.

During its first years Champlin & Haskins offered a variety of stock styles, but by 1971 had settled on the conservative "American classic" pattern. By 1970, Haskins had left the firm, and its name was changed to Champlin Firearms, Inc.

Champlin makes extensive use of aircraft-parts technology to produce many of its smaller rifle parts. Right-hand receivers are investment-cast, left-hand receivers are forged. Octagonal barrels are offered as well as round, and refinements such as multiple-leaf express sights and integral barrel ribs are available. Champlin stocks are made by hand, and the firm has enjoyed the services of such talented stockmakers as Clayton Nelson, Phillip Pilkington, and Maurice Ottmar.

In addition to the manufacture of rifles, the Enid, Oklahoma, company imports high-grade shotguns and buys and sells fine used rifles and shotguns of all makes.

charge See POWDER CHARGE.

charger A measure used to dispense a specific amount of black powder directly into the muzzle or cylinder of a firearm. Several kinds are commonly employed, the simplest being a small, open container of horn, brass, or iron that, when filled level, will dispense the proper charge. Some powder flasks are fitted with adjustable powder measures that also act as chargers.

Some black-powder shooters (mostly shotgunners) use dippers, and rifle or musket hunters who need not carry a large amount of powder but who must reload quickly dispense with a powder horn and carry individual premeasured charges in stoppered bottles that are suspended from a bandolier.

charger clip A clip designed to hold extra cartridges to supplement a loaded military rifle. When it is engaged in a rifle's magazine guides, its cartridges may be quickly transferred to the magazine.

Charter Arms (company) Founded in 1964, Charter Arms Company of Stratford, Connecticut, originally offered shooters small, inexpensive, and well-made five-shot double-action revolvers. The first

model was the Undercover, a .38 Special that weighs 16 ounces with a 5-inch barrel. Over the years, the line has been expanded to include models in chamberings from .22 rimfire through .44 Special, and Charter Arms also manufactures the AR-7 Explorer, a .22 survival rifle based on the Air Force AR-5.

checkering On a firearm, a form of decoration that also provides a nonslip surface for grasping. Checkering consists of intersecting rows of V-shaped grooves in wood, which produce pointed, raised diamond shapes or squares (English style). Generally, checkering is cut or impressed only into the portion of a long gun stock or handgun grip that the shooter holds when shooting.

The outline of a checkering pattern to be hand cut is first traced or drawn onto the wood, typically to fit the curvature of the stock. Then the outline is scribed into the surface. Next, two master guidelines are cut into the wood. These guidelines must be straight and true, for they serve to guide the start of the cutting process and essentially determine much of the result.

The cutting tool has two rows of V-shaped blades, one row serving to guide the tool by running in an already cut groove while the other does the actual cutting in the new groove. Many gunsmiths prefer to use power driven checkering tools. These utilize a variable speed electric motor to turn a small sharp-toothed wheel, which does the cutting. Alongside the wheel is a guide that rides in the previously cut groove. The cuts are repeated, deepening as the checkering progresses. If a groove were to be cut to full depth at the start, the points of the raised diamond shapes would be more susceptible to breaking during the process.

The space between parallel rows of grooves may vary from stock to stock, depending upon its owner's preference and the gunsmith's ability. This density or closeness of the lines is called line count and is indicated in lines per inch. For instance, 18-line checkering is composed of 18 grooves per inch. The coarser the checkering (18-line is quite coarse), the rougher and more positive the gripping surface. Too rough checkering can be uncomfortable to handle, while too fine checkering (more than 26 or 28 lines to the inch) lacks the functional nonslip surface. It takes a dense, close-grained piece of wood to accept a fine checkering pattern without chipping, even though not as much wood is removed from each groove in a fine-line pattern.

Not all checkering consists of evenly spaced grooves. The pattern may be broken, with certain areas within the pattern left uncheckered. This is referred to as skipline, or French, checkering.

Checkering grooves typically intersect between 30

and 45 degree angles, but on some older English guns the grooves are cut at right angles to each other, producing squares instead of diamond shapes, and the squares are often flat on top.

In the early 1960s, impressed checkering came into widespread use as an economical means of providing ornamentation to mass-produced guns. This method involves die-pressing the surface of the wood to stamp into it the appropriate pattern, which may be either negative or positive. Positive checkering produces raised pyramids similar to hand cutting, while the negative form produces pyramid-shaped depressions. Negative checkering, which is primarily ornamental, does not provide the nonslip gripping surface that positive checkering does.

In recent years vast improvements have been made in machine checkering, but the quality of the hand cutting method has not yet been duplicated. (See IMPRESSED CHECKERING.)

checkering, English See ENGLISH CHECKERING.

checkering, laying out of The process of tracing, drawing, and cutting a proposed checkering pattern onto a gunstock. Normally, the outline of a check-

ering pattern is traced or drawn onto a stock and then the two master guidelines that determine the pattern's form are started with shallow cuts. These master lines intersect approximately in the center of the pattern and are deepened by a single row of teeth on a two-row cutting tool. They then serve as guides for cutting all subsequent rows of grooves. (See CHECKERING.)

checkering, line count The number of lines or grooves per inch in a field of checkering. The coarser the checkering, the rougher and more positive the gripping surface. However, checkering that is too coarse, fewer than 18 lines per inch, can be uncomfortable to grasp, and checkering that is too fine, more than 28 lines to the inch, is not functional as a nonslip surface. (See CHECKERING.)

checkering, recutting of Undertaken to restore worn areas of a pattern, to repair damage or to correct errors in the original pattern. Through use, the raised points in a checkering pattern wear down, becoming less functional as a nonslip gripping surface. Checkering can also be gouged or damaged by a blow. Both problems can be corrected by recutting the original checkering, as can mistakes made in the original cutting (for example, when there are border runovers, the pattern can be recut and slightly extended to obliterate them). (See CHECKERING.)

checkering cradle A frame designed to support and firmly hold a gunstock while it is being checkered. Checkering cradles are of many different designs, but all must allow freedom of access to the working surface while holding the stock firmly enough to resist slipping under cutting pressures. (See CHECKERING.)

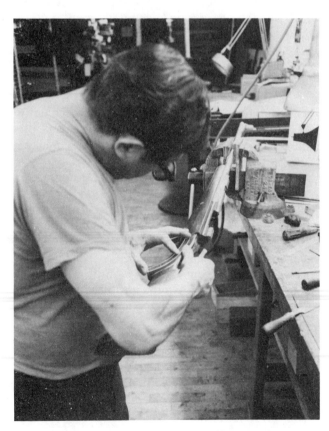

The first step in executing a checkering patterning is laying out the shape of the pattern by means of templates. Lines are drawn on the stock that follow the template, and then the lines are actually cut into the wood.

The checkering cradle must hold a stock absolutely steady, but must also be able to rotate to let the gunsmith work at different angles. This cradle can be adjusted to hold a shotgun stock or a rifle stock.

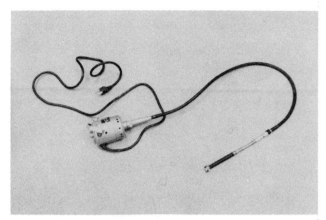

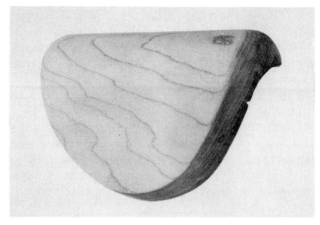

Today, many gunsmiths prefer a checkering machine to hand tools, claiming that it not only cuts faster, but cleaner as well. The device consists of a variable-speed electric motor, a driveshaft, and a cutting wheel.

For rifles that lack a cheekpiece, glue-on models are available. This one is made of wood, others are rubber or leather.

checkering machine   A power driven tool used to hand cut checkering on a stock or grip. Hand-guided machines with high-speed cutting heads occasionally replace the muscle-powered cutters. Also in use are elaborate computer-guided machines that cut checkering on a mass production basis. (See CHECKERING.)

checkering runover   A cut that extends from the checkering field past a boundary of the checkering pattern. It is a flaw resulting from a slip of the cutting tool, usually caused by excessive momentum. Runover does not occur in impressed checkering. (See CHECKERING; CHECKERING, RECUTTING OF.)

cheekpiece   A cheekpiece is an enlarged area on the inside surface of the buttstock of many modern rifles and some trap shotguns; the shooter rests his cheek against it while aiming and shooting. The cheekpiece was developed to aid eye/sight alignment

when the use of telescopic sights on hunting rifles became widespread. Its use on shotguns is rare and of dubious benefit; its advocates contend that cheekpieces aid trapshooters to align the front and rear sighting beads while aiming.

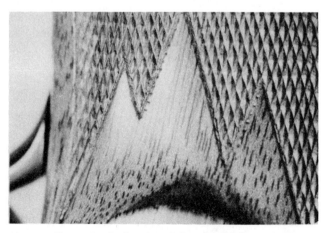

The small cuts at the border of the checkering pattern are runover. Considerable skill and care are needed to avoid making them.

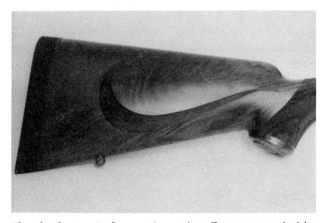

The cheekpiece in figure 1 is used on European and older American rifles. The kind in figure 2 is preferred by most shooters since it allows the face to slide away from the stock as the rifle recoils.

Until the 1920s, few rifles (outside of Schuetzen target guns) had cheekpieces; their presence in the next decades was essentially restricted to custom arms. After World War II manufacturers such as Winchester (on its Model 70 Super Grade) and Remington (on its Model 700) offered cheekpiece stocks. Today they are common.

Dramatic and often bizarre cheekpieces are a special feature of the so-called California stock design. Lace-on pad cheekpieces are available to facilitate scope use with old rifles or on those whose stocks do not have cheekpieces. (See CALIFORNIA STOCK.)

cheekpiece bead   See BEAD (CHEEKPIECE.)

chilled shot   Shot pellets that are hardened by the addition of antimony to the standard lead composition. Chilled shot deforms less in forcing cones and chokes of shotguns and therefore delivers tighter and more even patterns than does soft or "drop" shot. Also called hardened shot. (See ANTIMONY; COPPER-COATED SHOT; DROPPED SHOT.)

choke   Choke is a constriction at the muzzle of a shotgun barrel (usually expressed in "points" of .001 inch), the function of which is to compress the shot charge and therefore limit the dispersion of the shot after it leaves the gun. The object is to control the percentage of the pellets that will hit a target at a fixed distance from the muzzle. The inventor and the precise date of invention are not known. However, according to the late arms historian Harold L. Peterson, choking was in a state of evolution as early as the 1700s and reached its present form about 1850.

The effectiveness of the choke of a shotgun barrel cannot be determined by its nominal designation, nor even by the literal dimensions of the constriction at the muzzle. Powder charge, size of shot, hardness of shot, and wadding all have an effect on the patterns delivered by a particular barrel, and a shotgun barrel therefore may shoot at different degrees of choke when used with different loads. Further, because different manufacturers use slightly varying degrees of constriction to attain a given choke, it is impossible to give precise standard measurements. As an example, here are the amounts of constriction for the basic chokes used by two American companies for their in 12-gauge shotguns:

Full	.030-inch	.040-inch
Modified	.015-inch	.020-inch
Improved-cylinder	.006-inch	.008-inch
Cylinder	None	None

Choke markings are relative, since a variety of constrictions can be used by different manufacturers for the same designation. Here, a dial-readout gauge is used to determine the actual diameter of a shotgun barrel and, thus, the points of constriction.

The choke labels on American shotguns are determined by the average percentage of the total number of shot pellets from a given load that will strike within a 30-inch circle when fired from 40 yards. The following table shows industry choke standards for American shotguns:

CHOKE	PERCENT IN 30-INCH CIRCLE FROM 40 YARDS
Extra-full	80–100 percent
Full	70–80 percent
Improved-modified	65–70 percent
Modified	55–65 percent
Improved-cylinder	45–55 percent
Skeet #1, #2	35–45 percent
Cylinder	35 percent or less

Several of these chokes are highly specialized. Extra-full is used in guns intended for long-range

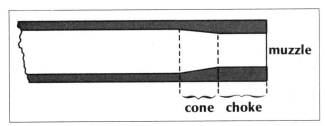

Shotguns control the density of their pattern by means of a constriction at the muzzle, known as the choke. A tapered section of the barrel leads into the choke, so as to compress the shot charge gradually and avoid pellet deformation. This is known as the cone, or forcing cone.

waterfowling, live pigeon shooting, and on a few trap guns. Improved-modified and skeet are employed only in trap and skeet guns, respectively. Cylinder is found most often on riot shotguns and in slug barrels. Optimum ranges for the common chokes—full, modified, and improved-cylinder—are as follows:

RANGE	CHOKE
Over 35 yards	Full
25 to 35 yards	Modified
15 to 25 yards	Improved-cylinder, cylinder, or skeet

With loads containing extra-hard copper-plated shot that is cushioned by the addition of granulated plastic to the shot charge, many shotgun barrels will shoot much denser patterns than industry standards for each choke designation. For instance, many full choke barrels will pattern 90 percent or higher with copper-coated shot.

The original intent of choke boring was to improve patterns over those obtainable from cylinder bored barrels, which were limited not only because their patterns became thin at comparatively close ranges but also because these patterns were uneven and often left large areas near their centers uncovered, through which game could escape. Used with modern ammunition, however, most modern cylinder bores deliver wide, dense, even patterns that are particularly useful for close-range shooting at such game as woodcock and grouse. This fact nicely illustrates the effect of today's ammunition on all degrees of choke in shotgun barrels. (See ADJUSTABLE CHOKE.)

choke, adjustable See ADJUSTABLE CHOKE.

choke adjustment The degree of choke in a shotgun barrel may be altered from that which was originally present. The user may want tighter or more open patterns or may require delivery of a particular pattern percentage with a specific shot size or load. Gunsmiths can adjust a choke to shoot either tighter or looser patterns.

choke marking Most shotgun barrels have engraved on them their nominal type of choke. These markings may be found on the side or upper surface of the barrel or on the barrel flats of side-by-side or over/under guns. Some makers use a word designation—full, modified, improved-cylinder, etc.—while others use such symbols as stars or dashes (the key to which appears in the brochure that accompanies new guns) or actual pattern percentage figures..

choke tube Adjustable shotgun choke devices such as the Cutts Compensator, Lyman Choke, Winchoke, and various custom systems employ interchangeable screw-in tubes to obtain different pattern percentages from one barrel or one set of barrels. Some of these systems incorporate a muzzle brake into their designs. (See ADJUSTABLE CHOKE; RECOIL BRAKE.)

chopper lump A chopper lump is a metal block, or projection, on the bottom of side-by-side shotgun barrels that fastens them to the action. (See SIDE-BY-SIDE GUN.)

chopper lump tube This term refers to a method commonly employed by London gunmakers to join barrels of side-by-side shotguns. Each barrel is forged with a lump at the breech end. When the barrels have been bored to approximate desired diameter, they are brazed together, which joins the lumps into a single unit. (See LUMPS; SIDE-BY-SIDE GUN.)

chromatic aberration In any optical device, a lens forms a real image by refracting the light passing through it. Since sunlight, or "white" light, is made up of light rays of several different colors and wavelengths, a single lens cannot bring the light rays of different colors to a common focus. That is, the images formed by different colors of light are at different distances from the lens and are of unequal sizes. These out-of-focus images form color halos around each detail of the image, blurring them together, and this is called chromatic aberration. Another way of explaining it is in terms of the refractive index of the glass of which the lens is made. The refractive index is not the same for light of different colors, i.e., different wavelengths.

Correction of chromatic aberration is usually accomplished by making doublet lenses of two different kinds of glass (usually crown and flint), cemented together. Having different refractive indices, properly selected, the result is to bring all colors to approximately the same focus. (Full color correction would result in an unacceptable increase in other kinds of aberrations.) A lens of this type is called "achromatic." (See ACHROMATIC LENS.)

chronograph As it applies to shooting, an instrument that measures and records the speed of projectiles over a fixed course. This distance, divided by the time of flight, is the velocity of the projectile,

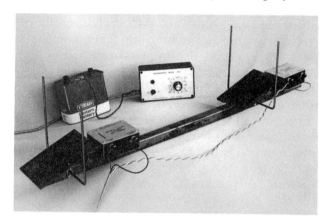

The chronograph measures the speed of a projectile by timing the interval of its flight between two points. This one employs an electric field between the pairs of opposing prongs. As the bullet passes between each pair, it breaks the field, and the interval between its passage is then translated into feet per second. In use, the device is mounted on a tripod; the shooter stands a measured distance away and fires.

expressed in feet per second. At one time, chronographs were costly, cumbersome machines that were impractical for the individual shooter to own and use. However, in recent years, chronographs have been made smaller, simpler, and more compact, and are at a price many shooters can afford.

The Boulengé chronograph, invented in 1855 by Paul Boulengé of the Belgian artillery, measured short time intervals, particularly at ordnance proving grounds. It was the first practical chronograph, and remained in use until the end of World War I. The distance of free fall under the acceleration of gravity is used as the basis for this instrument.

The Aberdeen chronograph was developed during World War I for the U.S. Army as a more accurate instrument than the Boulengé. A number of other kinds of chronographs then preceded the electronic-counter instrument that came into use during World War II and is most utilized by shooters today. This device was based on an electronic counting circuit first used in England in the 1930s.

The modern chronograph consists of four parts: a pair of photoelectric cells that react to the "shadow" of the bullet as it passes over them; a crystal-controlled oscillator that supplies consecutive pulses at a rate of 200,000-to-500,000 per second; a gate circuit, which is opened by the signal from the first photoelectric cell and is closed by the signal from the second one; and a counting circuit, which registers the number of pulses that pass through the gate while it is open.

Modern chronographs automatically translate the number of pulses that register during a bullet's passage between its photoelectric cells into feet per second, and some print out this information as well. There are chronographs that calculate high, low, and average velocities of shots in a series, as well as standard deviation.

A chronograph is an invaluable tool for the handloader. Not only does it give him the velocity of the loads he develops, but can reveal information about load uniformity and pressure as well.

Churchill, Winston Gordon (1939–) A master engraver, working principally on firearms and knives, Churchill also does high-quality stockwork. Churchill is unique among engravers in that he did not start his career until he reached his mid-twenties, yet was recognized as a master of his craft by the time he reached his early thirties.

He learned the basics of his profession under the guidance of Robert Kain and refined his skills during four and one-half years at Griffin & Howe, where he worked for the noted Austrian engraver Joseph Fugger. Churchill then returned to his native Vermont, where he currently resides and works.

A native of Vermont, Winston Churchill was recognized as one of the world's greatest gun engravers while still in his 30s.

Some engravers use a minimum of lines to suggest enough to the eye so that the mind fills in the figure or scene, much as a skilled caricaturist can characterize a person with a few sketch lines. Churchill's work displays countless tiny lines under magnification. Inlaid gold animal figures, sculpted to a depth of a few thousandths of an inch, show muscle and body structure as though carved in deep relief. Backgrounds are accurate in such minute details as clouds, knots, and even the irregularity of insect-eaten edges and holes in leaves. His stockwork, both inletting and checkering, exhibit similar mastery of form. (See CHECKERING; ENGRAVING; INLETTING.)

Churchill shotgun The Churchill shotgun became best known during the lifetime of Robert Churchill, "father" of the trend to short-barreled shotguns. His famed Churchill double with 25-inch barrels, introduced in the 1920s, created the greatest shotgun controversy in decades, Churchill maintaining that the short tubes would kill just as far away as, and handle much faster than, the longer-barreled guns then in conventional use. By and large, history has supported Churchill's shorter-barrel concept.

Churchill guns are still made in both sidelock and boxlock actions, the majority being side-by-side doubles. Although not generally considered in quite the class with Purdey and Holland & Holland, the Churchill is known worldwide as a very fine shotgun.

Cincinnati Milling Machine Co. See INTRAFORM PROCESS.

claw mount A kind of telescopic sight mount very popular in Europe and Africa, although rarely seen in the United States, a claw mount makes a scope quickly and easily detachable from the rifle. Invented in Europe, this mount is so named because of the "claws" on its scope rings that serve to hook the rings into the bases. The claws fit into carefully machined dovetails in the bases and are secured by spring loaded locks. Removal is achieved by lightly depressing a button on the rear ring, which in turn releases the claws of the rear base. The scope can then be swung out and the claws of the front ring will simply lift out of their cuts. (See SCOPE MOUNTS.)

clay target A dome-shaped disc aerodynamically designed to fly straight and to considerable distance when properly launched by skeet or trap machines or thrown by hand-operated launchers. Used for practice and competition by shotgunners, clays are often called "blue rocks" by old-timers or "birds" or "clay pigeons" by modern shooters. These terms come from the days when live pigeons were commonly used in competition; their modern replacement is made of composition pitch (not actually clay at all). When hit, the clay target shatters; if solidly hit it disappears into a cloud of dust. This is called "smoking the bird." (See SKEET SHOOTING; TRAP-SHOOTING.)

cleaning rod Despite the noncorrosive properties of modern primers and powders, firearms must still be cleaned regularly in order to remove metal fouling and powder residue. A cleaning rod is necessary for this operation. Cleaning rods consist of three parts: the handle (which, on rifle and handgun rods, is swiveled so that the rod can revolve and follow the rifling twist); the rod itself; and the tip, which can be a brush, jag, slotted tip, or swab.

Traditionally, the best rifle rods have been made of steel because its hard surface resists grit, which can act as an abrasive and damage rifling. Today, the steel rifle rod is being superseded by plastic-covered metal because it is believed that this material is less abrasive to a bore than steel. Quality shotgun rods are made of varnished hardwood, and handgun rods are usually made of aluminum or steel.

In selecting a cleaning rod, it is important to choose one of the proper diameter for the gun to be cleaned and to wipe the rod off frequently during use. Some older shooters still prefer solid brass rods, wiping them before each use, because they are softer than the barrel's steel rifling. (See JAG; RAMROD.)

clean-out plug Also known as the clean-out screw. It is a removable plug or screw employed in muzzleloading rifles that, when removed, allows cleaning of the breech recess, drum, and bolster. The device is also used in the gas cylinder assembly of some modern semiautomatic and automatic arms to permit cleaning of the assembly. (See GAS CYLINDER.)

click A single notch unit of sight adjustment, ranging from ¼ inch to 1 inch at 100-yard point of impact, in scopes and aperture sights. It is so named for the "click" that is felt or heard when a sight's adjustment knobs are turned. (See METALLIC SIGHTS; TELESCOPIC SIGHTS.)

clip A device (or box) of brass or steel holding cartridges in a single line or staggered formation to be used in loading a magazine with a single downward motion of the shooter's hand. (See MAGAZINE.)

clip lip A recess or cutout in a rifle receiver that accepts and guides a stripper-type clip for transferring cartridges from clip to magazine. Sometimes also called a clip slot.

clock system The face of an imaginary clock is often used in shooting to describe a sight picture, wind direction, and the location of a shot group on a target. In the employment of the clock system, 12 o'clock is at the top of the bull's-eye on a target sheet. A wind blowing directly into the shooter's face from behind the target thus comes from 12 o'clock, while a shot group at the bottom of the bull is at 6 o'clock. (See SIGHT PICTURE; SIX O'CLOCK HOLD.)

CO₂ gun A gun that utilizes liquid carbon dioxide as the propellant for the pellet it fires. The CO_2 is usually retained in a steel reservoir within the gun. A pull of the trigger opens a valve, discharging carbon dioxide to propel the projectile from the barrel. When propelling pellets of .17 or .22 caliber, velocities of 600 to 650 feet per second can be obtained, with an effective range of 30 yards. A CO_2 gun is similar to a pneumatic gun except that gas propellant is utilized instead of compressed air. CO_2 is often used in tranquilizer guns to propel the tranquilizing dart. (See AIR GUN.)

coarse bead See BEADS, FINE AND COARSE.

coated optics Optical glass lenses coated with a material that enhances light transmission are called coated optics. The usual coating material is magnesium fluoride, applied to an average thickness of .0005-inch, or a quarter of a light wavelength. Coating reduces the amount of light normally lost in reflection; a coated lens has its light transmission ability increased by up to 50 percent. Good-quality binoculars, spotting scopes, cameras, and scope sights have coated optics as a matter of course. (See BINOCULARS; LIGHT TRANSMISSION; MAGNESIUM FLUORIDE; SPOTTING SCOPE; TELESCOPIC SIGHTS.)

cock As a verb, the word means to place the hammer of a firearm in the firing position. As a noun it is synonymous with the hammer of a muzzleloading arm.

cocking dog A 19th-century term used to describe the cocking lever of a break-open shotgun. The cocking lever (or levers in double-barrel guns) is activated by a small rod in the fore-end as the gun is broken. The forward end is depressed, elevating the rear end of the lever and pushing the hammer, or tumbler, into cocked position.

cocking indicator A small projection, usually at the rear of a rifle action, whose function is to tell the shooter if his rifle is cocked. It is activated by cocking the bolt, and is often an extension of the firing pin. (See CARTRIDGE INDICATOR.)

cocking lever That part in a break-open rifle or shotgun that mechanically forces the hammer or firing pin to the cocked position when the action is opened.

cocking on closing Some older bolt-action rifles (notably Enfield designs) provide for the cocking of the firing mechanism as the final act of action manipulation, at the same time that the lowering of the bolt handle locks the breech. This is called cocking on closing.

cocking on opening The most widespread method of cocking the firing mechanism of all modern firearms is to have it occur at the beginning of action manipulation—in bolt guns when the bolt handle is lifted, for example. This is called cocking on opening.

cocking piece A knob or spur that protrudes from the rear of a bolt-action firing mechanism when the firearm is cocked. On some military rifles, most notably the Model 1903 Springfield, it is part of the firing pin and can be pulled back to manually cock the arm.

coefficient of expansion A mathematical expression of the rate at which powder gas, when affected by the heat of its own combustion, expands within a barrel. Coefficients of expansion are not a practical consideration for the average shooter or handloader; they are of use only to advanced students of interior ballistics. (See INTERIOR BALLISTICS.)

coefficient of form A numeral that provides an index indicative of the efficiency of a projectile's nose shape, or ogive. Generally, the sharper a projectile's point, the more efficient it is in flight because a given velocity produces less nose pressure and less drag. The more-pointed bullet better retains its velocity and therefore travels on a flatter trajectory.

The coefficient of form is one element used in the computation of ballistic coefficient, which also takes into account the weight and cross-sectional area of the projectile (sectional density), as well as air density at the time of firing.

The coefficient of form is sometimes referred to as the form factor. (See BALLISTIC COEFFICIENT; BULLET DRAG; BULLET VELOCITY; EXTERIOR BALLISTICS; OGIVE; SECANT OGIVE.)

coil spring One of two kinds of springs usually found in firearms, coil, or helical, springs are typically used in firing pin and cocking mechanisms. In addition to being easier to manufacture, coil springs are preferred in modern firearms because they are less subject to breakage than flat springs. (See FLAT SPRING.)

coincidence prism A complex optical arrangement, used in rangefinders, in which two images, formed by two separate objective lenses, are superimposed on each other.

The most familiar application of the coincidence prism is the camera viewfinder, where the superimposing, or aligning, of two halves of an image indicates that the lens is focused accurately upon it.

However, the problem with adapting this system to long-range shooting lies in the fact that, to be effective, there must be considerable distance between the two lenses to produce the dual image. Thus, any rangefinder that is truly accurate at long distances—where a rangefinder is most needed—must be large and therefore more cumbersome than most hunters are willing to tolerate.

cold weather malfunctions See MALFUNCTIONS, COLD WEATHER.

cold working Drawing, shaping, or forming a metal at room temperature, such as in case forming. Cold working alters the molecular properties of the metal and has a direct bearing on cartridge case life and elasticity.

Generally, cartridge case necks become brittle with repeated cold working and are prone to cracking or splitting. Cases that have been frequently cold worked, typically when reloading, are sometimes annealed to decrease the possibility of cracking. Most metals

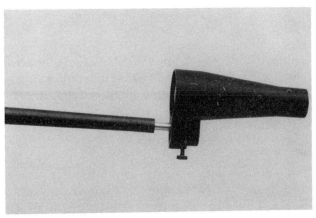

A collimator is a device that is used to align the axis of a rifle bore with the crosshairs of a scope.

harden when cold worked, but lead softens. (See ANNEALING; CASE FORMING.)

collet puller See BULLET PULLER.

collimator An optical instrument designed to facilitate making the line of a firearm's sights parallel to the axis of its bore. It contains a grid optical screen that has an X or a cross centered in its window, or is laid out in squares that usually subtend 4 inches at 100 yards. This part of the instrument is attached to a short spud, or rod, of the diameter to fit a given bore. (A different spud must be used for each bore size.) With the rod inserted into the bore and the collimator in an upright position, the rifle's sight, either iron or scope, is adjusted so that the front sight or reticle centers on the inter-

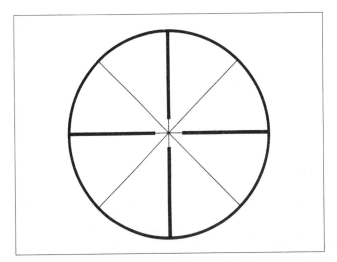

A collimator is used to align the reticle of a scope with the axis of the bore without the necessity of shooting. The collimator spud is inserted in the barrel, and the scope crosshairs are adjusted until their center is aligned with the center of the diagonal wires of the collimator.

section of the center cross line or X, or the center square. This zero adjustment will result in most rifles putting the first shot within a few inches of center at 100 yards. While the collimator is the ideal means of bore- or presighting, the rifle should *always* be zeroed in by actual firing. (See SIGHTING IN.)

Colt, Samuel (1814–1862)   Colt is perhaps the best known of the long list of men—Henry, Spencer, Winchester, Remington, Wesson, Ruger, to name but a few—whose names became synonymous with firearms in the complex history of the American arms industry. Born in Hartford, Connecticut, on July 19, 1814, Colt was from early boyhood a nonconformist. An eager learner and doer of things that interested him, he was stubbornly resistant to routine school and family disciplines. He was interested in guns, explosives, and chemical oddities, and he worked tirelessly to improve an ancient pistol, learned to make gunpowder and explode it from a distance via a galvanic battery, and learned to make and administer nitrous oxide, commonly known as "laughing gas." But these were extracurricular accomplishments, and young Sam soon found himself facing two choices: enter his father's business or go to sea. He chose the latter.

Colt spent the major part of two years, 1830–1831, as an apprentice midshipman aboard the sloop *Corvo*, enjoying shore leaves in such ports as Calcutta, London, and New York. Wherever possible, he visited museums featuring gun collections. On board ship, he spent his spare time whittling a prototype of a firearm that would accept six loads in a cylinder and fire them as each load came into line with a single barrel. He called it a revolver.

But applicants for patents need better than a whittled-out wooden model to show, and Colt did not have the money needed to build working models. His father, not impressed with the revolver, suggested that Colt either enter the family business or return to sea. Instead, the young man set himself up as a traveling entertainer—"Dr. Coult, of New York, London, and Calcutta"—with an act that consisted of persuading paying customers to amuse crowds by clowning under the influence of "laughing gas." It was a device that would have delighted P. T. Barnum: show business without having to pay the actors! Colt was just 18 years old at this time, and he grew a luxuriant beard to lend credence to his billing. He traveled widely with his act, hoarding the profits to pay for the making of the necessary models of his revolver.

The first Colt patents were issued in England, to ensure protection in the European markets. These were obtained in December 1835. In February 1836, patents for the Colt revolvers (both handgun and

Samuel Colt's revolvers, in addition to their significance as firearms, have entered into American folklore.

rifle) were issued also by the U.S. Patent Office. Colt then set up a stock company composed of New York and New Jersey investors, and established a factory in Paterson, New Jersey. This enterprise failed, but the guns produced there, the Paterson Colts, are among the most prized of modern collectors' pieces.

Impressed by the Colt guns for use as cavalry weapons in the Mexican War, General Zachary Taylor sent Captain Samuel Walker to Washington to urge the purchase of Colt guns for the Army. Early in 1847, the government ordered 1,000 pistols. Given a market, Colt now had no factory. He solved this problem by joining forces with Eli Whitney (of cotton-gin fame) to make the guns in Whitney's Connecticut factory. The Walker Colts produced there and later in Colt's own factory in Hartford are also collectors' gems.

Colt's death came on January 10, 1862, but the guns, famous now in their own right, found markets at home and abroad.

Sam Colt never learned to spell, but he made his name world famous, and his guns still rank among the leaders in world markets wherever repeating handguns are in use. (See COLT [COMPANY].)

Colt (company)   Samuel Colt was granted his first American patent for a pistol and rifle design in 1836, several years after he had carved his first pistol from a block of wood while at sea.

Upon receiving the patent, Colt established the Patent Arms Manufacturing Company of Paterson, New Jersey. The year 1836 also marked the beginning of the Texan war for independence from Mexico, a circumstance that created a considerable demand for weapons. The bulk of the arms manufactured at Paterson were five-shot pistols, though rifles, carbines, and shotguns were also made.

Many of Colt's business associates did not agree with his ideas of production and marketing. The internal struggles led to the company declaring bankruptcy in 1842. Fortunately the patents, according to agreement, reverted to Colt's control.

With the annexation of Texas to the Union, and the subsequent war with Mexico, Colt resumed manufacturing pistols. That took place in 1847, when, following suggestions made by Captain Samuel Walker of the Texas Rangers, Colt designed a new handgun, a .44 caliber with square-back trigger guard, hinged lever loading device, and a 9-inch barrel. The government placed an immediate order for 1,000 of these guns and Colt, having no factory of his own, arranged for Eli Whitney to manufacture the pistols at his plant in Connecticut.

As government orders grew, Colt separated from Whitney and late in 1847 began his own production in Hartford, Connecticut. A new factory was built and Colt's Patent Firearms Manufacturing Company was chartered. Colt continued to produce revolvers for the Army and also introduced a new line of .31-caliber pistols.

In the period just prior to the Civil War, two new military models were produced, a Navy model in .36 caliber, and a .44-caliber Army model. The Civil War brought about increased production, with Colt selling more than 385,000 revolvers to the government between 1861 and 1865. Samuel Colt did not live to see the end of the war; he died in 1862.

In 1877, Colt introduced its new line of double-action revolvers. Developments in Colt pistols have continued, with modifications made for sportsmen, military personnel, and law enforcement officers. (See COLT, SAMUEL.)

columbaire See LIVE PIGEON SHOOTING.

coma The comet-shaped blurring of the border of the total image viewed through a telescopic sight or a similar optical instrument, generally ascribed to spherical aberration of one or more of the lenses in the optical system. (See SPHERICAL ABERRATION.)

comb The upper edge of a buttstock of a shoulder arm. The shooter's cheekbone rests on top of the comb. For this reason, the height of the comb is very important in aligning the shooter's eye with the sights. With a comb of proper height, the eye is aligned with the sights automatically when the gun is brought to the face and shoulder.

In the usual stock, the comb slants downward toward the rear. If the shooter "crawls the stock" (places his head farther forward than usual), the eye is elevated above the line of sight. If he holds his head back farther than he should but his cheekbone is still touching the comb, his eye is too low. For this reason, many modern designers and stockmakers employ combs that are dead level and parallel to the barrel axis. With these stocks, the shooter's eye is at exactly the same height for every shot, no matter how far forward or back he places his head. A level comb also reduces felt recoil since it tends to slide rearward under the cheekbone instead of recoiling upward and rearward as many slanted combs do.

Comb height is very important to clay bird shooters who need to maintain precisely the same eye-barrel relationship from shot to shot. It is also very important to users of telescopic sights; when hunting, the need to place the eye quickly behind the scope is obvious.

Comb thickness affects how the eye is placed laterally behind the sights. If the comb is too thick, the eye of a right-handed shooter is too far to the left; if it is too thin, his eye is too far to the right.

For serious competitive shooting, the comb must fit the shooter's individual requirements. Combs can be lowered or thinned by cutting away some wood; they can be built up with layers of plastic material or glued-on wood shaped to fit. (See CHEEKPIECE; MONTE CARLO COMB.)

combination gun This kind of firearm has at least two barrels, one of which is a rifled tube for cartridges loaded with a single projectile, and the other of which is a shotgun barrel. All are break-action guns in which the barrels pivot downward to expose the breeches of the barrels for loading. These arms are used mostly in central Europe where bird hunting, small game, and big-game seasons are open at the same time. With this kind of gun, a hunter is able to shoot both flying birds and four-footed game.

In America, the most common combination gun is the Savage over/under with a .22 barrel on top (although a few centerfire offerings are available) and a shotgun barrel under, but in Europe, the most common arrangement with this combination is to place the shotgun barrel on top and the .22 or other smallbore tube underneath.

European combination guns include the following (names in German):

Drilling. A side-by-side shotgun with a rifle barrel centered below the shotgun tubes.

Vierling. Four barrels. Essentially, this arm is a Drilling with a smallbore barrel added. It is placed in the center of the triangle formed by the other three.

Schienendrilling. Basically a side-by-side shotgun with a rifle barrel placed in the rib on top of and between the shotgun tubes—an upside-down Drilling.

Büchsflinte. Two barrels, side by side. One is rifled, the other smoothbore.

Doppelbüchsdrilling. A three-barreled gun similar to the Drilling, but the two barrels on top are rifled, and the third barrel underneath is for shotgun shells.

Seldom seen is the over/under shotgun with a small bore (usually .22 rimfire) barrel at the side of and between the shotgun tubes.

The Drilling is the favored combination type in Europe. One shotgun barrel may be loaded with a small-shot cartridge for birds, the other shotgun barrel with bigger shot for four-footed small game and foxes; and the rifle barrel with a bulleted deer load.

In America, these combination guns are not as useful as they are in Europe because many of our bird and four-footed-game seasons do not overlap, but in certain situations they can be used to great advantage. For instance, a squirrel hunter with a .22/ shotgun combination is equipped to take sitting squirrels with the rifled tube and running ones with a shotgun. Where shotguns and rifles are both legal for deer hunting, a Drilling is handy. One shotgun barrel is loaded with buckshot, the second is loaded with a slug, and the rifle barrel, of course, is loaded with a bulleted cartridge. At close range on a moving deer, the hunter uses the buckshot load. For standing shots at medium range and in situations where firing a long-range rifle cartridge could be dangerous to others, he uses the shotgun slug. For long-range shots, where safe, he uses the rifled tube.

Some of these guns have disadvantages. The lock of a three-barreled or four-barreled gun is very complicated, and aligning the barrels during manufacture is difficult. Therefore, these guns are usually quite expensive. They also have tended to be rather heavy, though modern Drillings and Vierlings are surprisingly light in weight because it has become possible to employ shorter barrels than were formerly used. Drillings and Vierlings are complicated and rather delicate, and they are therefore difficult to repair. The average American gunsmith is unfamiliar with them. If repairs are needed, it is best to send them back to the manufacturer unless a capable European trained gunsmith can be found.

Another disadvantage is the lack of a magazine. A hunter who uses a Drilling is limited to one rifle shot. With a Doppelbüchsdrilling, the hunter has only one shotgun shell in his gun. Quick follow-up shots are unavailable. Using a combination gun amounts to hunting with a single shot in many instances.

The firing mechanism is also complicated. A Drilling typically has two triggers that fire the two shotgun barrels. To fire the rifled barrel, a selector switch must be used first, and then the rear trigger fires the rifled barrel. Some Drillings have been made with three triggers, one for each barrel. If a hunter is not really familiar with his gun, he may fire the wrong barrel in the excitement of a hunt. This is inconvenient, and it could be dangerous, for instance if the hunter mistakenly shoots a charge of small birdshot at a boar. Many Europeans, however, are one gun hunters and become so familiar with the arm that there is no difficulty.

Vierlings and other multibarrel combination guns are fired by means of two triggers, each equipped with selector switches.

Because combination guns must function both as shotgun and rifle, the sighting equipment must not interfere with the gun's performance as a smoothbore. The standard is an unobtrusive front iron sight and an open rear, usually one that folds flat. The better Drillings are equipped with levers that will flip up the rear sight instantly. Naturally, this kind of sighting equipment precludes precision use of the rifle barrel(s) at ranges of more than 250 yards or so.

In some European countries, the law makes it difficult for a hunter to own more than one firearm, and in that situation, a good combination gun is almost a necessity. (See DRILLING; HINGED FRAME; VIERLING.)

combination trap house See TRAP HOUSE.

combustion chamber See CONTROLLED COMBUSTION CHAMBERAGE.

compensator A device attached to or integral with the muzzle of a firearm; it counteracts the forces of muzzle jump resulting from recoil. This is accomplished by a series of slots in the compensator that direct the powder gases upon firing in a manner to force the muzzle in a downward direction counter to that imposed by recoil. The most widely known device of this type was formerly the Cutts Compensator used on shotguns.

Rifles and handguns are sometimes equipped with integral compensators to reduce recoil. However, while these may lessen kick to a certain extent, the fact that they direct the powder gas backward and upward results in greater noise. At this time, they are not widely used, but are becoming more popular for calibers that deliver heavy recoil. (See CUTTS COMPENSATOR; RECOIL BRAKE.)

component In firearms terminology, the word most commonly refers to an ammunition part. For instance, bullets, powder, and primers are ammunition components. (See HANDLOAD.)

compound bullet Sometimes called a composite bullet, the term refers to a projectile that is composed of two different alloys. The alloys are cast in separate molds, then the two sections are swaged together to form a single projectile. A compound bullet's softer base upsets to fill the rifling grooves upon firing while the harder front section rides the lands.

Compound bullets are used in black-powder rifle shooting. They provide superior velocity combined with good penetration. (See BULLET UPSET; LAND.)

compound lens A compound lens is a combination of two or more lenses used in conjunction to minimize optical aberrations. There are six kinds of aberrations that, unless corrected, will impair the performance of any lens or lens system: chromatic aberration; spherical aberration; coma; distortion; curvature of field; and astigmatism.

It should be understood that a "fully corrected" lens system, as sometimes advertised, is an impossibility. A "full correction" for one kind of aberration will cause an increase in another kind. A quality optical instrument is the result of its designer's skill in balancing optical corrections and qualities, good mechanical design, and precision manufacture.

compressed charge A compressed charge occurs when reloading centerfire rifle cartridges using large charges of slow-burning powder. The powder charge may fill the case to the point where it occupies space in the neck, and must be compressed sufficiently to enable a bullet to be seated. A slight degree of compression will have no adverse effect, but severe compression can crush powder granules, resulting in erratic pressures and poor accuracy.

compression formed shotshell Compression formed shotshells are fabricated of plastic under high pressure. The base wad and case are formed as one piece so that there is no separate base wad as in paper shotshells. This makes an extremely strong case with the potential to be reloaded many times.

Before the advent of plastic shotshells, the separate base wad could become dislodged from the head of the case, rendering it unusable for reloading. In addition, if a loose base wad became lodged in the barrel upon firing, it could obstruct the barrel on subsequent firing and create a condition that is hazardous to both gun and shooter. The advent of the plastic compression formed shotshell eliminated this possibility. (See BASE WAD.)

concave lens A negative lens that is thinner at its center than at its margin. Parallel beams of light entering the negative lens will be bent outward, diverging from the central axis of the lens. Concave lenses are used in combination with convex lenses to form optical systems. (See CONVEX LENS.)

cone See FORCING CONE; NIPPLE.

cone choke See TAPER CHOKE.

Continental Europe, guns and loads for hunting in Sport hunting in Europe is virtually unknown as it is practiced in the United States. There is, to be sure, plenty of hunting for large game and birds in most Continental countries, but it is on private grounds by the landowner and his invited guests. There is very little land open to public shooting. However, there is some hunting open to the visitor from abroad, usually obtainable through those travel agencies specializing in such excursions.

It isn't as easy to go hunting in some European countries as it is in America. An examination has to be passed in most countries, a test that can cover such things as game recognition and management, tracking, safety habits, conduct afield, and ability to shoot well. That last requirement entails a shooting trial for the novice, whether with rifle or shotgun. License requirements are most strict in Germany, perhaps, and the applicant for a certificate of proficiency must usually go to a hunting school. This *Jagdbrief*, as it's called in Germany, is good for life and it is often an aid to going hunting in other countries.

Certification aside, wherever one hunts in Europe, he'll have to fire a few shots to show the forester or guide that he is able to hit the mark—and it is not a big mark.

Hunting techniques. Most European bird shooting means drive shooting for the visitor, at least, and it's a common method for the residents, too. For the visitor it has advantages—he or she can get in a lot of shooting in a few hours or days that couldn't happen if "walking up" or rough shooting were the mode. On a well-organized drive hunt everything is arranged—the drivers are hired and ready to work, the shooter is assigned a certain "butt" or stand (these are rotated each drive, the first butt having been assigned by the luck of the draw)—and, once the birds appear, the shooting begins. It can be, if conditions are right, as exciting as any wingshooting in North America.

Red deer are frequently driven, too, and often enough on such drives various other game will appear—hares, foxes, roe, and the like. Depending on the rules laid down beforehand such animals may or may not be shot.

An elevated seat or platform, usually roofed over and closed on four sides, is used over much of Europe to conceal the hunter and lift his scent above ground level.

This *Hochsitz*, as the Germans call it, may be from a dozen feet above the ground to much higher, depending on such factors as visibility from the seat, the surrounding terrain and its lie, etc. They are mostly man made of local rough lumber, and a ladder to reach the seat is part of the structure. High seats are sometimes built onto a tree, should one of the right size and form be in a suitable location.

The standard routine for high-seat hunting involves a quiet predawn arrival at the scene, a noise-less ascent to the plank seat with a forester/guide, and near-silent sitting and waiting. It is often quite cool, even chilly, so a warm jacket is needed, as well as binoculars.

Unlike American hunting, where there are limits solely on the number and sex of the animal that may be taken in Europe, only a particular animal out of a herd may be collected. Immature males are excluded, as are exceptionally fine mature stages (these can be shot, but the trophy fees are exorbitant). The guide, basing his decision on an intimate knowledge of the local game population, will usually select a mature male with less than perfect antlers.

Wild boar (called *Keiler* in Germany) is sometimes hunted in full darkness. Arriving at the selected location around midnight, often carrying a warm fur-lined sack to slip into for what may be a long wait, the hunter and guide set themselves on a blind, some 10 feet or more above the field level. Both are armed with scope sighted rifles, the scope power at least 6X, possibly 8X, and the objective lens a big one for superior light gathering.

Soon or late, if all goes well, one hears the grunting of the pack as the boars root and feed in the potato or beet field near the perch.

In such conditions it isn't easy to place a shot exactly—it may be impossible—so your rifle should be of medium caliber. In Europe that's the 9.3×74R or the 9.3×62, but if you're bringing your own rifle, the .338 or the .375 H&H are good choices.

Game animals in Europe are judged and assigned values under a different system than in America. The rules in Europe are issued by an International committee (C.I.C.). For example, red deer antlers are measured at many places, the spread and length are assessed, the configuration is important (symmetrical or not), and the finished weight of the antlers is a prime factor. There are, in effect, four classes—the top three being Gold, Silver, and Bronze medal, with all lesser-count heads falling below the Bronze range.

Only certain individuals, appointed by the C.I.C., can assess and assign the points awarded officially.

A fair spread exists within the classes, of course. One could shoot a low Silver, or a high Bronze, and be charged accordingly. Depending on the country and its scale of fees, high-ranking trophy heads can cost several thousand dollars. The average rack, however, runs to a few hundred dollars.

Guns and loads. Autoloading and pump-action shotguns have made inroads in European hunting fields. Nevertheless, the break-open shotgun, rifle, or combination gun are preferred, especially on drive hunting.

For an excellent survey of virtually every firearm available in Europe, plus detailed ammunition tables, charts, etc., one can purchase a copy of *Der Ratgeber für den Jäger*, published by Waffen-Frankonia of Würzburg, West Germany.

The range of centerfire metallic cartridge calibers offered the Continental sportsman is large; almost as many as can be found on sale in the U.S. A 1990 catalog issued by Rheinische Westfälische Sprengstoff (RWS), a division of Dynamit Nobel, lists several metric-designation calibers, from the 5.6×50 Magnum, in rimless and rimmed case form, to the 9.3×74R (for rimmed case).

Most calibers available come in rimless or rimmed-case form, the latter intended for use in break-open rifles, a type much more popular there than here.

The most popular calibers in Europe today are the 7×65R (7×64 rimless) and the 9.3×74R or the latter's rimless near equivalent, the 9.3×62. The old 7×57, in both case types, is still a first choice of many hunters, and deservedly so. The 7×57 allows a lighter rifle and moderate to light recoil. The 7×57 is popular with chamois hunters for those reasons. The 6.5 Swedish is still popular for moose hunting in the Scandinavian countries.

Both 7mm cartridges are a good choice for European deer generally, though needlessly powerful for roe. The 9.3×74R is often the caliber of choice on moose or wild boar.

Most of the European calibers are offered with two or more choices in bullet weight and bullet form. The 6.5×57, rimless or rimmed—a popular choice for roe deer, chamois, and ibex—may be had with four different bullet weights, as may the 7×57 and the 7×65 and 7×64.

Bullet types offered by RWS include: the Cone Point, a recent design of small soft point form, with a quite flat trajectory; two "original Brenneke" bullets, these with a form of boattail base and a combination soft/hard lead core for controlled expansion; a standard roundnose soft point; and the famous H-mantle bullet, one with an internal belt that lets the front section expand reliably while the rear section and its thicker jacketing maintain their form for deep penetration. Also offered is a roundnose full-metal-jacket bullet for use on dangerous game. It is little used in Europe.

RWS supplies two worthwhile booklets—among many other pieces of literature—that will interest the sportsman who is Europe-bound. Both are in English, as are the data—a metric/English table isn't necessary.

Shotgun gauges in Europe are the same as they are here—12, 16, and 20 for most hunters. The 28 and the .410 see little use in the game fields. The 16 gauge was, before World War II, the favored size, but it has been losing ground for some years. A 12 bore is now the prime choice in most areas. Shotshell loads, too, are about identical with U.S. offerings. There is no need to buy shotgun cartridges before going abroad—suitable loadings are available everywhere.

If you prefer the 16 gauge and want to take your gun to Europe, by all means do so. The variety of loads offered for the 16 are more numerous than they are here. RWS has introduced a 2⅝-inch shell, designed to work satisfactorily in older 16-gauge guns, which had 2⁹⁄₁₆-inch chambers, and equally well in modern 2¾-inch-chambered 16s. (See COMBINATION GUN; DRILLING; GREAT BRITAIN, GUNS AND LOADS FOR HUNTING IN.)

contoured barrel   Rifle barrels are contoured because of two requirements: They must be thick at the chamber where the peak pressure of ignition occurs, yet they must not be unduly heavy. In order to achieve both objectives, a variety of tapering styles, or contours, is used.

Some sporter barrels employ a very straight taper, with no noticeable "step," from the breech to the muzzle, while others taper quite abruptly ahead of the chamber. Some foreign rifles employ two steps: one ahead of the chamber and another midway along the barrel.

Any tapered barrel is referred to as a contoured barrel. (See BARREL, RIFLED.)

controlled combustion chamberage (CCC)   This was the trade name coined by E. Baden Powell for the design of a kind of rifle chamber which he patented in the 1940s, with a group of cartridges made especially for it. Developed by Powell and Ralph Waldo Miller, calibers ranging from .22 to .30 were available. All of the cartridges were of large capacity, many based on the .300 H&H Magnum, but with little case taper. The controlled combustion chamber was unusual in that it utilized a venturi, or curved, cartridge shoulder (rather than the standard angled

one) and the chamber made use of the freebore principle, with the lands relieved for longer-than-standard distance ahead of the case neck.

The venturi shoulder, it was claimed, promoted more efficient combustion of the powder, while the freebore allowed the bullet to gain momentum unhindered by contact with the rifling, thus permitting higher charges without undue pressures.

Neither of these theories was proved effective. In general, pressures were high, barrel life was poor, and a 20 percent increase in powder charge resulted in perhaps a 10 percent increase in velocity. (See FREEBORE; LEADE; VENTURI SHOULDER; WILDCAT CARTRIDGE.)

convex lens   A convex lens is a converging lens, or positive lens, thicker at the center than at the edges. It may be double-convex (both sides bulge outward at the center), plano-convex (one side flat), or concavo-convex (one side concave and the other convex).

Convex lenses bend light toward the image point on a line through the center of the lens to form a real image. Convex lenses are combined with concave lenses to form lens systems. (See CONCAVE LENS.)

cook-off   The unintentional firing of a cartridge that results from the absorption of heat from the barrel. Generally, cook-offs are associated with early design, fully automatic military weapons.

copper-coated shot   The compression of a shot charge after ignition, as it travels through the shotgun barrel, tends to deform pellets, which in turn reduces the density of the shot pattern. A thin coating of copper protects against deformation in the bore, and various brands of shotgun cartridges that utilize copper coating are readily available. But the true quality of copper-plated shot depends upon the hardness of the lead core. Low-antimony lead cores will still permit the deformation of copper-coated shot, as copper is itself a rather soft metal. (See PATTERN.)

Corbett, Edward James (1875–1955)   As Jim Corbett he wrote *Man-Eaters of Kumaon*, first published in Bombay in 1944, later in America, in 1946. It is a gripping account of his stalking and shooting of tigers in India, and unusual for sporting books, it became highly popular generally. In 1948, Corbett's second book was published, called *The Man-Eating Leopard of Rudraprayag*. This book, which was not as popular as Corbett's first effort, covers his two-year pursuit and eventual killing of a deadly leopard that, by official records, had killed 125 people.

Cordite A kind of British double-base smokeless propellant manufactured by extruding a colloid into long cordlike strands, hence its name. The gunpowder, consisting of about 65 percent guncotton (nitrocellulose), 30 percent nitroglycerin, and 5 percent mineral jelly, was invented in 1889 by Frederick A. Abel and James Dewar, British chemists.

The first attempts to use nitrocellulose as a propellant were unsuccessful for several reasons, one of which was that the raw fibrous guncotton presented an excessive burning area to the flame front. When, in 1846, nitrocellulose was treated to form a colloid, this paved the way for shaping its granules to control burning. The first successful efforts, in 1885, included rolling the colloid into sheets and cutting the sheets into flakes. The extruded Cordite formed the basis for many currently used propellants. (See SMOKELESS POWDER.)

corrosion See BARREL CORROSION

corrosive primers An obsolete kind of primer that contains potassium chlorate or a mercuric compound, or both. These chemicals are hygroscopic (attract moisture) and if their residue is not carefully removed by thorough cleaning soon after shooting, bore corrosion will result.

The first practical nonrusting rimfire primer was used in the German .22R cartridge which was popular from 1910 to 1913. Shortly after World War I, Remington employed the noncorrosive Kleenbore primer in .22 Long Rifle cartridges as the company's first development in this area, and soon followed with noncorrosive centerfire primers. However, the military was slow to adopt noncorrosive primers, wanting first to see how the new kinds proved under field use. It was not until about 1952 that the American military establishment dropped the use of corrosive primers. All ammunition manufactured since that time has been noncorrosive, and no corrosive primers are currently used in American sporting ammunition. (See PRIMER.)

Cosmoline A patented liquid rust preventive material. It is used for protection of ferrous metal parts between stages of machine processing. The name is sometimes improperly applied to thick grease used as a protective coating on firearms when long storage is anticipated.

covert shooting This term, which probably originated in New England, refers to shooting in or hunting through a "covered" location where upland birds are found. For example, a grouse covert would be an apple orchard where the birds feed, or a group of pines where they would be likely to roost.

cratered primer This is a condition that exists when the metal of a metallic cartridge primer cup extrudes into the firing pin hole and creates a tiny ridge around the indent made by the firing pin. While it is often attributed to excessive pressure, it may also occur under mild pressures. A weak firing pin spring, a soft primer cup, a small firing pin point, and/or an overly large hole in the bolt face can all cause cratered primers.

crazy quail A generic term referring to a number of offbeat clay target shotgun games, none of which has official sanction or is used in formal competition. Excellent practice for upland gunners, the most common crazy quail setup consists of a pit housing a rotating trap machine (target launcher) and an operator who may turn the trap to face any direction. The shooter on the firing line cannot see the trap, and therefore does not know the direction or angle the target will take.

Perhaps the most difficult crazy quail range in America is located at Nilo Farms, a Winchester-owned shooting preserve near East Alton, Illinois. More than 200,000 rounds of 10-target competition have been thrown from this machine, and only about 20 shooters have been able to hit 10 clays in a row.

In the Southwest, portable crazy quail machines are operated from ground level with the operator protected, and hidden from the shooter's view, by a steel plate. The operator can swivel the trap to throw in any direction. Because of the rotational capability of the machine, Southwesterners often refer to the game as "whirling traps."

creep See TRIGGER CREEP.

crimp A crimp, in reference to ammunition, refers to the closure at the mouth of a shotshell, or to the turning in of the mouth of a metallic cartridge to grip the bullet. A primer is sometimes crimped into place in the primer pocket of a centerfire cartridge, but friction is generally depended upon to hold it.

In shotshells, a roll crimp is used for closing paper shells, while a pie crimp holds the top wad that seals plastic shells.

crimp die A loading die designed to force the mouth of a metallic cartridge case inward to grip the bullet. This kind of die is sometimes furnished as one in a four-die set for loading handgun cartridges. Some two- or three-die sets have a crimping constriction in the seating die.

Shotshell loading dies for tough plastic cases include a crimp starter, which starts the fold at the case mouth. A crimping plunger then presses the folds down and completes the shotshell crimp. (See HANDLOAD.)

crimped primer Specifications for loading United States military .30/06 ammunition at one time required crimping the primers in place. After seating the primer, crimping consisted of peening the brass surrounding the primer at the base of the case. This formed a slight lip at the edge of the primer pocket and locked the primer in. In almost all modern sporting ammunition, friction fit of the primer in the primer pocket is now relied on to retain the primer.

cripple stock   See CROSS-EYE STOCK.

Crosman (company)   The Crosman Arms Company, Inc. was formed in 1924 by the Crosman family of Rochester, New York, to produce a compressed air gun that operated on the pump-up principle invented by William McLean, the Crosman family chauffeur. The Crosman family was also the owner of the Crosman Seed Company in Rochester.

The company began operation with the manufacture of one rifle model—a very efficient design as originally manufactured, but too costly to be sold in volume in the United States. Sales, from 1924 through 1939, were low but sustained the company.

In 1940, Crosman was purchased by Philip Y. Hahn Sr. for $5,000. Hahn guided the growing firm and served as its chairman of the board until the company was acquired by Coleman Industries, a corporation specializing in the manufacture of recreational outdoor equipment, in 1971.

An initial order for 2,000 compressed air rifles from the Office of Strategic Services, the American intelligence organization in World War II, started Crosman toward its present position as the largest manufacturer in the world of compressed air and CO_2 guns.

Hahn anticipated that the constantly shrinking open areas in America would inevitably lead to restrictions on hunting and target shooting in this country as it had in Europe. He worked to manufacture products that could be used in more confined areas than would be safe or appropriate for conventional firearms.

Crosman had the distinction of producing the first modern CO_2 air rifle for the American market, and the company perfected the system of virtually leakproof seals for CO_2 rifles and pistols that today results in a high level of performance.

In 1978 the company changed its name to Crosman Airguns. It operates manufacturing facilities in Fairport and East Bloomfield, New York and sells its products throughout the United States and Canada as well as overseas. (See AIR GUN; CO_2 GUN.)

cross bolt   A cylindrical metal plug that is inlet in a rifle stock, usually behind the recoil lug, as reinforcement. The bolt is perpendicular to the lug, and its ends are sometimes concealed with wood plugs or are engraved. In very heavy-recoiling guns, two bolts are sometimes used; the second one is located on a line with the first, just ahead of the trigger guard.

cross-bolt safety   The kind of safety usually found on pump-action and semiautomatic rifles and shotguns. It is located at the front or rear of the trigger guard and consists of a bolt that is pushed laterally to release or lock the trigger.

cross-eye stock   When firing a rifle or shotgun, it is not uncommon for a shooter to have to compensate for a master, or dominant, eye that does not correspond with his dominant-handedness. One solution to this problem is the cross-eye, or cripple, stock, which is drastically bent under a combination of heat and pressure so that it is nearly semicircular in shape. It allows a right-handed shooter to place the gun butt against his right shoulder, while positioning the receiver and barrel in line with his left eye. The reverse of these positions can also be accomplished for left-handers.

Cross-eye stocks are expensive to make and regarded as unattractive. For this reason, they are rarely employed. (See MASTER EYE.)

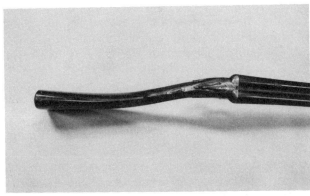

A cross-eye (or "cripple") stock enables a shotgun shooter who is right-handed, but has a left master eye, to shoot from the right shoulder while sighting with the left eye. This is done by bending the stock and tang of the gun. (A highly skilled gunsmith can even bend the locks to some degree.) This kind of stocking is rarely seen, since it is very expensive to execute.

crossfiring Mistakenly firing on another target shooter's target. Crossfiring can be detected by the use of backing paper placed approximately 5 yards behind the scoring target. In a comparison of the target and the backing paper, a crossfire will be obvious because it will stand away from the rest of the shot group on either the target or the backer because of the angle at which the errant shot will have gone through the two spaced pieces of paper.

crosshair See RETICLE.

Crossman, Captain Edward C. ("Ned") (1889–1939) Captain Crossman was one of the outstanding figures in the firearms field during the first half of the 20th century. As a civilian, he hunted in much of the western United States, from Oregon to New Mexico, and competed with rifle, pistol, and shotgun on the shooting ranges and trap and skeet fields of those areas as well as in National and International competitions.

A longtime director of the National Rifle Association, he was recruited by Colonel Smith W. Brookhart, then NRA president, and commissioned as captain in the U.S. Army to assist in organizing the first Small Arms Firing School at Camp Perry, Ohio, in 1918, for purposes of training rifle instructors for the wartime army. After World War I, his technical knowledge and long experience with small arms resulted in his being assigned to the group of ordnance engineers who conducted the firing tests of the .30/06 cartridge at Daytona Beach, Florida. These tests developed new knowledge of small arms ballistics and led to the development of the M1 .30-caliber cartridge and the use of the boattail bullet by the U.S. Army.

Crossman was also one of this country's early users of the comparison microscope in the science of forensic ballistics. A prolific writer, he wrote several books that remain classics in the firearms field (among them, *The Book of the Springfield*, Samworth, 1951), as well as a great many articles for publications ranging from *Ordnance Magazine* and *The American Rifleman*, through the range of sporting and general circulation magazines. His ability to compose technical articles about firearms in a manner that made the contents clear to the average reader, his honesty in writing, and his somewhat waspish humor endeared him to the shooting fraternity. (See BOATTAIL BULLET; NATIONAL RIFLE ASSOCIATION [NRA].)

crowning If the muzzle of a rifle or pistol barrel is cut off square at a 90 degree angle to the axis of the bore and left that way, contact with a hard object such as a rock or piece of metal is likely to deform

The purpose of crowning a barrel is to protect the rifling at the muzzle. One method is to simply round the muzzle off, recessing the rifling very lightly. The other method, which is more effective (and more expensive), is to recess the inner circumference of the muzzle.

the end of the bore, which will almost certainly lessen accuracy. The end of the muzzle is therefore rounded so that the edge of the bore is beveled, or the end of the bore itself is beveled so that it ends below the surface of the muzzle and is protected from damage. This process is called crowning.

Older rifles (and some custom ones) are crowned by spinning an abrasive-covered brass ball against the muzzle. A more modern method is to spin the barrel in the lathe, using a countersink to produce an angular bevel recess.

crusher gauge To determine the pressure produced by a metallic cartridge or shotshell during the firing process, a gauge is fitted to the chamber of a test gun, or universal receiver.

A hole is bored through the barrel into the chamber and covered with a steel piston. On top of the piston, a metal plug—copper for rifles and autoloading handguns and lead for shotguns—is butted against an adjustable yoke so that there is no slack. When the gun is fired, gas pressure exits through the hole and acts directly on the piston, causing it to crush the copper or lead plug slightly; the plug is then removed and its length measured. Comparing the

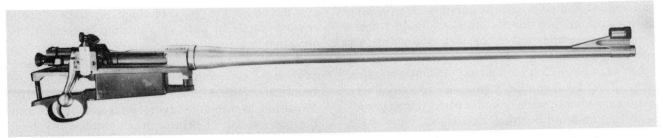

On occasion, a military action will be converted for sporting use. This Springfield Model 1903 action has been extensively reworked by fitting a new barrel, attaching a new bolt handle, fitting a new peep sight, and altering the safety and the trigger.

new length against standards listed on a reference chart tells the pressure (in copper units of pressure, or C.U.P., for rifles and autoloading pistols, in lead units of pressure, or L.U.P., for shotguns) that a given cartridge has generated. Since the metal plug is crushed during the firing process and it is used as a gauge, it has become known as a crusher gauge. (See CHAMBER PRESSURE; C.U.P. [COPPER UNITS OF PRESSURE]; L.U.P. [LEAD UNITS OF PRESSURE]; UNIVERSAL RECEIVER.)

C.U.P. (copper units of pressure) The system by which rifle and autoloading handgun chamber pressures are classified is referred to as copper units of pressure, commonly shortened to C.U.P.

To determine the C.U.P. of a particular load, a cartridge is fired in a special pressure gun that has a hole in its chamber. The hole is covered by a piston attached to a copper plug of a given hardness. Upon firing, the plug is compressed by the piston, acted upon by powder gas escaping through the hole in the chamber, and the measurement of the plug before and after compression is translated into a value according to a set scale to give the number of units of pressure. (See CHAMBER PRESSURE; CRUSHER GAUGE; UNIVERSAL RECEIVER.)

cupro-nickel A copper-nickel alloy used in the manufacture of rifle bullet jackets from the 1890s until the end of World War I. The alloy was composed of approximately 60 percent copper and 40 percent nickel. Because it fouled bores severely, it was replaced by gilding metal, an alloy of copper and zinc. (See BULLET JACKET; GILDING METAL.)

curvature of field When the center of the field of view in an optical instrument cannot be brought into focus simultaneously with the edges of the field, the instrument suffers from a form of aberration known as curvature of field. This deficiency is caused by improper spacing of the lens elements. (See ABERRATION.)

custom guns Before the mass production of firearms began in the middle of the 19th century, all arms were built by hand, individually, with tremendous variation in overall quality and price, as well as significant variance among arms that today would be regarded as virtual twins. The development of assembly line production, and the concomitant standardization and interchangeability of parts, resulted in firearms that were, on the average, of lower price and considerably higher quality than those that had been produced individually.

However, the practice of building a firearm to order has never died out and, in fact, has steadily increased over the past 50 years. Often referred to as custom guns, these arms are either production models that have been extensively modified or ones that have been made entirely on a to-order basis. Invariably, custom guns are expensive, as they reflect a very high degree of craftsmanship and many hours of hand labor.

Custom shotguns, almost always single shots or double barrels, are produced on a very limited basis and designed to a customer's specific requirements. They include the so-called London guns made by such firms as Boss, Holland & Holland, and Purdey, and the high-grade Continental arms from such makers as Fabbri, Merkel, and Famars. The price for one of these shotguns commonly exceeds $10,000 and may involve a waiting period of several years for delivery. Each of these guns is precisely fitted to its owner and may be had in any combination of barrel lengths, chokes, and gauge, and with elaborate engraving. The only American-made shotgun that meets these criteria is the Winchester Model 21 side-by-side, which is produced in extremely limited numbers on a to-order basis.

Until recently, comparatively little customizing of handguns was done, save for some modification of grips and sights. But with the growing popularity of silhouette shooting by handgunners, and the development of various "combat" pistol courses, an increasing amount of effort has been devoted by custom gunsmiths to tailoring production line revolvers and automatic pistols to these pursuits. So extensive is this customizing that the finished product bears almost no resemblance to the factory firearm that served as its basis.

For example, a Colt Model 1911 .45 automatic that is modified for a combat course has literally every part changed or reworked: a new barrel (target grade) with custom-fitted bushing, new sights, lengthened ejection port, squared trigger guard and stippled backstrap, new grips, customized trigger, redesigned safety, and hard-chrome finish are common modifications. It is possible to begin with a firearm that retailed for $125 and end with one that costs $15,000 and more.

Rifles, however, have been the traditional favorite for customizing. It is probable that this tradition stems from the days of the Pennsylvanias and Kentuckys, which were individually made and quite expensive, whether decorated or not.

The excellence and low price of mass-produced rifles tended to eclipse the custom versions in the first decades of this century, though a steady line of craftsmen kept the tradition alive. Among the most notable of these gunsmiths were Alvin Linden, Adolph Minar, and Thomas Shelhamer, as well as firms such as Griffin & Howe.

In the 1950s, a new generation of custom gunsmiths appeared: Al Beisen, Jerry Fisher, Dale Goens, Monte Kennedy, and Keith Stegall, among the more prominent. By the late 1960s, the craft had attained far greater popularity than ever before, with literally scores of first-rate craftsmen at work.

The appeal of the custom rifle is based on the widespread feeling that, while modern manufacturing methods produce accurate, sound, and reliable guns, the quality of fit and finish that was once present is gone, and that no matter how efficiently factory rifles may perform, they are "tinny" and lack aesthetic appeal and individuality.

Most custom rifles utilize factory bolt actions; the pre-1964 Model 70 Winchester and Mauser action (commercial and military) are two of the most popular. Formerly, the Model 1903 Springfield action enjoyed great popularity.

These actions are polished, or lapped, to ensure smooth functioning, and the locking lugs of the bolt are trued up so that they bear equally against their recesses in the receiver.

It is possible to purchase a custom action, which of course must be built to order, but at a very high price—often equal to that of a finished custom rifle.

Frequently, factory barrels are utilized, but since they are usually rather heavy, many custom gunsmiths turn them down to a smaller diameter. Alternatively, a custom barrel may be used.

If the original trigger is retained, it will be adjusted for a light, crisp pull, or a custom trigger will be installed.

Bluing is most often done by the "cold rust" process—a procedure that is time consuming and requires several exposures of the metal, after final polishing, to corrosive vapors. It takes skill to control the process, but it results in a nonreflective finish that is highly durable. If the gun is to be engraved, this will be done after the final polishing, but before the bluing.

Stock work usually consumes most of the hours of labor involved in completing a custom rifle. The typical stock wood is a variety of European walnut—*Juglans regia*—and the specific piece is selected by the customer for its color, figure, and weight. The stock is built to the customer's dimensions, checkered, and finished as he wishes.

This is the basic procedure. Extensive optional features range from the installation of a special sighting rib and iron sights and/or scope mounts to the fitting of a new bolt handle, safety, extractor, trap buttplate, and pistol grip cap.

On the whole, custom firearms are more attractive and function more smoothly than factory arms, and they appreciate in value at a rate that makes them worthy of serious consideration.

cut shell   A shotgun shell that the user partially cuts through—a dangerous practice that can burst the gun barrel at the muzzle. The cut, which circumscribes the outer surface of the cartridge in the plane where the wad separates the powder charge from the shot, causes the entire shot charge, when the shell is fired, to leave the muzzle as one slug confined in the forward section of the cartridge.

Cutts compensator   A patented muzzle attachment that acts both as a muzzle brake and a variable choke for shotguns.

The recoil reducer also provides the shooter with a selection of chokes through interchangeable sleeves of various sizes. It was developed by Colonel Richard M. Cutts (USMC, Ret.) as a muzzle depressor for the Browning Automatic Rifle and Thompson Submachine Gun. The Lyman Company acquired rights to the Cutts compensator in 1929 and has manufactured it since. (See ADJUSTABLE CHOKE.)

cylinder   A cylindrical multichambered gun part that holds the firearm's cartridges. In the modern shooting world, it is associated with revolvers, though a few rifles utilizing cylinders were produced before the turn of the century.

A revolver's cylinder is rotated by a pawl upon

the initial stage of trigger pull in double-action operation, or upon the cocking of the hammer in single-action operation, and locked in position during firing. The measured rotating action brings a live cartridge into firing position with each pull of the trigger or cock of the hammer. (See REVOLVER.)

cylinder choke   Also called cylinder bore, this refers to a shotgun barrel with no choke constriction. A typical modern shotgun with a cylinder choke barrel delivers 20 to 30 percent of its shot pellets into a 30-inch circle at 40 yards, producing a wider pattern than a choked bore. Cylinder choke guns are favored by users of rifled slugs, because the lack of constriction lessens the chance of the slug being deformed, and by hunters who take game at very close range, where a wide pattern is an advantage. (See CHOKE.)

cylinder crane   A hinged link joining a swing-out type of cylinder with a revolver frame, typically found in double-action revolvers. The cylinder release, when activated, permits the cylinder to swing out from the frame. In this position the cylinder can be loaded with cartridges or empty cases can be ejected. (See DOUBLE-ACTION REVOLVER.)

cylinder gap   The space—usually .006- to .008-inch—between the cylinder and the breech end of a revolver barrel. The larger this gap, the greater the escape of powder gases, unburned powder, and possible lead or bullet jacket particles. (See REVOLVER.)

cylinder indexing   A revolver cylinder is mechanically locked in position by the cylinder bolt, which engages notches machined in the outer surface of the cylinder. The notches must be accurately located and the cylinder rotating mechanism timed to assure precise alignment of each chamber, in turn, with the bore. The rotating action to provide chamber-bore alignment is termed indexing. (See REVOLVER.)

cylinder release latch   The cylinder release latch is found on double-action revolvers. When activated, it permits the cylinder to swing out to the left of the revolver frame for ejecting of empty cartridge cases, loading, or cleaning. (See DOUBLE-ACTION REVOLVER.)

cylinder stop   Also referred to as the cylinder bolt, this is a small stud, held under spring pressure, in the bottom of the cylinder space of a revolver frame. Activated by the trigger or hammer mechanism, it retracts as the cylinder is rotated. When the cylinder comes to rest, the cylinder stop, properly timed, raises to its upward position and projects into the cylinder stop notch. This action locks one of the chambers into alignment with the bore. (See REVOLVER.)

cylinder stop notch   A cut in the outer surface of a revolver cylinder—there is one for each chamber—that is designed to receive the cylinder stop in its projecting position and thereby lock the cylinder in place for the firing of the cartridge in each chamber. (See REVOLVER.)

Daisy (company) In 1888, Clarence J. Hamilton, a plant foreman for the Plymouth Iron Windmill Company in Michigan, invented an air-powered rifle. He showed his invention to the company manager, Lewis Cass Hough, who decided to give a free rifle to every farmer who purchased a windmill. The air rifle became more popular than the windmills, and in 1895 the firm's name was changed to the Daisy Manufacturing Company.

Through the first half of the 20th century, the company expanded its lines of nonpowder guns and ammunition. In 1957, the company moved its facilities from Plymouth, Michigan to Rogers, Arkansas.

Daisy became a subsidiary of Walter Kidde & Company, Inc., in 1977 and redirected its marketing program to appeal to adults as well as youngsters.

Daisy produces a full line of pneumatic arms, including BB guns, CO_2 pistols, and air rifles. The company also manufactures holsters and other air gun accessories as well as its own line of BB ammunition. (See AIR GUN; BB GUN; CO_2 GUN.)

Daly, Charles (company) The Charles Daly line of shotguns, while bearing the name of its American importer (based in New York City), was actually produced by several firms in Suhl, Germany, and an over/under model, the Commander, was made in Belgium. The Daly guns, whose importation began circa 1900, were of a modified Anson and Deeley boxlock design; they were offered only with double triggers, in all gauges from 10 to .410.

Five basic grades were available, starting with Superior and ascending to Regent Diamond. Daly also imported a single-barrel trap gun of standard design, a Drilling, and the Daly Sextuple Trap, which had no fewer than six locking bolts.

Import of the "Prussian" Dalys ceased in 1933, although the Belgian guns continued in the line for six more years.

In 1963, Sloan's Sporting Goods in New York City reintroduced a line of Japanese- and Italian-made over/under, double, and semiautomatic shotguns under the Charles Daly name. The venture met with only modest success, and the last of these guns was imported in 1976.

Today, the prewar Daly shotguns command high prices, as they are finely made and durable arms, excellent examples of German gunmaking. (See ANSON AND DEELEY ACTION; DRILLING.)

Damascus barrel During the latter part of the 19th century, the production of Damascus steel was an attempt to create thin but strong barrels for nonrifled arms. The process drew its name from the ancient Middle Eastern technique of laminating steel and iron to produce sword blades that were hard, yet flexible. These blades also had a highly distinctive pattern of different colored waves, or lines, in the steel, resulting from the folding and refolding of many layers of contrasting metals.

Damascus shotgun barrels were produced by wrapping alternating layers of steel and iron around each other (actually twisting them, so that Damascus barrels were also known as twist-steel barrels) and simultaneously wrapping the twisted metal around a core, or mandrel, of the desired bore diameter. The iron-steel laminate was then forged solid by means of heat and blows from a hammer, and the forged steel filed or drawn to shape. Polishing was the final step.

Damascus barrels were used on high-grade guns for the most part, and the higher the grade, the more elaborate the pattern of the lamination. So popular was the process and the result that even reputable makers such as L. C. Smith surrendered to buyer pressure and imitated Damascus patterns on non-laminated barrels.

The popularity of Damascus steel was ended by the emergence of smokeless powder and the higher pressures it generated. Damascus barrels, adequate for black-powder charges, burst under the force of the newer propellant, and the manufacture of this barrel steel had largely ceased by 1915.

A considerable number of Damascus-barreled shotguns survive, many of them of high quality. They should not be fired with modern shells under any circumstances.

Dardick revolver An open-chamber revolver invented by David Dardick. Three pilot models were made in 1956, and the Dardick Corp. then prepared for production in Hamden, Connecticut. However, the gun was not a commercial success, and only forty Dardick revolvers were manufactured in the four years of the firm's existence.

The gun and its ammunition were unique. Extremely compact and short-barreled, the revolver somewhat resembled an automatic pistol, since its ammunition—11 to 20 rounds, depending on caliber—was carried in the handle. The ammunition, produced in 9mm, .38, .380 ACP, and .22LR, consisted of standard conical bullets fixed in cases that were triangular in cross section (but with rounded corners) and called, appropriately, trounds. The cases were initially made of aluminum, but beginning in 1958 they were manufactured of polypropylene plastic.

A cylinder with three open-sided chambers, revolving within a sleeve, picked up rounds from the magazine in the grip frame. These rounds were rotated to the firing position, fired, and the cylinder then advanced to the next round. The fired cases were ejected to the side from the same opening in the cylinder sleeve through which they entered.

The advantages claimed for the Dardick revolver were compactness, rapidity of fire, and mechanical simplicity, since unlike an automatic pistol, the cartridges did not have to be pushed forward into a chamber or ejected to the rear. Despite this, the Dardick's unconventionality militated against its success, and the few completed pistols are today in the hands of collectors.

The tround concept still is evident today, as the U.S. military looks at ways to increase its firepower.

Darne shotgun Regis and Pierre Darne perfected their unique side-by-side shotgun in 1895. Instead of the usual break-action (hinged) arrangement of double-barreled shotguns, the Darnes' barrels are rigidly attached to the receiver. The breechblock is moved to the rear by means of a powerful lever on top of the receiver. To open the action, the lever is lifted and pulled to the rear. This movement also extracts fired shells. Two new shells are manually started into the open breeches, and the lever is pushed forward.

Darne shotguns are now being made under the name of Paul Bruchet, who bought the company from the Darne family. The new guns are sometimes called Bruchet-Darne.

dead center hold Aligning the sights of a gun precisely on the center of a target, or on the point the hunter wishes to hit. This sighting alignment is typically used with telescopic sights, or iron sights in a hunting situation; the six o'clock or sub-six o'clock hold is commonly associated with iron sights used in target shooting. (See SIGHT PICTURE; SIX O'CLOCK HOLD.)

decap To remove a fired primer from used ammunition—centerfire metallic or shotshell—before reloading the case. Decapping can be done with a punch and a small hammer, but most often it is accomplished as one of the functions of a multistage reloading press. A pin is forced downward through the mouth and flash hole of the shell and into the primer pocket to force out the fired primer cap. This operation is often combined with reforming (resizing) the case. One stroke of the operating lever drives out the fired cap and reforms the case to original dimensions. (See HANDLOAD.)

decibel A unit for expressing the relative loudness of sounds. A decibel is approximately equal to the smallest degree of sound detectable by the normal human ear. Noise in the range of 90 to 100 decibels is generally regarded as being injurious to human hearing, and most kinds of firearms produce noise equalling or exceeding that figure. For example, a .22 rifle produces slightly over 100 decibels; a 12-gauge shotgun with target loads, 140; and a magnum rifle, 170. (See EAR PROTECTORS; HEARING, SHOOTING DAMAGE TO.)

decoy An imitation animal or bird designed to lure quarry within range. Most common is the familiar waterfowl decoy, but many others are or have been used.

Before the invention of firearms, decoys were often employed to lure game within bow and arrow range or into pit traps or nets. American Indian hunters often placed buffalo skins or deer skins, with heads still attached, over their bodies in order to kill these animals with bows by approaching them closely or by luring them within range. This kind of combined concealment and decoying became dangerous after the introduction of modern firearms and the large increase in the number of hunters, as there was too much chance that the decoying hunter would be shot.

Though waterfowl decoys are best known, carved imitations of shorebirds, herons, and swans have also been used in America. Quite recently (1979), plastic facsimiles of wild turkey hens were placed on the market. This "sex" decoy imitates the female; its intention is to attract the male of the species. Since the wild turkey is the only American game bird that is hunted in the spring breeding season, the plastic hen is the only sex decoy in legal use in the United States.

Another kind of lure may be called the "prey" decoy. With this decoy, the hunter displays an imitation of a species customarily attacked by the quarry. For instance, a stuffed, carved, or molded plastic owl on a pole or in a tree attracts crows to within shotgun range because crows hate owls and customarily attack one seen in daylight. Using a live prey animal—a tethered water buffalo to bring tigers to a blind or a tethered goat to lure leopards into range—

is a form of decoying, akin to baiting, illegal in the United States.

Waterfowl decoys may be as simple as a mud mold used by Cree Indians or white sheets or newspapers spread in a grain field to imitate flocks of snow geese. The classic waterfowl decoy, however, is a carved and painted imitation of the game—in its highest form a work of art. Most used is cedar wood. Paints must be dull in finish so that the decoy will not reflect sunlight. Decoys must be properly weighted so that they will float naturally on the water, and the anchor (often a lead weight) and anchor line must be properly adjusted for the same purpose.

Field decoys used on land are of two kinds—the full-bodied decoy and the silhouette. A full-bodied field decoy is three dimensional like a floating one, but it is usually equipped with a stake or metal rod that is driven into the ground to hold it in place at the proper height. Silhouette decoys are essentially two dimensional. These flat wood cutouts, painted in realistic colors, are also mounted on stakes.

Oversized field decoys (full-bodied or silhouette) that may be four or five times the size of the real thing are sometimes used. Apparently, flying waterfowl recognize and come to them because they can be seen at a greater distance. Strangely enough, the birds are not alarmed by the decoys' great size.

The term decoy was once universally used for *live* decoys. For instance, the waterfowler maintained a flock of tame geese or ducks that were trained to bring in the wild birds, often by calling to them as well as simply by being present and moving about. Nowadays, live decoys are forbidden for all kinds of hunting by state and federal law in the United States.

An intermediate class of decoys exists when dead game, previously shot by the hunter, is propped up to attract live game. This is often done in Africa and has been used by North American Indians, for instance, when Crees propped up dead geese with willow sticks in their mouths.

Merely setting out decoys is not effective. To do the job for which they were intended, realistic decoys must be used in conjunction with a natural looking blind and true sounding calling.

deep-hole drilling   Deep-hole drilling is the method by which rifle and handgun barrel blanks are drilled to approximately the caliber of the finished bore. While many barrels have been drilled on a lathe, special barrel-drilling machines are usually used today.

The bit, welded to a drill rod, is specially ground so that it will drill a perfectly straight hole, and it has in it a hole through which oil is pumped under high pressure. The bit also has a straight groove running parallel to its axis to allow the barrel chips to pass to the rear under the pressure of the oil forced back from the drill point. The drilled hole is later reamed to exact bore diameter. (See BARREL, RIFLED.)

deer, guns and loads for   See MULE DEER, GUNS AND LOADS FOR; WHITETAIL DEER, GUNS AND LOADS FOR.

delay theory   The delay theory is used to explain the explosion and case rupture that sometimes occur when a reduced charge is used in a rifle cartridge.

The theory, which has not been conclusively proved, is often referred to as the secondary explosion effect (S.E.E.). Although there are disagreements among ballisticians regarding the precise mechanics of the theory, this is the commonly accepted interpretation: When the flame from a struck primer passes through a reduced charge of slow-burning powder, the propellant force is only enough to unseat the bullet from the cartridge, but not sufficient to propel it from the barrel. With the bullet wedged in the leade, the remainder of the powder charge continues to burn but does not develop enough force to drive the bullet from the gun. Pressure in the cartridge case and chamber continue to build to the point where the case ruptures. (See LEADE; REDUCED CHARGE.)

deloading   Sometimes a muzzleloading rifle will inadvertently be loaded without a powder charge, or the powder charge will get wet, necessitating that the gun be unloaded. This can be done in one of two ways, depending on whether the arm is percussion or flintlock

Flintlock rifles are best unloaded with a ball puller, a corkscrewlike device that attaches to the end of the ramrod and is twisted over the ball. When the puller firmly engages the ball, it should be withdrawn gently, in a straight line.

Percussion rifles can be cleared by removing the nipple and using a pick to work priming powder (FFFFG) behind the ball. The nipple is replaced, and the gun fired toward the ground. If the first attempt fails, repeat the process, after making certain that the ball is still seated firmly on top of the priming powder. Only a modest amount of priming powder (a fraction of a standard charge) should be used, since it creates great internal pressures.

dense powder   A modern hard-grained, controlled burning smokeless propellant that, unlike bulk powder, has a relatively high weight per volume. The term is used to distinguish this type of propellant from bulk powder, which has a low weight per volume. (See BULK POWDER; SMOKELESS POWDER.)

dent remover A tool used to remove dents from the barrels, receivers, or box magazines of firearms. Usually it is a steel bar or cylinder, with tapered ends, that can be driven into or through the dented part. Expanding mandrel swages operated by screw pressure, or two-part sliding swages, are used for removing dents in shotgun barrels.

departure See ANGLE OF DEPARTURE.

deplating Some firearms have electroplated metal surfaces that can become worn with use. Rather than replate them, some gunsmiths remove the electroplating and blue the deplated parts. The removal of plated metal can be accomplished by the use of an electroplating device with reversed anode/cathode wiring.

Deringer or derringer (firearm) The second spelling refers to any small pocket pistol. The first spelling is properly applied only to the original pistols invented and marketed by Henry Deringer of Philadelphia and bearing his imprint (H Deringer Philada.). The original Deringer pistol, which first appeared in the 1830s, was a rifled percussion single-shot pocket pistol with a back-action lock and very fancy engraving and stockwork. It rapidly became the most popular concealed firearm of the American frontier and is perhaps most famous, or notorious, as the gun used to assassinate Abraham Lincoln.

Because the Deringer was widely and successfully imitated, Henry Deringer sued to obtain sole use of the name for his own pistol line. Thereafter manufacturers such as Colt and Remington called their Deringer-type pistols by the variant spelling "derringer" to circumvent copyright laws.

The advent of cartridge pistols eclipsed the original percussion Deringers. But they are still prized by collectors, and any small pocket handgun manufactured today is commonly called a derringer. (See DERINGER, HENRY, JR.)

Deringer, Henry, Jr. (1786–1868) Maker of rifles, dueling pistols, and pocket pistols. Son of a German-American gunsmith, Deringer was born in Easton, Pennsylvania. After an apprenticeship in Richmond, Virginia, he established a plant in Philadelphia in 1806. He produced government contract pistols, rifles, and muskets and, for general sale, sporting arms, plains rifles, and duelers. Among his more than 20,000 contract arms, many were flintlock hunting rifles for the Indian tribes that were forced from their homelands to territories west of the Mississippi River. His fine dueling pistols brought him some fame, but until he perfected the small single-

shot handguns that made his name a synonym for pocket pistols, he was known primarily as a builder of shoulder arms.

Deringer's rifled percussion pocket pistols first appeared in the 1830s and attained their standard style by the end of the next decade. They employed back-action locks—with the firing mechanism inletted into the wood behind the hammer rather than in front—and featured checkered walnut bird's head stocks, German-silver mountings, foliate engraving, and a round, wrought-iron barrel, flattened on top and browned to simulate Damascus twist. Hammer, lock, and action-holding bolts were blued iron. Barrel length ranged from under 1 inch to over 4, caliber from .33 to .51. Lock and breech were marked "H Deringer Philada." Sales agents' names were sometimes stamped on the top of the barrel.

In 1859, Congressman Daniel Sickles used a Der-

The original Deringer was a large-caliber, single-shot percussion arm made by gunsmith Henry Deringer of Philadelphia. This arm, seen here, became so popular that it spawned a host of similar pocket pistols, and the name derringer, spelled with two rs, became generic. Probably the most successful of the later derringers was the Remington Model 95 two-shot .41 rimfire model, a favorite in the Old West.

inger to murder Philip Barton Key, son of Francis Scott Key. In 1865, John Wilkes Booth used one to assassinate Abraham Lincoln. But notoriety had come much earlier. Deringers and imitations were popular as concealed weapons in the South and West, particularly during the California gold rush. Henry Deringer successfully sued rivals, including former employees, for trademark infringement. The term "derringer" (any small pocket pistol) originated as a common misspelling, and competitors adopted it as a trademark evasion. Deringer himself became wealthy, though cartridge "derringers" were eclipsing his percussion guns when he died. (See DERINGER OR DERRINGER [FIREARM].)

detachable box magazine   See CLIP.

diaphragm   A partition or plate separating two compartments. In telescopic sights, and similar optical instruments, a diaphragm having a circular hole in the center may be used between lenses in the optical system to cut off marginal beams of light.

Aperture sights are sometimes fitted with an adjustable diaphragm so that the size of the aperture can be adjusted to suit the shooter's preference under different light conditions.

Also, the partition in a Mauser 98 action between the threaded front of the receiver and the rear part that contains the bolt is sometimes called a diaphragm. (See METALLIC SIGHTS; TELESCOPIC SIGHTS.)

Dickson, John, & Son   Famous Scottish gunmaking firm. The first John Dickson was born in 1806. After being apprenticed to James Wallace of Edinburgh for six years, Dickson started his own business in 1830, and in 1840 the firm was styled John Dickson & Son. In 1923 the last John Dickson died, the business then continuing under other managers. In 1938 the firm merged with Mortimer and Harkon, the address then 21 Frederick St., Edinburgh. John Dickson & Son is in business today at the same address, with branches in Aberdeen, Glasgow, and Kelso, all in Scotland.

Dickson is most famous for the "round-action" double-barrel shotgun made by the firm on patents granted in 1882 and 1887. This action was rounded in cross section with no flat surfaces left anywhere except on the bottom; the wood of the buttstock and fore-end carried out this treatment. The entire lockwork attached to the trigger guard plate. The first patent also claimed a three-barrel gun, the three barrels to be positioned horizontally, that is, side-by-side-by-side. A few Dickson three-barrels were so made and sold.

The quality of Dickson firearms is generally conceded to be the equal of the best London gunmakers

in all respects—fitting up, finish, performance and handling, long life, and esthetics. These compelling factors may have been the motivation for a wealthy Scot, Charles Gordon, to act as he did. During the last decade of the 19th century Gordon ordered from Dickson's more than 300 rifles and shotguns, all muzzleloaders. These "Charley Gordon" Dicksons are prized by collectors for their superb workmanship, beautiful stock wood, and handsome engraving in the tiny scrollwork typical of the period.

Today, Dickson's justly famed round action is being made anew. David M. Brown of Hamilton, Scotland (who worked in earlier years for John Dickson & Son and for Martin in Glasgow), is making the round action double guns to the same high standards of the originals—but at a price of £4500 apiece, which contrasts mightily with Dickson's 1900 price of 75 guineas for a single specimen.

diopter   See METALLIC SIGHTS.

diopter scale   Commonly found on the right eyepiece of a binocular, a diopter scale provides a means of bringing both of the observer's eyes into proper focus for clear stereoscopic vision. The scale is designed to reveal the degree of convergence or divergence of light as it leaves the eyepiece. Rotating the eyepiece counterclockwise from the scale's zero setting gives plus readings, and when rotated clockwise minus readings show. Emerging light that is convergent (plus readings) corrects for a myopic (nearsighted) eye, while divergent light (negative readings) corrects for a hyperopic (farsighted) eye.

Diopters are employed to measure the refractive power of a lens, and are equal to the reciprocal of the focal length of a lens in meters. For example, a lens with a focal length of -2 meters has a power of -0.5 diopters.

Director of Civilian Marksmanship (DCM)   A position established in June 1916, under the National Defense Act, and under the auspices of the National Board for the Promotion of Rifle Practice, whose purpose was to promote marksmanship among civilians. The DCM, a commissioned officer of the Army or Marine Corps, was detailed by the president to serve under the secretary of the Army. The DCM controlled the issue of rifles, ammunition, targets, and other equipment to National Rifle Association-affiliated gun clubs, and opened military ranges to civilian shooters.

Today, largely because of recent gun control laws and growing antigun sentiment, the importance of the DCM is greatly reduced. Functions of the office include administering a marksmanship program for junior rifle clubs. (See ARMY MARKSMANSHIP UNIT;

NATIONAL BOARD FOR THE PROMOTION OF RIFLE PRACTICE [NBPRP].)

disconnector The mechanism in an automatic, autoloading or repeating firearm that disconnects the trigger from the sear each time the action cycles, so that only one shot is fired for each separate pull on the trigger. In automatic arms capable of selective fire, the disconnector functions only in the semiautomatic mode of fire and is inactivated when the arm is in the automatic mode.

dispersion The scatter of shots on or around a target. Small dispersion corresponds to what shooters commonly call good accuracy, and large dispersion corresponds to what is called poor accuracy, though these terms are relative and not precise. In the statistical sense, dispersion is the term applied to the scattering of any quantitative values, such as the velocities or chamber pressures, measured in a series of shots. Some of the quantitative measures of dispersion are extreme spread (also called extreme variation or range), mean variation, mean radius (mean radical variation), standard deviation, and variance. Dispersion is the antithesis of uniformity. (See MEAN RADIUS.)

Distinguished Shooter's Badge, rifle and pistol Properly, the badge won with the rifle is called the Distinguished Marksman Badge and that won with the pistol is the Distinguished Pistol Shot Badge. These awards were established by the National Board for the Promotion of Rifle Practice. They are awarded to qualifying shooters of all branches of the armed services, and to civilians through the office of the director of civilian marksmanship.

Only scores fired with the service rifle or pistol in specific courses of fire at national matches, most regional championships, and some state championships may be used to qualify for the badge. A point system is used, with the open match winner being credited with 10 points, second place with eight, and third place with six, provided they have not previously reached Distinguished status. Those shooters ranking in the top 10 percent of the non-Distinguished competitors all receive points, with those below third place receiving six points each. A total of 30 points is required for a badge.

There is also an International Distinguished Shooter's Badge, awarded to shooters who take bronze, silver, or gold medals in the Olympics, World Championships, Pan American Games, or Championship of the Americas.

distortion In a lens or lens system, the result of failure of the lens to have uniform lateral magnification over its entire field. A round object near the edge of the field may appear to be oval; square or rectangular objects may produce an image in which the corners are elongated (pincushion distortion) or foreshortened (barrel-shaped distortion). It is one of the six kinds of lens aberrations. The others are: chromatic, spherical, coma, curvature of field, and astigmatism. (See ABERRATION.)

doll's head When a side-by-side shotgun is fired, a bending effect takes place on the action from the force of the upward torque of the barrels. Over time, this repeated stress can result in loosening of the barrels' fit against the standing breech, or even break the action bar.

One method of counteracting this force was devised by Westley-Richards. Based on earlier existing designs, this method employs a rear extension of the barrels consisting of a straight bar about ½-inch long with a circular swelling at its end. This "doll's head" extension fits into a corresponding recess in the top of the action and absorbs much of the strain of firing.

If the doll's head is to be effective, it must fit perfectly into the action recess, and achieving such fit is slow and costly. For this reason, plus the greatly increased strength of modern steels, it is not used on shotguns of current manufacture. (See ACTION BAR; SIDE-BY-SIDE GUN.)

dominant eye See MASTER EYE.

double (noun) When applied to shotguns, "double" means a side-by-side. In bird hunting, a double consists of two birds downed in immediate sequence.

double (verb) When the second barrel of a shotgun or rifle fires virtually simultaneously with the first because of mechanical failure, the gun is said to double. The recoil of the first shot normally unseats the sear of the second lock; thus, there is a span between shots, albeit a short one.

double-action A kind of gunlock mechanism in which the hammer can be drawn back and the gun fired in a single motion by pulling the trigger. The trigger pull force is usually between about 8 and 12 pounds, and the trigger movement required is about ⅜ to ½ inch when firing in the double-action mode.

Double-action mechanisms are found almost exclusively on handguns. In a double-action revolver, pulling the trigger in the double-action mode also serves to rotate the cylinder and thus bring an unfired cartridge into alignment with the barrel preparatory to firing. Many double-action handguns can also be fired in the single-action mode, by cocking

RUGER

Redhawk

Double-Action Revolver

Caliber .44 Magnum

STURM, RUGER & Company, Inc.

Southport, Connecticut 06490 U.S.A.

ALL RUGER FIREARMS ARE DESIGNED AND MANUFACTURED IN RUGER FACTORIES IN THE UNITED STATES OF AMERICA

The Ruger Redhawk is an unusual revolver that was built to handle the requirements of a specific cartridge—the .44 Magnum. It has fewer parts than most double-action designs and utilizes a massive frame, barrel, and cylinder to handle the stress caused by the .44 Magnum.

the hammer manually before pulling the trigger. The single-action mode allows a much lighter and shorter trigger pull, causing less disturbance of aim, and is therefore preferred when accuracy is more important than speed in firing the shot. (See DOUBLE-ACTION REVOLVER; REVOLVER; TRIGGER PULL.)

double-action revolver The first revolvers on the market were of the single-action type, i.e., it was necessary to cock the hammer for each shot. During and after the Civil War, percussion revolvers appeared that were of the double-action type, notably the Tranter, Adams, Cooper, Rider, Starr, Remington, and Pettingill. (Smith & Wesson and Colt did not produce double actions until after the advent of cartridge arms.)

Unlike the single action, double-action revolvers may be fired by merely pulling the trigger. It cams the hammer back almost to the full-cock position.

From there, the sear releases the hammer to strike the cartridge primer or a separate firing pin.

Trigger pulls of double-action revolvers are usually very heavy (8 to 12 pounds) when used in the double-action mode, but almost all double-action revolvers can also be fired single action by cocking the hammer with the thumb before pulling the trigger. When used in this manner, the trigger pull is fairly light. Because the lighter pull affords greater accuracy, almost all target shooters using double-action revolvers fire their guns in the single-action mode.

Double-action revolvers were once very popular for organized target shooting, but they have been almost entirely supplanted for this use by the autoloading pistol. The double-action revolver is still the official sidearm of many police organizations in America, but here too the autoloading pistol is slowly eroding the popularity of the revolver.

However, the double-action revolver has attributes that make it the logical choice for some purposes. It is a safer arm than the autoloader for use by untrained or, as in the case of many police organizations, poorly trained persons. For the same reason, it is the best choice for those who might have only occasional use for a handgun for purposes of self-defense. For handgun hunting, the revolver is not only a safer arm, but many revolvers chamber cartridges that are much more powerful than those available for all but a few autoloaders.

Double-action revolvers are manufactured mainly in the United States, although a few are of foreign origin. The largest volume of high-grade revolvers are made by Colt, Smith & Wesson, and Ruger. Charter Arms and Dan Wesson conclude the major lists. (See DOUBLE ACTION; REVOLVER.)

double-barrel shotgun In the beginning, all shotguns were single-barrel guns. The long-barreled flintlock fowling piece was used to kill upland game birds while they were on the ground and waterfowl before they had taken flight from the water. These guns were heavy and cumbersome, with stocks that extended to the muzzle. When the sport of taking birds on the wing became popular in the early 18th century, it became almost immediately apparent that having an extra shot available in case of a miss or to take an additional bird from a flock would be of great advantage. The answer was found in the double-barrel gun, with barrels joined by a central rib and with individual locks for each barrel.

When fine flintlock muzzleloaders by such English gunmakers as Joseph Manton appeared, wing shooting became a popular sport among the rich and landed gentry. The quality of powder improved, and William Watts developed the process of pouring melted lead through pans having holes of various sizes in the bottom to produce round shot. (Prior to this, shot was made by chopping up sheets of lead. This chopped shot was roughly square and a ballistic nightmare.) With the advent of the percussion lock with its faster ignition time, wingshooting became easier, especially in wet weather.

With the development of the Lefaucheaux pinfire cartridge, it became possible to make breechloading shotguns. Shortly thereafter, centerfire shells and shotguns designed for them came on the market. The first double-barrel breechloading shotguns had outside hammers like the percussion muzzleloaders that preceded them, and a few are still made with this feature. Choke boring became common during the last 30 years of the 19th century, and refinements such as the automatic selective ejector and single selective trigger brought the double-barrel shotgun to its peak of popularity around 1915.

Between World War I and the mid-1950s, changing economic conditions and the growing popularity of pump-action and autoloading shotguns brought the double-barrel to the nadir of its popularity in the United States. The high cost of the skilled handwork necessary to the production of a fine double-barrel had its effect, as did the retirement of the craftsmen with the skills required to build them. With the single exception of the Winchester Model 21, all new high-grade double-barrel shotguns sold in America are imports from England, Spain, Italy, Japan, Germany, and a few other countries.

There has been a perceptible increase in the popularity of the double-barrel shotgun with American shooters since the late 1960s. With decreasing bag limits on upland game and waterfowl, the advantages offered by the pump gun and the autoloader have faded. The sterling qualities of the double-barrel are being rediscovered by new generations of shooters. The double-barrel, in both side-by-side and over/under configuration, is the only shotgun that offers instant selection of two different degrees of choke. In the side-by-side style, it is the handsomest and quickest pointing of all shotguns, and the easiest to carry for a full day in the field. The over/under is favored by trap and skeet shooters. (See CHOKE; MALFUNCTIONS, DOUBLE-BARREL SHOTGUNS.)

double-base powder Single-base powders have nitrocellulose as the sole explosive base, whereas double-base powders have a dual base composed of nitrocellulose and nitroglycerine. (See SINGLE-BASE POWDER; SMOKELESS POWDER.)

double gun See SIDE-BY-SIDE GUN.

double pull The double pull, or two-stage trigger mechanism, is used on military rifles because of the greater safety and durability of the deep sear engagement. The first stage of the pull is relatively light and partially disengages the sear. The shooter then feels a distinct stop in the movement; a shorter and heavier continuation of pull disengages the sear and releases the firing pin.

Designed to accommodate the rough handling of combat conditions, the double pull is now often used in very light trigger mechanisms, such as those on free rifles and free pistols, to insure against accidental discharge and still provide a light and crisp final trigger pull. (See FREE PISTOL; FREE RIFLE; TRIGGER PULL.)

double rifle A British and European kind of rifled long gun with two barrels, either side-by-side or over/under. The German term for the side-by-side configuration is *Doppelbüchse,* and the over/under

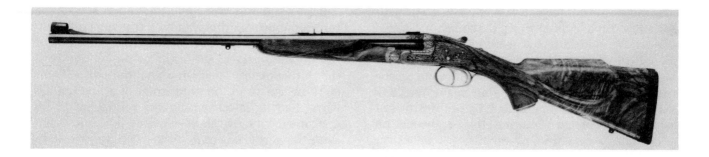

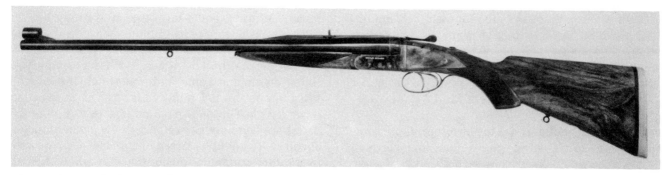

The London-made double rifle was at one time the standard arm for African and Asian hunters of dangerous game. It offered two fast shots and was the only action type that could handle the powerful cartridges required. These two are examples of the utilitarian and the ornate. The plainer gun is a Westley Richards boxlock with a case-hardened receiver and no decoration. The Purdey, built for an American customer, is a highly engraved sidelock with extra-fancy wood and skipline checkering. Few double rifles are made today, owing both to their extreme expense and the decline of the hunting for which they were designed.

combination is called *Bockdoppelbüchse*. There are also double guns with a rifle/shotgun combination.

Double rifles are expensive. There must be two barrels, two firing mechanisms, and two locks, all housed in one stock. Part of the high cost arises from regulating the barrels, i.e., getting both to shoot close to the same point of impact over most hunting ranges. It is a slow and tedious job, even for an experienced maker of double rifles. The barrel lugs must be welded or brazed together, then the barrels are held together at the muzzle with clamps and packing is inserted between the barrels. This packing is moved forward or rearward to see what positioning provides the best performance from each barrel individually, and then both barrels together. When both barrels are shooting in accord, the ribs are installed and the barrels are soldered together permanently. After the sights are fitted, minor adjustments may be made again at the muzzles. Guns regulated for use either with iron sights or with a scope will not usually shoot well when the other is installed, so the barrels have to be re-regulated.

A double rifle is regulated for only one load. If another bullet is used or another primer/powder combination, the barrels will not usually shoot to the same point of impact.

There is great dispute about the advantages and disadvantages of boxlocks and sidelocks on double

rifles. Some claim the boxlock is not as strong at the junction of the frame's bottom and the standing breech. On the other hand, the boxlock has a stronger stocking design. Likewise, there is dispute about single *vs.* double triggers. Whichever is correct, few would deny that the double rifle is well balanced and has a short overall length considering the length of barrel. This makes for a quick pointing firearm. The double rifle also has a fast safety, an instant second shot, and can be reloaded rapidly. Most important, the locks and barrels operate individually, so there is always a backup if one fails. For these reasons, the double rifle has earned quite a reputation in the game fields of Africa as an excellent dangerous-game rifle. (See AFRICAN DANGEROUS GAME, GUNS AND LOADS FOR; SIDE-BY-SIDE GUNS.)

doubles   Under Amateur Trapshooting Association rules, doubles refers to an event in which shooters fire at a pair of clay targets thrown simultaneously. The competitors always stand at the 16-yard line, not at handicap distance. Doubles is considerably more difficult than single target shooting because of the speed required to break the second target before it flies out of range. (See TRAPSHOOTING.)

double selective trigger   The ability to choose the firing order of a double-barrel shotgun is a decided advantage, since a shooter can instantly select the correct choke (barrel) for either a close or distant target. One means of providing this capability is the double selective trigger. This arrangement utilizes two triggers, with either one capable of firing both barrels in sequence. For example, some early Browning Superposed shotguns were equipped with double selective triggers that were arranged so that the forward trigger fired the upper barrel first, then the lower, with the sequence being reversed for the rear trigger.

Although the double selective trigger system is a perfectly workable one, it has not proved popular, and is rarely seen today.

double set trigger This is a very old device (the first examples appeared on crossbows) that allows a shooter to fire a rifle or handgun with a few ounces of pressure. Double set triggers employ a series of spring powered levers (usually three) that are cocked by pulling or pushing a first trigger and that are released by a pull on the second trigger. Some free pistols dispense with the two-trigger arrangement and employ a lever on the side of the gun for cocking the trigger mechanism.

Although double set triggers were quite common on Pennsylvania and Plains rifles, they are seldom seen on modern guns of American manufacture. They do, however, retain considerable popularity in Europe. The reasons for their decline in popularity are that they increase the lock time of a rifle, creating greater chance for aiming error, and that the vibration set up by the trigger's release can affect a rifle's accuracy. (See SINGLE SET TRIGGER.)

double-stage trigger Also known as a two-stage trigger, this mechanism is employed on military and some target rifles. A double-stage trigger incorporates a "slack" stage before resistance is encountered. This slack is the result of an extra hump, or knuckle, on the trigger, which engages the sear and which must be disengaged before the sear can be released. The double-stage pull increases the certainty of the rifle cocking, which is a consideration in a gun with a light trigger pull and subsequent light sear engagement. It also ensures against an accidental discharge, since the shooter must squeeze the trigger through the first stage.

Double-stage triggers are rarely, if ever, used on sporting rifles, which must be fired quickly on occasion. (See SINGLE-STAGE TRIGGER.)

doublet In optics, a system comprised of two lenses of different focal lengths, which are combined to reduce aberration. (See ABERRATION.)

double triggers Many over/under and side-by-side shotguns, as well as double rifles, are equipped with two, or double, triggers. The customary firing arrangement is: over/under, front trigger fires lower barrel, rear trigger fires upper barrel; side-by-side, front trigger fires right barrel, rear trigger fires left barrel. (See DOUBLE SELECTIVE TRIGGER.)

Douglas Barrels, Inc. (company). One of the nation's largest manufacturers of custom-rifled barrels—rifle, pistol, and muzzleloading. The company was founded by the late G. R. Douglas in 1947 in Charleston, West Virginia (its present location), and carries his name to this day.

Douglas began gunsmithing as a hobby in 1931. Then, 16 years later, the ex-Du Pont foreman decided to go into gunsmithing full-time. In 1954, he decided to focus attention on barrels alone.

Douglas had heard of experiments with the plastic flow of steel and its application to mass production of rifle barrels during World War II. Douglas applied this technology to rifle barrels, and after years of experimentation developed the patented "Ultra-rifled" process in the mid-1950s.

This button-rifling process allowed Douglas to produce high-quality rifle barrels at a reasonable cost.

The process involves pressing a carbide die through a carefully bored and reamed hole. The steel is heat-treated prior to the process. The carbide die carries the rifling impression to be swaged into the bore under some 6,200 pounds of hydraulic pressure.

Douglas also produces muzzleloading barrels by the conventional cut-rifling process whereby each rifling groove is slowly scraped by a cutting tool drawn through the bore. The cut-rifling process may require as much as an hour per barrel, while the button process takes about four minutes.

In January 1969, after the death of G. R. Douglas, William Gardner and A. L. Gardner, Douglas's foremen, purchased the company and it remains under their ownership to date. (See BARREL, RIFLED; BARREL MAKING.)

doves, guns and loads for Mourning doves are the most populous and widespread game birds in America and are so prolific that millions are harvested each season without adversely affecting the resource. In some states doves nest as many as three times a year, each time producing two young, and they thrive near civilization. Cities, in fact, have become dove rookeries in that the birds may nest in town trees (where they are not affected by predators or hunters) in some areas of prairie states where very few nesting trees exist except those planted by man.

The greatest boost to dove populations has been

increased small grain farming, which provides the birds with supplementary food on their migration. In some Latin American countries, notably Colombia, the dove population is said to have increased about 500 percent when previously brushy valleys were converted to agriculture. Undoubtedly this is what happened to dove populations in America as settlers began to till soil and thus produce the inevitable growth of weed seeds that comprise the basis of dove diet.

Since dove hunting conditions vary greatly from state to state, guns and loads must also vary, and there is probably no such thing as the perfect dove gun for hunting everywhere in America. The most versatile dove guns are over/unders and doubles, because they provide a selection of two chokes rather than just one. Of all choke combinations, improved-cylinder and modified or improved-cylinder and full may be the most practical, particularly in a gun with two triggers or a quick barrel-selecting mechanism—the long-range barrel can be used on the long shots, the larger pattern of the open barrel on the close ones.

In the deep South, where much of the shooting is pass shooting at birds flying to or from feeding fields, full-choked 12 gauges are popular. Some Southern shooters rely on No. 9 shot in the belief that this helps compensate for their tightly choked barrels, but No. 8 or No. 7½ in the same full choked 12 will generally kill cleaner, because the smaller shot lacks penetration capability at the long ranges for which the full choke was designed. Probably the best pass shooting combination for doves, bearing in mind that some will be close and some far, is a modified- or even improved-cylinder barrel loaded with trap-loads of No. 7½ or No. 8 shot. Traploads contain extra-hard shot, which patterns significantly better, and provides less recoil, than most field loads.

In some areas of the Southwest, much dove hunting is done around waterholes in the early mornings and late afternoons, and for this purpose a light-weight 20 gauge or even a 28 gauge can be a pleasure to shoot and perfectly adequate for the short, often quick shots that have to be made. The .410 is widely used; but it patterns so poorly at ranges past 30 yards that it becomes a crippler in most hands and should be used only by experts (and by them only at very short ranges). In general, the smaller the gauge and more open the barrel, the smaller the shot size that will give consistently dense "dove getting" patterns. A 28-gauge skeet barrel loaded with skeet load 9s is excellent for close-range waterhole shooting; the 20 gauge is large enough to handle 8s with almost the same density, and the 12 gauge handles 7½s very well. Small shot have the advantage of less destruction of birds shot too close to the gun, but

the disadvantage of leaving a lot of partly penetrating pellets in the meat, where they can become a problem at the dinner table. Because they normally drive through breast meat and lodge against the breastbone, No. 7½s are favored by many Southwestern dove shooters. It's possible to eat a dozen doves for every pellet found in the meat when 7½s are used at moderate ranges.

dovetail A wedge-shaped block, usually of steel, designed to fit into a correspondingly shaped slot, thus providing a means of attachment without the use of screws. This slot is also referred to as a "dovetail" slot. Its most common use is for attaching iron sights to rifles.

downhill shooting For correct bullet placement, a downhill shot is perhaps the most difficult of all shots on big-game animals. There are two main reasons for this. First, bullet drop is equal only to the amount it would be for the *horizontal* distance to the animal, not for the surface distance as seen by the hunter. Second, when you see an animal at a steep angle from above, you not only see the side but the back as well. It follows that the point that *appears* to be the center is actually up near the back line. With a higher point of aim and less bullet drop than the actual range indicates, the bullet will strike high. The point of aim should always be lower for downhill shots to allow for less bullet drop and the optical illusion. This applies also to uphill shots. (See TRAJECTORY.)

drag See BULLET DRAG.

dram A unit of weight equal to ¹⁄₁₆-ounce (avoirdupois). A dram also equals 27.34 grains. (See DRAM EQUIVALENT.)

dram equivalent This term is used as a unit of measure for designating the volume of powder in a shotshell. It derives from the period when the standard charge for a shotgun was 3 drams of black powder. The term has since come to mean a dram of black powder, and was retained to serve as a reference for shooters who were unfamiliar with the relative power of various charges of smokeless powder.

Today, the term is actually obsolete, since a 3-dram-equivalent charge of smokeless powder is far less in actual weight and volume than that amount of black powder.

draw-filing A method of smoothing a surface such as the exterior of a firearm barrel by stroking the full length of the barrel with a file. (See BARREL MAKING.)

Dreyse, Johann Nikolaus von (1787–1867) Pioneer firearms designer. In 1824, Dreyse founded the Waffenfabrik von Dreyse in Sömmerda, Prussia. There, in 1829, he designed the famous needle gun, the forerunner of the bolt-action rifle. Waffenfabrik von Dreyse produced rifles and handguns on the needle gun principle, as well as percussion revolvers, until the company failed in 1889. Several modern arms, manufactured by other companies, have been named after Dreyse. (See NEEDLE GUN.)

drift Lateral displacement of a bullet in flight in the direction of the twist. The effect of drift is so slight that it is of no consequence under normal shooting conditions at normal ranges.

Also, a cylindrical tool commonly used by gunsmiths to punch pins or other friction-tight parts.

drift pin A cylindrical or tapered pin that is tight fitting and must be driven into place with a drift. There are grooved pins and spring pins; spring pins are in the form of roll pins or spiral pins. When spring pins are driven into place, the resiliency of the spring pin material locks the pin into place. There are also flat, straight, or tapered keys that, for some purposes, serve the same function as pins, such as holding subassemblies of parts, such as triggers, in place. (See DRIFT.)

Drilling A European break-action long gun with three barrels. In the strictest sense of the term, a Drilling is composed of side-by-side shotgun barrels with a rifle barrel underneath and centered between the two. However, in more general terminology, the term has come to mean any combination of three barrels. For instance, a side-by-side shotgun with a rifle barrel on top is called a *Schienendrilling*. A gun with side-by-side rifle barrels with the shotgun barrel underneath is a *Doppelbüchsdrilling*. A single shotgun barrel with a single rifle barrel underneath and a second rifle barrel at the side, centered between the two others, is called a *Bockdrilling*. An over/under shotgun with a rifle barrel at the side is

called a *Bockdoppelflinte mit seitlichem Kleinkaliberlauf*.

Drilling-type guns are generally referred to as combination guns. Combination guns may have any combination of gauges and calibers with any number of barrels. For instance, a gun with a combination of four barrels is a combination gun and is referred to as a *Vierling*, not as a Drilling.

These kinds of guns are popular in Europe attributable, in part, to the hunting situations. Much of the hunting is done on preserves where large and small game and birds are encountered in the same hunting area. All are hunted at the same time, and the rules of sportsmanlike conduct—and sometimes the law—require that the hunter use a bullet, or a charge of shot, depending upon the quarry. The combination guns allow the hunter a quick choice. (See COMBINATION GUN; CONTINENTAL EUROPE, GUNS AND LOADS FOR HUNTING IN.)

drill round A dummy rifle cartridge used for practicing rapid loading and bolt manipulation. Drill rounds were used primarily by the military before the wide acceptance of automatic rifles.

drop at comb The distance between an imaginary line extending rearward from the shooter's line of sight when aiming the gun and the upper leading edge of the comb. (See TRY GUN.)

drop at heel The distance between an imaginary line extending rearward from the shooter's line of sight when aiming the gun and the rearmost top edge of the stock. (See TRY GUN.)

dropped shot Up to World War II, some shotgun shells were loaded with what was called dropped shot. This soft shot was made of almost pure lead with a trace of arsenic added as an aid in its manufacture. A shot tower was necessary for manufacture. (See SHOT; SHOT TOWER.)

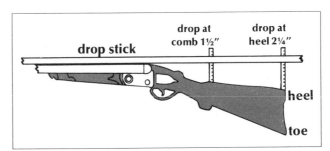

This diagram illustrates the drop at comb and heel on a shotgun. The measurements consist of the distance between a line drawn from the level of the barrels to the comb and the heel.

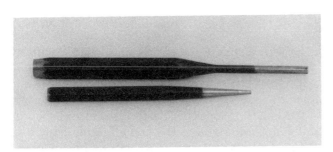

These are typical drifts, used to punch drift pins in and out of position.

dropping block action This term encompasses any firearm action employing a breechblock that moves in a vertical or near-vertical plane for loading and unloading. The first successful dropping block action was the Sharps; a modern example is the Ruger No. 1. (See ACTION; BREECHBLOCK.)

dross When impure metal is melted, the impurities and foreign matter that rise to the surface are referred to as dross. This refuse is skimmed from the surface and discarded. (See CAST BULLET.)

drum The drum was and is used in converting flintlocks to the percussion system of ignition. The vent in the flintlock was opened up to take a cylindrical piece of steel—this was the drum. It extended a bit from the vent and was tapped to take a nipple. A percussion hammer replaced the flintlock hammer.

This proved to be an efficient system for flintlock conversions, and is used a great deal today. Many shooters feel it to be less prone to misfires than the patent breech. (See CLEAN-OUT PLUG; FLINTLOCK; PATENT BREECH.)

dry firing The act of simulating shooting with an unloaded firearm, including cocking the firing mechanism and pulling the trigger. Dry firing is used to practice gun handling and trigger control and is not recommended for rifles chambered for rimfire cartridges. (See SNAP CAP.)

ducks, guns and loads for The proper choice of gun and load for ducks usually depends more on the shooting situation than the size or kind of bird. Most ducks killed over decoys are taken well inside of 40 yards, and many at 25. Thus, either a 20-gauge or 12-gauge shotgun is adequate, and with modern tight patterning ammunition an improved-cylinder choke is deadly, particularly with the 12 gauge. Doubles or over/unders bored improved-cylinder in one barrel, modified in the other, are excellent. Experts may take ducks over decoys with the 28 gauge or even the .410, but this is not recommended because of the likelihood of crippling. The heavy plumage of ducks, plus their great stamina and will to live, makes them more difficult to bring down than upland birds.

For all-around duck hunting, it is difficult to beat a modern 12-gauge pump or autoloader with 28-inch barrel and modified choke. With the best premium-quality, plastic-buffered magnums (or with steel shot) the modified barrel will sometimes throw very even full choke patterns. With ordinary nonbuffered high-velocity or magnum loads, shot patterns of the same 12 gauge will be about modified or even slightly less dense. Thus the shooter can, with one barrel, alter his choke for more pattern spread for close-range hunting (nonbuffered loads), or tighten the choke for pass shooting by using premium loads such as the Remington Nitro Mag, Winchester Super X Double X, or Federal Premium.

Magnum loads of these types contain more shot pellets of a given size, a heavier payload, and kill farther than standard loads. Latest tests of new steel shot loads show killing capability about the same as that of nonbuffered lead magnums, but with slightly less range (perhaps not more than 3 to 5 yards difference) than the best premium-lead magnums.

Tests on hundreds of pen-raised mallards, as well as field tests on wild birds, indicate that the best performance on large ducks is with No. 4 lead shot or No. 2 steel shot (with 12-gauge guns bored full choke). For more open chokes or smaller gauges, No. 5 or No. 6 lead and No. 4 steel may be better. Size 7½ lead is popular for close-range shooting in the South, but its best use is for small ducks and/or teal or for finishing off cripples because the higher pellet count offers more chance for a head shot. Many experienced shooters take 7½s or even 8s to the blind for this purpose. (The lighter shots lose penetration capability too quickly for long-range use.)

The best long-range pass shooting guns are heavy and long barreled, for maximum sighting plane and maximum burning of heavy magnum powder charges. Full choke and large shot are indicated. Many duck shooters would be surprised at what can be done with even No. 2 lead shot (commonly used on geese, not ducks) in a tightly choked gun using the newest buffered 3-inch magnum ammunition. For guns with standard 2¾-inch chambers, No. 4 "short magnums" with plastic buffering appear best for maximum range duck shooting. The deadliest long-range duck gun of all is the 3½-inch 10-gauge magnum with No. 2 shot in premium quality buffered loads. (See BLIND; DECOY.)

Ducks Unlimited A private, nonprofit organization founded by hunter-conservationists in 1937 to raise funds for acquiring and improving nesting habitats for wild waterfowl. D.U. has about 300,000 members and spends from $10 to $11 million each year on Canadian breeding grounds. It has contributed to the comeback of many waterfowl species, particularly in areas where some impoundment of flooded marsh by D.U. may be the only water by the end of nesting season.

The largest sources of D.U. funds are memberships and contributions raised at annual fundraising dinners. Memberships are $10 minimum; national headquarters may be contacted by writing to P.O. Box 66300, Chicago, Illinois 60666.

dud A cartridge or shotshell that fails to fire when the firing pin strikes the primer. Cause may be lack of priming compound or a primer rendered ineffective by oil or silicone absorption.

dum dum A term used in common parlance to mean an expanding bullet. It is derived from the .303 service cartridge for the Lee-Metford rifle, which was modified at the Indian Army arsenal at Dum-Dum, near Calcutta, in 1895. Before modification, the full-jacketed bullets did not expand and hence lacked shocking power. The Dum Dum modification removed the jacket from the tip, so that one millimeter of lead was exposed, allowing the bullet to expand upon contact with a target. Dum Dum ammunition was never adopted by the British Army, which employed a hollow point bullet. Today the term is usually rendered as "dumdum." (See EX-PANDING BULLET.)

dummy cartridge An inoperative cartridge or facsimile that is used to test firearms' functioning or is employed in training in the handling of arms. (See DRILL ROUND.)

dummy sideplate Dummy, or false, sideplates are added to double or over/under shotguns for purposes of decoration. They are usually engraved or otherwise ornamented, but have nothing to do with the locks. (See SIDELOCK.)

duplex loads Loads consisting of two different powders in one cartridge case, with the faster burning powder next to the primer, and the slower powder on top, closer to the bullet. Such loads have

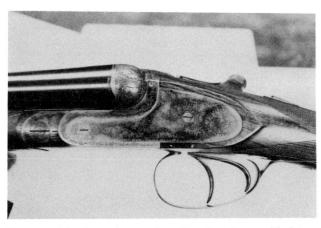

Dummy sideplates are nonfunctional and are added to a boxlock gun to enhance its appearance. They can be distinguished from true sidelock plates by the fact that they contain no pins for the action parts.

been tried by some handloaders in an attempt to obtain maximum burning efficiency and velocity from a sporting cartridge; the military experimented with such loads during World War II, notably the .50-caliber machine gun cartridge.

One version of the duplex loads utilized an extended flash tube to shift the ignition forward; this method required the powders to be loaded in reverse order, with the slower burning powder at the rear of the case. Igniting the powder directly behind the bullet first started the bullet moving through the barrel, while burning of the slower powder at the rear continued the acceleration over a longer time interval, reducing the pressure peak, ensuring more complete combustion of the powder, and in a few instances actually—but not materially—increasing the velocity.

Metallic cartridge black-powder shooters have also experimented with duplex loads, loading a small charge of smokeless powder next to the flash hole, followed by the regular black-powder charge on top of the smokeless. Usually reserved for match shooting, such loads tend to reduce the amount of black-powder fouling.

Du Pont de Nemours, E. I., & Company, Inc. Éleuthère Irénée du Pont de Nemours, the son of a French statesman, immigrated to the United States in 1800. Intrigued by the high prices and poor quality of American gunpowder, he decided to draw upon his training in chemistry and start his own gunpowder mill. In April 1801, after raising the necessary capital, he established E. I. du Pont de Nemours & Company; the first Du Pont powder mill was built on the banks of the Brandywine River near Wilmington, Delaware, in 1802.

In the spring of 1804, the first Du Pont powder was offered to the public. The government made its first purchase of military powder in 1805. Increased demand for the product prompted the company to expand its facilities in 1813.

Du Pont decided to augment his product line in 1832 by adding refined saltpeter, refined charcoal, pyroligneous acid, and creosote. E. I. du Pont died in 1834, leaving control of the company to family members.

Du Pont manufactured only black powder, in several granulations, until 1857. That year, the company developed a "soda powder" from sodium nitrate for industrial blasting purposes. In 1880, the company began production of two more explosives, nitroglycerin and dynamite, and smokeless gunpowder was marketed in 1890.

The Du Pont Company was incorporated in 1899. The corporation began an era of diversification, during which it added such products as lacquers, cements, finishes, chemicals, pigments, and paints. In 1917, Du Pont purchased Harrison Brothers & Company and several smaller concerns. During World War I, the company directed a large portion of its production toward the manufacturing of powder and explosives for the Allied forces.

As the corporation grew, its activities became even more diversified. In 1950, Du Pont accepted an assignment for the government to design, build, and operate production facilities for atomic materials. In 1968, several low-profit products were dropped from the Du Pont line, including black powder. However, until recently, Du Pont still manufactured smokeless gunpowder.

In 1987, the Du Pont Company sold the assets of its smokeless powder business to the IMR Powder Company, which presently manufactures the IMR line of powders in a plant located in Plattsburg, New York.

dust shot　A very small size of lead shot. Usually, No. 12 shot is referred to as dust shot. It is used primarily in the loading of .22 rimfire shot cartridges. (See SHOT.)

DWM　Trademark of the Deutsche Waffen and Munitionensfabrik (German Weapons and Ammunition Works). Various German ammunition manufacturing companies were reorganized into a new corporation under this name in 1896. At first, the company specialized in ammunition making, but it later also made rifles, pistols, and many military arms. Perhaps its most famous product was the Luger (Parabellum) military pistol, used by the Germans in two world wars. This pistol was also made by other German and some foreign companies.

The DWM corporate name has been altered to Industrie Werke Karlsruhe (IWK), which means Industrial Works, Karlsruhe (the city). But the DWM trademark is retained for ammunition, and these products were once imported into the United States by Speer, Inc. (DWM ammunition is now imported by Dynamit-Nobel of Northvale, N.J.)

DWM ammunition was once world famous for dependability and shot-to-shot consistency. The modern ammunition sold under this trademark is excellent, but many other companies now make quality ammunition, so DWM no longer enjoys the status it once had. (See LUGER [PARABELLUM] PISTOL.)

ear Any earlike projection, such as those situated on each side of the front and rear sights on the U.S. Model 1917 (Enfield) military rifle to protect the sights from damage or displacement by an accidental blow from the side. The term also is applied to the projecting thumbpiece on the breechblock of a rolling-block rifle.

ear protectors Products designed to prevent hearing damage resulting from excessive noise. It has long been recognized that exposure to the noise created by firearms causes hearing impairment, but not until the early 1960s were efficient hearing protectors widely sold or used.

Ear damage is caused by the high pressure produced by the concussive sound of firing. This pressure damages the ciliae, the microscopic hairs of the inner ear that transmit sound through the hearing mechanism, and impairs their ability to receive sounds. The function of an ear protector is to prevent this concussion from reaching the inner ear.

Basically, there are three kinds of protectors. The first, the mass-produced plug type, is usually made of soft rubber, and is inserted in the ear canal. This device offers only partial protection, since it is not an efficient barrier against intense noise.

The second kind of protector is also a plug, but is custom made to fit the outer ear surrounding the canal to the inner ear, and to plug the middle ear canal as well. This protector is made of semirigid rubber or plastic and creates an effective seal against sound. It is available from ear, nose, and throat specialists.

Earmuffs are the most effective kind of protection. These consist of two hard plastic shells, filled with sound-deadening foam and connected by a steel clamp that holds them tightly over the ears.

It should be emphasized that no one device affords complete protection under all conditions. The most efficient arrangement is a combination of plugs and headphones (earmuffs) worn simultaneously. However, it is thought by some otiologists that the vibration of the bones in the skull caused by severe noise is sufficient in itself to damage hearing, and that no amount of external protection will be totally effective. (See HEARING, SHOOTING DAMAGE TO.)

ebony A dark wood obtained from a tree widely distributed in the tropical parts of the world. Its color, durability, hardness, and susceptibility to polish make ebony attractive in custom firearms for such features as inlays, fore-end tips, and grip caps. Though it is difficult to work with, the heartwood of ebony is said to excel all other woods in the fineness and intensity of its dark color. Ebony's drawback is that it is structurally unstable; that is, prone to checking (cracking) or shrinking over a period of time.

Echeverria, Bonifacio (company) See SPANISH GUNMAKERS.

eject To throw out or expel. A cartridge case is ejected from the gun after it has been extracted from the chamber. (See EJECTOR; EXTRACTOR.)

ejecta Literally, this term means "that which is expelled." In regard to firearms, it refers to any part of the projectile, as well as any object accompanying it, that is not consumed by the combustion of the powder. For example, shotgun ejecta usually consists of the shot charge, the shot cup, and the wads. Rifle ejecta would include the bullet and any filler used to eliminate excess air space in the cartridge.

ejection port The hole in the receiver of a firearm through which the spent cartridge case is expelled. Ejection ports vary in size and shape depending upon the firearm and the cartridges used.

ejector The device that thrusts the spent cartridge case free of the firearm after it has been extracted from the chamber.

There are several basic kinds of ejectors. The simplest is the kind found in many rifles, and consists of a stationary strip of metal set in the bolt raceway. As the spent case is extracted, its base strikes the ejector, and the shell is kicked clear of the gun. A second, more complex kind is the spring and plunger. It is used in modern bolt-action rifles and double shotguns. The ejector is a spring powered plunger that is tripped by the opening of the action, and that strikes the shell under its own power, propelling it from the gun. The hand-operated ejector also uses a plunger, or piston, but operates by hand rather than spring power. This kind is employed on double- and single-action revolvers.

ejector rod In break-open rifles and shotguns, the push rod that activates the ejector when the firearm is broken. In revolvers, the rod that expels the cartridges automatically, as with Webleys or vintage Smith & Wessons, or by manual action, commonly seen on modern revolvers. (See EJECTOR.)

electronic transducer system See CHAMBER PRESSURE.

elevation Vertical adjustment, of any firearm sight, that alters the point of impact of the bullet on the target.

Eley-Kynoch (company) A British ammunition manufacturing company. It originated with the consolidation of Eley Brothers, a cartridge manufacturing firm that made paper cartridges as early as 1840, and the larger Kynoch Company, plus other smaller firms. The complex is now owned by Imperial Chemical Industries, Ltd., but the "Eley" and "Kynoch" names are used as trademarks. Eley rimfire .22 ammunition in fine target grades is imported into the United States. Kynoch was long famous for production of sporting ammunition, particularly the big-bore cartridges used in Africa and Asia for dangerous game, but ICI has ceased manufacture of these loads.

elk, guns and loads for A mature bull elk will usually weigh 600 to 700 pounds on the hoof, a far cry from the 1,000 to 1,100 pounds often attributed to him. Still, at 600 pounds, the American wapiti is considerably larger than his cousins, the whitetail and mule deer. He's tough by comparison and often gives no indication of being hit even when a bullet is placed in his lung region.

Any centerfire rifle cartridge in existence today will kill a bull elk, but not all are wise choices for elk hunting. In the years 1900 to 1945, many of the most skilled elk hunters in the West used such cartridges as the .25/35, .250/3000 Savage, .257 Roberts, and .30/30 Winchester. It was rare indeed that you chanced upon an elk hunter armed with a rifle chambered for a cartridge larger than the .30/06.

Today, a surprising number of hunters consider the .30/06 too small for elk, favoring instead such cartridges as the .300 Winchester, .308 Norma, 8mm Remington, .338 Winchester, and .375 H&H Magnums. In reality, both the .25/35 and .375 H&H Magnum represent extremes. In all fairness to the elk, the average hunter is better armed for the task with an 8mm Remington Magnum than with a .25/35.

All things considered, the .25/06 with the 120-grain Nosler Partition bullet is the smallest cartridge

Elk are large, tough, and must often be taken at very long range. These loads will cope with both circumstances (from left): .264 Winchester Magnum, .270 Weatherby Magnum, 7mm Weatherby Magnum, 7mm Remington Magnum, .300 Winchester, and .340 Weatherby.

that can be used reliably on elk. Some hunters have success with the .243 and 6mm Remington, but these are adequate only when the shot is perfectly placed. The .270 Winchester, .280 Remington, 7x57 Mauser, 7mm/08 .284 Winchester, .308, .30/06, and .35 Whelen are a few other non-magnum cartridges that perform well on elk.

In the magnum category, the .270 Weatherby, 7mm Weatherby, 7mm Remington, .300 Winchester, .300 Weatherby, and .308 Norma Magnums, the 8mm Remington, the .338 Winchester, and .358 Norma are good choices. The .25/06 and the .257 Weatherby are borderline.

Extreme differences in the terrain inhabited by elk (from the eastern slope of the Rocky Mountains westward) make choosing a particular cartridge and bullet weight very difficult. In some regions of the Rockies, elk hunting can involve long shots of 300 to 500 yards in large open parks, or even in sagebrush covered foothills. But in other regions, elk are commonly hunted in dense timber where a long shot is 150 yards, a more typical one no more than 75 yards. Since elk usually inhabit rough country, it's always to the hunter's advantage, whether he packs the meat out on his back or on a horse, to drop the animal in its tracks. A good lung shot is a sure killer, but the tenacious elk may travel 100 yards or more after being hit before he goes down. This is enough to put him into down timber or a precipitous canyon. In either instance, the pack job will be a nightmare.

To put a bull down quickly, the bullet has to break massive bone. A head or neck shot is excellent, but often beyond the marksmanship capabilities of the hunter shooting from an unsteady position. The answer, then, is to break the shoulder, a target that's not to hard to hit even at long range. To accomplish this, the bullet being used must hold together so that it breaks the heavy shoulder bone and then penetrates the vitals. Light bullets in any caliber won't do the job. They'll go to pieces when they hit bone, inflicting only a superficial wound.

The following table lists some of the more popular elk cartridges and the bullet weights recommended for elk hunting.

Cartridge	Recommended Bullet Weight
.25/06 Remington	120 grains
.257 Weatherby Magnum	120 grains
.270 Winchester	130–150 grains
.270 Weatherby Magnum	130–150 grains
7x57 Mauser	150–160 grains
7mm/08	150–160 grains
.280 Remington	150–160 grains
.284 Winchester	150–160 grains
7mm Remington Magnum	150–175 grains
.308 Winchester	150–180 grains
.30/06	165–200 grains
.300 Winchester Magnum	180–200 grains
.300 Weatherby Magnum	180–200 grains
8mm Remington Magnum	185–225 grains
.338 Winchester Magnum	200–250 grains
.35 Whelen	250 grains
.358 Norma	200 grains

Today, the bolt-action rifle equipped with a scope is by far the most popular arm among elk hunters. The need for powerful cartridges and precise shooting has made it preeminent. The most popular scope among elk hunters has traditionally been the 4X, but the variable-power scopes have gained greatly in popularity, since they are adaptable to both long- and short-range shooting.

For the hunter who goes on foot, a rifle sling is a necessity, since long distances must be covered.

Horseback hunters, on the other hand, carry the rifle in a saddle scabbard, and here a sling is actually an encumbrance, since it interferes with the speedy withdrawal of the rifle from its carrier.

end wad See FRANGIBLE TOP WAD.

energy formula The formula for calculating the kinetic energy of a bullet. It is based on the general equation for kinetic energy due to translatory motion in Newtonian mechanics, which is $E = \frac{1}{2}mv^2$. In the British Engineering System of dimensions, the mass of the body (m) is expressed in slugs, the velocity (v) is in feet per second, and the energy (E) is in foot-pounds. In European countries where the meter-kilogram-second (mks) system is in general use, the mass is expressed in kilograms, the velocity is in meters per second, and the energy is in meter-kilograms (mkg). Kinetic energy may also be expressed in Joules in some countries where the metric system is in use (1 mkg = 9.81 Joules).

Because bullet weights are usually expressed in grains, it is necessary to divide the bullet weight in grains first by 7,000 to obtain the weight in pounds, then by 32.17 (because 32.17 ft/sec^2 is the acceleration of gravity) to obtain the mass in slugs, if the general kinetic energy formula is to be used. The constants can be combined for the special case of calculating the kinetic energy of bullets more conveniently. In that case, the formula becomes $E = Wv^2/450,400$, where W = bullet weight in grains, v = velocity in feet per second, and E = energy in foot-pounds.

Enfield Founded in 1856, the Royal Small Arms Factory, Enfield Lock, England, has manufactured military arms since that time. The first issued to British troops was the Enfield Rifle Musket, 1852 pattern, a single-shot muzzleloader. Muzzleloaders, breechloading rifles, revolvers, and full automatic weapons followed. The latest developments are a rifle and a light machine gun chambered for the experimental 4.85mm cartridge.

Perhaps most famous is the Lee-Enfield rifle, a repeating bolt-action arm in .303 British caliber, used by British forces in both world wars. There were many "marks" or model variations of this bolt-action rifle.

The Enfield pattern six-shot revolver is also well known; it too has been made in several model variations and calibers. The rather complex design using the .455 Webley cartridge was abandoned in the late 1880s and was replaced by a Webley top-break design.

The name Enfield was also applied to a bolt-action Mauser-type rifle in .276 caliber, designed by the Enfield facility. This rifle was intended as a replace-

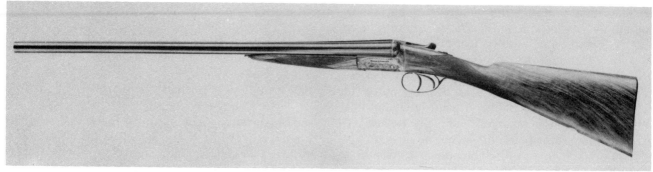

A typical English stock utilizes a straight wrist and narrow fore-end.

ment for the Lee-Enfield in .303, but because of the outbreak of World War I the attempt to convert to the more modern rifle and cartridge was abandoned. The design was subsequently adapted to the .303 British cartridge and to the American .30/06 military round. As manufactured in the United States, this Enfield .30/06 was issued to American troops in World War I and thereafter, but it was finally abandoned by the U.S. in favor of the Springfield .30/06. (See WEBLEY & SCOTT, LTD.)

engine turning The process of decorating a metal surface, such as a bolt, with a pattern of overlapping circular spots. This is accomplished by rotating an abrasive-coated rod against the surface. The work is then indexed to the proper point for the next overlapping application of the grinding or polishing bit.

English checkering This kind of checkering differs considerably from what is regarded as high-quality hand checkering in America. Good American checkering employs diamonds that are markedly longer than they are wide, and the top surface of each diamond comes to a point. English checkering, especially on old guns, employs diamonds that are squarish and often flat topped. In addition, English checkering patterns are frequently surrounded by border lines, which are seldom seen in American stockwork.

The influence of this style of decoration is still evident on modern British shotguns. (See CHECKERING.)

englishing On a side-by-side shotgun, the barrels are farther apart at the breech than at the muzzle, and some means must be used to adjust them so that they shoot to the same point of impact. Englishing refers to a painstaking method of making this adjustment that is used on the most expensive British guns. It is accomplished by both bending and beveling the barrel tubes as they are assembled on the center rib.

English stock A shotgun stock with a straight grip (no pistol grip) is often called an English stock. In a broader context, the classic English stock has no pistol grip, is oil finished rather than lacquered, has a length close to 15 inches—as compared with the 14-inch "standard stock" popular in America—and is considerably more cast-off. (See SHOTGUN STOCK.)

engraving Without doubt, the art of engraving and inlaying is the most difficult of all the skills pertaining to the construction of a firearm. The practice of engraving or otherwise decorating weapons is an ancient one and, when firearms made their appearance, the tradition of decoration was transferred to them. Very early in the development of the gun, engravers turned their art to it, often with exquisite results.

The process of engraving and inlaying is one that requires few tools but demands great artistic skill and mechanical ability of its practitioner. This is because the engraver is not working with a plastic substance, but with steel of an especially tough and resilient kind—one of the most difficult of all mediums.

The first step in engraving is to disassemble the firearm (assuming a factory arm is to be engraved) and to polish and true up all the metal surfaces to be engraved. The steel (which has not yet received its final heat treatment; or, if already heat treated, has been dehardened) is coated with a thin white paint, and the basic design, which has been drawn on translucent paper, is laid over the paint and scribed onto it.

With the basic design in place, the engraver cuts away at the metal, following the lines in the paint. The tool used for this cutting is called a chisel, scribe, or burin. It is pushed against the steel either by hand pressure or by tapping it with a small hammer. An engraver will have perhaps a dozen of these chisels, each with a different point, to make the various necessary cuts. The part being engraved is held in a heavy ballsocket vise that can be pivoted and locked in any position.

The engraver's vise is a pair of jaw clamps set on a rotating ball rest. The vise is heavy and provides solid support along with an unlimited number of working angles.

After the basic design is cut, the engraver adds shading, detail, or inlay, according to the kind of work to be done. Over the years, several distinct schools of engraving have evolved, and any design is likely to incorporate the characteristics of one of these:

English scrollwork utilizes extremely fine, detailed scrollwork that covers large areas of the gun. Usually no central motif or figure is featured. This kind of engraving can be seen on many of the best grade London guns such as Boss, Purdey, and Holland & Holland.

German/Austrian engraving employs very bold figures and scrolls done in deep relief. A leaf motif is common, and the engraving is often done in conjunction with elaborate carving of the stock.

Bulino or "banknote" engraving is a style that is popular in Italy and is gaining an increasing following in America. Bulino is executed with a very fine chisel, pushed by one hand, and features extremely

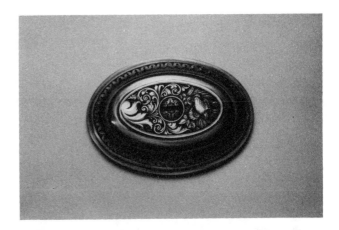

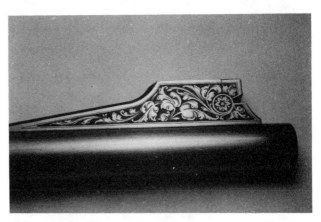

Floral engraving employs a flower-and-vine motif to cover small parts or to act as a background for larger scenes. Here, it is used on a pistol grip.

fine detail, shading, and the greatest subtlety of design in the depiction of hunting scenes or themes from classical mythology. It is often used in combination with fine scrollwork.

The best American engravers draw on elements of all three schools; indeed, most topflight engravers can do work of any type, although most will prefer one approach over the others.

Inlaying is a close adjunct to engraving. It consists of cutting deeply into the steel in the shape of the desired figure. The edge of the steel is undercut, and gold, silver, or platinum is hammered into the opening so that it flows under the bevels (undercuts), ensuring that the finished figure will be held in place. The excess metal is then trimmed away, and the inlay is given its final shape and form. Inlays can either be raised above the surface of the steel or made flush with it.

When the engraving and inlaying are complete, the steel is given its final finish. It is usually blued, although case hardening is commonly used, or it can be left "in the white."

Because of the extreme difficulty of engraving, there are very few truly first-rate engravers to be

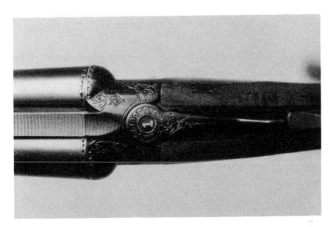

Engraving can be both decorative and functional. This Winchester Model 21 shotgun has floral engraving at the breech and on the top lever, while the gold 1 on the top lever marks it as gun number 1 of a two-gun pair.

found. While there are scores of topflight stockmakers in America at this writing, it is doubtful if more than three or four men could claim a similar rank as engravers.

Since so few shooters have the opportunity to examine superior engraving, it is difficult for them to judge the quality of the engraving they do see. Also, personal taste enters greatly into the picture. However, there are a few criteria that can be used in the appraisal of most engraving.

First, has the artist used a "coarse" or "loose" design in order to cover a large area with very little work? This is often seen on American factory engraved guns, where a single figure, or a large scroll device, will stand alone in a broad expanse of unengraved metal.

Conversely, has the engraver attempted a design that incorporates an obviously high degree of difficulty? For example, a master engraver can inlay a gold line only a few thousandths of an inch thick or do virtually perfect shading and detail work so fine that it must be viewed under a magnifying glass.

Are the figures, whether engraved or inlaid, lifelike? Poorly done figures, regardless of what they

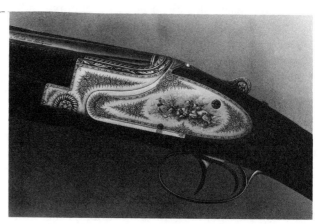

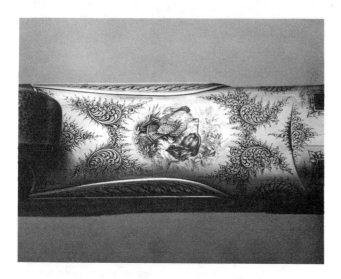

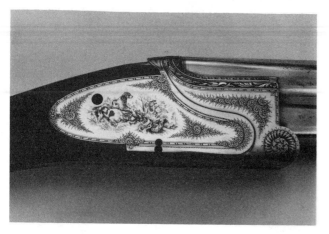

These four examples of the engraving of Winston G. Churchill can stand as supreme examples of the art. Note the minute and perfect detail, the variations in style and motif, and the photographic perfection of the animal and bird figures.

depict, will be stiff, artificial, and crude, almost as if a child had done them. Top quality figures are lifelike, realistic, and vibrant in appearance. Perhaps the simplest way to judge the quality of a figure or a scene is to envision it as if it were a drawing. If it would not appear well rendered on paper, then it should not be considered well rendered in steel.

Because of the difficulty involved, and the many hours invested, top quality engraving is extremely expensive. The tens of thousands of dollars such work costs places it out of reach of all but a few. Even a relatively small amount of coverage, such as the engraving and inlaying of a floorplate and trigger guard, is likely to cost more than a fine custom gun itself.

On the other hand, the work of a recognized master invariably appreciates in value. As an illustration, a rifle with extensive inlay and engraving that was completed by Winston G. Churchill in 1975,

Engraving and inlay work is likely to be either terrible or excellent, with little in between. The inlays in the shotgun are stiff and lifeless; they are out of scale to each other and do not fit the background engraving as a harmonious whole. The gold-inlay mule deer on the rifle floorplate blends with its background and is lifelike and realistic.

and sold for $10,000 then, can command half again as much today. Engraving, if done with the consummate skill that the art demands, is both a fine investment and a joy to the beholder. (See BLUING; CASE HARDEN; CHURCHILL, WINSTON GORDON.)

entrance pupil The circular area, bounded by a curve, that is the image of the front stop of an optical system, caused by the action of the objective lens. (See OBJECTIVE LENS.)

envelope In firearms usage, an envelope is a container. In bullet construction, for example, the bullet jacket would be the envelope for the bullet core.

epoxy A shortened term for a polyether resin. This relatively recently developed material has excellent adhesive qualities and is extensively utilized in fire-

arm repair and action bedding. Epoxy is also used in stock finishing because it provides a finish nearly impervious to moisture and hence lessens the chance of the wood warping.

eprouvette A device once used for testing black powder. The date and location of the development is unknown, but eprouvettes are mentioned in William Bourne's book, *Inventions and Devices Very Necessary for all Generalles and Captaines* (London, 1587). They were made and sold as late as 1866. Most eprouvettes were in the general form of a pistol, with a very short barrel or chamber that was filled with the powder to be tested. A wheel, usually serrated on the periphery, with a cap extending to fit closely over the end of the chamber, was suspended on a pivot below the muzzle. A friction spring pressed against the edge of the wheel or on the serrations, and the wheel was graduated. The chamber was filled with the black powder to be tested, the wheel rotated to close the cap, and the pistol fired. The amount of rotation of the wheel could be compared with that obtained from other lots of powder or with a lot accepted as a standard. Both flintlock and caplock models exist. (See BLACK POWDER.)

erector lens The objective lens of a telescope forms an image that is inverted, both top for bottom and right for left. The erector lens (usually a system of more than one lens) corrects these inversions and forms an image properly oriented, as seen by the user, through the eyepiece lens.

In prism telescopes and binoculars the function of the erector lens is performed by the prisms. (See OBJECTIVE LENS.)

erosion See BARREL EROSION.

escutcheon A metal piece that is inlaid into the forestock of a muzzleloading rifle to hold barrel keys. Iron, brass, and German silver are used. Some escutcheons are plain, some are highly ornamented and engraved. The sizes run from ½-inch to about 3 inches. Every gunmaker has his own favorite style of escutcheon, so they vary greatly.

On a Plains rifle the escutcheon accepts the barrel wedges. (See MUZZLELOADER; PLAINS RIFLE.)

estimated velocity Handloaders who do not have access to a chronograph to accurately determine bullet speeds must employ estimated velocities in developing their loads. Estimated velocities are based on the fact that, given identical barrel lengths, case capacity, bullet weight and diameter, and powder charges, firearms will often give similar velocities.

The experienced handloader can therefore consult a loading manual that lists all of these factors and interpolate for his own gun and load, but this practice is *not* recommended, nor should it be practiced by casual or beginning handloaders, resulting chamber pressures being uncertain. (See CHRONOGRAPH; HANDLOAD.)

Etchen Grip Developed and popularized by Fred Etchen, a champion trapshooter, the Etchen trap gun grip is a very tightly curved pistol grip that enjoyed considerable popularity from its inception in the late 1940s to the 1960s. Proponents of the grip claimed that it gave the right hand better control over the gun itself, and over the trigger, because of the "locking" effect it had on the right hand. (See PISTOL GRIP.)

etching A method of decorating metal firearms parts by means of an acid. An acid resistant coating is first placed over the surface, then certain portions of the coating are cut away in a decorative design to expose the surface of the metal. Acid is then poured over the piece and allowed to eat into the unprotected portion to a predetermined depth.

"excellent" (condition) See GUN CONDITION.

exit pupil The small bright circle of light seen in the eyepiece of a telescope when the instrument is held at some distance from the eye and pointed toward a light source. The exit pupil diameter is an important measure of telescope or binocular performance in dim light.

The exit pupil of the instrument must be at least as large as the pupil of the human eye, under the conditions in which it will be used, in order to see full detail. In a hunting telescope or binocular, a 5mm exit pupil will usually be adequate, although a larger exit pupil will allow full optical qualities with some error in placement of the eye. In a spotting scope, generally used under daylight conditions or in good artificial light, an exit pupil of 2mm to 3mm will be adequate. (See IRIS; MAGNIFICATION.)

expander plug Sometimes referred to as the expander ball, it is that portion of the decapping rod in the resizing die that expands the case neck back to the correct diameter to hold the bullet friction-tight after the neck has been resized from its fire-formed diameter. (See CASE RESIZING.)

expanding bullet A bullet that is designed to expand its original diameter on contact with any ob-

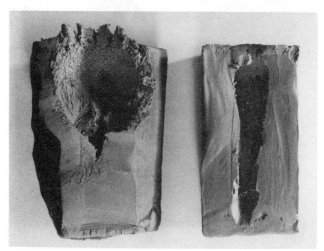

There are a number of ways to gauge the expansion of a bullet. One is to fire into clay and then section the material to examine the cavity. These two clay blocks were used to test a standard-velocity .22 bullet and a hyper-velocity projectile. The latter had by far the more violent expansion. A recovery box measures both expansion and penetration. This one is 12 inches square and 4 feet long. It is filled with a mixture of half silt, half rotted sawdust, moistened with water, and divided by cardboard spacers every 6 inches. The truck inner tube at the front simulates an animal's hide.

ject, particularly animal tissue. Expanding bullets are designed especially for hunting; when they strike the animal a greater amount of bone, tissue, and nerves is disrupted than with a nonexpanding bullet. This also creates a great deal of shock to the vital organs, and brings immobility and/or death quickly.

Expanding bullets are usually composed of a lead core encased within a jacket of copper alloy and structured so that the soft core expands the jacket when the bullet point encounters solid resistance. Some lead alloy bullets without jackets have a cavity in the point to facilitate expansion. (See HOLLOW POINT.)

This is a Trophy Bonded 500-grain softnose bullet shown in sectioned and expanded form.

These are both 160-grain 7mm Nosler bullets. The one at left expanded perfectly and retained 117 grains of its original weight.

expanding gas mechanism   See GAS OPERATION.

expansion ratio   The ratio between the bore diameter of a bullet of a certain caliber and the amount of space the powder capacity of the case provides. As the powder that fills this space is burned, the gas it creates expands to fill that space, and as the gas volume exceeds the volume of the powder it replaces, pressure is built up within the case so that the bullet is dislodged from the neck and started up the bore. The expanding powder gas continues to fill the increasing space and exert pressure on the rear of the bullet, thereby increasing velocity until the bullet exits the muzzle. The amount of expansion available to the powder gas is therefore not only governed by the capacity of the case, but also by the additional space within the bore of the barrel, which becomes greater as bore diameter is increased, thereby increasing the expansion ratio.

Expansion ratio is a relative, rather than a mathematical, expression, and is usually designated in terms of high or low. It is one of the factors considered when determining if a particular load is efficient or not. As a rule, a rifle cartridge with a low expansion ratio is inefficient (wastes considerable powder to achieve its velocity), while a cartridge with a high expansion ratio is efficient. The .22 Long Rifle rimfire cartridge, for example, has an extremely high expansion ratio while that of the .22/250 is extremely low.

express cartridge   A nearly obsolete term indicating higher-than-normal velocity from a specific cartridge, originally achieved by loading the cartridge with heavier charges of black powder than standard, and with lighter-than-standard bullet weights. The term was first applied to a number of British cartridges (called express train cartridges) in the 1880s, and began to fade from use after World War II. Some of the most popular of these cartridges, such as the .470 Nitro Express, are still in use. (See EXPRESS RIFLE; NITRO EXPRESS.)

express rifle   A British name for rifles made especially for high-velocity express cartridges. These rifles first appeared in the mid-1880s, and were mostly in the form of double-barrel guns, but sometimes were of single-shot design. The term has been carried over and applied to modern actions like the Remington bolt-action Model 30 Express. (See EXPRESS CARTRIDGE.)

extension stock   A stock, made of heavy wire, that slides in and out of the frame of a shoulder-fired arm. Extension stocks are most often used in military and survival arms, especially submachine guns and machine pistols.

exterior ballistics   The branch of ballistics pertaining to the motion of a projectile from the instant it leaves the muzzle of the gun until it strikes the target. During this interval, the bullet is constantly acted upon by gravitational and aerodynamic forces. The trajectory is determined by the initial velocity of the bullet and the resultant of gravitational and aerodynamic forces. Though the gravitational force is practically constant throughout the bullet's flight, the aerodynamic forces are constantly changing.

Sir Isaac Newton, who formulated and proved the law of gravity in about 1690, began his formal argument supporting that law with an example of the trajectory of a horizontally fired projectile. Newton introduced formal mathematical methods into the study of exterior ballistics, but he was handicapped by the lack of instrumentation for the accurate measurement of projectile velocities. The invention of the ballistic pendulum by Benjamin Robins in about 1740 provided the means of measuring projectile velocities with reasonable accuracy, and started the progressive refinement of aerodynamic laws that continues today.

Many mathematical schemes have been developed for the calculation of trajectories, but the most useful of these for small arms has been that of F. Siacci, an Italian ballistician, who formulated it about 1880. Tables for convenient computations using the Siacci Method were developed by Colonel James Ingalls in 1886. The Siacci Method was refined and greatly improved for application to modern pointed and boattail projectiles by H. P. Hitchcock and R. H. Kent of the U.S. Army Ballistic Research Laboratory during the 1930s, and their refinements of the Siacci Method provided the basis for most of the trajectory data now available on small arms bullets. (See BALLISTICS; INTERIOR BALLISTICS; TRAJECTORY.)

extract To withdraw a cartridge or case from a chamber. (See EXTRACTOR.)

extractor The firearm member that withdraws a cartridge or case from the chamber. The member, which incorporates some sort of hook or claw, is attached to the reciprocating member of the action to withdraw the case to the rear. In some kinds of break-action guns, such as a single-shot shotgun, the extractor consists of a plunger that engages the case rim.

extractor hook The clawlike member that engages the case rim to withdraw the cartridge or case from the chamber. It is that portion of an extractor that grasps the case for withdrawal.

extra-full choke See FULL CHOKE.

extreme spread See GROUP.

extruded primer A primer that protrudes from the primer pocket above the face of the case head. It is caused by, and indicates, excessive headspace between cartridge and rifle chamber. (See HEADSPACE; PRIMER.)

eyepiece The lens assembly or housing nearest the eye in a microscope, binocular, riflescope, or other optical instrument. The external eyepiece holds the ocular lens. Its configuration is important to the shooter because sharp edges could injure the eye if the firearm recoils hard enough and the shooter's head is held too far forward. (See TELESCOPIC SIGHTS.)

eye relief The greatest distance between the eye and the eyepiece of a telescopic sight at which a full field of view can be seen.

This primer has cratered, or flowed, around the firing pin because of excessive pressure.

The pencil is touching the edge of the extractor, a spring loaded hook that grips the rim of a cartridge case and pulls it out of the chamber after firing.

The proper eye relief for a centerfire rifle and appropriate scope is 3 to 4 inches. Some specially designed scopes allow even more.

Fabbri, Armi (company) Ivo Fabbri, with years of experience as a barrelmaker and a machine tool designer, went into business as a gunmaker in Brescia in 1964. Within months the unusually high quality of his break-open double-barreled shotguns became noted in the shooting world—particularly in the expensive European sport of live bird shooting, where very fast handling and uniform, nearly perfect patterns are mandatory.

Fabbri's guns met those difficult requirements, but at considerable expense. From the beginning, Fabbri doubles sold for at least twice the price of comparable guns.

Fabbri guns take a long time to make, longer by far than others of near-equal quality. Fabbri believes strongly that barrel quality is of supreme importance, with a completely reliable single trigger next in line. Fabbri barrels enter the shop as rough undrilled forgings in chopper lump form—that is, the pendant bits of steel, which will later become the locking area, are forged integrally with the barrels. These rough steel bars are then slowly drilled, reamed, honed, and polished internally, during which time the tubes are externally lathe turned progressively to final form. At frequent intervals these barrels are closely inspected, measured, and remeasured. At an early stage the barrels are magna-fluxed to guard against flaws or cracks, and the rejection rate is quite high at this point.

When finished, Fabbri barrels are of astonishingly uniform wall thickness throughout; measuring any point on their tapered length reveals an out-of-roundness of no more than a few ten thousandths of an inch.

All metal components (except raw barrels) of a Fabbri gun are made in the shop; only the stock and the engraving are done outside. The action-to-be enters the shop as a solid steel billet; the subsequent drilling, machining, and finishing are done by Fabbri artisans.

The action of the much favored Fabbri over/under gun follows closely the low-profile action system developed by Boss of London. Rather than having the standard hinge pin and under-barrel bolting, Boss uses trunnions attached to the action wall's interior, these receiving short stub sections lying alongside the lower barrel. This results in a decrease in height of the action, making the gun handier. Fabbri uses essentially the same design, but instead of screw-fastening the trunnions he forms them integrally with the action walls. He invented and built a milling tool to accomplish this difficult job.

Today, a Fabbri sold in Italy will cost about $10,000, the exact price depending on wood quality and engraving. However, the firm is some three years behind on deliveries, and the state of the market, inflation included, at the time the gun is ready will determine its cost. (See BOX PIGEON SHOOTING; CUSTOM GUNS.)

Fabrique Nationale D'Armes de Guerre The National Manufactory of Martial Arms, familiarly abbreviated to FN, is a very large arms company with facilities at Liège and Herstal in Belgium. It was founded in 1889 and at first manufactured Mauser-type rifles for the Belgian Army; later the company manufactured many other military rifles and machine guns as well as handguns, sporting rifles, and semiautomatic shotguns.

The American arms designer John M. Browning was long known as "Le Maitre" in Liège and Herstal because of his intimate connection with FN. Many of his Automatic Pistols were manufactured by FN under license, and his long recoil semiautomatic shotgun was and is made by this company. Another Browning design, the famous Browning Automatic Rifle (BAR), was also manufactured by FN for the European military market. (The BAR was also manufactured by American plants and used by the U.S. Army.)

FN also has an intimate connection with Germany. The company manufactured Mauser rifles of various patterns for many years. This culminated in production of a civilian version of the famous Mauser 98 bolt-action rifle, perhaps the most used bolt-action design ever developed. The design, however, calls for expensive and complex machining, and the Germans abandoned manufacture of this very durable and accurate rifle. FN still produces a slightly altered version for the civilian market, and it has been imported into the United States for many years. It has been produced in a wide variety of American, English, and Continental calibers and in several quality grades.

Current FN production is heavily committed to military weapons for various NATO countries, with one factory in South Carolina. (See BROWNING, JOHN M.)

"fair" (condition)   See GUN CONDITION.

falling block   A breechblock that moves vertically in a receiver mortise. The block is usually operated by a lever that is often integral with the trigger guard. When the lever is manipulated, the block drops into a well within the receiver to expose the chamber. (See BREECHBLOCK; FALLING BLOCK ACTION.)

falling block action   A kind of basic firearm action that consists of a breechblock that moves vertically in a receiver mortise, hence the name. The block is usually operated by a lever, which is often integral with the trigger guard. When the lever is manipulated the breechblock drops into a well within the receiver to expose the chamber.

The falling block action was popular in early cartridge rifles such as the Farquharson, Winchester, Stevens, Ballard, and Sharps-Borchardt. There were also a number of shotguns that utilized this action type. After lying dormant for a number of years, the falling block action has been revived in the form of the Ruger and Browning single-shot centerfire rifles, and in the reintroduction of the Stevens Favorite .22 rimfire. (See BREECHBLOCK; FARQUHARSON ACTION.)

false muzzle   An extension of the barrel, attached to the muzzle with the aid of pins for alignment. Its purpose is to facilitate loading from the muzzle, and it is usually associated with target muzzleloaders.

A false muzzle is usually a cut off barrel section that sometimes is tapered internally to reduce bullet deformation upon loading; it also protects the rifling at the muzzle origin. False muzzles are used only for loading and must be removed for firing. (See MUZZLELOADER.)

Famars, Armi (company)   Famars is an acronym for Fabbrica Armi Mario Abbiatico and Remo Salvinelli. Abbiatico manages and directs the business affairs of this 23-year-old company of gunmakers, and Salvinelli is the top craftsman who supervises the work force. Both men were trained as gunmakers in their youth, and Abbiatico, who is the firm's principal designer, spent some time learning the art of the engraver.

The mainstay of the Famars line is a quite conventional side-by-side gun, but its superb quality and matchless form were quickly recognized by discerning shooters and, soon after, by collectors.

Several years ago Famars introduced Abbiatico's idea of what a modern external hammer double gun should be. Called the Castore 270, this classically styled sidelock gun has ejectors and is self-cocking. The early Castores had a minimum of engraving—just enough to accent the gleaming surfaces of the chaste, unadorned Castore lock plates. Handsomely done in all respects, they come up to the shoulder with the balance and handling of a "best gun."

Later, Abbiatico produced a four-barrel 28-gauge gun. This *tour de force* has outside hammers for the top pair of tubes, but the barrels below are fired by internal strikers. A single trigger fires the four barrels in fixed succession—left top, right top, left bottom, right bottom. However, if the external hammers are not cocked the lower barrels fire in the usual order.

Famars recently exhibited in London two small-frame over/unders in 28 and .410; but as with all Famars orders these days, a wait of a year or more is normal. Famars has been largely responsible for the emergence in recent years of several master engravers, notably Angelo Galeazzi and Firmo Fracassi—both great workers in the difficult *bulino* technique. Abbiatico has also cowritten (with G. Lupi and F. Vaccari) a book on gun engraving entitled: *Grandi Incisioni su Armi d'Oggi* or, in English, *Great Gun Engraving Today.*

fanning   A technique of firing a single-action revolver with maximum speed. Most typically it is done as follows: A right-handed shooter draws his revolver, holding it level at about waist height, with the elbow of the right arm braced against the body, and pointing rather than aiming the gun. The first

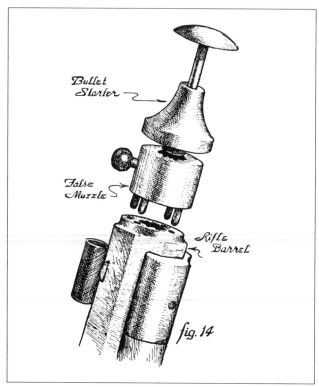

The false muzzle, along with its bullet starter, was employed on target rifles to prevent wear at the muzzle, which would ruin accuracy.

shot is fired by pulling back the trigger, then thumbing back and releasing the hammer. For subsequent shots, the hammer is struck backward and released by the outer edge of the left hand while the trigger remains held in the rearward position.

Using this technique, a skilled shooter can fire five shots in less than two seconds, but with minimal accuracy. Fanning was purported to have been a common technique among gunfighters of the Old West, but few reliable records of its use are in existence. (See REVOLVER.)

Farquharson action A kind of falling block single-shot rifle action. It was patented by John Farquharson in 1872 and was later manufactured by various English firms including Gibbs, Webley, Bland, and Westley Richards.

The Farquharson is an extremely strong action with a massive breechblock and recess. Original guns in good condition are desirable collector items. The Gibbs version is by far the most common.

Many of these actions have been rebarreled for use with modern big-game cartridges. The rifle's

hammer is enclosed and strikes a firing pin that angles steeply upward to the primer. The rifle's underlever wraps around the trigger guard.

Some features of the Ruger Number One single-shot action were derived from the older Farquharson. (See FALLING BLOCK ACTION; SINGLE-SHOT ACTION.)

farsightedness See HYPEROPIA.

fast draw A term used to describe the drawing of a handgun from its holster and firing with maximum speed, usually in a combat situation or in competition designed to simulate combat. A uniquely American skill, the fast draw had its origin in the Old West, although it was never employed with the frequency that Western lore would have. The favored gun for this pursuit was the Colt Single Action Army, a revolver that, through motion pictures and television, has practically become synonymous with the term.

Since the advent of sophisticated electronic timing equipment in the 1920s, shooters have measured

Jeff Cooper, a leading authority on combat shooting, demonstrates a fast-draw technique that is used when there is no time to aim the gun. The gun is jerked clear of the holster, and, as it clears, the body leans back to bring it into line.

their speed against electronically controlled stopwatches, and organized competitions have taken place to determine the "fastest gun."

Today, numerous law enforcement agencies teach the fast draw to their officers, and issue special holsters that permit a fast draw as standard equipment.

Fecker scope J. W. Fecker obtained his early training in Europe and after immigrating to America, worked at Bausch & Lomb in Rochester, New York. Ads in *Arms and The Man* show that he was in business in Cleveland, Ohio, about 1921, manufacturing both rifle telescopes and spotting scopes. The business was later moved to Pittsburgh, Pennsylvania. Fecker died in 1945, but the business continued until 1960.

The typical Fecker riflescope was of target type; using three-point suspension, micrometer, and mounts; a ¾-inch tube; and objective lenses of appropriate sizes to match the magnification. Fecker is credited with the introduction of high-grade, large objective, target-type telescopes to the United States. His scopes were unusual in that focusing was not accomplished by moving the objective lens, but by moving the erector lens assembly in the middle of the tube. (See TELESCOPIC SIGHTS.)

Federal Cartridge Corporation In 1916, the Federal Cartridge and Machinery Company was established in Anoka, Minnesota. The company soon folded and the facilities sat idle until 1922, when Charles L. Horn reorganized the business. The company name was changed, and Horn became the managing general partner of the Federal Cartridge Company. By late 1922, the new firm was selling shotgun shells, and in 1924, rimfire .22s were added to the line.

In 1941, the government contracted with Federal to build and operate a government-owned facility for the purpose of manufacturing military small arms ammunition. The plant, located in Brighton, Minnesota, and now known as the Twin Cities Army Ammunition Plant, was operated by Federal through World War II, the Korean War, and the Vietnam War. During this time, the sporting ammunitions branch of Federal was also enlarging its production. In 1963, the company introduced its brand of centerfire rifle and pistol cartridges to the market, and in 1988 it began importing ammunition loaded by the Swedish firm of Norma Projektilfabrik AB.

feed The process of transferring cartridges to the chamber, generally from a magazine. Also, the system employed for this process in a particular firearm.

Feed may be accomplished either manually as in a single-shot, or mechanically as in a repeating mechanism.

feeding guide Means for guiding cartridges smoothly into the chamber. It may consist of a portion of the magazine, receiver, or barrel.

feed ramp That part, integral with or adjacent to the breech of a gun, that guides cartridges from the magazine into the chamber. Generally it is a sloped and slightly concave surface leading from the upper front of the magazine to the chamber.

Feinwerkbau (company) Feinwerkbau Westinger & Altenburger G.m.b.H. Oberndorf am Neckar, West Germany. In English, Feinwerkbau means precision products. Westinger and Altenburger are family names, and G.m.b.H. is an abbreviation for one form of German corporation. Oberndorf is the armsmaking center made famous by Mauser. Feinwerkbau specializes in finely designed and made air rifles and air pistols for match competition, a quite popular sport in Europe and of growing importance in America.

After World War II, German manufacture of firearms was forbidden by the occupying powers, and a few arms firms turned their attention to air-powered arms. Much progress was made in a few short years, and German air rifles and pistols soon began to win most matches. The Feinwerkbau 300 Match Rifle is a single-shot .177-caliber pellet gun (does not fire round BBs). It develops 575 feet per second muzzle velocity. Barrel and receiver recoil together independently of the stock, completely eliminating felt recoil. In other words, the functioning parts of the air rifle work as completely independent units, recoiling the same distance and in exactly the same plane from shot to shot. If human error is absent, or almost so, the shooter is assured of consistency in placement of his shots on target. The Feinwerkbau 200 is almost the same as the 300, but it has a slight recoil effect. It develops 640 fps at the muzzle. With such high velocities, trajectory is very flat at competition ranges.

This company's air pistols are equal in quality to their rifles. The Model 65 is favored by many World Shooting Championship record holders. It is imported to the United States by Beeman Precision Airguns, Santa Rosa, California. (See AIR GUN.)

Ferguson Colonel Patrick (1744–1780) Ferguson, who served with the 70th Regiment of the British forces in the Revolutionary War, invented a breechloading rifle that saw limited use during that conflict. The action had a threaded plug, attached to the trigger guard, that engaged a vertically threaded section in the breech end of the barrel.

This idea was not new, but Ferguson greatly improved upon it by using fast threads so that the plug could be dropped with only one clockwise rotation of the trigger guard. Moreover, the plug was never detached from the barrel, and one counterclockwise turn easily returned it to firing position. In loading, the plug was lowered and the barrel tipped slightly downward. The ball was first dropped into the breech cavity where it rolled to a stop after striking the lands in the barrel rifling. The rest of the breech cavity was then filled with powder and the plug closed. These rifles were very easy to fire rapidly (for those times).

Although the Ferguson rifle was greatly superior to any rifle of its time, the British never capitalized on it. Colonel Ferguson was killed on October 7, 1780, while serving under Sir Henry Clinton in the Battle of King's Mountain in South Carolina. (See BREECHLOADER.)

ferrule   See RAMROD THIMBLES.

fiberglass floc   A fibrous material used primarily in action bedding compounds to thicken the liquid substance. The floc, or floccule, prevents the compound from running out of the action and allows easier, less messy manipulation of the substance until it hardens.

Fiberglass floc usually consists of extremely fine filaments of glass. (See BEDDING.)

fiddleback   Fiddleback is the kind of grain found in some individual pieces of wood used in gunstocks. The term is taken from the wood used in the backs of violins. It is actually a small wave in the grain structure that runs crosswise to the general grain direction, causing a streak of contrasting color

This wood pattern takes its name from that frequently seen in the maple used in violins. This walnut stock shows the typical vertical stripes of the fiddleback pattern.

that has a flamelike appearance under certain light conditions. (See STOCK WOODS.)

Field & Stream   Founded in St. Paul, Minnesota as *Northwestern Field & Stream* in 1895, *Field & Stream* magazine adopted its present title in 1898, the year it moved its offices to New York City, where it is presently published.

Over the years, *Field & Stream* established a dual tradition of featuring leading writers in its pages and of acting as an advocate of conservation. Among the writers of note who have appeared in its pages are Zane Grey, Erle Stanley Gardner, Ben Hecht, Theodore Roosevelt, Robert Ruark, and Corey Ford.

Pursuant to its role in conservation, the magazine has advocated such steps as season limitations on, and an end to the sale of, wild game; federal protection of migratory birds; the creation of the duck stamp; and the passage of the Game Refuge Bill. *Field & Stream* was also instrumental in the founding of Ducks Unlimited and the National Shooting Sports Foundation. (See DUCKS UNLIMITED; NATIONAL SHOOTING SPORTS FOUNDATION [NSSF].)

field gun   A term applied to any shotgun not specifically intended for waterfowl hunting or clay target shooting. Field guns are typically lightweight, short-barreled, open-bored guns for use on flying game birds where the average shot will be from 20 to 35 yards.

field load   Shotgun ammunition intended for use in open-bored field guns. The components used in field loads are less expensive than those used in high-grade target and waterfowl loads. Field loads deliver adequate performance at moderate ranges where the more expensive premium ammunition offers no advantage.

field of view   The area seen through a telescopic sight or binocular at a given distance when the eye is positioned at optimum eye relief. Field of view decreases as the magnification of the scope increases. For instance, a 2½X scope may have a 43-foot field of view at 100 yards while a 6X scope might only have a 20-foot field of view at the same distance. (See EYE RELIEF; MAGNIFICATION.)

figure-8 sight picture   See MIDDLE SIGHT.

filler (for metallic cartridges)   Handloads with reduced smokeless powder charges frequently end up with considerable vacant space in the cartridge case. A fibrous filler material may be used to take up space between the powder charge and the base of the bullet. This ensures that the powder charge is always in the bottom of the case and contributes to positive and uniform ignition from shot to shot.

filler (for shotshells) Some commercial shotshell loads make use of a special filler material dispersed among the shot pellets. This filler takes up the empty space between the round pellets. The purpose of the filler is to absorb some of the crushing force applied to the shot charge as it moves down the barrel and is further confined in passing through the choke at the muzzled end. This tends to lessen the deformation of the individual pellets, permitting truer flight and denser shot patterns, and enhancing the fluidity of the ejecta mass.

fine bead See BEADS, FINE AND COARSE.

finger lever See OPERATING LEVER.

finger rail The wide groove in the fore-end of a rifle or shotgun is known as the finger rail. Its purpose to to give the shooter's hand a better purchase.

finish See FIT AND FINISH.

finisher See CHAMBER REAMER.

firearm A device designed to expel a projectile or projectiles by the use of a chemical propellant that provides high-pressure energy. The propellant normally used is either smokeless or black powder and is ignited by use of a primer, thereby creating pressure behind the projectile by rapidly expanding gas.

Firearms Act of 1934 This act provided for a federal tax to be applied to such weapons as machine guns, submachine guns, sawed-off shotguns, silencers, pen guns, etc. It was derived from the power of the federal government to regulate interstate and foreign commerce and also from the taxing power of the federal government.

This act was intended to control these items through the imposition of a tax on persons engaged in the business of importing, manufacturing or dealing in such arms. In addition, a transfer tax was assessed each time such a piece was sold or transferred. For instance, a tax of $200 was levied upon the machine gun, no matter whether it was a purchase or a gift.

Furthermore, in order to enforce payment of these transfer taxes, all weapons covered by the act were required to be registered individually by serial number and description. Heavy penalties were provided for the possession of an unregistered machine gun.

This act marked the beginning of a serious na-

tional controversy over the right of a law-abiding citizen to keep and bear arms.

The act, in its original form, included pistols and revolvers, but because of a storm of protests, these were removed to ensure passage. The NFA 1934 was patterned after the previously enacted Harrison Narcotics Act, which was based upon the taxing power of the federal government and which had already been court tested as to its constitutionality.

Such an indirect approach in controlling the misuse of such firearms was necessary in the opinion of the then attorney general, Homer S. Cummings, because of two problems. First, there was no constitutional grant of police powers to the federal government, and secondly, there was the Second Amendment to the Constitution, combined with the appropriateness of machine guns to a militia.

Charles V. Imlay of the National Conference of Commissioners on Uniform Laws criticized the fact that the NFA 1934 was a mere contrivance to cloak a federal gun registration law with some semblance of constitutionality. Thirty-two years later, Imlay was proved correct. On January 29, 1968, in Haynes vs. United States, the U.S. Supreme Court invalidated the most important part of the National Firearms Act of 1934 on the grounds that it violated the constitutional guarantee of the Fifth Amendment against the self-incrimination to which a criminal would be exposed by forcing him to register his submachine gun.

fire forming A method of forming case bodies to fit a chamber of larger body dimensions. This is usually done when a cartridge is made into an "improved" version, where the body is expanded to provide more powder capacity than the original but the other dimensions are left the same or with a steeper shoulder angle. The Improved .30/06 is an example, and factory .300 H&H ammunition can be fired in the chamber of the .300 Weatherby to reform cases.

Cases can be fire formed by slightly reducing full-power charges and using bullets of the correct diameter, or with bullets of smaller diameter if the bore of the new cartridge is larger. Flour, fine-grained cereal, or plugs of rolled paper or wax can also be used with the correct charge of fast-burning powders. (See CASE FORMING.)

fire hole A fire hole, also referred to as a touch hole, is used in muzzleloading guns and is a small hole through the breech of the arm that runs from the ignition source to the powder chamber; in early muzzleloaders, a fuse led through the fire hole and was ingnited by hand with a match.

In arms using percussion caps, the hollow nipple

over which the cap fits forms part of the hole, with the hole drilled in the breech continuing on to connect the powder chamber with the igniting cap. (See MATCHLOCK.)

firelock   See MATCHLOCK; MUZZLELOADER.

firing line   At a target range, that line along which shooters are placed for firing. It is an imaginary line through the several firing points.

firing pin   The firing pin is the device used to ignite the primer by causing an indentation in the primer cup that crushes the priming compound between the cup and the primer anvil.

The firing pin has many forms. In bolt-action rifles it is often an integral part of the striker, or a jointed part of the striker, that is spring activated and held at ready by the sear until the trigger is pulled to release it. In some older guns, especially revolvers, it is part of the external hammer. In most lever-action rifles and modern revolvers, the firing pin is separate from the hammer and is activated when the hammer strikes it. Many firing pins of this type are known as rebounding firing pins; they have a spring that causes them to retract to the rear as soon as the pressure exerted by the hammer is released. Others are of the "floating" type and are free to move to the rear when the hammer is not in contact, but are not forced to do so, by spring tension. Many shotguns have used this firing pin system.

Many modern revolvers have a safety lever that is lifted between the hammer and the firing pin only while the trigger is held in the release position. If the hammer is accidentally dropped while the trigger is not in the fire position, it contacts the frame instead of the firing pin.

firing pin protrusion   The distance the firing pin tip extends beyond the bolt face. Some protrusion is required to ensure positive ignition, but it must not be too much or the primer cup is likely to be pierced.

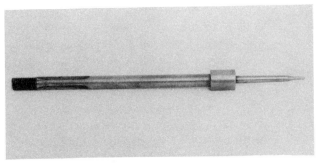

This is a rifle firing pin. It is driven by a powerful coil spring that fits around it.

firing point   At a target range, the point from which the gun is fired. It may consist of a bench for shooting from a rest position or simply a numbered location for a position shooter.

fishtail wind   A wind that blows first in one direction and then another, making it very difficult to estimate the potential drift of a bullet.

fit   See GUN FIT.

fit and finish   A term referring to the workmanship of a gun. More specifically, it refers to the fitting of metal to wood, and to the quality of the finish of wood and metal surfaces.

five-in-one blank   A specific kind of blank cartridge. It is called the "five-in-one" because it can be fired in five different arms: the .38/40 and .44/40 rifles, and the .38/40, .44/40, and .45 Colt revolvers. Another name is "movie blank," because of its common use in filmmaking. It is also sometimes designated "5 in 1." (See BLANK CARTRIDGE.)

flake powder   The term "flake" refers to the physical shape of the propellant grains, as opposed to spherical, granular, or extruded. The earliest smokeless propellant was rolled into sheets and then cut into small pieces or flakes. Flake powder is still used in some European cartridges. (See SMOKELESS POWDER.)

flange (British)   In British terminology, flanged refers to a rimmed cartridge case. British cartridge nomenclature sometimes includes this term, as in ".450/3¼ Flanged." The flange, or rim, is used for headspacing the cartridge, stopping the forward movement of the cartridge as it enters the chamber and to allow ample purchase for the gun's extractor.

flange (U.S.)   A projecting or raised edge, rim, ring, or collar on a shaft, pipe, machine housing, etc. It is cast or formed to provide additional strength, stiffness, or supporting area, to attach other objects to, or to allow easier insertion. A cartridge case mouth is sometimes belled to facilitate bullet insertion, particularly for cast bullets. This is accomplished by forcing the relatively soft ductile brass case mouth against a tapered expander ball, causing the brass to form outwardly and increasing case mouth diameter.

flash hole   A small hole in a cartridge case or shotshell case located in the bottom of the primer pocket and extending through the web into the powder reservoir. The flash from the primer passes through this small hole to enter and ignite the powder charge.

Its function is similar to the touch hole in a flintlock gun. (See FIRE HOLE; PRIMER FLASH.)

flash tube   See FRONTAL IGNITION.

flats   See BARREL FLATS.

flat shooting   A term applied to high-velocity cartridges that deliver a low bullet-trajectory arc. The velocity at which the bullet leaves the muzzle does not automatically make the cartridge a flat-shooting round in itself. The bullet must also have good ballistic form, that is, streamlined shape, combined with good sectional density to give it a high ballistic coefficient. This reduces air resistance and allows high-velocity retention, which decreases the bullet's time of flight to the target, making for less bullet drop. (See BALLISTIC COEFFICIENT; BULLET VELOCITY; EXTERIOR BALLISTICS.)

flat spring   A spring, in the mechanical sense, is a resilient member used to store, and then to release, energy. Cocking the hammer of a firearm stores energy in the hammer spring, which is released to do work by pulling the trigger.

A flat spring is made from flat metal, usually spring tempered steel, with a length several to many times its width and a width usually many times its thickness. When well designed, it is tapered from the fixed end in both width and thickness. A flat spring may be gently curved for space or functional reasons.

Today, flat springs are used in relatively few firearms; most notably, in the locks of European double shotguns and in some revolvers such as the Smith & Wesson. (See COIL SPRING.)

flier   In target shooting, especially rifle competitions, a flier is a shot that misses the scoring rings of the target completely. The term also describes a deformed shot pellet that flies completely outside the pattern.

flinch   Any involuntary movement or jerk of the hand or trigger finger, or even the arm, at the time the shot is fired. In mild cases of flinching, the shooter may jerk the trigger with the trigger finger instead of squeezing it. Very often in these cases the shooter does not even realize he is flinching, and the shot may land quite close to where it is intended to go. The worst form of flinching is when the shooter closes both eyes and yanks on the whole firearm with everything from the trigger finger to the shoulder with a violent jerk of the head and neck at the same time. Such shots may land a yard or more away from the target even at close range. Individual

flinching habits may run anywhere between these two extremes.

The main cause of flinching is the fear of recoil and/or the noise of firing. The anticipation of the jar of recoil or the noise is telegraphed from the brain to the muscular system and is reflected in the sudden tightening and jerking of the parts of the body involved.

To avoid flinching by the novice shooter, a great deal of shooting should be done with the .22 rimfire before shooting cartridges that develop even mild recoil. Going back to this same cartridge and doing a great deal of shooting will also often cure bad cases of "flinchitis" among experienced shooters.

flint   In a flintlock mechanism the piece of stone that strikes the steel frizzen to produce a shower of sparks, thus igniting the priming charge and, subsequently, the main charge in the barrel. The ability of a lock to produce an adequate shower of sparks, aimed in the right direction, is partially dependent on the shape and quality of the flint.

Flints were once made by hand from the hard quartz known as "flint" as it appeared in nature. Today, however, flints are sometimes cut from agate or Arkansas stone. (See FLINTLOCK; FRIZZEN.)

flintlock   Evolving in about 1600, and quite probably the design of French inventor Martin le Bourgeoys, the flintlock was an enormously successful system of firearms ignition, remaining in worldwide use for nearly 250 years.

The flintlock was not created from whole cloth; rather, it was a refinement of existing locks. The basic action prior to the flintlock was the snaphaunce, of which there were a number of variations. Minor differences aside, the snaphaunce utilized a piece of flint held in the jaws of a cock, or hammer. When the trigger was pulled, the cock snapped for-

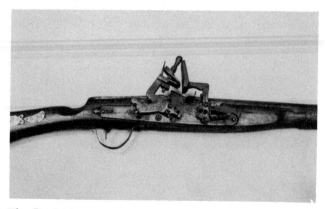

The flintlock, in its nearly 300 years of common use, was made with varying degrees of sophistication. This is a very crude example.

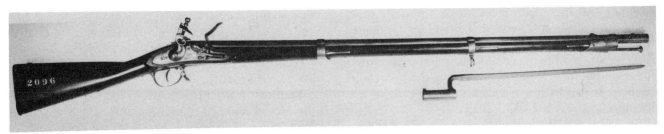

This typical military flintlock is the U.S. Model of 1816. It weighs about 9½ pounds and fires a .69-caliber ball. It is a smoothbore, with a lock patterned after the French Model of 1777.

ward, striking the flint against a striking plate, or steel. The resulting shower of sparks fell into a pan, igniting the priming powder in the pan, and the flame from the pan ran through a hole into the barrel, igniting the main charge.

In some variations of this system, the steel was separate from the cover of the priming pan. The pan had to be opened by hand, prior to firing or an extra part had to be added to the lock mechanism to open the pan as the hammer fell. Some locks had one-piece steel-and-pan-cover arrangements that eliminated this fault, but that lacked a safety device to prevent the gun from firing accidentally when the hammer was cocked. Still others had external springs that were subject to damage.

Le Bourgeoys's design internalized all the springs,

The flintlock is a simple and enormously successful ignition system. It consists of a hammer, or dog, that contains a flint in screw-tightened jaws; a frizzen, or striking plate; a pan, in which the priming charge is placed; and a touch hole, through which the flame passes to the main charge in the barrel. This lock is shown in fired position, with the dog forward and the frizzen up.

adopted the one-piece steel/pan cover and, most important, created a sear that operated vertically instead of horizontally and that engaged a notched tumbler attached to the cock. This tumbler permitted the use of half-cock position whereby the gun could be held ready to fire with only a half-pull of the hammer to the full-cock position.

By 1700, the flintlock was virtually the standard form of firearms ignition and retained this distinction until the development of the percussion cap more than a century later. Some flintlock rifles were used as late as the opening stages of the Civil War, and many flintlocks continued in use in primitive parts of the world where percussion caps were unobtainable. (See MATCHLOCK; SNAPHAUNCE; WHEEL LOCK.)

flip   See BARREL FLIP.

floating barrel   A floating barrel is one that does not touch the forearm of a rifle's stock anywhere along the barrel channel from the receiver ring of the action forward. However, many floating barrels are bedded firmly for the first 1½ to 2 inches forward of the receiver ring, which tends to stiffen the support of the action and the rear of the barrel somewhat. A floating barrel is not affected by stock warping caused by changes in atmospheric conditions, and therefore holds the original point of bullet impact better than barrels that are not floated.

Floating rifle barrels is common practice among gun manufacturers, since it offers superior performance without the added cost of carefully bedding the fore-end. It is also employed by custom makers of target rifles and hunting arms. Here, cost is not a factor, but uniformity of bullet impact is paramount. (See STOCKMAKING.)

floating chamber   A design by David M. ("Carbine") Williams in which the firearm's chamber is in the form of a hollow piston fitting into the rear of the barrel. This piston is allowed to move axially a short distance, but is held in place by a lip and groove on one side.

The design was used to adapt the .30 Browning machine gun for practice with the .22 Long Rifle rimfire cartridge, by installing a .22 barrel, bolt, and feed mechanism. When the cartridge is fired, the chamber slides to the rear, exposing the front end of the chamber to the gas pressure in the bore. This provides the force necessary to operate the massive breech mechanism of the Browning. This allowed the use of far cheaper .22 ammunition in target practice, a prime consideration in light of the enormous number of cartridges expended in training.

Another adaptation of the Williams Floating Chamber was in the Colt Service Model Ace, a replica of the .45 Service Automatic using the .22 LR cartridge. The power developed through the floating chamber moved the slide with enough force to give a recoil effect similar to that experienced with the .45 Service cartridge.

Remington used the floating chamber principle in the Model 550 .22 semiautomatic rifle. This design made it possible to use .22 Short, .22 Long, and .22 Long Rifle regular velocity or high-speed cartridges interchangeably, without any changes or adjustments to the mechanism.

floating firing pin   A firing pin that is not an integral part of a hammer or striker, but is suspended in a bolt or breechblock by means of spring or by engagement with other parts of the firing mechanism. (See FIRING PIN.)

Flobert cartridge   See RIMFIRE VARIATIONS.

floorplate   A metal plate covering the bottom of the magazine in a bolt-action firearm. When a latch is released, the floorplate hinges downward, allowing the cartridges to drop into the shooter's hand. In many rifles, the magazine spring and the cartridge follower are attached to the floorplate. In the usual arrangement, the shooter opens the bolt and loads the magazine by pressing the cartridges into the magazine against spring pressure; but it is also possible to open the floorplate, turn the rifle upside down, and load the cartridges by placing them in the magazine, and then close the floorplate with the follower pressing on the last cartridge loaded.

Many cheaper bolt-action arms and military rifles have fixed floorplates that cannot be removed without tools. In these arms, the rifle is always loaded through the top with the bolt open, and it must be unloaded by working the bolt to feed each cartridge in turn into the firing chamber and then remove it. (See BOLT ACTION; FOLLOWER; MAGAZINE.)

fluid steel barrel   Joseph Whitworth of England, around 1880, discovered that barrel steel, when compressed during its fluid state, would result in a finished barrel that was stronger than one produced by other available methods. Barrels so manufactured were stamped "Fluid Steel." This process is now obsolete. (See BARREL MAKING.)

flush-seating   Flush-seating is accomplished by adjusting the bullet seating stem in the seating die so that the base of the bullet is flush with the base of the case neck. This seating depth is considered by many reloaders to be the optimum for best cartridge performance. (See HANDLOAD.)

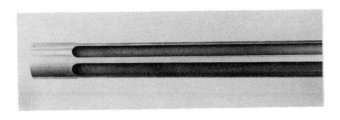

Fluting, or grooving, a rifle barrel lessens its weight without reducing its stiffness, and increases its cooling surface. This operation is performed almost entirely on target-rifle barrels.

fluted barrel Many rifle and pistol barrels have flutes, or rounded grooves, milled or shaped into them as a weight-saving measure. Fluting is often employed in large-barreled target arms in order to reduce weight while retaining the barrel's stiffness. (See BARREL MAKING.)

flux In connection with firearms, flux is any substance that will clean and facilitate the joining of metals. In the casting of metals, flux is a substance that causes impurities in bullet metal to rise to the surface so that they can be skimmed off as dross.

flyer In live bird shooting, the pigeons used are often referred to as flyers. (See LIVE PIGEON SHOOTING.)

focal length In a thin lens, approximately the distance from the center of the lens to the point at which light rays entering parallel to the axis are brought to focus at a point. In thick lenses, or lens systems composed of several lenses and/or elements, the term "equivalent focal length" is used, and it may be greater than the actual distance between the lens and the sharp image of a distant object. Thus, a 400mm lens on a camera may actually be much less than 400 millimeters in actual length.

focus (noun) The point at which light rays passing through a lens, or reflected from a concave mirror, are seen to converge. Also, the mechanism on an optical device that is adjusted to bring an image into focus.

focus (verb) To adjust a telescope, camera, or other such optical device so as to form a sharp image of the object being viewed.

folded crimp See SHOTSHELL CRIMP.

folding gun A firearm that folds up for compact storage and easy carrying. Almost all are break-action shotguns that hinge open in the normal manner, but in which the pivoting motion can be continued until the bottom of the barrel or barrels almost touches the toe of the stock. A few folding rifles have also been made.

With the barrel or barrels sawed off short, these guns are easily concealed, and none are currently offered on the American market because of various gun control laws. Folding guns are produced chiefly in Italy.

follower In repeating firearms equipped with a magazine and a magazine spring, this is the metal plate or plug at one end of the spring. With the magazine fully loaded, the spring pushes against the follower, which, in turn, pushes against the cartridges so that each one arrives at the proper position for insertion into the firing chamber.

In rifles, the follower is usually a metal plate shaped to conform to the shape of the cartridge and act as a cartridge platform. This is also true of some semiautomatic pistol magazines. In tubular magazines, the follower is a simple plastic or sheet-metal plug that contacts the bullet in the first cartridge loaded.

The follower is sometimes referred to as the magazine platform. (See MAGAZINE.)

follow through Follow through in shooting is analogous to follow through in golf or bowling. In shooting moving targets such as live or clay birds, most shotgunners come from behind and then swing ahead of the target in order to obtain the required lead before pulling the trigger. When a shooter follows through, he continues to move the gun in the proper plane even after he has fired. This is done to make absolutely sure that the shot has left the barrel properly before the shooter lowers his gun, and to impart smoothness and proper timing to the swing. (Dropping the gun's muzzle too early can and does cause misses.)

In shooting at a stationary target, mostly with rifles and handguns, the shooter tries to maintain the correct sight picture even after he has fired. Again, this is done in an attempt to ensure that the firearm remains in proper relationship with the target until after the bullet has left the barrel.

foot-pounds See BULLET ENERGY.

forcing cone The section in a shotgun or revolver barrel, just ahead of the chamber, in which the diameter is gradually reduced to that of the bore or lands. In shotguns, the forcing cone reduces the diameter from that of the chamber mouth to that of the bore. In revolvers, the diameter is reduced from that at the front of the chamber in the cylinder to that of the lands.

The basic function of the forcing cone is the same in both kinds of arms: in shotguns, to gradually compress the mass of pellets and prevent their deformation; in revolvers, to prevent deformation and stripping of the bullet and to permit it to align itself with the bore as it jumps from the cylinder upon firing. (See BORE DIAMETER; LAND.)

forearm   See FORE-END.

fore-end   The fore-end of a gun, also known as the forearm, is that part of the stock forward of the action. On most rifles, especially bolt actions, it is an integral part of the stock, but on the majority of lever and autoloading actions, and on all slide actions, it is separate. With the exception of a few bolt actions, the fore-end of a shotgun stock is separate from the buttstock. Its purpose is to afford a grip for one hand below the barrel or barrels to facilitate handling. (See RIFLE STOCK; SHOTGUN STOCK.)

fore-end hanger   A fore-end hanger is the device used to attach a shotgun's fore-end (or the fore-end of a rifle with a two-piece stock) to the bottom of the barrel. This can be done by a push-button device, a drop-down latch, or a screw attachment. (See FORE-END.)

fore-end latch   The mechanism used to hold the fore-end solidly in place on the barrel or barrels of a rifle or shotgun. While the fore-end of some guns of two-piece stock design is held in place on the barrel by a screw, nearly all guns that are readily dismantled into two pieces are equipped with a latch in the fore-end to quickly release it from the barrel. The wood of the fore-end is mounted on metal fittings that hold the latch, and the latch lever or button engages a matching stud or other projection on the bottom of the barrel. (See FORE-END.)

fore-end tension   One of the most important factors in the accuracy of a rifle is the uniformity with which its barrel vibrates from shot to shot. One method of achieving high uniformity is by inletting the fore-end of the stock so that it exerts a constant small upward pressure on the barrel. Usually, this pressure is applied by an inch-long section at the end of the forearm, and amounts to 5 or 6 pounds pressure. Such construction is commonly found only in custom rifles, since the care and expense required in carrying it out is considerable. (See FORE-END.)

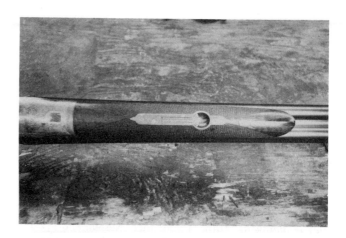

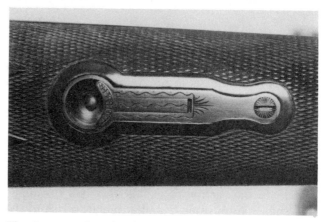

The Anson and Deeley fore-end latch has proved a highly effective design and has been used on all manner of break-action guns. In figure 1, it is employed on a British double-barrel shotgun; in figure 2, on an American single-barrel trap gun.

fore-end tip   A separate block or cap attached to the end of the fore-stock as a form of ornamentation was probably originated by the London gunmakers and dates from the early years of the 20th century. It is simply a piece of horn, plastic, contrasting wood, or metal cap attached to the fore-end of a rifle. Although horn has been used by British and Continental gunmakers, it is less than satisfactory because of its scarcity and instability and has given way to ebony as a favored material. Some stockmakers use other tropical hardwoods such as rosewood or plastics such as Bakelite. Older rifles often used metal caps.

Contrasting fore-end tips are attached by means of dowels and glue joints. They serve no functional purpose, being for decoration only. (See EBONY; FORE-END.)

foresight   See FRONT SIGHT.

form die   See FIRE FORMING.

form factor See COEFFICIENT OF FORM.

Forsyth, Alexander J. (1768–1843) Forsyth, a Scots minister, sportsman, and amateur chemist, patented the first percussion ignition system in 1807. Called the Scent-Bottle system, it was a gunlock mechanism in which fulminate of mercury was fed out of a magazine, then detonated by a hammer to ignite the main charge.

Until Forsyth's invention, all firearms had been detonated by a flame held outside the gun. The percussion system was quicker than the flintlock; it eliminated loose priming powder; and it led to the development of the metallic cartridge and smokeless powder. With the advent of the percussion cap, invented in 1814 by Joshua Shaw of Philadelphia, the percussion system of ignition made all other systems obsolete.

After securing his patents, Forsyth set up Alexander Forsyth & Co. in London to manufacture firearms employing his inventions. (See MERCURIC PRIMERS; PERCUSSION IGNITION.)

fouling shot Many barrels will place the first shot, when the barrel is clean and cold, at a different point of impact from subsequent shots fired after some powder has fouled the bore. Therefore most competitors in match shooting fire at least one "fouling shot"—if the rules allow—before firing for record, thus ensuring that all bullets will give the same point of impact.

fowling pieces The first true shotguns, as we know the term today. The earliest of these guns were made by the English and had bores of from .59-inch to 1½ inches in punt guns. Originally, fowling pieces had a heavy, wide butt, a flintlock ignition, and a single barrel 50 inches long with a heavy breec hat was designed to handle heavy loads. After small shot came into use, barrels became shorter, and by 1800 the long barrel had disappeared.

By the mid-1800s, barrels had been shortened to 30 or 32 inches, bore sizes had decreased, and the most advanced gunsmiths such as the Manton brothers of England were producing shotguns in essentially the modern form. (See FLINTLOCK; PUNT GUN; SHOTGUN.)

Fox, A. H. (company) Fox shotguns were manufactured by the A. H. Fox Gun Co. of Philadelphia, Pennsylvania, from 1903 until 1930. This boxlock design, like most American double-barrel guns of good quality, was produced in a number of grades. The plainest was the Sterlingworth; it was made in field grade as well as in Skeet, Upland, and Deluxe models. Above the Sterlingworth were seven ascending grades, commencing with Grade A and culminating with Grade FE. These models featured superior workmanship, select wood, engraving, and fancy checkering. In addition, a single-barrel trap gun was produced in four grades ranging from JE to ME.

In 1930, Fox was taken over by Savage Arms, then of Utica, New York (now of Westfield, Massachusetts). Savage ceased production of the higher grades and concentrated solely on the manufacture of economy models, which continue in production today.

Today, the high-grade Philadelphia Fox shotguns are of considerable value, especially the 20-gauge guns, which are priced up to 75 percent higher than comparable models in 12 and 16 gauge.

Franchi, Luigi (company) Established in 1868 in Brescia, Italy, Franchi manufactures both repeating and double-barrel shotguns of very high quality. Among its most notable guns are the Model 530 Trap, an autoloader of very advanced design that is supplied with interchangeable chokes and a target-grade trigger. Perhaps more distinguished is the Imperiale Monte Carlo Extra, a Holland & Holland-derived double shotgun that is available on custom order only and that presently sells for about $20,000.

Franchi guns have been imported to the United States since the 1950s by Stoeger.

Francotte (company) The Auguste Francotte Company of Liège, Belgium, made revolvers of many different kinds, as well as a semiautomatic pistol. Most Francotte revolvers were heavy military-style weapons; they included one very successful model patterned on the Lefaucheux pinfire, as well as hinged-frame centerfire types.

The original company went out of business during the German occupation of Belgium in World War I. A successor organization using the name A. Francotte began to make side-by-side shotguns after the war, and later the firm also made over/under shotguns. The side-by-sides were patterned on the finest English models and were made in all gauges; they are remarkable for a Greener cross-bolt that is entirely concealed within the standing breech. All Francotte shotguns were of the finest quality, and many were custom built on special order. Elaborate engraving was available. These guns were imported into the United States by Abercrombie & Fitch, but they are no longer made. Since manufacture ceased in the mid-1970s, prices for secondhand Francotte shotguns have steadily increased. (See GREENER CROSS-BOLT.)

frangible ball A .30/06 military cartridge developed during World War II for training aircraft gunners. It may be identified by the green tip and white band on the bullet. The bullet was made of powdered Bakelite and powdered lead in equal quantities, pressed into form, and was designed to break up on contact with the aluminum skin of an aircraft without doing damage. The bullet weighed about 108 grains and was given a muzzle velocity of about 1,360 feet per second. Guns had to be modified to use this low-power ammuntion. Many years ago, several firms offered .22 rimfire cartridges loaded with frangible ball for gallery shooting.

frangible top wad Before the advent of plastic shells, which employ a pie crimp, roll-crimp paper shotshells made by Federal Cartridge were equipped with frangible top wads, also called end wads, that were designed to disintegrate upon firing. This, it was thought, would lead to a more even pattern, as the wad would not interfere with the flight of the shot as it left the muzzle. (See SHOTSHELL CRIMP.)

Frankford Arsenal (FA) Located on Frankford Creek, about a quarter of a mile from the Delaware River, in Philadelphia, Pennsylvania, the Frankford Arsenal got its start as a center for ordnance activities on August 5, 1814, when Colonel Decius Wadsworth, then commissary general for ordnance, ordered one Lieutenant Baker "to establish and superintend the 'Laboratory' for providing and supplying of ordnance stores of all kinds."

The site was originally chosen for its access to navigable waters and was a purchase, storage, and distribution center. Land amounting to a bit more than 20 acres was purchased in 1816, and construction of the original six stone buildings and two workshops was completed in 1832. Between then and September 30, 1977, when Frankford Arsenal was closed, its size increased to 228 buildings and 58 storage facilities, covering 110 acres. The first power driven machinery was installed in 1853.

Although early documents refer to a "laboratory," laboratory work as generally understood did not begin until 1864, when experimental tests of the effects of powder explosions on the iron frameworks of buildings were conducted. Important contributions of the Laidley Laboratory, built in 1868, included the development of extruded, perforated, smokeless propellant powder grain, still in use today, and the development of progressive burning smokeless powder, patented in 1906.

During its active years, Frankford was the United States center for the development of explosives, small arms and major caliber ammunition, gauges, precision optical equipment (panoramic and telescopic sights as well as rangefinding equipment), fire control instruments, and fuses for artillery, missiles, and rockets, in a range from the simple developments of the early 1900s to the most complicated and sophisticated computer-controlled mechanisms of the guided missile age.

To the rifle and pistol shooter, the name Frankford Arsenal is synonymous with small arms ammunition, particularly of the match type, made for competitive target shooting. During the Spanish American War, FA produced about 37,000,000 rounds annually. This increased to 60,000,000 rounds just prior to World War I, and reached the staggering total of 8,000,000 rounds per *day* during World War II. (All of these figures are for service ammunition.)

For the rifle shooter and pistol shooter, the FA headstamp on .45, .30, or 7.72 NATO Match, National Match, or International Match ammunition meant the best in accuracy and reliability. The famous "tin can" .30/06 ammunition (so called because the bullet was tin plated to reduce metal fouling in the barrel) was developed at Frankford in 1921 and made almost a clean sweep of new records at the national matches at Camp Perry that year. The development, in 1922, of the 172-grain M1 boattail bullet, and its evolution in the following two or three years produced match ammunition giving a mean radius of 2.3 inches at 600 yards, the equivalent of 10 shot groups averaging 6 to 8 inches extreme spread at this range. Mass-produced match ammunition of current manufacture will not group substantially better than this.

Fraser, Daniel (1848–1901) The most famous of the Fraser gunmakers, he was the son of Lachlan Fraser, a master coach builder. Fraser worked for the rifle maker Alexander Henry until 1873, when he set up in business on his own in Edinburgh, Scotland.

His trade label reads "Dan'l Fraser & Co., Patentees and Manufacturers of Hammerless Guns and Telescopic Rifles," and states that he could also supply Express double, rook, roe, and rabbit rifles.

Fraser, a noted marksman, was holder of several patents, notably one for a falling block single-shot rifle, and another for a match rifle made with two widely separated triggers—one for prone shooting, the other for back-position shooting.

Daniel Fraser died in 1901, and his older brother Donald carried on the firm until it went into liquidation in 1917.

freebore The term freebore refers to the short portion of the barrel ahead of the throat in which the rifling has been cut away, leaving the bore smooth.

Freebore is measured in two different ways. With

the chamber measuring method, freebore is the distance between the forward end of the chamber neck and the rear of the lands, or leade. What this actually amounts to is the length of the throat, and some rifle manufacturers like Weatherby prefer to call it "long throating." The second method measures the distance between the forward end of the bearing surface of the bullet and the rear of the lands and is more accurately termed the free travel of the bullet rather than the freebore of the barrel chamber.

The purpose of the freebore is to allow the bullet to move freely for a short distance after it is released from the tension of the case neck until it engages the lands. This free travel alleviates initial pressure by allowing bullet velocity to build up before the engraving process of the lands and the friction of the barrel cause it to rise to the peak. This reduction of pressure makes it possible to increase the powder charge somewhat, which may increase velocity slightly.

Freebore may vary from only a fraction of an inch in length to several inches in extreme cases. (See LAND; LEADE; THROAT.)

Freedom Arms (company) Manufacturer of a line of high-quality, single-action revolvers. Most notable among the Freedom Arms chamberings is the .454 Casull cartridge, an extraordinarily powerful load that develops ballistics far in excess of even the .44 magnum. The company was founded in 1983 and is located in Freedom, Wyoming.

free pistol Any .22 rimfire pistol or revolver that meets the rules of the International Shooting Union or the National Rifle Association, which specify the arms to be used in free pistol competitions. "Free" means that there are a minimum of restrictions on the pistol and its appurtenances. The following specifiations summarize NRA rules:

A. There are no weight restrictions; however, the pistol must be capable of being held in one hand in the shooting postion without support.
B. The caliber may not exceed 5.6mm, using ammunition of internationally recognized specification, .22 caliber rimfire. Bullets must be of lead or similar soft material.
C. The grip of the gun may not be constructed in any way that would give support beyond the hand in which the gun is held.
D. The trigger pull is free and must be released by a finger of the hand in which the gun is held, and that finger must make physical contact with the trigger.
E. Sights. Telescopic, optical, and mirror sights are prohibited. If corrective lenses are used, they must be worn by the shooter and not attached to the firearm.

The result of these rules is that typical free pistols are of single-shot type with large, hand-fitting grips, often wrapping almost completely around the shooting hand; barrels 10 to 12 inches long; sensitive, light pull triggers; precision adjustable iron sights; and a firing mechanism giving very fast lock time. A top grade free pistol, with ammunition suited to its chamber and barrel, should group within one inch at 50 meters from machine rest; some will produce groups of half to three-quarters this size.

Free pistol shooting originated in Europe. Most of the early guns were built on actions of the falling block type, miniature Martini actions being especially popular because of their fast lock time. In many of the early guns, the grip shape followed that of dueling pistols, with finger rests extending from the trigger guard. Barrels tended to be long (2 to 14 inches) to gain sight radius, and consequently were of rather small diameter to keep weight to a usable level.

During the past 20 or 30 years, the general outline and grip angle of free pistol stocks has approached the shape of stocks commonly used on automatic pistols, although free pistol stocks usually wrap around the hand to provide large areas of contact and uniform support from shot to shot. The falling block actions are no longer generally manufactured, probably attributable more to the amount of handwork and fitting required rather than to inadequacies of performance. Several free pistols are essentially of bolt-action design. One Hammerli design is a toggle action, operated by a lever swinging out on the left side.

Set triggers have fallen out of favor for free pistols, as triggers capable of similar light, crisp pull but of faster operating time have been developed. A few guns are being built with electric triggers, in which the trigger movement actually closes a precision limit switch, completing an electric circuit from a battery in the grip to a solenoid, whose movement releases the sear. It is claimed that this design gives the most uniform trigger pull and the fastest lock time.

A free pistol target, designated the B-17 by the NRA, is fired on from 50 meters, and is divided into 10 rings, scoring from 10 at the center to 1 on the outer. Only rings 10 through 7 are black, and the 10-ring itself measures only 50mm. The course of fire allows unlimited sighting shots and 60 shots for record. The time allotted is 2 hours and 30 minutes, and shooters may take their "sighters" before any 10-shot string.

free rifle A rifle meeting the requirements of the International Shooting Union and generally used for competitive target shooting at 50 meters or 300 meters, depending on caliber.

Free rifles are made in both rim- and centerfire versions. The rimfire, which is used in the three-position 50-meter event, is chambered for .22 Long Rifle. It cannot weigh more than 8 kilograms (17.6 pounds), cannot employ optical sights, and must be capable of safe operation. Centerfire free rifles are fired in the three-position 300-meter match. The regulations governing their design are the same as those for the rimfire, with the additional stipulation that they cannot be of larger caliber than 8mm. Most centerfire free rifles are chambered for the 7.62mm NATO round or the 7.62mm Russian.

The ISU course of fire for the free rifle is a total of 120 record shots, 40 each in prone, standing, and kneeling positions. Shots are fired in series of 10 each, with 10 sighting shots allowed per position, either at the start of the competition or between 10-shot series. The free rifle and its attachments are designed to allow the highest standard of performance in these three positions on the difficult ISU targets. Shooting is done from a shooting station constructed so the shooter is sheltered from rain, sun, and wind, and may include screens forward of the station.

The free rifle and the positions from which it is fired are designed to utilize the bone structure of the human body as much as possible for holding the rifle in position, to minimize strain on the muscles used to hold the rifle, and to free the trigger finger, hand, and arm as much as possible from the effort of holding the rifle. This facilitates trigger release without disturbing aim. For example, in the standing position, the muzzle-heavy balance of the free rifle is controlled by the palm rest and the hook buttplate. The elbow or upper arm of the hand holding the palm rest is positioned against the hip or rib cage, acting as a support and pivot point for the rifle. The hook of the butt plate, held in the armpit, holds the rear end of the rifle in position, minimizing the amount of muscles in tension in the trigger arm and its appendages, and freeing the index finger for its fundamental job of moving the trigger.

The attachments and special features of the free rifle include the following:

Thumbhole stock to provide maximum support for the trigger hand and optimum control of the trigger.

Sling and sling swivel, which are removable and can be adjusted for longitudinal position.

Palm rest, which attaches to the fore-end rail, and which is fully adjustable for length below the fore-end and for positioning on several axes so that the shooter in the standing position may establish its best location for holding the rifle, as determined by his physique and the body position he assumes when firing.

Buttplates, which are adjustable or interchangeable for length of pull, vertical position, and sometimes to allow movement around an axis parallel to the barrel of the rifle. A flat or slightly curved buttplate is generally used prone and kneeling, and a hook type for standing.

Cheekpieces are sometimes adjustable for height, to provide proper head support on the stock for shooters of different physiques and in different shooting positions. Some shooters prefer detachable comb sections, using different ones for different positions.

Sights In the early years, the rules required the use of an open rear sight and a post or bead front sight. The aperture rear sight (called orthoptic in England and Europe) and aperture front sights with interchangeable inserts are now commonly used. Some competitors use a post insert, particularly in the less stable standing position, as they feel it makes it easier to coordinate aim and trigger letoff. A bubble level is frequently fitted to the front sight. This assists the shooter in maintaining the same vertical position of the rifle from shot to shot. Holding the rifle with the sights other than directly vertical over the bore is called "canting." Changes in the angle of cant will change the point of strike of the bullet on the target, even though the sights are properly aligned on the bull. Some shooters, particularly in the standing position, use a constant degree of cant because they find it results in a more stable position. One reason advanced for this is that the sense of balance resides in the canals of the inner ear, and holding the head level aids balance.

Triggers are two-stage, with a very light pull, ranging from a few ounces to a pound, with the final stage adjusted to a very clean, crisp pull. Set triggers increase lock time, and anything that increases lock time makes follow through more difficult.

The origin of the free rifle dates back at least to the middle of the 1800s, and quite possibly to the flintlock period. The first international free rifle championship was held at Lyon, France in 1897 and was won by F. Jullien of Switzerland with a score of 942 out of a possible 1,200 points. Switzerland, truly "a nation of riflemen," dominated free rifle shooting for the first half-century, its marksmen winning the world championship 18 times in the first 37 competitions. The 300-meter target has remained unchanged except for the addition of an X ring used to decide ties, so it is possible to trace the improvements in equipment and human performance down through the years.

Rifle shooting, and especially the 300-meter free rifle game, is among the most demanding in terms of human performance; it is very much a mental sport, where the mind and the will control performance, and strength and physique are of much less importance than in most other sports. In light of the rapidity with which other athletic marks have been bettered, it is possible that scores in the high 1180s to low 1190s are within the realm of human performance.

free travel The distance, traveled by a bullet, from its loaded position in the case to the point of contact with the rifling. Usually the bullet has some free travel with cartridges and chambers of standard dimensions, but benchrest and target shooters who handload are likely to seat the bullet so that it touches, or nearly touches, the rifling when the cartridge is loaded into the chamber.

The term "free travel" is probably used more often in connection with barrels having freebore. Freebore is an unrifled section of the barrel ahead of the throat. Free travel (through the freebore) permits the bullet to move without encountering the resistance of rifling engraving forces during the initial burning of the powder charge. Popular in magnum calibers, it permits the use of heavier charges of powder, which produce higher velocities at acceptable pressures. However, this is accomplished at the cost of shortened barrel life, attributable to the removal of lands near the mouth of the case, together with accelerated erosion and often some loss of accuracy. Also, there is a loss in efficiency, since the expansion ratio is in effect lowered, and proportionately more powder must be used for a moderate gain in velocity. Accuracy also often suffers because of the jump of the bullet before it engages the rifling, which results in greater bullet deformation during engraving. (See BARREL, RIFLED; FREEBORE.)

French checkering See SKIPLINE CHECKERING.

freshing out When a muzzleloading barrel has had much use, it sometimes has to be freshed-out because of the wear on the rifling and/or muzzle. Freshing out usually means using a reamer to recut the grooves and the lands, which in turn means an increase in bore size. A .32 caliber might have to be cut to .38 or even .40 caliber, depending on the condition and thickness of the barrel. (See MUZZLE-LOADER; REBORE.)

frettage The process of reinforcing the breech of a cast iron cannon by shrinking on hoops of wrought iron or steel. The hoops were bent around the barrel while still red hot and shrank as they cooled, producing an extremly tight fit.

frizzen In a flintlock, the frizzen is an upright steel plate against which the flint strikes, producing the sparks that ignite the powder. When a frizzen has become worn, it can be "shoed" (refitted with a new striking surface) by a good gunsmith, thus adding years to its life. However, a properly hardened frizzen should last for a long time. (See FLINTLOCK.)

frog See SLING HOOK.

frontal ignition The ignition of the powder charge in standard cartridges is from the rear of the case, where the flame from the primer makes contact with the powder through the flash hole in the web. With the frontal ignition system the powder charge is ignited forward of the center of the case. This is accomplished by the use of a "flash tube" that is threaded into the flash hole in the case head to carry the primer flame forward.

The theory behind frontal ignition is that if the powder charge is ignited near the front, the bullet starts to move sooner because the expanding gas originates nearer to it. As the flame spreads toward the rear, the gas pressure will be prolonged somewhat and will give a longer pressure curve to provide a continuous and more even push on the bullet than if the charge were ignited from the rear. It is reasoned that this lower but longer pressure peak will provide the sustained thrust to deliver higher velocity, especially with heavy bullets in any given caliber. However, frontal ignition has proven to be only marginally successful, and then only with certain powders in certain cases. Some of the OKH wildcat cartridges, called "duplex loading," were equipped with flash tubes. (See IGNITION; WILDCAT CARTRIDGE.)

front sight The forward sighting mechanism on a firearm, at or near the muzzle end. When placed in line with the target, the rear sight, and the shooter's

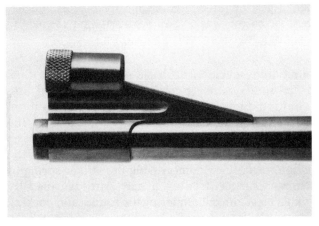

A hunting rifle's front sight should be protected by a removable hood.

eye, it establishes line of sight from the gun to the target.

The front sight may be constructed of any number of materials such as steel, brass, or plastic. It may take the form of a bead, post, blade, or any number of other shapes. It is sometimes adjustable for windage and/or elevation.

In Britain, the term "foresight" is commonly used instead of "front sight." (See METALLIC SIGHTS; REAR SIGHT.)

full charge When any cartridge or muzzleloading arm is loaded to the maximum safe limit, it is said to be loaded with a full charge.

full choke The tightest of all shotgun choke constrictions, full choke produces shot patterns of some 70 percent in a 30-inch circle at 40 yards. It utilizes 30 points of constriction at the muzzle. (A highly specialized variation, extra-full choke, can produce patterns of 80 to 100 percent. However, installation of this degree of constriction in a shotgun barrel requires the skills of a custom gunsmith who specializes in choke alteration.) It is generally agreed that full choke is excessively tight for all shotgun uses save handicap trap shooting and pass shooting at waterfowl. Most modern ammunition makers do not recommend tight full choke constrictions with steel shot loads larger than No. 1 shot, as steel BBs and T- or F-shot do not flow fluidly through a tight choke and could ring-bulge the barrel. (See CHOKE.)

full metal jacket (FMJ) See SOLID BULLET.

full patch See SOLID BULLET.

fulminate of mercury The explosive mercuric salts used in some now-obsolete primer compounds. Cases fired with mercuric primers quickly became brittle, and the primer residue also caused corrosion of the barrel and chamber, which led to erosion and excessive barrel wear. (See FORSYTH, ALEXANDER J.; MERCURIC PRIMERS; PRIMER RESIDUE.)

functioning cycle The basic operations that must occur in any firearm utilizing self-contained ammunition. Eight of the very basic steps are: ignition, normally by a firing pin blow; unlocking of the breechblock mechanism; extraction of the fired case; ejecting of the case from the action; cocking the action, usually by compressing the striker spring or hammer spring; feeding a new cartridge, usually from a magazine; chambering the round; and cocking

the action in preparation for firing and a recurrence of the complete cycle. The sequence of these events may be changed, depending upon firearm design and action type. Some of the events may overlap or occur simultaneously.

The cycle may be accomplished manually or automatically. A good example of a manual cycle is the simple break-action shotgun. The action is first unlocked by means of a thumb lever, the empty case is plucked out with the fingers, and the live round is inserted by hand. Then the action is locked and the hammer manually cocked with the thumb in preparation for firing.

In a fully automatic arm, after the mechanism is cocked, depressing the trigger to begin ignition starts a whole series of events to be completed without further action by the shooter. Ignition occurs, the action unlocks, the case is extracted, then ejected, while the action is simultaneously cocked, a fresh round is fed and chambered, and the action is again locked to begin the sequence anew.

The development of self-contained ammunition was followed by further refinement of gun and action types; these refinements consisted largely of advancements in the functioning cycle—from very simple single shot, to lever action, slide action, and automatic. As a result, the functioning cycle has improved from a very few rounds per minute in the case of the Trapdoor Springfield to 13 rounds per second with the M16 rifle.

furniture The term applied to any metal inlays—trigger guards, buttplates, ramrod thimbles, cap or patch boxes—on a muzzleloading rifle. They could be of brass, iron, German silver, mother of pearl, pure silver, or gold. Sometimes, as in the case of expensive presentation pieces, the furniture was tastefully engraved. In workhorses such as the Plains rifles the furniture was almost always iron, with no decorations.

In more modern parlance, a gun's furniture may include such items as grip caps, sling swivels, and swivel studs.

fused shot Shot pellets that are compressed in the bore to the point where they adhere to one another are referred to as fused shot. This condition is most common with softer grades of shot and is highly detrimental to uniform patterning. (See SHOT.)

fusil An early kind of flintlock musket. The early French *fusil-court* was in great demand among some American Indian tribes in the latter part of the 17th century. (See FLINTLOCK.)

Gabilondo (company)   See SPANISH GUNMAKERS.

gain twist   The rotation of the lands in a rifled barrel is known as twist, and is determined by the distance required to make a complete turn, one turn in 10 inches being a 1–10 twist. A barrel with gain twist is one in which the rate of twist increases between chamber and muzzle. For example, it may start at 1–16 and end up at 1–10.

Few barrels with gain twist have ever been made for jacketed bullets in this country except for experimental purposes, but many were made for lead bullet use, the famous Pope barrels being among them.

The predominant reason for using the gain twist was that when the bullet first engaged the rifling, the shock of rotation was less violent, decreasing the possibility that the bullet would skid as it entered the lands, perhaps affecting accuracy. With the gain twist the rotation of the bullet was gradually increased to the desired rate of spin while reducing the likelihood of deformation and loss of accuracy. (See BARREL, RIFLED; LAND; METFORD, WILLIAM ELLIS; TWIST.)

Galilean telescope   In 1609, the Italian scientist Galileo constructed the first working telescope in which the objective lens is always positive, the ocular lens, or eyepiece, is always negative, and the focal points of the two lenses are coincident. By adjusting the eyepiece out of coincidence, so that the emitted rays of light converge or diverge, there is accommodation for an eye that is nearsighted or farsighted. In the Galilean system the objective lens serves as both field stop and entrance pupil. Therefore, the field of the scope depends on the diameter of the objective lens. (See TELESCOPIC SIGHTS.)

gas check   A shallow copper-alloy cup fitted to the base of a lead-alloy bullet. It protects the bullet from the hot cutting gasses of powder combustion and permits loading higher-velocity loads than are recommended for bare-based lead bullets.

gas cutting   The expanding gases produced by the combustion of smokeless powder have a highly erosive effect on barrel steel; this erosion is referred to as gas cutting. One of the more common instances of gas cutting occurs with the use of boattail bullets

A gas check is a copper cup that is attached to the base of a chat-lead bullet to improve its upset quality in the bore.

that, because their tapered bases cannot expand to achieve perfect obturation, allow small amounts of gas to escape past them. This gas, which is compressed between the bullet jacket and the barrel, is under especially high pressure, and results in accelerated barrel erosion. (See BARREL EROSION; BOAT-TAIL BULLET; OBTURATION.)

gas cylinder   Gas operated semiautomatic arms obtain the power to function through means of a gas cylinder in which the powder gases are harnessed. A typical cylinder employs a bleed hole that leads to the barrel and that drains off a small amount of gas into the tube. This gas pushes a piston at the end of the tube to the rear, and the force of the piston in turn operates the bolt, pushing it to the rear. Most gas cylinder pistons require periodic cleaning to remove carbon deposits and ensure reliable functioning. (See GAS OPERATION.)

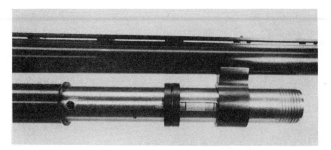

This is a typical gas cylinder design for a modern semi-automatic shotgun.

gas leak A gas leak results from any failure in obturation, either by a cartridge case or by a projectile in the bore. Gas leaks most commonly result from loose primer fit in the primer pocket, case necks that are too short for the chamber, an imperfect upset of a bullet or base wad, or an excessive gap between a revolver cylinder and the rear of the barrel. Gas leaks can cause loss of velocity or damage to the firearm. (See OBTURATION.)

gas operation In self-loading or automatic firearms, as distinguished from those operated by external power such as the Gatling and Vulcan, one source of power for functioning is the powder gas. Small semiautomatic pistols, and some self-loading rifles are straight blowback in operation. In the kind of self-loading or automatic arm designated as gas operated, a gas port or small hole in the barrel allows powder gas to enter a gas cylinder and to exert pressure on some kind of piston. Driven by the pressure of the gas, the piston is used (generally through some kind of operating rod or linkage) to unlock the breech mechanism, open the bolt, extract and eject the fired case, cock the firing mechanism, and compress a spring. The energy stored in the spring is used to close and lock the bolt and breech mechanism, loading a fresh cartridge from a magazine during the forward movement.

There are a number of ways in which the piston and its related mechanism can function. The most common arrangement is for the gas cylinder and piston to be located parallel to and mounted on the barrel, with a link or operating rod attached to the piston. The operating rod either contains or actuates a cam, which is used to unlock the bolt, by rotation, by tilting it out of locking recesses, or to move a locking block, strut, rollers, or cams out of locking recesses. In some mechanisms, the gas is fed to the breech by a long tube, and acts on the bolt, which is made in two parts, with one of these functioning as the piston and sliding on the other to perform the unlocking and locking functions and to store enough energy in bolt momentum to perform the rest of the functions.

The piston may be fixed, with the gas vented through it and driving the hollow cylinder, or, as in the case of the short stroke piston invented by David ("Carbine") Williams and used on the M-1 carbine, the piston may be allowed to move only a fraction of an inch and to act as a tappet, impacting on the operating slide and imparting enough energy for the mechanism to function.

Gas mechanisms are divided into impinging and expanding types. In the impinging type, the gas enters the cylinder through the gas port, and the piston is exposed to the gas pressure from the barrel until the bullet exits from the muzzle. This is the simpler type and the one most used, but it gives a rather harsh and violent action to the mechanism. In an expanding gas mechanism, the flow of gas to the cylinder is cut off by movement of the piston, and the gas trapped in the cylinder expands, giving a smoother and more prolonged impulse. It is more complicated and more subject to malfunctions caused by dirt, corrosion, and fouling.

The location and size of the gas port is critical and must be related to the ammunition used and to the pressure curve it develops. Located too close to the breech, near the point of maximum pressure, the violent forces developed may cause the extractor to tear through the head of the case during primary extraction, leaving the case in the chamber. Located too far forward, near the muzzle where gas pressures are lower, softer action is obtained—but the operating mechanism becomes longer and less rigid and the gun is more subject to malfunctions from pressure variations. Locations vary from that of the M-1 carbine, in which the gas port is a few inches from the breech, to those using a gas port forward of the barrel bore, as in the early Garand. In general, gas operation requires the use of ammunition that is loaded to a rather narrow pressure range and with powders developing similar pressure curves, although some of the gas operated shotguns handle a wide range of loadings without requiring any adjustments. Others, like some kinds of rifles and machine guns, have a variable gas port arrangement, so that the flow of gas to the cylinder can be matched to different ammunition or operating conditions.

Gas operated mechanisms have many advantages. For many years they have dominated high-power sporting and military rifle designs. In recent years they have come to dominate the shotgun field, and today they are entering the high-power pistol market. Gas operation generates only the amount of force needed, and this force can be applied where it is wanted. Instead of the heavy parts needed by blowback and recoil operated mechanisms, particularly with more powerful cartridges, the operating parts need only enough weight to carry them through the operating cycle. This reduces overall gun weight. It also reduces recoil effects, other things being equal, since the recoil is spread out over a longer time and is therefore less noticeable to the shooter.

gas port The small hole, through the wall of the barrel, that connects the bore with the gas cylinder in a gas operated semiautomatic or automatic firearm. It is sometimes called a "gas trap."

The term may also be applied to the vent hole often provided in the receiver ring or bolt of a rifle. In this case, the hole permits the escape of gas in the event of a ruptured case head or a pierced or blown primer. (See GAS OPERATION.)

gas pressure In firearms, the pressure exerted by the powder gases inside the barrel and cartridge case, if one is used. In the United States, it was formerly specified in pounds per square inch (psi), but today we use C.U.P. or L.U.P. for copper and lead units of pressure. In the British Commonwealth, it is expressed in long tons (2,240 lbs.) per square inch; and in countries using the metric system, in kilograms per square centimeter. Normally, it is given as the peak, or maximum, average pressure.

gauge See SHOTGUN GAUGES.

gauge adapter Gauge adapters are tubes chambered for shotgun shells that are smaller in gauge than the guns in which they will be used. In this way, .410-, 28-, 20-, and 16-gauge shells may be fired from a 12-gauge gun. These adapters are shorter than the full length of the barrels in which they are to be used, and choking of the shot charge is accomplished by the existing choke in the host gun. (See ADAPTER.)

Gebrüder Merkel (company) Gebrüder Merkel (Merkel Brothers), located in Suhl, Germany, is famous for break-action, side-by-side, and over/under shotguns. Prior to World War II, Merkel produced several varieties of over/under with two barrel extensions that are pierced by a transverse locking bolt on closing. This lockup resembles the single pierced extension of the Greener lock in a side-by-side double, but the twin lockups make the Merkel even stronger than the British gun. Other companies in Germany and Spain now use the same basic design.

After the Russian occupation, Merkel did not move to the western occupation zone like so many other arms makers. Rather, it remained in Suhl, and today continues to produce highly prized guns. Production is small, and any gun bearing the Merkel name commands a high price. They are very rare in the United States. (See GREENER CROSS-BOLT.)

geese, guns and loads for Guns for goose shooting can be divided into two general classes, guns intended for shooting over decoys and guns intended for long-range pass shooting. From 75 to 80 percent of all shots at geese will be taken at ranges of 40 yards and under, with the majority being at about 30 yards. These ranges are very similar to those encountered in upland shooting, and guns with chokes similar to upland guns are most effective.

Double-barrel guns bored modified and improved-cylinder and pumps and autoloaders with improved-cylinder chokes will be most efficient for this work. Some experienced goose hunters use double-barrel guns bored improved-cylinder in the right barrel and full choke in the left. These shooters like the full choke barrel for taking geese that have flared at the first shot or shots from the blind and are rapidly extending the range. Most of these guns were originally bored with modified and full chokes, with the modified barrel opened up to deliver improved-cylinder patterns for the first shot at geese.

Because heavy loads of powder and shot are required for efficient goose shooting, this kind of gun, though choked similar to those used in the uplands, should have sufficient weight to minimize the effects of recoil. Both gas operated and recoil operated autoloading guns slow down the speed of recoil and are more comfortable to shoot with heavy loads. For goose shooting from a field pit or water blind, these single-barrel guns are best fitted with improved-cylinder barrels.

Pass shooting at geese at ranges of from 40 to 60 yards comprises only about 20 to 25 percent of goose shooting in America. Most shooters cannot accurately estimate ranges of over 40 yards, and even fewer can make consistent hits at these ranges. Those few shooters who are skilled long-range pass shooters need little advice on guns and loads for this sport. The majority prefer full-choked autoloaders or pump guns chambered for 3-inch 12-gauge magnum shells. A few use similarly chambered double-barrel guns bored modified-and-full or full-and-full. A small minority use guns chambered for 3½-inch 10-gauge magnum shells.

Goose hunters who hunt over decoys from field and water blinds are best equipped with the 2¾-inch 12-gauge magnum shells containing 1½ ounces of shot. Some shooters use a gun chambered for the 3-inch 12-gauge magnum shells and fitted with a variable-choke device, which is set at one of the more open settings for decoy shooting. Some decoy gunners use shells loaded with No. 6 shot for the first shot, followed by No. 4s in the magazine or second barrel of a double gun. Most pass shooters prefer No. 4s for all shooting, or 4s followed by 2s for second and third shots. For pass shooting, No. 3

shot would be a better choice, but it is only available in handloads at this time. If steel shot is used, No. 2 pellets are the best choice. (See BLIND; DECOY.)

geometric center of lens The geometric center of a lens is located at the center of the outside diameter, while the optical center is determined by the curvature of the optical surfaces. Because the outside diameter of a lens is the mounting surface in the plane transverse to the optical axis, it is important that the optical center and the geometric center lie on the same axis through the lens. If they do not, the result is aberration in the lens system and poor optical performance. In the case of riflescopes, such lack of coincidence may also result in difficulties in mounting and sighting in, since the optical axis does not coincide with the mechanical axis determined by the outside of the scope tube. (See OPTICAL AXIS.)

German silver See NICKEL SILVER.

gesichert German for "safe" or "secure." It is a marking on some German-made guns that designate the safe position of the safety.

Gewehr German for "firearm" in the broadest sense. In modern usage, however, it almost always means rifle, such as the Gewehr 98, the Mauser bolt-action army rifle first issued in 1898. Narrowly, the word means military rifle. In sporting parlance, a rifle is a *Büchse* and a shotgun is a *Flinte*.

gilding metal The core of most modern rifle bullets is made of lead, which is too soft to withstand the hot gases and high friction developed by modern ammunition. Therefore, a harder jacket must be used to protect the inner core in high-velocity ammunition. The most common bullet jackets are gilding metal composed of 90 to 95 percent copper and 5 to 10 percent zinc.

Bullets for most semiautomatic pistol ammunition also have hard jackets, but they are employed to prevent deformation of the bullet in the semiautomatic mechanism and to assure smooth feeding from the magazine rather than to protect the core. (See BULLET JACKET.)

glass ball target Once used in England and America as a substitute for live birds in target shooting with shotguns. At first, two hollow glass balls were suspended at the ends of a rotating beam on a raised frame. The shooter tried to break the circling balls. Later, glass balls were thrown from a spring catapult (trap), but the glass often shattered during release, and lead shot often glanced off without breaking it.

Eventually, clay pigeons were substituted. (See TRAPSHOOTING.)

glass bedding The fit of the metal parts of a rifle into the wood of the stock has a very important effect on accuracy. At each shot, the metal parts move within the wood, first backward during recoil, then forward to a position of rest, because of the elasticity of the materials involved and the manner in which metal and wood are held together. With small surfaces absorbing recoil, the wood of the stock may compress with repeated firing, sections of wood may split out, or, as the guard screws come into contact with the wood, the stock may split through the screw holes and magazine opening. Thus, wood hardness, strength, and density are important in a rifle stock, and the manner in which the metal parts fit the wood is critical to accuracy and accuracy life. This is particularly important in the areas that control location of the metal in the wood and absorb recoil. Proper fitting of wood to metal is therefore a highly skilled and expensive hand operation.

The developments in the plastics industry during the late 1940s included commercial use of two-part resin-catalyst mixtures that were self-polymerizing when mixed in the proper quantities and that had high adhesive qualities to many materials, including wood and metals. As liquids in the mixed state, they could be poured and cast to conform precisely to any surface, had a shrinkage of only 1 or 2 percent, and could be filled with fibrous or powdered materials to increase mechanical characteristics and to thicken them so that they would remain in place while hardening. Hardness and strength were a great deal better than in the average stock woods.

It soon became apparent to those in the gun field that here was a material that had many advantages in providing proper fit of wood and metal, that its use would give greater areas of contact, and that its hardness, reinforced by fillers of glass fibers (hence the name, glass bedding) or powdered metals would better withstand the forces of recoil. The epoxy type rapidly came into use by both professional and amateur gunsmiths. Today some factory rifles are glass bedded, although the time and labor involved, and the necessity for keeping a bedded stock and action mated, limit this to the more expensive rifles.

A wide variety of glass bedding materials specifically designed for the gun field are now available. Some are furnished with the resin and catalyst in liquid form, with the filler as a fiber or powder; in others the catalyst is a powder; and some are furnished as two-part paste mixtures with the filler already incorporated.

The basic techniques of glass bedding are as fol-

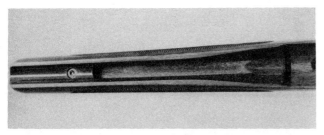

This stock fore-end was glass-bedded when a new barrel, smaller in diameter than the original, was fitted to the rifle. The fore-end channel was then hollowed out to save weight.

lows: Stock wood is cut away in selected areas to provide room for 1/16 to 1/8 inch of plastic; undercuts, holes, etc. in the metal parts are covered with tape or filled with modeling clay; a release compound is applied to the metal parts to prevent adhesion; the resin-catalyst-filler mixture is puttied or injected in place with a syringe; and the metal parts are put in and held in place while the mixture hardens. It is important to accuracy that the metal parts be held in an unstressed condition during hardening. After the plastic has polymerized, metal parts are removed and cleaned, excess plastic removed from the stock, metal parts sparingly oiled, and wood and metal parts reassembled.

Despite its many advantages, glass bedding is not a cure-all. It frequently improves accuracy, but it will not compensate for worn or neglected barrels or similar deficiencies to accuracy requirements. It is more stable than wood, but it is not entirely free from warpage during hardening. It will absorb some moisture and it will deteriorate in contact with some lubricants and solvents used in gun cleaning and maintenance. (See BEDDING.)

goat, guns and loads for See MOUNTAIN GOAT, GUNS AND LOADS FOR.

"good" (condition) See GUN CONDITION.

grain A unit of weight equal to 1/7000 pound avoirdupois.

grain equivalent A term formerly used to indicate that a particular charge of smokeless powder produced a muzzle velocity equivalent to a specified charge of black powder. Thus, a smokeless charge producing the same velocity as 40 grains of black powder in a particular cartridge would be called a 40-grain-equivalent charge. (See POWDER CHARGE.)

Grand American Trapshooting Championship The "Grand" attracts thousands of shooters each August to the headquarters of the sponsoring Amateur Trapshooting Association at Vandalia, Ohio. Events last 10 days and include 16-yard singles, doubles, and handicap trap. The earliest competition was on live pigeons; the present clay target competitions have been staged at Vandalia since 1924. The climax of each year's shooting is the Grand American Handicap, in which shooters compete from yardages determined by their scoring averages. Winners of major events usually earn several thousand dollars, depending to a great extent upon "options" (optional bets), plus purses and trophies.

In addition to the shooting, the "Grand" is a sort of shooters's country fair, featuring exhibits by gun manufacturers, dealers, accessory makers, food and drink concessions, etc. Thousands of shooters attend the Grand on their vacations, bringing along the family and camping in trailers, motor homes, and tents on the grounds, thus making the event also one of the largest campouts in America. (See TRAPSHOOTING.)

graphite A form of pure carbon notable for its lubricity. Graphite is used, either alone or in conjunction with other materials, as a lubricant for bullets and firearm mechanisms. The granules of smokeless powders are usually coated with graphite, because its lubricity facilitates the free flow of the powder during volumetric measuring, and its electrical conductivity prevents the accumulation of static electrical charges that might produce hazardous spark discharges.

graticule In British usage, the reticle of a telescopic sight or similar optical instrument. (See RETICLE.)

gravity The force by which every body in the universe attracts and is attracted by every other body. The law of universal gravitation, first formulated by Sir Isaac Newton, states that the attraction between two bodies is directly proportional to their masses, and inversely proportional to the square of the distance between their centers of mass. The force of attraction between the earth and any body upon it is the weight of that body. Gravity exerts a pull on every fired projectile, causing it to eventually fall to earth. (See TRAJECTORY.)

Great Britain, guns and loads for hunting in One does not go "hunting" in the United Kingdom—that term is almost exclusively reserved for riding to hounds, or fox hunting. In Britain, shooting is the proper term, whether on birds or other game.

A good variety of game is available to the visiting sportsman—red deer and roe for the rifleman; pheasant, grouse, partridge, the prized capercaillie or black game; ducks and geese, snipe, woodcock, pigeons, hares, and rabbits. Fallow deer and wild goats are found, too, in some areas—the Isle of Mull, off Scotland's western coast, is one such place.

Red deer are the prized big game, and the best shooting for them is to be had in Scotland, in the deer forests or on the rolling, heathered moors. Deer stalking in the Highlands is often a rugged test of endurance.

Such shooting usually calls for a "ghillie," or guide. There is little concealment for the stalker on the great moorlands except for a fold in the hills now and then. Once a suitable animal is spotted, one you *may* shoot, as in Europe, the chase really begins—frequently a long, wet and tiring one.

Until a few years ago, for some strange reason, roe deer were considered vermin—no season, no protection. Not so now. Roe bucks have become an important game animal, and the prize heads taken in Britain are among the best anywhere, rivaling or bettering those shot on the Continent. Wise game management has worked well, as it did in Spain in bringing the ibex back from near extinction.

For antlered game the scoped rifle does well. The .270 is a good choice on red deer. The Scottish stag is not as big as his Continental cousin, so the .257 or .243/6mm will serve if shots are accurate. The 7x57/7x64 or the .280 Remington are excellent choices, too. The .30/06 is a fine selection, of course.

There's no need for the larger calibers mentioned if the game is a roe buck, though they're usable. One of the 7mm cartridges, used with bullet weights of 140 to 150 grains in protected-point types—bullets that won't blow up too easily or expand too quickly—are good if only one rifle is available. However, the medium calibers noted above are a better choice on roe deer. Ask the outfitter which caliber he thinks suitable. He's familiar with the conditions in his domain, which can be 5,000 acres or more.

Drive hunting is the preferred and standard form for most bird shooting, though "walking up" with a dog is practiced, too, in season—usually in the winter months.

The break-open 12-bore double gun is much preferred in the British Isles. Pumps or autoloaders might get by for walk-up shooting, but they won't be entirely welcome.

Shotshells of all kinds are available in Britain. Shot size depends on the game being hunted, but all common sizes are readily available, as are 2¾ inch shotshells if the gun in use is so chambered.

Greener cross-bolt A bolting system used to increase the strength of hinged-barrel guns, invented

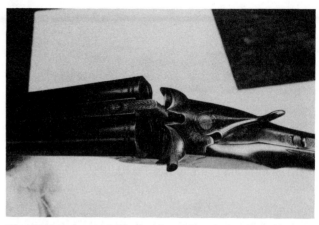

The Greener cross-bolt fits through a hole in the top extension of the shotgun's barrels. In the open position, the bolt slides to the side, as seen here. Closed, it fits flush with the receiver. In order to be effective, the bolt must be carefully fitted by hand. For this reason, it is seen only on the more expensive shotguns and double rifles.

by W. W. Greener in 1865, by means of which the barrel or barrels are secured in the closed position by locking them to the standing breech. It employs a bolt or wedge passing transversely through the standing breech, moveable from side to side by manipulation of the opening lever. The bolt passes through a hole in the rib extension that is fitted into a slot in the standing breech when the gun is closed.

The Greener cross-bolt has been widely copied by other manufacturers of hinged-barrel guns, especially in Europe. (See GEBRÜDER MERKEL; GREENER, W. W.)

Greener double lock See KERSTEN LOCK.

Greener safety Introduced on W. W. Greener shotguns in the mid-1870s, this safety was of the non-automatic type. It was conventional in that it blocked the trigger blades like other safeties, but was unconventional in that it was located on the left side of the stock to the rear of the action, whereas most double-barrel shotgun safeties are situated directly behind the top lever. It was not a popular variation and was not adopted by other makers. (See GREENER, W. W.; SAFETY.)

Greener, W. W. (company) This world-famous gunmaking firm was founded in Birmingham, England, by William Wellington Greener in 1841 after his father, William Greener (born in 1806), retired in that year.

Both men were inventive, particularly, W. W., and both were steady contributors to firearms literature. W. W. Greener's greatest literary effort was *The Gun and Its Development*, the first edition published in

1881. Nine editions in all were printed, the last, with 804 pages, in 1910. This last edition was reissued a few years ago (it is not dated) as a facsimile. French- and Russian-language editions were published in the 1880s, as were issues in other tongues. *The Gun and Its Development*, in its various editions, became an international best seller of its kind, and a monument to its author.

W. W. Greener obtained many patents for his designs; his Treble Wedge-Fast and bolting mechanism, also termed the "Facile Princeps," was strongly advertised and sold well, though Greener was sued (unsuccessfully) for alleged infringement of the Anson-and-Deeley-patented system. The Greener cross-bolt and his side safety are well known.

Although not considered quite the equal of the London-made "best guns," Greener breechloaders found ready acceptance around the world. At one time Greener had three importer-distributors in New York City alone. Greener guns won many awards over the years at the various matches and exhibitions held in England, France, America, and elsewhere. W. W. Greener died in 1921.

W. W. Greener went out of business, for all practical purposes, in 1964. The managing director then was Layton Greener, a nephew of W. W. Val Forgett, then and now the owner and operator of Navy Arms in New Jersey, bought the company assets. The title of the company was turned over to Webley & Scott of England, who still retain it.

For a detailed account of Greener guns and many others, plus a history of gunnery in general, *The Gun and Its Development* is highly recommended. Facsimile issues of some other Greener titles are also now available. (See GREENER CROSS-BOLT; GREENER SAFETY.)

Greenhill formula Developed by the British ballistician Sir Alfred Greenhill in the 1870s, this formula provided a means for determining the proper rate of rifling twist to stabilize a given bullet. Even though Greenhill's formula was originated at a time when velocities did not exceed speeds of 1,500 feet per second, it is surprisingly accurate when applied to today's bullet speeds.

To use the Greenhill formula in calculating the minimum or slowest rifling twist required to stabilize a bullet, divide 150 (constant) by bullet length (expressed in calibers) and multiply that number by bullet diameter (expressed in inches). Using a .257-caliber bullet of 120 grains and 1.125 inches long, dividing its length by its diameter gives us 4.38 calibers. In other words, the bullet's length is 4.38 times as great as its diameter. Next, we divide the constant (150) by calibers (4.38) and come up with

34.25. Multiplying 34.25 by bullet diameter (.257) gives us a recommended rifling twist of one turn in 8.80 inches. Taking this figure to the nearest standard rifling twist we arrive at one turn in nine inches.

Even though benchrest shooters consider the Greenhill formula a bit conservative, it is still one of the best to use when deciding on a rifling twist rate for a big-game rifle, because when shooting big game, bullet stability is extremely important. (See BULLET STABILIZATION; RATE OF TWIST.)

Greifelt (company) This German gunmaking firm was founded in 1885 at Suhl (Germany), where it remains in operation today.

Greifelt has long been known for high-quality sporting arms of various kinds, particularly Drillings (three-barreled rifle/shotgun combinations) and single-shot rifles. The firm was also an early proponent of telescopic-sighted rifles, working closely with the Zeiss Company on optics and mounting systems. Much the same range of firearms is made today, but Greifelt arms are rarely seen in the United States. (See DRILLING; ZEISS, CARL, INC.)

Griffin & Howe (company) Incorporated in 1923, Griffin & Howe was founded by Seymour Griffin and James Howe. The firm specialized at its inception in the conversion of military rifles (most notably Model 1903 Springfields) into high-grade sporting arms. James Howe left the company after only four months, but the operation was successful, and expanded its scope to include all kinds of gunsmithing, engraving, and the sale of high-quality imported arms.

Griffin & Howe was made a subsidiary of the sporting goods concern of Abercrombie & Fitch in 1932, and was bought by that company and dissolved as a corporate entity in 1961. However, in the mid 1970s, Abercrombie & Fitch experienced extreme financial difficulties, and Griffin & Howe was re-established as a company in its own right, under its present director, William Ward.

Today, the firm is noted as a dealer in fine guns and as a maker of distinctive sporting rifles. Many of the older Griffin & Howe sporter conversions, especially the highly engraved ones, are valued as collectors' items, and far exceed their original worth.

grip That portion of rifle and shotgun stocks gripped by the firing hand. On handguns, the grip is the complete stock and can be made of wood, plastic, horn, ivory, or other materials.

grip adapter A removeable filler, usually of plastic, inserted between the front grip strap and the rear of

Grip adapters enlarge the grasping surface of a revolver stock, giving a firmer purchase.

the trigger guard on a revolver. Grip adapters are furnished in various sizes to fit individual shooters' hands.

grip straps The metal parts of handguns to which the grips are attached. There grip straps house the mainsprings on revolvers and form the magazine well on most autoloading pistols.

groove In a rifled barrel, the grooves are the channels forming the major diameter of the bore, in between the lands, which form the minor diameter. Together, grooves and lands make up the rifling; they are formed in a helix to rotate the bullet as it passes through the bore and to give it gyroscopic stability in flight. (See BARREL, RIFLED; LAND.)

groove diameter The measurement of diameter of the bore, taken from the bottom of a groove on one side to the bottom of the groove on the opposite side. Barrel groove diameter is the same as the diameter of the bullet it is made to handle. It should not be confused with bore diameter, which is the diameter of the bore before the grooves are formed. (See BORE DIAMETER; GROOVE.)

group In the firing of any gun using a single projectile at vertical targets, the result of a series of shots is a two-dimensional pattern of shot holes or impact points. This is called a group. When done under constant conditions of weather, ammunition, and means of holding and aligning the gun, the group may be considered representative of the probable dispersion of gun and ammunition. Although the term accuracy is often used in connection with group size, accuracy also includes the deviation of a series of shots or groups attributable to changes in any of the circumstances that may affect the location of the impact or impacts, including the normal random location of the center of impact from group to group.

Groups are measured in several ways, the most common being extreme spread (ES), the distance in a straight line between the widest two shot holes. Military and ballistics people generally use mean radius (MR) and radial standard deviation (RSD). Some of the other measures are:

Extreme horizontal deviation (EHD) combined with extreme vertical deviation (EVD).

Mean horizontal deviation (MHD) combined with mean vertical deviation (MVD).

Diagonal (D).

The vast majority of shooters hold erroneous beliefs of the grouping capabilities of their guns, based on one or two lucky groups. Any serious student of firearms should acquire a basic knowledge of probability theory as applied in the firearms field. (See GROUP MEASUREMENT; IMPACT BEHAVIOR BALLISTICS; MEAN RADIUS.)

group measurement Group measurement is the distance between the bullet holes that are the greatest distance apart in a string of shots. Any number of shots from three up is considered a group.

Extreme spread, the most common group measurement, has been determined by a number of different methods. The distance between the inside edges of the bullet holes that form the extreme spread of the group has been used, while some measurements are taken from the outside edges of the same holes. Today, group size has been standarized and is taken from the center of the bullet holes giving the extreme spread. (Another way of making this measurement is from the inside of one hole to the outside of the other.)

Group measurement serves the shooter in many ways. It is, of course, used as the deciding factor in some forms of match shooting. In benchrest shooting, it is the smallest group that wins the match, even though the group may not be near the aiming point. In most other forms of match shooting the winning target is scored by the proximity of the center of impact to the center of the target, but if group size is not very small there is little chance the score will be high.

Group measurement is used to determine the accuracy of the rifle and/or the load. It is also used when checking the accuracy of a barrel and in finding the correct bedding of the stock for that particular barrel. (See CENTER OF IMPACT; GROUP.)

grouse, guns and loads for *Bonassa umbellus*, the ruffed grouse, is a bird of the woods and forests. Heavily muscled and feathered, it is an agile flier and is adept at screening itself from the shooter by dodging behind foliage. Because of its startling take-off and rapid, elusive flight, shots must be taken with extreme speed, and the prerequisites of an effective grouse gun are light weight and swift handling. An open choke (or chokes) is more effective than a tight one, since most of the birds are taken at close to moderate range.

Unlike woodcock, which are also dwellers in thick cover, grouse are sturdy birds with considerable vitality and require a sizeable shot pellet to bring them down. Experienced grouse hunters prefer loads of No. 6, 7½, or 8 shot, and some claim that the smaller sizes work best only in the late season when the leaves have fallen. While it is not necessary to use high-brass loads, they are more effective because of the extra velocity they offer.

Traditionally, double shotguns are favored for grouse hunting. Their shorter overall length, superior handling qualities, and instant choice of chokes offer significant advantages over a repeater. Twenty-gauge guns can be effective in the hands of a skillful shot, but a 12 gauge, if it is not too heavy for rapid handling, fires a denser pattern and gives a better chance of clean kills in most situations.

The Western grouse species such as the sage and blue grouse are hunted in the sage flats and foothills of the far West. Unlike ruffed grouse, these birds often congregate in large flocks. The technique for hunting them is usually to take first shots at birds breaking out of the flock, and then to hunt down the scattered birds individually.

Like the ruffed grouse, these western species are sizeable, and they are usually taken at long range, especially late in the season when they are nervous as a result of weeks of being hunted. A 12-gauge gun, choked modified, is probably the best choice. If a double is used, modified and full is an excellent combination. High base loads of No. 6 or No. 7½ shot are highly successful.

guard screws The screws that hold the rifle receiver and trigger guard assembly together and bind them to the stock. Most actions have two guard screws, one at the receiver ring and one at the tang, but some actions have another at the front of the trigger guard.

gun A generic term that is commonly applied to all kinds of firearms. In military terminology, the word refers to artillery pieces or naval guns (cannon), but in civilian usage this meaning does not hold.

gun care Gun care should start when the rifle is unpacked from its container and continue even after it is no longer used actively for hunting or target shooting. The former is to ready it for use, the latter to preserve it and protect it from rust and corrosive action caused by high humidity and/or changes in atmospheric conditions.

When purchased, most guns have some kind of rust-inhibiting preparation applied to the action, bore, and chamber, and this should be removed before the gun is fired. With most commercial arms, it is a simple matter to remove the preparation from all parts by ordinary cleaning of the bore and chamber; the action will not require internal cleaning unless the gun is to be used at low temperatures. Surplus military arms, and some imports, are a different matter. Cosmoline and similar preservative preparations are extremely difficult to remove, and the rifle should be completely dismantled and all working parts washed in gasoline, kerosene, or some other suitable solvent before use.

The reasons for this are that heavy grease can cause working parts to malfunction, and lubricating and preservative preparations in the bore may cause pressures to rise drastically. Even light lubrication of the chamber prevents the cartridge case from holding firmly against the chamber wall when it is expanded by firing and allows it to slide to the rear, exerting greater back-pressure on the bolt.

There is little need to say much about gun care for those guns used exclusively for competition shooting. Anyone who competes seriously in the shooting sports know how vital it is to care for guns used and keep them in perfect tune at all times. Also, the guns used are almost never subjected to severe weather conditions or rough treatment. But the hunter finds completely different circumstances and is often poorly informed as to how to cope with them.

To start with, if a hunt will take place in a very wet area, especially near salt water, the barreled action should be removed from the stock and coated with a good rust inhibitor to prevent rust from forming between metal and wood or between metal parts. As added insurance, the gun should again be stripped after the trip and thoroughly cleaned of any rust or other corrosion. This should include even the small metal parts such as detachable sling swivels and scope mount bases. (In regard to scope mount bases, it is not a good idea to put grease or any oily lubricant between the base and action when mounting the scope. Some gunsmiths, and many rifle owners, do this with the thought that it will prevent rust from forming, and they are right; but it will also prevent the base from making firm contact with the action, and after extended use it will almost certainly become loose. Light spraying with a thin Teflon oil, which is then wiped off so that no coating is formed, will help prevent rusting and not interfere with solid base/action contact.)

For hunting in these wet areas, the internal parts of the action should be lightly lubricated with some kind of very light rust preventive lubricant. Conversely, if the hunt will take place in temperatures below freezing, and especially in Arctic hunting, the lubricant should be removed from the action mechanism completely. If any lubricant is used it must have a proven capability of remaining solvent in very low temperatures.

One of the most important parts of gun care is cleaning of the bore while on a hunting trip. Shortly after the advent of non-corrosive primers, some rather misleading advertising engendered the belief that cleaning the bore was no longer necessary, which is completely untrue. While the priming compound does not in itself corrode the bore, neither does it prevent the bore from corroding when exposed to moisture. And moisture is more likely to remain or form in the bore under the powder residue than in a clean bore. Any time the gun has been fired during the day it should be cleaned before leaving it overnight. During damp weather, or when hunting in coastal areas, the bore should be wiped thoroughly even if no firing is done.

For bore cleaning on a hunting trip it is highly important that a good powder solvent be used, preferably something that is effective as a rust preventative as well and that will not cause the first shot to stray from zero if a little remains in the bore. The cleaning outfit should consist of a jointed rod, bronzed bore brushes, patches, the solvent, and some kind of light lubricant for external areas. The jointed rod not only does a better job of bore scrubbing, but if a case becomes stuck in the chamber it can also make the difference between success and failure of a very expensive trip.

In general, it is an excellent idea to clean the bore of any gun every day or two while on a hunting trip in order to remove moisture that may have formed in response to sudden changes of temperature or to remove deposits of abrasive dust in dry hunting areas. Even when the gun is stored at home it is an excellent idea to clean the bore occasionally—corrosion will be prevented and careful cleaning won't wear out the barrel.

In rifle shooting of any kind, accuracy is the prime requisite for success; continued and careful maintenance—to ensure that the highest degree of accuracy the individual rifle is capable of delivering is retained—is a vital part of gun care.

If accuracy seems to be going sour, the first place to check is the scope mount. The screws in mount rings are easy to keep tight if checked from time to time, but periodically the base screws should also be checked to make sure they are tight. Even 1/1,000 of an inch of play here can means several inches of error when shooting.

Whether the gun is used for hunting or not, the guard screws of a bolt-action rifle should be checked often and kept tight. This is particularly critical when the rifle is carried in a vehicle of any kind over rough terrain. Rifles with loose guard screws suffer loss of accuracy, and recoil is almost certain to split the stock if firing is continued with loose guard screws.

While bolt-action rifles have very few screws, aside from the guard screws, that can loosen and cause functional problems, most other kinds of actions do. Lever, slide, and autoloading rifle actions should be gone over occasionally, and especially prior to a hunting trip, and all screws checked for tightness. The same applies to slide and autoloading shotgun actions. Some revolvers have a tendency to jar screws loose, particularly when chambered for magnum cartridges, and autoloaders do the same thing. Autoloading actions, especially those that are gas operated, must be disassembled, cleaned, and relubricated regularly if much firing is done and occasionally even if it isn't.

When hunting under dry, dusty conditions, and especially if part or most of the hunting is done with some kind of vehicle that stirs up sand and dust, any type of action should be cleaned often enough to ensure that it does not ingest enough grit to cause a malfunction or wear the parts by abrasive action. Under these conditions, except where absolutely necessary to ensure proper functioning, no lubricant should be used that is not dry; any kind of oil or grease simply causes the dirt to collect in thicker layers.

Gunstock care will vary depending upon the kind of finish originally applied. If it is one of the hard epoxy or varnish finishes there isn't much the owner can do to care for it except to avoid scratches and bumps as much as possible. If it has any kind of oil finish it is a good idea occasionally to give it a very light coat of boiled linseed oil, rubbing it thoroughly with the hand until only a very thin coat is left. When a scratch appears, a drop of the same oil finish rubbed into the area will either restore the finish or, if it is too deep, make it less noticeable and seal it.

Guns that are to be stored for any length of time

should be cleaned thoroughly and coated with a light film of rust preventive grease (RIG has been the outstanding favorite for this use for decades), since light oil will evaporate. The bore must not be plugged, and the gun should be stored in a dry place where air can circulate over it. This prevents the accumulation of moisture and, subsequently, the formation of rust.

gun collecting   Collecting is a natural outgrowth of an interest in firearms. Collectors acquire guns for any number of reasons: to actually use them, as art objects, as investments, for their historical value, or as a combination of these elements. Just as there are numerous target shooters who never hunt, many gun collectors never fire a gun.

There is an almost infinite number of firearms types that can be collected. For example: Kentucky rifles, Hawken rifles, dueling pistols, early Colt revolvers, fine British shotguns, Parker shotguns, pre-1964 Model 70 Winchesters, Lugers, etc.

Whatever the kind of collection to be undertaken, it is important to refrain from buying any gun until the field is thoroughly understood. If one is collecting Parkers, for example, it should be kept in mind that these shotguns were made in many different grades, and that the plainest grades are simply old shotguns, with no collectors' value. Conversely, the top-of-the-line Parkers were made in very limited numbers; Parker's top grade, the Invincible, could conceivably be sold for more than $500,000 today, as only two were ever produced. Before investing in such a rarity, the most painstaking authentication should be undertaken—it would cost far less than $500,000 to make a fake Invincible.

Fine old guns—both antiques and arms of the modern era—are in extremely short supply, since the best have long since been absorbed into private collections or museums. Accordingly, the faking of antiques and collectors' pieces has become common, and many of these forgeries are done with extreme skill, so much so that it is impossible for anyone but an expert to detect the fraud. In buying modern arms, the possibility of encountering a fake is not so great, but there are still nuances to every market that must be understood. A Luger collector must know which manufacturers produced the most desirable models, and must check to see that all the gun's serially numbered parts match. A collector of British shotguns should be aware that some makes are far more desirable than others and should know enough about the way the guns function to ensure that he is buying a properly working firearm.

It should also be borne in mind that the desirability of many collectors' pieces is based on what the market will bear, not on any intrinsic value of the gun itself, and that what is valuable today may be out of vogue and nearly worthless in a few years.

Here are some general guidelines to follow:

Before investing in any gun for a collection, understand the market for that kind of gun thoroughly. Do not accept the initial price; check with several other sources to see that it is reasonable.

Do not buy guns that are in poor condition, that have parts missing, or that have been altered.

When buying any gun of considerable value, ask for a detailed bill of sale, vouching for the arm's authenticity and stating that the person selling is indeed the gun's legal owner.

If possible, have the firearm appraised by an expert before buying. Have the appraisal done in writing, and save it for insurance purposes.

If presented with a remarkable "find," bear in mind that the odds on uncovering such a rarity are very small and approach the deal with extra caution.

Collecting guns is a rewarding occupation and can also be highly profitable, but it must be approached with common sense and, above all, knowledge.

gun condition   Because the condition of used firearms varies enormously, the National Rifle Association has developed qualitative standards that enable a prospective buyer to know the approximate condition of a gun through a one-word description. The six NRA grades for used guns are as follows:

"Poor" condition denotes a firearm that is badly rusted and battered, has suffered major damage to the stock finish, and requires major repairs and/or alteration to be operable.

"Fair" indicates that the gun is in safe working condition, but well worn, perhaps requiring replacement of minor parts. A "fair" gun has no rust, but may have corrosion pits.

"Good" indicates no rust or pitting, no broken parts, some minor wear, and safe working condition.

"Very good" indicates perfect working condition, no appreciable wear on working surfaces, no corrosion or pitting, only minor surface dents or scratches.

"Excellent" indicates new condition, used but little, no noticeable marring of wood or metal, bluing perfect (except at muzzle and sharp edges).

"Perfect" means in new condition in every respect.

The NRA also sets condition standards for antique guns.

Gun Control Act of 1968   The Gun Control Act of 1968 consists of a comprehensive series of federal regulations and provisions affecting the sale, manufacture, importation, and transfer of firearms in the United States, and the licensing of persons engaged in the firearms business. The act is enforced and administered by the Alcohol, Tobacco, and Firearms division of the Internal Revenue Service, U.S. Treasury Department.

The major provisions of the Gun Control Act of 1968 are:

1. No one except licensed manufacturers, dealers, and importers may engage in the business of importing, manufacturing or dealing in firearms or ammunition, or in the course of such business ship, transport, or receive any firearm or ammunition in interstate commerce;

2. Standards for obtaining firearms licenses are considerably tightened and fees raised;

3. Licensees may not ship firearms or ammunition interstate to nonlicensees;

4. Licensees may not furnish firearms or ammunition to anyone they know or have reason to believe is a fugitive from justice, a convicted felon or anyone under indictment for a felony, an unlawful drug user or addict, or an adjudicated mental defective or one who has been committed to any mental institution;

5. Licensees may not sell rifles or shotguns or ammunition therefor to anyone they know or have reason to believe is under 18, or handguns or ammunition therefor to anyone under 21. However, 18-year-olds may purchase .22-rimfire ammunition;

6. Licensees may not sell firearms or ammunition to anyone who is prohibited from possessing or purchasing them by state or local law applicable at the place of sale or delivery, unless there is reason to believe the purchase or possession is not illegal;

7. Licensees may not sell firearms to persons who do not appear personally, unless the purchaser submits a sworn statement that his purchase is legal, a copy of which the licensee must forward to the chief law enforcement officer in the purchaser's locality seven days before shipment;

8. Licensees must note in their records the names, ages, and places of residence of firearms and ammunition purchasers (except purchasers of shotgun ammunition, ammunition suitable for use only in rifles, or component parts for the aforesaid types of ammunition);

9. Licensed importers and manufacturers are required to put serial numbers on all firearms;

10. Fugitives from justice, convicted felons or persons under indictment for a felony, unlawful users of certain drugs, adjudicated mental defectives, and persons once committed to a mental institution may not receive, ship, or transport any firearm or ammunition in interstate or foreign commerce, or receive any firearm or ammunition that has been so shipped or transported;

11. No one may provide a firearm to anyone who he knows or has reason to believe is a nonresident of the state;

12. No one except licensees may transport into or receive in their state of residence firearms acquired elsewhere;

13. No one may deliver a firearm or ammunition to any common or contract carrier for transportation or shipment in interstate or foreign commerce to persons other than licensed manufacturers, dealers or collectors, without written notice to the carrier that such firearm or ammunition is being shipped;

14. Carriers may not transport or deliver firearms or ammunition in interstate commerce with knowledge or reasonable cause to believe the shipment, transportation, or receipt would violate the act;

15. No one may make a false statement intended to or likely to deceive a licensee with respect to the lawfulness of his acquisition of a firearm or ammunition;

16. No one may import a firearm unless he satisfies the secretary of the treasury that it is "particularly suitable for or readily adaptable to sporting purposes" and is not surplus military firearm;

17. Nonlicensees may not transport, ship or receive in interstate commerce, and licensees may not sell or deliver to anyone, any "destructive device" (explosive, incendiary, poison gas, grenade, mine, rocket, missile, or weapon with a bore of ½ inch or more), machine gun, short-barreled rifle (barrel less than 16 inches), or short-barreled shotgun (barrel less than 18 inches), except as specifically authorized by the secretary of the treasury as consistent with "public safety and necessity."

Any person who knowingly makes any false statement or representation with respect to any information required by the Gun Control Act of 1968 shall be fined not more than $5,000 or imprisoned not more than five years, or both. Any person who ships, transports, or receives a firearm or ammunition with intent to commit an offense punishable by imprisonment for a term exceeding one year, shall be fined not more than $10,000, or imprisoned not more than 10 years, or both.

Additional information may be obtained by writing to any regional branch office of the Bureau of Alcohol, Tobacco and Firearms.

The Gun Control Act of 1968 was last amended on May 19, 1986 when Congress passed the Firearms Owners Protection Act, otherwise known as the McClure/Volkmer Bill (named after Senator James McClure and Representative Harold Volkmer).

To summarize the changes in the GCA of 1968, the FOPA amends the GCA in the following ways. Basically it:

Redefines crimes, misdemeanors, and commerce in firearms;

Relaxes commerce and trade in firearms;

Relaxes ammunition sales restrictions and eliminates ammunition sales recordkeeping;

Eliminates contiguous sales requirements for rifles and shotguns;

Eliminates restrictions on loaned or rented firearms;

Tightens controls on whom firearms should not be sold to. Changed restrictions from licensees to "persons";

Tightens definitions on whom firearms could not be sold to, i.e., illegal aliens, dishonorably discharged veterans, those who renounced citizenship, etc.;

Redefines "engaged in the business";

Bans transfer and possession of fully automatic firearms manufactured after May 19, 1986;

Defines how often a licensee may be inspected and for what;

Allows licensees to sell at gun shows;

Stiffens penalties for willful criminal violations, especially when violent or drug-related;

Makes the U.S. liable for frivolous prosecutions;

Grants relief avenues to those not specifically prevented from possessing, transporting, or receiving firearms;

Removes some of the secretary of the treasury's discretionary power;

Prevents centralized record keeping or accumulation of records;

Allows interstate transportation of firearms, when not readily accessible, even when prevented by state or local ordinances;

More clearly defines parts for full-auto conversions.

(See FIREARMS ACT OF 1934.)

guncotton A substance made by treating cotton with nitric and sulfuric acids. Guncotton was the explosive base of early smokeless powders. (See NITROCELLULOSE; SINGLE-BASE POWDER; SMOKELESS POWDER.)

Gun Digest The first edition of this well-known annual firearms publication was produced in 1944. The contents were divided roughly into two equal categories—feature articles and a catalog section reflecting the firearms and related products then available. The publisher was Milton P. Klein, then owner of the Klein's Sporting Goods store in Chicago. He had conceived the idea during World War II—when sporting firearms were extremely scarce—that frustrated customers for guns would welcome a publication dealing with such guns. He named Charles R. Jacobs, an employee of his, as editor. Jacobs produced the first four editions of *Gun Digest*. After the issuance of the fourth edition there was a short time gap before the fifth edition appeared in 1950.

The fifth edition was produced by John T. Amber, as were all subsequent annual issues, up to and including the 1978 edition. Under Amber's direction, *Gun Digest* flourished and gradually grew larger, recently exceeding 400 pages.

Gun Digest has featured articles by virtually all of the best gun writers, and in recent decades has had worldwide distribution. It currently reaches about one million readers. (See AMBER, JOHN T.)

gun fit A gun is said to "fit" the shooter when it comes smoothly to shoulder, with sights aligned naturally in front of the shooter's master eye, and without the shooter having to make extensive manipulations or contortions to feel comfortable. Fit is a combination of the right stock length, proper comb height, proper pitch of the stock, proper balance, and other factors related to the variances in physical configuration and dimensions of individual shooters.

Proper fit is generally conceded to be more important in shotguns than in rifles because shotguns have no rear sight and alignment of the shooter's eye is critical to placement of the shot. Good fit is important on any shoulder gun, however, and lack of it may create excessive recoil and poor shooting. (See COMB; MASTER EYE.)

gun metal The earliest cast gun barrels were made of bronze, an alloy of copper and tin, and the earliest makers were undoubtedly the bell founders, who had been practicing their craft since the 11th century. Copper and tin had been known since ancient times, and the technology of tin mining, smelting, and casting was much easier than that of iron and thus preceded it. Different works on the subject list the composition of this gun metal at proportions varying from 10 to 15 parts tin out of 100, the balance being copper. Given the primitive metallurgical knowledge of the times, the fact that barrels were often cast using metal from the bells and statues of captured cities and towns, and the impurities likely to be included in processing, it is probable that the composition varied widely.

Cast gun metal cannon barrels were still being manufactured well into the 19th century. The development of better gunpowder and the higher pressures resulting therefrom, forced the development of barrels made of iron. (See BARREL MAKING.)

gunpowder A term denoting black powder. It has also been erroneously applied to modern smokeless propellants. (See BLACK POWDER.)

gunpowder, shipping and storage of Gunpowder, as the term is properly used, refers only to black powder, though many of the storage and shipping regulations erroneously refer to all ammunition propellants as gunpowder. The primary difference between smokeless and black powder is that black powder will ignite easily and will burn explosively, even when unconfined.

This important distinction is the reason that black powder or gunpowder is so hazardous to handle. The slightest spark, reportedly even from static electricity, could ignite the propellant. Consequently, there are numerous federal regulations regarding the shipping and sale of black powder. Although they become quite detailed and involved, the regulations basically specify the amount of powder and kind of packaging and placarding required for shipment of black powder. It cannot be shipped by mail, United Parcel Service, bus, or by any other carrier that normally transports passengers. It must be shipped by freight in a properly marked vehicle with the powder in proper containers. The Department of Transportation classifies black powder as a class A low explosive. The "low" designation refers to the velocity of the exploding matter only.

The storage of black powder is regulated by municipal governments and varies from town to town. The National Fire Protective Association has established guidelines regarding the storage of powder, and many city governments have developed their regulations using these guidelines. Basically, the NFPA recommends that stored quantities of black powder be limited to 5-pound lots and that it should be stored in a Class II magazine, that is, a bullet resistant, fire resistant, theft resistant, and ventilated magazine. Construction of the magazine is also spelled out in the NFPA guidelines.

Historical accounts have not been without an occasional ignition of a powder flask by a spark from a flintlock rifle. The force is said to be powerful enough to sever a man at the midsection. At other times, however, the powder burns with a "whooshing" sound when a spark finds its way into a flask. At any rate, black powder should never be loaded directly from a flask, but from a powder measure instead, where only a small quantity is introduced to the bore. After measuring the powder from a flask, the container should be placed behind the body, or somewhere well away from the lock or muzzle when firing.

Several years ago Pyrodex was developed as a replacement for black powder. It met the D.O.T. class B explosive requirements and consequently could be shipped and stored with all the safety of smokeless propellant. It could be loaded volume for volume (but *not* by weight) in exchange for black powder, and it contained an additive that produced a grayish-white smoke to simulate black powder. It appeared that the problems associated with shipping and storage of black powder were solved with the mass production of Pyrodex—until the plant was consumed in an explosive fire along with the inventor, Dan Pawlak.

For the past several years, black powder has again filled the needs of muzzleloading shooters, but a new Pyrodex plant is in production.

The Federal Firearms License holder who deals in black powder is required to keep his stores of black powder locked in a magazine out of access to customers. He is also required to limit sale quantities to 50 pounds.

Shipment and storage of smokeless powder is also regulated and is subject to these provisions: Quantities of smokeless propellants not in excess of 25 pounds may be carried in a passenger vehicle. Commercial shipments of smokeless propellant in quantities not exceeding 100 pounds must be shipped in containers approved by the Department of Transportation. Smokeless propellants for personal use, in quantities of not more than 20 pounds, may be stored in the home in the original containers; quantities of 20 to 50 pounds must be locked in a wooden box. In addition, there are detailed regulations for the storage and display of powder by commercial establishments.

gut-shot An animal is said to be gut-shot if it is hit between the diaphragm and hindquarters. The term can also be applied when the bullet lands either to the rear of or forward of the intestinal cavity but passes through it. Gut shots should be avoided for two reasons: First, a gut-shot animal will nearly always live for a longer period after being hit and may be capable of traveling a great distance. Second, the meat of gut-shot animals is often contaminated and unfit for consumption.

gutta-percha During the late 19th and early 20th centuries, many handguns had handles made of gutta-percha, a black hard-rubber compound that was favored by many shooters because of its sticky feel, which lent a good grip to the hand, especially if the hand was sweaty. Gutta-percha was also favored by manufacturers, since it was inexpensive and could be molded at low cost.

Eventually, it was replaced by wood, which was more durable and better looking; and, on cheaply made guns, by plastic, which was less expensive.

gyro-jet A gun that fired a small rocket projectile that bears the same name. This molded plastic handgun was designed and produced in limited quantities by MBA Associates in the mid- and late 1960s. The loaded cartridge consisted of a long steel projectile with a solid-fuel rocket motor housed in its hollow rear. A conventional Boxer-type primer ignited the rocket motor. The solid-fuel gases were then exhausted through angled nozzles designed to propel the projectile forward down the smooth bore. These angled nozzles were also designed to provide rotation for stabilization.

The primary advantages of the system were inexpensive gun construction and practically no recoil. The gyro-jet offered a relatively high energy downrange, but was slow to accelerate. One critic claimed that the projectiles could be caught in the hand as they slowly exited the muzzle.

Even though the guns were cheaply made, they were produced in very limited numbers and were priced up to $300 each. The plastic guns more closely resembled toys than real guns, and ammunition was costly and not widely distributed. Consequently, the guns were not commercially successful. Today, both the guns and the rocket cartridges are considered collectors' items.

Several factors also prevented the Gyro-Jet from being seriously considered for military use. The primary reasons were the bulk and weight of the ammunition and the low short-range penetration. Several yards were required for the rocket to accelerate and build up velocity and energy. Thus it was ineffective for short-range police situations or combat use.

gyroscopic stability A bullet that spins perfectly around its axis and maintains a straight line of flight is said to have gyroscopic stability. To achieve this, the rate of twist in the rifle barrel must be correct for the diameter, weight, and length of the bullet for the velocity at which it leaves the muzzle. If the bullet does not maintain gyroscopic stability throughout its flight, it will start to yaw or weave and may eventually tumble.

A number of factors may cause the loss of gyroscopic stability: the wrong rate of twist; voids in the lead core; a jacket that is thicker on one side than the other; bullet points that are off center; bullet bases that are not square to the axis of the bullet or have an imperfect edge; and a bullet that is not perfectly round. (See BULLET STABILIZATION; BULLET YAW; INTERIOR BALLISTICS; TUMBLING; TWIST.)

hair trigger A popular term for a rifle or pistol trigger that can be released by very light pressure. It is commonly applied to double set triggers. (See DOUBLE SET TRIGGER; TRIGGER PULL.)

half-bent A British term synonymous with the American "half-cock" (position). (See HALF-COCK.)

half-cock A hammer position controlled by a notch at the midpoint of sear or hammer travel that forestalls accidental hammer fall. In some revolvers, the cylinder can be rotated only when the hammer is in this position. (See HAMMER.)

half-hand A British term for a semipistol-grip shotgun stock. (See SEMIPISTOL GRIP.)

half-jacketed Half-jacketed (often called short-jacketed or semijacketed) bullets feature short metal jackets crimped into the lead bullet cores, with the lead exposed from the midway point forward. (See PRACTICE BULLET.)

hammer That part of the firing system of some firearms that strikes the percussion cap in muzzle-loaders or the primer in cartridge arms. Some hammers directly strike the cap or primer to initiate ignition, while others strike a separate firing pin. Most hammers are exposed and are cocked by hand, by operating the mechanism of the firearm, or by both methods. Some hammers are internal and are cocked only by operating the gun's mechanism.

The hammer on flintlocks is called the cock; it is designed to hold the flint in a viselike screw-operated jaw. (See IGNITION.)

hammer burr Some hammers have a round wheel-like projection on their rear portions rather than the usual hammer spur. The burr is usually striated or checkered to prevent the thumb from slipping when cocking the arm. Burr hammers are employed on autoloading pistols that are to be carried concealed because there is less likelihood of their becoming entangled in the user's clothing. (See HAMMER SPUR.)

hammered barrel See BARREL, RIFLED.

hammerless A hammerless firearm is any one in which the firing pin is not struck by a hammer, but

obtains its force through the release of a spring acting directly upon it.

Hammerli (company) A firm in Lenzburg, Switzerland, well known since 1863 for high-quality target and sporting rifles and pistols. Originally Rudolph Hammerli & Cie, the anglicized name now would be Hammerli Hunting and Sporting Weapons Factory. For some time it has had a branch plant in Tiengen, West Germany.

From the early 1900s to World War II, Hammerli was best known in America for target guns built on Martini-type actions, particularly those designed for Olympic and International shooting at 50 and 300 meters. Swiss marksmen using Hammerli free rifles were so preeminent during this period in 300-meter competition that the U.S. International teams of 1928–1931 were equipped with Hammerli-Martini free rifles, although they were rebarreled at Springfield Armory. Hammerli free pistols were made on small Martini-type actions, and typically had four-lever set triggers with the operating lever working through the buttstock.

After World War II, Hammerli purchased manufacturing rights to the Walther .22 auto pistol, and their first auto pistols for the International Shooting Union rapid-fire course were Hammerli-Walthers. In addition to free rifles and free pistols on Martini, bolt, straight-pull, and other kinds of actions, Hammerli has produced a variety of lighter target arms, training rifles in .22 caliber that are duplicates of military arms, a variety of .22 auto pistols for the ISU rapid-fire course, CO_2 pistols, and hunting weapons. Hammerli guns are imported to the United States by Mandel Shooting Supplies. (See FREE PISTOL; FREE RIFLE; HAMMERLI-TANNER RIFLE; MARTINI ACTION; WALTHER [COMPANY].)

Hammerli-Tanner rifle A 300-meter free rifle made by Hammerli. A single-shot bolt-action design, it is a typical 300-meter rifle, with a thumbhole stock, four-level set trigger, adjustable palm rest, and adjustable buttplate. For the Swiss, it is chambered for the 7.5 Swiss military cartridge, but it has been offered in the United States chambered for the .30/06, .308, and 6.5×55. (See FREE RIFLE; HAMMERLI [COMPANY]; THUMBHOLE STOCK.)

hammer shoe When telescopic sights are mounted on rifles having outside hammers, it is sometimes difficult to cock the arm with the thumb because of the overhanging eyepiece of the sight. Hammer shoes fit over the hammer spur and have a projection to the right or left of the eyepiece. This allows the user to cock the arm without interference.

hammer spur The spur is the rear projection of the hammer on guns equipped with outside hammers. The function of the spur is to allow the shooter to cock the hammer with the thumb. The upper surface of the hammer spur is usually striated or checkered so as to present a nonslip surface to the ball of the thumb. (See HAMMER BURR.)

hand When a revolver, either single- or double-action, is cocked, the cylinder is rotated into battery by the hand, a part that is connected to the hammer by means of a lever and abuts the ratchet in the rear of the cylinder.

hand cannon Probably the earliest form of muzzle-loading gun, the hand cannon was purportedly invented around 1325 by the Chinese. It was simply a primitive iron tube joined by bands to either a straight wooden stock or to iron handles and was ignited by a lighted wick applied to the touch hole. The vent, or touch hole, was drilled directly into the powder chamber.

These hand cannons were so hazardous that sometimes condemned criminals were offered a choice of either summary execution or holding a hand cannon in battle. In current usage, the term "Handcannon" is associated with a line of custom handguns and accessories marketed by SSK Industries, of Bloomingdale, Ohio.

hand checkering A form of functional ornamentation applied to firearms by means of hand tools rather than by machine. It usually consists of rows

The very earliest portable firearms took the form of hand cannons, such as this one.

of intersecting grooves that provide a nonslip grasping surface. (See CHECKERING.)

hand ejector A Smith & Wesson model designation for a kind of revolver. It is a gun in which the cases are ejected from the cylinder by manually pushing them back with the ejector rod. (See EJECTOR ROD.)

hand guard The cover over a barrel, generally on a military firearm, that protects the hand from the heat generated by sustained rapid fire.

handgun Any firearm designed to be fired by one hand only, without the support of the shoulder, and without the cheek on the stock for aiming.

handgun barrel See BARREL, HANDGUN.

handgun bullet When handguns first came into common use after the French invention of the flintlock, and continuing through the percussion period up to the American Civil War, the most commonly used bullets for these arms were round lead balls. The cylindro-conoidal bullet similar in shape to modern bullets was being used in some rifles prior to the Civil War, and during that war, this kind of bullet was adapted for use in percussion revolvers. With the widespread adoption of the self-contained metallic cartridges and revolvers loaded from the rear of the cylinder, the round ball as a handgun bullet passed from the scene.

Modern handgun bullets are of three general kinds. Those intended for target shooting with light powder charges at ranges up to 50 yards are cylindrical in shape and have a flat nose that aids in cutting a clean hole in the target paper. For this reason they are called "wadcutters." Target-type wadcutter bullets are swaged or cast from lead alloyed with tin, antimony, or other hardening agents and are not jacketed.

Handgun bullets intended for military use under the provisions of the Geneva Convention are restricted to those with hard full-metal jackets. These bullets have rounded noses, as do the lead bullets intended for police use.

Handgun bullets for defensive use and for hunting are mostly of the semiwadcutter configuration. This kind of bullet is cylindrical at the base and for some distance along its sides. It then tapers—abruptly on some designs, gradually on others—to a flat nose that may be hollow pointed or solid. Some designs have a sharp shoulder where the cylindrical portion begins to taper toward the nose. Semiwadcutter bullets cast or swaged of lead alloys have been used for many years for hunting and defense and have proved to be highly efficient.

The most efficient handgun bullets for use in hunting game animals and for defense are properly designed cast bullets and some of the currently manufactured jacketed bullets. When driven at high velocity, unjacketed bullets can cause leading problems in rough gun barrels. Jacketed soft point bullets can be driven at high velocities consistent with safe pressures and give good accuracy with no barrel leading, although properly lubed and sized cast bullets provide more velocity with less pressure. Expansion of these jacketed handgun bullets can be controlled to some degree by the thickness of the jackets and by the alloys used in their lead cores. In this manner, such bullets can be constructed so as to expand within a given range of velocities. (See HANDGUN CARTRIDGES, HUNTING; HANDGUN CARTRIDGES, TARGET.)

handgun cartridges, hunting Any handgun cartridge may be used for hunting; however, over the years certain handgun rounds have proven to be outstanding for hunting use.

The .22 Winchester Magnum Rimfire is an outstanding cartridge for use on the smaller game species at normal handgun ranges of 50 yards and under. This cartridge will cleanly kill game up to the size of bobcats at these ranges. The best hunting cartridges are those loaded with 40–50 grain hollow point bullets.

The .38 Special, originally conceived as a police and defense cartridge, is a fine small-game round because of its outstanding accuracy and the fine targetgrade revolvers chambered for it. The target wadcutter load in the .38 Special is excellent for use on such game as rabbits, squirrels, and woodchucks. Special high-velocity handloads with jacketed soft point and hollow point bullets make the .38 Special usable on larger animals such as foxes, bobcats, and coyotes up to the maximum 50-yard range.

The .357 Magnum is really an elongated .38 Special and in fact was developed from that cartridge. It imparts higher velocities to and therefore delivers greater energy from the same bullets that are used in the .38 Special. While it has been used successfully on such medium game as deer and bear, it is a marginal cartridge for this use.

The .41 Magnum and .44 Magnum cartridges are so similar in the amount of energy delivered within normal handgun hunting ranges that they can be considered as being equally useful on medium game and, under special circumstances, on large nondangerous game such as elk and moose. The .44 Magnum has a slight edge because of the wider variety of ammunition that is available for this cartridge.

The .45 Colt, sometimes referred to as the .45 Long Colt, has been in use for more than a century. It made its debut in the Colt 1873 Single-Action Army Revolver. This cartridge made a fine reputation for itself as a stopper of game as well as men with the old 250-grain bullet and 40 grains of black powder. In the modern Ruger Blackhawk revolver and in the Thompson Contender single-shot pistol, the .45 Colt with special handloads in modern cases will perform near the levels of the .41 Magnum and .44 Magnum. At this time, these loads can only be used in these two handguns.

The .22 Long Rifle rimfire is popular for both formal and informal target shooting. In addition, in trained hands the Long Rifle in a good handgun is an excellent choice as a small-game arm at short range.

During the 1980s, an increase in interest in both handgun hunting and in silhouette shooting with handguns led to a rethinking of what constituted a handgun cartridge. Older standards of power, velocity, and acceptable levels of recoil were scrapped, and new cartridges began to appear.

Notable among these are the Herrett series of cartridges, and the .454 Casull. The former, designed by Steve Herrett and Bob Milek, utilize modified .30/30 cases and are intended for use in single-shot pistols. The Casull cartridge has been in existence for more than 20 years, but guns for the .454 cartridge were only custom modifications to existing firearms. However, it is now commercially loaded, and high-quality single-action revolvers are made for it by Freedom Arms. The Freedom Arms .454 is commonly seen in the field today from Alaska to Africa.

In some cases, single-shot bolt-action pistols are used for hunting. These are chambered for rifle cartridges such as the 7mm/08. (See HANDGUN BULLET; HANDGUN CARTRIDGES, TARGET.)

handgun cartridges, target The preeminent cartridge for formal target shooting with handguns is the .22 Long Rifle rimfire in special target loadings. Statistics show that a far greater number of .22 Long Rifle cartridges are used in competitive handgun shooting than the combined total of all other cartridges used for this purpose.

For serious match shooting, CCT, Federal, Remington, and Winchester-Western manufacture premium ammunition in the .22 Long Rifle case that is specially loaded for target shooting and is so marked. This ammunition is made with carefully selected components and subjected to rigid quality controls. The muzzle velocity developed by these cartridges is lower than that of ammunition intended for use in rifles, and the energy generated is just enough to operate the mechanisms of autoloading pistols chambering the .22 Long Rifle cartridge. This kind of ammunition will usually produce tighter groups from most handguns than will ordinary .22 Long Rifle cartridges. However, an occasional handgun will be found to deliver tighter grouping with standard-velocity ammunition or, in rare instances, with high-velocity cartridges. This fact serves to point out the value of testing various loads in a target handgun in order to select that ammunition that will deliver optimum results.

For many years, the .38 Special cartridge has been a favorite among target shooters competing in centerfire matches. Loaded with the wadcutter type of bullet, it delivers superb accuracy. It was originally a revolver cartridge, but as the advantages of the autoloading pistol for target shooting became apparent, custom-made and factory autoloading pistols designed for use only with the midrange wadcutter .38 Special loads became available. These target loads develop just enough velocity to get the bullets to the target without tumbling and with the required accuracy. Recoil is negligible with these loads, and they are particularly useful in the timed and rapid-fire stages as they allow the shooter to get back on the target and quickly pick up his sight picture for following shots.

Handloads in the .38 Special case that meet these criteria are used by many target shooters. These handloads are popular for practice shooting, but some of them in some handguns will equal the factory products. Because of these characteristics, more .38 Special cartridges are reloaded than any other cartridge.

The .45 Automatic Colt Pistol cartridge became popular as a target round primarily because it chambered in the U.S. Pistol, Model 1911, the official sidearm of the U.S. armed forces for almost 70 years. In addition, the cartridge is capable of excellent accuracy. Two kinds of matches are scheduled for this cartridge. "Hardball" or Service Pistol matches require the use of unmodified Model 1911 pistols with the full-jacketed military-type bullet.

In the .45-caliber matches, any pistol or ammunition may be used. Most shooters find that handloads with 185-grain and 200-grain semiwadcutter bullets give the best results. The .45 autoloading pistol is used by many shooters in centerfire matches in preference to the .38 Special cartridge. (See HANDGUN BULLET; HARDBALL.)

handgun sights Sights for pistols and revolvers can be broken down into three approximate categories: fixed, adjustable, and telescopic. More recently a fourth kind has been seen on target ranges or in the field and consists of a battery-powered electronic sight with limited or no magnification.

The first classification applies to those sights used on service revolvers and concealment arms where compactness and durability are paramount considerations. The front sight usually consists of a rounded blade that won't snag holster or clothing while the rear sight consists of a notched blade held firmly in the receiver or a simple notch milled in the top strap. These sights are not normally associated with arms intended for a high degree of accuracy, although excellent shooting is possible with them.

Adjustable sights generally consist of a sharper and larger front sight in conjunction with an adjustable rear sight. In some instances the front sight is adjustable as well. Most adjustable sights allow adjustment for windage and elevation, while a few are adjustable only for windage. When adjustable sights are found on a target arm, the front sight can consist of a Patridge pattern, which calls for a sharp blade with a perpendicular or undercut rear portion that presents a precise "post" sight picture when aligned with the rear notch or peep. Nontarget arms tend to feature a ramp front sight that will clear holster or clothing without snagging.

Telescopic sights are currently associated with hunting or silhouette arms and are used in applications where compactness isn't of concern. Modern handgun scopes range from nonmagnifying one-power scopes that feature noncritical eye relief to 7- or 10-power scopes and even variable-power scopes for long-range handgunning. These higher magnifications call for more critical eye relief and are used in specialized applications.

The electronic sight (commonly called the Aimpoint because it was so named by its initial manufacturer) appears to place a dot of light "on target" when the switch is on and one sights through the scope. As with telescopic sights, the advantage of the Aimpoint is that sight alignment is eliminated from the sight picture while both accessory sight systems are also much heavier and bulkier than are corresponding open sights. (See METALLIC SIGHTS; PATRIDGE SIGHT; TELESCOPIC SIGHTS.)

handgun stocks Stocks that provide the hand grip on revolvers and pistols. They are made of various materials including wood, plastic, and rubber. The stocks for service handguns are usually made with smooth lines and are unobtrusive in design. However, handguns used in some forms of target shooting are equipped with more sophisticated stocks that conform to the natural shape of the hand and include a thumb rest. Some handgun target stocks go so far as to provide the means of adjusting the fit to individual hands. (See GRIP; STOCKMAKING.)

handicap trap Trapshooting from any range greater than the standard 16 yards. Trap fields are laid out with shooting positions varying from 16 to 27 yards from the trap house. In handicap matches registered with the Amateur Trapshooting Association, each shooter must fire from his or her officially assigned handicap distance. This distance is determined by compiling the average of the shooter's scores in previous registered matches and by using known ability. Each shooter must display an official card, issued by the ATA and bearing a notation of the shooter's current handicap and averages, to a match official before shooting. The thought behind this system is to even out the odds on winning between the more skillful shooters and those less skillful.

In handicap shooting, the gun is moving through a shorter arc, but deeper concentration and more accurate gun pointing are required than when shooting from 16 yards. While a hold that is slightly off might result in a chipped target when shooting from 16 yards, such a hold will result in a lost target from the handicap distances. It has been noted that the majority of good handicap shooters are also fast shooters. Their speed gives them a decided advantage at the longer yardages.

Trapshooters who aspire to be good handicap shooters should practice fast shooting even at the shorter ranges, including 16 yards. Many of the best handicap shooters do all of their practice shooting from the handicap distances on the theory that if they can break targets consistently at these distances, they will have no trouble with the 16-yard targets. (See TRAPSHOOTING.)

handload Although reload is used as a synonym for handload, and the two words are equally descriptive, handload is the term preferred by most pistol and rifle handloaders. Until relatively recently in firearms history, most shooters made their own ammunition. The invention of the self-contained cartridge altered that, however, and now most of the ammunition used in firearms is loaded by ammunition manufacturers. Today, shooters who produce ammunition by hand for their firearms comprise an increasingly large and active percentage of those who shoot guns. At the turn of the century the ammunition companies were making every attempt to discourage handloading, because of the adoption of unfamiliar smokeless powder, but large companies and small concerns that specialize in loading tools and components are numerous today.

The intent of modern handloading is simple: to re-use the case, the most expensive and only recoverable component of a fired centerfire cartridge or shotshell. With special handloading tools, fired cases can be replenished with bullet, primer, and powder, or shot charge, wadding, powder, and primer in the case of a shotshell. There are three basic reasons for handloading. First, because the handloader purchases his components in large quantities, assembles his ammunition with his own labor, and re-uses the expensive case, handloaded ammunition is relatively inexpensive; handloaded ammunition can be as much as 75 percent cheaper than factory loads. Second, handloading allows a degree of control over the ammunition that cannot be had with factory ammunition. Handloaders have the widest possible choice of components to choose from. They can create special loads tailored to specific needs, such as low-power loads for hunting turkeys or squirrels with a big-game rifle. Careful experimentation can produce handloads that are particularly accurate, or pattern unusually well, in an individual gun. Most centerfire target shooters are handloaders for this reason. Third, a handloader can create ammunition for firearms that are obsolete and for which the big companies no longer load ammunition. Even if cases are not available, new cases can usually be made by modifying the cases of other cartridges.

With the acquisition of a set of tools—usually a manually operated loading press, set of dies, and a powder scale or measure—the handloader is ready to produce new ammunition from his spent centerfire cases (rimfire cases cannot be handloaded because the primer cannot be replaced). For rifle and pistol handloading, the steps are nearly identical. First the spent primer is discarded (a process called decapping) while the case is resized to proper dimensions in a sizing die made especially for that round. The case may be full-length resized if it is rifle brass and always is in the case of handgun brass. However, rifle cases that are to be used in the same rifle in which they were originally fired (not including autoloaders) can have their lives prolonged somewhat by neck sizing only—that is, resizing only the part of the case that grasps the bullet.

Repriming is done following decapping and resizing, and the case is then removed from the tool and filled with a weighed or measured charge of powder. The correct powder and charge are determined by referring to a loading manual and must be matched to a particular bullet.

Once the case is charged with powder, the bullet is placed in the case mouth and then seated to its correct depth in the case by putting bullet and case through a seating die. Handgun ammunition requires a further step that is not necessary with rifle cartridges, but is occasionally employed. The case mouth, which in pistol sizing dies is slightly belled during the sizing process, must be crimped tightly around the bullet in a crimping die, except in those autopistol cartridges that headspace in the mouth of a case. Many other procedures, such as case weighing, bullet weighing and spinning for concentricity, chamfering, neck trimming, are also practiced by accuracy-conscious handloaders.

Basic shotshell loading is similar to loading metallic cases, and the number of steps is about the same. After segregating cases by gauge and make (whether paper, plastic, high or low brass), resizing, decapping, and repriming are done just as in metallic case handloading. A suitable powder in a proper amount is selected from the loading tables for the gauge and shot charge one wishes to use. Once the powder charge is placed into the resized and primed hull, an over-powder wad (to prevent mixing of powder and shot), or a plastic shotcup and collar, is placed over the powder. When the shot charge has been delivered into the hull, the mouth is pie crimped in a crimping die, and the new shotshell is ready for use.

Handloading is a growing hobby and sport in the United States and around the world. It is entirely safe if proper caution in following loading tables and selecting and matching components is maintained; its economic and quality advantages have already been mentioned. Handloading also becomes, for most who try it, a very pleasant indoor hobby in and of itself. (See CASE RESIZING; LOADING DIE; LOADING PRESS; RELOADING DATA.)

Handloader, The The *Handloader* is a bimonthly publication devoted to the technical and experimental aspects of handloading. It covers handloading techniques and tips for loading ammunition for rifles, handguns, and shotguns. The magazine was founded in 1966 by Dave Wolfe, a founder of *Shooting Times* magazine. In 1970, editorial offices were transferred from Peoria, Illinois, to Prescott, Arizona.

hand stop Target rifles are generally equipped with an aluminum or plastic block attachment that projects down from the bottom of the fore-end of the stock. This block offers a convenient stop for the shooter's extended hand and is usually moveable, along a track recessed in the underside of the fore-end, so that the stop can be located in the best position for the individual shooter. It usually includes a swivel for attaching a sling strap.

hangfire A time delay in the ignition of a cartridge at the time of firing. Common in the days of flintlock arms and to a lesser extent in the caplock period, it is rarely encountered with modern cartridge arms and ammunition. Some of the test facilities in present-day ammunition plants report the firing of more than one million rounds without a hangfire.

Total time from ignition to bullet exit is a little

less than 4 milliseconds (ms) in modern rifles. The shortest delay in time recognizable to the average shooter is about 30 to 40 ms. From about 60 ms upward, a hangfire produces the typical "click-bang" of the impact of the firing pin, a delay, then fire. Older instruction manuals instruct a shooter to wait 10 to 15 seconds in the case of a misfire, as it may turn out to be a hangfire and the cartridge could go off with the action opened. Present-day tests indicate that this is unnecessary, as hangfires of more than 1/4 to 1/3 of a second (250 to 333 ms) are exceedingly rare, but nevertheless occasionally occur.

Old ammunition, ammunition exposed to heat or moisture for long periods, primers exposed to oil or some of the modern antirust compounds, and primers improperly seated in handloads are all possible sources of hangfires. Weak firing pin springs and heavy oil or grease in firing mechanisms are others.

Occasionally, delays in ignition, identified by the shooter as hangfires, are the result of mechanical malfunctions, improperly adjusted triggers, etc. (See IGNITION; MISFIRE.)

hardball A full-metal-jacketed bullet, usually weighing 230 grains, for the .45 Automatic Colt Pistol cartridge. Originally, all hardball bullet ammunition was manufactured at government arsenals and issued to the military services in order to comply with the provisions of the Geneva Convention which state that expanding or explosive small arms bullets will not be employed in warfare. The term hardball is used to differentiate these full-jacketed bullets from soft-nose jacketed bullets and cast or swaged lead bullets without jackets. (See HANDGUN CARTRIDGES, TARGET.)

hardened shot See CHILLED SHOT.

hard or "magnum"-grade shot In the modern shotgunner's lexicon, hard shot is birdshot that has a higher percentage of antimony to toughen it against deformation than does chilled shot. Hard shot, which is often called magnum shot, varies in its antimonial content according to size, with the clay target sizes of No. 7½ and 8 often having the most antimony at 5 to 6 percent while the hunting sizes may have 3 to 4 percent.

hares, guns and loads for See RABBITS, GUNS AND LOADS FOR.

Harpers Ferry armory In 1795 the second national armory was established at Harpers Ferry, in what is now West Virginia. By 1801 the Model 1795 musket, the first American military musket, was being manufactured at both the Springfield, Massachusetts, and Harpers Ferry armories. The first musket manufactured in quantity at Harpers Ferry was the 1803 Harpers Ferry Musket, a .54-caliber rifled flintlock. This was the model that was used by the Lewis and Clark Expedition. Many U.S. military rifles and muskets were made there over the years. They bear the Harpers Ferry and U.S. Eagle marks. (See SPRINGFIELD ARMORY.)

Harrington & Richardson (company) Established in 1871 in Worcester, Massachusetts, by Gilbert H. Harrington and W. A. Richardson, and incorporated in 1888, this company originally made only revolvers (including one model with a knife blade attached to the barrel as a bayonet), but gradually expanded its line to include .22 rifles and, during World War II, the Reising submachine gun.

Harrington & Richardson manufactured a variety of arms, including revolvers, single-shot shotguns, and .22 rifles. In the early and mid-1970s, H&R produced commemorative models of the .45/70 Springfield Trapdoor Carbine and imported the British-made Webley & Scott side-by-side shotguns. Harrington & Richardson went out of business in 1987. The company was located in Gardner, Massachusetts.

hasty sling The term hasty sling does not apply to the design of a gun sling, but to the manner in which it is used. In a hasty sling maneuver, the right-handed shooter inserts the left arm between the sling and rifle fore-end from left to right, brings the hand back around the sling so that it is wrapped around the forearm, and grasps the rifle fore-end. If the sling is adjusted to the correct length so that it is tight in this position, the tension exerted on the arm and rifle fore-end will help to steady the rifle.

This maneuver can be used with either a shooting sling or a carrying strap. (See SLING.)

Hawken rifle Hawken rifles were the definitive form of the Plains rifle style. Half-stocked, of large caliber (.52 was about the average), and octagon-barreled, they were made by Samuel and Jacob Hawken. Jacob Hawken established himself in 1820 at St. Louis, where his brother Samuel later joined him in partnership. Their rifles became famous during the last years of the Fur Trade era (1840–1860). Although their business only lasted until around 1860, a great many of these muzzleloading rifles were made.

A number of gunsmiths worked on the Hawken rifles on practically a production line system. The guns were in great demand because of their sturdy, no-nonsense qualities. Jim Bridger, Kit Carson, and

many of the famous mountain men used Hawken rifles.

Barrel lengths ranged from 26 to 38 inches, and the guns weighed from 6½ to 12 pounds or more. These guns were designed to fire heavy charges; thus the heavy barrels. There are a few examples of flintlock Hawken rifles, but the great majority were percussion guns. Many specimens survive and are highly prized as collectors' items. (See MUZZLELOADER; PLAINS RIFLE.)

headspace Headspace is the distance from the face of the breechblock to the part of the chamber that stops the forward movement of the cartridge when the breech is closed. The dimension of both chamber and case must be matched so that there is minimal movement of the cartridge under the impact of the firing pin. If the headspace of the cartridge case and chamber do not match, one of two things can take place: the cartridge moves forward in the chamber, lessening the impact of the firing pin enough so the primer is not detonated; or, if it does fire, the body of the case has to stretch to fill the extra space in the chamber. When the latter situation occurs, a stretch ring or thin spot forms inside the case near the head and weakens it at that point. In some instances the case will completely separate at this point, leaving the forward section in the chamber.

Actual headspace varies for cases of different designs. On rimmed cases it is the thickness of the rim of the case and the distance between the breechblock face and the shoulder of the end of the barrel. The belted case uses the same basic arrangement, except that the forward edge of the belt is used to stop the forward movement of the case when it is forced against the front of a matching recess in the chamber. Rimless cases that have a shoulder are headspaced against that shoulder, so headspace is the distance from the breech face, or cartridge head face, to a point on the shoulder of a specified diameter. On rimless pistol cases and rifle cartridges like the .30 Carbine, the case is headspaced on the mouth of the case, so headspace is the distance from the case head face to the mouth of the case. (These cases should not be crimped into a crimping cannelure on the bullet or they will not headspace correctly.) Cases with rebated rims, like the .284 Winchester, are also headspaced from head face to shoulder. Semirimmed cases should be headspaced from case head face to shoulder as well as on the rim because of the small contact of the narrow rim with the chamber face.

Headspacing of cartridges is a critical consideration for beltless or rimmed cases if they are to be used for reloading. These cartridges will fire reliably because the rim or belt holds the case head firmly against the face of the breechblock, but if the case shoulder does not make very close contact with the chamber shoulder, the case will stretch and cause a partial or full head separation. Therefore, the sizing die must be adjusted so that the case shoulder is left in very light contact with the shoulder in the chamber. This is exactly as it must be for the rimless case, which must be resized so that the shoulder is not set back and the headspace increased, as a misfire or head separation may result.

Because of variations in manufacture, cases are sometimes short in head-to-shoulder length, and/or chambers may be long in the same area. While the reloader can do nothing to change the head-to-shoulder headspace of belted and rimmed factory ammunition and unfired cases, he can make certain that after the case is fired the first time the head-to-shoulder headspace continues to fit the chamber of his rifle.

Headspace for all kinds of cartridges is extremely critical when reloading for any kind of rifle action that locks at the rear of the bolt—lever, slide, bolt, or semiautomatic. High-pressure loads cause the bolt to compress and/or the receiver to stretch slightly, which allows the case to stretch, To chamber easily, the reloaded case must have the shoulder pushed back to original length. If this is repeated many times, a head separation will ensue. Cartridges for these actions must be reloaded to pressures below where this occurs. (See CASE RESIZING; CASE SEPARATION; HANDLOAD; HEADSPACE GAUGES.)

headspace gauges Headspace is the distance between the face of the breechblock and that portion of the chamber against which the cartridge bears. It may be equivalent to the cartridge rim thickness, the distance from the cartridge head to a selected point on the shoulder of a bottleneck case, or the distance from the case head to the case mouth.

Because of manufacturing tolerances in both firearms and cartridges, minimum and maximum chamber headspace dimensions must be established. These dimensions are checked with headspace gauges, accurately made of hardened and ground steel for the headspace dimension and design of a particular chamber. The minimum gauge should allow the breech to be fully closed without binding. The maximum gauge should prevent the breech from fully closing. In practice, manufacturers work to standard minimum and maximum gauges.

Headspace tends to increase with wear. A field gauge, longer than the maximum, is used to determine the point at which wear requires repair to the gun. (See HEADSPACE.)

These gauges are used to determine the amount of headspace in a rifle. The ones shown here are for (from left) rimless, belted, and rimmed cartridges.

headstamp An identifying mark stamped onto the head of a cartridge case (around the primer pocket in centerfire cases; in the center of the case head in rimfire). In centerfire sporting ammunition, the marking usually includes the name of the manufacturer and the caliber. The headstamp on military ammunition often does not include marks identifying caliber, but does include the date of manufacture and identification of the manufacturer or arsenal.

hearing, shooting damage to If the human ear is exposed to excessive sound over extended periods of time, some loss of hearing will result. The hearing loss will not necessarily occur through all levels of sound, but rather becomes evident at certain frequency levels. That is, the damaged ear does not pick up sounds carried on some frequencies, while other sounds are not nearly as diminished. Of course, in the worst cases nearly all hearing can be lost, while being accompanied by a steady ringing in the ears called tinnitus. Once such hearing damage is sustained there is no road of return, and the best that can be hoped for is proper ear protection to effectively eliminate further hearing loss.

While doctors have long been aware of the damage to hearing by constant exposure to loud noises, it is only relatively recently that preventive measures have been taken by the introduction of hearing protectors. Many of these are made especially for shooters. Some are termed sonic and have sound-wave-activated valves that are supposed to eliminate the damaging sound of gunfire while allowing normal, low-level sound to come through. There is also the muff type, which has a lining of sound-deadening foam and a reflective outer shell. Some shooters prefer one type, some the other, but the consensus is in favor of the muff type. Some educated shooters wear both when doing a great deal of firing.

No shooter should routinely do any firing without wearing hearing protection, if possible. (See DECIBEL; EAR PROTECTORS.)

heel The uppermost rear portion of the butt stock: It is rounded in shape and wider than the toe of the stock on today's long arms.

The heel is very important on shotguns, where the drop at heel is measured from the top line of the barrel. A shotgun with a great deal of drop will tend to shoot low, while one with little or no drop will shoot high. Trap guns generally have a small amount of drop at heel, while skeet guns and field guns have more drop. Some older shotgun models tended to have excessive drop at heel and were noted for their punishing recoil as the stock slammed into the cheekbone. (See DROP AT HEEL.)

Henry rifle In 1855, Oliver F. Winchester became a major stockholder in the Volcanic Arms Company, a firm that produced the Volcanic rifle and pistol. These were lever-operated, rimfire arms that offered potentially superior performance, but that suffered from poorly designed ammunition. In 1857, Winchester became president of the New Haven Arms Company, which bought out Volcanic's assets.

However, the new firm suffered from poor management and the problems affecting the ammunition remained. Winchester sought help from B. Tyler Henry, his plant foreman, charging him with both a redesign of the cartridges and with redesigning the Volcanic guns. In October 1860, Henry patented an improved lever-action brass framed rifle that weighed 9¼ pounds (light for the time) and held 15 .44 rimfire cartridges in a tubular magazine. This rifle, called the Henry, made its debut in 1862.

In its time, the Henry offered breathtaking firepower, but despite this, Winchester was able to sell only 1,713 to the government. However, Henry's reputation was made by these guns, and Winchester's firm prospered. In 1866, the company became Winchester Repeating Arms Company, and the Henry was superseded by the Winchester Model 1866, an improved design.

Today, surviving Henry rifles are highly sought after by collectors and command considerable prices. (See WINCHESTER [COMPANY].)

Hercules Inc. Hercules Inc., originally known as the Hercules Powder Company, began operations in 1913 following a U.S. government antitrust suit against the Du Pont Company. At that time, Hercules was awarded eight black-powder mills, three dynamite plants, and several patents for the manufacture of smokeless sporting powder. The company set up operations in Wilmington, Delaware.

Hercules has become a diversified corporation with operations around the world. It manufactures such products as plastics, synthetic fibers, paper, explosives, and industrial products, as well as firearm powders.

Higgins, J.C. A trade name under which Sears, Roebuck & Co. marketed firearms produced by various American manufacturers. It has been discontinued.

high base A shotshell that employs a thick base wad is called a high base shell. This kind of shotshell is used for light powder and shot charges, some typical examples being light field loads and target loads. (See HIGH BRASS.)

high brass A shotshell that utilizes an extended brass base is commonly called a high brass load. High brass shells are used for heavy powder and shot charges, two common examples being buckshot and waterfowl loads. (See HIGH BASE.)

high house The taller of the two "houses" from which skeet targets are launched. The high house is on the shooter's left as he faces the skeet range. Targets from this house emerge at a higher angle and drop slightly as they lose launch velocity; targets from the low house are angled lower and tend to climb as they reach midfield. (See LOW HOUSE; SKEET SHOOTING.)

high intensity cartridge An old term describing high-velocity cartridges that is not often used today. When the term was in general use it applied to any cartridge that developed a muzzle velocity exceeding 2,500 feet per second. (See HIGH-VELOCITY LOAD.)

high power cartridge A term that was once used to describe any cartridge with a muzzle velocity exceeding about 2,000 feet per second. Today it is usually used to differentiate centerfire (high power) from rimfire cartridges, especially in match shooting.

High Standard Sporting Firearms (company) Founded in 1932 as High Standard Manufacturing Corp., this firm concentrated on the production of

.22 automatic pistols, as well as drills and tools, until World War II, when it manufactured sidearms for the military. After 1946 the company diversified and produced not only a wide variety of .22 automatic pistols, but .22 revolvers, .22 rifles, and repeating shotguns as well.

At present, High Standard no longer manufactures firearms.

high velocity load Any load, or cartridge, with higher than normal muzzle velocity. The term is most commonly applied to shotgun cartridges and is often used to denote high base loads, which, in 12 gauge for example, are loaded to muzzle velocities of around 1,330 feet per second as compared with 1,100 to 1,250 fps for most upland, skeet, and trap loads. (See HIGH BASE.)

hinged frame An action in side-by-side and over/under shotguns (and, rarely, in revolvers) that employs a top locking lever and a pivoting joint, by which the barrels can be tipped up for reloading, cocking, and ejection of spent shells. In some designs an underlever, usually located ahead of the trigger guard, is used.

hinged trigger In heavy recoiling arms with double triggers, the front trigger can cut into the index finger when the rear trigger is pulled. To prevent this, some high-grade double rifles (and some shotguns) hinge the front trigger so that it folds away from the finger under recoil. Also termed an articulated trigger. (See DOUBLE TRIGGERS.)

hip rest In rifle shooting in the standing position, the hip rest is a position in which the elbow of the arm supporting the rifle is placed against the rib cage. The term is something of a misnomer, as only a person with very long arms, and using a palm rest or supporting the rifle with the fingertips, can actually place the elbow on the hip bone. Generally, this is the steadiest standing position. (See PALM REST; POSITION SHOOTING.)

hip shooting Sometimes a handgun shooter, when wishing to fire with extreme speed, will shoot without aiming by merely bringing the gun to hip level, pointing it by instinct, and squeezing the trigger. Hip shooting is used only at very close range, since it allows little precision. The term is one of many from the shooter's vocabulary that have passed into common parlance; it has come to mean acting rashly, without thought. (See FANNING.)

Hodgdon Powder Company Inc. In 1950, Bruce E. Hodgdon, then an employee of the Kansas Gas Ser-

vice company, purchased a 50,000-pound lot of a surplus government gunpowder (4895) and, in his spare time, retailed it through an advertisement in *The American Rifleman*. The powder was packaged in 150-pound kegs, and cost $30 per keg.

The business prospered, and in 1952 Hodgdon resigned from the gas company and went into the powder and loading components business full time. In 1966, after considerable expansion, the powder business was detached from Hodgdon's other ventures and was incorporated as Hodgdon Powder Co. The firm is located in Overland Park, Kansas.

In addition to its success with the widely applicable 4895, Hodgdon has made other considerable contributions to the handloader. The slow-burning 20mm cannon powder, 4831, was the first commercially available powder that could be efficiently utilized in magnum rifle cartridges. In addition, Hodgdon was the first to offer spherical powders—most notably, Ball-C.

Because of the growing popularity of black-powder shooting, Hodgdon imported (beginning in 1971) British-manufactured Curtis & Harvey black powder, which sold under the Hodgdon name. In 1976, Pyrodex, a revolutionary replica black powder, was first offered to the public by the firm. (See BLACK POWDER; PYRODEX.)

holding off Under certain circumstances, a shooter must deliberately aim to one side of a target, or high or low, in order to compensate for such factors as wind drift or mirage. This practice is known as holding off. (See DRIFT; MIRAGE.)

hold over Aiming a gun so as to compensate for bullet drop. For instance, if a rifle is sighted to hit dead-on at 100 yards, and the shooter wants to hit a target at 300 yards, he must allow for bullet drop by holding high. If both the exact range and the bullet trajectory are known, the proper amount of hold over is a simple matter to calculate. In a hunting situation, hold over is usually nothing more than educated guessing, as neither the exact range nor the precise trajectory is usually known. (See TRAJECTORY.)

Holland & Holland (company) Founded in London in 1835, Holland & Holland has remained not only a premier name in the manufacture of the highest quality double rifles and side-by-side and over/under shotguns, but has also been an innovator in cartridge design.

All Holland & Holland shotguns are built employing back-action sidelocks, Southgate ejectors, and a self-opening mechanism that aids in breaking the action for loading. Although in past years H&H has manufactured several grades of shotguns, the best known and most coveted is the Royal grade; the top grade H&H double rifle is the Modele Deluxe.

Holland & Holland has devoted a significant part of its production over the years to the manufacture of bolt-action rifles and, in 1912, introduced a cartridge for this kind of arm—the .375 H&H—which revolutionized rifle ammunition design. This cartridge, the first belted magnum, was the ancestor of our present magnum cartridges. The .375 H&H remains extraordinarily popular throughout the world.

Holland & Holland is also noted for its shooting school, located in the suburbs of London. (See SOUTHGATE EJECTOR.)

hollow base   A bullet design with a cavity in the base. Today, it is most often found on wadcutter handgun bullets where it increases the bearing surface without appreciably increasing weight. It also moves the bullet's center of gravity forward to increase stability.

The hollow base is also used in some muzzle-loader projectiles, where it forms a skirt that allows a smaller diameter projectile to be used to facilitate rapid loading. Then, under the pressures generated in firing, the skirt flares out to serve the purpose of obturation and to hold the rifling. (See MUZZLE-LOADER; OBTURATION; WADCUTTER BULLET.)

hollow point   A bullet design with a cavity in the nose, generally formed to facilitate and hasten expansion. Hollow point bullets, when fired at high velocity, generally expand dramatically on impact.

Hollow points are found in both unjacketed lead and jacketed bullets. On jacketed bullets they are usually formed by not quite closing the mouth of the jacket in manufacture. The cavity size may vary from a pinhole in a small caliber, high-velocity bullet, to three-fourths of the bullet's diameter in a low-velocity lead bullet. (See EXPANDING BULLET.)

This .44 Magnum bullet employs a flat, hollow point to increase its expansion.

hollow-pointer   A device used for drilling a cavity in the nose of a conventional bullet to produce a hollow point bullet; the tool usually holds the projectile and aligns a drill with the bullet's nose for drilling the cavity.

Hollow-pointers were once commonly used to alter full-metal-jacket military ammunition to hollow point ammunition for hunting purposes. However, projectiles so altered performed erratically and did not always expand properly.

Another kind of hollow-pointer consists of a small steel pin, usually with a wood handle, inserted into special bullet mold blocks to leave a hollow point in cast lead bullets when the lead is poured. (See HOLLOW POINT.)

holsters   Prior to the invention of the Colt revolver in 1836, flintlock and percussion handguns were too cumbersome to adapt to holster carry and were either carried on the saddle, thrust through a belt, or placed in a pocket, as in the case of the Deringer. As the handgun became a compact and highly portable firearm, a variety of leather scabbards, or holsters, was developed to carry it on the person.

The first Colt revolvers enabled their users to carry a powerful, accurate, and rapid firing personal weapon that could be brought into play almost instantly and kept on the person at all times. Since the first users of these guns were military and paramilitary groups, the kinds of holsters they favored exerted a powerful influence on holster design. For many years, the revolver was the arm of the cavalry, but was accorded a place of less importance than the sabre. Holsters were worn on the left side, to leave the right, or sword, arm free. Since this arrangement made a rapid draw impossible, and since the gun had to be protected from the elements and from loss, the early military holsters "swallowed" the guns entirely, and covered them with a large flap. This design is still favored today for most military and many police holsters.

As the revolver evolved and came into wider use by civilians, a different requirement was added to the role of the holster—the ability to gain instant access to the gun. The flap was discarded, and the holster positioned on the right side where it was easily reached.

Despite the fact that the revolver was almost universally carried in the West for more than 60 years, the holsters in which it rode remained relatively crude and unsophisticated. Many were homemade, and most were simply leather pouches into which the gun was dropped. The so-called fast draw and the holsters with which it is accomplished on television and in the movies are of very recent invention.

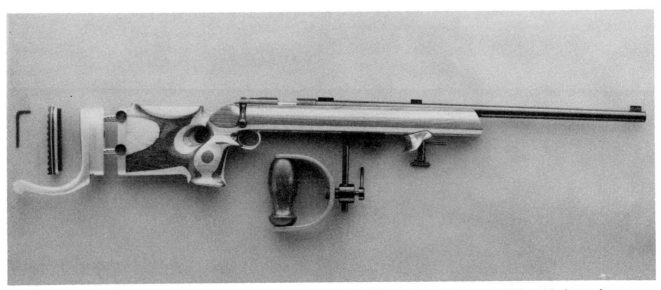

This Winchester Model 52 International Match rifle employs a hook buttplate, palm rest, and thumbhole stock.

Over the past four decades, however, the holster has gained considerable sophistication in design, and the following kinds are now commonly in use:

Concealment or "hideout" holsters are designed for law enforcement officers who must carry a small, short-barreled handgun for extended periods of time and with a maximum degree of concealment. These holsters offer a minimum of protection to the gun but afford a very fast draw. They can be worn shoulder style (hanging beneath the armpit), high on the waist, or strapped low on the ankle, under the trousers.

Military and police holsters exhibit a variety of designs. Most military holsters offer maximum protection to the gun, and cover it with a snap-fastening flap. Police departments employ styles ranging from the military design to those that are intended for a quick draw, and are raked forward, with the entire grip, the trigger, and much of the frame exposed for easy grasping. These designs rely on a tight fit, plus a keeper strap over the hammer, to hold the gun in place.

Some military personnel, such as tankers and pilots, whose duties require that they sit, employ shoulder holsters. In addition, police officers who work in plainclothes often favor a shoulder holster for concealing larger, heavier revolvers.

The last category could be called "sporting" holsters—those designs that are a compromise between protection for the sidearm and a rapid draw. As a rule, handgun hunters favor long-barreled, large-framed revolvers and automatic pistols, so the holsters for these arms must allow the user to carry them for long periods without discomfort, afford protection against damage and loss, and still allow reasonably quick access to the gun. A typical holster

of this kind will cover all of the gun but the grip and trigger guard and will employ a keeper strap to prevent the handgun from falling out. (See KEEPER.)

hooded front sight Because the front sights of rifles are subject to damage or displacement from rough or careless handling, they should be protected. This is accomplished by means of a steel hood that slides into a groove on the sight ramp and is removed when the sight is to be used.

Most of the better British custom big-game rifles are equipped with steel hoods that pivot over the sight ramp and rest on the barrel to the rear of the ramp when the front sight is in use. This arrangement is more reliable than the common version, but is more costly to produce. (See FRONT SIGHT.)

hook buttplate A rifle buttplate provided with a rearward projection that fits under the armpit. It may range from a simple prong, made as a part of the buttplate, to a formfitting projection that is adjustable in several planes. Used most often in the hip rest position, in combination with a palm rest, it is an aid to steady holding, especially with the muzzle-heavy rifles used in competition shooting.

Some of the older hook buttplates had hooks at both top and bottom. (See BUTTPLATE; HIP REST; PALM REST; POSITION SHOOTING.)

hooked breech See PATENT BREECH.

hook of lump A hook, or half-round cavity, put into the fore part of the forward lump, that is integral with and underneath the barrel on side-by-side and single-barrel break-action shotguns and rifles. The hook is machined to fit perfectly the cross or hinge pin in the frame, thus preventing forward movement of the barrel and acting as the pivot point for opening. (See LUMPS.)

Hornady Manufacturing Company Joyce Hornady, a handloader and big-game hunter, founded the company that bears his name in 1949. In the ensuing years, the company has become not only one of the largest American bullet manufacturers, but one of the most diverse.

Located in Grand Island, Nebraska, Hornady produces a full line of rifle bullets in all calibers from .17 to .458. In addition to supplying its bullets to major ammunition loading firms, as well as handloaders, Hornady has marketed its own line of ammunition under the name Frontier. The company's loading manual, one of the most complete in current use, is widely available at gun and shooting supply stores. Hornady also manufactures a complete line of reloading tools for shotshell and metallic cartridges.

house See TRAP HOUSE.

Hoxie bullet A lead bullet made by the Hoxie Ammunition Company shortly after the turn of the century. The bullet contained a steel ball in its point that was believed to facilitate expansion. The company purchased ammunition from both Remington and Winchester, pulled the original bullets, and reloaded with Hoxie bullets. The company operated for only a short period.

Hoyer wildcat cartridges See RIFLE CARTRIDGES, TARGET.

hull The empty casing of a round of ammunition, either metallic or shotshell, although the term is generally used to describe the casing of a fired shotshell. Many shotgunners save their hulls for reloading.

hunting, guns and loads for See ENTRIES UNDER INDIVIDUAL GAME SPECIES AND REGIONS.

Huntington, Fred See RCBS, INC.

Husqvarna Vapenfabriks Aktiebolag (company) Founded in 1689 to produce musket barrels, Husqvarna has since diversified into the manufacture of sewing machines, housewares, bicycles, chainsaws, motorcycles, and lawnmowers. Located in Husqvarna, Sweden, the company has also produced shotguns and bolt-action rifles for export. Few Husqvarna shotguns have been sold in America, but in 1954, Tradewinds of Tacoma, Washington, began importing the rifles, and during the late 1960s and early 1970s Smith & Wesson imported Husqvarna rifles that it marketed under its own trademark. Despite the high quality of the arm, sales were never profitable. Husqvarna later attempted to market it under the names Viking, Carl Gustaf, and FFV. These efforts were to no avail, and in the late 1970s importation of Husqvarna rifles ceased.

hyperopia Commonly called farsightedness, this visual defect is caused by an eyeball being too short, causing the image to focus behind the retina. Farsighted individuals can see well at a distance, but have difficulty focusing on close objects. The condition is more common among shooters over 40 years of age, attributed to loss of elasticity of the eye's lens.

Prescription glasses and other optical equipment having a convex lens to bend the light rays more so that they focus on the retina will correct farsightedness.

hypervelocity A term occasionally applied to bullet velocity that is extremely high. One cartridge imparting hypervelocity is the .17 Remington; another is the .220 Swift. The velocity of 4,000 feet per second, which both of these cartridges produce, is generally regarded as the threshold of hypervelocity.

ignition When applied to firearms, ignition means the firing of the powder charge to create the expanding gas that propels the projectile from the barrel. The rate and completeness of the ignition of the powder charge governs the amount and duration of the thrust on the bullet, which in turn controls the velocity at which the bullet is expelled from the barrel. Factors that affect ignition are the amount and duration of heat created by the primer; the burning rate of the powder; the position of the powder within the case (if the charge does not fill the powder space); and the size of the flash hole in the web or solid head portion of the case.

Some powders are more difficult to ignite than others; ball or spherical powders are considered the most difficult to ignite properly. Poor ignition will result in low and erratic velocities and may also cause a hangfire. Primers that create a hotter flame of longer duration, sometimes called magnum primers, are recommended for use with hard-to-ignite powders.

In cartridges where fairly fast powders are required for high velocity with light bullet weights, a good deal of air space is left in the powder space. If the powder charge is at the forward end of the case it will not ignite in exactly the same manner as if it is spread out full-length or at the rear, so ignition will not be the same, causing erratic velocity and a loss of accuracy. This is why nearly 100 percent loading density is considered optimum so that ignition will be uniform. (See HANGFIRE; IGNITION TIME; LOADING DENSITY; PRIMER.)

ignition time The interval of time that elapses from the moment the firing pin makes contact with the primer cup to the moment the bullet or shot charge is released from the case or shell.

illumination The quantity of light present in an image or passing through an optical instrument, such as a riflescope or binoculars. The optical quality of the glass has a bearing on illumination, as does the magnesium flouride coating or absence of it on the lenses. (See MAGNESIUM FLUORIDE; TELESCOPIC SIGHTS.)

image formation Most optical systems, such as a riflescope, spotting scope, binoculars, or monocular, have more than one refracting lens. (A refracting lens bends the light rays passing though it, causing them to diverge or converge.) Thus the image formed of the object by the first lens becomes the object for the second lens; the image formed by the second lens serves as the object for the third lens, etc.

Light travels in a straight line, so the image formed by the objective lens of a riflescope, for example, is inverted or upside down and smaller in size than the original object, in much the same way the image formed on the film in a camera is smaller than the object photographed and upside down. This upside-down image becomes the object for the second, or erector, lens system housed within the tube of the riflescope; the erector system reinverts, or makes erect, the image. Finally, the eyepiece assembly, consisting of the ocular lens elements, magnifies the second image to produce a larger erect, or virtual, image, which we actually see. (See ERECTOR LENS; EYEPIECE; OBJECTIVE LENS.)

impact behavior ballistics In the study of projectile ballistics there are three stages to be considered. They are interior ballistics, or what happens from primer ignition until the projectile leaves the muzzle of the firearm barrel; exterior ballistics, or what happens while the projectile is actually in flight from the muzzle of the barrel to the target; and impact behavior ballistics (or terminal ballistics, as it is more commonly called), that is, what happens after the projectile actually reaches the target.

What happens when a bullet impacts is extremely important to the manufacturer of bullets used for hunting, and to the hunter using cartridges loaded with such bullets. Does the bullet expand properly? Does it penetrate deeply or blow up on the surface? Does it hold together? Does it expend its total energy? These are all questions an impact behavior ballistician has to ask about a bullet design.

The use of live tissues as an aid to answering the questions is not practical in the laboratory, hence the use of a material called ballistic gelatin which behaves somewhat similarly to animal tissue. Shooting into the gelatin, coupled with high-speed photography, including X-ray photography, will provide some answers, possibly enough to warrant further testing of a bullet design in the field on actual game. But even then, there are many variables to be considered relating to the actual impact. (See EXTERIOR BALLISTICS; INTERIOR BALLISTICS.)

Imperial Chemical Industries (company)   ICI is a very large English conglomerate that controls many varied industrial units that manufacture a wide variety of chemical bulk products and finished products. These include explosives and ammunition. ICI owns Eley-Kynoch, the famous manufacturer of British sporting ammunition. (See ELEY-KYNOCH [COMPANY].)

impinging gas mechanism   See GAS OPERATION.

impressed checkering   Sometimes called negative checkering, this form of stock decoration is more decorative than functional. It is applied to a stock by using a master die with a regular checkering design, and a heating element. The combination of pressure and heat burns the design into the stocks; as a result, the diamonds of such checkering are sunken or impressed, unlike regular checkering where the diamonds are sharp and pointed to provide a gripping surface. Impressed checkering does not produce sharp-pointed diamonds and the impressions tend to fill easily with dirt and grease.

Many American arms manufacturers employ this kind of checkering, as it is quick, economical, and uniform. Good quality hand checkering requires a great deal of time and the talents of a skilled craftsman. Impressed checkering requires neither. (See CHECKERING.)

improved cartridge   An improved cartridge is a wildcat cartridge that is formed from a commercial cartridge case. Where many wildcat cartridges change the length and shape as well as the diameter of the bullet to be used, the improved cartridge remains the same length and caliber, with only the body dimension and (usually) the shoulder angle changed.

Many of the older cartridge cases have a good deal of body taper and rather mild shoulder angles. In the improved case, the body is blown out by fire forming to fit the improved chamber, and may or may not incorporate a sharper shoulder angle. Headspace remains the same as in the original cartridge, which makes it possible to fire a factory round in the improved chamber and form the improved case.

The results of this change in case form and dimension increases the powder capacity, which increases bullet velocity at the same pressure level, hence the term "improved." (See FIRE FORMING; HEADSPACE; WILDCAT CARTRIDGE.)

improved-cylinder choke   That degree of choke that lies between true cylinder and modified. It is supposed to produce patterns of 35 to 45 percent at 40 yards. Improved-cylinder is useful for moderate-range shooting on game and is a favorite all-around choke for sporting clays. (See CHOKE.)

improved military rifle powder (IMR)   Introduced by Du Pont in 1914, the IMR powders are single-base powders, consisting principally of nitrocellulose. With one exception, all the IMR powders are fundamentally alike, differing only in granulation and, to a limited extent, in the coating of dinitrotoluene (DNT) to slow initial burning. Potassium sulphate is added as a muzzle flash inhibitor and diphenylamine as a stabilizer, and the grains are glazed or coated with graphite to carry off static electric charges and improve the flow in powder measures. The IMR series of powders is widely used by both ammunition manufacturers and handloaders for all kinds of rifle cartridges. (See NITROCELLULOSE; SINGLE-BASE POWDERS.)

improved-modified choke   The degree of shotgun bore constriction between modified and full. Also called three-quarter choke, it customarily requires 25 points of constriction and produces a pattern of 65 to 70 percent of the short charge in a 30-inch circle in a 40-yard range. It is used almost entirely in trapshooting. (See CHOKE.)

incipient separation   The partial separation of the cartridge case just forward of the solid web section of the head. The first sign of this condition will be a stretch ring on the inside of the case. This ring can be felt on the inside by the use of a wire bent to form a 90-degree hook on the end, and it may be visible on the outside as a light-colored ring either partially or completely around the case. (Do not confuse this with the pressure ring that appears tight against the web.) In the more advanced stages, small cracks will appear with the ring.

If the same case is reloaded and fired again there may be a complete head separation that will leave the portion of the case forward of the separation in the chamber, with only the head section being extracted.

The cause of this condition may be excessive headspace, but it can also occur with rimless cartridges, the shoulders of which are improperly located or which offer insufficient bearing. (See CASE SEPARATION; HEADSPACE.)

indexing   In the firearms field, this term denotes the operation of dividing a circle, i.e., rotating an object a given number of degrees. Thus, in cutting a six-groove rifle barrel with a single cutter, the cutter is drawn through the barrel blank, cutting a groove to part of its finished depth. Then, either the cutter or the barrel may be indexed 60 degrees, and the next cut undertaken. This process is repeated until the barrel is completely revolved, and all six cuts are made to their final depth

Simple indexing for comparatively low numbers of divisions (such as barrel rifling) may be accomplished with a simple circular plate having properly spaced holes engaged by a pin. More sophisticated indexing, such as that used in making reamers with irregularly spaced flutes, other kinds of tooling, and cams, requires the use of universal dividing heads, employing a worm gear and a worm, driven by a crank, with the crank movement controlled by an index plate. (See BARREL, RIFLED; GROOVE.)

index mark A mark used to indicate the point or position at which two mating firearms parts are properly assembled. In the case of a gun barrel threaded into a receiver, a continuous line is scribed or cut into the two adjoining surfaces of barrel and receiver after proper assembly. After disassembly, the barrel and the receiver may be reassembled to the proper relationship by screwing them together until the index marks meet.

inertia block In the single-trigger mechanism used in double shotguns, an inertia block may function to shift the mechanism to fire the second barrel, but its main purpose is to prevent doubling, otherwise known as involuntary firing. (See INERTIA TRIGGER.)

inertia firing pin A firing pin that is shorter than the length of the breechblock in which it rides. Such a firing pin, when struck by the hammer, is given sufficient momentum to cause the primer to fire, although with the hammer forward and pushing on the firing pin, the front end of the pin will not reach the primer. The inertia firing pin is generally used for safety reasons; one of the more common examples of its use is in the Model 1911 .45 Colt Automatic. (See FIRING PIN.)

inertia puller See BULLET PULLER.

inertia trigger A single trigger mechanism, used in a double-barrel shotgun, in which an inertia block is used to shift the trigger mechanism to fire the second barrel. Such a mechanism may be selective, allowing the choice of which barrel is fired first, or it may be nonselective.

The single trigger mechanism of the Browning over/under is an easily understood example of a single selective trigger operated by an inertia block. Selection of the barrel to be fired first is made by positioning the safety to the right or to the left, on the upper tang, before shoving it to the "Off" position. The projection on the safety, which extends down to contact the trigger mechanism, is guided in slots in the tang and can only be moved sideways when the safety is in the "On" position.

The sears on the Browning over/under are pivoted in the upper tang of the receiver; the trigger is mounted in the lower tang; and a link pivoted in the trigger reaches up to engage the sears. An inertia block is attached to this link, and the link-inertia block assembly is spring loaded to bring the link forward into contact with the sears except when it is held out of contact by pushing the safety to the "On," or safe, position. The link has three projections that may engage the sears. One of these faces forward, toward the sears, and is on the centerline of the link. It may engage the sear for either the upper or the lower barrel, depending on whether the safety is positioned to the left or the right when it is pushed to the "Off" position. Pulling the trigger then causes the sear engaged by this projection of the link to pivot and disengage from the hammer, firing the selected barrel.

As the gun recoils, the link-inertia block assembly is forced to recoil with the gun. When the recoil of the gun is stopped by the shooter's shoulder, the inertia forces cause the inertia block to continue to pivot backward, freeing the sear of the fired barrel to pivot and move clear of the link projection with which it had been engaged.

The two other projections on the link are positioned opposite each other and at 90 degrees to that which fires the first barrel selected. As the link-inertia block mechanism is forced forward by the spring—after the gun has stabilized from recoil—one or the other of the two opposite projections will engage with the sear of the unfired barrel, so that this barrel may be fired by a second pull of the trigger.

Cocking the hammers by breaking the gun resets the trigger-link-inertia-block sear mechanism so that it is ready to repeat the sequence. (See DOUBLE SELECTIVE TRIGGER; INERTIA BLOCK.)

infinity In optics, a distance so far removed from an observer that the rays of light reflected to a lens from a point at that distance may be regarded as parallel. Also, a distance setting on a camera or telescope focusing scale beyond which all objects are in focus. For practical purposes, low-power hunting telescopic sights may be considered to be focused at infinity when focused at 100 to 150 yards, and high power target telescopes and spotting scopes when focused at 200 to 250 yards. (See TELESCOPIC SIGHTS.)

Ingalls tables A set of tables of constants, developed by Captain James M. Ingalls, First Artillery, U.S. Army, for making exterior ballistics calculations for direct fire. First published in 1886 under the title *Exterior Ballistics*, they were later published as *Artillery Circular M* and were used for many years by the U.S. armed forces.

Exterior ballistics considers the circumstances of motion of a projectile from the time it emerges from the gun until it strikes the object aimed at and, if calculated by pure mathematics, requires the use of calculus and many long, difficult, time-consuming equations. To the uninformed, the calculation of the trajectory of a bullet might seem to be simple, since the only factors involved are the resistance of the air (drag), the shape and mass of the projectile, and the effect of gravity. The problem is greatly compounded by the fact that the resistance of the air varies continuously with velocity, at a power of the velocity.

Ingalls's work was based on studies of several earlier works on ballistics, starting with Benjamin Robins's *New Principles of Gunnery*, published in 1742. Particularly important to the Ingalls work were experiments made at the Krupp Works in Germany in 1881, and studies of these experiments and additional experiments performed by Mayevski at St. Petersburg, Russia, in the period from 1868 to 1882. Also of importance were the discoveries of the Italian ballistician, Siacci, about 1880.

Although guns of several calibers were used, the Krupp experiments made use of a standard projectile, flat based, 3 calibers long, with a head ogive of 2 calibers. Mayevski constructed a mathematical model for the drag deceleration of this standard projectile. He concluded that the relationship of drag and velocity varied as a power of the velocity, to which he gave the symbol "n." His table of n is shown below. It is still accepted as being substantially correct. Note the sudden increase in drag in the area of the velocity of sound.

Velocities (feet per second)	n
Below 790	2
790 to 970	3
970 to 1,230	5
1,230 to 1,370	3
1,370 to 1,800	2
1,800 to 2,600	1.7
Above 2,600	1.55

From this mathematical model, Mayevski could calculate the elements of the trajectory, i.e., the curve in space occupied by the projectile from the gun muzzle to the target. This curve is a parabola.

Once the drag function and the effect of gravity

had been worked out for the standard projectile, which provided a basis for ballistics calculations, the data for projectiles of different form could be obtained by determining the relationship of their drag functions to that of the standard projectile. The relationship of the standard to the actual projectile is called the ballistic coefficient, symbolized by the letter "C." Since the standard projectile was given a C of 1, the C of the actual projectile becomes a decimal figure that is the drag deceleration of the standard projectile (1), divided by the drag deceleration of the actual projectile. The ballistics coefficient, used as a multiplier in the Mayevski formulas, makes it possible to determine the elements of the trajectory of any projectile, once the C is determined. (In the interests of accuracy, it must be stated that drag functions other than the original Mayevski have now been developed. However, recent tests have shown that the original still applies to most of the rifle bullets now commonly used.) The C of today's rifle bullets varies from a low of about .115 to a high of about .628. The C varies inversely with the drag or retardation, and a high C denotes a low drag. To put it another way, a high C denotes the ability of a bullet to maintain velocity.

Ingalls tables provide constants for a range of velocities from 800 to 3,200 feet per second for the standard projectile, and, once the C is known, a complete trajectory table can be worked out without resorting to calculus. For accuracy of results, C is usually established, or at least checked, by actual firings, measuring bullet velocity at two different distances. The development of the digital computer has made the use of Ingalls tables obsolete. (See BALLISTIC COEFFICIENT; EXTERIOR BALLISTICS.)

initial recoil Initial recoil is that portion of the recoil of a firearm that occurs before the bullet exits from the muzzle. Gas pressure from the burning of the powder exerts equal force in all directions inside the cartridge case. Because the bullet moves forward, propelled by the gas pressure, the gun moves backward in an equal and opposite reaction. The energy imparted to the gun is, for practical purposes, the same as that imparted to the bullet, but the velocity of the gun is much less because the gun weighs many times more than the bullet. Forward movement of the powder gases also contributes to initial recoil, and this is included in recoil calculations by taking one-half the weight of the powder charge and multiplying it by the muzzle velocity of the bullet. Initial recoil and its effects on a rifle are a determinant of accuracy. (See MUZZLE VELOCITY; RECOIL.)

inlaying See ENGRAVING.

inletting The portion of a rifle, shotgun, or handgun stock that is cut away to accept the metal parts of the arm is called the inletted area. Inletting is the process of cutting or removing the wood, although it is also used to describe the completed area. Hand inletting is a true test of a stockmaker's skill, but nearly all commercially manufactured arms today have the inletting done by machines routing away the wood, following a master pattern. Inletting should conform as nearly as possible to the contour of the metal parts being fitted. This perfect mating of the wood and metal is particularly important in recoil absorbing areas and in the barrel channel of rifles, where accuracy is affected by one side of the forearm exerting more pressure on the barrel than the other side. (See BEDDING; GLASS BEDDING; STOCKMAKING.)

inletting screw A headless screw, 2½ to 3 inches long, with a short thread of a size and pitch to fit the guard screw holes in the receiver of a rifle. It is used as a guide in the process of inletting the receiver and barrel of a rifle into the stock. If possible, the trigger guard and magazine box assembly is inletted first, then the front guard screw hole is used as a guide for the inletting screw, which has been threaded tightly into the receiver. The barrel and receiver are coated with a pigment, then placed into the roughed-out inletting of the stock and struck lightly with a wood or plastic mallet. The pigment will show on the wood, indicating those places where the wood must be cut and scraped away to obtain proper fit of wood to metal. (See GUARD SCREWS; INLETTING.)

inside lubricated bullet So called to differentiate it from an outside lubricated bullet, the inside lubricated bullet is simply a lead cast bullet that is seated into the case neck so that the grease grooves encircling it are covered by the case neck and not exposed to lint and dirt. It is common with certain handgun loads (the .38 Special wadcutter load, for example), because the outside lubricated bullet is messy to handle and can be stripped of lubrication under some conditions. (See OUTSIDE LUBRICATED BULLET.)

instrumental velocity The velocity of a bullet— measured by a chronograph—at any given distance beyond the muzzle. It is lower than actual muzzle velocity. (See CHRONOGRAPH; MUZZLE VELOCITY.)

interchangeable ammunition As a general rule of safety, it is prudent never to fire ammunition through a firearm that is not expressly chambered for the cartridge as its designation appears on the box or headstamp. However, the American system of cartridge naming is not in universal use. Europeans employ metric designations in their cartridge nomenclature. Below is a chart of cartridges that are actually identical, although the names are different:

Rifle

.22 Hornet	5.6x35R
7mm Mauser	7x57
.30/30 Winchester	7.62x51R
.308 Winchester	7.62 NATO
.30/06	7.62x63
8mm Mauser	8x57

Pistol

.25 Auto or ACP	6.35mm Browning
.30 Luger	7.65mm Parabellum
.32 Auto or ACP	7.65mm Browning
.38 Automatic	9mm Browning
9mm Luger	9mm Parabellum

In a comparatively small number of instances, two *different* cartridges will fire in the same firearm. However, in every instance the arm must be chambered and designed for the more powerful round of the two. For example, .38 Special ammunition will fire in a .357 magnum, but not vice versa, and the .44 Special will fire in .44 magnum revolvers, as well. In rimfires, the obsolete .22 WRF will chamber and shoot in .22 magnum guns. Actually, a .25/06 will fire in a .30/06 rifle, since the cases are identical. However, the .25-caliber bullet will rattle through the .30-caliber barrel, resulting in no accuracy. With shotshells, any gun chambered for long hulls, such as 3-inch magnums, will fire all shorter cases of that gauge. A shotgun chambered for 2½-inch shells will not chamber the longer hulls, however. (See BARREL ADAPTER.)

interchangeable barrels When a barrel can be removed from a handgun, rifle, or shotgun and replaced with a barrel of a different length, choke, or caliber, it is said to be interchangeable. Such barrels are common on pump and autoloading shotguns, but not to the same degree on handguns and especially rifles, where operating pressures are greater and the headspace is more important. Side-by-side and over/under shotguns and rifles do not accept interchangeable barrels readily unless the barrels were originally hand fitted to the frame at the factory. However, the majority of the repeating shotguns manufactured today, such as the Remington Model 870 pump and the Winchester Model 1500 XTR autoloader, do have interchangeable barrels of different lengths, different chokes, and even with or without ventilated ribs.

Currently there are no American rifles available

with interchangeable barrels, although several different models have been available in the past in which barrels chambered for different cartridges having the same head size, such as the .30/06, .25/06, or .22/250, could be interchanged. The German Mauser Model 660 is a bolt-action rifle that features interchangeable barrels of different calibers; in this design the bolt locks directly into the barrel extension.

A number of handguns feature interchangeable barrels. The Thompson/Center Contender single-shot break-action pistol is famous for its variety of barrels in calibers from 5mm rimfire to the .45 Winchester Magnum centerfire. Removal of a single pin permits the barrel of the Contender to be lifted out of the frame and a different barrel put in its place. The Dan Wesson revolver has interchangeable barrels of different lengths but the same caliber. Among autoloading pistols, interchangeable barrels are quite common, although usually of the same caliber. An exception is the Heckler & Koch HK-4, which features interchangeable barrels in four different calibers—.380 ACP, .32 ACP, .25 ACP, and .22 Long Rifle rimfire.

interchangeable chokes The first detachable shotgun choke was invented by an American, Sylvester H. Roper, in 1866. Consisting of a small ringlike device threaded internally, it simply screwed onto the threaded muzzle end of the barrel to provide a minimum amount of choke. Since it was detachable and could be replaced with a ring of slightly different internal diameter, it was the first interchangeable choke. (Contemporary reports indicate the Roper choke was less effective than a regular choked barrel.)

The firm of O.F. Mossberg used interchangeable choke tubes measuring 2 inches in length on its .410-bore shotguns for more than a quarter of a century (1940–1971), and the Cutts Compensator with interchangeable choke tubes has been in production for nearly half a century. More recently, interchangeable choke tubes have appeared on the market for a wide variety of hunting and competition shotguns. While most of the early detachable choke tubes screwed onto the muzzle of the barrel, or into a cage or compensator designed to receive them, the more recent designs are tubes, measuring from 1¾ to 3 inches in length, which slip down into the muzzle of the shotgun barrel and are retained either by screwing them into position, or by separate screws, such as on the Franchi Model 530. (See CHOKE; CUTTS COMPENSATOR.)

interior ballistics Interior or internal ballistics covers the events happening to a projectile inside the chamber and bore of a gun from the time of primer ignition until the bullet leaves the muzzle. Although much research has been done and a great deal of complex mathematical data developed, determination of events purely by mathematics is not reliable, and empirical methods are still relied upon for final results.

The gun is a heat engine using a high-energy fuel, most often smokeless single-base powder. The nitrocellulose powders commonly used today can theoretically develop about 180 foot-pounds of energy per grain weight of powder. In practice, only 20 to 30 percent of this energy is delivered to the bullet as it leaves the muzzle. The balance is lost in heat, forcing the bullet into the rifling, friction, rotation of the bullet, recoil, and in the energy of the powder gases lost as muzzle blast.

The blow of the firing pin on the primer ignites the priming composition, resulting in an intense blaze of hot gases and incandescent particles through the primer vent, filling the interior of the case and setting the entire powder charge to burning. It is desirable to ignite the whole powder charge at once, without such violence of ignition that powder granules are shattered or packed so as to change their burning characteristics. For this reason, a variety of small arms primers are manufactured to match case capacities, charge weights, and the ignition characteristics of a wide range of powders.

Smokeless propellant powders are made in a variety of sizes and shapes, as required by the gun, cartridge, charge weight, and bullet with which they will be used. Among the shapes that have been used or are still in use are: long flat strips; long cords; long tubes; short perforated cylinders; square and round flakes; thick, round perforated flakes, resembling tiny doughnuts; spheres; and flattened spheres.

Smokeless powder ignites and burns on the exposed outside, or surface, layer, and this burning continues, layer by layer of outer surface, as the granules decrease in size. Thus, the individual grain's thickness has the greatest effect on burning speed for any given composition. With shapes such as simple cylinders and spheres, the exposed surface gets smaller as the burning continues, and the speed of burning decreases as there is less surface left to burn. Such powder is called degressive burning and tends to produce high, peak pressure close to the breech, low muzzle pressure, and lowered velocities, relative to pressure, for a given grain size.

If a perforated or tubular shape of granule is used, the inside and the outside surfaces will be ignited at the same time and the area of the inside surface exposed to burning will increase as the outside decreases. This kind of granule is called neutral burning. Its performance is intermediate between degressive and progressive burning powders for a given grain size.

To slow the burning of the exposed surface, the powder granules may be given an outside coating that is more difficult to ignite and that burns at a slower rate. This coating is called a deterrent. Thus, burning will proceed more slowly, with a slower rise in pressure, until the coating is burned through, then the rate of burning increases and there is a faster rise in pressure. Such a powder is called progressive burning. For a given grain size, the peak pressure occurs farther down the bore, the powder burns for a longer time, breech pressure is lower, while muzzle pressure is higher, and the pressure-velocity ratio is better; i.e., higher velocity is obtained for the same maximum pressure. Work has also been done with double coatings of deterrent, with layers of powder of two kinds, and with methods of changing the density of the granule within the thickness of the web, to control the burning rate. Coatings are extremely important in small arms powders, and ball or spherical powder would be impractical for most propellant uses if uncoated. Double-base powders have a wider tolerance; that is, they burn well over a wider range of pressures, and are more often left uncoated than straight nitrocellulose. Uncoated powders are often used in pistol and shotgun loadings.

With the same charge weight, smaller granules expose more surface to initial ignition, the powder burns faster, pressure rises faster, and the powder is consumed in less distance of bullet travel than with coarser granules. In any gun, if the powder granules are too large, some of the charge will be blown out of the muzzle unburned. For each caliber of gun, case capacity, pressure level, weight of charge, weight of bullet, and density of loading, there is an optimum grain size and coating, if coating is required.

Unconfined in the open air, smokeless powders are difficult to ignite and, in small quantities, burn slowly. The rate of burning increases with heat, confinement and pressure. Confined inside the cartridge and chamber, the heat of burning of each granule communicates itself to adjacent granules, making them burn faster. The resistance of the bullet causes a rise in the pressure of the gases and increasing pressure raises both heat and burning rate. The complete charge may be burned in a .001-second, or less. With a heavy charge of fine-granule fast-burning powder behind a heavy bullet, the pressure curve may rise so steeply that the gun bursts before the bullet has time to move forward enough to keep the pressure within safe limits.

Other factors that affect the burning rate and consequently pressure and velocity are the loading density; weight, shape, and diameter of the bullet; force required to start the bullet out of the case neck; chamber and neck clearance; length and shape of the throat; and the design of the rifling. The potential for change in pressure from just one of these factors may be illustrated by a test in which 10 different .30-caliber bullets, all of 150 grains, were tested for pressure and velocity, with the same cases, powder, weight of powder charge, the same seating depth, and in the same test barrel. Pressures varied from 44,510 pounds per square inch to 51,900 psi, a difference of 7,390 psi, while velocities varied from 2,956 feet per second to 3,037 fps, for the averages of a 10-round series for each bullet.

Loading density is defined as the ratio between the weight of the powder charge used and the weight of the same powder that will just fill the powder space to the base of a seated bullet. In general, a decrease in the density of loading lowers the velocity and maximum pressure and moves the peak pressure toward the muzzle. From the viewpoint of uniformity of pressure and velocity, it is desirable to use a powder that just fills the case to the base of the bullet.

For practical purposes, all of the powder that is going to burn has burned by the time the bullet leaves the muzzle. The balance is mostly blown out the muzzle as unburned, or partially burned, granules, although some of these may be found in the bore or in the case after firing. This means that *all* of the powder that is burned in most centerfire rifle calibers is consumed in an inch or two of bullet travel, and, from that time until bullet exit, all of the work of pushing the projectile forward is done by expansion of powder gases. Because of this, a factor known as the "expansion ratio" is of major importance in determining the efficiency of the cartridge-gun combination. This is the ratio between the volume of the inside of the cartridge case to the base of the bullet and the total volume of the bore. It is a measure of the work that can be done with the expanding gases. For example, the .30/06 case has an inside volume about 22 percent larger than the .308 Winchester. In a 24-inch barrel, the expansion ratio of the .30/06 is about 7.5 and that of the .308 is about 9.1. Using the same 180-grain bullet in both, with a maximum charge of the optimum powder for each, the .308 with about 12 grains less of powder develops a muzzle velocity of 2,600 fps, against the 2,780 fps velocity. The large-case-capacity Magnum rifle cartridges are extremely inefficient for this reason, particularly in short-barreled sporting rifles. It is also a fact that there is nothing magical in case shapes or in shoulder contours.

The area of the base of the bullet is another important factor determining the amount of energy that can be imparted to the bullet at a given pressure.

Since the work is done by expanding gases, the amount of work that can be done is directly related to the area available for the gas to push on, known as the "piston effect." If the average gas pressure is known (in most rifles this can be taken as about one-third of the maximum pressure), together with the area of the bullet base, bullet weight, and the length of bullet travel to the muzzle, it is possible to make fairly accurate calculations of muzzle energy and muzzle velocity. If the bullet diameter is doubled, from .22 inch to .44 inch, the area of its base is quadrupled, and the amount of work that can be done at the same pressure increases accordingly. Doubling the diameter increases the area four times.

The internal ballistics of firearms using black powder are somewhat different from those using smokeless. Compared with smokeless, black powder is easier to ignite, burns at a much more constant speed regardless of pressure, and the burning rate is controlled almost entirely by the size of the granules and the density to which they have been compressed. Pressure and velocity curves are similar to smokeless in their general shape, but peak pressures range from perhaps 7,000 to 25,000 psi, and velocities are very much lower than those obtained with smokeless. More than half the products of combustion are solids, largely carbon or soot, and these are blown out of the muzzle, forming the cloud of smoke typically associated with black-powder shooting. Since less than half of the charge of black powder is turned into gases, to expand and do the work of bullet propulsion, large powder charges have to be used, thus black powder is much less efficient than smokeless; in addition, recoil is increased by the weight of the solids blown out the muzzle with the bullet. (See BALLISTICS; CHAMBER PRESSURE.)

International Benchrest Shooters (association) IBS was formed in 1970 as a result of a split among National Bench Rest Shooter's Association members. As a result, the IBS currently represents shooters primarily in the northeastern United States, while NBRSA is currently composed primarily of shooters in the Southeast, the Midwest, and the West. However, many members belong to both organizations. Like the NBRSA, IBS encourages a style of shooting that promotes extreme rifle shooting accuracy from the benchrest. Other than minor variations in the rules, the gun classes and courses of fire are virtually identical with NBRSA, so groups and records are comparable. The major difference is in Hunter Class. Here IBS allows the use of any cartridge, while the NBRSA limits it to a .236 bore diameter (6mm) or larger, with a case capacity not less than that of a .30/30.

The distances fired are 100, 200, and 300 yards.

Five-shot groups are recognized in all classes except Hunter which requires 10; 10-shot groups are also recognized in the Heavy Bench Rifle Class.

The IBS maintains headquarters at 411 North Wilbur Avenue, Sayre, Pennsylvania 18840. (See BENCHREST COMPETITION SHOOTING; NATIONAL BENCH REST SHOOTER'S ASSOCIATION.)

International Handgun Metallic Silhouette Association (I.H.M.S.A.) As an outgrowth of the popularity of *Siluetas Metalicas*, which had its first officially sanctioned American match in 1973, the First National Handgun Metallic Silhouette Championships were held near Tucson, Arizona, in 1975. Forty-six shooters participated, and the course of fire was 40 shots. A year later, in October 1976, during the second Championships, the International Handgun Metallic Silhouette Association was formed. Incorporated as a nonprofit organization, I.H.M.S.A. is headquartered at Box 368, Burlington, Idaho 52601-0368. According to the by-laws, one of the main purposes of the organization is to ". . . encourage organized silhouette pistol shooting," and to this end sanctioned matches are held by qualified clubs. A sanctioned match for centerfire competition consists of 40 rounds—10 rounds each at chicken, pig, turkey, and ram silhouettes located at 50, 100, 150, and 200 meters respectively. Firing is in five-round stages, two minutes time per stage, in a freestyle or standing position, without artificial support. (A rimfire match is similar, but the silhouettes are positioned at 25, 50, 75, and 100 yards respectively.)

For centerfire handguns, competition is in four categories: Production Single Shot, Production Revolver, Production Standing, and Unlimited. Basically, a production handgun is one that was a regular catalog item of the manufacturer as of January 1, 1977, in all features, except standard commercial stocks may replace the original stocks, if desired. The barrel length must not exceed 10¾ inches. The I.H.M.S.A. limits production guns to those that retail for less than a specified amount. (No optical sights are permitted.) Unlimited handguns are any handgun, other than production, with a maximum unloaded weight of 4½ pounds and a maximum barrel length and sight radius of 15 inches.

In 1979, .22 rimfire competition was introduced in three categories: Semiautomatic Pistol, Revolver, and Single Shot, with all handguns being standard catalog items on or before January 1, 1979. Only .22 Long Rifle cartridges are permitted in this competition.

As of mid-1989, I.H.M.S.A. had a membership of more than 50,000, with two permanent ranges, one in Idaho Falls, Idaho, the other in Oak Ridge, Tennessee. I.H.M.S.A. hosted more than 5,000 matches in 1989 with more than 180,000 entries recorded. In addition, there were 127 regional, state, and European championships held in 1989. (See SILHOUETTE SHOOTING [SILUETAS METALICAS].)

International Shooting Union (L'Union Internationale de Tir)   The official world organization for the shooting sports, formed in Zurich, Switzerland, July 17, 1907. It governs the kinds of shooting included in World and Olympic Shooting, the targets, equipment, clothing, and positions that may be used and provides standardized rules of conduct and organization. Decisions as to what countries shall host what matches, where and when, are decided by ISU committees.

There are records of shooting competitions in some European countries as early as the 11th century, but many of the national shooting organizations of those nations of the world where shooting developed into a major sport, such as England, Germany, Switzerland, and the United States, were not formed until the 19th century. International shooting competitions of the type of the Olympic Games and World Championships started in 1896, with the first modern Olympic Games at Athens, Greece, where representatives of four nations competed in a total of five events.

The concept of an international shooting federation was first discussed at a shooting competition in Milan, Italy, attended by representatives of six nations, in June 1906. The formation of the ISU occurred at the Zurich meeting mentioned above, with representatives of Argentina, Austria, Belgium, France, Greece, Holland, Italy, and Switzerland present. They adopted a constitution, general regulations, and special statutes, largely as drafted by the French delegation headed by Pierre Merillon, a distinguished lawyer who was the first president of the ISU. The first International matches fired under ISU regulations were hosted by the Austrian Federation in Vienna, July 1908, with nine countries competing. Interrupted sporadically by war, depression, and politics, and with changes in regulations and programs, the International and Olympic Matches have grown and prospered, with the shooting program encompassing men's, women's, and team competitions in the following courses of fire or kinds of shooting:

Free Rifle, 300 meters.
Free Rifle, smallbore, 50 meters.
Free Rifle, smallbore, prone position, 50 meters.
Free Pistol, fired variously at 30 meters, 50 meters and 50 yards, but standardized at 50 meters in 1912.
Rapid-Fire Pistol, fired variously at 25 meters, 20 meters and 30 meters, but standardized at 25 meters in 1924.

Running Boar, 50 meters. This superseded the Running Roebuck and Running Deer.
Clay Pigeon, Olympic Trap.
Skeet.
Army Rifle, 300 meters.
Smallbore Rifle, moving or disappearing targets, 25 yards and 25 meters, fired only from 1908 to 1920.
Live Pigeon Shooting. Not fired for many years.
Smallbore Standard Rifle, 50 meters.
Air Rifle, 10 meters.
Air Pistol, 10 meters.
Centerfire Pistol, 25 meters.
Standard Pistol, 10 meters.

The ISU has permanent quarters in Wiesbaden, Germany, and six times a year publishes a magazine, *International Shooting Sport*. It also has available an excellent and interesting history of the organization, *The International Shooting Union, Official History, 1907–1977*, written by A. J. Palmer of Great Britain. (See OLYMPIC GAMES SHOOTING EVENTS; WORLD SHOOTING CHAMPIONSHIPS.)

International skeet shooting   The form of skeet competition used in the Olympics and other world shooting events, and a form of skeet practiced in every skeet shooting country except the United States. More difficult than the American version, with targets thrown farther (thus faster), it requires the gun to be started with some part of the butt at hip level—rather than at the shoulder as permitted in American skeet. Only 12-gauge guns are used. A delay timer in the electrical mechanism that releases the targets provides an alternating delay up to three seconds after the shooter calls "pull" for the target to be thrown. The target may emerge instantly as the launching button is pushed or may delay up to three seconds; neither shooter nor referee knows precisely when the target will emerge.

Recent rule changes by the International Shooting Union have made the game even more difficult by taking out most of the easier targets and replacing them with doubles at stations 3 and 5, which in American skeet require only the shooting of singles. The shooter must move very quickly to break the doubles targets, which appear simultaneously and go in opposite directions at a launch speed of approximately 90 miles per hour.

The shooting discipline is as follows: The shooter starts at station 1, receives a high house target, then shoots doubles. Station 2 is a single target from each house, then doubles. Station 3, singles and doubles. Station 4, singles. Stations 5 and 6, singles and doubles. Station 7, doubles only. Station 8, one target from the high house, one from the low house.

International skeet can be practiced on any ordinary American skeet range by tightening the spring tension launching machines to provide the faster target that International rules require and by installing a delay timer or instructing the target puller to provide a varying delay before releasing the target. Increasing slowly in popularity in this country, International offers less tournament opportunity, but provides the shooter a chance at making some future team for world class competition. The game is being promoted in this country by the National Rifle Association, which is the official sponsor of all American teams for the Olympics, World Games, World Moving Target Championships, and Pan American Games.

International skeet is generally conceded to be better training for the field hunter than American skeet, primarily because of the low gun position and the fast gun mounting required.

Rule changes now require no more than 1 ounce (28 grams) of shot in International skeet. (See INTERNATIONAL SHOOTING UNION; SKEET SHOOTING.)

International trapshooting This shotgun game, popular around the world, uses clay targets that are harder, emerge much faster, and fly at wider variations of horizontal and vertical angles than in American trap. Rather than emerging from a visible trap house, International targets emerge at ground level from machines that must be capable of throwing the clay target 75 meters. The target must be thrown within an area bounded by angles of 45 degrees right and left, much wider angles than in American trap. The shooter is confronted by a target that may go high, low, right or left at a launch speed (depending upon humidity, air density, etc.) approaching 100 miles per hour. The shooter is permitted two shots at each target, with a hit scoring the same for either shot.

In most countries, International trap is shot over 15 trap "bunkers," with three machines recessed beneath each of the five shooting stations. The various traps are set to throw high, low, left, right, etc., and a complex programming system with a built-in selector mechanism determines which target will be thrown from which trap, so that at the end of 25 rounds each shooter will have fired at precisely the same number of rights, lefts, highs, and lows. This bunker layout is used in major competitions, but the International Shooting Union has now approved so-called "wobble traps," which duplicate the unknown angles, highs, and lows of the other system but require only one trap machine. This oscillates up and down, right to left, and throws its targets from whatever position it may be in when the shooter calls "pull."

International trap is often described as the most difficult of all sanctioned clay target competitions and is a fascinating test of shooting ability; but it remains little practiced in this country because of lack of ISU shooting facilities and the fact that most American trapshooters are interested in perfecting the American version of the game, which offers the prospect of more money, larger prizes, and more shooting events. Rule changes in 1988 require no more than 1 ounce (28 grams) of shot. (See TRAPSHOOTING.)

interocular distance Another term for interpupillary distance. (See INTERPUPILLARY DISTANCE.)

interpupillary distance The barrels of a binocular must swing on a hinge to provide for adjusting to the distance between the eyes of the user. This distance between the pupils of the eyes is known as the interpupillary distance, and the barrels of a binocular must be set to this distance so that the image seen by each eye will be correctly superimposed in order to form a single clear image. In better binoculars, the hinge is provided with an interpupillary scale, graduated in millimeters, so that the user may return to the same setting without trial and error. (See BINOCULARS.)

Intraform process Intraform was a trade name, copyrighted by The Cincinnati Milling Machine Co., to cover a rotary swaging machine and the process of doing work on this machine.

Rotary swaging machines of this basic type have been in use since the mid-1800s. The Intraform machine had provisions for holding a short mandrel, restrained from moving axially, located between the dies and inside the tube to be worked on. By making the mandrel the reverse of a rifle bore, including the rifling, rifle barrels could be blanked out from short, heavy-walled tubes. The workpiece put into the machine for a .30-caliber barrel would have a hole about .340 inch in diameter, an outside diameter of about 1⅜ inches, and a length of 20 inches. The rifle barrel blank, after swaging, would have a conventional .308-inch-groove diameter rifled bore, about 1¼ inches in outside diameter, and 23 inches long. Total forces developed by the dies in this process might run as high as 200 to 400 tons.

Because of the high initial cost of the Intraform machine, and the high cost and relatively short life of dies and mandrels, application of the machine was limited and only a few were produced. Similar machines, also used for barrel work, were made by Fellows-Appel in America and GFM in Austria. In the more sophisticated applications, the swaging operation formed the rifling, the complete chamber and throat, and also rough-contoured the outside of the barrel blank. (See BARREL MAKING; SWAGED RIFLING.)

investment casting Investment casting is a very old process, its origins probably going back to very ancient times, when it was used to produce jewelry and art objects of precious metals. It has been used to make dentures, inlays, and other items required in dentistry for perhaps hundreds of years, but has become a major manufacturing method in industry only in this country. The melting points of gold, silver, bronze, and the alloys of ancient times are all under 2,000 degrees Fahrenheit, and the use of investment casting, or the "lost wax process," as it is also called, had to await the development of ceramics and methods capable of handling the higher temperatures of steel and steel alloys (in the range of 2,500 degrees F.) before it became practical for the products of the steel age.

Investment cast products are of major importance in small arms manufacture, being used for receivers and bolts, frames of revolvers, and many small parts. The process can be used for many ferrous alloys, including stainless steels and the high-strength alloys required for receivers, bolts, and frames. The process is capable of great precision, dimensions of small parts being held to plus or minus .002 inch and double this on receivers, bolts, etc.

The first step in the process is to make a pattern of wax (or another thermoplastic material) that is an exact duplicate of the part to be cast, except that it has allowances for the amount of shrinkage of the material that will be used to make the part. For production work, patterns are molded in an automatic injection molding machine, using a mold with a cavity that is an exact negative of the finished pattern. The model may also be used as a hob and pressed into the metal of the mold to form the cavity. Multiple patterns are often molded, or several patterns may be joined by attaching wax "runners" (which provide flow channels from part to part in the finished ceramic mold) to form a cluster of patterns referred to as a "Christmas tree."

Patterns or pattern clusters are provided with gates and risers. A gate is an opening into which the molten metal is poured; a riser is an opening to release air and gases trapped in the mold as metal is poured. They are then dipped several times into a slurry, made with a ceramic or refractory material, with drying between coats. After curing, the wax pattern, with its coating of ceramic, is fired in a kiln, melting out the wax pattern and, with the high temperature reached by firing, burning out all traces

of wax. Hence the name "lost wax process." The result is a ceramic mold with an inside cavity (or cavities connected by runners) exactly duplicating the wax pattern, including the tiniest of details.

The ceramic mold is brittle and rather fragile, so it is supported in sand within a steel flask for the pouring of the melted metal. Melting is done in an induction furnace, the pour is made, then the molds are covered with a layer of powdered material to reduce oxidation and to provide more uniform cooling. After cooling, molds are broken away, leaving the cast parts attached to gates, runners, and risers. Abrasive cutoff wheels are used to separate the parts from these, then the parts are cleaned and inspected.

Scrap loss tends to be high on investment cast parts. In parts such as revolver frames, as much as 40 percent of the castings may be rejected. These rejects, and the gates, runners, and risers are remelted and used again, of course.

Investment casting is economical only where it saves machining time, broadly speaking. If a part must be machined all over, investment cast parts will likely be more expensive than ones machined from bar stock or forgings. They cannot compete in cases where parts can be machined on automatic screw machines. However, some very good quality guns are currently being made by this process and at very reasonable prices.

iris The opaque contractile diaphragm perforated by the pupil and forming the colored portion of the eye. The iris expands and contracts, changing the size of the pupil to match light conditions. The pupil of the human eye varies from about 2.5mm in bright sunlight to about 7mm in moonlight. It will be about 5mm in the dim light conditions of dawn and dusk.

A knowledge of this is important to sportsmen in selecting optical instruments, as the exit pupil of the instrument must be equal in size to the shooter's pupil, as determined by the iris. (See EXIT PUPIL.)

iris diaphragm An adjustable diaphragm of thin opaque plates that can be turned by a ring so as to change the diameter of a central opening. These are used to regulate the aperture of a lens in cameras, etc., and also used in adjustable aperture peep sights and front aperture sights on firearms.

The usefulness of a peep sight arises from the fact that when its aperture is smaller than the pupil of the human eye, it allows only rays that are nearly parallel to enter the pupil. The effect of this is to increase the depth of focus, just as a small "f" stop increases the depth of focus in a camera. Thus the shooter is enabled to see both the front sight and the object aimed at more clearly. The iris diaphragm in a peep sight allows for quick, simple adjustment of the aperture to the optimum size for existing light conditions.

An iris attachment, held by a rubber suction cup, is available for attachment to eyeglasses. Older shooters, whose eyes lack accommodation, find it helpful in giving better definition to both the sights and the target, when shooting a pistol.

A front sight with an iris aperture for target shooting is also available. This enables adjustment of the size of the aperture to match the size of the bull's-eye and existing light conditions. (See APERTURE SIGHT; METALLIC SIGHTS; PEEP SIGHT.)

irons See LUMPS.

iron sights Any nonoptical sight, either open or aperture, so called because all firearm sights were once made of iron. Today the term is interchangeable with "metallic sights," although many materials are used for modern sights. (See METALLIC SIGHTS.)

Ithaca Gun Company An outgrowth of the L.C. Smith Gun Company of Syracuse, New York, the Ithaca Gun Company began production in 1880 in Ithaca, New York. During the early years of the company, production focused on a line of double-barrel shotguns. Production was expanded in 1908 to include the Ithaca single-barrel trap gun.

The Model 37 Featherlight Repeater was introduced in 1937. The repeating model was a success, and the company continued development in this area. However, sporting firearm production was temporarily halted during World War II, when Ithaca geared its production to the manufacturing of military arms.

The clip-loading X-5 Lightning semiautomatic rifle was introduced in 1958. The following year, the Model 37 Deerslayer was marketed. The Deerslayer was designed and equipped for rifled slugs. In 1966, Ithaca introduced a new line of double guns imported from Japan.

General Recreation Inc. bought the Ithaca Gun Company in 1967. Facilities were improved and expanded, and in 1968 the Perazzi competition singles made in Italy and the LSA rifle from Finland were added to the product line. In 1979, the Model 51 gas operated semiautomatic shotgun was introduced. Ithaca affiliated with the German Erma-Werke firm in 1972 to produce the Model 72 Saddlegun. In 1976, Ithaca marketed a Bicentennial Commemorative Model 37, fashioned after the model introduced in 1937.

The company fell into bankruptcy in the 1980s and is now operating limited production lines. The Model 37 has been changed to the Model 87, to agree with its year of re-introduction.

Iver Johnson Arms (company) was founded in 1867 at Worcester, Massachusetts, and moved to Fitchburg, Massachusetts in 1891. Shortly after its establishment the company name was changed to Iver Johnson Arms and Cycle works because, in addition to inexpensive shotguns, .22 rifles, and rimfire and centerfire handguns, the firm also made bicycles. These product lines were maintained through the 1950s, but as market conditions grew more competitive Iver Johnson gradually dropped the bicycles and long arms, and produced only .22 and centerfire single-action handguns. In 1978 the company was moved to Middlesex, New Jersey. Iver Johnson is no longer in business, but several of its handguns are manufactured by American Military Arms Corp. of Jacksonville, Arkansas.

jacket See BULLET JACKET.

jacketed bullet Prior to the invention of smokeless powder and the resulting increase in bullet velocities, bullets were manufactured entirely of lead and given a suitable lubricant or patching to reduce friction and leading. The new powder boosted pressures and velocities, and the hot gases tended to melt away a portion of the base and sidewalls of the bullets, causing velocity loss, inaccuracy, and fouling of the rifle bore. To overcome these problems, the lead bullets were given a jacket or covering of a harder material, usually copper or an alloy of copper such as gilding metal.

For deeper penetration, and military use, the jacket completely covers the nose of the bullet and may be of steel covered with gilding metal; such bullets are called full-metal-jacket (FMJ) or solid bullets and may or may not have a tapered or boattail base section. Most jacketed hunting bullets have the jacket covering the base section, but leave the nose exposed, either as a soft lead point or with a hollow point or similar expanding design.

The early jacketed bullets were roundnosed, but around the turn of the century the sharp or ''spitzer'' pointed bullets were developed in Germany. Later, this design was copied in the United States and in various other countries. Today, pointed jacketed bullets are manufactured extensively in the United States for hunting and military use and for target shooting, while the round- or flat-nosed jacketed bullets are used mainly in handguns or rifles with tubular magazines. (See BULLET JACKET; GILDING METAL; SOLID BULLET; SPITZER BULLET.)

Jaeger rifle The early American gunmakers were predominantly German immigrants, and the influence of the German hunting rifles can be seen in the early American flintlock rifles. The Jaeger was the rifled arm of Central Europe in the late 1600s. It was a short weapon, with an octagonal barrel about 28 inches in length and a large bore (usually .60 to .70 caliber). The heavy stock extended to the muzzle and traditionally included a small patch box with a sliding wooden cover in the butt. The furniture was usually brass.

In America, the Jaeger was often referred to as the ''Yager'' rifle. It was the ancestor of the Kentucky rifle, and enjoyed its heyday in this country from the mid-1600s until after the Revolution, when the Kentucky pattern gained ascendance. The Jaeger's influence extended to the Harpers Ferry 1803 musket and to the Hawken rifle, which replaced the Kentucky in the West. (See FLINTLOCK; KENTUCKY RIFLE.)

jag The end portion of a cleaning rod. It has a series of grooves or ridges used to grip a cleaning patch, or similar swabbing material, wrapped around it. Jags may be constructed of brass, steel, nylon, aluminum, wood or plastic.

Janka test A test to determine the relative hardness of different species of woods. Hardness values are developed by recording the load in pounds required to embed a steel ball, .444 inch in diameter, to one-half its diameter in the wood. These values will vary in different samples, depending to a great extent on the soil and climate in which the wood grew. For example, American walnut grown in swampy bottomlands will have a soft, porous grain structure and is likely to be straight grained. Grown at higher elevations in thin, dry soils, it will be denser, be more likely to have curly or wavy grain, and will register higher Janka readings than the bottomlands wood.

Typical Janka readings, taken at the standard 12 percent moisture content, of some of the woods used for firearms stocks are listed below.

Apple	1,730
Birch, paper	910
Birch, yellow	1,260
Maple, sugar	1,450
Rosewood, East Indian	2,630
Walnut, American	1,010

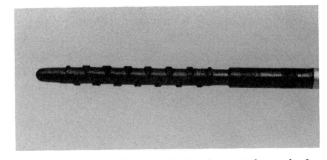

A jag is used to hold a patch in place at the end of a cleaning rod. With this kind of jag, the patch is wrapped around the pointed protrusions, which grip it.

Hardness, combined with other factors such as strength and light weight, is highly desirable in a stock wood. Thus the hardest woods, such as the walnuts, are the best. (See STOCK WOODS.)

javelina, guns and loads for   The javelina is a wild pig of the desert Southwest, found primarily in southern Arizona, Texas, New Mexico, and in Mexico. Even though classified as a big-game animal in Arizona, the javelina is relatively small; an average javelina weighs about 30-to-35 pounds when field dressed. (These animals actually do look much larger than they are because of their 4- to 6-inch-long hair.

Because of the pig's diminutive size, the smaller centerfire cartridges are entirely adequate for javelina. The Arizona Department of Fish and Game even allows the use of the .22 magnum rimfire and 5mm Remington Magnum for Javelina, but these two rimfire cartridges are marginal for effective use. Some javelina hunters prefer to use the high-velocity, rapidly expanding varmint cartridges and bullets, but this has the effect of destroying an excessive amount of meat on the small pigs. Probably the best cartridges for javelina are in the class of the .243 Winchester, 6mm Remington, and .250 Savage loaded with the heavier bullets designed for smaller big game.

Javelina are hunted in brushy country and are frequently taken at close to moderate range. If a rifle is used, it should be equipped with a low power scope, or a variable in the 1X-4X range. Some hunters prefer to take the animals with handguns. As with rifles, power is not needed, and a .357 Magnum or hot loaded .38 Special is adequate.

jaws   The jaws or vise on the hammer of a flintlock gun are used to hold the flint securely. A small piece of leather is placed over the base of the flint, and then the flint is placed in the jaws and the jaws are firmly tightened. (See FLINTLOCK.)

Jeffrey's (company)   Noted English gunmaking firm. W. J. Jeffrey opened his first London gunmaking shop in 1885. On his death in 1909, W. J. was succeeded by his brother Charles; in that same year the firm became a limited (incorporated) company. In 1960 Jeffrey's was acquired by Holland & Holland.

Large-bore double rifles, notably the .600 Nitro Express doubles, brought Jeffrey's their greatest fame.

Jorgensen, Erik   See KRAG RIFLE.

jug choke   Sometimes called a recessed choke, the jug choke is often used on shotgun barrels that have been shortened, thereby removing all the original choke. Two or so inches back from the muzzle of a shortened barrel, metal is removed from the walls of the barrel by boring (expanding reamers); this metal removal increases the internal diameter of the bore for an inch or more along the barrel, permitting the shot charge to expand slightly. The shot charge is then constricted by the remainder of the barrel, which is left at its original diameter. (See CHOKE.)

jump   See BULLET JUMP; MUZZLE JUMP.

Jurras bullets   In the mid-1960s, in an attempt to improve the bullet performance of the .38 Special cartridge, Lee E. Jurras, an Indiana experimenter, developed a 110-grain jacketed bullet design in two forms—one with a hollow point and one with a soft point. Tests conducted with these bullets by the Phoenix Police Department, and later by several other police departments, indicated that the bullets to be just what was needed to put some life into the .38 Special cartridge. Jurras then formed the Super Vel Cartridge Corporation to commercially load ammunition with the Jurras bullets for police use. Still later, additional Jurras bullets were designed for the .38 Special/.357 Magnum, .41 Magnum, .44 Magnum, 9mm Parabellum, .380 ACP, .38 Super, and .45 ACP cartridges, and ammunition was loaded to velocities determined to make the bullets perform as designed. Bullets were also made available commercially for handloading, along with ballistic data, prior to the original Super Vel firm going out of business in 1975.

Featuring thin jackets with lots of lead exposure at the nose, a truncated cone shape, and large hollow points, the Jurras bullets were the first commercially available bullets to produce suitable expansion when fired from handguns. The bullets intended for use in autoloading pistols had the jackets coming up to and slightly rounded into the hollow point to ensure positive feeding from the magazine and to prevent deformation of the nose. Later, the basic Jurras design was copied by many other manufacturers.

keeper A leather, plastic or metal loop, ring, or clamp used on a rifle sling to maintain tightness and prevent slipping. Military and Whelen slings are equipped with two leather keepers, while the modern web military sling has a single metal clamp. Regular leather sporting slings or carrying straps generally have a single leather keeper. For target shooting, one of the keepers on a leather sling may be replaced by a screw-tightened metal clamp. (See SLING.)

Keith, Elmer (1899–1984) Born in Missouri, Elmer Keith was for more than five decades a prolific and influential writer on hunting and firearms. Keith moved with his parents to Montana in his childhood and, during his twenties and thirties, was a cowboy, freight packer, big-game hunter, and competitive rifleman.

Keith began writing for such magazines as *Outdoor Life* in 1927, and shortly became a regular magazine contributor. In 1948, he became a technical editor on the staff of *The American Rifleman*. Among the books he authored are: *Shotguns by Keith* (Stackpole, 1950), *Sixguns by Keith* (Stackpole, 1955), *Big Game Hunting* (Little, Brown, 1948), and *Keith, an Autobiography* (Winchester Press, 1975).

A lifelong advocate of heavy-caliber rifles and handguns, Keith was influential in the development of cartridges such as the .41 and .44 Magnum.

Kellner eyepiece The Kellner eyepiece is known as an achromatized Ramsden eyepiece. The Ramsden eyepiece is made of two lenses of spectacle crown glass of equal focal lengths. To correct for lateral color, their separation should equal the focal length. When so located, the first focal plane of the

Long an advocate of big bores and heavy bullets, Elmer Keith has had a profound effect on the design of American firearms and the tastes of American shooters.

system coincides with the field lens, and any dust on the lens surface is seen in sharp focus. For this reason, the lenses are usually moved a little closer together, thus moving the focal plane forward at the cost of some lateral achromatism. The Ramsden eyepiece has the advantage of greater eye relief than other eyepiece (ocular) systems, together with much less spherical aberration and distortion.

The many desirable features of the Ramsden eyepiece led to attempts to correct its chromatic defects. The Kellner eyepiece is a Ramsden eyepiece with the eye lens made as a cemented doublet, one lens made of crown glass and one made of flint glass, to correct for chromatic aberration. (See CEMENTING LENSES; CHROMATIC ABERRATION; EYEPIECE; RAMSDEN EYEPIECE.)

Kentucky pistol   A kind of single-shot muzzleloading pistol that was popular in America from the Revolutionary War until about 1840. These pistols bore many similarities to the Kentucky rifle; hence the name. Most Kentucky pistols are flintlocks (percussion examples are almost always flintlock conversions), with locks that were imported from Germany or England, as were the barrels. The earlier guns were stocked in walnut or cherry, and the later specimens in maple. Invariably, the pistols were stocked to the muzzle, and many of them are found with a reddish wood stain—the so-called German violin finish.

Overall, the quality of these guns is not nearly so high as that of the Kentucky rifles, since they were intended only as backup arms to be used at close range and in an emergency. This is reflected in their large caliber—.36 to .50—and the fact that only the later specimens are rifled. (See FLINTLOCK; KENTUCKY RIFLE.)

Kentucky rifle   This uniquely American firearm evolved as a working implement, and became, in the process, an authentic art form. Although it is called "Kentucky rifle," the vast majority of these arms were made in Pennsylvania by gunsmiths of German and Swiss descent. However, the arm made its reputation on the Kentucky frontier in the hands of men such as Daniel Boone, Davy Crockett, and Simon Kenton; hence the usual name.

The Kentucky rifle traces its ancestry to the Jaeger rifle, a comparatively short-barreled, full-stocked flintlock arm of large caliber. In response to the demands of the time, the Jaeger underwent extensive modifications. The primary considerations in building a rifle for the American frontier were accuracy, lightness, and frugality with lead and power, since resupply was always a crucial problem.

In response, the Pennsylvania gunsmiths developed a new kind of rifle with a long barrel, of comparatively small caliber for the time, with open sights and a full stock. The typical Kentucky rifle was a flintlock, had a barrel of 44 inches, was about .45 caliber, had a blade front sight of silver, a nonadjustable rear notch sight, a maple stock with a patch box, and a weight of 8 to 9 pounds. The first specimens appeared about 1710.

This gun was exactly what the times required. It was powerful enough for both large game and hostile Indians and its long sight radius and rifled barrel made it highly accurate to 250 yards in the hands of a good shot, an astonishing range for the time. Using a .45 caliber rifle, a frontiersman could expect about 200 shots from 2 pounds of powder and lead.

It was not until the Revolution that the Kentucky achieved real notoriety. In that conflict, units of frontiersmen armed with these guns wreaked havoc with the British forces. The accuracy of the Americans' fire, combined with their tactic of shooting from ambush, both scandalized and awed the British, and the legend of the "long rifle" had its start.

In its earliest days, the Kentucky rifle was a plain arm. However, as it evolved, more and more attention was lavished on its ornamentation. Brass and German silver, worked in elaborate and distinctive patterns, were used for patchboxes and for trim. Striking blanks of fiddleback maple were used for

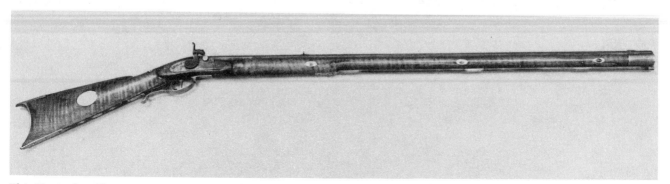

This Kentucky rifle was converted from flintlock to percussion ignition. It is unusual in that it lacks a patch box on the buttstock.

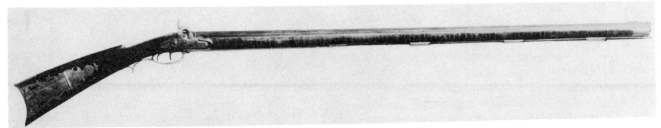

By the time percussion ignition was widely accepted, the Kentucky rifle had become garish—marred by excessive decoration. This example, despite an ornate patch box, did not suffer that fate.

the stocks. In the golden age of the Kentucky rifle (1775–1830), no fewer than 14 separate "schools" of the gun developed, each with its own distinctive style of stock profile and decoration. Kentucky rifles were still made largely in Pennsylvania, but they were also produced in Maryland, in large numbers, and as far south as North Carolina, west to Indiana, and north to New York.

Kentuckies made after 1830, when the percussion cap met widespread acceptance, are of poorer quality than earlier specimens, and the decoration is often garish. Calibers tend to be heavier, and the graceful appearance of the earlier guns is not present. Eventually, the Kentucky rifle was superseded on the frontier by the Plains rifle and the repeater, but during its prime it was a marvel of efficiency and grace—one of the purest forms of Americana. (See JAEGER RIFLE; PLAINS RIFLE.)

Kentucky windage An old shooting term derived from the American experience with nonadjustable sights on the Kentucky rifle, "Kentucky windage" refers to lateral hold-off to compensate for wind deflection. (See HOLDING OFF.)

Kenyon trigger A trigger for bolt-action match rifles, invented by Karl Kenyon of Ely, Nevada, in the mid-1950s. Available in pull weights as low as 2 to 3 ounces, or in the 3-pound pull required by National Rifle Association rules in some kinds of competition, it has a reputation for excellent workmanship and uniformity of pull. It is a three-lever single-stage trigger, in which the load of the mainspring on the cocking piece is stepped down through a system of three levers, so that the load on the engaging surfaces of the trigger and sear is only a fraction of that on the cocking piece. This permits very short engagement and a light pull, since friction between the trigger/sear surfaces is very low. (See TRIGGER PULL.)

Kersten lock Sometimes called the Greener double lock, the Kersten lock (named after its inventor, Gustav Kersten) consists of two perforated extensions projecting from the breech of the barrel—one on each side of the top barrel on over/under shotguns—into the upper portion of the standing breech. A cross-bolt, operated by the top lever, passes through the hole in each extension, securely locking the barrels to the receiver or frame. Examples of over/under shotguns, or rifle/shotgun combination guns, using the Kersten lock include Brno, Franz Sodia, Frankonia, Anson, and Merkel Bros. (See GREENER CROSS-BOLT; LOCKED BREECH ACTION.)

keyhole The imprint of an unstabilized bullet on a target. Instead of being round, the imprint will be longer in one direction, roughly similar to the keyhole in a lock.

Lack of stability in a bullet in flight may be caused by a rifling twist that is too slow, resulting in inaccuracy and wild shots. The rifling twist required to stabilize a bullet depends on its caliber, length, form, and the velocity at which the bullet is fired.

Keyholes may also be the result of the bullet striking some object prior to hitting the target.

key wedge On Plains rifles, a wedge-shaped metal piece that moves through a slot on the stock and a lug on the barrel's underside to fasten the barrel to the stock. Either one or two key wedges may be used. (See PLAINS RIFLE.)

kick A popular expression for perceived recoil. (See RECOIL.)

kicker A term applied to a shotgun or rifle that has a great amount of sensed recoil energy. In many instances, much of the recoil of such an arm is psychological, since the actual recoil energy is not as great as the sensed recoil. (See RECOIL.)

Kilbourne, Lysle See K-SERIES WILDCATS.

killing power The destructive effect of a bullet, both on the tissue and on the nervous system of the animal being struck. Killing power is dependent upon several factors, including the velocity, kinetic energy, weight of the bullet, shape of the bullet, type of nose on the bullet, sectional density, rotational velocity, and expansion qualities.

Killing power is frequently confused with bullet energy and/or shocking power. Bullet energy is a purely mathematical calculation and does not take into consideration any of the above factors except velocity and weight. Shocking power, on the other hand, is the ability to paralyze, not the ability to kill. Usually, however, a bullet with great shocking power also possesses great killing power.

There is no known way of measuring killing power. Efforts have been made to reduce this complex subject to a simple mathematical equation, but none has been completely successful. The best method for determining whether a cartridge is sufficiently powerful is to study the energy tables published by the ammunition manufacturers. If there's any doubt about killing power, it's always best to employ a cartridge possessing a greater degree of energy than is thought to be needed.

Bullet construction and performance are also very important in selecting the proper ammunition for the task at hand. For instance, a .30-caliber 180-grain pointed full-metal-jacket bullet traveling at 3,000 feet per second possesses 3,597 foot-pounds of energy. A pointed soft point of the same caliber and weight, traveling at the same speed, would possess the same energy. However, the full-metal-jacket bullet would very likely pass through a broadside-standing deer while transferring very little energy to the animal in the process. On the other hand, if the soft point bullet were to expand properly, a great deal of energy would be transmitted to the animal and would no doubt contribute to shock and killing power—but exactly how much can't be precisely measured and stated in finite terms.

Another aspect of killing power is hydrostatic pressure. When a high-velocity expanding bullet strikes game, the energy is transmitted from the point of impact through body fluids in the form of hydraulic pressure. This causes the rupture of arteries, veins, and other tissue.

Bullets traveling at a very high velocity may rupture the heart of an animal by hydrostatic pressure even when striking the animal some distance away from the heart. Likewise, when a high-velocity bullet strikes near the spinal cord, hydrostatic pressure may be transmitted to the spine and even the brain, resulting in great shock to the animal and even instantaneous death. (See BULLET ENERGY; ENERGY FORMULA.)

kinetic energy   Kinetic energy (K. E.) is the energy of a mass in motion. The kinetic energy of a bullet is the result of the mass of the bullet and the velocity at which it is moving.

The formula for the mass of a bullet is: $m = \dfrac{w}{7000g}$, in which w is the weight of the bullet in grains, and g is the acceleration of gravity, or 32.174 feet per second squared. There are 7,000 grains in a pound, and this factor converts bullet weight from grains to pounds.

The formula for kinetic energy of a bullet is: $K.E. = \dfrac{mV^2}{2}$, in which m is the mass of the bullet, and V is the velocity of the bullet at which the kinetic energy is to be determined. K. E., the result, is expressed in foot-pounds.

Thus, a 180-grain bullet at 2,600 fps has a K. E. of 2,700 foot-pounds. At 1,300 fps it would have a K. E. of 682 foot-pounds. The kinetic energy of a bullet is not necessarily a good index of its killing power on game, as there are many other factors to be considered. (See BULLET ENERGY.)

Kirksite bullet   Kirksite is a trade name, copyrighted by Morris P. Kirk & Son, Inc. of Los Angeles, California. The Kirksite alloy used for making cast bullets is Kirksite A, a zinc based alloy containing small quantities of aluminum and copper.

Kirksite A was developed for use as a material for forming dies. Cast bullet experimenters in the late 1930s and early 1940s found that it could be melted and molded with conventional bullet-casting equipment and techniques, although the melting point is in the range of 1,000 to 1,100 degrees Fahrenheit.

The hardness of this material is three to six times that of the usual lead-tin or lead-tin-antimony bullet materials, and its strength is correspondingly higher. A pointed spitzer lead-tin bullet, weighing about 170 grains in .30 caliber, weighs about 115 grains in Kirksite A and can be driven at velocities of 3,300 to 3,500 feet per second from a .30/06 rifle. Accuracy for five shot groups of about 1½ minutes of angle has been attained, out to 200 yards.

Experimenters who wish to work with Kirksite bullets, or with zinc or zinc-alloy bullets, should be aware that melting pots and dippers must be carefully cleaned of all traces of lead. Lead causes intergranular weakness in zinc alloys, the condition increasing with age. Because of the hardness of zinc alloys, bullets made from them should not be larger than the groove diameter of the rifle bore. Sizing of these bullets in the usual lead bullet sizing equipment is not possible; a mold must be found that will cast to the required size. (See CAST BULLET; HANDLOAD.)

knee joint   See TOGGLE JOINT.

kneeling roll   In competition rifle shooting, a small roll of leather, canvas or cloth, stuffed with a soft filler material, and used as padding under the instep of the foot supporting the body in the kneeling position. It cushions the instep, providing for greater comfort and a more stable position. (See POSITION SHOOTING.)

knockdown effect The term "knockdown" refers to a bullet's potential to deliver a blow of such intensity that a game animal or an assailant is stopped or felled instantaneously. The striking force of a moving projectile fired from a gun has been estimated in various ways, most commonly in foot-pounds of energy based upon a given bullet's weight and velocity at the impact point.

Actually, except in certain circumstances, bullets do not really knock animals off their feet.

John Taylor, the African ivory hunter, devised a system of measuring knockdown effect by considering not only bullet weight and velocity, but also frontal area. Knockdown power in pounds, according to his formula, equals the total of the bullet's weight, its actual velocity, and its diameter in decimals of an inch caliber, divided by 7,000: $KP = \dfrac{WVD}{7,000}$.

(See KILLING POWER; TAYLOR, JOHN.)

knockout die A knockout die is the simplest form of case-sizing die: The case is hammered in and then punched out. The term is also applied to the final

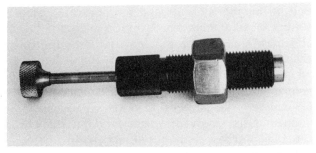

Knockout dies can have several functions. The plunger-equipped one is a point-forming die for bullets; the other is a case-sizing die. They derive their name from the fact that the bullet or case is knocked out of the die—literally—after it is formed.

bullet-shaping die in a home bullet-making set. (See CASE RESIZING.)

knockout rod The rod used to drive a case or bullet from a die. Also, a rod used to eject stuck cases from a rifle barrel.

knuckle On a double or side-by-side shotgun or rifle, the forward edge of the water table, or action flats, is referred to as the knuckle. This surface is rounded so that the forearm iron can pivot around it.

knurling The process of rolling lines, grooves, or diamonds onto metal objects, such as rifle safeties and revolver hammer spurs, by means of great pressure exerted on shaped rollers brought into contact with the metal surface. The finished surface can also be referred to as knurling, as well as knurled.

Krag rifle The creation of Ole H. Krag, a Norwegian army official who became Norway's master general of ordnance in the 1890s. He designed many pistol and rifle mechanisms, but his chief contribution to firearms history was his work with Erik Jorgensen, the works superintendent of the Königsberg Arsenal. This resulted in the Krag-Jorgensen rifle in 1889. A bolt action, the rifle has an unusual magazine that consists of a box on the right side of the receiver and a rather complex arrangement of follower springs. The magazine lid is opened with the right thumb by means of a large fin on the hinged lid. Cartridges are dropped into the box, and the lid is closed, activating the follower. The cartridges travel from right to left under the receiver. Manipulating the bolt strips a cartridge from the magazine and inserts it into the chamber.

The advantage of this magazine arrangement is that several cartridges can be fired and then additional ones inserted at any time without opening the bolt or completely emptying the magazine. Thus a soldier or sportsman can keep the magazine full at all times. This is not possible with most clip-loaded arms. Denmark, Norway, and the United States all adopted this rifle as an infantry arm, though there were slight model variations. The Danish rifles were 6.5 caliber; the Norwegian arms were mostly in 8mm; and the American version fired the .30/40 Krag cartridge, our last rimmed military round.

The U.S. Krag saw action in the Spanish American War and the Philippine Insurrection. The rifle is known for a very smooth bolt travel, much better than most other military bolt actions. Old Krags are still used by many hunters. (See MAGAZINE.)

Krieghoff (company) This manufacturer of fine sporting arms was founded as Sempert und Krieghoff in Suhl, Germany, in 1895. After World War II, the company again entered the arms field with headquarters in Ulm-Donau, Germany. Its current corporate name is Jagdwaffenfabrik H. Krieghoff (Hunting Arms Manufactory H. Krieghoff).

During the 1930s and World War II, Krieghoff made military small arms, notably Parabellum (Luger) pistols; but it has always been famous for sporting shotguns and rifles. The best selling product today is a Drilling with two side-by-side rifle barrels over a shotgun tube. The company also makes over/under rifles and shotguns, over/under combination guns, and others. Most Krieghoff break-action guns have one or two barrel extensions pierced by a transverse locking bolt. Their actions are famous for strength and durability.

For many years, Krieghoff's Model 32 has been a premier over/under shotgun. It was originally a Remington design, but when that company stopped production of its version, Krieghoff took it over, and still makes the gun. It is notable for separated barrels with no connection between the two except at the rear, and toward the muzzle in the form of a mechanical hanger that permits each barrel to expand and contract independently of the other. This prevents tension when one barrel overheats and the other remains cool. Some shooters claim that this unequal expansion can cause bending and change in the point of impact. The current skeet model has many improvements, including a funnel-type choke and a stock that is easily removable with a screwdriver so that different stocks with varying configurations can be used for different kinds of shooting. (See DRILLING.)

K-series wildcats Lysle Kilbourn, a longtime employee of the Lyman Gun Sight Corp., developed this series of wildcat cartridges in the 1930s and 1940s. Intended for varmint shooting, these cartridges were .22 centerfires based on a variety of cases such as the .22 Hornet, .25/20, .219 Zipper, and .22 Savage Hi-Power. A highly efficient series for the powders then available, the K cartridges utilized sharp shoulders and straight case bodies with little taper. Probably the most popular was the .22 K-Hornet. Today, few rifles are chambered for these rounds, since they have been replaced by more potent, and more readily obtainable, factory loads. (See WILDCAT CARTRIDGE.)

ladder sight A kind of open rear sight employed on rifles. Ladder sights are mounted on a rail in which steps are cut for varying elevation adjustments. The sight is moved along the rail to raise or lower the point of impact. (See METALLIC SIGHTS; MUZZLELOADERS, SIGHTS FOR.)

Lake City Army Ammunition Plant The Lake City Army Ammunition Plant is a government-owned installation at Independence, Missouri. Remington Arms Co. has been the operating contractor of the plant since its start in December 1940, operating the plant under the control of the U.S. Army Materiel Readiness Command.

Since starting production, Lake City has produced small arms ammunition in several types, in calibers .38 Special, 5.56mm, .30 carbine, 7.62mm, 7.62×39mm, .30(.30/06), and .50, as well as 20mm and 30mm cannon ammunition. The plant produced more than 5.5 billion rounds of ammunition during World War II, was deactivated to standby status in August of 1945, and was reactivated in December 1950. From that time through September 1978, the plant produced 26.3 billion rounds of ammunition.

In addition to service ammunition, Lake City has, since 1958, produced millions of rounds of match ammunition in 7.62 NATO and .30 caliber for use in the National Matches and for marksmanship training and competitions.

laminated barrel A gun barrel made from strips of iron and steel welded together. The proportions of iron and steel varied from equal parts in the cheaper barrels to eight parts steel and two of iron in the more expensive and stronger barrels. Rods of iron and steel were piled together into fagots, then welded together, then rolled to shape, heated, and twisted on its long axis so that the turns might be as many as 12 to 18 to the inch of length. In turn, these twisted rods were welded, usually two to four of them, to form a rod of rectangular cross section; then this was heated and rolled to form a riband. The riband was coiled around a mandrel in a helix so that the narrow edges touched, and was heated to welding heat in the forge, then "jumped" on the floor to start the joining of the edges. Then the welding was completed, a few inches at a time, using a mandrel for support on the inside of the barrel and formed swages and anvils on the outside.

When the finished barrel was browned, the exposed edges of the alternating layers of iron and steel produced repetitive patterns on the surface, as the iron and the steel did not react equally to the browning. The figure was controlled by the number and shape of the iron and steel rods, the amount of twisting, and the manner in which welded and twisted rods were joined into ribands. The more expensive barrels not only contained a higher proportion of steel, but much more intricate patterns, showing remarkable uniformity from end to end of the barrel.

A barrel made by this process is simply a mass of welds, with nonferrous inclusions and tiny seams. Such barrels are not only much weaker than steel barrels made by other processes, but the imperfections provide places for the initiation of corrosion, particularly over long periods of time. Such corrosion can proceed, unobserved, to the point where the barrel wall is seriously weakened. For these reasons, laminated barrels should never be used with smokeless powder, and many of them are unsafe with black powder.

In general usage, the term "Damascus barrel" is synonymous with laminated barrel. Nineteenth-century gun writers, such as Greener, differentiate between laminated and Damascus barrels, naming several varieties on the basis of the relative amounts of iron and steel, the manner in which the twisting is performed, and the number of welded rods made into a riband. (See BARREL MAKING; DAMASCUS BARREL; GREENER, W.W. [COMPANY].)

laminated case A metal cartridge case that has weak areas where the metal has separated in layers because of scaly inclusions. It is the result of slag, dirt, or foreign material being in the ingot from which the strip material that was used in making the case was rolled. As the blanks are punched out of the strip and drawn, the inclusion is drawn out to form a thin section, resulting in a seam or discontinuity between layers of metal. This weak spot in the wall of the case is cause for rejection if anything other than minor.

In present day usage, the term "scaly case" is often used.

laminated stock A stock made of layers of wood that have been glued together. The layers, or laminations, generally range from about 1/16 to 1/4 inch in thickness, although thicker laminations are sometimes used. Usually the joints of the laminations lie vertically on lines paralleling the long axis of the butt, but horizontal laminations have also been used. Laminated stocks, properly made, are stronger and less susceptible to warpage than one-piece stocks.

A tree grows in layers, adding an annular ring each year, the ring being composed of a harder, thin section of winter growth and a softer, thicker layer of summer growth. In any piece cut from a tree, the loss of moisture in drying and the arrangement of the annular rings results in warpage toward the outer layers. In an object made of seasoned or kiln-dried wood, changes in atmospheric humidity result in changes in the moisture content of the wood, and the object tends to warp toward the bark or toward the center. It may also twist, with irregular grain structure, or burl. Thus, the ideal one-piece stock should be cut with the annular rings at right angles to the long axis of the butt and with the bark toward the barrel channel. A laminated stock, for minimum warpage, should be assembled of laminations so arranged that the warpage tendencies of the laminations are balanced off against one another. (See STOCK WOODS.)

Lancaster, Charles W. (18?–1878) Charles W. Lancaster was the son of Charles Lancaster, who had been a barrel borer for Joseph Manton for many years. In 1826 the father opened his own shop in London; Charles W. succeeded his father, who died in 1845, and later became world famous for his advocacy of oval bore rifles. In these there are no conventional grooves and lands, simply a slight ovalizing of the bore interior that describes a spiral from breech to muzzle, as with ordinary rifling. Lancaster was also a strong believer in the merits of gain twist rifling. The Lancaster firm, which was bought out in 1890, was primarily known for shotguns of superior quality.

Charles W. Lancaster was the author of a highly popular book, *The Art of Shooting*, first published in 1887. It went into at least 13 later editions. (See GAIN TWIST; MANTON, JOSEPH.)

land On the inside of a rifled barrel, one of the ridges, standing above the groove or major diameter, that is formed in a helix and that engraves the bullet, causing it to spin on its axis. Lands of many shapes, dimensions, and numbers have been tried since the invention of rifling. The number of lands and their shape have relatively little effect on accuracy, so long as their size and shape is such that the bullet does not strip or skid badly in entering the rifling, although it is desirable to engrave the bullet with a minimum of distortion for best results. Land design

can have an appreciable effect on barrel life, however, since lands that are relatively high and wide resist erosion better than shallow, narrow lands. (See BARREL, RIFLED.)

lapping In mechanics, a process in which a lap, made of a softer material than the part to be polished, is charged with an abrasive and used to provide a better finish, better fit, or more accurate shape to the part lapped. The abrasive may be suspended in an oil or grease, creating a mixture that is called a slurry, or the lap may be charged with dry abrasive and the lubricant applied before use.

Common applications in the firearms field include the lapping of barrel bores and lapping of action parts against one another to provide smoother and easier working. In the lapping of rifle barrels, a lead lap is cast on the end of a rod inserted inside the bore. The lap is thus a negative of the bore. Charged with an abrasive slurry, the lap is pushed and pulled through the bore to create a smooth surface and uniformity of shape and dimensions. In general, the most accurate rifle barrels have bores finished by lapping. (See BARREL MAKING.)

Lapua bullet In the United States, this term refers to the match bullets made by the Lapuan Patruunatehdas Company of Finland. The bullets are full-jacketed, boattail, closed point target bullets, in which the boattail is rebated. That is, the boattail starts from a step, or slightly smaller diameter, at the rear of the parallel portion of the bullet body. In 7.62 (.30) caliber, Lapua bullets are made in weights of 170 and 185 grains and in diameters of .308 inch and .309 inch so that they can be matched to the throat and groove diameters of individual barrels. In 6.5, they are available in 140-grain weight. Accuracy of these bullets is excellent, and the jacket alloy and thickness makes them better adapted to the heavy powder charges, high pressures, and high velocities of the usual long-range target loads than some other makes of target bullets. (See BOATTAIL BULLET.)

lead (metal) A heavy, soft ductile metal, lead is used as a base for nearly all projectiles suitable for use in small arms ammunition. No other metal performs as efficiently as lead when used as the core for modern jacketed bullets. Its great specific gravity gives the bullet the sectional density necessary for retained energy and velocity over longer shooting ranges, while at the same time providing the malleability needed for the correct expansion of the expanding bullet. It also provides the weight that gives deep penetration on heavy animals when jacket expansion is properly controlled.

Lead cores in jacketed bullets, as well as cast and

swaged lead bullets, are usually alloyed with other metals like tin and antimony to increase hardness and toughness. Lead is also used, either straight or alloyed, for various kinds of shot loaded in shotshells.

lead (shooting) The forward allowance required to hit a moving object; the distance ahead of a moving object that a projectile must be placed so that its arrival coincides with that of the object. Factors involved with calculating leads are speed of the load, speed of the target, angle of the target, time of flight of the load, and distance to target. In practical application, the most important elements for the shotgun shooter are angle and distance; the greater the distance and more acute the angle, the more the lead required. Rifle shooters also must lead moving targets; although their bullets may be moving twice as fast as the shotgunner's pellets, rifle shooting distances are normally greater.

leade The rearmost edge of the rifling lands. The lands are removed completely at the extreme rear of the bore and to a lesser degree as they angle forward until bore diameter is reached.

The purpose of the leade is to prevent stripping of the bullet jacket when it engages the rifling. (See FREEBORE; LAND.)

leading Deposit left in the barrel by soft lead bullets caused by one or a combination of the following: improper bullet sizing; improper lube; improper alloy; or a rough bore. Jacketed bullets leave almost no metal in the bore. With modern hard shot, very little leading is left in the bores of shotguns.

lead poisoning A disease induced by absorption of toxic lead into the system. In waterfowl, the result of ingesting spent lead shotshell pellets. Ducks and geese apparently mistake pellets for weed seeds or "grit," which the birds eat to provide the grinding substances in the gizzards required for them to digest food. The U.S. Fish & Wildlife Service estimates that about two million ducks and geese succumb to lead poisoning each year; hence the present regulations requiring steel shot loads in certain designated areas.

lead shot Spherical pellets made of lead alloys and, in some top grades of shot, hardened by the addition of small percentages of antimony. Lead shot is customarily made by pouring molten lead through a sieve from sufficient height that the resulting droplets of molten metal harden into round balls as they reach a cooling solution below. The most common lead pellets used by American shooters are sizes 9, 8, 7½, 6, 4, 2, and BB (the larger the number, the smaller the shot). The largest lead pellets are called buckshot; these come in No. 4 "buck" up to size 00. (See SHOT.)

lead styphnate A high explosive that will detonate when struck. Since the late 1930s it has been the basis of most of the noncorrosive, nonmercuric primer mixtures used in small arms. Used alone, it would be much too violent and would not give good ignition to smokeless powder, so other chemicals are added to the primer mixture to control sensitivity and to improve ignition. In modern priming mixtures, lead styphnate amounts to about 40 percent of the mixture, with a small amount of tetracene added to give the proper sensitivity. Another 40 percent is barium nitrate, used as a moderator and oxidizer. The balance of the mixture, depending on the maker, includes lead dioxide, antimony sulfide, PETN (pentaerythritol tetranitrate, another high explosive), aluminum, zirconium, calcium silicide, and ground glass.

Because of their proven stability and long storage life, potassium chlorate primers were used by the U.S. military until the early 1950s, at which time lead styphnate primers were accepted as meeting these requirements also. The modern styphnate primer is both nonmercuric and noncorrosive and is very reliable and very stable. (See PRIMER.)

lead tape Self-adhesive material containing enough lead to be quite heavy, used primarily by golfers for weighting clubs. Shooters also use it to change the balance of shotgun barrels and to reduce recoil.

lead wool A lead-based product that looks much like steel wool and is available at many hardware and plumbing equipment stores. Used primarily by plumbers, it also is sometimes used by shooters because it can be compressed into small openings in the buttstock or elsewhere to add weight to the gun without modifying the stock.

leaf safety On bolt-action rifles, a safety that is pivoted in the cocking piece sleeve (also called bolt plug) on an axis parallel to the bolt axis and that swings through an arc from a horizontal position on one side to a horizontal position on the other. Most safeties of this kind have three usable positions, provided with detents. In the first position, the trigger may be pulled to fire the gun. The intermediate position retracts the cocking piece from the sear, so that the gun may not be fired, but the bolt may be worked to eject cartridges, etc. Usually, this position also provides for unscrewing the cocking piece sleeve from the bolt, as the firing pin and cocking piece are held back to clear the cocking cam recess. The third position holds the cocking piece retracted and locks the bolt in the closed position.

This safety was invented by Peter Paul Mauser in 1870 and first appeared on the Model 71 Mauser. In one form or another, it was used on almost all subsequent bolt-action Mausers and on many of the military and sporting rifles based on the basic Mauser-type bolt-action. (See COCKING PIECE; MAUSER, PETER PAUL; SAFETY.)

leaf sight   See MULTIPLE LEAF SIGHT.

Lee dot   A small black dot, alone or in conjunction with cross hairs, used as a reticle in a telescopic sight. T. K. Lee of Birmingham, Alabama, became famous for his Lee Dot installations. In today's usage, the term refers to any dot reticle. (See RETICLE.)

Lefever Arms Co.   From 1880 until 1892, Daniel M. Lefever manufactured shotguns in Syracuse, New York. In 1892, the firm changed its name to Lefever Arms Company. The Lefever sidelock double-barrel shotguns were produced until 1915, when the firm was purchased by the Ithaca Gun Company and the Syracuse factory closed.

"Syracuse" Lefevers were, like most American doubles of the time, manufactured in a wide variety of grades; in this case, no fewer than 20, ranging from the DS grade at the low end to the Thousand Dollar Grade at the top. These guns were made in 10, 12, 16, and 20 gauge and were available with many combinations of choking, stock styles, engraving, etc.

In 1921, Ithaca introduced a boxlock Lefever, the Nitro Special, and single-barrel models were made from 1927 to 1942. Production of all Lefever shotguns was discontinued in 1948.

In 1901, D. M. Lefever, the original founder, organized D. M. Lefever, Sons & Co.—later changed to D. M. Lefever Co.—and commenced manufacture of a new Lefever boxlock and single-barrel shotgun in Bowling Green, Ohio. Production ran only from 1904 to 1906, and ended with the death of D. M. Lefever. These guns were manufactured in eight grades ranging from the 0 Excelsior Grade to the Uncle Dan Grade. Generally, these boxlock guns do not command the prices that the sidelock Lefevers bring. (See ITHACA GUN COMPANY.)

Leitz, Ernst (company)   Ernst Leitz/Wetzlar GmbH (Ernst Leitz, Inc., Wetzlar, Germany), a maker of precision optical equipment since 1840. Among its first products were excellent microscopes, and the company is still known for these instruments. Later in the firm's history, it brought out and still produces the famous line of Leica cameras.

Since World War II, Leitz has produced cameras and binoculars that are very useful to the hunter, fisherman, and sports spectator. The line includes Trinovid binoculars, which employ an optical system that permits great reduction in the side-to-side bulk. The system eliminates the right-angle offset employed by most prism systems. Externally, each tube is straight, which gives the binoculars a novel appearance as well as vastly reducing bulk. These binoculars are made in 7×42, 8×32, 8×40, and 10×40. Even the 10X model weighs only 23 ounces, and extreme dimensions are 6.5 inches and 4.9 inches. Trinovids are equipped with "eye guards"—extension eyepieces that are pushed in if the user wears eyeglasses. This properly adjusts the distance to the rear lens from the eye so that the binoculars are much easier to use when wearing spectacles. (See BINOCULARS.)

Leman prism   A Leman prism is a kind of roof prism. Roof prisms are used in some binoculars and telescopes to provide for smaller and lighter instruments than are obtainable using Porro prisms with the same optical characteristics. (See PORRO PRISM; ROOF PRISM.)

length of pull   The distance, on a shoulder arm, from the trigger to the rear of the butt. For American arms, the standard length of pull for rifles is 13½ inches; for shotguns, 14¼ or 14½ inches.

lenses, cleaning of   To clean an optical instrument, dust is best removed with a lens brush or pressurized air. Oil or grease marks, such as from fingerprints, can be removed with lens cleaner and lens tissue. Brushes, cleaner, and tissues are available at camera stores. Do not rub the surface of the lens with cloth or use cleaning solvents, such as acetone, which can damage the lens coating.

Lesmok   An obsolete powder developed by Du Pont and used mainly in the loading of .22 rimfire ammunition. Lesmok was a semismokeless powder and

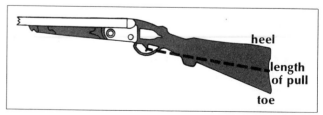

The length of pull is the distance from the trigger to the end of the stock. Most American rifles have lengths of pull of 13¼ to 13¾ inches; shotguns vary from 14¼ to 14¾ inches.

enjoyed some popularity. However, it was extremely dangerous to manufacture and handle. It was marketed from 1890 until the mid-1930s.

Leupold & Stevens, Inc. Precision instrument firm noted for its riflescopes. The company was founded in 1907 in Portland, Oregon, to manufacture and repair surveying instruments. Production of riflescopes did not begin until after the firm was incorporated in 1949. The first model manufactured, the Leupold riflescope, had a reticle that could be adjusted for elevation and windage.

The scope line eventually grew so popular that, in 1960, the firm sold the surveying instrument line and concentrated on the production of riflescopes. In 1968, Leupold & Stevens moved its facilities to Beaverton, Oregon. In order to expand the sporting products line, the firm became affiliated with Nosler Bullets in 1969 but discontinued the association in 1989.

lever action A design utilizing an underlever-operated breechblock. There are three classes of levers, with each class depending on the location of the effort applied, the resistance overcome, and the fulcrum or pivot point. All three classes are common, and in a complex machine such as a rifle, shotgun, or handgun, there are often many different levers, and sometimes several of each classification.

The general use of the term brings to mind a finger or loop lever beneath the receiver and around the trigger of a rifle or shotgun; the downward movement of this lever operates the action mechanism, such as in the Winchester Model 94 carbine, the Marlin M1895 rifle, the Mossberg Model 472 rifle or the Browning BLR, all of which have finger loop underlevers.

The Model 94 is a good example of an accepted underlever operated design that uses all three classes of levers in its operation. Initial movement of the underlever is an example of a second class lever, where the effort is applied to the loop of the lever, the fulcrum or pivot is at the opposite end, and the resistance is the link, which is pinned to the underlever near the middle. Movement of the link, fixed to pivot at the forward end, is an example of a third class lever, with the resistance the locking bolt at the rear end, while the effort is applied between the two by the underlever. Finally, as the link reaches the limit of its travel, and unlocking is complete, the underlever is cammed to a position where it acts as a first class lever; pivoting is around the link connection, the effort is exerted at the lower end, and the resistance is at the upper end in moving the breechbolt to the rear, extracting the fired case and cocking the hammer.

In normal use the underlever, which is often but not always a part of the trigger guard, is pivoted at or near its forward end; it is swung downward in an arc, and then returned. In the earliest lever arms, this operation merely lowered and raised the breechblock, or caused the barrel to tip downward, exposing the chamber for loading. In the single-shot models this was satisfactory, but as designs improved and magazines were added, the lever movement had to extract and eject the fired case, cock the hammer, and chamber a fresh cartridge.

The first lever-action arms were percussion models using a variety of cartridge types, including paper and rubber designs. Examples of early (1856–1865) lever-action percussion rifles include the Gallager, Maynard, and Sharps models, all single shots. After metallic cartridges were developed, breechloading lever-action rifles included the single-shot Peabody (later Martini-Henry), plus the repeating Henry, Spencer, and Volcanic designs. (The Volcanic design was also produced in a pistol form, one of the few lever action handguns ever manufactured.)

There were many variations among early lever action single-shot breechloading rifles, but one of the most common designs was the falling block. In this design, a massive breechblock moved up and down behind the chamber in a sort of tongue-and-groove arrangement, with the operation directly dependent on the movement of the under- or finger lever. Examples of such rifles include the English Farquharson, on which today's Ruger No. 1 is based, Ballard, Winchester, various Stevens models, Sharps, Sharps-Borchardt, Farrow, and Hopkins & Allen, plus today's Browning 78. Some of the falling block designs were hammerless, while others featured an outside hammer that required manual cocking.

A lever-action single-shot design which the underlever is separate from the trigger guard is the Peabody. The breechblock is hinged at the upper rear, and downward movement of the lever only tilts the breechblock down at the front to permit sliding the cartridge into the chamber. Originally patented in 1862, this design is still being manufactured as the Martini action.

A unique lever-action design was the Remington-Beals, in which movement of the finger lever simply slid the barrel forward for extraction and loading. It was somewhat similar to the percussion Gallager design.

The first practical lever-action repeater to survive for any length of time was the Henry, which was the first of a long line of Winchester lever action designs. The M1866 Winchester was basically an improved Henry. Featuring a tubular magazine beneath the barrel, operation of the underlever unlocked the breechbolt, moving it to the rear, extracting the fired case, and cocking the hammer; at the same time, a cartridge was picked up from the magazine and moved upward toward the chamber, to be rammed home as the lever swung back, moving the breechblock forward and locking it into the battery. Somewhat similar designs were manufactured by Marlin and Mossberg. Today, besides the Marlin, Mossberg, and Winchester designs, there are several foreign firms manufacturing lever-action repeating rifles based on expired Winchester patents.

Today's Browning BLR is still another kind of lever action, in which the arcing movement of the underlever causes a longitudinal movement of the breechbolt via a rack-and-pinion mechanism similar to the old Ballard. While the majority of lever-action repeaters have tubular magazines—the Winchester M95 had a fixed box magazine—the BLR has a detachable box magazine, as did the Winchester Model 88. Locking of the BLR breechbolt is accomplished by rotation of the bolt head to engage seven lugs in corresponding recesses.

Another unusual early lever action was the Evans, which featured a two-piece buttstock surrounding a tubular steel magazine having a rotating inner mechanism. The Evans was chambered for a .44-caliber centerfire cartridge, and it has the record for having the largest magazine capacity—up to 38 cartridges—of any lever-action rifle ever mass produced and distributed in the United States. The Evans also featured a concealed hammer.

The Savage M1895, which later became the famous Model 99, is a hammerless design in which the rear of the breechbolt is lifted upward to seat against the edge of the receiver or frame during locking, thus permitting the use of more powerful cartridges. Unlike the Winchester and Marlin designs, which have tubular magazines, the Savage features a rotary or a box magazine directly beneath the breechbolt.

Over the years, other firms have manufactured hammerless lever-action rifles, or concealed-hammer rifles, including the Winchester Model 88 (introduced in 1955) and Sako's Finnwolf, plus rimfire models by Marlin, Mossberg, and Winchester. Remington even produced a lever-action version of their Nylon 66 rifle.

The lever action is usually found in rifles, but Winchester manufactured two lever-action repeating shotgun designs, the Model 1887 and the Model 1901, and following World War II there was a hammerless lever-action shotgun called the Kessler. In addition, Ithaca produced a single-shot break- or hinge-action shotgun that used an under-lever in place of a top lever to operate the barrel-locking mechanism.

Today's Thompson/Center Contender single-shot pistol is, unusually, underlever operated. In the Con-

tender, upward movement of the trigger guard unlocks the pistol, whereas use of an underlever in unlocking is normally downward.

light gathering power In a very general way, this term expresses the ability of binoculars or telescopes to transmit enough light to provide an image sufficiently bright for seeing detail in dim light. In fact, if there is not enough light falling upon an object for clear viewing, no telescope or binocular is capable of "gathering light" or making it possible to see an object clearly. The impression of greater brightness of the object when viewed with a telescope or binocular is attributable to the magnification such an instrument provides, assuming proper optical qualities in the instrument. The magnification makes it possible to see greater detail, giving an impression of greater brightness.

To do this, such an instrument must have an objective lens diameter, related to power, that will provide an exit pupil as large or larger than the pupil of the human eye under dim light conditions. In general, this would be 5mm or larger. Also, all air-to-glass surfaces must be treated with an antireflection coating of magnesium fluoride to provide high light transmission. (See EXIT PUPIL; LIGHT TRANSMISSION; OBJECTIVE LENS.)

light transmission In optical instruments such as telescopes, field glasses, and binoculars, the term "light transmission" refers to the percentage of light that actually gets through the optical system to the eye. It depends on the number of air-to-glass surfaces in the optical system, the absorption of the glass, the amount of reflection loss inside the optical system, and the quality of the glass, lenses, and prisms. The development of antireflection coatings to reduce reflection losses marked a great advance in optical instruments and greatly increased light transmitting capabilities, cutting light loss by as much as 50 percent. A coating of magnesium fluoride .00004-inch thick, applied to all air-to-glass surfaces, increases light transmission and improves image contrast and detail. A well-made binocular with coated optical surfaces will have a light transmission in the range of 70 to 80 percent. (See COATED OPTICS; MAGNESIUM FLUORIDE.)

line count See CHECKERING, LINE COUNT.

line of bore An imaginary line drawn through the center of a barrel. It is a consideration in rifles and handguns, as the sights must be aligned in respect to the line of bore.

lipfire cartridge Invented in 1860 by firearms designer Ethan Allen, the lipfire metallic cartridge consists of a metal case with a small lip, containing a fulminating charge, projecting beyond the circumference of the case. This lip, when struck by the hammer of the firearm, detonates the cartridge. Calibers of the cartridges produced included .25, .32, and .44, all for use in Allen & Wheelock revolvers. (These single-action revolvers, manufactured from 1856 to 1865, could not compete with Colt, Remington and Smith & Wesson revolvers.) (See RIMFIRE VARIATIONS.)

live ammunition Ammunition that is ready to fire is considered to be live regardless of whether it is metallic or shotshell, and whether it has a case or is caseless.

live pigeon shooting The sport from which modern trapshooting evolved, hence the term "clay pigeon." Due to the unpredictable flight of real birds as compared with the relatively straight flight of clay targets used in trap and skeet shooting, this is our most difficult competitive shotgun sport. The game originated in the mid-18th century in England. Now often called Flyer Shooting it remains very popular in some areas of Europe, notably Spain, Portugal, and Italy, and is practiced in many Latin American countries. The first record of live pigeon shooting in the U.S. is in 1831, and a few private shoots are still staged in this country.

There are two basic kinds of live pigeon shooting: box shooting; and the "Columbaire" style, in which the birds are released by hand by professional throwers (Columbaires) from the center of a 100-meter circle. Birds must be dropped within the 100-meter ring to score. No shooter in the annals of the international Tiro Al Pichon Association (TAPA) has been able to maintain a registered average of hits much in excess of 80 percent, and average competitors do well to score 60 percent. This version of pigeon shooting originated in Spain and is very popular in Mexico. Some shoots feature large prizes in money or merchandise, and wagering between competitors is not infrequent. (See BOX PIGEON SHOOTING; TRAPSHOOTING.)

Llama pistols See SPANISH GUNMAKERS.

load As a noun, a particular combination of case, primer, powder, and projectile. As a verb, to charge a firearm with either fixed or nonfixed ammunition.

loaded chamber indicator See SIGNAL PIN.

loading density The relationship of the amount of propellant in a fire-formed case to the amount the case would hold when filled to the base of the bullet. If the space is 75 percent filled, then the loading density may be said to be 75 percent. Loading density can vary with bullet seating depth and case construction. (See CASE CAPACITY.)

loading die In handloading, that portion of the loading tool that actually forms the cases and seats the bullets. Most conventional die sets consist of either two or three dies. In loading Boxer-primed bottleneck cases, the set is composed of a sizing die and a bullet-seating die. The sizing die performs its primary function of resizing the case to the proper dimensions. This die also contains a decapping pin that knocks out the spent primer, and an expanding plug to round out the case mouth. A second die, the bullet-seating die, presses the bullet into the sized neck and, if necessary, crimps the case neck into the bullet's cannelure or crimping groove.

A three-die set is generally employed in the loading of straight-walled cases and/or for use with cast bullets. The set consists of a sizing die, a neck-expanding die, and a bullet-seating die. The expanding die bells the case mouth slightly for insertion of bullets. Dies have adjustments to control the amount of sizing, bullet-seating depth, crimping, and, in the three-die set, neck expansion.

The loading dies mentioned above are most commonly used in conjunction with bench-type loading presses. Some hand tools contain other combinations of dies. One type, the Lyman tong tool, consists of a five-die set: decapping die, sizing die, neck expanding die, priming die, and bullet-seating die. (See CANNELURE; CASE RESIZING; CAST BULLET; LOADING PRESS; HANDLOAD.)

loading gate In a revolver, the hinged portion of the standing breech or recoil plate that allows insertion of ammunition or ejection of fired cases. With the revolver at half cock or by lowering the loading gate, the cylinder is free to rotate. Then, as each chamber is lined up with the loading port, feeding or extracting can be accomplished. Extraction is accomplished by pushing the empty case to the rear by means of the ejector rod.

On some rifles, the loading gate is the hinged cover of the loading port. Found on lever-action rifles such as the Model 94 Winchester and Marlin Model 336, the spring loaded gate is usually located on the side of the receiver and allows easy insertion of cartridges into the magazine. The gate is pushed open by cartridge pressure, and then the cartridge is pushed into the tubular magazine against spring pressure. When the cartridge is inside the magazine, the loading gate swings shut, allowing cartridges to be cycled to the rear through the action. In the Winchester, the fired cases are then ejected through the top of the receiver; in the Marlin, through the side of the receiver, just above the loading gate. (See EJECTOR ROD; LOADING PORT; MAGAZINE.)

loading port A slot, usually oval in shape, cut into the receiver or magazine of a firearm to permit insertion of cartridges. An example is the loading port on the right side of the receiver of many lever-action rifles. The port is covered by a spring operated loading gate that is forced aside by the cartridges as they are fed through the port into the magazine. (See LOADING GATE.)

loading press A tool that provides means for forcing cases into and out of dies during loading operations. It consists of a moveable ram with a shellholder and a seat for the dies. Most presses designed for loading metallic cartridges are bolted to a bench or table top; they may be any of several designs, such as the "C," "O," or "H," the letters referring to the basic shape of the frame casting.

Dies are usually threaded into a receptacle in the press to perform the necessary loading functions. A shellholder, which sits atop the press ram, grasps the case rim, allowing the cases to be removed from the various dies. The ram is operated by a linkage and lever system to provide a mechanical advantage to the operator. (Generally, hand tools used in loading operations are not referred to as loading presses. However, hand tools are often used in conjunction with a press to provide mechanical advantage.)

The sturdy cast iron or cast aluminum construction of most bench-type reloading presses allows them to be used in case forming and bullet-swaging operations.

The bench-mounted reloading press is by far the most widely used kind of tool for reloading ammunition. (See BULLET SWAGING; CASE FORMING; LOADING DIE; SHELLHOLDER.)

loading rod A superior kind of ramrod. Loading rods are made of stainless steel, with a jag attached at one end and a wooden handle at the other end. A plastic or brass collar that exactly fits the bore of the gun is attached to the rod's shaft. The collar takes the ball down the bore, without the steel rod touching the bore. These rods are almost universally used by muzzleloading match shooters. They help prolong the life of a gun because they do not cause as much wear as conventional ramrods. (See JAG; MUZZLELOADER; RAMROD.)

lock The working mechanism of an early firearm was the lock. It constituted one of the three major parts—lock, stock, and barrel. Included in the lock were the lock plate to hold the various parts, the hammer or cock, the sear bar to disengage the tail

of the cock, the tumbler, and springs. (See FLINTLOCK; MATCHLOCK.)

locked breech action An action in which the barrel and breechbolt, breechblock, or standing breech are secured or locked to each other during the moment of firing. In high power bolt-action rifles of the turn-bolt design, this is usually accomplished by the use of from one to nine locking lugs, which rotate into receiver or barrel recesses cut to receive them. In pump-action and autoloading shotgun designs, the locking is generally accomplished by the tilting up of the rear of the breechblock by a camming movement or by a moveable lug within the breechblock or bolt. In break-action shotguns of the over/under and side-by-side design, locking is often accomplished by a sliding bolt and one or more lumps beneath the breech of the barrels, or by a cross-bolt through or over a barrel extension. (See BOLT ACTION; BREAK-ACTION; BREECHBLOCK; BREECHBOLT.)

lock energy Any moving part has an amount of kinetic energy, dependent on the mass of the part and the velocity with which it moves. In the lock mechanism of a firearm, this energy is mainly dependent on the mass of the hammer-firing pin assembly, or striker, and the power of the spring or springs providing the propelling force. If the combination of spring and hammer is such that the lock energy is low, misfires may occur. Accumulated grease and dirt, low temperatures, and other factors may also decrease the lock energy. (See KINETIC ENERGY.)

locking lug Projections on the forward circumference of the bolt or breechblock of a rifle, shotgun, or handgun that rotate into recesses or slots to secure the action during the firing sequence. Such lugs may also be located toward the rear of the bolt, as in the

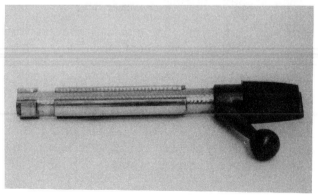

Many modern bolt actions utilize more than the customary two locking lugs. This Champlin bolt employs three; others use up to nine. The three long lugs running the length of the bolt are bolt guides.

Lee-Enfield and Remington Model 788 designs, on top of the breechblock, below the breechblock, or even around the barrel, as in the M1911 autoloading pistol. On break-action rifles and shotguns, such as side-by-side or over/under designs, lugs on the underside or breech of the barrels secure the barrels to the frame via a locking bolt. On regular turn-bolt rifles, the number of such locking lugs will vary in number from one (U. S. Krag) to nine (Weatherby Mark V, Browning BBR, etc.), although the usual number is two lugs spaced 180 degrees apart. (See LOCKED BREECH ACTION.)

lock plate The plate on the outside of a lock on a muzzleloading gun. It serves as the carrier for the lock mechanism. (See MUZZLELOADER.)

lock time Lock time is the total time taken by the trigger and the firing mechanisms, from the release of the trigger until the firing pin strikes the primer, crushing the primer pellet and causing it to ignite the priming mixture. It is primarily a function of the length of travel of the firing pin (or hammer), the weight that the mainspring must accelerate, and the power of the mainspring. Friction of the moving parts is a factor, and the kind of trigger mechanism can also influence lock time. For example, in a set trigger mechanism, the time required for the striker to release the sear adds appreciably to lock time.

Lock time on modern bolt actions varies from 2 to 6 milliseconds, in older bolt actions it may reach 9ms or 10ms, and in the pivoting hammer systems of some of the lever actions, pumps, and automatics, it may be even longer. Barrel time for the bullet ranges from 1ms to 3ms in both rifles and pistols, so lock time is the major part of the total time.

Assuming that the resultant firing pin impact on the primer is sufficient for good ignition, the shortest possible lock time is an advantage. No person can hold a gun absolutely still in any position; in the less stable positions, such as shooting a rifle offhand or in pistol shooting, the movement of the gun between the time the shooter's senses tell him the sights are aligned and that the trigger has been released, and the actual time of bullet exit from the muzzle, may be substantial in terms of point of bullet impact on the target. A short lock time will help prevent involuntary movement. (See BARREL TIME.)

lockwork A general term applied to all of the moving parts—hammer, firing pin, sear, mainspring, and trigger—that serve to discharge the cartridge in a modern firearm.

logwood dye A brownish or blackish dye formerly used to stain gunstocks. It was made from the dark heartwood of the logwood tree, found in South America. (See STOCK FINISH.)

Long (.22) Introduced in the early 1860s, only a few years after the introduction of the .22 Short rimfire, the .22 Long rimfire cartridge has a longer case with the same bullet as the .22 Short. Originally loaded with black powder, then Lesmok, and eventually with smokeless powder, the Long has survived well over a century. Available in both standard and high velocity at various times, the Long has usually been loaded with a plain lead bullet with an outside lubrication of grease, wax, graphite, copper plating, or other suitable material. In addition, hollow point bullets have been available, as have shot cartridge versions. Today, only the high-velocity Long load, with a 29-grain solid bullet having a velocity of 1,240 feet per second, is manufactured in the United States. (See LESMOK; LONG RIFLE [.22]; SHORT [.22].)

long gun This term is used to refer primarily to rifles and shotguns, and in general to an arm that is fired from the shoulder. It is synonymous with "shoulder arm."

long recoil principle In some types of semiautomatic and automatic gun mechanisms, the barrel and breechbolt remain locked together during recoil, until the bolt has reached its fully rearward position, or nearly so. At that point, the bolt is held in the rearward position by a latch, while the barrel is allowed to move forward to its normal position, impelled by a return spring. (In some cases, the bolt is unlocked from the barrel, just as the barrel starts forward.) As the barrel approaches its full forward position, it trips a lever, releasing the bolt latch. The bolt then moves forward into battery, propelled by its return spring, stripping a cartridge from the magazine or feed mechanism, and feeding it into the chamber.

Among firearms employing the long recoil principle are the first successful semiautomatic shotgun (the familiar Browning Automatic-5, still being made) and the Remington rifles, Models 8 and 81.

The long recoil principle has been practically abandoned in modern gun design. In a shoulder weapon, recoil forces are greater than with a gas operated design, and it produces a two-stage recoil, particularly noticeable in a rifle. The initial stage of recoil is the result of normal recoil forces on the barrel and bolt, and the second stage is the result of these impacting on the rear of the receiver. In machine guns and machine rifles, a long recoil mechanism results in low cyclic rates of fire, heavy impact loads on the gun mechanism, and difficulty in holding the gun on target as the recoiling masses move back and forth. (See RECOIL.)

Long Rifle (.22) Introduced by the J. C. Stevens Arms Co. in the mid-1890s, the rimfire .22 Long Rifle cartridge combined the .22 Long case with a longer and heavier (40-grain) bullet and an increased velocity. The new cartridge proved to be a big improvement over the .22 Long in several ways: It was more accurate, and its bullet more stable in flight and more effective on small game.

Originally loaded with black powder, then Lesmok, and eventually with smokeless powder, and still later with the noncorrosive priming developed by Remington and adopted by all American manufacturers, the Long Rifle has become the standard rimfire cartridge of the world. It has been manufactured in indoor, standard, and high-velocity loading, and with solid bullets, jacketed bullets for military use, hollow point and semi-hollowpoint designs, and even in shot loads.

Recent versions utilize a lighter bullet for still higher velocities. (See LESMOK; LONG [.22]; SHORT [.22].)

Long Tom shotgun At least one low-priced break-action, single-shot shotgun is so named (Ithaca), but this term is generally used to denote any shotgun with a barrel length of 36 inches or more. (See SHOTGUN.)

lost The term for any moving target that is shot at and missed completely, generally applied to a clay target missed in skeet or trap. The term originated with live bird shooting. (See SKEET SHOOTING; TRAP-SHOOTING.)

lost wax process See INVESTMENT CASTING.

lot number Powder, bullets, ammunition, and many other articles are manufactured and packaged in runs, batches, or lots, each of which is assigned a recorded lot number for control purposes.

Loverin design H. Guy Loverin, a leading authority on cast bullet design for rifle calibers, designed bullets that generally had a semiround nose section, many narrow grooves for lubricant, and gas check bases. Calibers ranged from the .225438 for the .22 Hornet through larger calibers, and molds for more than a dozen of the designs have been produced by the Lyman firm. (See CAST BULLET; LYMAN PRODUCTS CORP.)

low base A shotshell that has a thin base wad, allowing for a larger powder charge. Magnum shotshells typically employ low bases. (See LOW BRASS.)

low brass A shotshell that utilizes a short brass base, typically a target or light field load. (See LOW BASE.)

low house The lower of the two houses from which skeet targets are launched. The low house will be to the right of the shooter facing the skeet field. (See HIGH HOUSE; SKEET SHOOTING.)

low power cartridge In rifles, a cartridge producing a muzzle velocity of less than 1,850 feet per second is considered low powered. Thus, the .44 Magnum cartridge fired in a rifle is classed as low powered, as is the .45/70, while the same cartridges fired in a handgun are considered high powered. In handguns, cartridges having muzzle velocities of less than 850 fps are considered low powered. In shotguns, the lowest dram equivalent load for a particular gauge is generally considered low power; in the 12 gauge, a 2¾ dram equivalent or less is considered a low power cartridge. (See DRAM EQUIVALENT; HIGH POWER CARTRIDGE.)

lubricator-sizer The lubricator-sizer is a widely utilized handloading tool for casting bullets. It has two functions: to size the bullet to an exact and consistent diameter, and in the same motion to fill the grease grooves of the bullet with lubricant. Like the standard loading press, which it resembles, the lubricator-sizer accepts dies for a wide assortment of cast bullet sizes. To grease the bullets, it is filled with a semisolid lubricant. (See CAST BULLET; HANDLOAD; LOADING PRESS.)

Luger (Parabellum) pistol An Austrian by birth, Georg M. Luger entered the employ of arms manufacturer Ludwig Löwe in Berlin in 1891. He collaborated with Hugo Borchardt to redesign and improve Borchardt's semiautomatic pistol. The result (in 1902) was the famous Luger (Parabellum) pistol used by German soldiers in two world wars. (In Latin, *para bellum* means "for war.")

The Borchardt pistol was sound mechanically but was clumsy and awkward in use. In the Luger version, the external lines were redesigned for better appearance and convenience. In particular, the long overhang of the receiver on top of the shooter's hand was sharply reduced. The unique feature (present also in the Borchardt pistol) is a toggle bolt that holds the cartridge in place in the chamber. On firing, the stiff toggle resists rearward gas pressure until it has dropped to safe levels. Moving to the rear, the toggle is finally "broken" upward by a hump in the receiver cavity. The toggle's joint bends upward, opening the breech, and the spent case is ejected. Spring pressure moves the bolt forward again, stripping a cartridge from the clip in the magazine and straightening the toggle joint.

The Luger pistol was made in many model variations, with and without a grip safety. It was chambered for the 7.65 Luger cartridge and for the 9mm Luger, or Parabellum, round. This last is one of the most successful semiautomatic pistol cartridges and is used in many different pistols and submachine guns.

In 1943, the Luger was replaced as the Wehrmacht sidearm by the Walther P-38. By that time, it is likely that more than two million Lugers had been produced. Manufacturers included German firms such as DWM, Simson, Krieghoff, Erfurt Arsenal, and Mauser, as well as Vickers of England and the Swiss government arsenal in Bern.

The quality of these guns varies widely. Those made prior to World War I and between the wars are generally the best. Older Lugers are still used by shooters and are avidly sought by collectors.

The Luger has a certain mystique, but it has disadvantages. The toggle bolt is complex and requires close machining. Because of that, the pistol jams easily when dirty, in marked contrast to many other military pistols such as the U.S. Colt .45. The trigger pull has considerable creep and can be gritty unless an expert gunsmith has tuned it.

luminosity The word luminous implies emission of light, and derivatives of this word are used to describe degrees of brightness in the field of astronomy and for some applications in optics. Because of the connotations suggestive of brightness, the word luminosity is sometimes used in advertising optical instruments, such as telescopes and binoculars, with such phrases as "high luminosity." In this usage, the word has no scientific standing. Image brightness in instruments of these kinds should be described in terms of light transmission and relative brightness. (See LIGHT TRANSMISSION; RELATIVE BRIGHTNESS.)

lumps Also referred to as irons, lumps are the rectangular projections, on the underside of the breech end of double or over/under shotgun barrels, that serve to lock the barrels to the action. Two lumps are commonly used, one behind the other; they are referred to as forward lump and rear lump. (See BARREL, SHOTGUN; BIFURCATED LUMP.)

L.U.P. (lead units of pressure) In America, pressures inside the chambers of firearms are typically measured with a radial crusher gauge, although work has been done with strain gauges and piezoelectric gauges. The radial gauge consists of a yoke mounted on the barrel, and containing an anvil, adjustable by means of a screw. Opposite the anvil is a piston,

free to slide in a tight-fitting hole through the yoke and barrel wall. To measure pressure, a crusher is placed in the yoke between the anvil and the piston, and the anvil is adjusted to support the crusher. When the gun is fired, pressure generated by the powder gases forces the piston against the crusher, which is compressed, since it is restrained from moving by the anvil.

For rifle and autoloading pistol cartridges, the crusher is made of copper. For determining pressures in shotguns, the crushers are made of lead, because of the low pressures involved. In all cases, the dimensions and material of the crushers are closely controlled and samples are calibrated in physical testing machines so that the amount of compression can be measured and related to the pressure. Since this method does not measure pressures directly, it is customary to refer to the pressure figures as C.U.P. (copper units of pressure) or L.U.P. (lead units of pressure). (See CHAMBER PRESSURE; CRUSHER GAUGE; C.U.P. [COPPER UNITS OF PRESSURE]; UNIVERSAL RECEIVER.)

Lyman Products Corp. William Lyman, dissatisfied with the metallic rifle sights of his day, experimented with and secured his first patent for a tang sight in 1878. The Lyman Gun Sight Company was founded in the same year in Middlefield, Connecticut.

Previously, shooters looked *at* the aperture for sighting; with a Lyman sight, the shooter looked *through* the aperture. Mounted on a tang close to the shooter's eye, a small disc housed the aperture with a faint rim through which the shooter focused. The concept was accepted, production increased, and the company moved its facilities to a larger building in Middlefield in the early 1880s.

In 1885, William Lyman secured a patent for the ivory bead front rifle sight. The sight consisted of a bead of ivory set in a steel holder on top of a slim blued-steel stem. The flat rear face of the sight reduced light reflection. Bead sights were later offered in gold and red. Shotguns were fitted with the sights in 1888. In 1896, William Lyman died. The business stayed in the family, and shortly after his death the firm began production of revolver sights. These included a rear sight and the common flat-faced bead.

The increased use of bolt-action guns in the early 1900s made tang-mounted sights impractical. Lyman solved the problem by marketing a receiver sight in which the aperture was mounted on an arm across the rifle's action. Lyman also introduced a folding leaf sight that could be left on the gun when a scope was being used.

During World War I, Lyman sights were used on American military armaments. In 1918, Charles Lyman, William's brother, purchased the company from the remaining heirs and began a reorganization of the business. In 1925, the company purchased the Ideal Manufacturing Company. Telescopic sight rights from both Winchester Repeating Arms and J. Stevens Arms and Tool were acquired in 1927. Lyman began producing its own line of telescopic sights in 1938.

In 1969, Lyman was purchased by the Leisure Group, Inc., of Pasadena, California. After the acquisition, the company continued to modify and expand its sporting goods lines, which include loading equipment and black-powder arms in addition to its line of scopes and iron sights. Lyman separated from the Leisure Group in 1978, and is now a privately held company. (See APERTURE; METALLIC SIGHTS; TANG; TELESCOPIC SIGHTS.)

Lyman tong tool See LOADING DIE.

machine rest   A mechanical device in which a rifle or pistol may be mounted for the purpose of testing the gun with ammunition of known grouping quality, or of testing ammunition with a gun and rest of known performance.

The design and use of a machine rest capable of producing reliable results is difficult and becomes more difficult as the muzzle energy of the cartridge increases, with a consequent increase in the force of recoil. During the very short time from the fall of the firing pin to bullet exit from the muzzle, a firearm is subjected to the acceleration forces of recoil, and the metal parts, particularly the barrel, vibrate and whip in a most complicated manner. The position of the axis of the muzzle and, consequently, the path of the bullet at the instant of exit are determined to a large degree by the way in which the firearm is restrained in its recoil movements, since these restraints also affect barrel whip and vibration. The rest must also have the capability of returning the gun to exactly the same firing position from shot to shot, as well as supporting and restraining it in the same way from shot to shot. Because of differences in dimensions and configuration, as well as movement, it is often necessary to build a machine rest for a particular model of gun.

In some machine rests, such as the early ones employed with muzzleloading rifles, there was no forearm on the rifle, and the barrel was positioned in a V trough and allowed to slide in recoil. The famed barrelmaker, Harry Pope, used the same kind of rest with single-shot rifles, removing the fore-end. This method was successful with the low energies, light recoil, and simple construction of these rifles; but mounting the barrel and action of a high power bolt-action rifle in such a rest may not give a good indication of what that action and barrel assembly may do when mounted in the stock.

Machine rests for pistols and revolvers are much easier to construct than those for rifles. The more common of these have a clamp arrangement on the end of a pivoting arm. The grips are removed from the gun and the frame is held securely in the clamp. The arm of the rest may be restrained in recoil by a spring or stopped by the hand of the operator. Other rests have a cradle, sliding on rods, with the barrel of the pistol or revolver clamped to the cradle. The Ransom rest is such a device.

The most successful machine rests for testing a high power rifle complete with stock are those of the Woodworth cradle type. (See MANN V REST; WOODWORTH CRADLE.)

McKenzie, Lynton (1940–)   One of the world's foremost firearms engravers, McKenzie was born in Queensland, Australia, and educated at Kings College, Sydney. In 1964, he left Australia to seek additional training in antique firearms restoration, in which he had developed considerable skill. Settling in London, he restored antique arms and, relying upon early training as a photoengraver, did gun engraving for James Purdey and Sons, Holland & Holland, Rigby, and Westley Richards.

In 1970, McKenzie left Britain and moved to New Orleans, Louisiana, where he was employed by New Orleans Arms, a firm that specializes in the creation of ornate presentation rifles, handguns, shotguns, and replica Bowie knives. In addition to his engraving, McKenzie developed a wide range of skills, including color case hardening, wire inlaying, charcoal bluing, and browning.

McKenzie moved to Flagstaff, Arizona, in 1980, where he presently works independently. (See ENGRAVING.)

magazine   In a repeating firearm, the container or reservoir in which cartridges are stored before loading, one by one, into the chamber of the arm. There are many kinds. In rifles, the magazine is often a well in the stock under the receiver. It is equipped with a magazine spring and a follower. Cartridges are loaded through the top of the rifle with the mechanism open by pressing them against the follower and the pressure of the spring. Some long firearms have a tubular magazine underneath the barrel, also with follower and spring. In some Savage and Mannlicher rifles, the well under the receiver contains a spool-like mechanism. Cartridges are inserted into semicircular cuts in the spool, which rotates to feed cartridges into the chamber.

The detachable box magazine (commonly called a clip) is a magazine, separate from the gun, that contains the spring and follower. Cartridges are loaded into the magazine, and then the magazine is loaded into the gun. This type is commonly used in automatic and semiautomatic rifles and handguns. Some box magazines are hinged permanently to the receiver. Many submachine guns and some automatic rifles employ large capacity detachable box magazines or circular drum magazines.

A revolver's cylinder is not usually considered to be a magazine, but it serves the same basic purpose. (See FLOORPLATE; FOLLOWER; MAGAZINE SPRING.)

magazine cut-off A common feature on military bolt-action rifles around the turn of the century, the magazine cut-off consists of a sliding or rotating mechanical device which prevents cartridges from feeding into the chamber from the magazine. When the cut-off is in the "off" position, cartridges will feed from the magazine in the normal loading sequence. Examples of rifles with magazine cut-offs include various marks of the Lee-Metford and Lee-Enfield, and the M1893 Turkish Mauser. In more recent times, the Browning BPS pump-action shotgun, introduced in 1976, has a magazine cut-off. (See MAGAZINE.)

magazine follower See FOLLOWER.

magazine platform See FOLLOWER.

magazine plug In the United States, the federal laws governing migratory birds, as well as some state hunting laws, require that shotgunners must not be able to fire more than three shots from their guns without reloading. Since many pump and autoloading shotguns have magazine capacities of five rounds or more, a wooden or plastic plug is placed inside the magazine tube by the manufacturer or shooter to decrease its length; this magazine plug prevents more than two rounds being loaded in the magazine.

magazine spring In repeating firearms, the magazine spring provides the force to feed cartridges up in line with the breechbolt as the action cycles. In tubular magazines, the spring is a coil type; in all others, it is a flat spring. The spring bears on the magazine at one end and on the follower at the other. (See FOLLOWER; MAGAZINE.)

Maggie's drawers Formerly, on high power rifle ranges in America, a red flag was waved by the target puller in the pits to signal a miss. The term "Maggie's Drawers" arose from the flag's resemblance to red flannel underwear. High-powered spotting scopes have since taken over the puller's function.

Mag-Na-Port See RECOIL BRAKE.

magnesium fluoride Magnesium fluoride is the substance usually applied to lens surfaces of modern optical instruments to provide an antireflection coating. A coated lens is readily recognizable by the color, ranging from straw to purple, of its surface. In a riflescope, lenses coated on all air-to-glass surfaces will increase light transmission by about 50 percent over an identical scope with uncoated lenses, providing a much brighter image and greater clarity of detail to the eye of the user. Without coating, each air-to-glass surface reflects 4-to-6 percent of the light striking it, and this reflected light not only results in dimming the image, but is re-reflected back and forth, causing "flare" in looking toward the sun or another strong light source and degrading image contrast.

The process of coating with magnesium fluoride was developed and perfected in the early 1940s. Lenses to be coated are very carefully cleaned, then placed in a vacuum chamber; the coating, .00004-.00006-inch thick, is deposited by molecular bombardment. (See COATED OPTICS; LIGHT TRANSMISSION.)

magnification In an optical system, the term "magnification" is used to mean the number of times the image seen through the instrument is larger than the object appears to the unaided eye. Another way of defining magnification is that it is the ratio of the diameter of the entrance pupil of the optical system to the diameter of its exit pupil. As a formula:

$$\text{Magnification} = \frac{\text{Entrance pupil diameter}}{\text{Exit pupil diameter}}$$

A telescope having an entrance pupil of 20mm (the diameter of the free aperture of the objective lens through which light passes) and an exit pupil of 5mm (the exit pupil is the small clear circle of light seen when the scope is held at some distance from the eye and pointed at a light source) will have a magnification of four power (4X) and a relative brightness of 25 (the square of the exit pupil). (See BINOCULARS; ENTRANCE PUPIL; EXIT PUPIL; TELESCOPIC SIGHTS.)

magnum The term "magnum" has been applied to a wide variety of cartridges from the 5mm Remington Magnum rimfire to such massive cartridges as the .577/.500 Magnum Nitro Express. In many cases, the term is used largely for advertising and sales promotion purposes, to take advantage of the reputations of some magnum cartridges for high velocity, flat trajectory, and killing power on game.

It is generally agreed that the term, as applied to cartridges, originated in England and that it came into use from the association of the relative size and shape of large bottlenecked cartridges to other cartridges, in the same manner as a magnum of champagne related to other champagne bottles of smaller size. It is not possible to determine with certainty just when the term was first applied to a rifle cartridge, nor what was the cartridge first so named. It does date back to the 1890s, and among the early cartridges to which the term was applied were the .500/.450 Magnum Black Powder Express developed about 1880, and the .450/.400 Magnum (3¼ inch), which was developed at about the same time and was later renamed the .450/.400 Magnum Nitro Express (3¼ inch). The term magnum was included in the caliber and name designations of many of the large-case-capacity English cartridges in small, medium, and large calibers, that were developed in the 1890s and early 1900s. The British were in the forefront of both high-velocity and heavy-caliber, heavy bullet big-game cartridges at that time.

In America, magnum is more often associated with belted cases, such as the .300 Holland & Holland, introduced into this country in the mid 1920s, which spawned a host of belted magnum cartridges, both wildcat and factory. In a belted case, the case head has been left the same, generally, but the body has sometimes been shortened, blown out, the taper changed, and the neck sized down. The first of the belted cases was apparently the .400/375 H&H, introduced in England about 1905. (See BELTED CASE; WILDCAT CARTRIDGE.)

mainspring A term usually applied to the spring in a firearm that drives the firing pin or hammer.

maintained lead See SUSTAINED LEAD.

Malcolm scope A riflescope made by The Malcolm Telescope Mfg. Co. of Syracuse, New York, founded by William Malcolm in 1855. Typically, these were full-length scopes, reaching from the muzzle to behind the breech at a position for proper eye relief. Power ranged from 3X to 20X, the tube was ¾ inch in outside diameter, and effective lens diameter was about ½ inch. Malcolm pioneered the use of achromatic lenses in riflescopes, made improvements in lens design, was among the first to provide for focus for the individual eye, and improved mounting arrangements and sighting adjustments. The Malcolm Company was out of business by 1951. (See TELESCOPIC SIGHTS.)

malfunctions, cold weather Cold weather malfunctions of firearms can usually be attributed to one of two causes: thickening or congealing of the lubricant used, or freezing of moisture in the action. Although some modern lubricants remain fluid over a wide temperature range, other lubricants are similar to automotive oils and tend to become almost solid when the temperature starts dipping below zero.

When the lubricants do thicken, any or all of four major areas may be involved—the trigger, hammer, firing pin, and bolt mechanism. If the bolt is involved, it may be difficult to operate the mechanism, and in an autoloader it may fail to eject the fired case or chamber a fresh round. When lubricant on the hammer axis congeals, movement of the hammer may be slowed to the point where it will not impart enough energy to the firing pin to detonate the primer. Congealed lubrication on the firing pin can prevent it from moving forward with enough momentum to even dimple the primer, producing a misfire, and such congealed lubrication on the trigger-sear assembly can prevent the trigger from being pulled.

Similarly, moisture that has gotten into the action area of a warm firearm can freeze as the arm cools and prevent the arm from functioning properly. Such malfunctions tend to occur when an arm is taken inside a warm building after having been exposed to the colder outside temperature, and then taken back outside before the moisture has had time to evaporate. (See GUN CARE.)

malfunctions, double-barrel shotguns Side-by-side and over/under shotguns, unlike repeating shotguns, are dependent upon the correct functioning of relatively complicated actions that are made to very close tolerances. In addition, there are other factors that make these guns somewhat less sturdy than pump or autoloading arms. Double-barrel shotgun malfunctions occur most frequently in these four areas:

Double-barrel shotguns that are equipped with single triggers frequently suffer from doubling, in which one pull of the trigger fires both barrels simultaneously, or balking, in which one or both barrels fail to fire when the trigger is pulled. Doubling is also fairly common in double-trigger shotguns. In these, it is caused by too light a pull on one trigger or too long a stock, which can cause the shooter to inadvertently pull the second trigger. In single-trigger guns, it can be too light a pull, or a failure of the selector mechanism. Balking can be caused by too heavy a trigger pull, or by the failure of the selector mechanism (in single-trigger guns) to set itself for the second pull.

Ejectors, in order to work properly, must be timed so that they propel the shell from the barrel only when the action is fully opened. If they are not correctly timed, the gun will eject prematurely, and the shells will strike the standing breech rather than being expelled cleanly.

Firing pins can be broken by dry-firing—that is,

allowing the pins to fall on an empty chamber without using snap caps or a block of wood to cushion their impact. The repeated shock of the pin falling against the standing breech can cause the pin to weaken and snap off.

The barrels of a side-by-side or over/under are joined by a solder joint at the center rib, and this joint, either through repeated firing or improper bluing, can loosen. Although the gun can be fired with its barrels not firmly attached to the rib, the condition can result in serious damage to the arm and injury to the shooter.

It should be stressed that repairs made to double-barrel guns should be attempted only by qualified gunsmiths who have the specialized training required to make delicate adjustments to complex mechanisms. (See DOUBLE-BARREL SHOTGUN.)

Mann, Franklin See MANN V REST.

Mannlicher, Ferdinand, Ritter von (1848–1904) An Austrian arms designer, Count Mannlicher bridged the gap from single-shot guns to modern repeaters, and many of his arms were innovative. He began with the repeating rifle and designed several before achieving his first great success, the Austro-Hungarian Model 1886 military rifle in 11mm. This rifle was based on his Model 1884 straight-pull action, in which the shooter merely pulled the bolt back and shoved it forward, with no up-and-down motion. An internal cam mechanism revolved the bolt head to lock the breech. In 1887, Mannlicher developed a new rifle on the turn-bolt principle and adopted a rotary magazine for it that was developed by Otto Schoenauer. The Mannlicher-Schoenauer rifle, in different forms, was adopted by many countries as a military rifle, and it saw world-wide use as a sporting rifle as well.

Mannlicher's pistol designs included a blow-forward semiautomatic in which the barrel recoiled forward from the standing breech to operate the action and reload the chamber. His more conventional Model 1901 and Model 1903 pistols were among the earliest successful semiautomatic handguns. Mannlicher also designed an automatic rifle.

Most of the successful Mannlicher arms were manufactured by Österreichische Waffenfabrik Gesellschaft (Austrian Arms Manufacturing Company) of Steyr. This company after several amalgamations became Steyr-Daimler-Puch; it is still manufacturing at least one Mannlicher design, the turn-bolt rifle with rotary magazine, which is the Austrian army's sniper rifle and is also sold in slightly altered configuration as a sporting rifle. (See BLOW-FORWARD ACTION; MANNLICHER RIFLE; STRAIGHT-PULL ACTION.)

Mannlicher rifle Ferdinand, Ritter von Mannlicher designed many rifles, including a straight-pull bolt-action arm adopted by the Austro-Hungarian army in 1886, but his most successful design was a turn-bolt rifle with a rotary magazine. This rifle, which usually has a split receiver bridge, butterknife bolt handle, and full stock with cheekpiece, is the one commonly referred to as a ''Mannlicher'' by American and European sportsmen.

The rotary magazine is a spool with slots in the forward and rear rims for the cartridges. The shooter opens the bolt and inserts a cartridge in the topmost slots. Then he rotates the spool against spring tension to bring a new pair of slots to the top and inserts another cartridge, and so on, until the magazine is full. This rotary magazine was originally designed by Spitalsky and was later improved by Otto Schoenauer; the turn-bolt rifle employing it is often called the Mannlicher-Schoenauer. It is a very dependable system of loading, and a version of it was also used by Savage in its well-known lever-action rifle. Mannlicher rifles have also been made with clip-loaded magazines, and many military rifles employ this Mannlicher design.

Another distinguishing characteristic of Mannlicher rifles is a split receiver bridge. When the bolt is closed, the root of the bolt is forward of the receiver bridge; but when the action is opened by lifting the bolt handle and moving the bolt to the rear, the root of the handle passes through a slot in the top of the receiver bridge. At rest, the bolt handle serves as a safety lug. This is in marked contrast to almost every other bolt-action rifle, in which the bolt handle is behind the receiver ring when the action is closed. This split receiver bridge gives Mannlicher rifles a very smooth bolt travel—much smoother than is possible with the usual Mauser arrangement—but it has the disadvantage that the

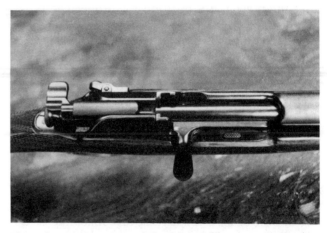

The split rear receiver of the Mannlicher action allows a very smooth bolt throw, but creates difficulty in mounting a scope.

rear scope mount cannot be placed on top of the receiver bridge. To overcome this difficulty, many Mannlichers are fitted with a plate, screwed to the left side of the receiver, on which the scope is mounted.

Most sporting Mannlicher rifles also have a flat butterknife bolt handle that makes the rifle easier to carry and store. Also, most sporting Mannlicher arms are stocked to the muzzle, and the stock has a high comb and a cheekpiece.

Mannlicher rifles are manufactured by Steyr-Daimler-Puch, headquartered at Steyr, Austria. One version with rotary magazine is used as the Austrian army's sniper rifle. The latest Steyr version of the Mannlicher for sportsmen encloses the redesigned rotary magazine in a separate assembly that is inserted in the rifle from underneath much like a detachable box magazine. This makes it possible to load and unload very quickly. (See BOX MAGAZINE; MANNLICHER, FERDINAND, RITTER VON; MANNLICHER STOCK; ROTARY MAGAZINE.)

Mannlicher stock   A full-length one-piece rifle or carbine stock in which the wood reaches all the way to the muzzle, sometimes capped with a decorative horn or plastic finial. The true Mannlicher stock is also characterized by a cheekpiece and a raised, usually level comb.

The full-length stock protects the barrel. But, because wood warps as moisture content changes, often affecting a rifle's accuracy and because this warping tendency is greatest with very long stocks, the Mannlicher stock is most often used for carbines or short rifles.

Though he did not invent it, Ferdinand R. von Mannlicher popularized this stock form by using it in many of his designs. (See MANNLICHER RIFLE.)

Mann V rest   The Mann V rest was invented by Franklin W. Mann in 1901 for testing rifle barrels and ammunition. It consisted of a heavy cast-iron member, about 4 inches high, 6 inches wide, and 36 inches long, arranged with flanges so that it could be bolted to a concrete pier. A V-shaped groove was planed down the length of this piece. The rifle barrel to be tested was equipped with two concentric bushings, or rings, of the same size on the outside and with inside diameters for a tight fit at two selected places on the outside of the barrel. When the barrel, with the bushings installed, was placed in the V-groove, stops were arranged so that the barrel could be returned to the same location in the groove for each shot. Mann used a "concentric action," a simple round cylinder screwed onto the barrel, which contained a firing pin and spring. The firing pin was held cocked by a wire inserted through a hole in the

pin, and the wire was pulled to release it. The barrel was allowed to slide on the rings in the V-groove under the forces of recoil.

Improved versions of the Mann V rest are still used for testing ammunition today. For this purpose, the rifle barrel used is from 1¼-to-1½ inches in diameter and up to 30 inches long. The two bushings may be integral or fitted to the barrel. The barrel is usually equipped with a standard bolt-action receiver, bolt, and firing mechanism. The advantage of the Mann rest for testing ammunition is that the recoil forces cause the barrel to slide in a straight line, so there is no jump or whip and little or no vibration. Thus it is possible to determine the grouping ability of ammunition free from errors of the rifle.

In order to use the precision of the Mann rest in testing completely assembled rifles, Al Woodworth, an ordnance engineer at Springfield Armory, designed the Woodworth cradle. This consists of two heavy steel blocks joined together by two heavy steel bars, with the underside of the blocks rounded to fit the V-groove in the Mann rest. The blocks are contoured and equipped with clamps so that a rifle may be held immoveably in them. The whole assembly is mounted in the V-groove of the Mann rest, in much the same manner as a barrel with rings would be. (See MACHINE REST; WOODWORTH CRADLE.)

Manton, Joseph (1766–1835)   Joseph Manton was widely considered the greatest gunmaker of his time, and that reputation still stands.

Manton's craftsmanship was excellent, but his enduring reputation is based on much more than that. He brought the fowling flintlock to a state of near perfection, excelling in the production of beautifully balanced, light, handy firearms, their dimensions hardly improved on even in modern times. His older brother, John, was also a noted gunsmith, but lacked Joseph's genius.

Joseph Manton's guns and pistols, the latter mostly paired dueling types, were in heavy demand during his working years, and a list of his noble customers alone is a very long one. During his good years, his shop produced about 400 shotguns, rifles, and pistols a year. He asked and got 70 guineas for a double gun when a similar common gun could be had for 15.

Manton was also a prolific inventor, in and out of the arms field. He patented many of his ideas, but left others without protection.

mark   An X-shaped scratch, made on a flat board or stump, that muzzleloading riflemen used as a target in shooting matches. Also, a method of nomenclature used by some manufacturers and governments to distinguish a particular model of arm or cartridge, such as the Weatherby Mark V rifle or the Western Mark 5 shotshell. (See MUZZLELOADER.)

marker   A stake, post, or flag that indicates a distance or the boundary of a particular area. On a high-power shooting range, for example, there may be markers to indicate yardage, such as 200 yards, 300 yards, etc., while on a skeet range there are shooting boundary markers, target distance markers, and even a marker to indicate the target crossing point for doubles.

Marlin Firearms (company)   John M. Marlin was born in Connecticut in 1836 and served an apprenticeship as a tool and die maker. During the Civil War, he worked at the Colt arms plant. With the experience gained in these two fields, he started the Marlin Firearms Company in 1870 in New Haven, Connecticut, and immediately began manufacturing his own line of revolvers, pistols, and derringers.

Impressed with the idea behind the Winchester repeating rifle, the Marlin company developed its own repeating lever-action rifle in 1881, first offered as the .47/70 Government Model. In 1893, Marlin produced a new action for the Marlin-Ballard .32/40 and .38/55 cartridges. When the .30/30 was introduced, that caliber was added to the company's line.

When John Marlin died in 1901, his two sons took over the business and began a diversification program. They bought the Ideal Cartridge Reloading Manufacturing Company, which was later sold to Lyman. Other products were a combination shoe-horn-buttonhook, decoy anchors, and handcuffs.

With World War I in progress, a New York syndicate bought the company and renamed it the Marlin Rockwell Corporation. After the war, Rockwell lost interest in manufacturing firearms, and the company was put up for auction in 1923. Frank Kenna, a lawyer, bought Marlin, added razor blades to the arms business, and the company starting showing a profit. In the 1960s, razor blade production was phased out to devote full attention to sporting firearms. In 1970, increased production prompted the company to build a modern plant in New Haven to meet the demand for its line of shotguns and rimfire and centerfire rifles.

Martini action   Patented in 1868 by Friedrich von Martini, an Austrian lace manufacturer, the Martini single-shot, lever action is an enclosed striker-fired modification of the American-designed Peabody action. Whereas the Peabody action was designed for rimfire cartridges and employed an outside hammer mounted on the right side of the receiver, the Martini was designed for centerfire cartridges and utilized a

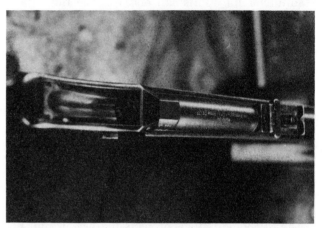

The Martini falling block action was at one time incorporated in the British service rifle and is still employed in some British target arms. This example is a .22 made by the Birmingham Small Arms Co.

spring powered firing pin passing through the center of the breechblock. Lowering the under-lever automatically lowered the breechblock, worked the ejector, and cocked the striker or firing pin. The Martini action has been manufactured in the United States, England, Belgium, and France in three sizes, for rimfire and centerfire metallic cartridges and for shotshells. It is still being manufactured in England, where it gained fame as the action portion of the Martini-Enfield and Martini-Henry rifles in the 1860s and 1870s. Today, it is made for the BSA Martini ISU .22 rimfire target rifle. (See ENFIELD; LEVER ACTION.)

master eye Sometimes called the dominant eye, it is the eye that controls both eyes when pointing toward or picking out an object, such as a clay target in flight. Normally, right-handed shooters will have a right master eye, and left-handed shooters a left master eye, but this is not always the case. When a right-handed shooter has a right master eye, he or she can shoot with both eyes open; without a dominant master eye, or with a master eye in opposition to the normal pairing, such as a left-handed shooter with a right master eye, the right eye would have to be closed to prevent interference with correct pointing.

To check for the master or dominant eye, point at something in front of you with both eyes open, sighting along your index finger at arms length. If left-handed, now shut the right eye; you should still be pointing at the object, indicating that your left eye is the master. If the object at which you were pointing appears to have shifted location, quickly shut the left eye and open the right eye. If the object now appears in the original location, your right eye is the master eye, and you have probably been missing moving targets in the past. For right-handed shooters the procedure is reversed. (See CROSS-EYE STOCK.)

match The fuse, wick, or smouldering cord used in matchlock firearms was known as a match. The term also refers to a competition among shooters to determine their skill. (See MATCHLOCK.)

match ammunition Match ammunition is ammunition specifically loaded for match, or competitive, shooting, and is hence loaded with greater care and with better components than service or hunting ammunition. Components for match ammunition are generally made on a line of machines carefully set up and maintained for this purpose, and the cartridges are charged and loaded on a special line, similarly maintained. This care in manufacture results in ammunition giving consistently smaller groups and better accuracy than standard commercial or service ammunition fired under similar test conditions.

matchlock The earliest form of firearm ignition, the matchlock—also known as firelock—can be dated accurately to the middle decades of the 15th century.

The earliest matchlocks utilized the principle of the touch hole and pan that would be retained by the wheel lock and flintlock. That is, a hole was drilled in the barrel near the breech, and a pan affixed to the stock next to it. The powder charge and ball were rammed in place and a small amount of powder was placed in the pan. A lighted match—usually a cord impregnated with saltpeter—was then touched to the pan, igniting the powder charge, which in turn shot its flame through the touch hole to detonate the charge in the barrel. In later matchlock designs, a vise called a serpentine was used to hold the match; it pivoted down toward the pan when pressure was applied to a spring loaded trigger.

While simple, the matchlock also had serious drawbacks—most notably, slow ignition time and extreme sensitivity to weather. Although the wheel lock, which superseded the matchlock, appeared early in the 16th century, the matchlock continued in use into the 17th century in many parts of the world because of its extreme simplicity and the ease with which matchlock guns could be manufactured. (See FLINTLOCK; WHEEL LOCK.)

matte finish Many shooters consider a dull, nonreflective finish on firearms to be desirable. Such finishes, whether applied to wood or metal, are referred to as matte finishes.

Gunstocks are matte finished by rubbing with very fine abrasives as the final step in their manufacture, or by coating with a nonreflective substance such as tung oil. Metal parts can be glass-bead-blasted, stippled or rust-blued. Military and other service arms are Parkerized, a process by which a chemical coating is bonded to the surface of the steel. (See METAL FINISH; STOCK FINISH.)

Mauser, Peter Paul (1838–1914) German arms designer and manufacturer. He was born into a family of gunsmiths at Oberndorf am Neckar, the famed arms center. Paul Mauser designed what became undoubtedly the most successful turn-bolt rifle. It has been made in many configurations as both a military rifle and as a sporter. Many different nations have adopted Mauser rifles, and many non-German gun designers have used the basic Mauser concepts in their designs, so much so that the term "Mauser rifle" is often used to designate any turn-bolt rifle of the Mauser type, no matter who designed it or where it was made.

The basic characteristics of the Mauser rifle came to the fore in the world-famous Mauser 98, adopted by the German army in that year, though Paul Mauser designed many predecessor rifles. (His first successful military design was, in fact, a single-shot bolt-action for black-powder cartridges.) The Mauser

98 cocks on opening and employs dual opposed locking lugs that fit into opposed recesses machined into the walls of the receiver. The magazine is a well below the bolt. In military rifles, cartridges are inserted from the top with the bolt open while held in a strip clip that fits behind lips in the receiver. In sporting Mauser 98s, cartridges are inserted singly from the top with the bolt open. The Mauser firing pin is a very sturdy one-piece unit that projects rearward when the action is cocked. This serves as a cocking indicator. The Mauser extractor is also heavy and is a separate unit mounted on the side of the bolt. The extractor body is its own spring. In unaltered Mausers, cartridges cannot be single-loaded into the chamber because the extractor will not jump over the rim of the cartridge; all cartridges must be fed into the magazine.

In general, all Mauser rifles are very sturdy and simple, and they are easy to disassemble in the field for repair and cleaning. Few shooters realize it, but the famous Springfield .30/06 rifle used by the U.S. Army in two world wars is merely a redesigned German Mauser rifle, and the U.S. government paid the Mauser Company $200,000 in royalties during the early years of manufacture. (Why the designers of the Springfield replaced the one-piece Mauser firing pin with a complicated three-piece pin remains a puzzle, since the Springfield pin is famous for breakage, and that defect has resulted in many burst rifles and injuries to shooters.)

Almost all German military Mauser 98s are chambered for the 7.92x57 cartridge. Sporting Mausers have been chambered for an extremely wide variety of cartridges. Usually, altered Mauser designs involve replacement of the turning wing-type safety on the cocking piece with a forward-back safety at the side or on the tang, and use of an extractor that snaps over the cartridge rim so that the rifle can be single-loaded directly into the chamber.

The Mauser 98 is no longer manufactured in Germany because it involves very expensive machining and because the design mandates a very slow lock time, perhaps the only real defect of the rifle.

Paul Mauser also designed an unsuccessful revolver and several automatic rifles. His company manufactured the well-known Mauser Military ("broomhandle") semiautomatic pistol. (See BOLT ACTION; LOCK TIME; MAGAZINE; SAFETY.)

maximum charge In any cartridge, with any given bullet weight, a certain amount of powder may be used within the limits of tolerable pressures. The most powder that can be loaded short of producing excessive pressure is referred to as a maximum charge or maximum load.

As a rule, it is advisable for handloaders to use maximum charges with extreme care, since the factors governing the behavior of a cartridge are somewhat variable, and maximum charges can produce excessive pressures with dangerous results. (See HANDLOAD.)

Maynard tape primer The invention of Edward Maynard, a Washington, D.C., dentist, this ignition system was developed in the mid-1850s to overcome the weaknesses inherent in percussion cap ignition. Maynard's system consisted of a paper tape (very similar to the caps in a modern cap pistol) impregnated at regular intervals with fulminate of mercury. The tape was coiled in a receptacle under the nipple of a firearm, and as the hammer was pulled back an arm moved the tape forward, placing a new cap over the nipple.

The Maynard system was used on the Model 1855 Harpers Ferry rifled musket. However, the tape was extremely sensitive to moisture and proved inferior to the percussion cap. It was not used again after that model issue. (See PERCUSSION IGNITION.)

mean radius One of several methods of measuring the grouping abilities of rifle and pistol ammunition, and the method commonly used by the military.

To determine the mean radius of a group of shots, draw a long vertical line through the center of the shot farthest to the left in the group and a long horizontal line through the center of the lowest shot. From these lines, measure at right angles to each shot, total the measurements, and divide the total by the number of shots, one set of figures for horizontal measurements and the other for vertical. Find the center of impact by measuring the results from the respective lines. Then measure from the center of impact to the center of each shot in the group, add these figures together, and divide by the number of shots. The result is the mean radius, or the average distance of all the shots on direct lines from the center of impact.

To obtain an approximate figure for extreme spread of a group (the distance on a straight line between the centers of the two widest shots) when the mean radius is known, multiply by 3.2 for 10-shot groups. For five-shot groups the constant is 2.7, and for 20-shot groups, 3.6. (See CENTER OF IMPACT; GROUP; GROUP MEASUREMENT.)

mechanical trigger A kind of single shotgun trigger, either selective or nonselective, that does not rely on an inertia block for its second shot. There are a variety of mechanisms for achieving this, but basically all of them use a spring-urged mechanism (as opposed to an inertia block, thus the name) to bring the trigger into battery for the second pull after allowing a delay for the involuntary pull.

A mechanical trigger gun can be differentiated from an inertia block model by pulling the triggers when the gun is unloaded. A mechanical trigger will fire a second time after being pulled and released; the inertia block trigger will not fire unless the gun is deliberately jarred to activate the block. (See IN-ERTIA BLOCK; THREE-PULL SYSTEM.)

medium bore   In present American usage, a medium bore rifle is one of over .30 caliber, but less than .375. This includes guns using such cartridges as the .338 Winchester, .340 Weatherby, 8mm Remington Magnum, and .358 Norma Magnum.

medium bore rimfires   See RIMFIRE VARIATIONS.

meplat   The small flat on the point of a spitzer rifle bullet. From the viewpoint of manufacturing and handling, a small flat is desirable, since it provides a surface for the knockout punch to eject the bullet from the forming die. (An exception to this is the famous Ross 180-grain .280-caliber match bullet, which had a very sharp point. The point was shaped on rotary swaging machines instead of in conventional bullet-forming dies.)

Contrary to popular opinion, an extremely sharp point does not give the lowest drag. A meplat of about 10 percent of the diameter of the bullet gives the lowest drag. This is attributable to the manner in which the air flows around the point of the bullet in flight, involving turbulence and shear. (See EX-TERIOR BALLISTICS; KNOCKOUT ROD; SPITZER BULLET.)

mercuric primers   The basis of the mercuric primer is fulminate of mercury, which chemists call mercuric isocyanate, a violently explosive salt. Fulminates, used alone, are extremely sensitive and detonate violently. A combination of potassium chlorate and mercuric fulminate makes an excellent primer, the fulminate providing sensitivity and the chlorate making it less dangerous to handle. In addition, many of the early priming compounds included antimony sulphide.

Along with other explosive metallic salts, fulminate of mercury was certainly known in the late 1600s, and perhaps much earlier, but its use as a priming compound to ignite gunpowder is credited to Alexander John Forsyth, a Scots clergyman, chemist, and firearms enthusiast, whose patent is dated April 11, 1807. (Forsyth's first priming compound was composed of potassium chlorate, charcoal, and sulphur in powdered form, but the patent covers both oxymuriatic salts and fulminating metallic compounds.)

Mercuric primers have a tendency to become inert in long-term storage, and they have another very serious drawback if cartridge cases are to be reloaded: The residue of ignition contains metallic mercury, which amalgamates with many other metals, including brass. Amalgamation starts first with the mercury penetrating between the brass crystals, destroying their cohesion and weakening the brass. The action proceeds most rapidly where the brass is hardest from cold-working—at the head of the case—and it is accentuated by higher pressures. Cases fired with mercuric primers, then reloaded, may rupture disastrously in subsequent firing. This was not a problem of consequence in black-powder days, but the advent of smokeless powder made mercury embrittlement of fired cases a serious problem and forced the development of nonmercuric primer mixtures.

The U.S. military stopped using mercuric primers in 1898; commercial companies soon followed suit. Mercuric fulminate is no longer used in primer mixtures. (See FORSYTH, ALEXANDER J.; FULMINATE OF MERCURY; PRIMER.)

Merillon, Pierre   See INTERNATIONAL SHOOTING UNION.

metal-cased bullet   See SOLID BULLET.

metal finish   The finish on the metal parts of sporting and military arms are of eight main kinds. Its purpose can be decorative, protective, or (usually) both. Bluing is the most common finish. Bluing consists of a controlled rusting of the surface area of the steel parts of a firearm. The surface may have been given a high polish prior to bluing, or it may have been sand- or vapor blasted to provide what is known as a matte finish. Bluing may be applied hot in a bath, by a slow-rust process, or cold for a temporary touch-up.

On military arms, the metal surfaces are often given a finish known as Parkerizing by turning the metal to crystalline iron phosphate. This finish provides a non-reflective gray or gray-green surface somewhat similar to the matte finish seen on sporting arms.

Many handguns, and fewer long arms, are plated with nickel to reduce the surface wear and resist rusting, while the bores of many foreign shotgun barrels are chrome plated for the same reason. Chrome-plated parts on pump and autoloading shotguns and autoloading rifles include the bolt, the lifter or carrier, and the charging handle. In addition, such parts as backstraps, buttplates, nose caps, and even frames are often brass, silver, or gold plated.

The nonferrous parts of arms, such as aluminum-alloy frames, trigger guards, etc., cannot be blued, and are generally given a hard surface coating called an anodized finish. Such a finish may be black in color, or pink, gold, silver, green, or even turquoise.

Some major steel parts of rifles and shotguns, such as the receivers, barrels, etc., are given a Teflon or electroless nickel coating to make them more resistant to rusting under adverse weather conditions. Teflon coatings tend to be green or olive drab in color and are not as durable as metal plating.

The frames of many single-action revolvers and single-shot break-action shotguns are given a mottled red-blue-gold case-hardened finish by heating the parts to a high temperature and treating them with carbon that is absorbed into the surface. Originally cyanide was used, but it has been discontinued recently in favor of less toxic material.

On some lower priced arms the metal surfaces are simply painted with a bluish-black or black paint, which is then permitted to dry or is baked on like the finish on an automobile. Arms of this kind often have a zinc-based alloy for the frame.

The metal surfaces of black-powder arms were originally browned, which is similar to bluing, but chemically different; a browned finish resembles reddish-brown rust more than the Prussian blue color. The more authentic of the modern black-powder arms have browning on the metal parts. (See BARREL MAKING; BLUING; BROWNING [PROCESS]; MATTE FINISH.)

metallic sights   The earliest firearms had no sights, the shooter simply taking aim by eye along the top of the barrel. As accuracy improved, metallic or "iron" sights of the simplest kind came into use. These consisted of a projecting stud or blade at the muzzle and a groove in the top of the breech plug or rear end of the barrel. The aperture sight, first used on crossbows, was adapted to firearms as early as the 1500s. The representative types of metallic sights can be divided into the following somewhat arbitrary classes:

Front sights. An incredible variety of shapes and sizes of bead, blade, post, and inverted V (barleycorn) front sights have been used on rifles, pistols, and shotguns, with the bead-type including a true bead, fixed on a cross-wire inside a hood or sunshade. In addition to the blade or post, military rifles often have front sights incorporating protective "wings" along each side of the blade. Aperture front sights for target shooting came into use soon after the appearance of round bull's-eye targets, a result of the understanding that it is easier to center a round bull's-eye in an aperture by viewing a uniform ring of white around the bull than it is to hold a uniform relationship of post or bead to bull. Soon after their adoption, aperture front sights were provided with interchangeable apertures of different sizes and, later, with spirit levels to reduce the tendency to cant the rifle while aiming. Refinements also included lateral or windage adjustments, often with vernier graduations.

Open rear sights. Used on rifles, pistols, and shotguns (for slug shooting), open rear sights have been commonly supplied on factory rifles, most military rifles, and nearly all pistols and revolvers. On pistols and revolvers, they may be located on the barrel or at the rear end of the slide or frame. On rifles, they are located partway down the barrel, usually 10 to 14 inches from the position of the eye of the shooter while aiming. The reason for this is that the human eye, like any optical system, can actually focus only at one distance at a time and has a limited depth of focus. In sighting with metallic sights, the eye must rapidly accommodate its focus from target to front sight to rear sight, and the rear sight must be located far enough from the eye to make this possible. Young

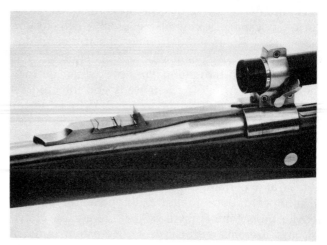

Two of the more effective metallic sights are the adjustable aperture and the multiple leaf. The latter is quite expensive, since each leaf must be painstakingly regulated to a particular range.

eyes can make this accommodation rapidly; but as the eye lens stiffens with age, the rear sight becomes fuzzy, then the front sight, to the point where the shooter of threescore years, who may still do well with aperture front and rear sights, will do very poor shooting with an open rear sight and a front bead.

A variety of shapes of open rear sights have been used. The better ones are those with a flat top and a V or U notch sufficiently large for the shooter to get a clear picture of the front sight. Sights of the buckhorn and semibuckhorn kind (once popular, but less seen today) are to be avoided; the projections serve no useful purpose, they obstruct the view, and they tend to cause the shooter to shoot high on a quick shot. Rear sights with a square or rectangular notch, called Patridge sights from the name of the inventor, are often used with post or flat-topped blade front sights, particularly on revolvers and pistols. The notch should be of a width to give the shooter a clear lie of white on each side of the blade. An older shooter will need a wider notch than a young one.

Some open sights have no adjustments for either windage or elevation. Most have adjustment for elevation, ranging from a screw through the flat spring section of the sight and bearing on the barrel, to a simple stepped elevator slide, all the way to micrometer click adjustments for both windage and elevation. Some have a series of leaves, such as the English express sights used on big-game rifles, with each leaf dimensioned to provide the elevation for a certain range when it is turned to the vertical position.

With the development of smallbore, high-velocity military rifles usable for volley fire at long range, rear sights capable of being elevated some distance were required. This led to the development of the vertical leaf sight, with a slider held by a thumb screw or notches. A typical example is that used on the Model 1903 Springfield. Others, such as many of the Mauser military models, have a tangent-curve sight adjustment in which the slider moves horizontally in contact with a cam surface; this provides elevation adjustment to match the bullet trajectory. A relatively few open rear sights are provided with windage adjustments through a cross-sliding member, often just held in place with screws, occasionally equipped with an adjustment screw to move it sideways. On most open sighted rifles, it is necessary to drive either the front or rear sight sideways in its slot to make windage corrections in sighting in.

Aperture rear sights. Aperture rear sights have several advantages. Since the front sight is centered in the aperture when sighting, and the aperture appears brightest at the center, there is a tendency for the shooter to center his view and the front sight automatically at the brightest point, aiding in quick,

accurate sight alignment. Except under conditions of very poor light, a small aperture can be used, much smaller than the entrance pupil of the eye, and this increases depth of focus and sharpens the vision, since the entering light rays are parallel and stray light is excluded. Another advantage results from the longer sight radius, which reduces the effects of alignment error.

Many of the early aperture rear sights provided only elevation adjustment; windage adjustment was provided in the front sight. Aperture rear sights on early muzzleloading target rifles were often only a fine-pitch screw, threaded vertically into the tang, with a flattened head pierced with a small hole. With this kind, the minimum adjustment was a half turn of the screw, and the peephole had to be well centered on the screw axis to avoid a windage change in using a half-turn of elevation. The logical development of this sight led to the folding tang sights typical on single-shot rifles, where a slide was mounted on the sides of a long, rectangular opening, usually clamped in place by the peep disc itself. Better sights of this kind were provided with long fine-pitch screws and vernier graduations for accurate and repeatable elevation adjustments. A few had windage adjustments, some with verniers.

Tang sights of the Lyman and Marble type had a round stem projecting vertically from a base mounted on the tang. The outer member of the stem is actually a nut, restrained from vertical movement. Turning this raises or lowers the inner member, which is restrained from rotating and which carries a peep disc at the upper end. With an aperture of $3/32$ to $1/8$-inch diameter and a disc outside diameter of $1/4$-inch to $5/16$-inch, they are an ideal hunting sight for many of the single-shot and lever-action rifles—quick to sight with, more accurate in sight alignment than open sights, and the disc gives a minimum of interference of view. Some of these sights had a windage slide, holding the disc, at the top of the stem. Others, mostly used for target shooting, had the stem mounted in a windage slide on the base.

A few bolt-action rifles were equipped with cocking piece sights, a small folding sight of the Lyman tang type that was mounted on the cocking piece. While they had an advantage of being close to the eye when sighting and moving forward upon firing, so as to reduce the chance of striking the shooter during recoil, they were somewhat fragile, and accuracy suffered from play between the cocking piece, bolt sleeve, bolt, and receiver.

The most common aperture rear sight today is the receiver sight, in which the sight base is mounted on the side or top of the receiver of the rifle. A slide, moving vertically in the sight base, is constructed with a right-angle member carrying a windage slide.

With the exception of low priced sights where the sliding members are adjusted with the fingers and clamped in place with screws, both hunting and target receiver sights have micrometer screw adjustments. Many of the hunting sights and most of the target sights have moveable index plates that can be set to zero after sighting in the rifle. Some also have moveable knobs or rings on the screws, so that the graduations on these may also be set to zero. Thus any accidental movement from zero can be detected. The use of screws for adjustment is almost universal, but cams and scrolls have also been used.

Tube sights. Tube sights extending the full length of the barrel, and equipped with an aperture at both front and rear, were tried out on target rifles in muzzleloading days. Both in full-length form and in short forms (from 6 inches to 14 inches in length and serving only as a rear sight), they were tried again on small bore (.22 rimfire) target rifles in the 1930s and '40s. Although some users have the opinion that the reduction of stray light gives a clearer sight picture and a more distinct bull's-eye, sight alignment is highly dependent on the eye locating the center of the rear aperture from brightness alone. The reason for this is that with nearly all tube sights, the dimensions of the circle of light seen by the eye are bounded by the front end of the tube and not by the opening in the sighting aperture. Because they were made using target telescope mounts, tube sights offered some advantages to the small bore target shooter: They had the same line of sight at the same distance above the rifle bore and the comb of the stock, they were convenient to adjust, the aperture could easily be positioned close to the eye, and the mount design gave an accuracy of adjustment and freedom from play and backlash not common to receiver-mounted sights of that era. They enjoyed a brief resurgence in the '50s and '60s when Redfield brought out a tube sight adaptation for their target receiver sight, but tube sights are not often seen in use on rifle ranges today.

Accuracy of aim with metallic sights. Under hunting conditions, particularly in the woods and under poor light conditions, even a riflescope of only 2 or 3 power has a definite advantage over any iron sights in accuracy of aim. On bull's-eye targets under fair light conditions, there is very little difference between good aperture target sights, front and rear, and high power target telescope in accuracy of aiming. Perhaps the greatest advantage with the scope in target shooting is that one can see mirage and follow changes in wind conditions while aiming, and alter the point of aim accordingly. With metallic sights, it is necessary to view conditions through a spotting scope, and conditions may change substantially while one is aiming and firing the shot.

NRA definition of metallic sights. For many years the NRA rules defined metallic sights as: "Any sight not containing a lens or system of lenses; except that a single lens may be attached to the rear sight as a substitute or in addition to prescribed spectacles. A colored filter-type lens may be attached to either front or rear sight."

In recent years, with the exception of matches shot under International rules or unless otherwise specified in match conditions, diopters are permitted. The diopter is a very compact telescope of about 1.3 power, not containing a reticle, and is mounted in the rear sight. It can be focused to give the shooter with poor eyesight, or the older shooter with poor accommodation of focus, a reasonably clear view of both the front sight and the target. It has disadvantages, particularly under dusty or rainy conditions, and it is not something that is going to give the shooter with good eyesight an advantage.

Metford, William Ellis (1824-1899) W. E. Metford, an English civil engineer, devoted much of his life to the scientific study of rifles and ammunition, and was probably England's greatest authority in that field in the last half of the 19th century. Although generally remembered for his developments in rifling, he made many other contributions to the knowledge and development of rifles and ammunition.

As early as 1853, Metford suggested that the hollow based Minié ball would expand and take the rifling without the use of a taper plug in the cavity, and he later proved that hardened flat base bullets of lead and tin would expand to take the rifling, when muzzleloaded, and that they were more accurate than ones of soft lead. Also: He was perhaps the first to adopt the solid, drawn cartridge case; as an early user of hollow point bullets, he correctly stated the reason for their greater accuracy; his engineering knowledge enabled him to correctly explain the gyroscopic action of the elongated bullet, the effect of air pressure in keeping its axis tangent to the trajectory, and the phenomenon of drift; and he was probably the first person to understand the whip of a rifle barrel and something of its vibrations during firing.

Metford is best remembered today for his rifling designs. Rifling of the mid-19th century was deep, and black-powder fouling in the bore was a problem, both in loading the bullet from the muzzle and in its effects on accuracy. Metford's contribution was his discovery that shallow rifling, only about .004 inch deep, was entirely adequate to spin the bullet; that a bullet hardened with tin would upset sufficiently to take such rifling and shoot with greater accuracy than a soft one because it did not upset as badly at the point; and that the shallow rifling gave less of a problem with fouling.

Metford's first rifling design in 1865 was basically the Enfield type, which is the general design most used today. It was .004 inch deep, had five lands and grooves of equal width, and sharp corners. His later development, the type called Metford rifling, had seven shallow segmental grooves, narrow lands, and a gain twist. Metford felt that the gain twist, first used with long, muzzleloaded, paper-patched projectiles, sheared the patch just enough to ensure its coming off the bullet at exit from the muzzle. With no sharp corners, this design was less subject to fouling problems, and barrels of Metford design won many of the long-range matches in England. The design lasted into the smokeless powder era, but gave short life with Cordite powder and was replaced with Enfield rifling of slightly deeper groove. (See BARREL, RIFLED; BULLET UPSET; ENFIELD; GAIN TWIST; LAND.)

micrometer A mechanical instrument for measuring small distances or movements accurately. In principle, it depends on a precision fine-pitch screw, turning in a nut, with means to count the turns of the screw and precision graduations to divide each turn into increments.

The first micrometer was patented in France in 1848. In the firearms field, the basic system had been used since the late 1800s for accurate, repeatable setting of sights and for sight adjustment to change the point of impact as required from shot to shot. (See METALLIC SIGHTS; MICROMETER ADJUSTMENT; TELESCOPIC SIGHTS.)

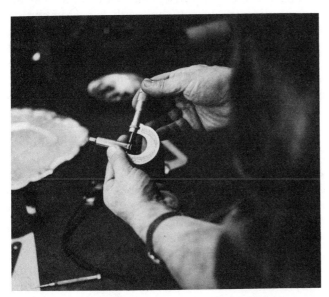

One of the many uses of a micrometer is checking case head expansion.

micrometer adjustment Some mechanical devices, such as the iron sights on target rifles and pistols, are equipped with a micrometer to provide adjustment or location. The micrometer graduations are usually in minutes and fractions of minutes of angle in America; in countries using the metric system, the micrometer on sights may be graduated to coincide with the ring dimensions of the standard metric target used at a specified distance in meters.

Rifle telescopes also have micrometer adjustments, although only the target types have provision for counting the number of turns of the screw, as well as the fractions per turn. (See METALLIC SIGHTS; MICROMETER; TELESCOPIC SIGHTS.)

middle sight A small metal or plastic bead situated on the rib of a shotgun roughly halfway down the barrel. Primarily used by trapshooters, the purpose is to help the shooter perceive whether his gun is straight rather than canted to one side, and how much barrel he is seeing.

The standard sight picture looking down a trap gun is for the center bead to be at or near the base of the front sight; this is called a "figure 8" sight picture. If the shooter sees some rib between the two beads, the gun will normally shoot higher than if the two beads are aligned perfectly one behind the other. If the middle sight is horizontally out of line with the front sight, the gun is canted or the shooter's head position is not properly aligned with the barrel, indicating need for changes in the stock. (See SHOTGUN SIGHT; SIGHT PICTURE.)

middle wad See OVER-POWDER WAD.

mid-range load In target shooting, a revolver cartridge that is considerably less powerful than the full-power or service load. These cartridges are used mostly for paper target shooting at 25 or 50 yards, where there is no need for the full-power load. The reduced charge results in less recoil and greater accuracy. Special flat nose wadcutter bullets are often employed. The most familiar is the .38 Special mid-range target or match load.

Any centerfire cartridge can be underloaded so as to reduce recoil and improve accuracy for target shooting at short ranges. But cartridges for semiautomatic pistols and rifles must retain enough energy to function the action. If not, the arm will not function as a repeater and must be single-loaded. A few semiautomatic target pistols have been specially designed to function well with mid-range target loads, such as the Smith & Wesson Model 52 or the Walther Centerfire .32 GSP.

mid-range trajectory height   When a firearm's sights are adjusted so that the gun will hit a distant target, the barrel is actually tilted slightly upward at the muzzle. A bullet therefore rises at first, but then drops back toward the line of sight. Mid-range trajectory height is the height above the line of sight attained by the bullet halfway between muzzle and target. For instance, a 150-grain .30/06 is a little less than 2 inches high at 100 yards when the rifle is sighted in to be dead-on at 200 yards.

Unless otherwise specified, all published ballistics tables give mid-range trajectory height at the mid-point. Also, unless otherwise specified, mid-range trajectory height is given in terms of height above line of sight, not line of bore. Modern high-velocity arms have flat trajectories when compared to the high or looped trajectories of older low-velocity arms. A low or flat trajectory aids the shooter since he is not required to allow for extreme bullet rise or bullet drop at reasonable hunting ranges. (See SIGHTING IN; TRAJECTORY.)

mild steel   This is a general term used to describe a steel with a carbon or alloy content below the point at which a steel becomes self-hardening when heated above the critical temperature and quenched. Such a steel, unheat-treated, is often used for the parts of a gun not requiring great strength and wear resistance, such as a rimfire rifle barrel. However, by increasing the carbon or nitrogen content of the outside layers of mild steel, then heating above the critical point and quenching, a hard, strong, wear resisting outer surface is obtained, combined with a tougher, more ductile core. Receivers, bolts, hammers, etc. on many firearms are made of mild steel.

military creep   See TRIGGER CREEP.

military sling   For many years, the military rifle sling was constructed of 1¼-inch-wide heavy leather with punched pairs of holes for adjustment, two leather keepers, a metal ring or loop for the rear portion, and two metal end pieces with claws to fit into the adjustment holes. Today's military sling is constructed of heavy webbing; the claws have been dispensed with, as have the pairs of punched holes, and adjustment is via a friction buckle and a metal clamp. (See KEEPER; SLING.)

Miller trigger   See SINGLE SET TRIGGER.

Minié ball   In 1851, Captain Claude-Etienne Minié of the French army developed a method of expanding a bullet to fit the grooves of a rifled barrel. The bullet consisted of a three-groove hollow base design in which the base cavity was filled with tallow and plugged with a sheet iron cup. On firing the powder, gases drove the cup into the base of the bullet, expanding it to fit the barrel grooves. Later, an American, James H. Burton, determined that the use of the iron cup was not necessary for expansion, and American Minié balls did not have this feature.

The Minié ball received its greatest use in the Civil War, when it was the universal rifled musket projectile for both sides. However, with the introduction of practical fixed ammunition toward the end of the war, the Minié rapidly became obsolete.

minute of angle (MOA)   A measurement used in shooting to express group size or sighting adjustment, one minute of angle equals ¹⁄₆₀ of one degree of angle. With a distance of 100 yards between shooter and target, one minute of angle subtends 1.05 inches; at 200 yards, 2.10 inches. Any rifle that shoots minute of angle groups, measuring between centers of the holes of the widest shots, is considered very accurate. (See GROUP MEASUREMENT; MICROMETER ADJUSTMENT.)

Miquelet   The Spanish version of the Snaphaunce was known as the Miquelet. It used a heavy mainspring and cocking mechanism outside the lock plate. The frizzen contained the pan cover in one piece. When the flint struck the frizzen, the pan automatically uncovered in order to allow the spark to ignite the priming powder. (See SNAPHAUNCE.)

mirage   An optical phenomenon resulting from the distortion of light by alternate layers of hot and cold air. As applied to shooting, it is produced by heat waves generated by a rifle barrel made hot by continued firing coming in contact with the cooler air surrounding the barrel; the result is a shimmering effect that distorts the view of the target. The illusion is also noticeable on very warm days when heat waves rise from the ground surface and create a distorted view of the target, even making it appear to be in a different location. Mirage, also called shimmer, is a cause of concern among large bore, smallbore, and black-powder target shooters. Shotgunners shooting in competition will also be subject to the phenomenon. Ventilated barrel ribs aid in reducing mirage, and over/under shotguns without side ribs tend to cool faster than those with ribs, thus reducing the amount of heat generated.

misfire   The complete failure of a round to detonate following the usual ignition process (the fall of the hammer or the striking of the primer by the firing pin) is called a misfire. Misfires may be caused by any number of situations, but usually are the fault of the charge or cartridge rather than the firearm.

Misfires are common with flintlock mechanisms because of the susceptibility of the priming powder to moisture. Similarly, moisture or oil that seeps into a nipple flash hole in a percussion gun, or into the primer of a metallic cartridge, can cause a misfire. In rare instances, the flash of an old primer may be too weak to ignite a heavy charge of slow-burning powder. Occasionally, excessive headspace in rimfires, or a weak firing pin mainspring in any gun, will produce misfires. (See HANGFIRE; HEADSPACE; IGNITION.)

modified choke Halfway between maximum choking of a shotgun barrel (full choke) and no choke at all (cylinder choke). Most modified chokes in American shotguns utilize approximately .015 inch of constriction and produce patterns with ordinary hunting loads of 40 to 50 percent into a 30-inch circle at 40 yards. Trap loads and premium plastic buffered or hard shot magnum loads frequently deliver slightly higher shot percentages.

One of the most versatile and usable of chokes, particularly for the dove and waterfowl shooter, the modified choke is a bit too much for most upland game, at least in 12-gauge guns. (See CHOKE.)

modified clay pigeon This American trap game is designed to encourage participation in Olympic or International trapshooting, but without the expense of building a 15-trap ground level installation. Ideally, the roof of the trap house should be at ground level, or at the same level as the regular five trap stations, although the standard house can be used.

International clay pigeon or Olympic trap has 15 traps, in five groups of three traps each, installed in a trench at ground level. The five shooting stations are arranged in a straight line parallel to the trench, unlike the arc shape of American trap. There are fewer than a dozen such installations on the North American continent. Thus, the modified clay pigeon game is a compromise game to simulate International trap, using the facilities available on a standard trap range.

The standard trapshooting stations are used, and a squad consists of six shooters—five on the line, and the sixth shooter to the rear of station one, ready to move onto station one. The squad members rotate to the next station as soon as the shooter at that station has fired, and two shots are permitted at each target. (As soon as shooter number five has fired, he immediately moves to the standby position for station one.) Thus, there is always a shooter in the process of moving from one station to the next.

The single multioscillating trap may be manually or automatically loaded, mechanically or electrically operated, and capable of throwing targets at random.

The angles and elevations must be continually changed within the official limits designated by the National Rifle Association and the Amateur Trapshooting Association. (Modified clay pigeon is sometimes called the NRA International Clay Pigeon, or NRA Modified Clay Pigeon, since it originated with this organization.) (See INTERNATIONAL TRAPSHOOTING; TRAPSHOOTING.)

mold See BULLET MOLD.

monobloc A form of barrel construction used in manufacturing over/under and side-by-side shotguns, and rifles. The barrel breech section is machined from a one-piece steel forging, with all locking surfaces and extractor/ejector cuts therein. This monobloc is then bored to receive the breech ends of the barrels, which are either threaded or brazed in place. Such construction is considered to be more economical to produce, and stronger, than the traditional chopper lump or designs that have the lumps brazed on separately. (See BARREL MAKING; CHOPPER LUMP; LUMPS.)

monobloc barrel See BARREL, MONOBLOC.

monocular A monocular is an optical device for one-eye use, in somewhat the same manner as a telescope but in a much smaller package. Monoculars are generally manufactured by firms producing binoculars, and basically a monocular is half a binocular, at about half the cost, with half the weight, and taking up half the space, but with the same quality of prisms and lenses as a regular set of binoculars. A good quality 8X monocular, for example, might measure 5¼ inches in length and weigh 8 ounces, complete with case, while binoculars of the same brand and power might measure only 4¼

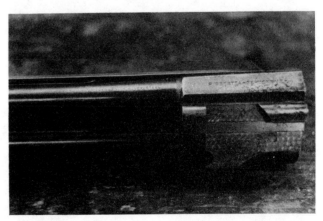

Using the monobloc system, the lumps of a shotgun are forged from one piece of steel, and the barrels are then brazed to it. The knurled strips on this Beretta over/under show where the barrel joint is located.

inches in length, but will also be 4¼ inches in width and weigh 19½ ounces, complete with case. The disadvantage to a monocular is a loss in depth perception. (See BINOCULARS.)

Monte Carlo comb   Rifles that have stocks designed for use with open or iron sights require a higher comb when used with a scope because the scope's line of sight is above the normal line of sight. The cheek, and thus the eye, is raised by the addition of an elevated comb, called a Monte Carlo. The Monte Carlo extends from the nose of the comb to just ahead of the heel of the stock butt; the top surface of the Monte Carlo may be parallel to the bore line, or even raised slightly at the heel on some high power rifles, such as the Weatherby designs, so that the stock comb will recoil away from the cheek.

Trap grade shotgun stocks are often fitted with a

Monte Carlo comb in order to cause the shot charge to pattern high for rising targets. Another reason for installing the Monte Carlo comb on shotguns is to place the shooter's eye on the same level regardless of where his cheek meets his comb.

moose, guns and loads for   Moose are the largest North American big-game animals, both in size and weight, and the largest Alaskan-Yukon bulls may weigh as much as 1,800 to 2,000 pounds when fat and stand 7 feet or more at the shoulder. Considering this size, and the great variety of terrain moose are hunted in, the ideal moose cartridge is of fairly large caliber—from 7mm up—and capable of handling long, heavy bullets at velocities of 2,500 feet per second or more. These heavy bullets of high sectional density should be of the controlled expansion design, so that they will drive through heavy bone

Despite their truly enormous size, moose can be readily taken with guns in the .30/06 category. This British Columbia bull was dropped with a .300 Magnum.

and muscle and give very deep penetration, while expanding enough to tear up a lot of vital tissue and nerves along the way. The best moose cartridges, for shooting in all areas where moose are found, are the modern magnums from 7mm up. For hunters who are a bit sensitive to recoil, the .30/06 and .35 Whelen are excellent moose cartridges.

Rifles suitable for hunting moose include all kinds of actions that chamber cartridges that are powerful enough to kill cleanly an animal of this size and weight. Few modern lever-actions chamber such cartridges, and only one slide-action, but some autoloaders, like the Browning BAR that is chambered for the 7mm Remington Magnum, the .300 Winchester Magnum, and the more powerful .338 Winchester Magnum, are good moose guns. Bolt-action rifles are generally best because they are chambered for all the best moose cartridges.

The best scope for hunting these giant deer is probably a variable, since moose may either be stalked and/or called in to very close range or, in the case of the Alaska-Yukon moose, be shot at long distances across a lake or meadow. Much moose hunting is done at dawn and twilight, so a Duplex-type reticle or a medium cross hair should be used. Since it seems to rain more often than not on the Alaska Peninsula, hunters who seek a moose there will find lens caps worth their weight.

Mosee, Phoebe Ann   See OAKLEY, ANNIE.

Mossberg, O. F., & Sons, Inc.   Oscar F. Mossberg was born in 1866 in Sweden. He immigrated to the United States in 1886 and, in 1894, began his career in the firearms industry at the Iver Johnson Arms and Cycle Works in Fitchburg, Massachusetts. While at Iver Johnson, he developed his own revolver action. After working for the Shattuck Arms Company of Hatfield, Massachusetts, for a short while, he went to the J. C. Stevens Arms and Tool Company in Chicopee Falls, in 1902, where he stayed for 13 years. There he designed a small four-barrel .22 novelty pistol called the Unique and patented it in his name. With the help of his two sons, Mossberg converted an old barn into a shop and began producing the pistols.

In 1919, Mossberg and his two sons launched their own full-time arms manufacturing concern in New Haven, Connecticut. Their first gun was the Brownie four-shot .22 caliber semiautomatic pocket pistol. In 1921, they purchased a target factory, and in 1922 began production of the .22 Mossberg rifle, a pump-action hammerless repeater.

The Mossbergs incorporated in 1926. In 1935, the company expanded into the field of telescopic sights, spotting scopes, and scope stands. O. F. Mossberg died in 1937.

During World War II, the firm produced parts for .50-caliber machine guns and for Lee Enfield rifles used by the British military. Expansion of the sporting firearms line continued after the war. In addition to bolt-action shotguns in 12, 16, and 20 gauge, a new line of .22 rifles was introduced.

With the outbreak of the Korean War, Mossberg did subcontract work for the Browning Automatic Rifle. Mossberg manufactured its first pump shotgun, the Model 200, in 1957. Since that time, the firm has introduced a wide variety of pump-action and autoloading shotguns and is now one of the world's largest producers of shotguns. (See INTERCHANGEABLE CHOKES.)

mountain goat, guns and loads for   It is likely that no other big-game species presents the hunter with so many conflicting requirements as to rifle and cartridge as does the mountain goat. These animals are found in the high reaches of the American and Canadian Rockies and in the mountains of Alaska. Their natural range is above that of the wild sheep and taking them at altitudes of around 12,000 feet is not uncommon. The difficulty of negotiating this kind of terrain requires the goat hunter's rifle to be as short and light as possible and to have little felt recoil as shooting positions are often precarious.

However, the mountain goat is a sizable animal—a big billy will weigh 300 to 350 pounds—and is solidly built as well. Add to this the need to drop a goat in its tracks, lest it plunge over a precipice, wrecking its horns or precluding recovery altogether, and the need for a powerful rifle is evident. And while most goats are taken at moderate range, the occasional shot must be taken from a long distance.

With all these considerations in mind, it is reasonable to say that the minimum goat rifle would be a .270 or .280 Remington loaded with controlled expansion bullets of 130 to 160 grains and fitted with a 4X scope in a solid mount. A 7mm or .300 magnum would offer more power and flatter trajectory at long range, but would necessarily weigh more, and would need a longer barrel. Added recoil, too, would be a factor. Any rifle bigger than .300 magnum would be a handicap, as would any rifle, regardless of caliber, that weighed more than 9 pounds or had a barrel longer than 24 inches.

A sling is an absolute necessity, and the hunter should ensure that the swivel studs are secure. A good pair of binoculars in any power from 7X to 10X is likewise necessary.

Heavy, well-broken-in climbing boots are re-

The mountain goat is a creature of the highest altitudes and roughest country. It is large, tough and phlegmatic, and requires a rifle of adequate power, such as this 7mm Magnum.

quired, and the hunter should be sure that he himself is in the best possible physical condition.

mule deer, guns and loads for   Not so many years ago a deer rifle, whether it was to be used for hunting whitetail, blacktail, or mule deer, was a lever-action chambered for a cartridge like the .30/30 Winchester, and it carried iron sights. There were also a few slide- and autoloader actions chambered for cartridges in the same power range. But as the bolt-action rifle that was chambered for high velocity and flat trajectory cartridges came into general use in the West, it gradually took over as the gun best suited for hunting mule deer.

One factor that had much to do with the switch from lever- to bolt-action rifles for mule deer hunting was the transition from horse to motorized transportation for the great majority of hunters. The Win-

chester M-94 carbine, the Savage M-99, and a few other light, compact rifles fit well on the side of a pony; a bolt action was not ideal. With wheeled transportation, the bolt action is as handy as the lever gun and it fires cartridges with the long-range capability needed for much mule deer hunting. Bolt-action rifles are also ideally suited for use with telescopic sights—which are superior to iron sights of any form for all mule deer hunting—while rifles like the 94 Winchester are not.

Another point in favor of the bolt action as a mule deer rifle is the fact that in many areas where mule deer are hunted, elk are also hunted on the same trip and often seen the same day in the same place. Under these circumstances, the rifle used should be chambered for a cartridge that is adequate for shooting elk at all hunting ranges. This means more powerful cartridges than needed to cleanly kill a mule

Mule deer are larger than whitetails and are usually shot at longer ranges. However, they can be hunted with the same cartridges (from left): .308, 7×57mm, .270, .280, .30/06, 7mm Remington Magnum, .300 Winchester Magnum, and .338. The last three are too powerful for mule deer alone, but double well as elk cartridges.

deer, and few rifles except bolt actions are chambered for such cartridges. Also, as mule deer are hunted in such a wide variety of terrain—anything from cactus-bearing desert and sage-covered rolling hills to thick juniper, fir, and pine thickets, and up into the subalpine basins near the timberline—the ideal mule deer rifle should be light and compact, yet highly accurate. Many bolt-action rifles possess all of the above requirements, while few others do.

Mule deer, which inhabit the western third of the United States, are not especially large animals, even the larger bucks weigh in at no more than 350 to 400 pounds, so the cartridge required to kill one cleanly need not be in the class of a good elk cartridge. But the same cartridges will do very well for taking both animals. The old adage that most deer are killed at ranges under 100 yards does not hold true for hunting mule deer, especially when trophy hunting. It is more realistic to place the average range at 200 yards. The open nature of much mule

deer habitat often makes it impossible to stalk to close range. Also, when hunting in rough mountain country, many shots must be taken from one side of a wide canyon to the other.

The ideal mule deer cartridge is one that develops velocities approaching 3,000 feet per second. If no heavier game is to be hunted at the same time, the bullet need not be of large caliber—anything from 6mm up will do—but the bullet must have a high ballistic coefficient so that it will not only shoot flat but will also retain high terminal velocity and energy at long range. This means a spitzer bullet with good sectional density. The bullet design should make expansion certain out to over 400-yard velocity retention for the long-range shot, yet the structure should be strong enough to give sufficient penetration at close range. Such cartridges as the .270 Winchester, the .280 Remington, and 7mm magnums are the ideal for all-around mule deer hunting.

multigroove rifling   Consisting of many lands and grooves, multigroove (sometimes called polygroove) rifling services to spread the torque stresses and engraving more favorably over the bullet surface. Marlin Firearms Co. adopted what it termed Micro-Groove rifling, in which the lands are half as wide as the grooves; the number of grooves on Marlin sporting arms varies from 12 to 20 depending on the caliber of the arm. Other manufacturers have experimented with such rifling, and barrels with up to 24 grooves have been produced. (See BARREL, RIFLED.)

multiple leaf sight   A sight with two or more leaves graduated for different sighting ranges, such as a three-leaf sight with one leaf graduated for 100 yards, the second leaf graduated for 200 yards, and the third leaf for 300 yards. Generally considered a British invention. (See METALLIC SIGHTS.)

musket   A smoothbore military long arm, either flintlock or percussion. When rifling came to be used, this class of guns was referred to as rifled muskets.

muzzle   The forward, or frontal, end of a barrel, from which the projectile exits.

muzzle bell   A bell, flared or funnel-shaped at the muzzle of a barrel can be produced in any arm by continuous and overzealous use of a bent cleaning rod, or a ramrod in muzzleloading arms. Belling is simply the wearing away of the metal in the muzzle area, and when rifling lands are involved, the accuracy of a rifle can be affected. On shotguns, this belling will have a less noticeable effect, but it will open patterns somewhat.

A muzzle bell is more common in arms that are cleaned from the muzzle and in muzzleloading arms; it can be prevented by the use of a straight rod and a rod guide or, in the case of muzzleloaders, a steel loading rod. (See CLEANING ROD; LOADING ROD.)

muzzle blast   Muzzle blast occurs when the gases that propel a bullet or shot charge emerges from the barrel and expand into the open air. The blast is registered as both heat and noise and is governed by the length and diameter of the bore and the kind of powder burned. As a rule, the longer the barrel and/or the smaller the powder charge, the less the muzzle blast, since the propellant is more completely burned and its force dissipated before it clears the muzzle. For example, a .30/06 with a 22-inch barrel would have a moderate amount of muzzle blast, but a rifle chambered for the same cartridge, but with an 18-inch barrel, would have a quite severe muzzle blast. (See HEARING, SHOOTING DAMAGE TO.)

muzzle brake   See RECOIL BRAKE.

muzzle cap   A small rubber device that fits over the muzzle of a rifle or shotgun barrel to prevent moisture or foreign matter from entering. The term is also sometimes used to indicate a cuplike device fitted to the muzzle of recoil operated arms to provide a rearward assist to the recoiling barrel. Expanding gases leaving the muzzle and entering the cap push the barrel to the rear as the bullet exits.

muzzle energy   The energy of a projectile as it leaves the muzzle of the gun from which it is fired. The figure is expressed in foot-pounds.

muzzle flash   When the burning gas that propels a projectile emerges from a firearm barrel, it creates a bright flash. In sporting arms, this flash is normally not visible during daylight, but at dawn or dusk it can be quite noticeable. Muzzle flash is of concern

Flash is one of the adjuncts of muzzle blast. Not that apparent in daylight, it can be extreme at night. As a rule, the greater the powder charge and/or the shorter the barrel, the greater the flash. Shown here are a percussion .50 Hawken firing 100 grains of powder, a .45-caliber flintlock pistol firing 25 grains, and an 18-inch-barreled .308 firing 49 grains of smokeless powder.

to designers of military arms, and many of these guns are equipped with flash hiders.

muzzle jump   The backward and upward movement of the gun before the bullet or projectile leaves the muzzle. When a shoulder arm or handgun is fired, the rapidly expanding gases push the projectile forward and the butt or grip of the gun rearward. This is further exacerbated by the release of bullet and powder gas from the muzzle. Since this rearward push is exerted below the line of the axis of the bore, the tendency for the barrel to move upward. This jump is most noticeable at the muzzle because it is the point farthest from the rearward point of resistance—the shoulder if a rifle or shotgun is being fired, the hand in the case of a handgun.

Muzzle jump makes a second aimed shot more difficult to get off. This can be a major disadvantage

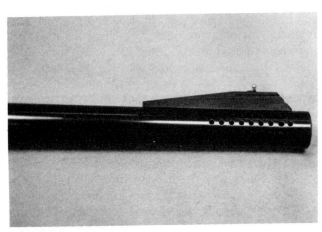

The barrel of this .458 has been drilled with a series of ports designed to direct the gas that propels the bullet up and to the side to counteract the force of recoil. (This particular design is executed by the Pendleton Co.) While kick is lessened, the muzzle blast is increased.

in shooting situations where a fast second shot is necessary, such as trap doubles or pigeon shooting. Muzzle jump can be controlled by the use of a long, heavy barrel and/or a muzzle brake. (See RECOIL BRAKE.)

muzzleloader Any gun—long arm or handgun—with a solid breech, which must be loaded through the muzzle by charging first with black powder, followed by the lubed or patched projectile, is called a muzzleloader. (In the case of muzzleloading shotguns, wads are charged over the powder, followed by the shot charge and an overshot wad.) The muzzleloading family of arms consists of matchlock, wheel lock, flintlock, and percussion designs, with some minor variations. The flintlock and percussion are the best known, and the past two decades have seen a renewed interest in these black-powder arms.

muzzleloaders, cleaning of Unlike the propellants used in modern arms, the powder (and some percussion caps) used with black-powder guns is highly corrosive and creates considerable fouling. Therefore, it is extremely important that a muzzleloader be cleaned thoroughly after every use. If the fouling is not removed, accuracy will suffer (in rifled arms) and the barrel may be ruined.

One effective method of cleaning black-powder guns is as follows: First, mix a water-based cleaning solvent. This consists of 1 ounce of liquid dishwashing detergent, 1 ounce of water-soluble oil, and enough water to make a pint of solution when the three are mixed. (Note: This solvent must be shaken before use.)

If cleaning a percussion arm, the nipple must first be sealed. This is done by seating a live percussion

cap on the nipple and very carefully lowering the hammer to hold it in place. For flintlocks, simply plug the vent with a sharpened wooden matchstick.

Pour enough cleaning solvent into the barrel so that the bore is filled to within 8 inches of the muzzle (1 inch in pistols). Plug the muzzle with a finger, and upend the gun half a dozen times so that the whole bore is completely soaked. Stand the gun upright and let it soak for 5 minutes. Upend the gun several times more and then pour out the solution. Wipe out the bore, and unplug the nipple or vent.

Now, run dry patches through the bore until they come out a light gray. Follow this with a patch heavily saturated with a lubricant such as WD 40, let the gun stand for a few minutes, and follow with a dry patch. This one should emerge nearly white. Finally, coat the bore with any good nonsilicone gun oil, and oil any exposed metal parts. Before shooting the gun again, remove the oil in the bore with an alcohol-soaked patch. Do not attempt to "shoot" it out; this method is ineffective.

Both the drum on a percussion gun and the vent on both percussion guns and flintlocks should be cleaned regularly. The vents can be gotten to with a section of a pipe cleaner and solvent, while the percussion drum can be cleaned with a cotton swab. Before reassembling the percussion drum, place a tiny bit of grease or oil in the threads; this will keep it from "freezing."

It is wise to periodically disassemble and clean both percussion guns and flintlocks. (Some flintlock shooters clean their locks after each use. Otherwise, it is felt, the priming powder can get into the lock and interfere with its operation.) After cleaning, lightly oil all parts before reassembling.

Stocks should be periodically wiped with a one-foot square of burlap saturated with pure linseed oil. Be sure to wipe the ramrod as well, and store the burlap in a plastic bag between uses.

Finally, in humid areas, it is advisable to use a heavy gun grease such as RIG rather than oil to insure against rusting.

muzzleloaders, dating of Affixing a date, specific or approximate, to an antique arm is to skill that requires genuine expertise and considerable experience. Not only were few records kept of the manufacture of many black-powder guns, but many of those records that were kept have not survived the years. To complicate matters, the great rarity and subsequent high value of antique arms has prompted a wave of forgeries, many of them quite skillfully done, and detecting such a bogus specimen requires the consultation of an expert.

Should the reader wish to pursue the matter himself, some reference works that are recommended are: *One Hundred Great Guns*, by Merrill Lindsay (Walker & Co., 1967); *The Kentucky Rifle in Its Golden Age*, by Joe Kindig, Jr. (George Shumway, 1960); and *The Plains Rifle*, by Charles E. Hanson (Stackpole, 1960).

It must again be stressed that the only sure means of dating and/or authenticating an antique arm is actual inspection by a recognized expert.

muzzleloaders, match On the American frontier, where the ability to direct a single shot with precision was often literally a life and death matter, accurate muzzleloading arms were developed rapidly. Tests of shooters' skill were popular, the most common being matches such as the turkey shoot, where a small target (sometimes actually the turkey's head) was fired at for a prize.

With the advent of percussion ignition and the development of the slug, or bullet-shaped projectile, accurate arms became more common, and target matches became more formalized. The first muzzleloaders built expressly for competition made their appearance in about 1840 and reached their peak in the 1880s with the emergence of highly sophisticated arms that employed such refinements as Vernier sights, false muzzles, set triggers, and heavy, very precisely made barrels.

Today, with the resurgence of interest in blackpowder shooting, there is considerable interest in match shooting. Informal matches are held, usually of the turkey shoot variety, utilizing standard hunting rifles with no particular refinements. These guns are opensighted and usually of .32 to .40 caliber. On a more formal level are the so-called Free Rifles, which closely resemble the Schuetzen rifles of the turn of the century. These guns, designed for offhand shooting, employ peep sights and retain the elaborate Schuetzen trigger guards. Light and Heavy Bench guns are the equivalent of the modern benchrest rifle. Fired only from solid benchrests, they are equipped with ¼-minute click aperture sights, globe front sights, false muzzles, and, in some cases, sealed ignitions that prevent gas escape and ensure more consistent velocity. The most common bore sizes are .50 to .54, although .60 is not uncommon. Weight limits are 14 pounds for Light Bench guns and 60 pounds for Heavy Bench. (See FALSE MUZZLE; SCHUETZEN RIFLE.)

muzzleloaders, sights for The earliest sight for muzzleloading rifles was a simple bead at the muzzle. By the time the Kentucky rifle evolved (c. 1750) rifle sights had developed into a low silver blade at the muzzle and a rear notch. The extremely long sighting radius of these guns minimized errors in sight alignment, and the fact that these arms were intended for offhand shooting (where the steadiest hold is not possible) and were not used at long range made the crude sights adequate for their intended use.

Muzzleloading handguns and shotguns, because of the extremely short ranges at which they were effective, were either equipped with a crude front sight or no sights at all. (The one exception to this was the dueling pistol, which could be fired with precision and was fitted with both front and rear sights of the blade/bead front and open rear variety.)

As the range and effectiveness of rifles increased, the need for more accurate sights became apparent. These consisted of adjustable open rear sights, finely adjustable rear peep sights, and even crude telescopic sights.

Probably the most popular forms of sighting equipment were a blade or bead front sight, combined with either a "ladder" rear sight adjustable for elevation by means of raised steps in the rail on which it was mounted, or with a Vernier rear sight. This latter was a tang-mounted aperture fitted to a finely threaded stem and could be adjusted for windage by raising or lowering. Most Vernier sights were combined with windage-adjustable front sights that could be moved laterally. (See METALLIC SIGHTS.)

muzzleloaders, stock types While military muskets were made to strict and unvarying patterns, American civilian rifles, most notably the Kentucky or Pennsylvania specimens, developed distinctive styles according to maker and place of origin. The vast majority of these rifles were stocked in curly maple, although plain maple, cherry, walnut, and a very few ash stocks were used. The earlier examples of the Kentucky rifle had thick butts and were rather heavy in overall lines. As the form developed, the stocks became slimmer and more graceful, and distinct styles emerged. Thus, a rifle made in Lancaster County (Pennsylvania) would differ from one made in Bedford or York County. Similar stylistic variations are found in the design of the brass patch boxes that adorn the rifles' stocks.

The form reached its peak in the decade of 1790. Eventually, the classic long rifle evolved into the Plains rifle, which was shorter in overall length, heavier both in caliber and barrel weight, half-, rather than full-stocked, and less ornate. (See KENTUCKY RIFLE.)

muzzleloading barrels The rifle barrels of the 1700s were mostly hand fashioned on a mandrel. This mandrel was then withdrawn, and the barrel was rifled by a broach-type cutter. Many of these old rifles are being shot to this day, and most of them show a high degree of accuracy.

Twist in a muzzleloading rifle barrel is of vital importance, and a number of different twists are used. In a slug gun a 1-in-20 rate of twist or less is common. For a round ball gun, this twist is much too fast; 1-in-48 is a popular twist, much used by custom barrel makers. This twist will use a relatively light load when compared to the slower twists, such as 1-in-56, 1-in-60, 1-in-66, and 1-in-72. With a very slow twist, such as 1-in-72, you can use a much heavier charge of powder, an advantage at long ranges.

Lengths of muzzleloading barrels vary greatly, from 20 inches to 50 inches and more in the big guns. An average offhand .45-caliber full-stocked gun will be anywhere from 38 inches to 44 inches.

Most muzzleloading rifles have octagon barrels, but there are a number of variations—swamped barrels, tapered barrels, round barrels (used on Trade rifles)—with the straight barrel most popular. Except for Muskets, muzzleloading barrels are all browned.

The Heavy Bench Barrels are from .47 to .64 caliber, and more, and weigh in the neighborhood of 40-to-60 pounds. They range in barrel length from 38 to 50 inches and more. These are extremely accurate guns, even when shooting a round ball.

muzzleloading matches At Friendship, Indiana, home of the National Muzzle Loading Rifle Association, a great many matches are held during the spring and fall National Championship Shoots. They include matches for slug guns; muskets; flintlock bench guns; percussion bench guns; both percussion and flint Light Bench or Buffalo guns (14-pound limit); squirrel rifles (.40 caliber, 10-pound limit, open sights); offhand rifles in both flint and percussion (all weights); caplock pistol; flintlock pistol; percussion revolver (25 and 50 yards); and both flint and percussion trap, skeet, and other shotgun matches.

The Primitive matches sometimes require costumes of the 1790–1840 period, or earlier. The guns are mainly flintlocks, although there are some Primitive matches for percussion rifles. All sorts of targets are used, including X-centers, ax blades, playing cards, and skillets. The matches are very colorful, especially the Seneca matches. These are running matches, one for percussion, one for flintlock. Five shots are fired offhand from five stations at various targets from various distances, with a 10-minute time limit on the approximately 300-yard course.

Target distances in muzzleloading matches vary from 25 yards for small offhand guns to 300 yards for slug guns.

muzzleloading pistols The idea of a gun that could be fired with one hand occurred to firearms inventors very early; the first pistols appeared in the early 14th century and were matchlocks. If the long guns of the muzzleloading era were limited in range and accuracy, the pistols were even more so. Thus, they were limited to use as weapons and largely defensive weapons at that.

Muzzleloading pistols took two essential forms: concealment arms, which were made in a variety of small calibers; and the large "horse pistol" designs of major caliber (.60 to .70) that could be readily used as clubs should their user miss.

Some of the smaller handguns were exquisitely made, especially those turned out by the better English, German, and French gunsmiths. Those made for the nobility were highly ornate, and it is doubtful whether they were ever intended for use as weapons.

The muzzleloading pistol reached its peak of development in the form of the dueling pistol. The *code duello*, which heretofore had been practiced with the sword, became the realm of the pistol toward the end of the 18th century, and a specialized kind of gun arose to meet the need for genteel bloodletting. The typical dueler was a percussion arm with a 12-inch barrel, open iron sights, a light, finely tuned trigger, and a caliber of .45 to .50. Duelers were always cased in pairs with cleaning and loading accessories, and the cases themselves are things of beauty.

Muzzleloading pistols had a shorter life than did their long gun counterparts. The appearance of the Colt revolver in 1835 marked the beginning of the end for the muzzleloading pistol. By the beginning of the Civil War, which was fought largely with muzzleloading muskets, the muzzleloading pistol was already an antique, and the percussion revolver was the standard sidearm.

muzzleloading shotguns Before the modern breechloading concept was developed, shotguns were loaded by pouring the powder and shot into the barrel via the muzzle. A wad was used to separate the two and pushed home with a lengthy ramrod. The ignition was provided by either flintlock or percussion ignition.

The earliest muzzleloading shotguns were single-shots, with few exceptions, as the double shotgun did not appear until the mid-16th century. As only the wealthy could afford these arms, the surviving specimens are all of a superior grade.

The single-barrel shotgun, or fowling piece, was one of the most popular. In its various forms, either in flint or percussion, it was used to fire all kinds of projectiles from gravel and small rocks to shot of different sizes at all varieties of game.

The gauges of these early shotguns varied widely,

ranging from 6 gauge or even 4 to .410 with the 10 and 11 gauge being the most used. The guns were simple in nature and were repaired without difficulty.

Many shotguns were made in England and imported to this country. This continued into the late 1800s. Some of these doubles were strictly functional, while others, such as the London "Best" guns, were superbly made.

The greatest number of surviving muzzleloading shotguns are percussion, since many of the earlier flintlocks were converted to this form of ignition. If you are planning to shoot an original muzzleloading shotgun, it is most important that you have it checked for safety by a competent gunsmith. A great many of these old arms have pitted and cracked barrels and are not safe to shoot.

muzzle velocity　The velocity of a projectile as it leaves the muzzle. Muzzle velocity is of prime concern to rifle shooters, who must deal with problems of trajectory over long distances. Knowledge of a gun's muzzle velocity will give an idea of its trajectory and, hence, its useful range, amount of holdover necessary at a given range, etc. (See INSTRUMENTAL VELOCITY.)

myopia　Commonly called nearsightedness, myopia is caused by an eyeball that is too long for the lens of the eye to focus the image cone on the retina. To a shooter, this means the target will be blurred, although items that are very close, such as the receiver of a rifle or shotgun, will be in focus. Myopia is correctable by wearing prescription glasses having concave lenses.

National Bench Rest Shooter's Association The NBRSA was organized in 1954 for the encouragement of extreme accuracy in rifles, ammunition, equipment, and shooting methods. It formed the basis of a program whereby targets, ranges, scoring methods, records, and match procedures would become uniform.

Under NBRSA rules there are five separate classes in which various rifles may be fired: Hunter, Sporter, Light Varmint, Heavy Varmint, and Unlimited. The differences are those of rifle weight, caliber, barrel bedding arrangement, scope magnification, fore-end design, etc. The kind of rest used with the rifle and the targets also differ. All rifles are fired from the sitting position with the aid of a solid table or benchrest.

The shooter, in most classes, does not fire at a particular point on the target for score. Rather, he attempts to fire the smallest group or cluster of shots possible. The Hunter class is the exception to this, however; there the shooter does fire at a bull's-eye target for score.

The NBRSA is headquartered in Akron, Ohio. (See BENCHREST COMPETITION SHOOTING; BENCHREST RIFLE; GROUP MEASUREMENT.)

National Board for the Promotion of Rifle Practice (NBPRP) The National Board for the Promotion of Rifle Practice was established in 1903 by the Dick Act, during the administration of Theodore Roosevelt. Successive congressional legislation in 1905, 1916, and 1918 further defined the structure and duties of the NBPRP.

The various acts of Congress, and the regulations formulated by the War Department in accordance with those acts, established the following:

1. The continued existence of the NBPRP to carry out its program.

2. That the purpose of the NBPRP is to further marksmanship training among the armed forces of the United States, including the National Guard and the organized militia, and among the civilian population.

3. That for purposes of civilian marksmanship training, the War Department is to encourage the organization of civilian rifle clubs. (The Office of the Director of Civilian Marksmanship was established for the purpose of organizing and carrying out the civilian program.)

4. That yearly National Matches be held for members of all branches of the armed services and for civilians. This is to include all requirements of holding the matches, including awards, the issuance of rifles, pistols, and ammunition, a Small Arms Firing School for instruction, and the transport and support during the matches of National Guard and civilian teams from each of the states and territories.

5. Construction, equipment, operation, and maintenance of indoor and outdoor ranges.

6. The loan of rifles and pistols, and the issuance of reasonable quantities of ammunition, targets, and supplies to civilian rifle clubs.

7. The sale to members of the National Rifle Association, at cost to the government, of rifles, pistols, ammunition, components, and supplies.

8. That a club wishing to enroll in the DCM program must hold membership in the NRA.

The number of members on the NBPRP varies from 21 to 32. The members are appointed by the Secretary of the Army.

The founding of the NBPRP and the office of the DCM, and the establishment of the markmanship training program, was a recognition that it takes time to train competent marksmen, that time is not available when war comes, and that men untrained in markmanship are less likely to survive in battle, lessening the effectiveness of the armed forces for their primary purpose. Thousands of civilians have received marksmanship training as a result of NBPRP, DCM, and NRA programs.

Despite the fact that the legislation establishing the NBPRP and the DCM and providing for their continued existence is still in effect, most NBPRP and DCM programs have been virtually eliminated since 1968. In large part, this has been caused by increasing antigun sentiment and the resulting gun control laws of recent years. (See DIRECTOR OF CIVILIAN MARKSMANSHIP [DCM]; NATIONAL RIFLE ASSOCIATION [NRA]; ROOSEVELT, THEODORE.)

National Match ammunition Special match-grade ammunition with superior accuracy characteristics is manufactured by or for the government for use in the National Rifle and Pistol Matches. When such ammunition is especially loaded for National Match use, the cases are headstamped NM; if it is selected for such use from already loaded lots of ammunition, the packing is either relabeled to indicate it is ''For

National Matches,'' or the existing label is stamped "Match Grade."

Currently there are two standard National Match loadings, all loaded to the highest possible standards of accuracy under existing methods of production. These loadings are: Cartridge, Match, Caliber 7.62mm M118; and Cartridge, Ball, Match Grade, Caliber .45 M1911. (See NATIONAL MATCHES.)

National Match Course The National Match Course for high power rifles consists of 50 fired shots, including 10 shots of slow fire at 200 yards from the standing position, 10 shots rapid fire at 200 yards either sitting or kneeling from a standing position, 10 shots rapid fire at 300 yards prone from the standing position, and 20 shots slow fire at 600 yards from the prone position. Time limits are one minute per shot during slow fire, and 50 seconds for a semiautomatic rifle at 200 yards during rapid fire (60 seconds for manual arms), with 60 seconds permitted from the prone position during rapid fire (70 seconds for manual arms).

The pistol section of the National Match Course consists of two strings of five shots per string at 50 yards, with five minutes time allowed per string, plus two strings of five shots each in 20 seconds at 25 yards, and two strings of five shots each in 10 seconds at 25 yards. All timing starts with the command to "Commence firing."

National Matches Annual rifle and handgun matches held each summer since 1907 at Camp Perry, Ohio, under the direction of the National Rifle Association. The course for handguns consists of firing 30 rounds, 10 each of timed fire, rapid fire, and slow fire with a single gun, for a possible score of 300. A full aggregate consists of firing the same three stages with each of three handguns—.22 rimfire, any centerfire caliber, and the .45. (A centerfire handgun is any revolver or autoloader of .32 caliber or greater; many shooters use the .45 autoloader for both the centerfire and the .45 stages.)

The rifle course consists of firing 10 rounds slow fire at 200 yards from the standing position, 10 rounds rapid fire at 200 yards from the standing to kneeling or sitting position, 10 rounds rapid fire at 300 yards from the standing to prone position, and 20 rounds slow fire at 600 yards from the prone position.

Bolt-action rifles used to be the standard service rifle used at the National Matches, but since World War II the military autoloaders—M1, M14, and more recently the M16—have been permitted in rapid-fire matches. If both manual arms and autoloaders are permitted in the same match, the time limits that apply are those for the manually operated rifles, unless otherwise indicated. Time for the slow fire segment is 60 seconds per shot at ranges up to 600 yards, while on the rapid fire the time is 60 seconds for 10 shots at the kneeling or sitting position, and 70 seconds for the prone position; shooters firing autoloaders have the time limit cut 10 seconds in rapid-fire matches. (See NATIONAL MATCH AMMUNITION; NATIONAL MATCH PISTOL; NATIONAL MATCH RIFLE.)

National Match pistol In the Service category of the National Matches, and U.S. military pistol, caliber .45 M1911 or M1911A1, may be used. The same kind and caliber of commercially manufactured pistol is also permitted, but it must be equipped with issue or factory stocks without thumbrests, it must not have a trigger pull of less than 4 pounds, and it must have open sights consisting of a nonadjustable front and an adjustable rear sight, either an open U or a rectangular notch; the sight radius must not exceed 7 inches. The frontstrap of the grip may be checkered, and the mainspring housing may be the flat or arch type. Trigger stops—internal or external—are permitted, as are trigger shoes. No other external or internal alterations are permitted, except that internal parts may be specially fitted to improve functioning and accuracy, provided such fitting does not impair the operational safety of the pistol.

There are three non-Service categories. For the .45-caliber semiautomatic pistol match, any .45-caliber semiautomatic may be used, provided the trigger pull is not less than 3½ pounds, the sight radius does not exceed 10 inches, and all safety features function properly. Any sights may be used, including telescopic.

For the "Any Centerfire" matches, the pistol or revolver must be of .32 caliber or larger, with a barrel length, including the cylinder if a revolver, not exceeding 10 inches. The sights may be of any kind, including telescopic, but the radius must not exceed 10 inches nor the trigger pull be less than 2½ pounds (3½ pounds on the .45-caliber semiautomatic). All safety features must function properly. Many shooters use the .45 caliber for both categories.

The same basic rules apply to the .22-caliber pistol or revolver category, including barrel length, sight radius, and sights, but the handgun must be chambered for a .22-caliber rimfire cartridge no longer than the standard Long Rifle cartridge, and the trigger pull must not be less than 2 pounds. (See NATIONAL MATCH AMMUNITION; NATIONAL MATCHES.)

National Match rifle Currently three rifles are sanctioned for use in the National Matches under the Service category. These are the U.S. Rifle, Caliber .30 M1; U.S. Rifle, Caliber 7.62mm M14; and the

U.S. Rifle, Caliber 5.56mm M16 series, as issued by the U.S. armed forces; or the same kinds and calibers of commercially manufactured rifle, having a trigger pull of not less than 4½ pounds, and the rifle must be incapable of automatic fire without changing parts. The gas systems must be fully operational, although special bedding of the action and barrel are permitted, provided such bedding does not interfere with the safe operation of the rifle.

Sights must be of military issue design, but may vary in dimensions. (Front and rear sights on the M16 must be as issued.) On the M14 and M16 rifles, the 20-round box magazine (or 30 round on the M16) must be attached during all courses of fire and in all positions. On the M14, the hinged buttplate must be used only in the folded position. (See NATIONAL MATCH AMMUNITION; NATIONAL MATCHES.)

National Muzzle Loading Rifle Association (NMLRA) Founded in 1933, the NMLRA is the parent club for many smaller clubs throughout the United States and abroad. Originally headquartered at Portsmouth, Ohio, the organization was later moved to Friendship, Indiana, where it is presently located.

The purpose of the NMLRA is to promote safety and proficiency with muzzleloading arms, to support the use of these guns in target matches and in hunting, and to act as the sanctioning body for muzzleloading matches. It has a membership of 26,000.

The NMLRA sponsors two major shoots each year at Friendship. The first is the National Spring Championship Matches, which draws about 2,000 registered shooters, and the second is the National Fall Championship Matches, which lists about 1,000 competitors.

The NMLRA offers yearly, multiyear, or life memberships and publishes *Muzzle Blasts,* a monthly magazine.

National Rifle Association (NRA) The National Rifle Association of America was incorporated in New York City on November 17, 1871. Its founders were almost all men who had served as officers in the Civil War. Their fundamental purpose in founding the NRA was to promote marksmanship training in all branches of the armed services and among civilians.

The NRA bylaws, as amended October 28, 1978, state the purpose and objectives of the organization as follows:

1. To protect and defend the Constitution of the United States, especially with reference to the inalienable right of the American citizen guaranteed by such Constitution to acquire, possess, transport, carry, transfer ownership of, and enjoy the right to use

One of the prime functions of the NRA is the sponsorship of shooting programs in summer camps and schools.

arms, in order that the people may always be in a position to exercise their legitimate individual rights of self-preservation and defense of family, person, and property, as well as to serve effectively in the appropriate militia for the common defense of the Republic and the individual liberty of its citizens;

2. To promote public safety, law and order, and the national defense;

3. To train members of the law enforcement agencies, the armed forces, the militia, and people of good repute in marksmanship and in the safe handling and efficient use of small arms;

4. To foster and promote the shooting sports, including the advancement of amateur competitions in marksmanship at the local, state, regional, national, and international levels;

5. To promote hunter safety, and to promote and defend hunting as a shooting sport and as a viable and necessary method of fostering the propagation, growth, conservation, and wise use of our renewable wildlife resources.

After the incorporation of the NRA in 1871, the first objective of its leadership was to establish a rifle range on which its program could be carried out. The first range, at Creed's Farm, on Long Island, was purchased and built partly with funds furnished by an act of the state legislature, partly from NRA funds, and partly by donations from business interests in the area. The range, called Creedmoor, had 20 targets usable from 200 to 1,000 yards. The first shot was fired on it April 25, 1873, and the first official match was held in June of that year. Creedmoor was the scene of the first international rifle match held in America, on September 26, 1874, with the American team the winner. The Great Centennial Rifle Match, forerunner of the Palma Matches, was first held there in 1876.

Creedmoor was at its peak in the late 1870s, but the NRA was still largely a state organization, led by New Yorkers with a military background, and both Creedmoor and the NRA were dependent on the National Guard of New York and on the financial support of the state. Political changes in the state and personnel and policy changes in National Guard resulted in the loss of state support, and Creedmoor was deeded to the state in 1890. The NRA Board of Directors met in June of 1892, the last formal meeting of that century, voting to place the organization's records in storage and to ask the New Jersey State Rifle Association if NRA matches could be transferred to that organization's range at Sea Girt. With the transfer, the New Jersey organization assumed, in effect, the functions of the NRA.

Shooting at Sea Girt was broadened to include revolver and Schuetzen matches, and by 1900 it had assumed the status of a national match site. Inspired by the editorials of A. C. Gould, publisher of *Shooting and Fishing*, Lieutenant Albert S. Jones, secretary of the New Jersey State Rifle Association, began a campaign for a new national rifle association. The resulting meetings in the fall of 1900 brought about the rebirth of the NRA and culminated in its establishment as a true national organization. NRA headquarters were in Passaic, New Jersey, for a short period, returned to New York City in 1907, and then moved to Washington, D.C., where the NRA is headquartered today, in 1908.

Of major importance to the NRA was the founding of the National Board for the Promotion of Rifle Practice in 1903. With this, and with the federal legislation enacted in 1916 and 1918, the NRA undertook the responsibilities of the leadership of marksmanship training in America. The programs of the National Board for the Promotion of Rifle Practice and the Director of Civilian Marksmanship, carried out largely by the NRA, have trained millions of Americans in marksmanship. The NRA was also instrumental in developing and establishing hunter safety programs, now required by the majority of states as a prerequisite to obtaining a hunting license.

In its early years, the NRA had no official journal. The organization acquired the rights to *Arms and the Man* (formerly *Shooting and Fishing*) in July,

1916, and this became its first official publication. The name was changed to *The American Rifleman* in June 1923. The NRA has published hundreds of different pamphlets, booklets, and instructional manuals on subjects related to firearms and shooting. *The American Hunter* was started in October, 1973, to meet the interests of sportsmen more involved with hunting than with the target shooting sports covered by the *Rifleman*. To obtain better coverage of tournament activities once covered in the *Rifleman*, the NRA has for some years published a monthly, first called *Tournament News*, now called *Shooting Sports USA*.

One of the concepts of the founders of the NRA was that it should be a major duty of the organization to promote target shooting on a national scale, to establish courses of fire, rules covering the conduct of matches and the equipment permitted, standardize targets and ranges, keep records of scores, and all other matters related to this activity. Originally, this was confined almost entirely to the field of military rifle shooting. In the early 1900s this was expanded to include pistol and revolver shooting, mostly from the military standpoint. (The U.S. Revolver Association, formed in 1899, was already active in civilian revolver and pistol shooting.) With the advent of the .22 rimfire rifle for target shooting, particularly in its field of use as a training rifle in preparation for military high power shooting, this also became a field of interest for the NRA. The first International match with the .22 was the Dewar, fired in 1909, with Great Britain, the United States, and Australia competing. The first national smallbore match in America was fired at Camp Perry, Ohio, in 1920. (Camp Perry, built on the shores of Lake Erie as a National Guard range and encampment, became the scene of the National Matches in 1907 and, with the exception of a few years, the National Matches have been held there since then.) In high power shooting, the NRA was an inseparable part of the National Matches, conducted by the War or Defense Department, through the National Board for the Promotion of Rifle Practice from 1903 until 1968. Since 1968, the NRA has carried on the National Matches with its own funds and with volunteers, although participation by the armed services in the competitions has greatly declined. As the official governing body for the shooting sports in America, the NRA is in charge of all programs in the shooting sports in the International competitions. These include the Olympics, the World Championships, the Pan American Games, and the Championship of the Americas. The interests and participation of the NRA now reaches into all of the different kinds of the shooting sports, fired with any kind of rifle, pistol, or shotgun. News of these events is carried in its periodicals, and it maintains close ties with other national shooting organizations, such as the National Muzzle Loading Rifle Association.

To much of the general public, the NRA is best known today for its stand on the right to keep and bear arms, and for its legislative activities in this field. The original charter and bylaws make no reference to this. But with the increase in public disarmament proposals, the NRA inevitably found itself involved, and formed its Legislative Division in 1934. NRA officials gave testimony and helped shape the National Firearms Act of 1934 and the Federal Firearms Act of 1938. In 1975, after a decade of increased gun control activity, the NRA Board of Directors established a separate division in the NRA, the Institute for Legislative Action (ILA), solely responsible for administering the legislative, legal, informational, and fund-raising activities of the NRA relating to the defense or promotion of the right to keep and bear arms. Since then it has grown to a force of nearly 50 people, including four registered lobbyists. It is supported financially by contributions of the gun-owning public and is involved with federal, state, and local legislation.

At its headquarters building, completed in the mid-1960s, the NRA maintains a firearms museum, displaying about 1,000 firearms of all kinds, starting with examples of the hand cannon of the 1300s and extending to the latest arms of the 20th century. It now covers virtually the complete history of firearms, and almost every major American and European manufacturer of sporting arms is represented.

In 1971, NRA directors, worried about the loss of rifle ranges, the curtailment of the programs of the NBPRP, and the difficulty of obtaining firm, long-term commitments for the use of the National Guard range at Camp Perry, Ohio, voted in favor of a proposal to look for land suitable for a national shooting center. This resulted in the purchase of about 33,000 acres of land near Raton, New Mexico, in 1973, now named the NRA Whittington Center. Ranges are under construction, and the National Metallic Silhouette Championships have already been held there, as well as numbers of state and local matches and muzzleloading events of the Primitive and Rendezvous types.

Today, membership of the NRA numbers nearly 3,000,000. (See AMERICAN RIFLEMAN, THE; DIRECTOR OF CIVILIAN MARKSMANSHIP [DCM]; NATIONAL BOARD FOR THE PROMOTION OF RIFLE PRACTICE [NBPRP]; NATIONAL MATCHES.)

National Shooting Sports Foundation (NSSF) Chartered in 1961, the NSSF consists of approximately 110 member companies connected with the shooting sports. It is a private nonprofit organization whose function is the education of both shooters and the nonshooting public in the role that these sports play, and in furthering shooter safety and proficiency. The NSSF distributes a variety of booklets, brochures, and films, sponsors shooting leadership courses in colleges and universities, and sponsors National Hunting and Fishing Day, an annual event designed to introduce new participants to the shooting sports. The NSSF is located in Riverside, Connecticut.

National Skeet Shooting Association (NSSA) Subsequent to its development in the 1920s, skeet shooting grew steadily in popularity, until the need for a governing body to regulate the sport became apparent. This body, the NSSA, was formed in 1935, and the first national championship held under its auspices took place in Cleveland, Ohio, in August of that year. The NSSA continued in operation until 1942, when World War II temporarily eliminated skeet shooting as a sport.

In 1946, the NSSA reorganized and was incorporated in December of that year. Originally headquartered in Washington, D.C., after its reformation, the NSSA moved to Dallas, Texas in 1952, and to San Antonio, Texas in 1973.

Today, the organization lists approximately 20,000 members and is the governing body for all organized skeet shooting in America. The National Championship, highlight of the competitive year, is held at the National Gun Club in San Antonio. (See SKEET SHOOTING.)

nearsightedness See MYOPIA.

neck expansion The process of expanding the neck of a cartridge case, after it has been resized, so that the inside diameter will be of the correct size to receive and hold the bullet in reloading. The expan-

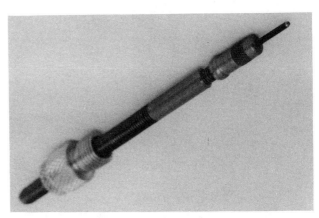

Actual expansion of the case neck is performed by the bulge in the decapping stem that is just above the knurled section. It is sometimes referred to as the expander button.

sion is accomplished by pushing or pulling a steel plug of the correct diameter through the neck of the case. (See CASE RESIZING.)

neck resizing The process of reducing the diameter of the neck of a cartridge case by forcing it into a die of appropriate diameter. The purpose of neck resizing is to reduce the inside diameter of the case neck sufficiently to hold a bullet securely when it is reloaded.

The term is sometimes used in contradistinction to full-length resizing, in which not only the neck but also the case body are reduced approximately to the dimensions that they had before being expanded by firing. (See CASE RESIZING.)

neck turning The process of reducing the wall thickness of a cartridge case neck by removing metal from the surface. Outside turning is usually accomplished by means of a small tool having a mandrel that fits inside the case neck, and a cutter on the outside that operates in the same manner as a tool-bit in a lathe. Inside turning, as usually accomplished, is not truly turning in the technical sense, but rather reaming or boring.

Neck reaming or turning is sometimes required to thin the case neck to acceptable dimensions for the chamber, but more often is done to improve the uniformity of wall thickness around the neck, thus

Rifle case necks are seldom of uniform thickness, a factor that is of little importance to the hunter, but that may be critical to the benchrest competitor. This device is twisted around the neck and shaves off brass until it is all of the same thickness.

improving the concentricity of the bullet with the reloaded cartridge case. (See CASE RESIZING.)

needle gun One of the significant developments in the evolution of firearms in the 19th century. Invented by the Prussian designer Johann Nikolaus von Dreyse in 1829, the needle gun featured the idea of a turn-bolt action as well as a revolutionary ignition system. It was the forerunner of the modern bolt-action rifle.

In a needle gun, the priming compound was affixed to the base of the bullet. The gun's long needle-like firing pin pierced the paper envelope containing the powder charge, penetrated the powder, and then hit the priming compound, which exploded and set off the main charge. The bullet, in other words, was used as an anvil on which to detonate the primer.

Because it was a breechloader and had a relatively fast operating time, the needle gun was far superior to the ordinary arms of its day. It was superseded by arms with true internal ignition, but continued to be produced until 1889. (See DREYSE, JOHANN NIKOLAUS VON; IGNITION.)

negative checkering See IMPRESSED CHECKERING.

New Orleans Arms (company) See MCKENZIE, LYNTON.

Newton Arms Company The Newton Arms Company was organized by Charles Newton in Buffalo, New York in 1914. The rifles he produced were among the first true American high-velocity sporters

Neck resizing is most commonly used on shells to be fired in varmint and benchrest rifles where ease of chambering is not important, but precise fit of case to chamber is. Here, the neck has been resized, but the case remains in as-fired condition.

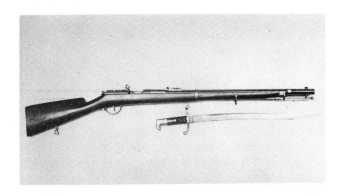

The Prussian Needle Gun, Model of 1871, was the fore-runner of the modern bolt action. An effective arm, it had a telling effect in the Franco-Prussian War. The needle of the Model 1871 pierced the base of the cartridge and detonated a priming compound located in the front of the powder charge. The drawback to the system was the fragility of the needle, compounded by the fact that it became corroded and weakened by repeated firing.

and were far ahead of their time. Between the date the company was organized, and the production date of the first rifles (1917), Newton purchased German rifles built on the Model 98 Mauser action, and these rifles were apparently the first rifles to bear the Newton name. The start of World War I prevented delivery of all but a very few of these Mauser rifles.

It was not until early 1917 that quantity production of the Newton rifle commenced. After about 2,400 rifles were manufactured, the company went into receivership in April 1918.

In May 1918, Newton established another company, known as the Charles Newton Rifle Corp., but no rifles were ever made by that company. It did eventually lead to the organization of the Buffalo Newton Rifle Company in the spring of 1923, and later that year the operation was moved from Buffalo, New York to New Haven, Connecticut. The rifles made by the Buffalo Newton Arms Co. were of somewhat different design than the original Newton

rifle, and were called Buffalo Newtons. Approximately 1,000 Buffalo Newton rifles were produced by both the Buffalo Newton Rifle Co. and by the Meeker Arms Co., which took control in 1925. Charles Newton was never able to interest anyone in financing another operation to make Newton rifles; he died in 1932.

nickel silver   There is no silver in nickel silver, or German silver as it is sometimes called, although it does have the appearance of silver. Often used for decoration on the stocks of muzzleloading rifles and shotguns, nickel silver is an alloy of approximately 55 percent copper, 25 percent zinc, and 20 percent nickel, depending upon the manufacturer.

night glasses   The amount of light entering the eye is dependent upon the dilated size of the pupil, which government tests have determined to be a maximum of 7.1mm in almost total darkness. Thus, the eye cannot admit any more light than can pass through a pupil measuring 7.1mm in diameter. Binoculars classed as "night glasses" are generally of the 7×50mm size, having an exit pupil of 7.1mm and a relative brightness of 50.4mm. Such an instrument is designed for use in darkness, and the 7.1mm exit pupil will provide all the light the eye can use at night. (See EXIT PUPIL; RELATIVE BRIGHTNESS.)

Nilo Shotshell Effectiveness Test   During the fall and winter of 1972–73, Winchester-Western ran a series of tests at Nilo Farms in Illinois to examine the relative killing efficiencies of lead, copper, and steel shot pellets on mallards at ranges of between 30 and 80 yards. These tests came about as a result of a 1965 report compiled by the Mississippi Flyway Council, which in effect stated it was time to discontinue the use of lead shot on waterfowl, and a 1968 test by the Fish and Wildlife Service that concluded, "The performance of soft iron [steel] shot was close to that obtained with lead loads" between 30 and 65 yards.

The Nilo tests showed that at 30 yards, all three metals were quite similar in effectiveness, but at 40 yards lead's superiority over steel began to show. (Copper was more effective than steel beyond 30 yards, but was found in later tests to be toxic, and thus was eliminated as a possible lead substitute.) When the tests were completed and the data analyzed, the conclusion was that at 40 yards and less, a steel shot load can be a good duck load. But to shoot at ducks—and especially geese—beyond that yardage is going to significantly increase waterfowl crippling losses. The results of this test are now questioned by many in the field. Experience with steel loads has improved our knowledge. (See PA-TUXENT TEST.)

nipple A cone-shaped device that is the seat on which a percussion cap is placed and detonated by the hammer of a muzzleloading arm. The nipple is bored completely through, usually narrow in the middle and wider at both ends, to permit passage of the cap flame to the powder charge in the barrel. It is manufactured in several sizes and generally threaded so that it can be screwed into the bolster or barrel breech of a rifle or shotgun or into the cylinder of a revolver. A nipple is occasionally referred to as a cone, but that use is archaic. (See PERCUSSION IGNITION.)

nipple charger In normal use of a percussion firearm, the nipple is not charged with powder, but in the event of a misfire this may be necessary. A small brass cylinder and piston device, called a nipple charger, is filled with FFFF black powder, which is then forced into the nipple. With a fresh cap, and the additional powder in the nipple, enough force

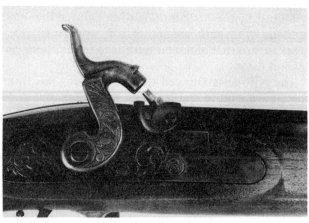

The nipple of a percussion arm serves as the anvil on which the primer is detonated and as the flash hole through which the primer flame passes. Nipples are replaceable, since in time they will become corroded and fouled.

is normally generated to cause ignition of the powder charge in the barrel. (See MISFIRE; NIPPLE; PERCUSSION IGNITION.)

nipple wrench The nipples on percussion muzzle-loading arms eventually become rusted, corroded, and battered to the point where they must be replaced. A special socket-type wrench of hardened steel, often with a T-shaped handle, is slipped over the nipple and turned to remove it and is also used to reseat the new nipple. Nipple wrenches come in three sizes—handgun, rifle, and musket. (See NIPPLE.)

nitrocellulose The principal ingredient of practically all smokeless propellant powders. It is a chemical compound produced by the action of nitric and sulfuric acids on cellulose, which is a vegetable fiber found in cotton, wood, and many other plants. Cotton and wood are the principal raw materials used in the manufacture of nitrocellulose for propellant powders. The nitrogen content of nitrocellulose may vary from about 8 to 14 percent, and the chemical energy that can be derived from the nitrocellulose upon burning depends upon the nitrogen content. A typical nitrocellulose for powder manufacture might contain about 13.15 percent nitrogen and have a potential energy content of about 1.55 million foot-pounds per pound. Although nitrocellulose can be detonated by a sufficiently powerful initiator, it is not a very useful high explosive. When ignited by a primer in a cartridge, nitrocellulose burns rather than detonating.

nitro express "Nitro" is a term referring to smokeless powders that contain nitrocellulose and, sometimes, nitroglycerine. "Express" is a term formerly used to describe a black-powder cartridge having unusually high velocity. The term "nitro express" therefore refers to a cartridge, loaded with smokeless powder, that develops unusually high velocity for a cartridge of its particular kind.

nitro solvent A liquid used in cleaning guns, so named because it was once thought to be especially effective in removing the residue left in the bore by firing smokeless ("nitro") powder.

In the early days of smokeless-powder ammunition, gun bores were found to be much more susceptible to rusting than they had been when black powder was used, and this was widely attributed to some residue of the smokeless powder. Nitro solvents were therefore much in demand. It was found subsequently that the rusting was largely attributable to the corrosive residue of the primers then in common use, and that smokeless powder itself leaves very little residue in the bore. Nevertheless, nitro solvent is useful in removing the residue left in the bore by modern primer compositions, bullet metal, and some additives used in smokeless powders, so its popularity has continued, notwithstanding that its name is based on a misunderstanding of its function. (See GUN CARE.)

Nobel, Alfred B. (1833–1896) A Swedish engineer and chemist who invented dynamite and the first smokeless powder, Nobel was born in Stockholm but reared in Russia. In 1862 he began to experiment with nitroglycerin (invented 16 years earlier) and gunpowder to make blasting caps. Liquid nitro was so extremely brisant, however, that his Swedish factory was rocked by frequent explosions, one of which killed his brother. In 1867, through the accidental escape of some nitro into the siliceous sand packing around it, Nobel discovered how to tame the substance by adding an inert filler—*kiesel guhr*—and produced dynamite. In 1887, he developed the first smokeless powder by combining guncotton (nitrocellulose) with an equal portion of nitroglycerin. Nobel also took out a patent on Cordite, but lost it through a lawsuit.

Realizing the military uses of his inventions, Nobel became interested in peace preservation and, as a consequence, established the first of his Nobel prizes.

Nock, Henry See PATENT BREECH.

node of vibration Vibrating objects, such as a rifle barrel just after the cartridge is fired, produce standing wave patterns or vibrations according to certain laws of physics. The maximum distance the wave pattern vibrates away from the normal stationary position of the barrel is the maximum amplitude, while the point where the wave pattern returns to the stationary position of the barrel is the node. Thus, the node of vibration is a point at which the barrel is always at rest or is not vibrating.

Locating nodes of vibration is of great concern to riflemakers, since, if a barrel is to be firmly bedded in a stock fore-end, it should be bedded at those points where the nodes occur.

nonselective trigger A single trigger that permits the firing of both barrels of an over/under or side-by-side shotgun, but only in a set sequence. On shotguns having two different chokes, the more openly choked barrel is always fired first. (See DOUBLE TRIGGERS; SINGLE SELECTIVE TRIGGER.)

Norma (company) Norma Projektilfabrik was founded in Oslo, Norway, in 1895, by Johan Enger, an editor, competitive shooter, and industrialist. A second factory was established in Amotfors, Sweden, in 1902, and a third (which was started in conjunction with the gunmaking firm of Schultz & Larsen) began operation in Otterup, Denmark, in 1911.

Norma is a major manufacturer of ammunition and handloading components. It is noted for the development of the .308 Norma Magnum and .358 Norma Magnum cartridges, as well as for its manufacture of metric cartridges such as the 6.5mm Japanese, the 7.7mm Japanese, and 6.5mm Mannlicher-Schoenauer. The company's rifle powders were once valued by handloaders, especially its slowest burning propellants, N-205 and MRP, which give especially good results in magnum cartridges, but are no longer available.

Norma is represented in the United States by Federal Cartridge Corp. (See SCHULTZ & LARSEN.)

North-South Skirmish Association A club, founded in 1950 and headquartered in Omaha, Nebraska, that sponsors authentic re-enactments of Civil War battles, as well as many shooting contests. The skirmishes are held at Fort Shenandoah, Virginia.

The guns used in the contests are mostly .58-caliber Remington-Zouaves or Springfield types. The ammunition for these percussion muskets is sometimes a Minié ball, sometimes a .575 pure lead round, and sometimes a wadcutter. Civil War period revolver and artillery contests are also held.

nose cap A metal cap, made of iron, brass or German silver, that is located on the fore-end of a muzzleloading rifle. It is decorative and protects the end of the stock. The forearms of some lever-action rifles such as the Marlin models 336 and 39A terminate with a steel nose cap.

Noske scope Advertised as "field telescopes" during the 1930s, the riflescopes by R. Noske of San Carlos, California, were the first such scopes to have internal adjustments for windage and elevation. Featuring ⅞-inch diameter tubes, a wide field of vision and long eye reliefs—up to 6 inches—the Noske scopes were available in two magnifications, 2¼X and 4X. (In the 1940s, a 2½X scope was introduced.) Costing nearly twice as much as the Weaver scopes later available, the Noske scopes weighed 9½ ounces or less and were considered to be the equal of the German Zeiss scopes. The line was discontinued in the early 1950s. (See TELESCOPIC SIGHTS.)

Nosler Bullets, Inc. The Nosler Partition Bullet, widely regarded as the premier hunting bullet presently available, was developed by John A. Nosler in 1947. Nosler, a hunter and handloader, sought a kind of bullet construction that would allow both reliable expansion and deep penetration at all practical ranges. His solution was a "dual core" bullet, in which two lead cores were separated by a heavy partition. The front core would expand, but the rear one, protected by the partition, would remain intact, retaining much of the bullet's weight and, therefore, penetrate deeply.

By 1948, Nosler could no longer continue making bullets as a hobby and began selling them under the name of Nosler Partition Bullet Co. The original line included only .30-caliber projectiles, but was almost immediately expanded to include bullets in .25, .270, and 7mm. By 1952, the line encompassed all popular calibers, up to and including .375.

In 1967, Nosler added a solid-base single-core bullet to the company's line; it was marketed under the name Zipedo. These were eventually discontinued, but in 1975, the firm introduced an improved bullet of the same type, which is designated Solid Base.

In 1969, Nosler affiliated with Leupold & Stevens, Inc.; but the two parted company in 1989. In 1972, the company introduced a newly designed partition bullet, which it claims, delivers both superior accuracy and performance on game. The company is located in Bend, Oregon. (See LEUPOLD & STEVENS, INC.)

no target　Sometimes called a "no bird," the term "no target" means a clay pigeon that comes out of the trap in pieces, or in an illegal flight line. If the shooter does not fire at one of these targets, he is permitted to call for another target as a replacement.

novelty matches　During the days of the Colonists and up through the times of the Mountain Men, a number of unusual competitions were developed, and these are still engaged in at muzzleloading matches today.

Novelty matches involve such oddities as snuffing out a candle in the dark; shooting a pipe out of a dummy's mouth; splitting a rifle ball on the edge of an axe so that the halves break a target on either side of the blade. Such events are fired from the offhand position, and usually at 25 yards.

Nydar sight　A shotgun sight manufactured by Swain Nelson Industries of Glenview, Illinois, the Nydar sight was based on the aircraft gunsights used in World War II. It was a tube mounted on a shotgun by drilling and tapping two holes, and after installation it could be adjusted for windage and elevation so that the center dot of the sight would coincide with the center of the shot pattern at the distance desired. In use, the shooter looking through the reflector plate of the Nydar sight saw a ring with the center dot projected in space in the vicinity of the pattern area.

Oakley, Annie (1860–1926) Born Phoebe Ann Mosee near Greensville, Ohio, she became one of the best known figures in the annals of superlative marksmanship. By the time she was 15, Phoebe, using a long cap-and-ball Kentucky rifle that had belonged to her father, was selling game to the general store in Greensville, and later to a hotel in Cincinnatti. It was through the manager of that hotel that her shooting skill first came to public notice. Matched against an itinerant exhibition shooter, Frank Butler, and using the old cap-and-ball rifle, Phoebe scored 50 hits on 50 trap-thrown targets. She won $50, and she and Butler were married in June 1876. They became a popular team of exhibition shooters, and Phoebe assumed the stage name of "Annie Oakley."

The team of Butler and Oakley shot with stock and vaudeville companies, with the Four-Paw and Sells Brothers Circus, and with the Buffalo Bill Cody Wild West Shows, in such skilled company as Buffalo Bill, Pawnee Bill Lillie, and Sitting Bull, who adopted Annie as his daughter and called her "Little Sure Shot." One of Annie's stunts was to shoot bullet holes into customers' tickets, making them take-home souvenirs; and because complimentary tickets had holes punched into them for identification, free tickets to any show became known as "Annie Oakleys."

Annie continued with the Wild West Shows in their travels in Europe, thus becoming internationally famous. Both as a performer and as a teacher of shooting, she retained much of her skill, even when forced to shoot from a wheelchair, until her death in 1926.

objective lens In an optical instrument, such as a riflescope, there are two basic lens assemblies readily visible to the observer—the ocular lens, which is closest to the eye, and the objective lens, which is the assembly furthest from the eye and closest to the muzzle of the rifle. The objective lens forms the first image of the object being viewed. (See TELESCOPIC SIGHTS.)

obturation The sealing of, or obturation, of the breech of a gun from the gases produced during firing is normally accomplished by the use of a brass cartridge case, or plastic or paper shotshell casing. In some modern replicas of breechloading percussion arms, small brass or aluminum chamber seals are used, since commercially loaded cartridges for such arms are not available.

O'Connor, Jack (1902–1978) Widely regarded as America's foremost writer on guns and hunting, John Woolf O'Connor was born in Nogales in what later became the state of Arizona. He was educated at the University of Arizona and at the University of Arkansas, from which he graduated in 1925. He earned a master's degree in journalism from the University of Missouri in 1927.

O'Connor began his career as a teacher of journalism and wrote about his hobby to supplement his income. He became a successful novelist and, in 1941, was selected as gun editor of *Outdoor Life* magazine, a position he was to hold for 31 years. Shortly after leaving *Outdoor Life* in 1972, O'Connor became executive editor of *Petersen's Hunting* magazine. In the course of his career, O'Connor wrote 15 books on hunting and firearms, the most noted of which was *The Rifle Book*, published in 1949 by Knopf and revised and expanded in 1964 and 1977.

Although O'Connor hunted on four continents and collected all the significant trophy species, it was as a hunter of the North American wild sheep that he

Jack O'Connor began as a professor of journalism, novelist, and screenwriter but found his greatest fame as shooting editor of Outdoor Life *magazine.*

was most noted. He was the fifth man to achieve a grand slam of sheep—desert bighorn, bighorn, stone, and Dall rams.

From 1948 until his death, O'Connor lived in Lewiston, Idaho. (See OUTDOOR LIFE.)

ocular lens The rearmost lens in an optical system, i.e., the lens closest to the eye. The ocular lens can consist of one or several elements. (See EYEPIECE.)

offhand shooting This term, applied to rifle and handgun shooting, denotes firing from a standing position without support for the gun, other than the shooter's body. In rifle shooting, a sling is often used to lend steadiness.

offset mount This kind of scope mount, which is affixed to the side of the rifle receiver, is intended for use on rifles where upward ejection of fired cases prevents mounting the scope on top of the receiver. (see SCOPE MOUNTS.)

offset sights Sights that are offset, generally to the left of the gun barrel, to permit use of the master eye or sighting when shooting from the opposite shoulder, or made necessary by use of a top mounted magazine, as in the case of some submachine and machine gun designs. (See MASTER EYE.)

ogive Bullets normally have a curved, rounded, or pointed nose section forward of the main bearing surface; this is called the ogive regardless of the shape. Wadcutter, truncated cone, and Keith-type bullets have flat or straight tapered nose sections and are not considered to have an ogive as such.

oil dent In the process of resizing a metallic cartridge case for reloading, a lubricant is used to reduce friction. If excessive lubrication is used and some of the lubricant is trapped between the die and the case, pressure will force the case to flow around the incompressible lubricant, producing an oil dent in the shoulder or case wall. (See CASE RESIZING.)

Olin (company) See WINCHESTER (COMPANY).

Olympic Games Shooting Events The quadrennial Olympic shooting events are governed by the International Shooting Union, and International rules are followed. The National Rifle Association has been sanctioned to govern International shooting in the United States.

All Olympic events are fired with metallic sights except the running boar (running game) event, and all measurements are metric. The events include the following:

Free pistol. As the name implies, there are few restrictions on the firearm, but it must be a .22. The event is fired at 50 meters at a bull's-eye target with a 5.08cm 10-point ring. Sixty shots are fired within 2½ hours.

Centerfire Pistol. Pistols or revolvers of 7.62mm to 9.65mm are used in the 25-meter competition. Six five-shot groups are fired at a bull's-eye/silhouette target. There are two stages in this event, Precision and Duel. In the Precision phase, 6 minutes are allotted for each five shots. In the duel portion, the target is faced toward the shooter for 3 seconds and then away for 7 seconds. This continues until all shots are fired.

Ladies' Smallbore Pistol. Fired under the same rules as the open centerfire match, except that the women and junior shooters must use .22-caliber pistols.

Standard Pistol. A .22 competition conducted in slow, timed, and rapid fire.

Rapid-Fire Pistol. A .22 match fired from 25 meters at a bank of five silhouette targets.

Air Pistol. A 10-meter match with an air- or gas powered pistol having a .177 bore.

Air Rifle. An air- or gas powered rifle with .177 bore and weighing not more than 5 kilograms is fired from the standing position at 10 meters.

English Match. A rifle event for .22 Long Rifle and smaller calibers. The rifle cannot exceed 8 kilograms; it is fired from the prone position at 50 meters.

Smallbore Standard Rifle, Prone. For women and juniors only, this event is similar to the English match except that the rifle cannot exceed 5 kilograms.

Smallbore Free Rifle, Three-Position. Fired with a .22 rifle from the standing, kneeling, and prone positions at 50 meters.

Smallbore Standard Rifle, Three-Position. Fired by women and juniors only with standard rifles.

Free Rifle, 300 Meter. Rifles can include palm rests and buttplates but can weigh no more than 8 kilograms, and nothing larger than 8mm is allowed. Fired from three positions.

Big-Bore Standard Rifle. A 300-meter event formerly fired with service rifles. Now, 5-kilogram rifles are used with a 1.5 kilogram minimum trigger pull and no palm rests, thumbhole stocks, etc. It is fired from three positions.

International Skeet. An event similar to American skeet.

Clay Pigeon. A kind of trapshooting competition.

Air Rifle. A 10-meter "running circle" moving at right angles to the shooter.

(See INTERNATIONAL SHOOTING UNION.)

open bolt fire Most firearms fire with the bolt in the forward or closed and/or locked position, depending on a hammer to strike the firing pin for ignition of the cartridge; but some autoloading and automatic arms fire with the bolt in an open or rearward position. In the open bolt design, firing occurs just as the bolt reaches the forward position. Such designs have a separate firing pin, or simply a tip, machined on the face of the bolt, to serve as a firing pin or striker.

Many submachine gun and machine gun designs incorporate this method of firing to prevent cook off of a cartridge in a hot chamber, and several open bolt autoloading rimfire rifle designs have been manufactured, including models by Savage/Stevens and Gevarm. (See COOK OFF; IGNITION.)

open sights   See METALLIC SIGHTS.

operating lever   Sometimes called the finger lever, this part is located behind or as a part of the trigger guard, or it may encircle the trigger guard; it may be enclosed or open, S-shaped or a loop. Movement of the operating lever up and down opens and closes the action.

Examples of lever operated actions included the Winchester Model 94, the various Martini designs, and the Sharps rifles. (See LEVER ACTION.)

operating slide   The bar, rod, or similar structure on a pump-action or gas operated rifle or shotgun, connecting the bolt operating mechanism of the arm to the forearm handle or the gas piston. There may be one such bar, or two, and the nomenclature will vary—action bar assembly, fore-end tube assembly, operating handle bar assembly, slide, or operating rod—but the operation is basically the same.

optical axis   The axis corresponding with the line of vision as it passes through a lens assembly (of a riflescope or binoculars) and the cornea of the eye. This is the axis along which light travels in a straight line, without retraction or bending of the light rays. (See TELESCOPIC SIGHTS.)

optical glass   High-quality glass of crown or flint grade, completely homogeneous, free from strains, bubbles, striae, and seeds, with high refractive and dispersive powers. It is used in binoculars, riflescopes, and prescription shooting glasses.

optical stop   See STOP, OPTICAL.

Outdoor Life   A monthly national magazine devoted to hunting, fishing, and allied subjects. It was founded in 1898 in Denver, Colorado, by John A. McGuire, who was also its first editor. His son, Harry, succeeded as editor in 1929, and the editorial offices were moved to Mt. Morris, Illinois. In 1934, the publication was purchased by Popular Science Publishing Company and the offices were moved to New York City. Present paid circulation is approximately 1,500,000.

Outdoor Life has always been in the forefront of movement for constructive conservation.

outside lubricated bullet   A bullet with lubrication applied to the outer or exposed surface is called outside lubricated. Minié balls and conical bullets used in muzzleloading arms are so lubricated, as are some cast lead bullets used in handloading. Commercially the .22 rimfire cartridges are the best example of cartridges with outside lubricated bullets. The lubricant may be a wax, solid grease, or even Teflon. (See INSIDE LUBRICATED BULLET.)

overall cartridge length   The length of the cartridge case, measured from the base or head to the tip of the bullet inclusive in metallic cartridges, and from the rear to the tip of the unfolded case mouth in shotshells. Generally for metallic cartridges, the overall length is quoted as the maximum length measured to the nearest thousandth of an inch, or the nearest hundredth of a millimeter; any cartridge loaded to a greater length than the maximum quoted will not feed through the magazine of a rifle or pistol and may not chamber in a particular arm. In revolvers, the use of cartridges loaded to greater than the quoted maximum overall length may not permit rotation of the cylinder.

overbore capacity   This term is applied to large capacity cartridges that hold more powder than the bore can handle efficiently. Many wildcat rifle cartridges have been of overbore capacity, and an example of a commercial overbore cartridge is the .300 Weatherby.

The term is often used in a negative sense, since an overbore cartridge recoils more heavily, has more muzzle blast, and causes shorter barrel life than a nonoverbore load. However, comparing the .300 Weatherby to the .30/06, one sees that the Weatherby, using nearly 80 grains of powder, can propel a 180-grain bullet at 3,150 feet per second, while the .30/06 fires the same bullet as 2,700 fps using 60 grains of powder. This is a very large increase in powder for a comparatively small increase in velocity, yet that increase is tremendously effective in increasing muzzle energy and flattening trajectory. Overbore capacity, therefore, is not a condemnation in itself.

overbored barrel   Barrels for American shotguns, rifles, and handguns are supposedly manufactured to industry specifications for a particular caliber or gauge. For example, a .30-caliber barrel should be bored to have an internal diameter of .300 inch, prior to rifling, while a 12-gauge shotgun barrel should have .729-inch internal diameter. Yet some .30-caliber barrels may be bored to have a diameter of .302-inch or more, while some 12-gauge barrels have an internal diameter of .733-inch or larger. Such barrels are considered overbored, or oversized.

Overboring, in the modern connotation, most commonly refers to shotgun barrels that are deliberately bored or reamed oversize in order to improve patterning characteristics.

overboring   An increasingly popular barrel modification among clay target shooters, overboring increases the bore diameter of a shotgun, which reduces recoil and improves patterns. It accomplishes this by reducing the friction applied to the ejecta as it is forced forward by powder gases. A nominal overbore runs 0.010-inch to 0.015-inch, although some experimenters have taken it much further. For example, a standard 12-gauge bore runs about 0.729-inch, and a 0.010-inch overbore would take it to 0.740-inch. However, the 12 gauge has been taken to an overbore of 0.760- to 0.775-inch with excellent results. The reduced friction and the broader base upon which the powder gases can work actually increase the velocity.

Another popular term for overboring these days is "backboring." (See CHAMBERLESS GUN.)

overignition   When coated smokeless powders were originally introduced, the available primers had difficulty igniting them, because the coatings had a slower burning rate than the powder. New primers developed to ignite the coated powders properly were often too hot for uncoated powders, and overignited them, literally causing an explosion rather than rapid burning. Today, with modern primers and powders, overignition is almost unheard of, although some primers may be hotter than necessary for some powders. (See BURNING RATE; IGNITION; SMOKELESS POWDER.)

over-powder wad   Also called the middle wad. Formerly, the over-powder wad (between powder and shot) in a shotgun shell was composed of two or more components to form a wad column. Immediately over the powder was a stiff cardboard wad coated to make it impervious to grease; next was one or more cork or fiber cylinders impregnated with grease. The grease was intended to lubricate the bore and prevent the heavy accumulation of lead and powder fouling and making cleaning easier. The coated card wad prevented grease from reaching and ruining the powder charge.

The total length of the wad column could be adjusted by adding or subtracting greased wads. For instance, a 1-ounce load in a 12-gauge shell required a longer wad column to fill the space inside the shell than a 1¼-ounce load in the same case. Wad seating pressure was important, and handloaders had a great deal of trouble adjusting wad pressures for varying kinds of loads.

Today, these multi-unit over-powder wad columns have been almost completely replaced by single-unit plastic shotcup wads. Because of alterations in smokeless shotgun powder and other components, wad seating pressure is no longer very important, and the new plastic wads are much easier to load into the case. (See SHOT COLLAR; SHOTCUP WAD; WAD PRESSURE.)

over-shot wad   Also called the top wad. It is the circular cardboard wad placed over the shot in a shotgun shell to keep the shot in place within the case. It is used with the roll crimp in which the case wall is turned down all around its circumference on top of the wad to hold it on top of the shot. Overshot wads are seldom used today, since the old-fashioned roll crimp has been largely replaced by the folded pie crimp in which no top wad is needed. (See SHOTSHELL CRIMP.)

overtravel   The distance that a trigger moves rearward after the sear has been released. In rifles, considerable overtravel can adversly affect aim, as the continued movement of the trigger finger can cause the muzzle of the gun to move before the bullet has cleared the barrel. Excessive overtravel is sometimes called "slap" or "backlash." (See ADJUSTABLE TRIGGER; TRIGGER STOP.)

over/under gun   A double-barreled firearm in which one barrel is placed on top of the other. This is in contrast to the traditional double-barrel, in which the barrels are placed side by side. Over/unders are usually shotguns, but they may also be double-barreled rifles, or combination guns in which a shotgun tube is placed on top of a rifle tube or a rifle barrel is superimposed on a shotgun barrel.

The over/under shotgun is currently the most popular double used in trap and skeet competition and is becoming increasingly popular with hunters. Claimed advantages are a more precise single sighting plane than the side-by-side double, and minimal horizontal whip of barrels from recoil. Normally the lower barrel fires first.

Over/under guns are often called under/over guns in Britain. (See COMBINATION GUN; DOUBLE-BARREL SHOTGUN; SHOTGUN.)

Pachmayr Gun Works (company) Frank Pachmayr opened a small gunsmithing shop in downtown Los Angeles, California, in 1929. In the 1930s, Pachmayr brought his younger brother, John, into the company, and together they operated Pachmayr Gun Works to build and sell high-quality firearms.

During World War II, the Pachmayr gun business was kept busy producing military armaments. A second company was formed and was both prime and sub-contractor for millions of aircraft parts. In 1958, the aircraft company was sold, and Pachmayr concentrated on the production of sporting arms. The company also began to market such products as grip adapters, pistol cases, scope mounts, and rubber recoil pads.

Pachmayr is best known for its custom sporting rifles, engraved shotguns, and conversion work on the Model 1911 .45 Colt Automatic. More recently, Pachmayr's nonslip grips for automatic pistols have become very popular. One of the firm's recent projects has been the restoration and reconstruction of old Parker shotguns. Pachmayr has also introduced a flush-mounting sling swivel and offers more than 750 models of rubber recoil pads.

Page, Warren (1910–1977) One of the nation's best known and most respected sportsmen and gun writers, Warren Kempton Page was born in New Bedford, Massachusetts, and was educated at Harvard. He was a secondary school English teacher for 17 years and served in the U.S. Navy during World War II.

In 1947, Page became the shooting editor of *Field & Stream* magazine, a position he held for 24 years until resigning in 1971 to become president of the National Shooting Sports Foundation. He retired in 1976.

As a hunter, Warren Page recorded a list of accomplishments for which he was internationally recognized. He was the first hunter in the modern era to take a western bongo, and his blue glacial bear hunt in Alaska resulted in the first specimen taken since the beginning of this century. Page was awarded the Weatherby Big Game Trophy in 1958, was the first living American named to the Hunting Hall of Fame (1973), and was elected Winchester-Western's Outdoorsman of the Year in 1975.

An accomplished shotgunner and rifleman, Page contributed significantly to the technical knowledge of firearms and ammunition and helped pioneer the

A one-time English teacher and naval officer, Warren Page was shooting editor of Field & Stream *for a quarter of a century.*

introduction of a variety of today's high-velocity cartridges, including the .222 Remington, the .243 Winchester, the 6mm Remington, and the 7mm Remington Magnum.

Page produced more than 450 major articles relating to sporting arms, hunting, ballistics, benchrest shooting, and other shooting subjects. He was also the author of two books, *One Man's Wilderness* (Holt, Rinehart & Winston, 1973), and *The Accurate Rifle* (Winchester Press, 1975). (See FIELD & STREAM; NATIONAL SHOOTING SPORTS FOUNDATION [NSSF].)

Paine sight Consisting of a U-shaped rear notch and round bead front sight mounted on a thin blade, this revolver sight combination was designed and popularized by a famous competition and exhibition shooter of the 1880s, Ira Paine. It has long been obsolete. (See HANDGUN SIGHTS; METALLIC SIGHTS.)

Palma Match In 1876, the National Rifle Association, as a part of the American Centennial celebration, invited many nations to participate in a long-range shooting match for the championship of the world. Among the invitees were England, Ireland, Scotland, France, Germany, Austria, Canada, the

South American countries, and all other countries having rifle clubs or associations. The trophy was a $1,500 full-size replica of a Roman legionary standard, executed in silver, gold, and bronze by Tiffany & Co. and bearing the single word PALMA, the Latin word for palm tree. (The Romans used the palm to signify honor and excellence.)

The Americans won the 1876 match, and the trophy, initially called the Grand Centennial Trophy, soon became known as the Palma Trophy and the match as the Palma Match. It remains one of the most exciting of all International shooting events.

The annual Palma Match is presently open to teams from the United States and the British Commonwealth. The course consists of two sighting shots and 15 shots for record at 800, and 900, and 1,000 yards. The participating countries host the shoot on a rotating basis and provide the ammunition for all shooters. Members of the American team are selected on the basis of their performance at the National Matches.

palm rest Authorized for use in certain International rifle matches, the palm rest is a hand rest attached to the underside of the rifle forearm at approximately the balance point. To steady the rifle, the rest, which can be in the form of a ball, a D-shaped shovel handle, or contoured like a glove, is grasped by the off hand with the elbow wedged against the hip bone of the shooter. It is used primarily in the hip rest position. (See HIP REST; POSITION SHOOTING.)

pan On matchlock, wheel lock, and flintlock guns, a small receptacle for priming powder. It is mounted at the vent, or touch hole, just above the lockplate. The later flintlock guns also had a pan cover. (See FLINTLOCK; PAN COVER.)

Pan American Games Shooting Events The Pan American Games are a series of sports competitions much like the summer Olympic Games except that entrants are restricted to citizens of North and South America.

The first Pan American Games were held in Argentina in 1912. The only shooting match was the three-position International at 300 meters, 40 shots for each position. Rifles were restricted to the service rifles of the competing countries, except that receiver sights were permitted. Minimum trigger pull was 5½ pounds. The United States won.

The Pan American Matches of 1913 were fired at Camp Perry, Ohio, in combination with the Internationals, and included the 300-meter course, long-range matches, and pistol matches. Argentina won the 300-meter team match.

The next Pan American matches were fired in Peru in 1924. Rules remained the same, except that the minimum trigger weight was reduced to 3½ pounds. In addition to the 120-shot 300-meter course, individual and team, there were a variety of individual single-position matches at 300 meters, together with long-range team matches and a revolver match. The United States was the big winner in both team and individual matches.

Over the years, the shooting competitions, rules, and equipment of the Pan American Games have come to closely resemble those of the Olympics. The 300-meter shooting events have been dropped at most meets because of the lack of available ranges for this distance. The most recent Pan American Games in the summer of 1987 included the following events, fired as individual and team competitions: 50-meter Free Rifle Three-Position .22, 50-meter Free Rifle Prone, 10-meter Air Rifle, Women's Standard Rifle Three-Position, Womens' Standard Rifle Prone and 10 meter Air Rifle. Pistol events consisted of 50-meter Free Pistol, 25-meter Rimfire Pistol, Centerfire Pistol, Standard Pistol and 10-meter Air Pistol, Women's Sport Pistol and Women's 10-meter Air Pistol. Shotgunning events consisted of International Trap and International Skeet. In addition, there was a 50-meter Running Target and 10-meter Running Target event.

At present, the Pan American Games are scheduled to be held in the year prior to an Olympics. (See OLYMPIC GAMES SHOOTING EVENTS.)

pan cover On a flintlock gun, the pan cover is situated at the base of the frizzen. When the frizzen is brought to the firing position, this cover fits over the pan to prevent priming powder from falling out or becoming wet. (See FLINTLOCK; FRIZZEN; PAN.)

pantograph See STOCKMAKING.

paper cartridge In order to give greater speed of fire to their troops, armies of the muzzleloading era manufactured paper cartridges. These consisted of a charge of black powder and a ball wrapped in heavy paper tied off at both ends. The paper was usually waxed or greased to make it waterproof. In use, the soldier bit off one end of the paper, dumped the powder into the barrel, then tore the ball from its wrapping and rammed it home.

Paper cartridges were in nearly universal military use until the advent of metallic ammunition. It is claimed that they were responsible for the Sepoy Mutiny in India, when a rumor spread among native soldiers that the cartridges issued by the British *Raj* were greased with pork fat. Biting such a cartridge was a violation of the sepoys' religion.

paper patch bullet Made from high-quality, high-rag-content bond paper, the paper patch was and is used with many of the older black-powder, large caliber rifles, such as the .50 sharps. Cut so that the paper grain is perpendicular to the bullet axis, the wet patch is carefully rolled twice around the lead bullet's bearing surface, leaving a small amount of overlap at the bullet base to permit folding over, or twisting, to protect the base. Such patches are generally shot dry, although some are waxed or otherwise lubricated.

paradox rifling During the period 1870–1910, when big-game hunting in Africa and India enjoyed considerable popularity among British citizens, a system of rifling was employed in double-barrel shotguns that would enable an arm to function both as shotgun and rifle. The invention of Colonel G. B. Fosberry, V.C., it consisted of a 4- to 6-inch section at the muzzle rifled with numerous deep grooves. The remainder of the bore was unrifled. Originally made in 8 and 10 gauges by firms such as Rigby, Jeffrey's, and Purdey, the guns were sold under the trade names Explora, Paradox, and Jungle Gun. They patterned acceptably and fired a heavy, conical lead slug with moderate accuracy at short ranges.

Late in the period, the 8- and 10-gauge models were replaced by 12-gauge guns, and the short, heavy rifling grooves were superseded by "invisible" rifling—very shallow grooves that ran the length of the bore, spun the slugs acceptably, yet did not disrupt shot patterns.

parallax A condition in optical instruments, caused by nonalignment of lenses, that causes the image to appear in other than its true location. In telescopic sights, parallax is usually caused by the reticle not being in proper focus with the objective or erector lens.

The condition is easily seen by resting the scope (or firearm with scope) on a table or bench, with the reticle on a mark, and then moving the eye across the eyepiece to see if the reticle appears to move on the mark. Such movement indicates parallax. It is normally corrected by screwing the objective lens in or out to change the internal focal length—the distance between reticle and objective. With proper adjustment, the reticle will not move on a mark when the viewer moves his eye across the eyepiece. (See EYEPIECE; OBJECTIVE LENS; RETICLE; TELESCOPIC SIGHTS.)

Parker Bros. (company) Established in 1832 as a manufacturer of coffee mills by Charles Parker, the company that was to become famous as a maker of fine shotguns did not produce firearms until the Civil War, when it turned out Springfield muskets for the Union Army. Known during the war as Meriden (Conn.) Mfg. Co., the firm was joined by Wilbur, Charles, and Dexter Parker, sons of the founder, and in 1868 they changed the name to Parker Bros. and devoted the company's production to double-barrel shotguns.

In 1874, Charles A. King moved to Parker Bros. from Smith & Wesson and was to be the guiding force behind the development of the Parker shotgun. From the first, the company established a reputation for excellence; Parker guns were known for simplicity, reliability, and excellent handling qualities.

Over the years, Parker Bros. was a major innovator in shotgun design. Among the developments that Parker introduced were the 28-gauge gun, the ventilated rib, a unique bolting mechanism, and the concept of the luxury single-barrel trap gun. The Parker line was extensive, ranging from the Trojan, a utilitarian model that sold for $60 in 1934, to the A-1 Special, which cost $825. Shooters could select numerous options, such as single triggers, fancy wood, special engraving and checkering patterns, and automatic ejectors. As of 1934, the ascending grades were as follows: Trojan; VH; VHE; G.H.; G.H.E.; D.H. D.H.E.; C.H.E.; B.H.E.; A.H.E.; A.A.H.E.; and A-1 Special.

Increasing costs drove Parker Bros. into financial difficulty, and in 1934, Remington Arms assumed control of the company. Production continued at Meriden until 1937, when the manufacturing facilities were moved to the Remington factory at Ilion, New York. Parkers continued to be made on an extremely small scale through the World War II years, but in 1947, all Parker production ceased.

Today, Parker Bros. shotguns have appreciated greatly in value and are thought of highly both as collectors' pieces and as working guns.

Parker-Hale Ltd. Established in 1880, this company is located in Birmingham, England. It specializes in the manufacture of sights and shooting accessories, although it has produced some sporting rifles in the past, and presently offers the Super 1200 centerfire bolt-action rifle, imported to America by Jana International Co. of Denver, Colorado.

Parkerizing See METAL FINISH.

partition bullet See NOSLER BULLETS, INC.

patch (cleaning) Used in muzzleloading arms for wiping the bore between shots and for final cleaning, patches come in different sizes to accommodate the various calibers. They are usually made of soft flannel and are usually round. (See MUZZLELOADER.)

patch box A receptacle, usually in the buttstock of a muzzleloading long gun, for holding patches, grease, and small tools. It is closed with either a hinged or sliding lid. The metal covering and bordering the patch box is usually silver, brass, or iron; it is often formed into an intricate design and is sometimes engraved. (See MUZZLELOADER.)

patch knife A kind of small knife developed by American frontiersmen for trimming patches for their muzzleloading rifles. The typical patch knife had a 3- or 4-inch blade and a wooden or staghorn handle. These knives were often carried in a sheath sewn to the carrying strap of a hunting bag. (See PATCH [CLEANING].)

patch puller The conventional patch puller looks like a corkscrew and is screwed onto the end of a ramrod or loading rod. It is used to remove cleaning patches lost in the bore of a muzzleloading rifle. Great care should be exercised in inserting and withdrawing the patch puller, as its point is sharp and could scratch the rifling. (See LOADING ROD; MUZZLELOADER; RAMROD.)

patched ball When a round ball is employed in muzzleloading arms, a patch is fitted around the circumference of the ball in order to provide a gas seal and to impart a spinning action to the ball. The patch is lubricated, then seated down the bore onto the powder charge.

The correct fit of a patch/ball combination is of great importance. It should fit snugly enough for the patch to seal off the gas from the breech.

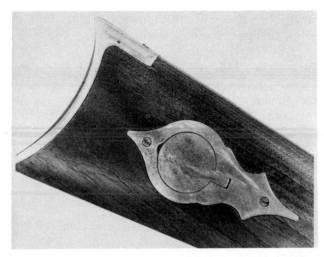

Inletted into the side of the stock and fitted with a flip-up cover, the patch box is a repository for cut patches. This is a plain one of the kind found on Plains rifles; others, such as those used on Kentucky rifles, are quite elaborate.

Match shooters use a very tight patch/ball fit, usually lubricating the patching with Teflon.

This very tight fit should not be used with a light rifle, as it creates pressures that are dangerous in thin walls. (See MUZZLELOADER; PATCHING.)

patching The material used for patched balls in muzzleloading guns comes in various thicknesses, from .005-inch (airplane cloth) for shallow groove rifles, through .010-to-.012-inch (Indian head), .015-inch (pillow ticking), .017-inch (pocket drill and some striped ticking), and .020-to-.022-inch (heavy ticking). In frontier days, deerskin was much used for patching, as was linen. Today's patching is usually 100 percent cotton, with no additives; blue denim is very popular. Some commercial patching is impregnated with Teflon. (See PATCHED BALL.)

patent breech The patent or hooked breech is found on many Plains rifles, and on all double-barrel muzzleloading shotguns. It was invented by Henry Nock, an Englishman, in 1787.

The patent breech consists of a bolster-type plug that is fitted over the barrel and is separate from the tang. The plug has a hook on its bottom and is made so that once the wedge or pin has been removed from the barrel, the barrel is very easily removed by raising it to a 45-degree angle so that the hook on the bolster will unhook from the tang.

Improvements in Nock's original design were made by others, the most notable being Joseph Manton's "recessed" breech, patented in 1792. This used Nock's principle but reduced the ignition time by placing the lock nearer to the center of the barrel. Chamber-type breech plugs did much to speed the ignition. This kind of breech is found on the Hawken-style Plains rifle and on the finer percussion dueling pistols. (See MANTON, JOSEPH; PLAINS RIFLE.)

Patridge sight A rifle or handgun sight consisting of a thick front sight, flat on top with parallel sides, in conjunction with a square notch rear sight. It was developed in the 1880s by E. E. Patridge. (See HANDGUN SIGHTS; METALLIC SIGHTS.)

pattern Pattern is a term applied to the shot charge distribution of a shotgun. All shotgun gauges in the United States, England, and Canada are patterned at a standard distance of 40 yards (except for .410, which is patterned at 30 yards); at this distance, for a full choke barrel, regardless of the gauge or shot size, at least 70 percent of the shot should be circumscribed by a 30-inch circle. Thus, if a 12-gauge shotgun having a full choke is patterned using a load containing 1⅛ ounces of No. 7½ shot, or approximately 394 pellets, it should place 70 percent of these pellets, or at least 276 pellets, in the standard 30-inch circle at 40 yards.

However, the .410 bore, which is not considered a true "gauge," is tested at 30 yards into a 20-inch-diameter circle.

A good pattern is uniformly distributed in all sections, but not all shotguns produce uniform patterns. Some patterns may have more shot in the center area, and hence have dense centers with fewer pellets in the outer portions, while other patterns may have holes in the center and be dense on the outside, like a ring. Some patterns have holes at random, and are patchy, and even oval-shaped patterns have been observed. (See PATTERNING.)

pattern board In patterning a shotgun, some ballisticians in the past have used a large steel plate instead of paper sheets. This plate measured 4 feet square and was bolted securely to a heavy framework to hold it in a vertical position. In actual use at 40 yards, or any other yardage desired by the shooter, this plate, or pattern board, was painted with whitewash or similar white coating, and a shot was fired at the center of the plate. The pellets striking the plate produced a gray mark.

The use of this kind of pattern board is very time consuming, since each pattern must be counted and analyzed before the next shot can be fired. Most ammunition factories today use sheets of paper tacked against a suitable backboard, such as cardboard; as soon as one shot is fired, the sheet is either rolled up or removed and replaced with another sheet for the second shot, etc. This pattern sheet is still referred to as a pattern board. (See PATTERNING.)

patterning The practice of determining the point of impact of a shot charge and its dispersion over a given area at a particular distance. Patterning a shotgun can be considered the equivalent of sighting in a rifle. Because of variables in stock design or the straightness of its barrel(s), a shotgun can center its pattern high or low of the desired point of impact, or to the right or left. Similarly, the pattern may be too dense for the use intended, too open, or may have "holes"—areas through which a target could escape unscathed.

Patterning is customarily done as follows: A pattern board is erected, and a 30-inch circle, the standard size for pattern measurement, is drawn on it, and the circle is then divided into quarters. The shotgun is aimed at the center of the circle from a distance of 40 yards (12-, 16-, and 20-gauge guns are patterned at 40 yards; .410s are patterned at 30 yards) and fired.

After each shot, several factors can be observed: the location of the shot charge (high, low, etc.), the presence of holes in the pattern, and the actual percentage of the pattern. To obtain this last, the pellet punctures in the 30-inch circle are counted and divided by the number of pellets in the shot charge. For example, in patterning a 12-gauge trap gun marked full choke, a standard trap load of No. 8 shot contains approximately 460 pellets. If 325 pellets strike within the circle, then the gun has a 70 percent pattern, which is satisfactory for a full choke gun.

It is standard practice to fire five shots, each time at a clean patterning sheet, and then to take the average of all five.

It should be noted that the 40-yard patterning distance is a general one and may be impractical for some guns. For example, a shotgun that is to be used for skeet shooting, or for grouse or woodcock at close ranges, should be patterned at 20 or 25 yards, while retaining the 30-inch circle. In Continental Europe, the patterning is done at about 35 meters, using a circle 75cm in diameter. One of the best pattern forms is the 16-field pattern used in Germany. The 75cm circle has a 37.5cm inner circle; the inner circle is divided into four quadrants of equal area, while the outer ring is divided equally into 12 areas, each of which is the same as each of the four quadrants in the inner circle. Thus, the 16 fields all have equal areas, and the distribution of the shot charge can be easily analyzed.

Deficiencies brought out by patterning can be corrected by altering stock dimensions to change the point of impact, by adjusting the choke, or by changing the load itself. (See CHOKE; PATTERN; PATTERN BOARD.)

Patuxent Test An evaluation of steel shot, made by the Bureau of Sport Fisheries and Wildlife in the spring of 1968, at Patuxent, Maryland, in which tethered game farm mallards were shot at measured yardages with 1-ounce steel shot loads in No. 4 shot, and results compared with mallards shot with 1¼ ounces of lead shot in No. 4 and No. 6. Although the heavier lead loads killed the most birds, the difference was statistically small, particularly at ranges out to 40 yards where the lead killed 75 percent of birds shot and steel killed 71 percent. This surprised and confused ballisticians, including E. D. Lowry, then Winchester's chief ballistician, because the steel pellets had only 70 percent the density of lead in the same shot size.

This test led to an extensive study, entitled *Analysis of the Performances of Lead and Steel Shotshell Loads*, which was done by Lowry for Winchester under a grant from the Sporting Arms and Ammunition Industry (SAAMI). In this study, Lowry concluded that the surprisingly good performance of the light steel loads was to a great extent attributable to their highly efficient form factor (roundness), and that lead loads were actually slightly less effective than had previously been believed because of their tendency to deform with the setback of ignition.

Lowry's report has never been formally approved by SAAMI, but appears (to some observers) to have been borne out in more recent field tests. (See NILO SHOTSHELL EFFECTIVENESS TEST.)

Pauly, Samuel Johannes (1766–c.1820)   In 1812 this Swiss inventor, working in Paris, developed the first successful centerfire cartridge. He used an obturating, or sealing, metallic head cartridge not unlike the brass head of a modern shotgun cartridge. The powder charge and ball were contained in a combustible envelope, and the primer consisted of a pellet placed in the primer pocket of the brass head, thus producing a centerfire cartridge.

Pauly also developed and patented a system of ignition that used a jet of heated compressed air, plus several other firearms designs. The majority of his designs were not successful, or were not recognized for their worth until long after his death, as was the case with the jet air ignition; Daisy/Heddon used this method of ignition in 1964, when introducing the VL caseless cartridge rifles.

PB powder   A single-base (nitrocellulose) powder in the form of very small thick washers, PB was introduced by Du Pont in 1954 to replace the earlier MX, which was a multibase powder. It has proved highly successful in 12-, 20-, and 28-gauge target and medium field shotshell loads. PB stands for "porous base." (See NITROCELLULOSE.)

Peabody action   A breechloading, single-shot, tipping-block action that was granted a patent on July 22, 1862; it was the invention of firearms designer Henry O. Peabody. This action, which utilized a back-action lock with a large outside hammer, was later modified and improved by a concealed striker design by Friedrich von Martini, and thereafter the action became known as the Martini.

Rifles using the original Peabody action design were manufactured in Providence, Rhode Island, by the Providence Tool Company. Although Peabody's rifle was not adopted by the U.S. government, it was purchased by the Connecticut State Militia in .45/70 caliber, and some Peabody rifles in other calibers were sold to foreign governments, such as Turkey. (See MARTINI ACTION.)

peak pressure   The maximum chamber pressure that occurs upon firing a gun. Peak pressure is usually determined by means of a pressure/time curve

as shown on an oscilloscope tracing, recorded by means of a piezoelectric crystal, or strain gauge.

The older crusher system of pressure measurement does not provide a true evaluation of peak pressure for the crusher's deformity is a measurement of pressure over time. The longer the pressure is applied, the greater the deformity, even though the amount of pressure may remain constant. Since the advent of the newer system, with oscilloscope tracings, a more accurate evaluation of pressure and time is possible. (See CHAMBER PRESSURE; CRUSHER GAUGE; PIEZOELECTRIC CRYSTAL.)

Pecar scope   A riflescope made in Berlin, Germany, and at one time imported into this country. It was a quality scope and was available with an interchangeable reticle feature. Reportedly, repeated changes of the reticle by the shooter did not change the rifle's zero. The scopes were available in both variable and fixed magnifications. (See RETICLE; TELESCOPIC SIGHTS.)

peep sight   A rear sight that utilizes an aperture. Although some front sights employ aperture inserts, they are not referred to as peep sights. (See METALLIC SIGHTS.)

pendulum chronograph   Often called a ballistic pendulum, this device consists of a bullet catcher of known weight hanging by a chain or wire of known weight, much like a plumb bob. A bullet is fired into and stopped by the weight. The distance of rearward travel of the block is recorded and is used to compute bullet velocity and energy. The ballistic pendulum has been replaced by today's more convenient chronographs. (See CHRONOGRAPH.)

Pennsylvania rifle   See KENTUCKY RIFLE.

pepperbox pistol   During the percussion period (c. 1820–1870), a kind of small handgun evolved that utilized three to six barrels revolving around a central axis. Of small caliber—.31 to .36—these guns became known as pepperbox pistols because of their resemblance to a peppermill of the time.

Many were fired double action only, but some, like the highly popular Sharps pepperbox, could be used single action. Pepperboxes were invariably employed as concealment arms and were effective only at close range. With the perfection of the revolver they became obsolete, and few were in use by the 1870s.

Perazzi, Manifattura Armi (company)   Founded in 1964 in Brescia, Italy, Manifattura Armi Perazzi has established a reputation for high-quality over/under, side-by-side, and single-barrel shotguns. Daniele Perazzi, the company's president, was born in 1934, and underwent early training in all phases of shotgun manufacture with a number of Italian firms. His chief talent was as a designer and, in 1964, he collaborated with Italian shooting champion Ennio Mattarelli in the design of an over/under shotgun with which the latter won a gold medal in International Trap at the 1964 Olympics.

Gaining financial backing, Perazzi founded his company, which employs a unique combination of the most modern manufacturing techniques and considerable hand labor. Although Perazzi produces a number of high-grade hunting shotguns, the company's principal efforts have been directed to competition arms. Using simple, highly sophisticated designs that hold up extremely well under the rigors of competitive shooting, Perazzis are distinguished by interchangeability of stocks, trigger groups, and chokes.

Perazzi shotguns were imported into the United States by Ithaca from 1968 until 1979, when their import was taken over by Winchester. They are now imported independently by Perazzi.

percussion cap An early form of primer. It was an external ignition device comprised of a small metal cup containing a priming mixture (originally fulminate of mercury). It was placed open-end-down over a nipple containing a vent hole leading into the main powder charge in the barrel. When struck by a hammer, the cap sent a small jet of flame into the powder charge, igniting it. (See PERCUSSION IGNITION.)

percussion ignition A system utilizing a percussion cap and hammer to ignite the charge in a firearm. The percussion ignition system was developed and patented by Joshua Shaw in the early 1800s; by the 1850s it had largely replaced the flintlock as an ignition system.

The percussion system had many advantages over the flintlock. It offered the first truly waterproof method of firing a gun and virtually 100 percent

Percussion caps are copper cups filled with priming compound. They fit over the nipple and are detonated by the impact of the hammer.

reliability. But in spite of its great advantages, the percussion system was nothing more than a stepping-stone in the development of the primer used in self-contained cartridges. (Actually, the modern primer is a form of percussion cap, in that it is detonated by percussion from the hammer or striker.) (See IGNITION; PERCUSSION CAP; PRIMER.)

"perfect" (condition) See GUN CONDITION.

pest cartridge See SCHONZEITPATRONE.

Peters (company) The Peters Cartridge Company, a manufacturer of rifle, pistol, and shotgun ammunition, was founded in 1887 in Kings Mills, Ohio. Its products were sold throughout the United States. In 1934, the company was absorbed by Remington Arms (in turn owned by Du Pont), and its machinery was moved to the Remington plant at Bridgeport, Connecticut. Remington kept the Peters name alive as a trademark, but in actuality for years there was little or no difference between the products offered under the Peters and the Remington labels.

Currently, however, product differentiation has been reinstated with the introduction of the Peters Blue Magic shotgun shells. These cartridges are produced with the reloader in mind. The cases are made of compression-formed plastic in one piece with a metal head added to provide the rim, but the Peters case walls are not corrugated like the Remington RXP shells (which were also introduced primarily for the reloading market). Corrugation in a shotshell makes for easy feeding from magazine to chamber, but it does make the case mouth subject to fraying and splitting during reloading. The RXP shell has a long reloading life, but it usually finally fails when the case mouth frays or splits along corrugations. (See HANDLOAD; REMINGTON [COMPANY].)

Peterson, Harold L. (1922–1978) A preeminent firearms historian and author, Harold L. Peterson was born in Peekskill, New York, in 1922. Peterson's interest in his life's work developed early; he began collecting arms and armor at 10 years of age; in college, he was a varsity fencer with both foil and saber. In 1949, Peterson became the editor of *Military Collector and Historian*. This marked the beginning of a remarkably prolific career as an editor and writer. In addition to numerous magazine articles, Peterson was the author of 22 books, among the most notable of which are *The Treasury of the Gun* (Ridge Press, 1962), *Pageant of the Gun* (Ridge Press, 1967), and *The Book of the Continental Soldier* (Stackpole, 1968).

In addition, Peterson was a member of 19 historical societies, both in the United States and abroad.

He was a founder and governor of the Company of Military Historians, and was a chief curator of the National Park Service.

pheasant, guns and loads for Most hunters use a 20-, 16-, or 12-gauge shotgun for pheasant, though a few pride themselves on their ability to kill these rather large game birds with a .410 or a 28. The 12 gauge is most widely used. With a 20, magnum shells are useful.

There is considerable argument about shot size, but No. 6 is used by most shooters for all regular hunting of pheasants. In the early season, before the birds have developed heavy feathers, No. 7½ works well; during the late season, when feathers are thick and the birds tend to flush at a distance, No. 5 is frequently used. Shooters of double-barreled guns often carry two different sizes in their guns and use either as required, the smaller shot in the barrel with the more open choke.

Most pheasant hunters prefer a modified choke in a pump or an autoloader. Adjustable chokes help the hunter to adjust to changing conditions in the field. In a double, improved-cylinder in the first barrel and modified in the second is a practical combination for pheasants. Above all, a pheasant gun must fit the shooter well so that he can get it into action quickly at the flush.

Pheasants are found in open country (they especially favor cornfields) in parts of the Northeast and Midwest. Hunting them without a dog is possible, although the birds' tendency to run rather than fly makes a flushing breed, such as the springer spaniel, a great asset.

pie crimp See SHOTSHELL CRIMP.

piezoelectric crystal A mineral crystal, usually of quartz, that is used in the electronic transducer system recording chamber pressures. This crystal will generate its own electricity when subjected to pressure from an outside source. In use, it is arranged so that the pressure exerted on the chamber walls when the cartridge is fired creates a minute electrical wave that is transferred through an amplifier to a cathode-ray oscilloscope, where the pressure peak and pressure curve is displayed on a graph screen. (See CHAMBER PRESSURE; STRAIN GAUGE.)

pigeon shooting See BOX PIGEON SHOOTING; LIVE PIGEON SHOOTING.

pill lock The pill lock was an ignition system invented by Joseph Manton, the famous British gunmaker, in 1816. In the pill lock system, a pellet of fulminate of mercury was placed in a tube that

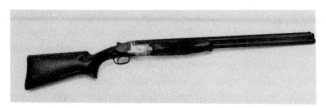

Most pigeon guns are over/unders, and all are 12 gauge. This one is a Perazzi, equipped with interchangeable screw-in chokes in the upper barrel.

employed a floating firing pin. The fulminate was usually coated or varnished. When the firing pin hit the fulminate it would ignite the main charge in the breech of the gun.

The pill lock was in vogue for only a short period of time because of the clumsy mechanism of the breech and other malfunctions. This system was used before the invention of the copper percussion cap, which proved to be more simple and efficient. (See PERCUSSION IGNITION.)

pinfire cartridge Invented by B. Houiller of France in 1847, this was the first self-contained cartridge. It was distinguished by the "pin" that extended above the base of the shell. This pin, when struck by the hammer of the lock, strikes a small percussion cap inside the case detonating the fulminate of mercury. The case expanded upon firing to create a gas seal. (See CARTRIDGE; PERCUSSION CAP.)

pinhole A tiny hole burned through the case wall of a shotshell. Usually occuring with paper hulls after several reloads, the pinhole will be found just ahead of the metal overlay. Shells with pinholes should be discarded.

pinwheel In target shooting, a shot that hits dead center in the bull's-eye, so called because the wrinkles in the paper radiating from the circular bull make the whole target look like a child's pinwheel.

pipes See RAMROD THIMBLES.

pistol Any handgun, rifled or smoothbore, not including revolvers, that is intended for use with one hand. In the United States, revolvers are usually considered to be a separate type of gun and are not included among the general class of pistols. The English, however, often call semiautomatic pistols revolvers.

pistol grip Any curved grip on a rifle or shotgun is called a pistol grip, as it is patterned on the sharply curved grips employed on revolvers. It permits a relaxed position of the hand and allows good trigger control. (See GRIP; SEMIPISTOL GRIP.)

pistol grip cap   Positioned at the base of a pistol grip, the cap is employed both as decoration and to protect the wood from splintering. Pistol grip caps are made of steel (usually blued and knurled), plastic, or contrasting hardwood, such as rosewood or cocobolo. As a decorative touch, some custom rifles employ skeleton pistol grip caps that cover the circumference of the grip and leave the inner part bare. (See PISTOL GRIP.)

pistol rug   A soft carrying case for a handgun. It is made of leather or plastic, lined with cloth or fleece, and sometimes equipped with a carrying handle.

pit   See TARGET PIT.

pitch   When applied to shotguns, this term means the angle of the butt and is expressed as the measurement of the intersection of the line of bore and the line connecting the heel and toe of the stock. In rifled arms, pitch is a synonym for rate of twist; as it applies to handguns, it is the relationship of the grip to the frame.

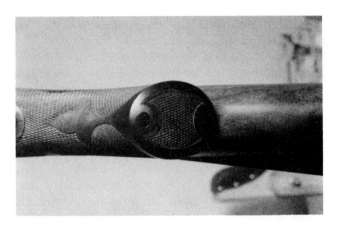

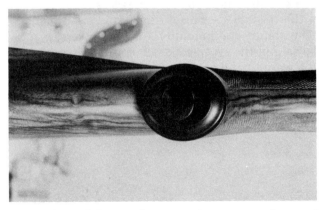

The purpose of the pistol grip cap is to protect the wood of the stock. However, there are other uses as well. A skeleton grip cap can be a decorative touch, while a trap grip cap can offer a receptacle for a spare front sight, pull through, or extra cartridge.

pitting   Ferrous metal (iron and steel), when exposed to moist air, can be eaten away by oxidation. The usual manifestation of this condition is rust, and deep rust produces a condition known as pitting, wherein small pits are formed in the surface of the metal.

Light pitting can be removed by filing, sanding, and polishing. Deep pitting often cannot be removed and permanently damages the gun it affects. The condition can be prevented by correct storage, handling, and cleaning of firearms. (See GUN CARE.)

Pittman-Robertson Act   Enacted in 1937, the Pittman-Robertson Act was designed to put state fish and game agency funding on a secure basis by creating a "federal aid to wildlife restoration fund." The purpose of the fund, comprised of revenues from an 11 percent excise tax on sporting arms and ammunition, was to assist states with specific wildlife restoration projects. To be eligible to receive allocations, states had to pass legislation that prohibited the diversion of hunting license fees for any purpose other than the administration of the state's fish and game department.

The program is administered by the Fish and Wildlife Service, with individual states submitting proposed wildlife projects for approval and funding. Such projects typically involve habitat acquisition and development, wildlife related research, and surveys and other management programs. The states pay for at least 25 percent of each project.

In 1970, an amendment to the P-R Act created the Hunter Education Program, using one-half of the excise tax on handguns as the source of revenue for the program. In addition, an amendment in 1972 added one-half of the excise tax on archery equipment as a further revenue source.

The P-R Act has become a key factor in strengthening the ability of state fish and game agencies to restore and manage their wildlife resources.

Plains rifle   As the western frontier expanded across the Mississippi and onto the Great Plains and Rocky Mountains, the trappers and explorers who led the way discovered that the rifles they carried were ill-suited for the new country. The changes made to the Kentucky rifles that they carried led to the development of the Plains rifle.

The Mountain Men discovered that ranges were greater, game larger and tougher, and that the ornate brasswork of a Kentucky rifle could be seen from far off, with sometimes fatal consequences. In addition, travel was now by horseback rather than on foot, which meant that a heavier rifle, as well as more powder and shot, could be carried.

A typical Plains rifle would be a percussion arm

of .52 caliber (they were seldom less than .45 or more than .58). It would be half-stocked in walnut, equipped with double set triggers, and would have all metal parts browned. (Occasionally, a pewter nose cap was used, pewter being suitable because of its dull finish.) Barrels tended to be quite heavy—an inch across the flats—and 36 inches long. Iron sights were standard.

Overall, the Plains rifle was a strictly utilitarian gun. The emphasis on aesthetics in the Kentucky rifle had been abandoned in its design. A Plains rifle was designed for hard use and could be loaded with extremely heavy charges of powder. The definitive Plains rifle is the Hawken.

The heyday of the Plains rifle was short—from 1825 to 1845. By the latter date, the fur trade was already in decline, and the time of the Mountain Man, who favored the Plains rifle, was nearly over. (See HAWKEN RIFLE.)

plastic bullet Originally designed to permit economical indoor practice at short range with center-fire metallic handgun cartridge cases, plastic bullets resemble hollow base wadcutters in construction. Later, plastic cases—with a primer pocket for large primers and a larger-than-standard flash hole—were designed for use with the plastic bullets. No powder is used; the primer provides all the propelling force for the bullets.

Plastic bullets have also been designed, manufactured, and loaded into centerfire rifle cartridges for riot control; such bullets have a poor sectional density and tend to tumble, producing a sting but seldom doing any permanent damage—unless driven at exceptionally high velocities. Plastic projectiles at extremely high velocities will defeat military armor.

plastic shotshell First introduced to the American market in 1962 by Remington Arms Co. as the SP (steel-plastic) shotshell, the plastic shotshell had already been in commercial production in Europe for several years. The Remington shell consisted of a ribbed polyethylene tube, a fiber base wad, and a brass-plated steel head. The earlier European shells, such as the R. Pinto from Italy and the Carplast from France, had been extruded all-plastic shells without a metal head. The European plastic shells had a tendency to split on firing or the head portion would crack.

The Remington shell took advantage of a development called compression forming, whereby plastic dust was molded to shape under heat and pressure. Winchester followed shortly with its own plastic shells, and these, along with the Remington SP, revolutionized shotgun ammunition. The plastic shells were immune to moisture (a major problem to waterfowl hunters) and could be reloaded far more often than paper shells. Today, plastic shells are the standard for shotgun ammunition.

plastic stock The stocks of firearms have for centuries been manufactured almost universally of wood. Recently, stocks have been produced in increasing numbers from synthetics, mainly in response to demand from the consumer. Synthetic stocks can be molded ready to fit to a barreled action with no labor-intensive hand fitting required. Even though such stocks are often made of nylon, fiberglass, Kevlar, and other exotic man-made materials, they are often referred to as plastic stocks.

Savage was one of the first large manufacturers to use a synthetic stock. Following World War II, it introduced Tenite stocks on several different models of the Stevens shotguns and rimfire rifles, as well as the Model 24 combination gun. Tenite becomes extremely brittle and cracks easily during extremely cold weather, and for this reason its use as a material for making gun stocks proved to be a total failure.

To refer to today's synthetic stocks as plastic is to do them an injustice. In addition to being many times stronger than wood, the modern synthetic stock is also far more stable and less likely to cause a rifle to lose its zero during extremes in ambient temperature and humidity. About the worst that can be said of the synthetic stock is that it doesn't have the warmth and beauty of wood.

Weatherby was the first to introduce a factory big-

The first commercially successful arm using a plastic stock (actually structural nylon) was the Remington Model 66, a .22 autoloader.

game rifle with a modern synthetic stock and offers the Mark V Fibermark and Vanguard Weatherguard in a variety of chamberings from .223 Remington to .416 Magnum. Remington, Winchester (U.S. Repeating Arms), Sako, Ruger, Savage, and others offer various rifles so equipped. One of the longest-lived and therefore most successful synthetic-stocked firearms is the Remington XP-100. A number of firms also sell synthetic stocks or will install them on the customer's barreled action. They include McMillan, Brown Precision, Bell & Carlson, and Ram-Line. Custom rifles with synthetic stocks are available from Jarrett Rifles, Inc., Brown Precision, Shilen Rifles, and numerous other shops.

plated shot Lead shot is alloyed with antimony— from 0.5 to 6.0 percent, depending on the manufacturer and the intended use—in order to make it hard. However, the use of antimony will only increase hardness to a certain point. If additional hardness is desired, such as for live bird shooting or some waterfowl hunting, the shot must be plated with a harder substance to decrease wear caused by friction with the barrel bore. Winchester-Western plates its shot with a coating of a copper-zinc alloy called Lubaloy, which has excellent lubricating qualities. Other shot manufacturers, particularly those in Europe, prefer nickel plating. Plating or coating the lead pellets with plastic has also been tried, not to increase the hardness, but to make the pellets more resistant to the digestive acids of waterfowl and thus reduce lead poisoning; this use of plastic as a coating has not proven satisfactory.

plinker Commonly used to describe a shooter who takes shots at informal, random targets such as tin cans, clumps of dirt, and sticks, a plinker can also be a rifle or handgun used for such shooting. The choice of the plinking arm is left entirely up to the plinker. To be thought of as informal target shooting.

In 1961, the Speer Products Co. (now CCI-Speer Operations of Omark) of Lewiston, Idaho, introduced a low-priced half-jacketed .30-caliber 100-grain roundnose bullet to the handloading market; these bullets were called "Plinkers."

plug When the muzzle of a rifle, shotgun, or handgun barrel is fouled with dirt or some other foreign debris, it is said to be plugged. The word also refers, in slang usage, to a firearm bullet. (See BREECHPLUG; MAGAZINE PLUG.)

plunger A plunger is a metal or synthetic shaft or rod sliding in a recess that is used to power, or activate, another part. Small ejector plungers, powered by springs, are commonly found in the breech-

bolt just behind the extractor. In the Ithaca Mag 10 autoloading shotgun, a large plunger is used to compress the action spring as the slide and bolt recoil rearward. On other arms, plungers are used in connection with sliding safeties, hammers, and even the bolts in some revolvers.

PMVF magnums In the late 1930s, Ralph Waldo Miller, in cooperation with E. Baden Powell, developed a line of wildcat cartridges with a Venturi shoulder, many of them based on the belted .300 H&H Magnum case. The PMVF nomenclature translates as "Powell-Miller-Venturi-Freebore." Later, the idea for the PMVF line of cartridges was sold to the Hollywood Gun Shop, and the name was changed to CCC, which stands for "Controlled-Combustion-Chamberage." The Weatherby line of cartridges is similar to the original PMVF design, except for having two curves, or radii, instead of only one.

point blank That distance to which a bullet will not rise or drop below the line of sight by more than a specified distance, commonly 3 inches. Zeroing for the longest practical point-blank range allows a hunter to hold his sight on the animal's body, instead of holding over, out to the maximum distance, making accurate range estimation in the field less critical.

In common parlance, point-blank range means, simply, extremely close range.

point of aim The spot at which a shooter aims is the point of aim.

point of impact This term refers to the spot where a projectile strikes.

points of constriction The narrowing down or constriction of the bore of a shotgun generally occurs at two different points—at the beginning of the forcing cone and at the beginning of the choke. At the forcing cone, the chamber diameter is constricted to the bore diameter considered standard for that particular gauge. At the choke, the bore diameter is constricted so many points, degrees, millimeters, or thousandths of an inch, depending on the desired choke, the manufacturer, and the particular system of measurement being used. (See BORE DIAMETER.)

polygroove rifling See MULTIGROOVE RIFLING.

"poor" (condition) See GUN CONDITION.

Pope, Harry M. (1861–1950) An American gunsmith of note, Pope was preeminent as a barrel maker during the heyday of the muzzleloading and

Schuetzen rifle in the late 19th century. His reputation was especially high among Schuetzen riflemen, and Pope himself was noted as a competitor with that kind of rifle. Many of the accuracy records set with arms that he had barreled are remarkable even by today's standards, and rifles that he built are highly prized by collectors. (See POPE RIB; POPE RIFLING.)

Pope rib A small bar, or rib, of metal, fixed to a telescopic sight tube. It engages the front mount of a target- (sliding) type scope to prevent the scope from turning in the mounts. Named for Harry M. Pope, famed rifleman and gunsmith, who is credited with originating the system. (See POPE, HARRY M.)

Pope rifling A kind of rifling developed by gunsmith Harry M. Pope for breechloading match rifles. It consisted of eight wide, shallow grooves with relatively deep rounded corners. This rifling would grip the lead bullets of the day, and the shallow grooves aided considerably in cleaning the barrel, which was then a crucial factor in obtaining top accuracy. (See POPE, HARRY M.; RIFLING.)

Porro prism Most commonly used in binoculars, the Porro prism is more properly termed "Porro system," since it consists of two reflecting prisms employed as a unit. These two prisms reflect light of the four surfaces within the system and act as an erector lens system.

The advantage of the Porro system is that it allows a shorter instrument to be designed than is possible with other lens systems. Porro prisms are used in many high-grade binoculars, such as those made by Zeiss, Leitz, and Bausch & Lomb. (See BINOCULARS; ERECTOR LENS.)

position shooting Match rifle shooting where a certain specified shooting position is required to fire a string of shots. Four positions are recognized: standing or offhand; kneeling; sitting; and prone. The course of fire in some matches may require shooting in all positions, while in others only one position is used.

The rules for position shooting have changed somewhat over the years, and some differences exist in the rules governing the various positions in different countries and in some domestic matches and international matches. Rules about firearms used also differ.

The standing or offhand shooting position affords a classic example of what is allowed in one match and not another. Some of this pertains to the rifle and its appendages, some to the position assumed in shooting. Back around the turn of the century, the Schuetzen rifle was in great favor for offhand match shooting, both in this country and in Europe. These rifles had very heavy barrels, single-shot actions, palm rests, heavy, high cheekpieces, buttplates with long hooks that fit under the arm and a shorter hook that went over it to hold the rifle tightly to the shoulder, double set triggers, and sometimes false muzzles or any other gadget the maker deemed necessary to increase accuracy and steady holding. These rifles were used in special Schuetzen matches, but were barred from some other matches where more conventional rifles were used.

Modern rifles that are similarly equipped are used in todays free rifle matches, but are not allowed in some conventional rifle matches. When shooting both the Schuetzen and free rifle and using a palm rest, the elbow of the arm holding the rest is placed on the hip, and the shooter leans backward somewhat from the hips. This hip rest position is used by many shooters, except that the hand holding the fore-end is placed back near the action, with the rifle resting on the thumb and fingers. With this variation of the offhand position the shooter must lean even farther to the rear than when using a palm rest.

The second position is kneeling. There are some modifications of the standard kneeling position. One way of using the kneeling position is with the elbow either directly under the rifle or bent past center slightly to put tension on the arm. The elbow is rested on the knee, with the joint extended just beyond the knee cap. This eliminates the rolling motion that is present if the elbow joint and knee cap are in contact. Normally, the other knee and the toe of that foot are in contact with the ground, with the weight of the upper body resting on the forward elbow and knee, but some shooters sit on the heel to form a partial sitting position. The latter method is a little steadier but is not allowed in most matches. The kneeling position is not overly steady because it allows a good deal of horizontal sway as well as some vertical movement.

The sitting position is the steadiest position except prone, especially if a good shooting sling is used. The shooter sits solidly on the ground facing about 45 degrees away from the target, and with one foot pointing toward the target. The knee is bent comfortably so that there is no strain. The other leg is in the same position except that it is facing more with the body. Both bent knees form a solid support for the two elbows, which are placed with the joints slightly forward of the knee caps to steady them. This forms a solid support that slants from the rifle to the ground in an inverted V formed by the forearms and lower legs, and is further steadied by the inverted V of the bent legs on both sides. With a little practice, this position is capable of delivering very tight groups on either a paper target far down the range or on an animal on the other side of a wide canyon or meadow. Add the tension of a shooting sling adjusted to fit properly, and the hold becomes even steadier.

A modified form of the sitting position is to sit with the legs crossed with the feet pulled back against the body and the knees up. This is the sitting position preferred by many competition shooters.

The steadiest of all shooting positions is prone. While it is possible to shoot from the prone position without a shooting sling, it is not usually done. The shooter faces about 30 degrees away from the target, with the body flat on the ground except for that portion that is raised up so that the elbows are bent to form two V supports for the rifle. If a sling is used, most shooters prefer to place the forward elbow so that it is under the rifle, causing a great deal of tension to be exerted on the sling. If no sling is used, it is better to slant the forearm outward from the rifle to the ground. The other elbow is placed out from the body to steady both body and rifle, as well as to place the shoulder correctly behind the stock. The feet are usually spread wide apart with the arches facing down, but some shooters use modifications of the basic foot position to relieve unwanted tension.

One secret for steady holding in prone shooting is to move around until the body is perfectly relaxed and seems to fit the ground on which it lies. If everything is done correctly, the reticle of a powerful target scope will show very little movement on the target. Shooters who practice from the prone position over long periods of time can shoot groups that are nearly as tight as those fired from a benchrest over sandbags. (See FREE RIFLE.)

possible   A term used to indicate a perfect score in target shooting.

post sight   A kind of iron front sight or scope reticle that, when seen from the rear, resembles a post or upright rectangle. Some posts are pointed at the top end. (See METALLIC SIGHTS.)

potassium chlorate   A crystalline salt used as an oxidizing agent in various kinds of explosives. It has been used in the manufacture of primers, but makes them highly corrosive. The modern noncorrosive primer does not contain potassium chlorate.

pot shooting   Shooting game for the pot—to eat it—with no concern about sportsmanship. A pot shooter's goal is to kill game as efficiently as possible. For instance, a true pot shooter prefers to "ground sluice" a covey of quail by shooting the birds on the ground. When the birds are closely bunched, one charge may kill more than a dozen. And, of course, a pot shooter shoots sitting ducks.

powder charge   The quantity of powder contained in a metallic cartridge, a shotshell, or in a muzzle-loading arm when loaded with a measured amount of propellant.

powder efficiency   The degree to which a propellant achieves its maximum potential for velocity within a given cartridge. The efficiency of a given powder is not absolute, but is dependent upon a variety of factors, chiefly case capacity and shape and bullet weight. For example, a slow-burning powder such as 4831 is efficient only in a case of large capacity, with little body taper, a sharp shoulder, and propelling a bullet that is heavy relative to its diameter. This combination of elements will allow the powder to be almost entirely consumed while it is still pushing the bullet. Were 4831 used in a .30/30 case, which is tapered, has little shoulder, and uses relatively light bullets for its bore size, the powder would still be burning when the bullet emerged from the barrel, and a significant amount of it would be consumed in the open air. The .30/30, and similar cartridges, require fast-burning powder that can be converted to propellant gas in the case and barrel.

powder flask   Any field receptacle that holds and measures out black powder. Powder flasks have been made of wood, leather, bone, and other materials, but are mostly of metal, with a spout on one end and a lever at the side that opens the flask to pour out a measured amount of powder.

The size of the spout controls the amount of powder measured, and spouts for pistols, revolvers, and rifles can be had in most any practical measurement. For the .58-caliber Springfield Musket, the famous Peace flask was used. Its spout measured 60 grains of FFG (2F) black powder, the conventional load for the musket.

Shotgun flasks usually have two or three spouts graduations, e.g. 2½ drams, 2¾ drams, and 3 drams, although you can find smaller spouts for the light shotguns and larger spouts for heavier guns.

Powder flasks hold anywhere from 100 grains of priming powder (FFFFG-4F), to 1 pound, the average being ½ pound or less. (See POWDER HORN.)

The alternative to the powder horn, the powder flask is normally made of cast copper or brass and equipped with a measuring nozzle.

powder horn Before the invention of the metallic cartridge, black powder for muzzleloading arms was commonly carried in powder flasks, or, in North America, in powder horns. (The military, for whom rapid fire was a necessity, carried fixed ammunition, consisting of a premeasured charge of powder and a ball wrapped in a paper cartridge. These cartridges were carried in a leather bag.)

Because most American colonists could not afford powder flasks, they turned to a readily available material—horn—and turned it into a highly serviceable container. The horn would be cut from the animal's skull, scraped to remove as much cartilage and skin as possible, and then boiled to clean it completely. The large end was sealed with a tight-fitting wooden plug, and the narrow end fitted with a removable wooden stopper, which was usually attached by a string to prevent its loss.

Powder horns were worn slung at the side. In use, the stopper was removed, and the powder poured either directly into the barrel, or into the palm of the hand first to get a rough measurement.

Many powder horns were decorated with the owner's name, artistic motifs, or patriotic slogans. Today,

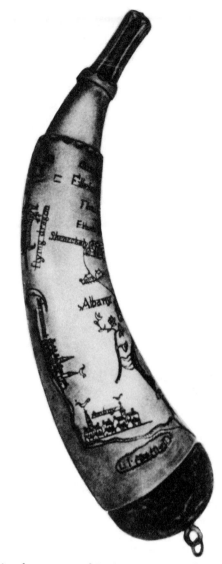

Made in about 1750, this American powder horn is decorated by various motifs, including a map of New York state, partly visible at one side.

highly decorated horns are valued as examples of American folk art. (See POWDER FLASK.)

powder measure A device for metering quantities of propellant volumetrically. It allows a precise amount of propellant to be dispensed, usually into an individual cartridge when handloading.

The most widely used powder measures consist of an adjustable drum or slide into which the powder is fed by gravity from a larger receptacle. In use, the drum is first adjusted, usually by checking with a scale, to throw a specified amount. Coarse-grained propellants are usually cut by a shearing motion of the edge of the drum, causing the hand-operated measure to function with a gritty motion, while spherical propellants generally meter smoothly and accurately.

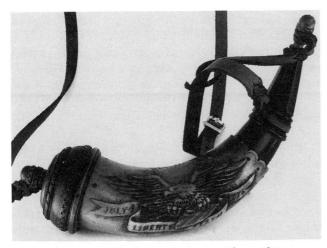

Civilian users of black-powder guns (the military employed paper cartridges) carried their powder in horns such as this. This horn is fairly elaborate, although such decoration was quite common. The stopper at the narrow end is removed to pour the charge.

The simplest powder measure consists of nothing more than a small cylinder, adjustable for depth, into which powder is poured until the cylinder is full. (See POWDER TRICKLER.)

powder residue The substance remaining in the cartridge case, chamber, and barrel as a result of the burning propellant. All propellant powders leave a residue to some extent, but black powder leaves copious amounts.

Black-powder residue can result in very rapid and very pronounced loss of accuracy, which is why the guns that use it must be cleaned after each shot, or each few shots. Smokeless powder residue has the same effect, but over a longer period. A highly accurate modern rifle will begin to exhibit a falloff in accuracy after 15 to 20 shots, while a less accurate arm will show the effects of powder residue over a longer period.

powder storage regulations See GUNPOWDER, SHIPPING AND STORAGE OF.

powder trickler A device for dispensing very small quantities of propellant. Used in handloading, it

This powder measure is made with an adjusting thimble and a set-screw to hold it in place.

generally consists of a small hopper through which runs an inside-threaded tube open at one end and with a small hole in the tube's side. When covered with powder in the hopper, the hole allows propellant to enter the tube, and when the tube is turned via a knob on the closed end, powder is slowly augered out by the threads onto the pan of a powder scale.

power The term commonly used to denote the degree of magnification of a telescopic sight, binocular, or spotting scope. For example, a seven-power binocular (also expressed 7X) would magnify a given object seven times. (See MAGNIFICATION.)

practice bullet Any inexpensive projectile fired from a rifle or handgun can be called a practice bullet. Quite often, cast lead bullets are used for practice. Plastic bullets are also utilized. These are loaded into special plastic cases that are primed, but not charged with powder. Plastic bullets are intended primarily for indoor use, as they offer a very low noise level and are safer than metal projectiles. (See PLASTIC BULLET.)

practice shotshell A shotgun cartridge, loaded with less shot and powder than normal, used for practice shooting with minimal expense and recoil. Many trapshooters load practice shotshells containing 1 ounce of shot and the equivalent of 2½ drams of powder for practice at 16-yard events. (The standard trap load is 1⅛ ounces of shot and either 3 or 2¾ drams of powder.)

press-type die See LOADING DIE.

pressure barrel See PRESSURE GUN.

pressure curve The rise and fall of pressure in a firing cartridge, shown on a graph as a rapidly ascending and descending curve. The safety of ammunition depends on controlling the loading in such a way as to make pressure rise slowly enough to give the bullet time to start moving and to move far enough so the peak pressure will not reach a dangerous level. (See PEAK PRESSURE.)

pressure estimation There are a number of ways to estimate pressure; by visible marks on the case, case head expansion, and difficult opening of the bolt.

Flattened and/or cratered primers have long been considered as indicators of high pressure but are unreliable unless the shooter knows what to expect from that particular brand and lot of primers, the cases being used, and the rifle they are fired in. A shiny mark where the brass has been forced into the ejector slot or hole in the bolt face is a sure indication of high pressure. If the cartridge is being reloaded and the bolt starts to resist opening, pressures are too high and the powder charge must be lowered.

pressure gun A special appliance for the measurement of internal pressures when a cartridge is fired. The pressure gun is normally built with a special receiver so that barrels can be changed readily, the universal receiver being the one most commonly used. The barrel is bored and chambered to rigid specifications as set forth by the Sporting Arms and Ammunition Manufacturers Institute (SAAMI). It may be equipped with any of several measurement systems to determine the pressure developed by the expanding powder gas with the cartridge case, chamber, and bore. Normally, however, when the term pressure gun is, used, it refers to one set up for the copper crusher system. (See CHAMBER PRESSURE.)

pressure peak See PEAK PRESSURE.

primer The primer is the part of a cartridge or shotshell that ignites the powder charge. Primers have two or three components: priming compound (an explosive chemical); an anvil against which the compound is crushed by the blow of the firing pin; and the cup, which contains the two.

There are two kinds of primers for metallic cartridges in use today—Boxer and Berdan. The Boxer primer, named for its English inventor, Colonel Edward Boxer, is the primer used in all American cartridges. It is composed of three parts—cup, priming mixture, and anvil. When the primer is hit by the firing pin, the cup is dented, smashing the priming mixture against the anvil and causing an explosion. The resultant flame shoots through the flash hole in the case and ignites the powder charge.

Berdan primers are used extensively in Europe and differ from the Boxer design in that they contain no anvil—only the cup and priming mixture. The anvil is an integral part of the brass cartridge case. Cases made for Berdan primers have two flash holes, which offer no advantage or disadvantage over a single hole; it is simply the way they were designed.

The basic ingredient in early primers was fulminate of mercury, a violent explosive that is very dangerous to handle. A further disadvantage of its use was that free mercury in the compound amalgamated with the brass in the cartridge cases; this made the brass brittle, weakening it so that it was useless for reloading.

Just before the turn of the century, mercuric primers were abandoned for a compound whose main ingredient was potassium chlorate. The hazard to brass no longer existed, but potassium chlorate created another problem: When burned, the compound broke down into a salt that was deposited in rifle barrels. The result was corrosive rust. The chloride salt was soluble only in water, and rifle barrels had to be scrubbed and oiled immediately after firing to prevent rust and corrosion.

After about 1931, American commercial primers became nonmercuric and noncorrosive when manufacturers changed to a priming compound made of lead styphnate and special sensitizers, which made the chemical easier to ignite. This compound has no detrimental effects on either the case or the barrel. The military was slow to change, however, and continued to use corrosive primers until the early 1950s. But by 1954, all military arsenals had made the change to the lead styphnate compound.

There are two sizes of primers used in American brass cartridge cases. Large primers, both pistol and rifle, have a diameter of .210-inch while small pistol and rifle primers measure .175-inch. While pistol and rifle primers have the same diameter, pistol primers should not be used in rifle cases, and vice versa. Rifle primers are usually thicker than pistol primers. If used interchangeably, a pistol primer will seat too deeply in a rifle primer pocket and a rifle primer will protrude from a pistol primer pocket, causing a "bugged" primer condition. When seated too deeply, a primer won't be dented enough by the firing pin and may not fire. A bugged primer condition is dangerous because it presents a remote but real danger of premature firing from contact with the handgun's bolt face or standing breech.

Secondly, because the firing pin blow of a rifle mechanism is usually much heavier than that of a handgun, rifle primer cups are made of harder metal. A rifle firing pin may puncture a softer pistol primer cup, resulting in a backflash that could burn the shooter, whereas a weaker pistol firing pin blow may not crush a rifle primer sufficiently to initiate detonation.

To further complicate the primer picture for metallic cartridges, we now have magnum and benchrest primers with which to contend. Magnum primers, both rifle and pistol, contain priming mixture for-

These primers are, from left: shotgun (in its battery cup), large rifle and small rifle.

mulas that produce a more intense and longer-lasting flame than standard primers. They are intended for use in large capacity cases containing heavy charges of slow-burning powder. Magnum primers are also advantageous in standard-capacity cases when used with the new spherical powders which, because they are denser, are difficult to ignite. Benchrest primers for small rifle cases are assembled with special attention to every detail to guarantee the most uniform results possible.

Because shotgun shells are made of paper or plastic with a thin brass head, they lack the strength to support primers such as those used in rifle and pistol cases. Therefore, shotgun primers employ what is called a battery cup design. The battery cup is a separate brass cup containing the primer and flash hole. In reloading shotgun shells, the entire battery cup and primer unit are normally replaced (See BERDAN PRIMER; BOXER PRIMER; IGNITION; LEAD STYPHNATE; MERCURIC PRIMERS.)

primer flash The explosion of the priming compound and the subsequent flame that passes through the flash hole to ignite the powder charge. (See PRIMER.)

primer indent The circular or rectangular mark left on the soft primer by the blow of the firing pin.

primer leak A primer leak involves powder gases escaping past the primer cup. Such leaks are potentially dangerous, and are caused either by excessive pressure or by a loose fit of the primer in the primer pocket. A primer leak, if severe enough, can damage a firearm or cause injury to the shooter.

primer lock The crimping of the case head around the top of the primer pocket so that the primer cannot be easily removed. Crimped primers are found mostly in cartridges manufactured for military use.

primer pocket The recess in the base of a centerfire cartridge case for receiving and holding the primer. A lip around the edge of the pocket—the primer lock—is often included in military ammunition to prevent primer dislodging. Commercial ammunition, which is not subject to the abuse military ammunition commonly receives, does not require this feature. (See PRIMER.)

primer protrusion A primer that is not seated to its full depth will protrude above the top of the case head. This is also known as "bugged primer," and is potentially dangerous. (See PRIMER.)

The primer pocket of a case is the receptacle for the primer. At its center is the flash hole.

primer residue The material left in the bottom of the primer pocket when the primer is fired. This is what remains of the priming compound. It should be removed before seating a new primer.

primer seating The procedure used to insert the primer in the primer pocket of the cartridge case. Some primer seating tools push the primer into the pocket, others force the case down onto the primer. A primer must be seated properly—not high or low—to ensure efficient detonation. (See PRIMER; PRIMING TOOL.)

primer tape See MAYNARD TAPE PRIMER.

primer tube A tube that feeds the primers into the priming cup on some loading presses and priming tools with automatic primer devices. (See LOADING PRESS; PRIMER SEATING; PRIMING TOOL.)

priming horn The average priming horn is about 4 inches long and constructed and plugged like a powder horn or flask. It is used to hold and pour the priming powder (FFFFG-4F) that is necessary to fire a flintlock firearm. Priming horns hold anywhere from 100 grains of powder up.

The priming horn is customarily slung on the hunting bag straps a few inches above the main powder horn. (See POWDER FLASK; POWDER HORN; PRIMING POWDER.)

priming pan See PAN.

priming powder The very fine-grained powder that is used in the pan of a flintlock, and which, when set off, ignites the main charge of powder.

FFFFG (4F) black priming powder should be used. Do not use (4F) powder as a main charge, as it builds up excessive pressure and is very dangerous. (See MUZZLELOADER; PAN.)

priming tool A small, hand operated tool designed to prime rifle and handgun cartridges (shotshells are always primed on a reloading press). The tool consists of a main body, a lever that is squeezed against the tool body, and a shellholder that fits over the base of the case to be primed. Inside the main body is a springloaded plunger. A primer is dropped into a recess in the shellholder, and the case is inserted on top of it. when the lever is squeezed, the plunger moves against the primer, forcing it into the primer pocket. (See PRIMER; PRIMER POCKET.)

primitive hunting, guns and loads for The term "primitive hunting" refers to hunting with muzzleloaders. Many states now have a "muzzleloader only" deer season, and other game species are taken with the old guns as well. This has led to an enormous increase in muzzleloading hunters.

Primitive hunting requires a caliber and load to fit the particular species you may be hunting. For instance, the .32, .36 and .40 caliber are fine squirrel rifles. For deer-sized game, anything from a .45 caliber up to a .58 is used. The .45 is sufficient for brush hunting, where shots are within 25 yards most of the time. For long ranges in open country, where power and distance are needed the .50, .52, .54, and .58 caliber are very popular. These heavy calibers are mostly half-stock guns, but some larger calibers are to be found on many "originals," with .50 probably being the most used.

A flintlock is used for true primitive hunting; but for reliability, a percussion gun is preferred, particularly in damp weather. Many hunters use replicas

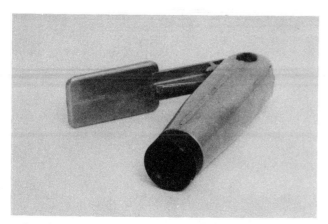

A hand priming tool such as this is probably the best, since it offers the reloader the maximum amount of feel during the operation.

of the old guns, and a lot of deer are taken annually with both flint and percussion muzzleloading rifles.

primitive shooting See MUZZLELOADING MATCHES.

prism This term refers to a wedge-shaped piece of glass that bends light, but does not bring it to a focus as does a lens. Prisms are most commonly used in binoculars to erect the image before it enters the ocular lens. (See BINOCULARS.)

progressive burning powder See INTERIOR BALLISTICS.

projectile When the term is applied to firearms, a projectile is any solid material propelled through the gun barrel by the power source—a bullet, shot charge, shotgun slug, sabot, ball, pellet, etc.

pronghorn antelope, guns and loads for Rifle selection for pronghorn antelope is dependent upon hunting style. A few modern hunters prefer bows, or muzzleloaders, which demand careful stalking or much waiting at waterholes to close within 100 yards or less. In some states, handguns of the .357 magnum, .41 magnum, and .44 magnum class are legal, and these are effective out to 200 yards when equipped with telescopic sights.

However, antelope hunting as it is most commonly practiced places a heavy emphasis on long-range marksmanship. Antelope are creatures of open country and rely on their eyesight to detect danger and on their great speed to take them to safety. Most hunters use powerful binoculars of 8X to 10X and/or spotting scopes of 20X to 60X to locate the animals from afar and, at the same time, pick the most desirable trophy out of the band. From that point, a stalk is made that brings the hunter within rifle range. While most North American game is taken at ranges of between 100 and 200 yards, the range at which antelope are shot is between 200 and 500 yards. This great distance, plus the creature's relatively small size (an average buck weights 90-to-100 pounds), makes the antelope a difficult target.

To be effective, a rifle for antelope hunting must fire a relatively fragile, quick-expanding bullet at a velocity of at least 3,000 feet per second and must be able to place three shots in a 1-inch group at 100 yards. Two of the most popular cartridges for antelope hunting are the .30/06, loaded with a 150-grain bullet at 3,000 fps, and the .270, loaded with a 130-grain bullet at 3,150 fps. Sighted in to strike 3 inches high at 100 yards, these loads will hit only a few inches low at 300, requiring no holdover until 325 yards or so.

Another class of calibers well suited to hunting

This photo (taken in eastern Montana) shows typical pronghorn country—vast plains, broken by timbered buttes. Binoculars and a spotting scope are a necessity in such terrain. The pronghorn, despite its remarkable speed and eyesight, is neither large nor hard to kill. This fine trophy was downed with a 7mm Mashburn Magnum, which is far in excess of what is required. A better selection of antelope cartridges is, from left: .243, 6mm Remington, .240 Weatherby, .250/3000, .257 Roberts, .25/06, and .257 Weatherby.

the "prairie goat" is the .24-25 family. The .243 Winchester and 6mm Remington, which both fire bullets of 100 grains at 3,000 fps, are superb antelope cartridges. The .250/300 Savage and .257 Roberts, when handloaded to their maximum capacities, fire slightly heavier bullets at similar velocities and are equally excellent.

A third class of pronghorn cartridges to be considered is the "hot" .25 group—the .25/06 and the .257 Weatherby. Both fire 100-grain bullets at considerably higher velocities, and eliminate the need for holdover out to 375 yards.

As for rifle types, the bolt action is by far the most popular because it is capable of the greatest accuracy. However, a modern single-shot rifle is also an excellent choice, provided it shoots within bolt-action standards.

The best scope for pronghorn hunting is one that delivers relatively high magnification and excellent definition. A 4X scope is generally considered to be the acceptable minimum, with some hunters opting for as high as 10X. The 6X scope is an excellent choice, and 2X-7X and 3X-9X variables have a great many adherents.

proof In firearms nomenclature, when a gun has been proofed it means that it has been tested by firing a load or loads that develop more pressure than the standard ammunition used, thus ensuring that the arm can withstand detonation forces.

proof house   A place where firearms are tested and proofed to determine whether the individual firearm meets industry standards. In Europe, proof houses are under governmental control, and every firearm and part proofed receives a stamped proof mark and in some instances a certificate of proof.

In America, there is no law governing the proofing of firearms, therefore each manufacturer decides whether to proof its arms or not. Some manufacturers do proof-test their firearms in their own facilities, but others do not.

proof law   Proofing is the method by which a firearm is tested to ensure that it is capable of withstanding the forces of detonation attendant to firing. This is performed by firing with a heavy proofload, or "blue pill," to demonstrate the margin of safety. Firearm proofing has been fairly common since at least the 16th century, but compulsory proof required by law is only a recent development in most countries and does not exist at all in others.

Some sources give Belgium credit for originating compulsory proof. England did not have an effective proof law until the middle of the 19th century, and Germany not until the end of the century. Arms manufacturers in America have resisted government proof regulations, and proof their arms privately and independently—or not at all. (See PROOF HOUSE.)

proof mark   A symbol stamped into the metal of a gun barrel to certify that the firearm has been proof-tested and that it strong enough not to burst when fired. Most European countries maintain one or more proof houses where all guns manufactured in that country must undergo proof. The United States does not maintain a government proof house and thus there are no government proof marks on American-made guns. (See PROOF HOUSE.)

proof master   The head of an official government proof house. (See PROOF HOUSE.)

proprietary cartridge   Starting in the last decade of the 19th century and continuing into the present, a number of English arms makers—those that specialized in the manufacture of heavy-caliber sporting rifles—sold ammunition for their arms on a proprietary basis. That is, a cartridge for which there would be a limited demand, such as the .577, .470, .600, etc., would be manufactured in a lot of several thousand by an ammunition manufacturer such as Eley-Kynoch, and then sold to the company that designed the cartridge for resale. Thus, such a firm as Rigby, which designed the .416 Rigby, would be the sole source of the cartridges for its rifles.

Because the decline in the sale of British big-bore

rifles and the lessened demand for ammunition for them, the number of proprietary cartridges is quite small, and prices are high.

As it is most often applied at present, a proprietary cartridge is simply one that was designed by a particular firearms company and that carries the name of that company as well as a caliber designation.

protected point bullet   A bullet that has the lead core of the soft point protected by some means so that it does not deform under recoil while in the rifle magazine. The Winchester Silvertip bullet has a protected point, and many years ago Winchester made a similar bullet with a sharper point called the Protected Point. Nosler also makes a Partition bullet, in which the lead core is covered by the jacket to form a small flat point on a spitzer bullet, that it calls the Protected Point.

psi (pounds per square inch)   In America, the highest degree of pressure developed within a firearm chamber is expressed as pounds per square inch, or psi. The maximum pressure in a modern high-velocity centerfire rifle can be as much as 55,000 psi; a .22 rimfire will generate 25,000 psi, as will a magnum

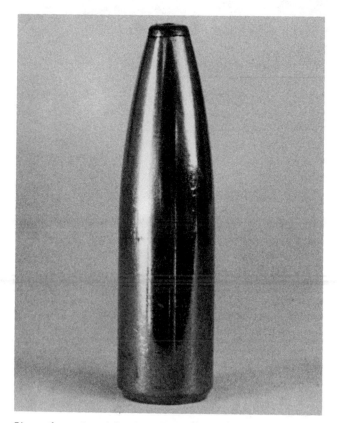

Since the pointed lead tips of rifle bullets are subject to battering and deformation in a magazine, some manufacturers cap them with harder metals or, in the case of this Nosler bullet, leave the lead tip nearly flush with the jacket.

handgun cartridge. Shotgun chamber pressures are considerably lower, ranging in the area of 12,000 psi. (See CHAMBER PRESSURE.)

pull The command given by the shooter for the release of a clay target. Also, the length of a gunstock from the trigger to the butt, usually referred to as length of pull. Also, the weight required to release hammer from sear, usually referred to as trigger pull.

pull, bullet See BULLET PULL.

pull-through On occasion, it is necessary for hunters to clean the bores of their shotguns or rifles in the field, where it is impractical to carry a cleaning rod. For this purpose, a pull-through is used. It consists of a string with a small weight at one end, and a loop in the other through which an oiled patch can be inserted. The weighted end is dropped into the barrel, grasped at the opposite end, and pulled through it; hence the name.

pump action Sometimes called a slide action or trombone action, a pump-action firearm is operated by the manual movement of a horizontal bar connected to the breechbolt. Usually this bar has at its forward end a handle or grip section, known as the forearm, the rearward movement of which unlocks the breech bolt, extracts and ejects the fired casing, cocks the hammer, and in some arms releases a fresh cartridge from the magazine for loading. The forward movement of the forearm then chambers the cartridge and locks the breechbolt into the receiver or barrel extension.

Pump actions were around as early as 1854 in England, when a patent was issued to Alexander Bain, but it was not until 1882 that an American—Christopher Spencer—received a patent for a pump-action design, followed by Sylvester Roper in 1885 and John M. Browning in 1888 and 1890. The Spencer-Roper patents were the basis for the Spencer pump-action shotgun, and although the Spencer firm went out of business in 1892, the New York firm of Francis Bannerman continued to market the Spencer shotgun until World War I. Another early pump-action shotgun was the Winchester Model 1893 designed by Browning. One of the most unusual pump-action designs was that of Andrew Burgess. Instead of the sliding forearm, the Burgess design employed a longitudinally sliding pistol grip and trigger guard assembly. The design functioned so well that it was purchased by Winchester in 1899 to get it off the market. Today, pump-action shotguns are manufactured by a number of American firms.

Pump-action rifles have never enjoyed as much popularity as other designs. Rimfire pumps have sold fairly well over the years, but at present only one centerfire pump-action rifle is made, by Remington. This lack of popularity is probably attributable to the "sloppy" feel of the moveable fore-end, and the fact that pump actions are less accurate than other kinds. While a pump can be fired as rapidly in the hands of a practiced shooter as an autoloader, the latter is easier to operate.

punkin ball The large caliber lead balls used in early muzzleloading muskets had trajectories somewhat similar to those of hand lobbed pumpkins, and in the slurred speech of the back country they became known as punkin balls. The term has also been used to describe the lead ball used in 12 gauge, and smaller, shotshells prior to the advent of the rifled slug. (See MUZZLELOADER.)

punt gun Before regulated waterfowling came about, it was common to use a large bore, single-shot smoothbore gun mounted on a punt, or specially designed boat, to shoot flocks of ducks and/or geese sitting on the water. These punt guns were capable of firing charges containing from 6 ounces to 1½ pounds of shot, and the recoil produced was absorbed by the boat on which the gun was mounted. Punt guns often weighted from 70 to 120 pounds with barrels as long as 9 feet.

The early punt guns were muzzleloaders, fired by a flintlock or a percussion lock. Later, breechloading punt guns became fashionable; and in England, where punt gunning is still legal provided the bore diameter at the muzzle is no more than 1¾ inches, screw-breech punt guns capable of handling 6 ounces of shot are still produced on occasion. Black powder was used in both the muzzle loading and breechloading punt guns, and the shot size was generally BB, although No. 1 might be used by some punt gunners.

Purdey, James, & Sons, Ltd. This London firm has, since its inception, manufactured rifles and shotguns which are regarded as some of the finest in the world. Founded by James Purdey the Elder in 1814, the firm was originally located at Leicester Square. Purdey was a craftsman who had learned his skills from Joseph Manton, and in 1826, he took over the Manton works on Oxford Street. As was the custom, Purdey passed on his training to his son, James the Younger, and with the elder Purdey's death in 1863, the second James Purdey built Audley House (57 & 58 South Audley Street), which has remained the firm's home since then.

Although Purdey has always made only Best grade guns, it has produced a wide variety of them. For many years, it made double rifles and magazine rifles based on the Mauser bolt-action. These arms have not been made for many years, and the double rifles are quite valuable.

Purdey shotguns are made in over/under and side-by-side configuration, and there have been single-barrel models produced for American trapshooting. All gauges are available from .410 bore to 12. Of particular note are Purdey's over/under shotguns, which are made with markedly shallow frames. These arms are generally regarded as models of the type because of their grace, light weight, and lack of bulk, and have served as the inspiration for other fine over/under shotguns.

Today, Purdey produces very limited numbers of shotguns to order. The delivery time may typically run several years and the prices are extremely high. Although it can be argued that some competitive shotguns hold up better under hard use, the fact remains that many Purdeys are giving good service after 50 and 60 years in the field, and no maker's mark carries more prestige than that of James Purdey & Sons, Ltd.

Purdey sidelock   Patented in 1880 by F. Beesley, a Purdey employee, this highly successful break-open action is still employed in Purdey shotguns. Basically, it is a bar-action sidelock, but it differs from similar actions in three ways: The tumblers are revolved into the full-cock position by the upper arms of the mainsprings as the gun is opened; the mainsprings are compressed on closing, not on opening; the upper arms of the mainsprings actually push the barrels up when the action bolt is swung aside, resulting in a self-opening movement.

The Purdey sidelock is a neat, reliable action; its self-opening feature and excellence of manufacture have made it highly popular with makers of fine shotguns. (See BAR-ACTION SIDELOCK.)

Pyrodex   Invented by Dan Pawlak, Pyrodex is a relatively safe powder for muzzleloading guns. Since it is not classed as an explosive, it can be shipped freely, which is a boon for those shooters who are not near a black-powder source.

Pyrodex comes in three grades: RS for rifle and shotgun, P for cap-and-ball revolvers and CTG for black-powder cartridges. The loads for Pyrodex are the same, in *bulk*, as the amount of black powder you would use. However, Pyrodex is lighter than black powder, so charges by weight should be recalculated. When loading Pyrodex, the ball should be pressed very tightly against the powder charge, compressing it. This, and "hot" percussion caps are recommended for good ignition. Pyrodex is much harder to ignite than black powder, and for this reason works poorly when used by itself in flintlocks. However, if black powder is used in the flash pan, and about 10 grains of 4 FG black powder is used as a starter charge followed by Pyrodex as a main charge, the propellant is satisfactory.

Pyrodex burns cleaner and produces less fouling than black powder, and it is neither necessary nor recommended that the bore be cleaned after each shot, as with the older propellant. However, its residue is highly corrosive, and after each use, the bore must be cleaned with a water-based solvent, as with black powder, dried, and oiled before storage. (See BLACK POWDER.)

quail, guns and loads for   Quail guns are commonly shorter of barrel, more open of choke, and often smaller in gauge than guns used for waterfowl because quail are normally shot at shorter ranges and lack the heavy plumage and tough skin of waterfowl. In general, the most popular choke is improved-cylinder or skeet, the most popular barrel length is 26 inches or less, and most popular gauges are 20 and 12.

The deadliest of all quail guns for the shooting conditions most commonly encountered in America is a short-barreled 12 gauge of 24 or 25 inches and with no choke at all (true cylinder). These provide large patterns that with modern shotcup loads are adequately dense for clean kills. The major advantage is a slightly greater margin of error for the shooter. Under certain conditions, the 28 gauge and .410 gauge are fine for quail, particularly on pen-raised birds on shooting preserves and in very close cover. Doubles and over/unders are often used by quail hunters because of their shorter overall length than pumps or autoloaders of the same barrel dimension.

Low brass No. 9 and No. 8 shot are probably the most commonly used loads for quail, although in open terrain No. 7½ may offer advantages on wild-flushing covies in the wind. Some Southwesterners use No. 6, particularly on the tough scaled quail, on the theory that one large pellet will do more to stop the bird than multiple hits with smaller shot. An excellent close-cover load is Winchester Special Skeet in No. 9 shot (12 gauge only); it has no shotcup wad

Quail country is basically open. These Florida palmetto flats are typical cover.

and its soft No. 9 shot opens its pattern quicker than most hunting loads. Thicket loads (spreader loads) are popular in some parts of the South, but probably 90 percent of quail are taken with ordinary hunting loads in 8s or 9s.

Quail are one of our most numerous game birds and are found throughout most of the United States. They adapt well to open country or to heavy brush, depending on terrain and hunting pressure. It is difficult to generalize about hunting techniques; however, the one universal tactic involves searching out a flock, "breaking" it, and then hunting the singles. Whatever kind of hunting, a dog is invaluable, and the pointers and setters are by far the most popular for this bird.

Queen Anne pistol   See TURN-OFF BARREL.

quick draw   See FAST DRAW.

quickloader   This tubular device, usually made of brass or plastic, is used to load tubular magazine rifles rapidly rather than one cartridge at a time. In common use in shooting galleries for many years, it has never caught on with field shooters to any great degree. Models designed for .22 rimfire cartridges, and holding a dozen or more Long Rifle cartridges or nearly 20 Shorts, are the most often seen form of quickloader. The same principle is employed today when speedloaders are used to rapidly reload a revolver cylinder.

rabbits, guns and loads for Cottontail rabbits are usually hunted with shotguns or .22 rimfire rifles or handguns. The cottontail is easily killed, and heavy shotgun loads are not required. Most hunters use a 20-, 16-, or 12-gauge shotgun with low base shells. No. 6 is the preferred shot size, and modified choke is usually preferred. With the .22 rimfire, most hunters use the Long Rifle cartridge with a hollow point bullet. Sitting targets provide challenging shooting requiring accuracy. For shooting them on the run, a pump-action or a semiautomatic rifle is best, as several quick shots may be needed.

For big western and northern hares (often erroneously called rabbits), the same loads work fairly well, but many hare hunters use something a bit more powerful—such as 1¼ ounces of No. 5 shot in a 12-gauge shell, or a .22 Magnum rimfire rifle or handgun.

raceway See BOLT RACEWAY.

radial pressure gauge The gauge used in the copper or lead crusher system for determining the chamber pressure of a cartridge is often referred to as a radial pressure gauge. The gauge is composed of a yoke that fits around the pressure barrel and is placed over a hole drilled in the barrel over the chamber. When the cartridge is fired the case wall ruptures, allowing the gas to escape through the hole leading to the gauge. The gas pressure pushes the gauge piston upward against a premeasured copper or lead cylinder (crusher) that is held between the piston and an adjustable stop. The crusher is then measured again with a micrometer caliper, and the amount it is shortened referred to a tarage table for translation into pounds per square inch (psi) or copper units of pressure (C.U.P.). (See CRUSHER GAUGE.)

radius shoulder See VENTURI SHOULDER.

ramp See FEED RAMP.

ramrod A ramrod is needed to load and clean any muzzleloading gun. Straight grain hickory is the most widely used wood for the ramrod. It should be well oiled with linseed oil and must be rubbed down frequently. This gives it strength and resiliency. The standard diameters of ramrods are: ¼-inch, ⁹⁄₃₂-inch,

A radius case shoulder takes the form of a curve (left) rather than an angle. Weatherby is presently the only manufacturer to use this design.

⅜-inch, ⁷⁄₁₆-inch, and ½-inch. Larger ones are sometimes used. Some shooters use the ramrod cut off flush with the muzzle, while others prefer an inch or so protruding from the muzzle. The longer rod is much easier to handle, especially when shooting in cold weather. (See MUZZLELOADER.)

ramrod thimbles Also called pipes or ferrules, these are short metal tubes used to secure the ramrod under the barrel of a muzzleloading rifle. There are usually two upper thimbles, which resemble pipes, and one entry thimble that is inlet in the part of the stock where the ramrod enters. Engraved thimbles are common on the fancy rifles. They can be made of iron, brass or German silver.

Ramsden eyepiece A positive optical eyepiece making use of two plano-convex lenses of equal focal length. The two lenses are separated by two-thirds of the focal length. The positive image is formed in the eyepiece, which when removed from the optical instrument, can be used as a magnifier to examine a real object. (See EYEPIECE; TELESCOPIC SIGHTS.)

rangefinder An optical device used to estimate the distance between shooter and target. Rangefinders come in many sizes, price ranges, and levels of efficiency. They consist of an oblong housing with a viewfinder, two viewing windows, and a focusing wheel. Some are highly accurate instruments, some next to worthless. Those that are made to be used in connection with rifle shooting and hunting are of necessity small and, therefore, of limited accuracy potential.

Based on the split-image principle, which in turn uses triangulation, the two viewing windows of a rangefinder are focused on a single point (the target) to give a range reading. The greater the distance between the two viewing windows, the higher the degree of accuracy. At very close distances the spacing of the windows can be quite close and still give good accuracy, as in some rangefinder cameras; but when the distance is in excess of 100 yards, accurate rangefinding becomes more complicated.

To check the range, the focusing dial is turned until the two images seen in the eyepiece lens blend into a single perfect image; then the range in yards is read on the calibrated range dial. Some rangefinders made for hunting have a magnifying eyepiece that enlarges the image for quicker, more accurate focusing.

Most rangefinders that are small and light enough to be carried easily by the big-game hunter have such a close viewing lens spacing that accuracy falls off badly at over 300 yards, which is in reverse of what it should be.

rangefinder reticle A kind of reticle employed in a telescopic sight. The design of a rangefinder reticle allows the shooter to estimate the distance between rifle and target by comparing some facet of the reticle with the size of the target or another object. The first American-made scope to advertise a rangefinder reticle was made by Weaver during the 1940s. The principle used by Weaver (still the most common design) consisted of regular cross hair with a finer horizontal crosshair slightly below it. The spacing between the two hairs subtended 6 inches at 100 yards. The theory in using this system is that the hunter knows the approximate size of the animal he is shooting at and can estimate the range by comparing the distance between the horizontal hairs with some part of the animal's body. Example: The average adult buck deer is supposed to measure 18 inches from the top of the back to the bottom of the chest. Thus, if the Weaver rangefinder's horizontal hairs just bracket him, the range will be 300 yards; if the space is only half-filled, the range is 600 yards, etc. Obviously, for animals of different sizes and shapes, and for various distances, the shooter will need to do a bit of fast calculation.

Some other scopes have used a number of short horizontal hairs projecting from the vertical hair to estimate various ranges, and some use dots for the same purpose. Some scope makers—Redfield being an example—use stadia wires that are connected to the power change mechanism of a variable power scope, and are used in connection with a visible calibrated range guide. In use, you adjust the power change ring until the stadia wires span the part of the animal you know the approximate dimension of, then you read the range on the range guide. The range guide will appear within the field of the scope.

The latest innovation is to estimate the range by the stadia wire method, then set the range on the elevation adjustment dial. These scopes have special elevation adjustment knobs that are calibrated in plainly marked 100-yard increments up to 500 or 600 yards. In use, the range is estimated by the spacing of the stadia wires as compared to the size of the animal or other target, and the elevation dial is then set for that range. With this method the reticle is placed at the exact spot the bullet is intended to hit. Several dials furnished with the scope are calibrated for loads falling within a certain trajectory curve. Blank dials are also available; these can be marked by the user for a specific cartridge or load to compensate for the bullet drop at various ranges.

The obvious drawback of rangefinder reticles is that they depend entirely upon correct estimation of the size of the animal being fired at. As the various

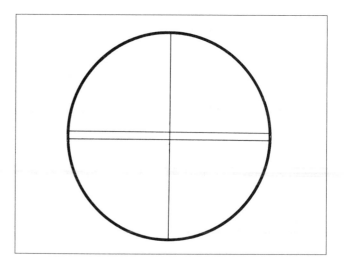

This is an example of a simple rangefinder reticle. The two horizontal crosshairs, or stadia wire, subtend a known depth at a given range. In use a target whose approximate depth is known is fitted between them, and the distance to the target can be determined by how much of it fits between the wires.

species of animals come in many sizes, and often do not stand still while adjustments are made, there is room for a great deal of error when using rangefinder reticles. (See RANGEFINDER; RETICLE.)

rapid fire The rapid-fire handgun phase of the National Match Course is shot in strings of five rounds, with 10 seconds allowed for each string. Normally, a rapid-fire phase will consist of two five-round strings, each fired in 10 seconds at a range of 25 yards.

In the high power rifle National Match Course, rapid fire consists of 10 shots taken from the sitting position at 200 yards and 10 shots taken from the prone position at 300 yards. These stages have time limits of 60 and 70 seconds, respectively. If the match is one for military autoloaders, the times are reduced to 50 seconds and 60 seconds. (See NATIONAL MATCHES.)

rate of twist The rotation rate of the grooves and lands in a rifled barrel; it is expressed as the distance required for a projectile passing through the bore to make one complete revolution. For example, barrel rifling that causes a bullet to make one complete turn in 10 inches is a 1-10 twist; one turn in 24 inches is a 1-24 twist, and so on.

The rate of twist that gives the best accuracy in a certain bore diameter with one cartridge may be entirely wrong for another cartridge using the same bullet. Also, the lightest bullet available for any cartridge may require a different rate of twist for the highest degree of accuracy than the heaviest bullet, and a spitzer bullet a different twist from a round-nose in the same weight and diameter. The longer the bullet in a given caliber, the faster the rate of twist that will be required. For example: 220-grain spitzer bullet will require a faster twist in .30 caliber than a 200-grain roundnose, and both will need a faster twist than the 110 grain .30 for the highest degree of accuracy. Big bores like the .45 caliber use slower twists than small bores, even though the bullets are of heavier weight.

The rate of twist must be sufficient to fully stabilize the bullet around its axis over its useful range of flight.

As a rule, the rate of twist of a rifle or handgun is of little concern to the average shooter, since manufacturers determine the twist that will give the best result with the widest range of bullets. Only in the case of a custom gun, built for a highly specialized purpose, would a deviation from standard rates of twist be a consideration. (See BARREL, RIFLED; GAIN TWIST; INTERIOR BALLISTICS; TWIST.)

RCBS, Inc. RCBS, Inc. was founded by Fred Huntington in 1943 in Oroville, California and later became one of the world's largest manufacturers of reloading equipment. The name RCBS is derived from the name of the dies the company was founded to produce: "Rock Chuck Bullet Swage."

As few good varmint bullets were produced prior to the early 1940s, Huntington decided to make his own and designed dies to swage .22 rimfire cartridge cases to form jackets for those bullets. (See HANDLOAD; LOADING DIE.)

real image An image formed by light that actually passes through an image point. The image seen through a window, for example, is a real image. On the other hand an image viewed in a mirror is a virtual image. Light rays passing through a convex lens converge; this is a positive lens and forms a real image. Light rays passing through a negative lens diverge, and form a virtual image between the eye and the lens.

rear sight On a firearm equipped with metallic sights, the sight nearest to the shooter's eye is the rear sight. Its purpose is the alignment of the shooter's eye with the front sight. (See METALLIC SIGHTS.)

rebarrel To replace the barrel in a firearm. A rebarreling job may consist of replacing the barrel with a new factory barrel chambered for the same cartridge, or with a custom barrel chambered for the same cartridge or for any other cartridge that will function properly with the action.

rebated bullet A bullet with a base section, or heel, that is smaller than the body of the bullet. The term could be applied to the common boattail, to the Lapua or to a cast bullet designed to accept a gas check that requires a rebated heel. Though the rebated shape is most usually used on boattail bullets, not all boattails are rebated. (See BOATTAIL BULLET; GAS CHECK; LAPUA BULLET.)

rebated head case A case that has a rim diameter that is smaller than the base diameter of the body is called a rebated head case (or a rebated rim case). The .284 Winchester cartridge, for example, has a rebated head with a rim diameter of .473-inch and a body base diameter of .500-inch. Rebated heads are primarily used in military machine arms.

rebated rim A cartridge rim with a diameter smaller than that of the case itself is said to be rebated. The purpose of this construction is to allow a large-diameter case to function in a standard-size rifle

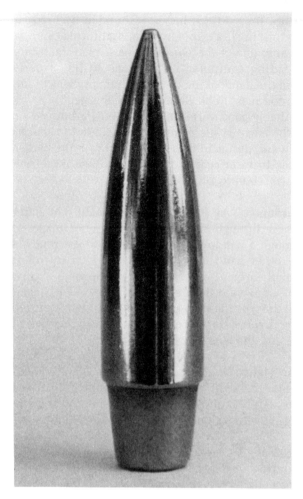

Bullets designed for target competition at long ranges are sometimes made with rebated sections at their rear. This smaller-diameter profile lessens wind drag and makes a flatter trajectory possible.

action with a non-magnum bolt face. The most notable use of a rebated rim in recent cartridge design is the .284 Winchester.

rebore To enlarge a gun barrel by drilling it to larger bore diameter. This is done to restore worn-out rifles to use. For example (depending on barrel thickness), a worn-out .300 Winchester barrel could be bored out to .338. With muzzleloading arms, reboring is often called "freshing out."

rebounding firing pin See FIRING PIN.

rebounding hammer A firearm hammer constructed to return to a partially retracted position after striking—some even return to a safety notch. A rebounding hammer is considered a safety factor in exposed hammer arms. (See HAMMER; REBOUNDING LOCK.)

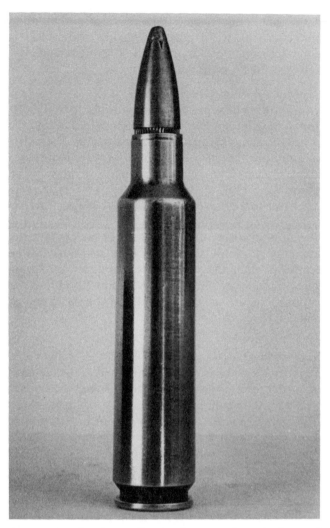

A case rim that is smaller in diameter than the base of the case is said to be rebated. This design is rarely used. The .284 Winchester case shown here is one of the few to employ it.

rebounding lock A lock that has the top of the mainspring and crank of the tumbler lengthened, so that when the trigger is pulled the hammer delivers its force and immediately rebounds to the half-cock position. (See HALF-COCK; LOCK.)

rebound slide In order to prevent accidental discharge, some revolver designs incorporate a device known as a rebound slide, whose purpose is to prevent discharge of the gun except by a deliberate, steady pull on the trigger. A typical rebound slide consists of a bar, under spring tension, to which a stud is attached. The stud blocks the rearward movement of the trigger against a casual or accidental pull. When the trigger is pulled deliberately, the bar, and hence the stud, is moved out of the way, and the revolver is capable of firing.

receiver Basically a frame for the action parts of a gun, the receiver is the part of a firearm around which the rest of the arm is built. The barrel is screwed or locked into the receiver, and the receiver also accepts the bolt, magazine, trigger mechanism, etc. The stocks of rifles and shotguns are also attached to the receiver.

receiver bridge See BRIDGE.

recessed bolt face A bolt face that is bored out so that the cartridge head is enclosed within the bolt head. The recessed bolt face fully encloses the brass case head in a ring of steel to contain the rupture of the head under excessive pressures. (See BOLT FACE.)

recessed choke See JUG CHOKE.

rechamber Rechambering a barrel involves reaming the chamber to accept a larger cartridge case, but one that accepts the same size bullet as the original case. For example, a .30/06 barrel of sufficient thickness can be rechambered to accept the larger .300 Winchester case, since both are of the same length and both use bullets of .308-inch diameter. Rechambering for the latter case permits the shooter to use more powder, and therefore to obtain a rifle of considerably more power than the .30/06 without the expense of fitting a new barrel.

recoil All firearms have recoil, which is the rearward movement of the gun in reaction to the forward movement of the projectile and powder gas emerging from the muzzle.

The amount of recoil developed by a given cartridge depends on a number of factors: the weight of the projectile and the propellant charge, called the ejecta mass; the muzzle velocity of the projectile;

Some modern bolts, such as the one at left, completely enclose the cartridge head when it is chambered. The older Mauser design at right leaves part of the case head unsupported, but enjoys the advantage of a larger extractor.

the velocity of the gas that emerges behind the bullet, called the jet thrust; and the weight and configuration of the firearm.

Considering these factors, it is obvious that a cartridge like the .30/06 will have far less recoil than the .300 Weatherby when using bullets of the same weight. Even if a 220-grain bullet is used in the .30/06 and a 100-grain bullet in the .300, the recoil of the .300 will be greater because of the greater weight of the powder charge and the higher muzzle velocity of the bullet and gas. However, if you compare the .300 Weatherby with the .458 Winchester, the .458 will develop much more recoil. Using the 180-grain bullet in the .300 Weatherby gives it a muzzle velocity of more than 3,100 feet per second, while the 500-grain bullet in the .458 starts at only 2,150 fps. Here the added inertia of the 500-grain bullet far outweighs the difference in velocity.

All of the foregoing is related to free recoil as developed by the cartridge, and assumes that the firearms used are of exactly the same weight. The weight of the arm determines the amount of inertia or resistance to movement, which acts to reduce the foot/pounds of recoil passed on to the shooter. Everything being equal, a 7-pound rifle will transmit much more recoil than one weighing 10 pounds. The amount of free recoil developed by a cartridge can be measured by mechanical means such as a dynamometer, or calculated by mathematical formula. While the dynamometer automatically takes firearm weight into consideration, weight must be included in the mathematical formula.

Recoil energy, which is expressed in foot-pounds, can be determined by the following formula. (One constant in the formula, C, is the velocity of gas escaping from the muzzle. It is equal to 4,700 fps.)

$$RE = \frac{1}{2GW} \left[\frac{bwbv + cwC}{7000}\right]^2$$

RE equals recoil in foot-pounds; G equals gravitational constant of 32.2 foot-seconds; W equals weight of the gun in pounds; bw equals the bullet weight in grains; bv equals bullet velocity in feet per second; cw equals the weight of the powder charge in grains; C equals 4,700 fps, the velocity of the charge.

Many shooters confuse *actual* recoil with *perceived* recoil, and are unable to understand why two rifles of the same weight, and firing the same cartridge with the same load, appear to have different levels of recoil. They don't, but the shape of the stock makes it feel that way.

To understand this, consider that the ejecta mass and the gas thrust travel on a course directly in line with the center of the bolt or breechblock. The stock is secured to the bottom of the action, with the grip also dropping down to about the same level. The comb of the stock is somewhat higher, with the point still being below the axis of the bore. Normal stock design drops the rear of the comb downward to place the heel of the butt another inch or so below the bore axis. As recoil is generated in line with the bore, and is above the center of the butt of the stock by several inches, the tendency is for the barrel to lift upward while it moves rearward, which causes a sharper thrust on the shooter's shoulder as well as on the cheek placed against the comb. This action increases *felt* recoil. To compensate for this, stocks that are made for rifles chambered for heavy recoil cartridges are very straight, with little or no more drop at the heel than at the comb. Also, if the butt of the stock is wider than normal it will spread the recoil over a larger area of the shoulder, delivering less felt recoil.

Another factor that will reduce perceived recoil—where two rifles have exactly the same stock design and the same weight with the same cartridge and load—is if one rifle has a heavy action and light barrel, while the other has a lighter action and heavier barrel. The one with the heavy barrel will have less felt recoil. The same situation is true of long and short barrels, the long one having less felt recoil. The reason in both instances is, that the weight near the muzzle causes less muzzle jump, and brings recoil back on a lower line to the shooter. (See INITIAL RECOIL; MUZZLE JUMP; RECOIL ABSORBING SYSTEM.)

recoil absorbing system In the broadest sense, any means of reducing either perceived or actual recoil could be said to be a recoil absorbing system. This includes the simple recoil pad. However, the term is usually applied to devices whose sole purpose is the absorption of recoil by mechanical means. One example is the use of spring loaded metal cylinders that are installed in a cavity in the buttstock of a shotgun. The rebounding effect of these cylinders, plus their weight, reduces both perceived and actual recoil. Another example is the Hydro-Coil stock, a two-piece plastic buttstock that employs hydraulic action (not unlike that of an automobile shock absorber) to reduce perceived recoil. (See RECOIL.)

recoil bolt In order to reinforce rifle stocks at their points of greatest stress, some gunmakers employ recoil bolts—steel bolts that are inletted transversely through the stock just behind the inlet for the recoil lug. Recoil bolts absorb some of the force generated by recoil and help prevent the stocks from splitting. On occasion, more than one bolt is used; a second

As a stock reinforcement in heavy recoiling guns, some gunsmiths use a recoil bolt—a steel bolt that traverses the width of the stock in the recoil-lug inlet. The bolt here can be seen as a dark strip in the lower rear surface of the inlet.

steel bolt or a hardwood dowel may be inlet ahead of the trigger mortise where the wood is thin.

Some manufacturers reinforce the recoil mortise with fiberglass, others with a steel block inlet with fiberglass just behind the mortise. (See RECOIL LUG.)

recoil brake Also known as a muzzle brake, a recoil brake is a device that directs recoil gases to the rear and upward in order to compensate for recoil. Recoil brakes can either be attached to the barrel or can be a modification of the barrel produced by slotting or drilling it at the muzzle. While recoil brakes do have some effect in reducing recoil and muzzle jump, some increase the muzzle blast felt by the shooter, since the propellant gas is directed at him.

recoil lug The recoil lug is the part of the action that contacts the recoil abutment (inlet) of the stock and allows the stock to absorb the recoil of the barreled action without splitting. On most bolt-action rifles the lug is an integral part of the bottom of the receiver ring, but on others it is a separate plate fitted between barrel shank and receiver. Some heavy-recoil rifles have an extra recoil lug on the barrel.

recoil operation See LONG RECOIL PRINCIPAL; SHORT RECOIL SHOTGUN.

recoil pad A recoil pad is a device, fitted to the butt of a rifle or shotgun, that absorbs some of the perceived recoil. Some recoil pads, mostly of older manufacture, consist of a rubber or leather boot that laces or slips over the stock butt and contains padding of some kind. Most modern recoil pads are made of soft rubber and joined to a hard rubber

When building rifles of extremely heavy recoil, many gunsmiths feel that reinforcement is necessary to keep the stock from splitting under the stress of firing. To solve this problem, Griffin & Howe has fitted this bolt action with a special sleeve on its barrel. The sleeve includes a forward lug fitted with its own fore-end screw, an open rear sight and a rear bearing surface that will also take up the strain of recoil.

backing that is attached to the stock by screws, glue, or both. The pad normally has a thickness of about 1 inch. A few have a layer of foam rubber that acts as the absorbant material, but most are molded with thin layers of soft rubber forming an X or V framework between the hard rubber base and the solid soft rubber area contacting the shooter's shoulder. (See RECOIL.)

Redfield Gun Sight Company   Founded in Denver Colorado, in 1909 by gunsmith John Hill Redfield, the Redfield Gun Sight Company initially produced iron sights and did gunsmithing work of a general nature. In 1958, the firm acquired the Kollmorgen line of Bear Cub scopes. These optical sights were highly successful under the Redfield management, and the Bear Cub and Kollmorgen names were replaced by Redfield's after a short time.

Redfield rapidly became an innovator in its field and expanded its facilities in 1968. Among the products it pioneered are the constantly centered non-magnifying reticle, the fixed-mount target sight, the wide-angle scope sight, and the high-powered variable scope. Today, the firm offers a wide variety of target and hunting scopes, spotting scopes, mounts, binoculars, and iron sights.

reduced charge   A powder charge that is lighter than that normally used in a particular cartridge with the same bullet weight is known as a reduced charge.

refraction   The bending, or deflection, of a light ray as it passes through a substance such as water or glass. Optical systems are designed around this principle; the angle and direction of refraction is controlled by the curvature of the lens. (See TELESCOPIC SIGHTS.)

regulating   The process of adjusting the barrels in a double rifle or shotgun so that both barrels shoot to the same, or nearly the same, point of impact. Regulating consists primarily of trial-and-error shooting while alternately driving wedges or inserting packing between the barrels at various points along their lengths. The ribs and barrels usually must be shifted and resoldered often before the barrels will shoot together reasonably well. It is usually a time-consuming and difficult process, and requires no small amount of experience.

If the barrels are regulated for iron sights, they sometimes have to be re-regulated when a telescopic sight is fitted, because this may change the point of impact. Likewise, a rifle regulated for scope usage may have to be re-regulated for iron sight usage when the scope is removed.

A rifle is regulated with a particular load, and changing the load may result in the barrels again not shooting in accord. The reason is that the shooter is dealing with two barrels of entirely different vibration characteristics. Changing the load may cause the point of impact to be higher or lower from one or both of the barrels, or the bullet paths from the individual barrels may cross or may diverge. However, by handloading, shooters can suit the load to the gun, rather than regulating the gun to the load. (See DOUBLE RIFLE.)

reinforce   The thick rear portion of a barrel, just ahead of the threaded portion in the receiver ring. This large-diameter section is designed to withstand the high pressures attained near the gun's throat.

relative brightness   The square of the exit pupil diameter in millimeters. For example, if a 6X scope has an objective lens diameter of 30mm, then its exit pupil is 30 divided by 6, or 5mm, and the relative brightness of the instrument is 25. (The square of the exit pupil is used because relative brightness deals with light within a given area.) A scope or other instrument with high relative brightness is desirable, but only up to a point. Since the maximum opening of the human eye is about 7mm, its ability to admit light is distinctly limited. (See EXIT PUPIL; LIGHT GATHERING POWER.)

release trigger   A shotgun trigger that works in the reverse of an ordinary trigger. Pulling back on a release trigger engages the sear; when released, the trigger moves to the forward position under spring pressure and the hammer is released to fire the gun. Release triggers are used by some trapshooters because it is thought that the releasing motion is more natural than pulling, and that it is effective in combating flinching.

relining See BARREL RELINING.

reload Although "handload" is the word preferred by most shooters who create their own ammunition, the synonymous term "reload" is found in many loading manuals, gun books, and magazine articles. (See HANDLOAD.)

reloading data Information regarding the components to be handloaded into a cartridge. In the case of a rifle or pistol cartridge it includes the brand and caliber of case, the brand and kind of primer, the powder type and charge weight, and the bullet brand, weight, and shape. Shotshell data would include hull, primer, wad column, and shot size and weight. For example, data for the .338 Winchester might appear as follows: case: Western .338; primer: CCI 250; charge/powder: 71 grains IMR 4350; bullet: 210-grain Nosler spitzer.

Reloading data can be obtained from the pages of various loading manuals. In the case of wildcat or obsolete cartridges, when no published data are available, the handloader may develop his own data via trail and error shooting while following accepted procedures. The inexperienced handloader should never attempt to develop his own data. (See HANDLOAD.)

reloading die See LOADING DIE.

reloading press Usually referred to as a loading press, it is a tool for holding dies and providing mechanical advantage to size and load ammunition. (See LOADING PRESS.)

Remington (company) At an early age, Eliphalet Remington II demonstrated a mechanical ability that made his homemade rifle a favorite in his Ilion Gulch, New York, community. Recognizing the business possibilities contained in the rifle's popularity, Remington built a gun and tool shop three miles from his farm in 1816. Demand for Remington's products, especially his rifles, grew until in 1828 he was forced to expand his operations. He built several small buildings at Ilion on the banks of the Erie Canal, which is still the site of the company's present-day plant.

Further enlargement of the plant became necessary when Remington began supplying military carbine rifles to Zachary Taylor's troops during the War with Mexico.

Remington's three sons became involved in the business, and in 1856, the firm of E. Remington and Sons was formed. His sons took over management in 1861 when Remington died. Developments at Remington continued, and in 1926 the company introduced Kleenbore, a noncorrosive priming. Shortly thereafter, Remington produced the first waterproof shotgun shells.

Remington merged with Union Metallic Cartridge in 1912; in 1933, Remington was purchased by Du Pont. In that same year, Remington acquired the business of Chamberlin Cartridge and Target Company, manufacturers of traps and clay targets. The Peters Cartridge Company of Kings Mills, Ohio, was acquired in 1934.

It was after World War II that Remington enjoyed its greatest success. Realizing that hand labor was prohibitively expensive on a large scale, the company modernized its manufacturing methods, and developed rifles and shotguns that could be produced inexpensively and were attractive and efficient. Some of these guns made use of "families" of parts—parts that were employed in several different models. Some of the more outstanding successes are the Model 700 centerfire rifle, the Model 1100 autoloading shotgun, and the Model 870 pump shotgun. Remington also introduced a large number of successful cartridge designs in the same period, most notably the .222, .22/250, and the 7mm Remington Magnum.

In addition to firearms, ammunition, traps, targets, tungsten-carbide-coated abrasive products, and powdered metal products, Remington has manufactured many other items over the years. These include bicycles, cash registers, typewriters, sewing machines, electric lighting systems, farm implements, cutlery, and power tools.

reprime In handloading, to seat a fresh primer in a fired cartridge case after the case has been decapped and resized. (See DECAP; HANDLOAD.)

residual pressure The exit of a bullet or shot charge from the muzzle following the firing of a round is extremely rapid and often occurs before the pressure curve inside the chamber has reached zero. Residual pressure is that pressure left inside the chamber following the projectile's exit. In fully automatic arms, residual pressure must drop to a safe limit before the mechanism will chamber another round. (See PRESSURE CURVE.)

resizing See CASE RESIZING.

resizing die See TUNGSTEN-CARBIDE DIE.

resolving power The ability of an optical system to resolve detail, or to form separate and distinct images that are adjacent to each other, is the resolving power of that system. This ability is dependent on two factors: correction of aberrations that degrade image quality; and objective lens diameter. Normally, a larger objective lens will resolve finer detail than a smaller objective lens, but for low power scopes, such as a riflescope, the human eye is the limiting factor of resolution. Put another way, the eye can resolve 15 seconds of arc in the field using a 4X scope. A good objective lens of 7.5mm diameter will resolve this 15 seconds of arc, but any objective lens larger than 7.5mm diameter for a 4X scope produces a theoretical resolving power greater than the ability of the eye to see it. (See TELESCOPIC SIGHTS.)

retained energy at target The amount of kinetic energy (measured in foot-pounds in America) retained by a bullet when it impacts on a target. At long range, retained energy is considerably less than the muzzle or peak energy. For instance, one factory .30/06 rifle load with a 150-grain spitzer bullet develops 2,820 foot-pounds of energy at the muzzle. Retained energy is only 876 foot-pounds when the bullet hits the target at 500 yards. Retained energy is important to the hunter since the energy available largely determines the effective killing range of the rifle or handgun. (See BULLET ENERGY; KINETIC ENERGY.)

retaining catch Any mechanism that holds part of a firearm in place, but is readily released, is termed a retaining catch or latch. One example is the spring activated latch that retains the base pin on single-action revolvers; another is the latch that holds the fore-end to the barrels of a double-barrel shotgun.

retarded blowback action See BLOWBACK ACTION.

reticle The aiming device in a telescopic sight is today universally called a reticle, but in former years it was also known as reticule and graticule. It is arranged within the lens system of the scope so that it is in perfect focus on the target when other elements are correctly assembled and adjusted.

The reticle itself can be constructed by any of three means: it can consist of spider web strands arranged in a cross hair; it can consist of metal wires soldered to a mounting disc; or it can be etched on a separate lens. Over the years, a wide variety of reticles has been offered: crosshair (in various thicknesses), crosshair and dot, dot, crosshair and post, post (flat-topped or pointed), rangefinder, and Duplex crosshair.

In past years, the reticle presented two significant problems to shooters. The first concerned the fact that reticles, when adjusted for windage and elevation, would be moved badly off center of the image, and in order to maintain a centered reticle the scope

would have to be shimmed (adjusted by inserting small metal wedges under the bases), a tedious process. And, in variable power scopes, when the magnification was adjusted higher, the reticle increased in size, often to the point where it blotted out the target. These problems were solved by shifting the placement of the reticle from the focal point of the objective lens (where adjustments could be most conveniently placed) to the focal point of the eyepiece. This development was introduced by Redfield in 1960.

The actual focus of the reticle is attained by adjusting the eyepiece (ocular lens housing) so that the reticle stands out sharply and clearly against the target. This is accomplished by loosening the lock ring at the front of the eyepiece and turning the eyepiece forward and back until the reticle is sharp against the target or sky to the eye of the shooter. The lock ring is then retightened against the eyepiece to hold it securely.

When parallax is present, the reticle image will move on the target when the eye is moved in any direction behind the ocular lens.

Scopes of fixed power are usually free from parallax up to about 6X and have only small amounts of parallax up to 10X. However, scopes of higher power ratings must have a parallax adjustment if accuracy is to be maintained. Variable-power scopes of more than 3X–9X usually have parallax adjustment. Either the reticle itself is moved by the sight adjustment knobs on the scope, or the lens arrangement is moved so that the reticle image is moved on the image of the target to shift bullet impact.

The most common riflescope reticle is the crosshair, and all of today's scope manufacturers supply some models of their scopes with this reticle type, regardless of how many exotic shapes some of their other reticle styles may take. A few years back, the post reticle was almost as popular as the standard crosshair, but today the post is rare. The theory behind the post was that it gave a broad, flat top that resembled the top of the iron post front sight, and would appeal to riflemen who used that kind of iron sight. It was also believed by many hunters that the post could be seen in poor light where the crosshair would fade out. This is true of very fine crosshairs, but is not true of medium crosshairs. Tests on the same object at the same time with identical scopes, one with a post reticle, the other with a medium crosshair, show that even when it is impossible to see the top of the post on the side of an animal in fading light, the crosshair is visible around the target so that the hunter knows where the intersection is.

One of the most popular reticles today is actually a crosshair that is formed by four very heavy hairs or small posts, with a fine crosshair center section.

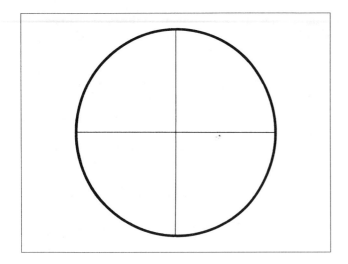

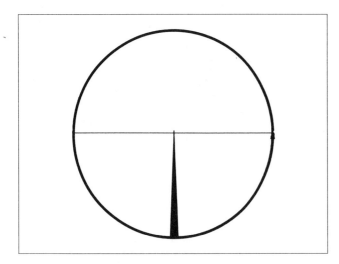

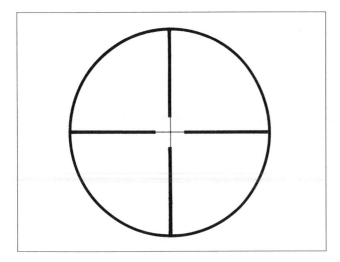

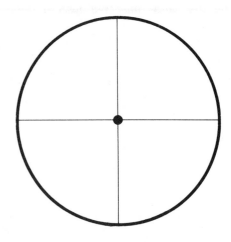

The most commonly used scope reticles are: crosshair, Duplex crosshair, crosshair and post, crosshair and dot, rangefinder (shown here in a wide-angle ocular lens).

center. Other reticles of similar configuration have a number of steps leading from the center to the outer field, making the posts larger by abrupt changes in thickness. These post/crosshair arrangements can be used as range finders by comparing the distance between certain points, or by comparing the thickness of the posts with the size of the animal. The same thing can be done with the dot reticles in various dot sizes. (See LEE DOT; PARALLAX; RANGEFINDER RETICLE; TELESCOPIC SIGHTS.)

retina   The sensory membrane of the eye that receives the image formed by the lens of the eye. It is linked by optic nerves to the brain.

retracting spring   Any spring (but almost invariably a coil spring) that returns a moving part to its original position can be termed a retracting spring. One example is the retracting spring used on the firing pin of some firearms. The firing pin is enclosed within a retracting coil spring, and when forced forward under pressure of the hammer or striker, it emerges from a hole in the breech face to strike the primer and is then withdrawn by the retracting spring.

reverse choke   A condition in the muzzle end of a shotgun bore with the interior walls tapering away from the bore axis in hopes of throwing a wider pattern than that produced by a straight cylinder bore. It is the opposite of a constricted choke, being instead a relieved dimension.

revolver   A revolver is basically a handgun in which a cylinder with a series of chambers or, rarely, a series of barrels, revolves around a central axis so that each chamber or barrel in turn aligns with the

This is generally known as the Duplex system. It has the advantage of being fast and easy to see on the heavy section, and the center section covers very little of the target. The tapered cross hair is also very fast to use for similar reasons, as the tapered cross hair also leads the eye to focus quickly on the exact firing mechanism. However, those handguns with a series of revolving barrels are commonly called pepperboxes, while the term revolver is applied to the handgun with a revolving cylinder and one or more barrels. (Two- and three-barrel revolvers are not common, but some have been produced; the Le Mat of the Civil War era is one of the most famous of the two-barrel designs.)

The concept of the revolver dates from the mid-16th century. A 1548 matchlock handgun with three revolving barrels survives in Venice, and in Copenhagen there are two surviving Snaphaunce revolvers, one of which is dated 1597. These early revolvers were plagued by design problems, mainly ignition and barrel-cylinder alignment, and it wasn't until the Puckle gun of 1718 that any large scale promotion of revolving arms was attempted. Mounted on a tripod, with a hand turned cylinder, the flintlock Puckle design did not obtain any notable degree of success either, and it was another century before the revolver achieved fame.

On June 10, 1818, Captain Artemus Wheeler of Concord, Massachusetts, was granted a patent for a flintlock revolver, which was later manufactured (in England) for gunsmith Elisha Collier of Boston. The Wheeler-Collier design sold quite well, but it was not until Alexander Forsyth perfected the percussion system of ignition that the revolver became a really practical arm. A number of inventors around the world worked on developing new percussion revolvers, with the Collier system being the first to appear in quantity. Quickly following were revolvers by Peder Rasmussen of Denmark, Jonas Offrell of Sweden, and Samuel Colt of America. Colt, in 1835, obtained an English patent for his design, and in 1836 he was issued an American patent. The basis for the Colt patent was the automatic rotation of the cylinder when the hammer was cocked, and although this in itself was not new—other designs preceded it—the Colt method was more reliable, simpler, and definitely stronger, thus ensuring its success.

The Colt revolvers were single-action designs, requiring the hammer to be cocked manually in order for the cylinder to revolve; with the cylinder chamber aligned with the barrel, the trigger was pulled, and the process repeated in order to fire a second shot. In 1851, in England, Robert Adams patented a large double-action revolver that required only that the trigger be pulled to automatically move the hammer to a cocked position, rotate the cylinder, and fire the gun; a second pull on the trigger would again rotate the cylinder and cock and trip the hammer, firing a second shot, and this could be continued as long as the chambers in the cylinder were loaded.

The Colt patent expired in 1857, and immediately Horace Smith and Daniel B. Wesson began producing the first successful cartridge revolver, based on a Rollin White patent of 1855. The White patent, acquired by Smith & Wesson in 1856, was essentially for a revolver with the chambers bored all the way through to accept a cartridge; coupled with the new Smith & Wesson rimfire cartridge—the .22 Short—the S & W revolver was the most successful cartridge revolver design until, when the patent expired in 1869, Colt and Remington introduced new designs.

In 1872, Colt designers created a handgun that is perhaps the quintessential American revolver—the 1873 (the first year of production) Model P single-action revolver, also known as the Peacemaker. Originally intended for the Army, this revolver was produced in a variety of calibers, but the one most famous was the .45 Long Colt. The Model P was rugged, quick to get into action, and could deliver a crushing blow at close range. It was the favorite handgun of the Old West. However, the Peacemaker, and other single actions, had several faults. They could carry only five shots in everyday use, since the hammer had to rest on an empty chamber for safety's sake, and they were slow to reload and fire repeatedly.

Both Smith & Wesson and Colt developed double-action revolvers that eliminated the faults, and by the time the United States became involved in the Spanish-American War, the standard Army sidearm was a .38 double-action Smith & Wesson or Colt.

In 1911, the Army phased out the .38s in favor of the Model 1911 Colt .45 Automatic Pistol, which was more powerful, more reliable, and faster firing. Since then, the U.S. Army as well as most of the world's armies have favored automatic pistols, while the revolver has remained a favorite in America among hunters, police, and some target shooters.

Today, revolvers are manufactured in nearly every industrialized country of the world, with many different variations of the original designs, mainly in the lock mechanism and the method by which the cartridges are loaded and extracted. The single-action mechanism, on which the famous Colt Single Action Army is based, is still manufactured, as are a host of double-action designs. In America alone, well-known firms manufacturing revolvers include Charter Arms, Colt Industries, Freedom Arms, Smith & Wesson, Dan Wesson Arms, and Sturm, Ruger, & Co. (See COLT, SAMUEL; SMITH & WESSON, INC.)

revolver timing In a revolver, the rotating cylinder must be positioned so that each chamber is aligned with the bore of the barrel at the instant of firing. If the alignment is off slightly to one side or the other, the timing is said to be off, and lead or jacket material will be shaved off the bullet, causing lead buildup at this point, and inaccuracy. (See RE-VOLVER.)

rib Existing in several forms, including solid and ventilated, with a variety of surface finishes—checkered, matted, smooth, and grooved—a rib is generally considered to be a raised area on a rifle, shotgun, or handgun barrel. It is usually situated on top of the barrel, and it leads the eye to the muzzle, serves as a sighting plane or base, or simply acts as decoration. Ribs are also used to fill in the space between the barrels on over/under and side-by-side shotguns or rifles. Thus, a side-by-side shotgun commonly has both a top rib and a bottom rib, while an over/under shotgun often has side ribs. (See SOLID RIB; VENTILATED RIB.)

ricochet A bullet's departure from its original trajectory caused by collision with a relatively unyielding object, causing it to glance off at a tangent. (See TRAJECTORY.)

rifle A rifle is a shoulder arm with a barrel into which longitudinal and spiraling grooves—rifling—have been cut to impart spin to a bullet as it passes up the bore. Of all shoulder arms, rifles have the longest range and the greatest accuracy potential. Modern rifles fire projectiles ranging in size from .14-inch in diameter to over .60-inch.

Rifle, The Sister publication to *The Handloader,* *The Rifle* was founded in 1969. It is a bimonthly magazine devoted exclusively to rifles, scopes, ballistics, and riflesmithing. *The Rifle* has a reputation of being the intellectual journal of the firearms field and is the official publication of the National Bench Rest Shooter's Association. Editorial offices are presently located in Prescott, Arizona.

rifle barrel See BARREL, RIFLE.

rifle bullet A conical object designed to be propelled through a rifled barrel. In flight it is called a projectile.

Ballistic enhancement was the primary motive behind the evolution from round ball to conical bullet. Conical projectiles for rifles were in use as early as the 1840s. The Flobert CB Cap (conical ball) and the hollow base cone-shaped Minié ball used during the Civil War are early examples.

Because of the relatively high velocity of modern rifle cartridges, rifle bullets for full-power use are now made of lead alloys rather than pure lead, and are enveloped in a copper or gilding metal jacket. These jacketed bullets are manufactured by cold-forming or swaging and are designed to fit a bore

tightly. For velocities under 2,200 feet per second, handloaders can cast lead-alloy bullets that are lubricated and slightly oversize, for the bullet must seal the bore completely to prevent gas escaping around its sides.

Rifle bullets are produced in many specific diameters and designs for a wide assortment of calibers and uses. There are armor-piercing bullets with steel cores and jackets; fully jacketed lead-core bullets for minimum expansion and deep penetration; boattail bullets to reduce air drag; frangible bullets with light jackets for no-ricochet, deadly varmint performance; sharp-pointed or spitzer bullets that perform well for long-range use; roundnose bullets for timber hunting; flat nosed bullets for tubular-magazined rifles; small hollow point designs for precision target shooting; and large cavity hollow points for quick expansion. A bullet's level of aerodynamic performance as a projectile is determined by combining its characteristics—point shape, weight, caliber, and length—to produce a rating called a ballistic coefficient.

The proliferation of good bullet makers has made it possible to obtain a bullet for virtually any shooting purpose. Of all bullets, the two most difficult to manufacture are match-grade target bullets, which must be entirely consistent and uniform for best accuracy; and the controlled expanding hunting bullet, which must expand enough to impart shock but still hold together and penetrate into the vital areas of big-game animals. The most successful bullet of this type has been the Nosler/Partition bullet.

Exotic bullets have been made with fins, explosives, and even—in one called the Gyrojet—with their own propulsion fuel. A type called the Glaser Safety Slug features a shot charge core rather than one of solid lead alloy. (See BITTERROOT BULLET; BOATTAIL BULLET; COMPOUND BULLET; EXPANDING BULLET; FRANGIBLE BALL; HOLLOW POINT; JACKETED BULLET; MINIÉ BALL; PAPER PATCH BULLET; SOFT POINT BULLET; SOLID BULLET; SPITZER BULLET; WADCUTTER BULLET.)

rifle cartridges, target In smallbore rimfire matches the only cartridge used is the .22 Long Rifle. In this sport, it is actually load rather than cartridge that is important. Most of the major ammunition manufacturers produce special match-quality Long Rifle ammunition for small bore target shooting.

Benchrest shooting for minimum groups rather than X-rings, at distances of 100 to 200 yards, has spawned a plethora of highly tuned cartridges. Many of these have been wildcats, and some of them have become commercial cartridges: the .22/250 was an early benchrest cartridge that did, the .219 Donaldson Wasp a successful one that did not. Benchrest shooting is primarily a sport of small caliber cartridges. Currently the holder of most of the records in the Light Varmint and Unlimited categories is the 6mm PPC.

Big/bore matches at 200 and 600 yards are commonly fired with the 7.62 NATO, the 7mm/08, and the .30/06 cartridges. At the National Matches at Camp Perry and other long-range big/bore shoots, however, where the targets and shooters are from 600 to 1,000 yards apart, the favored cartridges are those that shoot long, heavy bullets at high velocities. Favored commercial rounds for these matches are the 7mm Remington Magnum, and the .300 Winchester Magnum. The .30/06 is still used by some, and Winchester's .264 Magnum by a few. Many wildcats are used in the various long-range shoots. Al Hoyer, a gunsmith and shooter, has developed a line of small caliber magnum wildcats, based on modified Weatherby cases, that were much used by long shooters. His 6.5 Hoyer was the most popular of them. Other experimenters have produced similar wildcats by necking assorted big magnum cases to 6.5mm and 7mm, as there are some very fine heavy target bullets in these calibers, with high ballistic coefficients and superb ranging qualities conducive to putting shots in the 1,000-yard X-ring.

rifled barrel See BARREL, RIFLED.

rifled slug See SHOTGUN SLUG.

riflescope A common term for a telescopic sight used on a rifle. (See TELESCOPIC SIGHTS.)

rifle sights The metallic sights or optical devices attached to rifles that enable them to be aimed. Since the intent of a rifle is to deliver a single projectile to a target with precision and accuracy, the sights are an extremely important part of any rifle. It is a cliché, but true, that no rifle is better than its sights. Put another way, a poor rifle with good sights will usually outshoot a high-quality rifle with inferior sights.

This is a 12-gauge rifled slug, shown next to a dime for comparison.

Historians believe that sights were not used at all on shoulder arms until about the 15th century. Prior to that time, firearms were simply pointed in the direction of the target and fired. With the advent of improved ignition systems, such as the firelock, which enabled the shooter to use both hands to hold the piece while firing, the first crude sights could be employed. The later advent of rifling and long-range accuracy brought on related refinements in sighting equipment. Unlike earlier sights on arquebuses and muskets, which usually consisted only of a single bead or blade at the barrel's end, rifle sights employed a rear sight as well. With the alignment of a front and rear sight on a rifle, real shoulder arm accuracy was born.

In modern times, two basic kinds of rifle sights are in widespread use: iron sights, which can be subdivided into standard iron sights and aperture or peep sights; and telescopic sights. Any good rifle sight is expected to be easy and fast of alignment in aiming, readily adjustable (and preferably in fine increments), and rugged and reliable in holding its adjustment under field conditions. The success with which the various kinds of sights perform these functions differs markedly, causing considerable disagreement as to the superiority of any one over the others.

The standard open sight is the oldest and simplest of the three. It consists of a rear bar with either a V-shaped or U-shaped notch cut into it, and a front blade or bead. Aiming is accomplished by aligning the notch in the rear sight with the front blade or bead and superimposing that alignment on the target. The eye is thus called upon to focus on three aiming points at three different distances—an optical feat performed by rapidly focusing the eye back and forth between the three. This kind of sight seems fast, but is easy to misuse, for the tendency is to fail to pull the front sight down in the notch in poor light or in quick use. One other disadvantage is that most standard open sights have crude sight adjustments, even requiring the use of a mallet or hammer for windage adjustments. Nonetheless, this is the kind of sight furnished as standard equipment on almost all sporting rifles.

The other kind of iron sight, favored by the military and by target shooters, is the aperture sight, commonly called a peep sight. This sight differs from the standard open sight in that an aperture rear sight is utilized. The sight operates on the principle that in aiming the eye will automatically and reflexively center the front bead at the point of strongest light, which is at the center of the rear aperture. To use an aperture sight correctly, one simply looks through the aperture and places the front bead on the target. This makes it faster than a standard open sight. Rear aperture sights commonly mount on the receiver of a rifle, increasing the sight radius and enhancing accurate aiming. Virtually all aperture sights employ micrometer adjustments for easy sighting-in and sight picture changes.

The third kind of sight utilized on rifles is the telescopic sight. It is a tube containing magnifying lenses and an aiming reticle. Actually, telescopic sights are a fairly old concept, having been used in England, Germany, and the United States prior to 1850. In the American Civil War, both Union and Confederate sharpshooters utilized scope sights, made by Davis, Vollmer, Malcolm, and others. The first hunters to make widespread use of them were the buffalo hunters of the Great Plains.

The telescopic sight has evolved into a very satisfactory kind of rifle sight for both hunting and target shooting. Its advantages are numerous. The magnification (available from 1½X to 30X) allows the shooter to see better, make more telling shots, particularly at long distances, and avoid tragic mistakes. All scopes, or their mounts, are readily adjustable for focus, eye relief, and sighting. Scopes place both aiming point and target on the same focal plane, eliminating the tricky focusing between sights and target. The main disadvantages of scopes are weight and expense. But they are rugged enough for hunting and target shooting, if not military use, and most good-quality rifles now utilize them. (See METALLIC SIGHTS; TELESCOPIC SIGHTS.)

rifle stock   A rifle stock is the wood (either natural or laminated), plastic, fiberglass, or aluminum part of a rifle into which the mechanism is bolted and that provides a handle for the shooter to hold and fire the piece. The rifle stock may be in one piece or may consist of a separate buttstock and fore-end, but in either event its handlelike design provides four suspension points between shooter and firearm: shoulder, cheek, grip hand, and fore-end hand. These are also characteristics of shotgun stocks, but because of the deliberation of rifle shooting and the stress on high accuracy, the proportions and features of rifle stocks are decidedly different.

The dimensions and adornments of rifle stocks vary, but all have these basic features: the butt, which is the rear portion extending beyond the mechanism; the fore-end, extending under and providing a bed for the barrel; the grip, upon which the trigger hand rests; and the comb, the raised part of the buttstock that acts as a rest for the cheek. The top rear of the buttstock is called the heel, the bottom the toe. Rifle stocks may also have a carved and raised cheekpiece, a curved pistol grip, and most have a buttplate of some kind to provide a secure nonslip surface for the shoulder. In rifles that recoil

heavily, solid or partitioned rubber recoil pads are often used in lieu of steel or plastic buttplates. Fore-ends also vary in design, depending upon intended use. Most fore-ends on hunting rifles are made in an oval or U shape, but rifles for target shooting and varmint hunting have fore-ends that are broad and flattened on the bottom for shooting from rests. For accepting the mechanism of the rifle, stocks are precision cut, or inletted, and the mechanism is attached by means of through bolts.

Correct proportion in a rifle stock depends considerably upon the physical stature of the shooter and the kind of sights that are installed. Proper length of pull is very important, because a buttstock that is too long makes for a clumsy rifle, while one that is too short kicks hard and may jam the thumb of the grip hand into the nose during recoil. The correct length of pull for an individual who is 5 feet 8 inches to 5 feet 10 inches is about 13½ inches from butt to trigger. The amount of downward slant, or drop, from comb to heel is dependent upon the sights used. A stock with considerable drop may be comfortable for shooting offhand or with low-mounted iron sights. But for prone or sitting positions, or for use with the higher line of sight of a telescopic sight, drop should be only slight—as little as ½-inch from comb to heel, because the comb must be high enough to support the cheek during firing. A fairly straight stock also tends to minimize muzzle jump by taking the recoil thrust back rather than up. One compromise in rifle stock design intended to make a rifle comfortable with either open or scope sights is the Monte Carlo comb. Strictly for scope use is the rollover comb, which provides a broad, comfortable surface for the cheek on a raised cheekpiece.

In general design, stocks with clean, simple, straight lines are often called classic stocks; those with dramatic angles and curves are sometimes called California designs. These may feature Schnabel fore-ends, thumbhole grips, or other exotic characteristics. Stocks on factory made rifles are necessarily compromise affairs. Most of those on bolt-action rifles have in recent years been made for scope use, while those on other action types, particularly lever actions, have retained open sight dimensions. Actually, the average man with no peculiarities of build, who shoots in the conventional manner, should be well fitted with the factory stocks.

In materials and decoration, as well as design, rifle stocks have undergone a long evolution. The traditional material for rifle stocks has always been wood, but in the 20th century several other materials have been employed, none of which, despite their practicality, appear to possess the warmth and individuality of a high-quality wooden stock. Stocks have for centuries been decorated and embellished with elaborate carving and inlays, and with grip and fore-end caps of exotic materials. Checkering designs on grip and fore-end, intended to improve the shooter's grip, provide elegance as well as practicality. For both protection and beauty, stocks for rifles are finished with several coats of varnish, epoxy or, for the ultimate in richness, with hand rubbed oil stock finishes.

rifling Rifled bores differ from smooth bores in having a regularly spaced system of spiral raised ridges, or lands, that are produced by forming grooves down the length of a barrel bore. In a rifled system, the raised lands tightly grip the projectile, which is commonly made to correspond with the larger groove diameter of the bore.

Prior to the middle of the 16th century, all firearms had smooth bores regardless of whether they fired one or several projectiles at a time. Around 1550, grooves began to be cut into bores to facilitate the seating of the bullet. When some unknown designer conceived the idea of making the grooves spiral down the bore to impart spin to the projectile, rifling was born. With it came many advantages, including the ability to handle increased detonation pressures, a potential for greater power, and dramatically improved accuracy and range. Additionally, rifling made possible the use of conical, cylindrical bullets that offered ballistic superiority. An important innovation in rifled arms came in the early 18th century, when German gunsmiths discovered that a greased patch of cloth would form a seal around a projectile that was slightly smaller than bore diameter, while allowing the lands to grip tightly for accuracy and spin. German-American gunsmiths in the American colonies carried the practice to a high degree of refinement in the 18th century with the Kentucky rifle. Bulleted cartridges and the subsequent demise of muzzle loading made this technique obsolete.

Rifling systems vary in the shape of lands and grooves, and rifled barrels have been made satisfactorily with as few as two and as many as 20 or more lands and grooves. Most commonly, barrels have four or six grooves. However, at least two rifle manufacturers, Marlin and Sako, have produced barrels with a greater number of narrower grooves. This is claimed to give better obturation and reduce bullet deformation. However, it is thought by some that the advantages of this multi-groove system are outweighed by the shorter barrel life of the smaller grooves.

Rifling is achieved by four different mass-production methods. The oldest involves the pushing or pulling of a knife-edged scraper through the bore to cut each groove, an approach used by arms makers up until the end of the 1950s. Another cut-rifling

This sectioned rifle barrel shows three lands and grooves in the half; this means the barrel employs six lands and grooves, a standard number.

method, called the broaching system, utilizes a series of cutters that cut all the grooves at once. A third method, called button rifling, is produced by pulling a small carbide slug (the button) through the barrel to press the grooves into the steel. The fourth rifling technique in current use is the hammer-forging technique, whereby rifled barrels are formed by using heavy machinery to literally hammer the barrel blank around a tungsten-carbide mandrel carrying a reverse image of the grooves and lands. Already in use by some large manufacturers, hammer-forging is probably the wave of the future in rifling barrels.

Each system of rifling has its advocates. Manufacturers who use the hammer-forging or button method claim that these processes produce more uniform bores and that the stresses of forging create a harder bore, with resultingly longer life. Advocates of cut-rifling cite the fact that some of the finest barrels made are produced by this means. In fact, high-quality barrels can be turned out by all four methods, but it is considerably cheaper and faster to produce quality work with the button or hammer-forging methods.

Another critical factor in rifling is the rate of twist of the rifling, determined by how quickly the rifling completes a full spiral. Rates of twist range from one turn in eight inches (very fast) to a single turn in 50 inches or more of bullet travel. The longer and heavier the bullet in relation to bore size, the faster the twist must be to stabilize it in flight. A gain twist accelerates the rate of twist toward the muzzle, but no advantage has been proved for this system.

With only a couple of exceptions, small arms barrels are rifled to the right. This imparts a right-hand drift to the bullet, but it is constant and can be compensated for. (See BARREL, RIFLED; BARREL MAKING.)

rifling head In cutting the rifling into a gun barrel, that portion of the cutting tool that holds the actual cutting edges. (See RIFLING.)

rifling marks See BULLET ENGRAVING.

Rigby, John Renowned Dublin riflemaker and rifleman. In 1858, following the death of his father, Rigby became head of the Dublin-London gunmaking firm begun by his grandfather. Rigby match rifles became famous during the many years of long-range target shooting at Wimbledon, England. In 1865 his rifles were selected, after trials against such other makers as Whitworth, Alexander Henry, et al., for firing the second stage of the Queen's Prize. Rigby was selected to form the Irish Eight Shooting team 28 times. He led the Eight to victory in 1878 with the highest score made to that time—215 points at 800, 900, and 1,000 yards. In 1887 he became the superintendent of the Royal Small Arms factory at Enfield, where he saw the birth of the famed .303 Lee Enfield.

John Rigby closed the original Dublin shop around 1896 and, retiring, turned over the London John Rigby and Company operation to his son. In subsequent years, particularly in the early decades of this century, Rigby sporting rifles—and their reputation for ruggedness, accuracy, and reliability—became favorably known all over the world, in bolt-action or double rifle form. A much-liked cartridge for medium-game shooting was the Rigby .275 (a 7mm), as was the Rigby .256 Mannlicher for smaller hoofed game.

rimfire The first successful self-contained metallic cartridges were rimfires; that is, the primer was contained in a fold (rim) at the base of the cartridge, which was struck by the hammer to ignite the powder charge.

Today, the only rimfire cartridges are .22s, as this system is no longer used in larger case sizes. (See CENTERFIRE; RIMFIRE VARIATIONS.)

rimfire variations It is a little-known fact today, but nonetheless an important part of firearms history, that the rimfire design was once produced in many styles and calibers. The heyday of the rimfire was from the early 1850s through the 1870s. The original Flobert cartridges, designed by Louis Nicolas Auguste Flobert in the late 1840s, were eventually manufactured in four calibers—5mm, 6mm, 7mm, and 9mm—and were made with both round balls and conical bullets. In Europe, a 4mm rimfire was loaded for awhile for indoor target shooting.

During and after the Civil War, American manufacturers produced rimfires not only in .22 caliber, but also in .25, .30, .32, .38, .41, .44, .46, .50, .52,

.56, and .58 calibers. Many of these featured both Short and Long loadings. The .41 Short was the cartridge used in most of the hideaway derringers carried in the Old West. The .44 Henry rimfire was the cartridge chambered in the Henry Volcanic repeater, from which descended the present company of United States Repeating Arms Co.

Many of the smaller cartridges were offered even after World War I. Rimfires were definitely an advance over percussion arms, but their soft cases and the fact that they were not reloadable spelled the demise of all but the .22s.

rimless case The rimless case is currently the standard design of centerfire metallic rifle cases. It has a rim that is the same diameter as the case body. This necessitates forming a groove between the rim and case body to allow for extraction.

Rimless cases came into prominence with the development by the Germans of the 7mm and 8mm Mauser cartridges, and by the Americans of the .30/06. The primary advantage of the rimless case is that it feeds easily through rifle magazines, as there are no projecting rims.

rimmed case The first successful design of the solid case head came with the rimmed cartridge, so called because the case head or rim is of larger diameter than the case body.

This design was universally employed in rifle and handgun cartridges after the Civil War, but was overshadowed in the early 20th century by the development of such cartridges as the 7mm Mauser and .30/06, both of which are rimless. Its primary advantage as a case design is that the protruding rim permits easy extraction. A disadvantage in repeating guns is that with box magazines the rim of each round must be in front of the rim of that below, or jamming will result.

Today, the rimmed case is still employed in all .22 rimfire ammunition, in revolver cartridges, and in cartridges designed for lever-action rifles. It is occasionally used in a new design, such as the .444 Marlin or the .375 Winchester.

ringed barrel A barrel with a readily visible bulge resulting from the discharge of the arm with an obstruction blocking the bore. Shotgun barrels bulge more readily than rifle barrels because the barrel walls are thinner. With shotguns, the usual obstructions are smaller gauge shells or wadding debris from a previous shot. If pressures become high enough, or if the barrel walls are weak, a rupture may occur at the ring point.

More rarely, a rifle barrel can develop such a ring from firing with the bore blocked by mud, a cleaning patch, or other foreign matter. Invariably the ring will occur at the point of the blockage and may seriously impair subsequent accuracy.

ring trigger A variation of the standard trigger, the ring trigger receives its name from its shape, which is an enclosed circle in the form of a finger ring. This kind of trigger was found on some early revolvers, but is not in use today.

rising block action The rising block is a lever operated single-shot action type for light European calibers of metric designation and for some .22s. It has seen little use except in the Flobert-Warnant rifles, and certain early 20th-century German rifles. The design is unusual. The breechblock and barrel are connected by two arms that are integral with the breech and attach to the barrel by the use of pivot pins. Upon opening the action, the rising breechblock activates the extractor.

Rockwell scale See BRINELL HARDNESS SCALE.

rolled edge crimp See CRIMP.

rolling block The breechblock on the Remington-Rider single-shot action, which pivots (rolls) backward on a large hardened pin to open the breech, and rolls forward to close the breech. The hammer on this action has as its base a similar large block that rolls forward under the hammer to lock the breech closed at the instant of firing. Cocking the hammer rolls the hammer block back to allow the rolling breechblock to be opened.

rollover comb A modern variation of the Monte Carlo comb, in which the cheekpiece extends (rolls) beyond the top of the comb, forming a ledge on the off side. The rollover permits a high comb without an edge that will gouge the shooter's face. (See CALIFORNIA STOCK; MONTE CARLO COMB.)

roof prism There are two assembly systems generally used in prismatic binoculars. The most common, the Porro prism, has the objective and ocular lenses offset so that two lens barrels are actually formed, with the image going through the objective lens to one prism in a housing directly in line, then back to another prism that directs it to the ocular lens on the same line. This prism/lens assembly makes the binocular wide, bulky, and heavy.

With the roof prism principle, both the objective and ocular lenses are mounted in the same barrel, and the prisms are located so that the light channel forms a complex but narrow path that allows for a slender, compact, and light instrument. (See BINOCULARS; PORRO PRISM; PRISM.)

Roosevelt, Theodore (1858–1919) Rancher, cowboy, Rough Rider, big-game hunter, naval secretary, political reformer, author, governor of New York, vice president, 26th president of the United States, first recipient of the Nobel Peace Prize, the astoundingly energetic "Teddy" Roosevelt is also revered today by hunters and nonhunters alike as the father of American wildlife conservation. His accomplishments in this field include the establishment of the first federally protected bison herds; creation of the Wichita and Grand Canyon game preserves; establishment of five national parks, four big-game refuges, and 51 national bird sanctuaries; passage of the National Monuments Act; increasing the national forests by more than 43 million acres; one of the founders of the American Museum of Natural History; and setting a very visible example of hunting sportsmanship.

This studio photograph of Roosevelt was taken during his ranching days in Roosevelt's mid-twenties. Roosevelt was a lifelong hunter and conservationist.

Roosevelt was also a directing force in the early years of the National Rifle Association and was instrumental in the creation of the National Board for the Promotion of Rifle Practice. In 1966, a panel of leading American conservationists, sportsmen, and journalists named him "Sportsman of the Century."

Roper, Sylvester H.   See INTERCHANGEABLE CHOKES.

rotary magazine   Also known as a spool magazine, the rotary is a box-type magazine in which the rounds revolve around a center shank or rod. Each cartridge has its own separate cradle and its own follower, rather than a common follower as in the standard box magazine. The functioning of the action causes the rounds to revolve around the center shank, bringing each one in line with the upper part of the magazine, there to be engaged by the bolt and delivered forward into the chamber for firing and extraction of the empty case. The rotary magazine is especially useful for rimmed cases, because each round has its own compartment and cannot become hooked on another cartridge, rendering a relatively jam-free operation.

Although it is efficient, the rotary magazine has been incorporated in only a few rifle designs, most notably the Mannlicher bolt action and the Savage Model 99 lever action. (See BOX MAGAZINE.)

rougher   See CHAMBER REAMER.

rough shooting   The British equivalent of American uplanding, meaning to walk up the birds rather than waiting for driven birds to fly past.

round   A synonym for cartridge or shotshell. Also, in skeet and trapshooting, a round is 25 shots fired at clay targets.

roundball   Simply, a round projectile. Usually of lead, but sometimes made of alloy with tin or antimony, the roundball is normally fired from a muzzleloading rifle or pistol, but can be used in modern arms—shotguns and pistols as well as rifles. Roundballs are formed by molding or by swaging and are usually fired with a cloth patch when used in a muzzleloader.

roundnose bullet   A bullet whose tip is round, as opposed to pointed or sharply tapered. Roundnose bullets lack the ballistic efficiency of spitzer bullets, but offer better penetration, because they are less subject to deformation on impact.

Ruger, William B.   See STURM, RUGER & COMPANY, INC.

rule of three   The rule of three refers to sighting a rifle so that the point of bullet impact is 3 inches high at 100 yards. This sighting procedure is optimum for all high-velocity, flat trajectory cartridges to attain the longest accurate range. Using the rule of three, mid-range trajectory height of the bullet will not be more than 4 to 5 inches above the line of sight at the highest point, and the bullet will be right on the aiming point at somewhere between 250 and 300 yards, depending upon velocity and bullet shape. This allows a center hold on the side of a deer-size animal to give a vital hit out to 300 to 350 yards.

The late Warren Page coined the term and popularized the system. (See PAGE, WARREN; TRAJECTORY.)

Running Boar   A form of moving target shooting based initially on an appeal to those who find position or similar competition lacking in excitement, Running Boar shooting had its origin in Europe, as did the events it evolved from, and currently enjoys official status as an international competitive shooting sport. Running Boar shooting evolved from Running Deer shooting, a kind of target shooting that involved deer silhouette targets and big bore rifles used over a range of 100 meters. In 1964, a modification, the Running Roebuck, was introduced to popularize moving target shooting by making it more accessible. Running Roebuck competition featured .22-caliber rifles (either rimfire or centerfire) fired from a distance of 50 meters. Within a few years it was replaced by the Running Boar, which retains the firing distance of 50 meters, but is reserved in competition only for .22 rimfire rifles weighing not more than 11 pounds and having a minimum trigger pull of 1.1 pounds. In International Shooting Union competition, specialized rifles such as the Walther Moving Target Match Rifle and the Anschutz 1407 Match 54 Rifle are used. Scopes are allowed and preferred; for International competition the scopes are usually equipped with multiple vertical reticles to establish proper lead. Lead requirements vary from about 10 inches with high-velocity ammunition on the slow runs, to 24 inches on the fast runs if standard velocity ammunition is used. The standard course of fire consists of 60 shots fired in three series each of slow (5-second) and fast (2½-second) runs of a boar silhouette across a 10-meter opening. There is also a Mixed Speed category that features mixed fast and slow runs so that the shooter cannot anticipate either the speed or the direction of the boar target. Because of the expense involved in constructing ranges for these games and the lack of widespread shooter support in this country, the only examples are found at military bases; most notably,

Fort Benning, Georgia. (See INTERNATIONAL SHOOTING UNION; OLYMPIC GAMES SHOOTING EVENTS.)

runover   See CHECKERING RUNOVER.

Russian choke   Also known as Tula choke, this skeet choke design has so far been used only in 12-gauge guns; it features a "blunderbuss" muzzle larger than 10-gauge barrel diameter. The idea is to open patterns wider and more quickly and to lengthen the shot string. This kind of choke is found on the over/under German Rottweil and the Russian Baikal.

The choke chamber is approximately 6 inches long, and there is a slight amount of choke where true barrel diameter enters the enlarged area. This is said to slightly check the wad, permitting the shot pellets to open out into the greatly enlarged choke chamber, in which they encounter approximately .008-inch constriction (said to give some pattern control), and then open out into a belled section at the muzzle.

The Russian choke has little effect on common American shells with plastic shotcup wads, but it does significantly open patterns and lengthen shot strings when used with non-shotcup loads such as the Winchester Special Skeet load and many European cartridges. Dimensions of the Russian choke in one Russian Baikal were as follows: .731-inch bore diameter, increasing to .869-inch in the 6-inch choke chamber, then constricted to .782-inch at a point ⅜-inch from the muzzle, then opened to .813-inch at the muzzle. (See CHOKE.)

rust   Rust, the oxidation of iron or steel, causes deterioration of the surface and will continue to penetrate until the mass is completely consumed if the action is not terminated. Rust may appear as a brown oxide powder or as a reddish, brittle coating.

Rust on the steel of firearms can arise from many causes, but all are tied to moisture. When moisture is found in connection with any saline substance such as salt air or body perspiration, oxidation of the metal is much faster than with pure water.

Rust will form on most steel (except stainless) parts if left uncleaned, especially under the metal fouling and powder residue in the barrel. Modern rust-inhibiting compounds will prevent and remove rust on firearms if applied before and after exposure to moisture. (See GUN CARE; PITTING.)

RWS (company)   Short for Reinische Westfälische Sprengstoff und Munitionensfabrik (Rhenish-Westphalian Explosives and Munitions Works, Karlsruhe, Germany). Before and during World War I, this company supplied large quantities of munitions to the German armed forces, including small arms ammunition for rifles, machine guns, and handguns. The company also made a great reputation as a manufacturer of high-quality sporting ammunition.

After the war, the company's name was changed to IWK (Industrie Werke Karlsruhe or Industrial Works, Karlsruhe), and it later became part of the enormous Dynamit-Nobel industrial conglomerate. RWS was revived as a trade name for the unit's sporting ammunition, and it is still in use today. RWS ammunition is still among the best in the world, but other companies produce ammunition of equal quality and uniformity, so RWS products are no longer the standouts they once were.

SAAMI See SPORTING ARMS AND AMMUNITION MANUFACTURERS INSTITUTE (SAAMI).

sabot A sabot (pronounced sáh-bow) was originally a soft metal ring attached to a projectile to engage the rifling in a muzzleloading firearm. In smoothbore arms the sabot was a wooden disc, slightly hollowed to accept a portion of the ball, which was attached by iron bands. Currently, a sabot is a lightweight carrier surrounding a smaller caliber projectile, permitting that projectile to be fired in a larger diameter bore; the sabot falls away soon after leaving the muzzle, while the main projectile proceeds to the target.

saddle ring A heavy metal ring, permanently attached to the receiver, that is used to tie a rifle securely into its saddle holder. It is found primarily on lever-action rifles of the late 19th and early 20th centuries.

safety A device that prevents a firearm from being accidentally fired. The majority of safeties consist of a projection of some sort that must be activated manually, but there are also automatic safeties that are set whenever the action of the firearm is oper-

This experimental Winchester .375 bullet employed an unusual sabot. The bullet is solid steel, but has a copper jacket welded to its rear half to grip the rifling. The front half of the bullet is smaller than bore diameter so it won't contact the rifling.

ated, an example being a shotgun in which breaking the action automatically pushes the safety to the "safe" or "on" position. The half-cock feature found on many rifles and handguns may also be considered a safety device, in that while the arm is on half-cock it will not go off despite trigger activation. The safety normally blocks the sear, trigger, or the hammer function and it may lock the bolt or lever on some arms as well. On some modern handguns there is an additional safety in the form of a small metal projection that rises when the hammer is pulled back. As it rises, it blocks the hammer from striking the firing pin, and only falls out of the way when the hammer is pulled back fully to fire the arm. (See HALF-COCK.)

safety adjustment The act of correcting the safety mechanism. The adjustment may be made to a half-cock notch, such as those found on muzzleloading arms when the notch in the tumbler has smoothed and is no longer allowing full engagement, thus allowing the hammer to fall. Or it may be the adjustment, usually by recutting, of a smooth sear where merely moving the safety to the "on" or "off" position could fire the arm unintentionally. (See SAFETY.)

safety lever Normally, the safety lever refers to that part of the safety mechanism that is operated by the thumb or finger to move the safety to the "on" or "off" position; it is also known as the safety button, safety catch, and safety slide.

Some safety mechanisms have a rod connecting the external safety button, slide or whatever to the safety blocking device, which is also called a safety lever. (See SAFETY.)

Sako (company) Oy Sako AB is a Finnish corporation, located in Riihimaki, that manufactures rifles of high quality. The company's best known sporting product is a bolt-action rifle of modified Mauser type that is made in many model variations. In addition to good design, these turn-bolt rifles benefit, as do most Finnish arms, from expertise in metallurgy. Each part is made from a steel that is precisely right for the job it does, and machining and finishing are excellent.

Sako made its first success overseas with a miniature action that was designed especially to handle

.22 centerfire cartridges such as the .222 Remington. With the majority of other rifle makers, rifle actions for these small cartridges are merely modified full-size designs really intended for larger military or sporting cartridges. The resulting action is excessively heavy and bulky for the intended use. With the miniature Sako actions, the mechanism is built from the outset for the small varmint or benchrest cartridges. Sako also makes medium-length actions and full-size bolt actions, notably the Forester, the longest in the line. The Forester handles cartridges up to .375 H&H. Heavy bull barrels are available for target versions, and the company also makes a single-shot turn-bolt benchrest rifle. Sako also manufactures the Tikka bolt-action rifle.

At one time, the Sako Finnwolf rifle was imported into the United States. This is a hammerless lever-action rifle with a gear operated short-throw lever. It uses a detachable four-shot box magazine. In spite of the novel and very dependable action design and the convenience of the extremely short lever movement, this rifle did not succeed with American shooters.

Sarasqueta, Victor (company) See SPANISH GUNMAKERS.

Saturday night special An imprecise term used to describe any cheap, easily concealable handgun carried for criminal purposes. The term was allegedly coined by police, who often encountered such guns in bar fights on Saturday nights.

Sauer, J. P. & Sohn (company) J. P. Sauer & Sohn (J. P. Sauer and Son), arms makers, was founded in 1751 in Suhl, Germany, and the company was instrumental in the rise of the town as an arms-making center. After World War II, the Russians seized the company's assets, but company personnel who fled to West Germany reorganized it at Eckerenforde.

The company has always concentrated on sporting firearms, though it has also made military and police handguns. It is well known for its Drillings with two side-by-side shotgun tubes above a rifle barrel. These are of very high quality and traditional design. The company also makes under/over and side-by-side shotguns and break-action rifles, in several models.

In 1938, the company introduced one of the most remarkable handguns ever made, the Model 38H. This 7.65mm pistol was conventional in appearance and employed a detachable box magazine in the grip and had a concealed hammer. Unique was the decocking lever on the left side; with a round in the chamber and the hammer cocked, pressing this lever allowed the hammer to drop safely, so that the gun could be carried without fear of accidental discharge, but with a round in the chamber. In this mode, the pistol could be fired merely by pulling the trigger through the full cycle to cock and drop the concealed hammer. This enabled the shooter to get off a fast first shot just as though he were using a double-action revolver. Thereafter, the gun fired the rest of the shells in the magazine as a semiautomatic. If, on the other hand, the shooter wished to take deliberate aim, pressing the decocking lever again cocked the hammer so that the shooter could fire with the light single-action trigger pull. This design was sold to civilians before 1939, but then all production went to the German armed services.

At present, Sauer makes two double-action semiautomatic pistols incorporating the decocking lever. These are the P-220 and the P-230, which differ in detail. (These pistols are Sauer-SIG designs. SIG stands for Schwierische Industrie Gesellschaft—Swiss Industrial Company. Sauer manufactures some Swiss pistols so that SIG can avoid Swiss export regulations on handguns, but Sauer has helped in the design of both these pistols.) The P-220 is a locked breech pistol for heavy cartridges, principally the .45 ACP and the 9mm Luger Parabellum, but conversion kits are available so that it can be used for practice with the .22 Long Rifle and other lighter cartridges. The P-330, similar in design, is chambered for the 9mm Police cartridge, a new round. This cartridge is more powerful than the 9mm Short (.380 automatic), but less powerful than the 9mm Parabellum. The idea is evidently to provide a fairly powerful police double-action handgun without the power to penetrate of the full Luger round. Too much penetration and a tendency to ricochet is, of course, dangerous to innocent bystanders. The pistol is also capable of firing 9mm Short (.380 automatic), .32 ACP, and .22 Long Rifle cartridges by means of conversion kits. (See S.I.G. [COMPANY].)

Savage Arms (company) Arthur Savage of Utica, New York, organized the Savage Arms Company in 1894 and immediately started production of a lever-action centerfire rifle he had invented. This rifle, the Model 99, remains essentially unchanged today. Savage also marketed other sporting firearms.

In 1915, Savage Arms merged with the Driggs-Seabury Ordnance Company. Manufacturing at this time was concentrated on high power rifles and ammunitions, several .22 rifles, and an automatic pistol. With the onset of World War I, the company produced Lewis machine guns. After the war, the company reorganized as the Savage Arms Corporation and resumed the manufacturing of sporting arms.

The J. C. Stevens Arms & Tool Company was purchased by Savage in 1920. The corporation con-

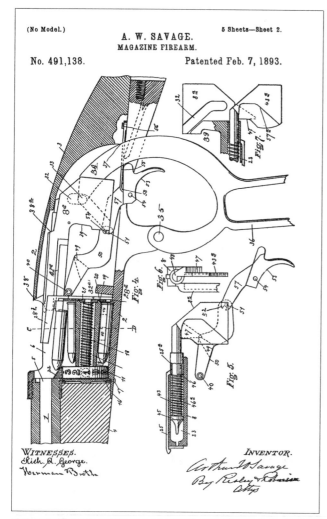

Here, Arthur Savage, inventor of the rifle that bears his name, is shown holding one of his early actions. Patent rights for the lever action—now known as the Model 99— were granted in 1893. The design was a remarkable one, surviving to this day, and proving perfectly suitable for modern cartridges.

tinued its growth by buying the assets of the Page Lewis Company, the Davis-Warner Arms Corporation, the Crescent Firearms Company, and the A. H. Fox Company. Both the Savage and the Stevens plants were converted to the production of machine

guns, submachine guns, military rifles, and fuses during World War II.

In 1947, Savage met increased production demands by moving the entire sporting arms division to Chicopee Falls, Massachusetts, where it was integrated with the Stevens plant. In 1963 Savage became a division of the American Hardware Corporation, now Emhart Corporation. Savage Arms now produces a variety of field rifles.

scabbard Also known as a boot, this device is used for carrying a rifle on a horse or ATV and is attached to the saddle by straps. Scabbards are usually made of leather, though there are some plastic designs. There are many styles of scabbard, depending upon the shape of the rifle and preference of the user. Some models are long enough to offer leather support up around the rifle butt, while others are much shorter, leaving the major portion of the buttstock protruding; a hood of leather may then be placed over the protruding buttstock for protection of the finish.

scaly case See LAMINATED CASE.

scatter load See SPREADER LOAD.

Schnabel fore-end tip A curve on the fore-end of a rifle stock that falls down and away from the main line of the fore-end, and then sweeps back up to that line to form a beak-shaped tip (Schnabel means "beak" in German). Sometimes this kind of fore-end is carved; usually it is left plain in appearance, with a slightly dished portion at the point where the Schnabel begins its departure from the main lines of the stock.

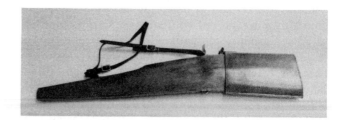

A saddle scabbard is designed for carrying a rifle on horseback. It should protect the gun, but still enable it to be gotten at quickly. The hood is removable. Ordinarily it is used only when the gun is being shipped.

The addition of the Schnabel affords no practical purpose and is considered decorative only. It is seen on a few American made arms, notably the Remington Model 7.

Schönauer, Otto See MANNLICHER, FERDINAND, RITTER VON.

Schonzeitpatrone In German, this word means "off-season cartridge." An English equivalent would be "pest cartridge." The term refers to any cartridge loaded with a nonexpanding bullet at low velocity, which is used to control pests on shooting preserves in the months when hunting is not allowed. These animals, usually small predators, are killed by gamekeepers, and their pelts are sold, hence the need for a nondestructive load.

Schuetzen rifle The Schuetzen rifle was built around a single-shot action and designed especially for offhand match shooting. These rifles took their name from the German *Schuetzenfest* (shooting fair), which had begun in Germany in the 14th century with crossbow matches. When German immigrants came to the United States, they carried the tradition—and their target rifles—with them, and over the years, the term "Schuetzen" came to mean a particular kind of rifle used for these traditional matches. These rifles were very popular both in Europe and America during the early part of this century. They were mostly chambered for blackpowder cartridges, like the .32/40, which gave outstanding accuracy with little recoil in a heavy rifle.

The Schuetzen barrels were much longer than we are accustomed to today and were also very heavy—thus most of the weight was placed forward to dampen sway and tremor. They were equipped with target sights of the finest quality, mostly with a tang peep sight and a front sight with various kinds of blades, beads, or apertures, depending upon the taste of the shooter.

The fore-end was equipped with a palm rest that was usually adjustable to suit the requirements of the individual shooter and that allowed the elbow to rest on the hip to further reduce sway and tremor for steadier holding.

Double set triggers were the rule—the rear trigger being pulled to the rear to set the sear mechanism, and the front trigger acting as the shooting trigger. A good double set trigger can be adjusted so that the lightest touch will release it, an advantage in offhand match shooting.

The comb of the Schuetzen rifle was very high because of the erect head position used when the eye was aligned with the sights. The comb normally dropped off quite steeply to the heel of the butt to give considerable heel drop, which was necessary for the position assumed by the shooter (leaning somewhat to the rear). The buttplate had a very long hook that rested on the deltoid muscle, and another hook that fit below the arm. The buttplate hooks often had ends that were rolled back in ornate fashion.

Some of the Schuetzen rifles were also equipped with false muzzles so that bullets could be seated from the muzzle, even though the rifle was chambered for a breechloading metallic cartridge. Famed riflemaker Harry Pope made many Schuetzen rifles with false muzzles.

Schuetzen rifles were usually highly prized by their owners and were often stocked with the finest wood and intricately engraved metal. Buttplates and action levers were also sometimes of highly polished brass of decorative design.

Schuetzen rifles and matches enjoyed considerable popularity during the 19th century, with the peak of the sport occurring about 1900 and the few years thereafter. The pastime was brought to an abrupt halt by the wave of violent anti-German feeling that swept over the United States during World War I. (See FREE RIFLE; POSITION SHOOTING.)

Schultz & Larsen (company) Schultz & Larsen Gevaerfabrik is located in Otterup, Denmark, and is best known in America for target rifles and for its Model 60 (redesigned as the Model 65 DL), a centerfire bolt-action rifle that the company exported during the late 1950s and 1960s. This gun had four locking lugs at the rear of the bolt, a highly unusual feature, and was chambered for a variety of cartridges. Although well made, it was never a commercial success partly because of lack of public confidence in its locking arrangement.

scope See SPOTTING SCOPE; TELESCOPIC SIGHTS.

scope mounts Primitive telescopes were in existence prior to the time of Isaac Newton (1643–1727), and no doubt some enterprising individual attempted to attach such a telescope to the barrel of a musket of that era. However, it was not until the mid-1800s that rifle-mounted scopes were seen to any degree, and then only on sniping rifles, such as those used by Berdan's Sharpshooters during the Civil War, and on the large bore single-shot rifles used by buffalo hunters. Both the scopes and the mounts of that era were crude, and other than the long, low power scope designs used by the buffalo hunters, mounted scopes were seldom seen on the rifle of a hunter in the field.

The German optics industry produced some excellent scopes following World War I, and in the period between the wars, the American scope and mount industry really began to develop. (A number of American firms had produced scopes and mounts around the turn of the century, but they were mainly

Before scope sights attained their present high state of reliability, some shooters preferred mounts that would allow the scope to be instantly detached for iron sight use. Shown are the Griffin & Howe double-lever mount (with a leather carrying case for the scope), the Griffin & Howe top mount, and a G&H double-lever mount with a windage adjustment dial.

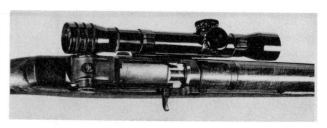

The solution to mounting a scope sight on a top-ejecting rifle such as this M-1 is to mount it to the side of the receiver. This particular offset mount was manufactured by Griffin & Howe.

low power target scopes.) The German mounts were high affairs, with tunnels through the bases to permit the use of iron sights. In addition, the majority of these mounts used a claw method of attachment in which one or two L-shaped hooks slipped into recesses in the receiver ring-mounted front base; the scope was pivoted down onto a post or into a recess in the receiver bridge-mounted rear base and locked with a lever or screw. Such mounts have never been popular in America, although since the mid-1970s a number of see-through scope mount designs have been manufactured here. Modern scope mounts are basically of two kinds—for target scopes or for hunting scopes. Target scope mounts are generally of the micrometer type, in which all windage and elevation adjustments for the scope are built into the rear mount, and the scope is free to recoil within the mounts. The rear base of such mounts is usually located on the receiver bridge, while the front mount base is attached to the rifle barrel. Examples of such mounts are those manufactured by Unertl.

Hunting scope mounts exist today in two basic forms—side-bracket mounts and top or bridge mounts. Each has certain advantages and disadvantages.

The top mounts are usually the easiest to install on a rifle, since factory rifles today are drilled and tapped for such mounts, and only a screwdriver or hex wrench is needed for installation. The base section, which may be a two-piece design, or a one-piece bridge, attaches to the receiver ring and bridge, and the rings holding the scope are attached to the base section via thumbscrews or a similar means. Scopes in such mounts can often be removed and replaced without losing zero, if the base sections are not moved. Examples of such top mounts include models by B-Square, Buehler, Burris, Bushnell, Conetrol, Leupold, Redfield, Weaver, and Williams.

The side-bracket mount usually attaches to the left receiver wall of rifles designed for right-handed use, and on some models the iron sights can still be used with the scope installed. On bolt-action rifles, some wood has to be removed in order for the mount base to be installed, and with the exception of the lever-action Winchester Model 94 rifle, most rifles are not drilled and tapped for side-bracket mounts. (Many such mounts, once installed, can be removed and replaced quickly if necessary.) Examples of side-bracket mounts include models by B-Square, Griffin & Howe, Jaeger, Kwik-Site, Redfield, Weaver, and Williams. One rather unusual scope mount, which is available in a choice of side-bracket or top mount models, is the Pachmayr Lo-Swing. This mount has a hinge on the left side, permitting the scope to be swung over to the left side of the rifle to allow use of the open sights, and back again when it is desired to use the scope. Windage and elevation adjustments are built into the Pachmayr mount.

A third kind of hunting scope mount, the V-block top mount, was once fairly common, but is not much seen since Bausch & Lomb discontinued its model. On such mounts, most of the adjustments are in the base, and if similar adjustments are in the scope, a maximum amount of adjustment is available; however, most V-block mounts were used with scopes having no internal adjustments.

The majority of American-made scope mounts are manufactured to fit scopes having 1-inch tubes. (German and other European scopes often have 26mm tubes.) And 30mm tubes are becoming more common. Such scopes are intended mainly for use on centerfire rifles and handguns. Scopes intended for use on rimfire rifles often have ⅞-inch tubes, and a one-piece tip-off mount is commonly used with such scopes. This kind of mount clamps onto a male dovetail machined into the top surface of the rifle receiver, and when being removed, is lifted off.

Scope mounts for handguns are mainly of the top mount type, and the same comments apply as for rifle mounts. Handgun scope mounts are intended to be installed and left in place, rather than being detachable as on some rifles. (See TELESCOPIC SIGHTS.)

scope mounting height The height the scope is mounted above the receiver is usually governed by the rings that hold the scope tube and attach it to the mount bases. Most mounts are made with rings in low, medium, and high, and the deciding factors as to which height is used depend upon the scope used, the rifle action, and the tastes of the shooter.

Scopes with very large objective bells such as target scopes of high fixed power or the larger variable-power scopes require medium or high rings, while the smaller hunting and varmint scopes can be used with low rings. (Some bolt handles, or a barrel of large diameter, can interfere with a low-mounted scope.) For most shooters, the lower the scope mount, the more convenient it is to use. (See SCOPE MOUNTS.)

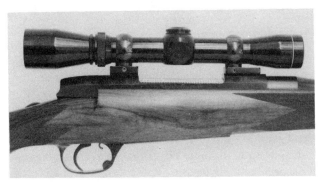

The scope in figure 1 is mounted considerably higher than the one in figure 2, since it must clear the higher bolt handle lift of the Mauser action on which it rides. Ideally, the lower a scope can be mounted the better, since it comes into the line of sight more readily when the head is on the stock.

scope sight See TELESCOPIC SIGHTS.

scoring gauge Any of several kinds of devices used for indicating the location of bullet holes in a paper target or for measuring the distance between holes. In centerfire rifle matches, templates with small flags show the location of holes, while benchrest targets are scored with a kind of dial caliper that measures the distance between holes in ten-thousandths of an inch.

scoring plug A metal plug, with a flange of a specific diameter, that is inserted in bullet holes in paper targets to ascertain the exact shot placement and/or whether two bullets have gone through same hole.

scoring ring A black or white paper target ring used to separate scoring areas of differing value.

screw-in choke See CHOKE TUBE.

scroll guard A scroll guard is an elaborate form of trigger guard usually found on the Schuetzen or other "free" rifles with which the shooter uses a hip rest position. Scroll guards extend below and in back of the trigger, with a place for each finger. They are often made of brass or German silver.

Elaborate scroll guards are often found in the early muzzleloading Kentucky rifles. The school of gunsmithing, and sometimes the maker, can be identified by the configuration of the scroll guard.

scrollwork A kind of motif employed in the engraving of metal firearms parts or the carving of stocks. Scrollwork usually consists of floral patterns—vines, flowers, leaves, etc.—and can be done either in a light, delicate style or with a heavier bas-relief effect. (See ENGRAVING.)

sear The sear is a mechanical link between the trigger and the hammer, or striker. Pressure on the trigger causes a disconnection of this link, allowing the spring loaded hammer to fall upon the firing pin. Close-tolerance notching connects trigger and sear, sear and hammer. This notching is one element of crisp, clean trigger pull and a gunsmith can hone the sear to create a smoother break in its connection with trigger and hammer; amateur tampering with the sear can result in insufficient engagement between sear and hammer, which could result in an accidental discharge when the gun is jarred or jolted. (See TRIGGER.)

season crack A crack that occurs in brass cases that have been exposed to the air for a long time (literally, as it seasons), often observed as a split neck. Season cracks are usually caused by the deterioration of the brass because of oxidation. These cracks may be prevented by storing brass cases in a sealed container, such as a rubber-lined military ammunition box, and also by coating the brass with some form of lubrication that retards oxidation.

seating depth The length of the bullet that extends into the cartridge case neck below the mouth and sometimes into the body of the case. Seating depth affects both accuracy and chamber pressure and varies according to the length of the leade. Normally bullets are seated so that they just clear the beginning of the lands in the barrel when the action of the gun is closed. Seating depth of the bullet is also dependent upon the length of the firearm's magazine.

secant ogive The kind of ogive that has a radius twice that of the normal tangent radius ogive. The secant ogive is normally considered to have less contact with the walls of the barrel, hence less bearing surface and less friction in the bore. (See OGIVE.)

secondary explosion effect (S.E.E.) A term synonymous with delay theory, which refers to the cause

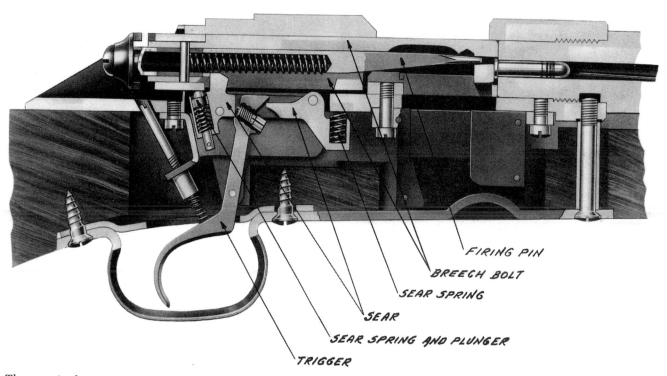

The sear is the connecting link between the trigger and the firing pin. This diagram of a Winchester Model 52 rimfire rifle shows a typical sear arrangement.

of a rupture of a rifle cartridge case that has been loaded with a reduced charge of slow-burning powder. (See DELAY THEORY.)

sectional density   The weight of a bullet in pounds divided by the square of its diameter in inches. Sectional density provides a weight length ratio for comparing bullets made of similar materials.

Bullets of the same shape, but with greater weight in relation to their diameter, retain their velocity longer. For example, two .308 spitzer bullets of 150 and 180 grains, respectively, will perform quite differently. The 180-grain bullet, which has a higher sectional density, will retain its velocity better and shoot flatter over long distances than will the 150-grain bullet, even though the latter can be given a much higher muzzle velocity.

self-loading action   See AUTOLOADING ACTION.

self-loading pistol   A repeating handgun that will fire the cartridge in the chamber, extract and eject the fired casing, and chamber a fresh cartridge, from the magazine each time the trigger is pulled. (There have been self-ejecting pistols manufactured; these are not called self-loading.) Self-loading pistols are also called semiautomatic pistols.

semiautomatic   Often termed self-loading or autoloading, semiautomatic arms are those that fire the cartridge in the chamber, extract and eject the fired casing, and chamber a fresh round from the magazine with each pull of the trigger.

semiautomatic action   See AUTOLOADING ACTION.

semiautomatic pistol   See SELF-LOADING PISTOL.

semibeavertail fore-end   On a shotgun or rifle, the width of the fore-end of the stock is generally equal to, or slightly less than, that of the stock surrounding the receiver or action. If the fore-end is much wider than standard, it is referred to as a beavertail, i.e., flat and wide. When the fore-end is only slightly wider than standard, in order to provide a better grip or to protect the hands from the hot barrel or barrels, it is called a semibeavertail.

semibuckhorn sight   An open rear sight for a rifle, with smaller "ears" than the full buckhorn sight. Though encountered on some older rifles, it is not popular today because the ears restrict the field of view and even cover much of the target. (See BUCKHORN SIGHT.)

semijacketed   See HALF-JACKETED.

semipistol grip   A compromise between the straight long gun stock, as exemplified in the famous Model 94 Winchester .30/30, and the full pistol grip. The full pistol grip places the hand almost perpendicular to the ground as it grips the stock, and the straight stock puts the hand nearer the horizontal; the semipistol grip comes between the two. Although it enjoyed considerable popularity on both rifle and shotgun stocks in the late 1800s, the semipistol fell gradually out of fashion. It was employed on the Belgian-made Browning shotguns as recently as the late 1960s, but is seldom used on arms of current manufacture. (See PISTOL GRIP.)

semirimless case   A case with a rim that is somewhat narrower than the rim of a standard rimmed case. The semirimless case also has an extractor groove in conjunction with the rim to ensure a secure hold by the extractor. The .220 Swift is an example of the semirimless case. (See RIMLESS CASE; RIMMED CASE.)

semismokeless powder   Today's powders for handloaders consist of black powder in various grades and smokeless powders. But at one time there was an intermediate powder known as semismokeless, which was a mixture of black and smokeless. Two such powders were Lesmok by Winchester, and King's Semi-Smokeless. (See LESMOK.)

semiwadcutter bullet   This bullet design, commonly abbreviated SWC, consists of a truncated cone with a sharp lip or edge at the base section. The flat nose tends to create a greater shock effect than a roundnose, while the edged base section is supposed to cut a clean hole in game, in somewhat the same manner as a regular wadcutter design cuts a hole in target paper; this hole prevents tissue from sealing the wound cavity and thus promotes greater bleeding. (See WADCUTTER BULLET.)

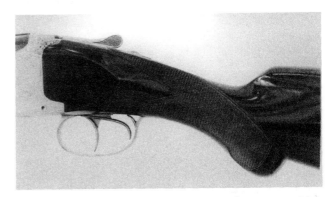

The semipistol grip is seldom seen on modern guns, which use a full pistol grip or a straight grip.

sensitivity The term "sensitivity" can be applied to firearms in a number of ways. An example is primer sensitivity; a "sensitive" primer is easy to detonate. It can also relate to the resistance to movement of any moving part of the mechanism, as in the sensitivity of the trigger to pressure.

serpentine A manually operated S-shaped clamp that held the fuse on early flintlocks. It was the forerunner of spring operated matchlocks. (See FLINTLOCK; MATCHLOCK.)

serrated trigger A serrated trigger is a trigger that has milled parallel grooves running longitudinally along its face to provide the finger with a nonslip bearing surface.

setscrew A screw, usually headless, used to set or lock two metal parts together so that they cannot change relative position accidentally.

setting back See BARREL, SETTING BACK OF THE.

set trigger See DOUBLE SET TRIGGER; SINGLE SET TRIGGER.

shank See BARREL SHANK.

shaping Making something into a desired form or shape, as in shaping a stock or grip. (See STOCK MAKING.)

Sharps rifle The invention of American firearms designer and manufacturer Christian Sharps, the Sharps Long Rifle and carbine were single-shot breechloaders that utilized paper cartridges and a separate disc-shaped primer that was automatically

A set trigger allows the gun to be discharged with an extremely light pressure—usually only a few ounces. The rear trigger is pulled first, cocking a series of levers that connects to the sear. When the front trigger is touched, the levers release the sear and the gun fires.

fed into position when the breechblock was closed.

Sharps's design, which was patented in 1848, employed a breechblock that rode in vertical cuts in the receiver. The trigger guard, which acted as the lever, lowered the breechblock. The shooter then inserted a cartridge in the exposed breech. Raising the lever sliced open the rear of the cartridge by means of a knife edge on the breechblock, sealed the breech, and fed a primer into position.

The system was strong, foolproof, and, above all, rapid, when compared to the muzzleloaders of the time. The federal government purchased 9,141 Sharps Long Rifles and 80,512 carbines for cavalry use during the Civil War. These guns, which were manufactured by Sharps's company in Philadelphia, wrought havoc on battlefields such as Malvern Hill and Gettysburg. Their long-range accuracy and blistering fire made a profound impression on the Confederate troops who faced them.

After the Civil War, the Sharps design was employed in the Sharps buffalo rifle and in the hammerless Sharps-Borchardt target rifles. Despite the soundness of their design, Sharps rifles were rendered obsolete by the perfection of the self-contained metallic cartridge and the repeating rifle. Sharps's company went through several reorganizations and ceased production in 1881.

Shaw, Joshua See PERCUSSION IGNITION.

sheath trigger Also known as a spur trigger, it is a trigger enclosed completely at the rear, and partially at the sides, within a slot in the gun frame. The trigger is usually housed in an integral projection, or spur, on the frame. Sheath triggers are not ordinarily surrounded by a trigger guard, the frame itself affording the necessary protection for the trigger. Sheath triggers are most commonly found on the small single-action pistols or revolvers that were popular during the late 19th and early 20th centuries.

sheep, guns and loads for While North America's four species of wild sheep—bighorn, desert bighorn, stone, and Dall—are not especially large or tenacious of life, the terrain in which they are hunted is difficult to negotiate and thus places its own demands on a hunter's equipment.

The mountainous country in which these sheep are pursued requires long hours spent at high altitudes, climbs of great duration, precarious footing, and shots taken at odd angles. Thus, the first requirement of a sheep rifle is light weight, preferably not in excess of 8 pounds with scope. The sight can be a 4X or a 2X–7X variable.

Magnum calibers are not advised for this kind of

North American wild sheep are not creatures of the crags, nor are they shot at long range in most instances. Any rifle of an adequate caliber for mule deer, equipped with a good scope, will suffice for sheep. The two shown here are an Idaho bighorn and an Alaskan Dall.

hunting. Their power is not required, the barrels that give them their velocity are too long, and the rifles that fire them are too heavy. The best cartridges for the purpose are the 7×57, .270, .280, .284, and .30/06. In all calibers, heavy bullet weights should be avoided. For the 7×57, .280, and .284, bullets of 140 or 150 grains are best; the .270 performs well with the 130-grain bullet, and the 150- or 165-grain bullets give the best results in the .30/06.

Experienced sheep hunters place great emphasis on quality binoculars and/or spotting scopes as part of a successful hunt. With the exception of the white-coated Dall, these animals can be exceedingly difficult to spot because they blend so well with their surroundings; once spotted, high magnification is required to judge the size of their horns. The best method is for the hunter to carry binoculars of at least 7X and for the guide to carry a spotting scope of 20X or more.

shell conditioner A mechanical device, separate from the loading press, used to return the outside dimensions of a fired shotshell casing to the original factory dimensions. The conditioner does this by using a steel sizing ring or a collet device. The conditioner may also decap the case at the same time, forcing out the fired primer.

shellholder During the reloading process, a device that holds a metallic case or shotshell must be held securely in a device that will aid its withdrawal from the sizing and/or capping die. This device is called a shellholder. Manufactured of steel to just over the head dimensions of the case for which it is intended, it is cut away along the edge enough to permit the case to be inserted, so that the upper portion of the holder grips the top surface of the rim or fits into the extractor groove. There are shellholders for virtually every cartridge available today, plus at least two "universal" shellholders that will fit a variety of case head sizes.

Sheridan Products, Inc. In 1945, E. N. Wackerhagen, an engineer and amateur gunsmith, designed and built an air rifle for his son. In that same year, he incorporated Sheridan Products in Racine, Wisconsin to manufacture the rifle, which he called the Sheridan Super-Grade. As the popularity of pneumatic firearms increased, the company added the Sporter, Silver Streak, and Blue Streak Models to its line.

The Benjamin Air Rifle Company of St. Louis, Missouri, acquired the assets of Sheridan Products in January 1977.

shim A shim is a thin piece of material, usually of steel, brass, wood, or plastic, that is used to raise an object or increase its thickness. In gunsmithing, a shim can be used to raise a scope mount base to make it level, to check the amount of headspace in a rifle, to restore misaligned parts, to check the cylinder clearance or gap on a revolver, and even to build up worn parts.

shimmer See MIRAGE.

shocking power See KILLING POWER.

shoe See TRIGGER SHOE.

shoot (noun) The gathering of individuals into a group for the purpose of firing at a predetermined set of targets with any number of firearm kinds within the framework of an accepted set of rules.

shoot (verb) To discharge a firearm.

shooting glasses Eyeglasses designed for all kinds of shooting and hunting, these protect they eyes from debris blowing on the wind, possible gasses from the rare cartridge or shotshell rupture, and fouling. The glasses range from comparatively cheap models with plastic lenses to tempered ground-glass types. Both are designed for a maximum of eye protection, not only from shooting, but also from other hazards, such as branches of bushes and trees, that could injure the hunter.

The better models of shooting glasses are light of frame and free from distortion. Often these glasses come in one of three tints, yellow, green, or gray. The yellow glass filters out ultraviolet rays, intensify contrast, and can improve visibility, especially on cloudy or hazy days. The yellows are frequently used for target shooting, especially at clay birds against a hazy background. Green and gray lenses filter out a large degree of the ultraviolet but yield more normal color rendition and are often preferred for hunting.

shooting glove Two kinds of shooting gloves are commonly employed. The first is used by riflemen; it is a heavily padded fingerless glove made of leather and canvas that is worn on the hand that grasps the fore-end. Its purpose is to protect the hand and wrist from the rifle sling.

Another kind of shooting glove is worn by trap and skeet shooters. It is made of thin leather or leather and elastic cloth. The purpose of such gloves, which can be worn on one or both hands, is to provide a more secure grip on the gun and to protect the forward hand from the heat of the barrel.

shooting jacket Competitive riflemen employ shooting jackets as an aid in steadying themselves

Part of the paraphernalia necessary to any competitive rifle shooter is a shooting jacket and glove. The jackets are made of either canvas or leather and are padded at the shoulder and elbows. The glove is also heavily padded and extends partway up the forearm. It is designed to protect the wrist from cutting by the sling and is sometimes made without fingers.

and as a complement to the rifle sling. Traditionally, a shooting jacket is made of canvas and has heavily padded elbows with an additional pad at the shooting shoulder and one on the upper arm that fits under the sling loop.

Shooters who compete under ISU rules wear tightly fitted all-leather jackets that are equipped with a series of tightening buckles. These specialized jackets act as a brace for the entire upper body and are invaluable in maintaining a steady hold.

shooting preserve The birth of the shooting preserve dates back to the 18th century when private grounds were stocked with game to allow for a steady supply of prey. The object of the preserve is to raise animals and birds in a controlled environment, usually with special feeding programs, and to keep the quarry in confinement until release time.

Today there are both public and private shooting preserves. The public preserves are on land owned by national or state governments, while the private preserves are on land owned by individuals, groups of owners, or corporations. The popularity of the shooting preserve is based on the fact that some hunters have found their favorite grounds too crowded and that the preserve owner can ensure that only a certain number of hunters will take to the field at a given time. If run properly, the shooting preserve can be a sporting proposition; however, it can also be abused when game is set out into the field only moments before the arrival of the shooters, given no time to disperse and grow used to the habitat.

The most popular quarry of shooting preserves is the ringneck pheasant. The pheasant is used so often because it has a tendency to revert to its wild state very quickly after release, offering the hunter a challenge rather than a condition of gunning for a tame specimen. Another bird that has gained in popularity is the chukar partridge, though it does not seem to revert to its wild nature as rapidly as does the pheasant.

The shooting preserve has become a home ground for the raising of fine dogs as well. Many field trials are held on shooting preserves today. Dog training on these grounds has also gained in popularity, and often the preserve will have a professional dog trainer on hand.

The big-game preserve is far less prevalent than the small game or bird preserve, although on some bird farms it is possible to purchase entrance to the land to hunt native species of large (and small) game during the open seasons. Big-game preserves may offer exotic game, including African species. This kind of preserve tries to maintain a habitat for the game animal, rather than attempting to confine the game and feed it. If the terrain is right, this game can revert to its wild state in a short time and be as difficult to locate and kill as it was in its natural state.

shooting school The shooting school is basically a short course of gun instruction given by experts. The school may begin with the basics, and may or may not award a certificate of completition. The major areas of instruction are usually safety, firearms handling, target shooting, best shooting form, and other facets that make the shooter more proficient.

Often a shooting school will be held on a private shooting preserve where the participant, at the close of his basic class instruction and practice sessions, has an opportunity to hunt. When this activity is a part of the school, the student has an opportunity to learn field safety and manners.

shooting stake A stake set into the ground at the target range that bears a shooter's identification and indicates his shooting position and target.

shoot-off In trap or skeet shooting, when two or more participants end their shooting round in a tie, a shoot-off round is held to decide the winner. One round of 25 targets may decide this event, or as many as 100 rounds may be fired. Informally, a shoot-off may also be held in any competition where two or more persons have ended their firing in a tie.

Short (.22) A rimfire .22 cartridge with a straight case .423-inch in length. It is loaded with a lead bullet, sometimes plated, usually weighing 27 grains in the hollow point and 29 grains in the solid point variety.

The .22 Short was first introduced in 1857, when Smith & Wesson brought out its first revolver, and was intended for close-range self-defense. It soon became a popular small-game and target load. Many revolvers, pistols, and rifles have been designed to chamber the .22 Short. It is effective for squirrel, rabbit, and pest shooting at close range and is still used for some forms of target shooting. (See LONG [.22]; LONG RIFLE [.22].)

short action A bolt action designed to handle cartridges shorter in length than usual. The Mauser short action is the best known, it handles cartridges shorter in length than usual with the standard 57mm Mauser cartridge case. Short bolt actions have the advantage of shorter bolt throws, which makes the action easier to operate, and the short action also reduces the weight and overall length of the rifle. (See BOLT ACTION.)

short recoil shotgun A recoil operated repeating shotgun employs recoil energy to eject a fired case, cock the action, and move a new shell from the magazine into the chamber. With a short recoil action, the usual arrangement is to lock the barrel and the breechbolt together at the instant of firing so that they recoil together for a distance less than the length of the breechbolt. During this movement, the pressure of the powder gas drops to safe levels. Then the barrel and the breechbolt separate. The barrel returns to firing position, but the breechbolt continues rearward and operates an ejector for the fired case, and a mechanical carrier brings an unfired shell into position for loading. When the breechbolt returns under spring pressure, it pushes the new cartridge into the chamber for the next shot. The gun is also cocked by the moving breechbolt. (In a long recoil action, the barrel and the breechbolt recoil together for a much longer distance.)

shot Pellets used in shotgun cartridges. Normally these are spherical, or as nearly as possible so, and the more of them in a load that remain spherical through the traumas of firing and passage through the barrel, the tighter the load tends to pattern.

Until recently, almost all shot was lead. To make lead shot harder, and thus more resistant to deformation, manufacturers add antimony. Some top this

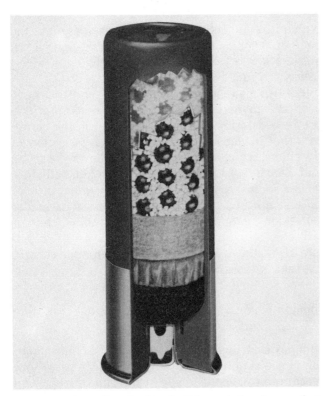

To protect the pellets in this shell from deforming on their passage through the barrel, Winchester has padded them with a granulated plastic called Grex.

with a thin plating of copper or nickel, although tests indicate that the plating is actually too thin to have much effect on pellet performance. The most critical aspect is pellet hardness, or how well it can be protected against setback deformation at the instant of firing. In modern plastic buffered shotshell loads containing finely ground plastic mixed with the shot, the plastic reduces deformation by filling the interstices between pellets.

Experiments are underway to determine if it is economically feasible to produce shot pellets of a teardrop shape to give them a higher ballistic coefficient, better flight characteristics, and more efficiency downrange. This could be of particular advantage to the new steel pellets, which are approximately one-third larger than lead pellets. Steel pellets have proved surprisingly effective on game, despite their lighter weight, because of their hardness and excellent retained "form factor" (they remain round, without deforming as does lead). Combining this feature with a better aerodynamic shape could result in further increasing steel shot performance.

shot, bridging of Spherical bodies, such as shot pellets, sometimes jam when poured through a narrow circular opening. The pellets actually form arches or "bridges" by contacting each other under the pull of gravity as the opening narrows. This occurs in loading press reservoirs, which are usually in the form of upside-down plastic flasks. The condition should be noted and corrected (usually by tapping the reservoir) as soon as possible or it will result in an empty or underloaded shell. This normally happens with pellets larger in diameter than No. 7½.

shot collar A ring of thin but tough plastic loaded into a shotgun shell between the shot and the wall of the case. When the cartridge is fired, the shot charge moves down the barrel with the plastic between the shot and the barrel wall. This protects the shot from "scrubbing" and produces more even patterns. Reduction of the number of deformed pellets also prevents "fliers"—pellets that fly completely outside the main circular shot pattern. Shot collars are often incorporated into one-piece shotcups. (See SHOTCUP WAD.)

shotcup wad Shotcup wads are plastic one-piece shotgun wads incorporating a recoil reducing wad that seals the bore against gas blow by, and a shotcup or shot pouch to hold the pellets. The walls of the shotcup also act as a shot collar and protect the pellets from deformation by the bore. One-piece shotcup wads are easier to load into the cartridge case than old-fashioned multi-unit wads. (See SHOT COLLAR; SHOT POUCH.)

shotgun A smoothbore firearm that usually fires a charge of small pellets rather than a single projectile. In earlier times, the distinction did not exist, a smoothbore gun was used to fire both charges of shot and single round balls. After the introduction of rifling, however, the rifled arms were used exclusively to fire single projectiles, while smoothbores continued to be used with single bullets or shot charges. In modern times, shotguns have become specialized arms designed for use with shot pellets, but even today shotguns can be used to fire single round balls or conoid slugs at low velocity for short-range big-game hunting. (It is also true that special shot cartridges are made or can be handloaded for use in modern rifled arms.) The primary distinction, however, remains valid: Modern rifles are primarily intended for bullets; shotguns for charges of shot.

Ironically, the very best shotguns are more complex than rifles, incorporate more intangible qualities of style and handling, and cost far more than the average fine rifle.

shotgun ballistics Shotgun ballistics are radically different from rifle ballistics, not only in the actual speeds of the various projectiles involved, but in the scope and purpose of the projectiles themselves. The ballistics of bulleted cartridges have changed dramatically since the introduction of metallic cartridges. Velocities have nearly doubled on the average; acceptable chamber pressures are far greater; and accuracy is greatly improved. Shotshells, however, have exhibited far less change.

The limiting factor in shotgun ballistics is the shot pellet. Being a sphere, it is self-stabilizing; i.e., it does not need rifling to fly on a true course. But at the same time, it has far less aerodynamic efficiency than a bullet and loses velocity at a far greater rate. In theory, it is possible to drive a shot charge at rifle speeds. However, this would require a pellet material other than lead, as the shock of the expanding gases would deform most of the pellets in the charge. And, to date, no other material save lead has both the ballistic properties and the low cost to serve as satisfactory shot over the wide range of uses required. (Steel shot, although satisfactory, is far too costly for protracted use in sports such as skeet and trap, and is ballistically inferior to lead.)

The earliest shotshells were loaded with black powder, and produced chamber pressures of about 5,000 pounds per square inch to 7,000 psi. Pressures in modern shells range from 11,000 psi to 13,000 psi. In contrast, modern rifle ammunition gives pressures of 40,000 psi to 55,000 psi.

Not only are pellet velocities much lower, but there is a far lower variance in velocities than occurs in rifle cartridges. As an example, here are some typical velocities of modern shells:

12-gauge trap	1⅛ ounces, No. 7½ shot	1,200 feet per second
12-gauge (high velocity)	1¼ ounces, No. 6	1,330 feet per second
12-gauge 3-inch magnum	1⅝ ounces, No. 6	1,315 feet per second
12-gauge field load	1⅛ ounces, No. 6	1,225 feet per second

These velocities (all of which are taken at the muzzle) hold true for all gauges; only the weight of the shot charge varies appreciably. From the above, it can be seen that while it is possible to significantly increase the number of pellets in a shot charge, it is impossible to substantially increase their velocity.

A skilled rifle shot equipped with a telescopic sight can deliver accurate fire to 400 yards under hunting conditions, and big bore target riflemen compete at 1,000-yard ranges. The shotgun, however, has a maximum effective range of 70 to 80 yards. The speed of the shotgun's projectiles assumes secondary importance to the shape and density of the pattern they form and the consistency with which they form it. A number of factors are involved: the kind of shot used; the pressures to which it is subjected upon firing; the amount of the charge that is deformed before it leaves the barrel; and the kind of choke that shapes the charge as it leaves the gun.

The two major advances in shotgun ballistics have been the invention of the plastic shotcup, which prevents deformation upon firing and in the barrel, resulting in denser patterns; and the perfection of the choke, which allows great control over the shape and density of the pattern. In shotgun ballistics, factors such as velocity and trajectory are of little or no concern. The "best" ballistics for a particular gauge, or for a particular kind of hunting and/or target shooting, must be thought of in terms of pattern size, shape, and density. (See CHOKE; PATTERN; PATTERNING; SHOT.)

shotgun barrel See BARREL, SHOTGUN.

shotgun cartridges, target Modern shotgun shells for target shooting take advantage of most of the recent improvements made in shotgun cartridges for hunting. Reloading results in considerable savings, and the target shooter can therefore shoot more often. The case life of a plastic case is about 10 times greater than that of a paper shell, depending on the individual brands involved.

For trapshooting, the standard load is 1⅛ ounces of shot in a 2¾-inch 12-gauge shell. (It is possible to use 1⅛ ounces of shot in a 16-gauge gun, but few shooters do it. The smaller gauges simply do not perform well in trap because it is a comparatively long-range game.) Shot sizes used for American trapshooting are Nos. 7½, 8 and 8½.

Formerly, shooters of International Trap preferred 1¼ ounces of shot in 12 gauge, but now 1 ounce of shot is mandated by I.S.U. rules. For live bird shooting, the 1¼-ounce load in 12 gauge is preferred, and copper- or nickel-plated shot is often used for better penetration.

For 12-gauge skeet, the 1⅛-ounce load is standard, and the rules provide that shot smaller than No. 9 cannot be used in any gauge. Smaller shot would be useful at some close-range stations (Station 8 particularly) where wide patterns work well.

In a four-gun skeet tournament, the shooter must fire all four skeet gauges: 12, 20, 28, and .410. The maximum allowable weight of shot for these gauges in skeet is respectively: 1⅛ ounces, ⅞-ounce, ¾-ounce and, in .410, 11/16-ounce or ½-ounce. In some .410 events the 3-inch shell with 11/16-ounce of shot is illegal. A 16-gauge gun firing 1⅛ ounces is allowable in the 12-gauge class, but few shooters use one.

With skeet ammunition, some shooters use single-unit plastic shot pouch wads, but others prefer a separate plastic wad to protect the shot form deformation in the barrel. Still other skeet shooters prefer shells without any plastic device to protect the shot. They like to have as many deformed pellets in the pattern as possible because they disperse widely. (Square shot or deliberately distorted shot is forbidden by the rules. At one time, the Russians were very successful with square shot in skeet tournaments, but it was outlawed.)

The improvements in modern target loads have enabled trap and skeet shooters to steadily push their scores upward. Scores shot by average competitors today would have won many tournaments only 30 or 40 years ago. This has gone so far that longer and longer shoot-offs to decide ties have become commonplace and very time-consuming. In shoot-offs, the gunners may fire 400 or 500 shells at skeet birds without a disqualifying miss.

shotgun gauges This system of measurement goes back to the days before rifled barrels. In those times, any firearm was expected to fire a single round bullet or a charge of shot. The most convenient way to designate the size of the bore (inside diameter of the barrel) was to weigh the round lead projectile it fired. For instance, a 12-gauge gun fired a ball of lead that weighed 1/12 pound, a 16 gauge fired a ball that weighed 1/16 pound, etc. In English-speaking countries, this system is still in use for shotguns, except that the smallest shotgun bore, the .410, is measured in decimal parts of an inch. Properly speaking, one should refer to the .410 as the .410 *bore*, not gauge. The gauges and the approximate equivalent inch measurements are given below:

$$
\begin{array}{l}
\text{4 gauge} = .935\text{-inch} \\
\text{8 gauge} = .835\text{-inch} \\
\text{10 gauge} = .775\text{-inch} \\
\text{12 gauge} = .729\text{-inch} \\
\text{16 gauge} = .670\text{-inch} \\
\text{20 gauge} = .615\text{-inch} \\
\text{28 gauge} = .550\text{-inch} \\
\text{.410 gauge} = .410\text{-inch}
\end{array}
$$

The inch designations in the table are approximate. Many manufacturers deviate slightly over or under these measurements. A convenient rule-of-thumb index is that a dime is almost exactly .729 inch in diameter—12 gauge.

The metric system is seldom used to designate shotgun bores, even in metric countries such as Germany. If millimeters are used, it almost always turns out that the metric designation merely reinterprets the old gauge measurements. A 9mm shotgun, however, was once very popular in Europe, and the bore was developed as a true 9mm without reference to the gauge system. It should be remembered that before metrics were introduced in European countries, they used pounds and ounces, and the gauge system was developed long before the metric system.

Use of guns larger than 10 gauge is forbidden in America.

shotgun sight This is usually a simple bead or post on top of the muzzle or between the muzzles of a double-barreled gun. On traditional shotguns, no rear sight is provided. It is often said that the gunner's shooting eye is the rear sight. He merely uses the front bead as an indicator of where the barrel is pointing, and the eye lines up behind the whole top and rear surface of the gun.

A shotgun is used mostly to fire pellets at flying targets, and fast movement of the targets makes it impossible to align a front and rear sight precisely, as is done with rifles and handguns firing single projectiles. It is also true that the large area of the circular shot pattern makes very precise alignment unnecessary. In any case, that would be too slow for wingshooting.

Some shotguns do have a middle bead or sight, however. It is usually located halfway down the barrel, and it is smaller than the front bead. Proper

The plain bead sight is commonly found on field shot-guns.

alignment with most guns of this kind is to place the rear bead below the front bead in a figure-8 configuration. Many shooters believe that shooting this way is too slow, but some use the method with success, particularly in trapshooting (clay birds), where the shooter aligns the sights with the gun on his shoulder before the target appears. Various V-notches are also machined into the top of shotgun receivers to serve as rear sights in much the same manner.

Some shotguns are also equipped with rifle sights of various kinds, including telescopic sights, when they are used to fire single projectiles (slugs) in big-game hunting. (See BEAD [SIGHT]; METALLIC SIGHTS; MIDDLE SIGHT.)

shotgun slug   A one-piece conoid projectile fired from a smoothbore gun. It is used for big game at short range. Effective range for a 12-gauge slug on deer does not exceed 100 yards, and most experienced hunters regard 80 yards as maximum. Slugs in smaller gauges have shorter effective ranges; the .410 slug should be used only for small game and varmints.

The usual American slug is made from soft lead. It is hollow based, but the nose of the projectile is thicker than the walls. This provides a weight-forward balance that keeps the nose pointing forward in flight. The soft lead skirt at the hollow base of the slug expands on firing because of gas pressure and seals the bore fairly well against gas blow-by. Also, the soft skirt walls are compressed by any

Rifled slugs can take highly differing forms. At right is the traditional design Foster slug; at left, a BRI sabot slug. The BRI projectile has a plastic shoe that encloses it until the slug has cleared the shotgun barrel.

choke in the shotgun's muzzle, so these slugs can be used in tightly choked guns. Shallow, angled vanes are present on the exterior of the slug, and these are intended to spin it axially in flight, providing gyroscopic stabilization. In actuality, these vanes provide little if any spin.

All of the above applies to the American-style slug. A German shotgun slug, the Brenneke, has several thick wads attached to its base, which provides a longer projectile and somewhat more stable flight. Spool-shaped slugs are sometimes used. The narrow waist provides a longer projectile within weight requirements. The French make a slug—the Blondeau—that is essentially a hollow tube with hellical vanes inside the tube. Air rushing through the tube in flight provides spin. The American BRI slug is wasp-waisted and employs a fallaway plastic sabot.

Slugs replaced round balls in shotguns. Balls were unsatisfactory because they had to be made as small as the tightest choke in any shotgun of the given gauge. Being so small, they literally bounced down the bore and were highly inaccurate. (See BLONDEAU SHOTGUN SLUG; BRENNEKE SHOTGUN SLUG.)

shotgun stock   The most critical aspect of the gun in terms of handling, fit, and even placement of the load downrange. The portion of the stock that fits against the shooter's shoulder is the butt—the top of which is called the heel, and the bottom the toe. The area where the shooter's cheek touches the stock is the comb. If the comb of a stock is too high the gun will tend to overshoot; if the stock is too crooked (excessive drop), recoil to the face is accentuated. A too long stock may cause the gun to come away from the face when the gun is swinging at a sharp angle. Too short a stock may cause the shooter to raise his head from the comb or even bump his thumb against his nose during recoil. Custom stocks can be ordered for most guns, or gunsmiths can shorten, lengthen, raise or lower combs as required.

Most shotguns now have a pistol grip; those without it are commonly called English grip, English or straight grip stocks. Advantages claimed for the pistol grip are better control of the gun and absorption of some recoil by the hand and arm, resulting in less perceived recoil at the cheek and shoulder. Advantages claimed for the English grip are sleeker, more attractive lines, a higher elbow position, and quicker pointing characteristics.

Shotgun stocks are usually made of wood (usually walnut), although synthetics are now used as well. Shotgun stocks are attached to the receiver either by a through-bolt inserted into a hollow in the stock, or by screws in the tang, which is called the Birmingham system.

As a rule, the typical American shotgun stock is longer than a rifle stock and has more drop. (The exception to this is the trap stock, which has very little drop.) Dimensions vary from maker to maker, but most field and skeet stocks have a 14¼-inch length of pull, 1½ inches of drop at comb, 2¼ inches of drop at heel, and a fraction of an inch of cast-off. Trap stocks average about 14½ inches length of pull and correspondingly less drop at comb and heel. (See CAST STOCK, DROP AT COMB; DROP AT HEEL; LENGTH OF PULL; PISTOL GRIP; STOCKMAKING.)

shot pattern See PATTERN.

shot placement A term used by riflemen to describe the accuracy (or lack of) of their shooting. Good shot placement means hits on the intended target; poor shot placement is synonymous with improper choice of aiming point or misses.

shot pouch Shot pouches are used for carrying bird shot for use in a muzzleloading shotgun. They come in several styles, the most popular being a leather pouch that resembles a pear-shaped powder flask in dimensions and use. This kind of pouch has two or more adjustments to throw premeasured amounts of shot. Another style is the kidney-shaped pouch that has an automatic measure in the stopper, adjustable for 1½ ounces to 2 ounces, or more.

Shot pouches are seldom, if ever, made of metal. Some are made of canvas, but leather predominates. (See POWDER FLASK.)

shotshell A cartridge containing a charge of pellets, intended for use in a shotgun. A shotshell consists of a plastic or paper case, a brass head, base and middle wads, a powder charge, primer, and, in the case of paper shells, a top wad. In Britain, the term shotshell is rarely used; "cartridge" is common British parlance for shotgun ammunition.

shotshell crimp The method used to close a shotshell's mouth after primer, wad(s), and the shot charge have been loaded. Formerly, the roll crimp was universal. With this crimp, a circular cardboard wad was placed on top of the shot and then the case mouth was rolled down all around the circumference to hold the top wad in place so as to seal the shot in the case. This crimp was used with paper cartridges, and it is still used in some of them. With the coming of plastic shotshell cases, the folded crimp, or pie, became almost universal. In this crimp, the mouth of the case is folded and then forced flat over the shot to hold it in place. Another name is star crimp because the six or eight folds form star-shaped creases in the mouth of the loaded shell. The folded crimp has the advantage of eliminating the top wad, which often caused irregularities in the shot pattern, and it is easy for a handloader to form again in a fired case. But for certain special loads, such as shotgun slugs, the roll crimp is still used.

The crimp is also important because it holds against primer thrust and early powder gas expansion to produce the proper pressure curve.

shot string When a charge of shot emerges from the muzzle, it is a tightly packed cylindrical mass, almost exactly the same length as the charge in the cartridge before firing. In flight, however, the charge lengthens because some pellets weigh more than others and some are rounder than others. This creates a shot string. In some cartridges such as the .410, this string is quite long even a short distance from the muzzle; in others, it is short.

Ideally, the shot should form a circular pattern very shallow in depth so as to cover the largest possible area with a densely packed pattern, but shot stringing cannot be entirely eliminated. With the introduction of more uniform shot, shotcup wads and shot collars, improved powders, etc., the shot string has been reduced in length and is no longer considered to be an important cause of misses caused by late arrival of some shot.

Steel shot throws a shorter shot string than lead shot because steel pellets don't deform.

shot tower A tower, approximately four stories high, for the formation of lead shot by the drop process. At the top of the tower, molten lead is poured through holes in a metal plate. The plates can be changed to provide holes of the right size to produce the various shot sizes. The droplets of molten lead fall through the air inside the hollow tower and assume a globular form (though some retain a slight teardrop shape or other irregularities). At the bottom of the tower is a tank of cold water. The shot drops into it and hardens. As a final control of shot size, the shot is put through sieves of varying sizes to sort the shot into uniform lots. Looking at shotgun shot through a magnifying glass will demonstrate that the pellets are not perfectly round. This process is used for birdshot, not buckshot. (See DROPPED SHOT.)

shoulder See CASE SHOULDER.

shoulder arm See LONG GUN.

side-by-side gun Also known as a double gun. The side-by-side arrangement of barrels in a single arm is a very old form, and was one of the first solutions to the problem of providing repeat shots without reloading. The side-by-side configuration is almost invariably used in shotguns, since the difficulty involved in aligning two rifle barrels so that bullets fired from them converge at a given distance is very great.

From the evolution of the modern shotgun in the late 18th century until the perfection of the repeating shotgun in the early 20th century, the side-by-side was the preferred shotgun. Since then, however, it has lost ground to automatic and pump models, which are less expensive, and to the over/under, whose narrower sighting plane has won many adherents. Today, comparatively few side-by-side shotguns are made (although their popularity is increasing), and double rifles are extremely rare. (See DOUBLE-BARREL SHOTGUN; OVER/UNDER GUN.)

sidehammer Hammers were frequently affixed to the right side of the actions of many of the firearms of the middle and late 19th century. The Trapdoor Springfield is an example of a sidehammer rifle of the period. Sidehammers were superseded by central hammers and by hammerless actions. (See HAMMER.)

side lever Generally located on the right side of the frame or receiver, the side lever is a breech unlocking device often found on older single-shot rifles and handguns, from the 4mm on up. More recently it has been used on economy priced sporting arms, such as the Savage Models 220-L and 940 shotguns, and the Model 24-S rifle/shotgun combination gun.

sidelock A sidelock is any lock mechanism in a double or over/under gun that is located on either side of the gun behind the action. The two kinds of sidelock are the bar action, in which a part of the mechanism extends to the front and is let into the bar of the action, and the back action, in which the entire mechanism is located behind the action body.

It is thought by some that the back-action design is superior in strength, since it avoids the cutting, and subsequent weakening, of the bar in order to intercept the mainspring. (See BACK-ACTION SIDELOCK; BAR-ACTION SIDELOCK.)

side screw Sometimes referred to as a side pin. Side screws pass through the action of a sidelock shotgun to fasten the lock plates to each other.

Sierra Bullets (company) Founded in 1947, this Santa Fe Springs, California, firm manufactures a wide variety of bullets for the handgun and rifle shooter, but has gained special recognition for its target and benchrest bullets. Sierra has long been an advocate of the boattail bullet design, and its prod-

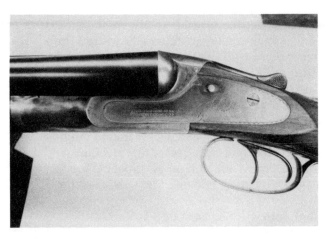

A sidelock gun is one in which the action parts are held in place by plates on either side of the action. This is a Lefever sidelock, a very simple design.

ucts have achieved great success in both American and International competition. Sierra is a division of Leisure Group, Inc., which acquired the firm in 1970. (See BOATTAIL BULLET.)

S.I.G. (company) Schweizerische Industrie Gesellschaft (Swiss Industrial Company), located in Neuhausen am Reinfalls, was founded in 1853 and at first manufactured railroad rolling stock. In the 1860s, it entered the arms field with an army rifle that was never adopted, but later it made the well-known Vetterli military rifle in .41 rimfire, as well as many other military arms.

The company also produced the SP 47/8, a locked breech semiautomatic pistol that was adopted by the Swiss Army. Civilian and police versions have also been marketed. One remarkable feature is that the entire lock mechanism, including the hammer, is contained in a single cased unit that is easily removed from the weapon for cleaning and repair. This arm is available in 9mm Parabellum with conversion kits for the 7.65 Parabellum and the .22 Long Rifle (rimfire). This is one of the finest pistols ever manufactured, but the cost is high—more than $700 in the United States. At present, this pistol is known as the P-210 and is made in four different model variations, ranging from the standard with wooden grips and plain blue finish to a target version with micrometer sights. The target version is used throughout the world for serious competition. A special feature that improves accuracy is the mounting of the slide, which moves on rails inside the frame instead of the more common system in which the slide envelops the frame and rides on it. The S.I.G. arrangement results in a more rigid pistol that can be machined to closer tolerances. S.I.G. now cooperates with the J. P. Sauer company in Germany in the manufacture and export of pistols.

sighter A preliminary round that is fired with the arm supposedly sighted directly on target. It helps the shooter make the necessary corrective measures to ensure subsequent hits.

sight hood See HOODED FRONT SIGHT.

sighting in Adjusting the sights on rifle or handgun so that the projectile strikes where intended is sighting in, also known as zeroing in.

In sighting, whether with metallic or telescopic sights, the first step may be to boresight the arm. This is accomplished by fixing the firearm in position so that it will not move, and then looking directly down the bore of the arm at some target. The sights are then moved to correspond with this point, until both the bore and the sight are looking at the same target. This step is also quickly and easily accomplished with an optical aid called a collimator.

The firearm is then shot from as stable a position as possible, preferably a benchrest. The object is to shoot groups of three or five shots, and then—by calculating the center of those groups—to determine where the arm is shooting as an average condition. Once this is established, the sights are moved to correspond to the correction needed to bring the point of impact of the bullets to the desired point on the target.

For example, if the arm is shooting 3 inches below the desired point of impact, and 2 inches to the left at any given distance, the sights must be moved so that the average striking point on the target is 3 inches higher and 2 inches to the right. Telescopic sights will be adjusted according to the value of each "click" of the adjustments, or each mark indicted on the turrets. A value of 1 minute of angle would be 1 inch for each 100 yards. If a firearm is to be moved 2 inches to the right in its point of impact when a scope has a value of 1 inch per each 100 yards per click, then only 1 click should bring the bullet 2 inches to the right at 200 yards.

Iron sights are different. If the rear sight is moveable, and most are on firearms today, the rear sight is to be moved in the direction in which the point of impact is desired. If the rifle is shooting to the left, moving the rear sight to the right will move the bullet's impact to the right. If the arm is hitting low, moving the sight up will bring the point of impact up. On rifles with fixed rear sights, such as the replicas of many muzzleloading arms, the front sight is used to change the point of impact on the target. In this case, however, the front sight is moved in the direction opposite the desired point of impact change. If the rifle is shooting to the left, the front sight is moved to the left, which will bring the impact to the right. If the arm is shooting too low, the front sight is filed off slightly, and this lowering of the sight will cause the barrel to be tipped, bringing the point of impact of the bullet up.

The rifle is ideally sighted so that the bullet follows a path that strikes the line of sight twice. The handgun is sighted the same way. Since the bullet will cross the line of sight twice, the arm can be sighted in at close range and then refined at the desired longer range. For example, a flat shooting cartridge may be sighted to strike the bull's-eye at 25 yards, which will allow the bullet to rise, striking high at 100, probably high at 200, and on the line of sight again somewhere between 275 and 300 yards, taking the advantage of this flatness of trajectory. Should the arm be sighted to strike at 100 yards, it would be low at 200 and of course beyond that, robbing the ballistic capability of that round. (See BORESIGHT; COLLIMATOR; TRAJECTORY.)

sight insert An interchangeable blade or aperture, usually used in a target-type hooded front sight for a rifle. The shooter changes the element to suit his preference as well as the particular shooting conditions. The insert is often provided with a circular seat that will accept a metal or plastic ring into which is placed a variety of shapes and sizes of sighting elements.

There are also open front sights with interchangeable inserts, as well as an open rear sight with interchangeable blades to offer various notches, such as the V-, U-, British, or Target notch. (See METALLIC SIGHTS.)

sight malfunctions See TELESCOPIC SIGHTS.

sight picture The visual image that the shooter perceives as he lines the sights of his firearm on the target is the sight picture. With open sights, a gen-

This "lollipop" sight insert can be removed and replaced with one of a different configuration.

erous amount of front sight bead showing in the notch of the rear sight would constitute a coarse bead sight picture, while a front bead fully nestled in the notch of the rear sight would be called a fine bead sight picture.

Sight picture also has to do with the relationship of the front sight bead and the bull's-eye on the target. If the target appears to be resting fully on top of the bead, this is the target sight picture, a six-o'clock hold. If the sight bead seems to be centered right on the bull's-eye, this is the hunting sight picture.

sight radius   The distance between the rear sight and the front sight is called the sight radius and is expressed in inches. A long sight radius offers greater accuracy than a short one, but is slower to use. (See METALLIC SIGHTS.)

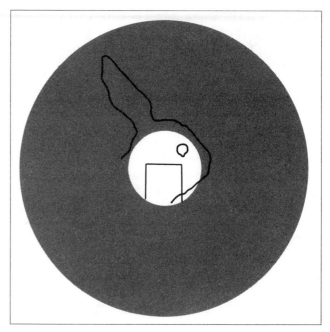

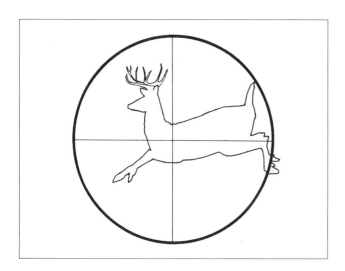

These are correct sight pictures for peep, open, and scope sights. Because of the limitations of the human eye, perfect focus of both sight and target can be achieved only with the scope, since both are in the same optical plane. With iron sights, either the sight or the target must be slightly out of focus. Of the two, the peep is superior in this respect, since the eye looks through it, and not at it, as with an open rear sight.

sights, handgun   See HANDGUN SIGHTS.

sight tube   A longitudinal metal tube enclosing the front sight of an iron-sighted target rifle is called a sight tube. The purpose of the tube is to minimize glare and the tendency of bright sidelighting to form a false center on the front bead. (See METALLIC SIGHTS.)

signal pin   A pin that indicates by its position whether or not a rifle is loaded, or whether or not it is cocked. In the first instance, the signal pin is sometimes called a loaded chamber indicator, and in the second instance it is sometimes called a cocking indicator. The signal pin is normally arranged so as to protrude when the chamber is loaded, or when the gun is cocked. The condition can therefore be determined by touch as well as by sight.

silhouette shooting *(siluetas metalicas)*   An unusual form of rifle competition that originated in Mexico, silhouette shooting began as a kind of informal contest at which shooters fired at live animals. A regular course of fire evolved, with a series of four life-sized metal silhouettes placed at the following distances from the firing line: chicken, 200 meters; javelina, 300 meters; turkey, 385 meters; wild sheep, 500 meters. The metal figures are ar-

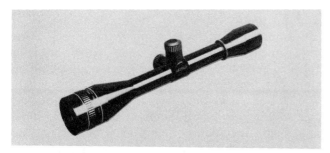

Scopes designed for silhouette shooting are equipped with click-adjustment dials that can be set at the firing line for each distance encountered. This is a Leupold 10X with an adjustable objective lens.

Silhouette shooting was originally intended to be fired with hunting rifles, although the guns now in actual use bear little resemblance to a hunting arm. This competitor is using the standard hip-rest stance and is aiming at the ram silhouette, an example of which is in front of his position. A telephoto lens reveals the scale of the targets. The rams in the background are 547 yards away; the middle row is 385 yards and the near row is 200 yards.

ranged in banks of five, and a competitor has 2½ minutes to fire at the five targets. No sighters are allowed. Placement of shots does not count; all that matters is that the target falls.

Siluetas was an informal game that could be competed in by a hunter with his field rifle. The sport's popularity spread, and in 1973, the National Rifle Association initiated the first National Championship Match for silhouettes. At that time, the kind of rifle that could be used was standardized. It is any rifle that weighs no more than 10 pounds, 2 ounces including sights. Scopes are permitted. *Siluetas* is fired entirely from the off hand position, but no palm rests, hook buttplates, slings, or shooting jackets are allowed. Most silhouette rifles are chambered for cartridges such as the .30/06, .270, .280, 7mm/08, and .308. There is no restriction on trigger pull, and most of these rifles have triggers set at 2 pounds or less.

Despite the original intent of the sport, a distinct kind of silhouette rifle has evolved, and target-type scopes as well. These guns are ill-suited for hunting, and a person competing against one with a true hunting rifle would be at a disadvantage. For this reason, in 1985 the NRA introduced a category of silhouette rifle known as the Hunting Rifle Class, which requires that the rifle be of standard factory origin, and unaltered, except that it may be glass bedded, and have its trigger pull set to 2 pounds (not less).

Silhouette shooting has enjoyed considerable popularity. Its major limitation is the fact that it requires a rifle range of major proportions. As a result, a .22 rimfire variation of *siluetas* has been developed, where the shooters fire at scaled-down targets at greatly reduced ranges with rifles that closely resemble their centerfire counterparts. In addition, there is also a kind of competition in which centerfire handguns are fired at scaled-down silhouettes at shortened ranges. (See INTERNATIONAL HANDGUN METALLIC SILHOUETTE ASSOCIATION [I.H.M.S.A.].)

single action In revolver design, a single action is a handgun that must have its hammer cocked for each shot. A single action automatic pistol is one in which the hammer has to be cocked either by the gun's action or manually, before a shot can be fired.

single-base powder A smokeless propellant whose single explosive base is nitrocellulose, a substance made from the action (nitration) of concentrated nitric acid on cotton or other cellulose products—hence the term "guncotton." In this stable and mildly erosive cartridge propellant, the burning rate is controlled by changing the size of the individual kernels and by adding deterrent coatings. (See NITROCELLU-LOSE; SMOKELESS POWDER.)

single selective trigger A mechanism on some side-by-side and over/under shotguns that permits the shooter to determine which barrel will fire with the first pull of the gun's trigger. Some single selective trigger mechanisms employ the safety as the selector. Others use a separate button located in the trigger itself or on the side of the receiver. Advocates of the single selective trigger claim that it increases the versatility of a shotgun by adapting it to all shooting situations. Others claim that it only complicates what is already a fairly complex mechanism and decreases the reliability of a gun, and that it is useful only under very rare conditions.

single set trigger A set trigger that combines the functions of both triggers of a double set mechanism into just one. This kind of trigger is used to allow a very light pull (from a pound to a few ounces) while still providing for safe engagement with the sear. These triggers are used on target, varmint, and hunting rifles, and on free pistols. They employ their own spring loaded locks that, when cocked, supply the energy to release themselves and the sear.

A typical single set trigger, and presently the most popular, is the Canjar, which can be employed as a standard trigger or as a single set. For the latter use, the trigger is pushed forward, cocking the gun and causing a small spur or tab in the middle of the trigger to extend forward. A touch on the spur releases the trigger, which in turn fires the rifle. The Miller trigger, another single set, functioned with a double-stage pull in normal use, but could be pushed forward, cocked, and, when touched, it released the sear with a few ounces of pressure. (See DOUBLE SET TRIGGER.)

single-shot action Single-shot actions are made for rifles, shotguns, and pistols, and are actions that are capable of firing no more than one shot without being reloaded. A few actions can be converted instantly from repeaters to single shots, but these are not true single-shot actions. The bolt-action Krag Jorgensen and Springfield rifles have magazine cut-off levers that block cartridges from feeding from the magazine, and are examples of the repeater/single-shot design.

Many bolt actions, especially those on .22 rimfire rifles, are of true single-shot design. Single-shot bolt actions are also used for shotguns and pistols, as well as for big-bore target rifles.

The most popular single-shot actions for all kinds of firearms are either of break-open type or have a sliding breechblock; the rolling block action was also popular many years ago. These actions nearly all use some kind of lever to open the breech. Most shotgun break-open actions open with a top-lever release, and some single-shot break-open pistol actions are also released from the top. A few single-shot actions have side levers, but the majority use the underlever system. Some modern sliding block single-shot actions are nearly as strong as bolt actions, but do not have as much camming power to seat or extract a tight cartridge case, and are not therefore quite as well suited to handloading.

Today, there are few practical uses for single-shot actions. Their most frequent use is in trap guns, where only one shot is allowed per target at 16-yard and handicap distances. Here, a very strong massive action can be employed in a single-shot arm. Similarly, single-shot handguns such as the Thompson-Center can be chambered for cartridges far more powerful than an automatic or revolver could employ, since they are not limited by action length or cylinder wall thickness.

True single-shot rifles are fairly popular, but their appeal is more aesthetic than practical. They lack the accuracy and extracting power of bolt actions and make follow-up shots difficult as well. (See FALLING BLOCK; FALLING BLOCK ACTION.)

single-stage trigger The kind of trigger used on almost all sporting firearms is the single-stage. It is so called to distinguish it from the double-stage trigger favored for military guns. First employed on shotguns, and then on the Winchester Model 70 bolt-action rifle, the single-stage trigger employs one short, crisp motion to release the sear or hammer. Adjusted properly, it displays no slack or "takeup" and releases cleanly with little or no overtravel.

single trigger A trigger that serves to fire each barrel of a double-barrel shotgun in succession. With a single selective trigger, the user may preselect which of the barrels is to be fired first. With a nonselective single trigger, the firing sequence is inherent in the trigger design and cannot be changed at will. Nonselective single triggers usually first fire the right barrel of a side-by-side gun, or the lower barrel of an over/under gun.

six o'clock hold In target shooting, the six o'clock hold means aligning the front sight directly below the bull's-eye, as if the bull's-eye were resting atop the front sight. If the target were imagined as the face of a clock, the front sight would be directly below the numeral 6. (See SIGHT PICTURE.)

sizing lubricant Since resizing metallic cartridge cases to original or near-original prefered dimensions requires severe metal-on-metal pressure, a special lubricant must be used to reduce friction. Sizing lubes have a high film strength that will not break under the pressure of die/case contact; they are usually petroleum based products, but may also be a soap or lanolin. (See CASE RESIZING.)

skeet choke   A bore constriction employed in skeet guns to throw a wide pattern at close range, normally 15 to 20 yards. It is close to a cylinder bore, and in some skeet guns actually has a reverse-choke dimension. At one time, double-barreled skeet guns had a No. 2 skeet boring, which was about a tight improved cylinder or a loose modified choke. The guns were then spoken of as having Skeet-in (skeet No. 1) and Skeet-out (skeet No. 2), but those combinations have fallen by the wayside in skeet competition as modern ammunition is extremely effective over skeet ranges from basically skeet or cylinder barrels. The Skeet #1 and #2 doubles, however, are beautifully matched to much upland bird hunting. (See CYLINDER CHOKE; IMPROVED-CYLINDER CHOKE.)

skeet gun   Almost any shotgun can be used for shooting skeet, but the most successful competitive guns have a weight-forward balance to ensure continuation of a smooth swing. Barrels are normally 26 to 28 inches long, with longer barrels, which add weight at the muzzle, being increasingly favored by top competitors using over/unders.

The most popular skeet guns are gas-operated autoloaders, particularly in the 12-gauge events, because they reduce recoil and cut down on shooter fatigue. But there is a trend to over/under 12 gauges with interchangeable barrel tubes—which convert the 12 gauge to fire 20, 28, and .410 shells. With a "tube set," the serious competitor can fire at every target with the same gun, same trigger pull, etc. Many top shooters now shoot the small-gauge events with a tubed over/under 12, then switch to a gas operated 12 for the grueling 12-gauge event. (See OVER/UNDER GUN; SKEET SHOOTING.)

skeet shooting   Skeet is the only competitive shotgun game involving the use of small-gauge guns (20, 28, and .410) in addition to the 12 gauge. Invented in 1915 at Andover, Massachusetts, by Charles E. and Henry Davies, and popularized by outdoor writer William Foster, it was originally designed as practice for bird shooting in the field and was first called "Shooting Around the Clock." Clay targets are thrown from the same position each time, but the shooter moves from one position to another, as the hands of a cock move from one hour to the next, so the target angle to the shooter changes. Thus, although targets are thrown from the same high house and low house

and travel the same trajectory and direction each time, the skeet shooter's relation to them changes the amount of forward allowance required; some shooting stations are more difficult than others.

The modern skeet field resembles one-half of a clock's face, and station 1 (first shot in a round of competition) is located directly beneath the high house at 9 o'clock to the center of the field. In American skeet the shooter fires at one high house target (high house is always fired first), one low house, and one pair of doubles at station 1, then moves to station 2 and repeats that process. At stations 3, 4, and 5, he fires at one target from each house. At stations 6 and 7, he shoots singles and doubles. At station 8 (center of the clock face), he fires at one high and one low house target, both of which must be taken as incomers before they reach the field's center stake.

Skeet teaches the hunter the importance of reading the angle of a target in flight. Although the target is the same distance away—21 yards to the center of the field from any shooting station other than the center station—the forward allowance required to hit targets at station 4 is about twice that required to hit targets at station 2, because the angle is twice as great.

The fact that four different gauges are required for a skeet championship has proved to be a handicap to the sport's popularity, since few shooters can afford the arms or the ammunition. Another problem is the fact that extremely high scores are quite common, with "straights" going into the hundreds of birds, and shoot-offs becoming little more than endurance contests. For these reasons, skeet has declined in popularity as a competitive sport in recent years, but it remains invaluable as a teacher of proper shotgun handling.

The term "skeet" is a modification of a Norwegian word meaning "to shoot." (See CLAY TARGET; HIGH HOUSE; INTERNATIONAL SKEET SHOOTING; LOW HOUSE; SKEET GUN.)

skeleton buttplate   On some custom rifles, instead of a solid buttplate only the perimeter of the butt is fitted with a metal skeleton, the purpose being to expose the wood in the center of the skeleton so that it can be carved or checkered to the taste of the stockmaker and arms owner. (See BUTTPLATE.)

skelp barrel   Another name for twist or Damascus barrels. (See DAMASCUS BARREL.)

skipline checkering   Also called French checkering, this is a pattern of checkering on a rifle stock, usually at the fore-end and grip, in which narrow intersecting bands are left uncut to produce areas of

This is an example of skipline, or French, checkering, as popularized by the Weatherby rifles.

clean wood amidst the checkering. If the skipping is done at specific places, a diamond effect will appear. (See CHECKERING.)

slap See OVERTRAVEL.

slave pin A pin used to hold gun parts in place during assembly. The slave pin may be slightly undersize to easily fit the orifices into which it is inserted. It is later replaced with the pin that is to remain in the firearm.

sleeved action A past trend in assembling match or benchrest rifles was to encase the action in an aluminum or steel "sleeve" that provides rigid bedding while allowing both action and barrel to vibrate freely. All bedding and scope pressures are thus absorbed by the sleeve rather than the barreled action.

With the introduction of a number of benchrest actions, the art of sleeving actions is dying.

slide lock In pump-action guns, a slide or bar lock locks the slide in the forward position when the gun is cocked, so that the action remains fully closed during firing. The lock release must be operated manually if a cocked action is opened without firing.

sling A strap, normally made of leather or canvas, and typically ⅞ to 1¼-inches wide, though sometimes much wider where it makes contact with the shoulder while carrying the rifle. The sling is at-

tached to the rifle stock and forearm by swivels, which are either permanent or quick-detachable, the latter preferred for storage in a gun cabinet or compact case and to allow display of the rifle's lines. The front swivel is usually placed 2 to 3½ inches behind the fore-end tip, except on very high recoil rifles, where it is mounted on a sweated barrel band in front of the fore-end to prevent it from gouging the hand holding the fore-end.

The sling serves as a carrying and shooting aid. For carrying, a simple strap is adequate and often preferred for its clean lines. The carrying strap can be used to steady the rifle with the "hasty" method by looping the arm through the strap and around, and back to the fore-end. This will put pressure from the left hand onto the forearm.

Military-type slings are equipped with metal claw hooks that allow for adjustment and for detaching the rear part of the sling from the rifle. The front section is looped tightly around the shooter's left bicep; the left hand is then passed over the sling and grasps the fore-end.

Target slings operate in a similar manner, but dispense with the rear loop—since they are never used for carrying the rifle—and utilize a heavily padded collar to make the front loop more comfortable over long periods.

A third style, the Whelen sling, was developed by Colonel Townsend Whelen. Its construction is similar to that of the full military sling, but it lacks the metal claws, and the rear loop does not detach from the front when the sling is employed as a shooting aid.

The carrying strap should be wide enough to distribute the weight of the rifle over a large area of the shoulder, preventing its digging in. However, a narrow sling may be used to carry the rifle when the shooter uses a packframe that has a metal hook attached to it. The strap loops right over the hook. Muzzleloaders equipped with metal ramrod thimbles and no place to attach a front swivel can use a special carrying strap that slides over the ramrod thimble.

There are many designs and styles of slings and carrying straps in one- and two-piece models, some straight, having the same width all of their length, and others tapered, becoming wider over the shoulder contact area, the latter often referred to as torpedoes.

sling hook Sometimes referred to as a frog, a sling hook consists of a pair of brass prongs that fit tightly into holes punched through a sling. Employed solely in military and target slings, the hooks provide a rapid and secure means of adjusting the sling to a particular length. (See SLING.)

sling swivel The swivel is a loop of metal that holds the sling on a rifle; it is mainly of two kinds, the permanent, which remains on the rifle at all times, and the quick-detachable, which can be removed from the rifle, thereby taking the entire sling off the arm. One swivel is generally placed on the fore-end, except on heavy recoil rifles, in which case the swivel is mounted on the barrel in front of the fore-end to prevent injury. The second swivel is placed a few inches up from the toe of the stock. (See SLING.)

slippage See BULLET SLIPPAGE.

slot See CLIP LIP.

slotted jag A cleaning tip, with a longitudinal slot, that is screwed onto the end of a cleaning rod. A cleaning patch is fitted into the slot and twisted onto the jag's rough surface, where it is held in place while being worked up and down the bore of the arm. The patch can be quickly freed from the jag and discarded when it becomes dirty. It is also called a wiper. (See CLEANING ROD; JAG.)

slow fire A phase of handgun competition in both National Rifle Association matches and in International matches. In the NRA Slow-Fire event, 10 shots are fired at a target, indoors or outdoors, with a time limit of 10 minutes. International rules require that 60 shots be fired at 50 meters, and the time limit can extend to several hours.

slug This term has several meanings. The most common is a generic use of the word as a synonym for bullet. Properly used, slug denotes a single projectile designed to be fired from a shotgun.

Slug also refers to a device for gauging the dimensions of a rifle bore. A slug, or lead plug of groove diameter, would be driven through the barrel at the end of a steel rod, which was pushed by the barrel-maker or gunsmith. This individual could tell by the amount of resistance encountered whether the bore was uniform in diameter for its entire length. Today, the slug has been replaced by the bore gauge, which can give a far more precise reading. (See BARREL MAKING; SHOTGUN SLUG.)

slug gun A heavy, highly accurate muzzleloader that is fired from a bench. The slug gun evolved in the late 1800s and was used for long-range target shooting, sometimes at ranges of up to 1,100 yards. Weighing 12 pounds and more, slug guns ranged from .36 to .50 caliber and were equipped with false muzzles and plunger-type bullet starters.

Slug guns are still fired in black-powder matches,

This Ithaca Model 87 is typical of a modern slug gun. It is a 12 gauge with a high-comb stock, a full-length-rifled barrel, and a scope sight. With modern design slugs, it is accurate at ranges up to 100 yards.

most notably at the National Championship matches at Friendship, Indiana. The guns are fired at ranges of 100, 200, and 300 yards. They are equipped with telescopic sights of 16X to 20X and are capable of extreme accuracy, even by modern standards.

In recent years, the term "slug gun" has taken on an additional meaning. It is also used to refer to pump-action and semiautomatic shotguns that are designed for use with rifled slugs. These guns are almost invariably 12 gauge, and have high-comb stocks for use with telescopic sights. Some have iron sights, while others have none. Two rifling systems are used to impart spin to a slug: The first involves a smoothbore barrel with a rifled choke tube screwed into the muzzle; the other, a barrel that is rifled for its entire length. In addition, some slug guns have their barrels permanently fixed to the receiver to gain greater rigidity and shot-to-shot consistency, unlike conventional repeating shotguns, whose barrels are detachable. (See SLUG.)

smallbore Smallbore is a rather nonspecific term, the meaning changing with both geography and history. For the English who hunted Africa, a small bore was a rifle roughly beneath .375 caliber. Hence, a .30/06 would be a smallbore rifle on a British safari, with .375 to .400 caliber being medium bore, and over .400 getting into large bore weapons. Earlier in time, the .45 would have been considered a small bore for the same Britishers who hunted Africa with guns ranging in gauges 12, 8, and even larger. In America, the term smallbore generally refers to the .22-caliber arm, both rimfire and centerfire.

Smith, L.C. (company) In 1877, Lyman Cornelius Smith established the L.C. Smith Gun Co. at Syracuse, New York, to produce a line of double-barrel sidelock shotguns. In 1890, Smith sold his interest in the business to Hunter Arms Company of Fulton, New York, which for the next 55 years manufactured a highly popular line of shotguns under the name L.C. Smith.

L.C. Smith shotguns came in a wide variety of grades, ranging from the utilitarian Field model to the top-of-the-line Premier. Smiths were made in 12,

16, 20, and .410 gauge; some were offered with automatic ejectors, single triggers, and a variety of borings. The fancier grades were stocked with select woods and were elaborately checkered and engraved.

In 1946, Hunter Arms Company was purchased by Marlin Firearms Company of New Haven, Connecticut. Marlin continued to produce the L.C. Smith guns until 1951 when their manufacture ceased. (In 1968, Marlin reintroduced the L.C. Smiths Field grade and offered it until 1973.)

Today, the high-grade L.C. Smiths made by Hunter Arms are highly desirable guns, especially in the smaller gauges.

Smith & Wesson, Inc. A pioneer among American firearms manufacturers, this company was founded in 1855 in Norwich, Connecticut by Horace Smith and Daniel B. Wesson as the Volcanic Repeating Arms Company. Volcanic manufactured rifles and handguns for the revolutionary self-contained metallic cartridge and thus ushered in the era of the modern repeating arm.

In 1856, the partners moved to Springfield, Massachusetts (where Smith & Wesson is still located) and opened a new firm under their own names. Their first gun, sold as the First Model Revolver No. 1, was chambered for the .22 Short which was specially designed for this gun, and was produced from 1857 to 1859. During the Civil War, Smith & Wesson was overshadowed by Colt and Remington, whose large-caliber, solid-frame arms (the S&W revolvers were then top-breaking) were universally preferred.

In 1869, Smith & Wesson introduced the American model, a .44 centerfire revolver with a sturdy top-break frame. The American was followed by the Schofield and Russian models, also .44s. The Russian revolver was produced under Russian military contract and occupied Smith & Wesson's efforts until 1877, when it introduced its first double-action revolver, a .38. The first solid-frame double-action Smith & Wesson was the Model 1902 Military and Police. This arm, a .38 Special, was the first truly modern revolver design and established Smith & Wesson revolvers as favorites of the police as well as the armed services.

Notable among the company's more recent innovations have been its development of handguns for the .357 Magnum (1935) and the .44 Magnum (1955). These two cartridges set new standards for handgun performance in two separate eras.

Today, Smith & Wesson manufactures a wide variety of revolvers and automatic pistols for service, sport, and target use, in calibers ranging from .22 to .45.

smokeless bulk powder See BULK POWDER.

smokeless powder Any propellant that produces less smoke on explosion than black powder; it typically consists of gelatinized cellulose nitrates (nitrocellulose) either alone or mixed with nitroglycerin or other ingredients, and it is produced in various forms (solid, perforated tubes, cylindrical grains, flakes, pellets, or spheres), depending on the desired burning rate. Actually, the term smokeless *powder* is a misnomer, as the propellant normally is used in one of the forms mentioned above rather than as a powder.

Black powder was the chemical propellant used in firearms from the mid-1300s until the late 1800s. However, less than half of a black-powder charge is converted to hot gases on firing; the rest is smoke-producing, and it results in a significant amount of residue that fouls the firearm.

Smokeless powder was the successor to black powder. It derives its name from the fact that nitrocellulose is converted to nearly 100 percent hot gases upon firing, producing very little smoke and residue.

Guncotton, the earliest known form of nitrocellulose, was first described in 1846 by Christian Frederick Schonbein, who experimented with its explosive nature and suggested its use in firearms. The first attempts were unsuccessful, however, because the material was chemically unstable because of residual acid in the fibers, and the raw fibrous nitrocellulose presented an excessive burning area. Later, the residual acid was removed from the nitrocellulose fibers and chemical stabilizers were added.

Schonbein then treated the nitrocellulose with alcohol and ether to form a colloid. Paul Vieille, a French chemist, utilized this material to mold the now homogeneous mass into controlled shapes and dimensions; this laid the groundwork for the development of successful single-base smokeless propellants.

In the late 1880s, Alfred B. Nobel of Sweden developed a double-base propellant called Ballistite. The new propellant was termed double base because it contained both nitroglycerin and nitrocellulose. (Single-base powder does not contain nitroglycerin.)

In 1889, Frederick A. Abel and James Dewar, British chemists, invented another colloidal double-base propellant—cordite. The Cordite colloid was extruded into long cords (both Vieille and Nobel had rolled their colloids into sheets and cut the sheets into smaller pieces). Cartridges developed in England during the early 20th century were designed for this Cordite powder.

In 1896, the U.S. Navy adopted a single-base smokeless powder called pyrocellulose or simply pyro.

By 1900, the changeover from black powder to smokeless was well under way all over the world, for both military and civilian applications. World War I was fought with both single- and double-base smokeless propellants.

The advantage of a smokeless powder for both wartime and sporting use is obvious; it neither gives away the shooter's location nor does it foul his firearm. Smokeless is also much safer to manufacture than black powder, because it will not explode when unconfined. Instead, it will simply deflagrate, or burn. Smokeless powders, in fact, are extremely difficult to bring to detonation; they are intentionally imbued with this property by the colloiding discussed earlier. (The ingredients, nitrocellulose and nitroglycerin, will detonate readily in the absence of the colloiding process.) This stability makes smokeless powder much safer to store and transport than black powder. (See BLACK POWDER; BULK POWDER; DENSE POWDER; GUNPOWDER, SHIPPING AND STORAGE OF; NITROCELLULOSE.)

smokestack An obsolete term for a gun barrel. Sometimes a jam in a semiautomatic where the fired case is not completely ejected might also be called a smokestack.

smoothbore Any firearm whose barrel is not rifled is a smoothbore. Modern arms that fire single projectiles are usually rifled, so the term is used as a synonym for shotgun. (See SHOTGUN.)

snap cap A small cover, usually of leather with a metal top, used to protect the nipple of a percussion muzzleloading firearm. Also a protective device, shaped in the form of a shotshell or cartridge, that is inserted into the chamber to prevent damage of the firing pin when dry firing (shooting the arm without any ammunition in it, an excellent practice method). The fall of the firing pin is stopped by a spring loaded button located in the mock cartridge or shell. (See DRY FIRING; NIPPLE.)

snaphaunce The earliest form of the flintlock. The hammer struck upon a piece of sulfurous pyrite. This produced sparks that fell into the priming powder and ignited the main charge. The frizzen had a separate pan cover. (See FLINTLOCK.)

snap shot A shot taken hurriedly, where the gun is simply pointed and fired without deliberate aim or lead.

soft-jacketed See HALF-JACKETED.

soft point bullet A jacketed bullet whose tip is exposed. This exposed lead tip may have a sharp point before firing, but it is generally flattened upon impact with the atmosphere when fired from high-velocity arms and arrives on target already somewhat blunted.

solid bullet The term "solid" bullet is generally considered British in origin and originally applied to bullets used in large bore arms for the biggest game in Africa. The solid is a lead core projectile with a metal jacket, usually cupro-nickel or steel covered with a softer alloy, extending to and covering the nose section, with the base being exposed lead.

Solid bullets have one main use today. Large solids such as the 500-grain .458 bullets available today, are used for the best possible penetration and bone-breaking performance on very large, and usually dangerous, game. The measure of a large solid is its ability to maintain its form after striking the target. (See JACKETED BULLET.)

solid rib A steel bar permanently affixed to a barrel to serve as a sighting plane. Solid ribs were commonly used on shotguns and handguns, rarely on rifles except some double rifles. They are more durable than ventilated ribs, but less effective in offering a mirage-free sighting plane when the barrel has heated from firing. (See RIB.)

Southgate ejector Invented by F. Beesley and patented in 1893 in Great Britain, the Southgate is a highly successful design that is widely used in double shotguns. It employs a tumbler that is rotated by a special limb projecting from the knuckle of the action. As the gun is opened after firing, this limb presses against the lower part of the tumbler; when the tumbler passes into the over-center position, it kicks the leg of the ejector and propels the shell from the gun. (See EJECTOR.)

spacer Usually a white piece of plastic, wood, or rubber—although other materials and colors may be employed—that is shaped to fit between various parts of the gunstock, such as between the buttplate and the wooden butt of a rifle, between the pistol grip cap and the wooden base of the grip, or between the fore-end tip and the fore-end of the rifle. It is primarily decorative; however, when placed between the buttplate and butt of a rifle stock, a spacer will add to the length of pull. (See STOCKMAKING.)

spacer wad A cylindrical wad, usually composed of fiber, that is placed within the shotshell to occupy some of the usual wad space. Normally, the spacer wad is used where reduction of shot and/or powder, or both shot and powder, have foreshortened the normal wad length; the spacer wad brings this length back to normal so that the shotshell can be crimped. (See SHOTSHELL CRIMP.)

Spanish gunmakers The firearms industry in Spain concentrates largely on the manufacture of shotguns and handguns of derivative design; few rifles are produced. The principal Spanish firearms manufacturers are as follows:

Aguirre y Aranzabal, located in Eibar in northeastern Spain, manufactures a wide variety of shotguns, ranging from expensive high-quality copies of the Merkel over/under and Purdey side-by-side to very inexpensive doubles employing Anson and Deeley-type actions. Most AyA guns are purchased domestically, but an appreciable number of moderately priced Matador models were imported by Firearms International. At present, AyA shotguns are available through IGI Domino in New York City and William L. Moore in Westlake, California.

Astra handguns are produced by Unceta & Co., in Guernica. This firm has traditionally specialized in compact handguns, whose importation is now severely limited by the Gun Control Act of 1968. The one Astra gun presently imported is the Constable model, which is closely patterned on the Walther PP series; it is imported by Interarms of Alexandria, Virginia.

Ignacio Ugartecha, like AyA, produces quality reproductions of German and British shotguns. Some Ugartecha shotguns are available from dealers in the U.S.

Llama pistols are manufactured by Gabilondo y Cia., in Vitoria. The firm specializes in a single-action automatic pistol based on the Model 1911 Colt, and a double-action service revolver that closely resembles the Smith & Wesson Model 19. Gabilondo has recently introduced a .44 magnum double action that is not derivative. Both the revolvers and automatic pistols are available in highly engraved as well as plain grades and are imported by Stoeger Industries, Hackensack, New Jersey.

Victor Sarasqueta, S.A., of Eibar, manufactures an extensive line of side-by-side shotguns, ranging from unadorned models to heavily engraved guns. The price for all models are modest by American standards. Sarasqueta guns are not currently represented by an American importer.

Star handguns are produced by Bonifacio Echeverria of Eibar. The firm specializes in a wide variety of single-action automatic pistols, both service and concealment. At present, only two models, the PD and BK, are imported; the importer is Stoeger Industries.

spanner In British usage, any wrench, but particularly one having fixed jaws. In American usage, a special kind of wrench designed to engage and turn a nut or screw that cannot be engaged by a conventional parallel-jaw wrench or a screwdriver. A common spanner has two or more projections that engage two or more holes or notches cut into the surface of the nut or screw in diametrically opposite positions. Spanners are used to tighten or loosen such parts as recoil bolts and firing pin plates in double-barrel shotguns.

speed of rotation The revolutions per second of the bullet in flight is the speed of rotation. To determine the speed of rotation, simply divide the figure 12 by the twist, multiplying the result by the velocity of the bullet. Speed of rotation is governed, then, by the twist of the rifle and the velocity of the projectile. This factor has a definite and measurable effect upon accuracy because of rotational stabilization. A round lead ball for muzzleloaders requires very little speed of rotation, hence very little twist in the bore, while an elongated missile demands much more twist and speed of rotation for stabilization. Hence we find excellent ball-shooting arms with only one turn in a full 72 inches, or an even slower rate of twist, while many modern arms firing long bullets will have a rate of twist of one turn in 10 inches or even faster, such as one in 9 or one in 8. As little as a quarter-turn of a round ball on its journey through the barrel will stabilize it for normal ranges, while a long bullet may turn completely on its axis several times in the rifle barrel before exiting. (See BULLET STABILIZATION; RATE OF TWIST.)

Speer, Inc. Early in World War II, when most commercial ammunition manufacturers converted to military products, a Lewiston, Idaho handloader named Vernon Speer began manufacturing his own bullets, using spent .22 rimfire cases as jackets. These early Speer bullets, all .224s, usually showed the headstamp of the case manufacturer on their bases.

At the end of the war, as the market for civilian shooting equipment increased and gilding metal for jackets again became available, Speer expanded his line and moved into a modern plant in Lewiston. By 1956, the new plant had been expanded to 12,000 square feet, and the Speer line included 49 different bullets in calibers from .22 to .375.

Half-jacketed pistol bullets were added in 1958, and in 1961, Speer perfected its double swaged, hot core hunting bullet, a design that offers great accuracy and maximum weight retention upon expansion. The Fourth of July Bench Rest Matches, which Speer inaugurated in 1962, are a major event on the benchrest shooter's calendar.

In 1976, Speer, Inc. merged with Omark Industries, also based in Lewiston.

Spencer rifles Spencer rifles and carbines were manufactured under patents issued to Christopher M. Spencer and were generally rated as the best infantry weapons in use during the Civil War. They were lever-action seven-shot repeaters, roughly .50 caliber. Approximately 200,000 Spencers were purchased during the Civil War for distribution to Union troops. Spencer arms were loaded through the butt, at first one cartridge at a time, later with tin tubes carrying seven cartridges. They were continued as sporting rifles in several models and calibers after the war.

The Spencer Rifle Company of Boston, Massachusetts, was sold in September 1869, to Winchester. Arms on hand were sold by Winchester during 1869–1872.

spherical aberration This condition is present in an optical instrument when a lens does not have the same focal length at its center position as at its outer zones. Instruments in which spherical aberration is present lack definition.

spin See BULLET SPIN.

spin energy The rotational energy of a bullet in flight. (See KINETIC ENERGY.)

spitzer bullet A generic term indicating a bullet that has a sharp-pointed nose shape. In a spitzer bullet, the ogive departs from the shank of the projectile to form a sharp anterior section, as opposed to the blunter form of the roundnose, wadcutter, or flat nose bullet.

splash See BULLET SPLASH.

splinter fore-end A wedge-shaped, narrow fore-end used on side-by-side shotguns and double rifles. It is narrower in width than the barrels and acts largely as a framework for the fore-end iron. Splinter fore-ends are commonly used on British shotguns, while American shooters have shown a preference for beavertail fore-ends.

split receiver bridge The rear portion of a rifle receiver that lies over the bolt channel, often acting as a surface for the mounting of the rear telescopic sight bracket, is called the bridge. When this receiver bridge is split so that the arm of the bolt may pass through it during extraction, it is known as a split receiver bridge. An offset telescopic mount is necessary with a split receiver bridge, otherwise the uplifted bolt, when passing through the split, would make contact with the scope mount at the rear.

spool magazine See ROTARY MAGAZINE.

sporterizing The process of converting a military rifle to sporting use. There are many ways of sporterizing a military rifle, some of which depend on the design of the original rifle.

The first step is usually to replace the military sights with sights more suitable to hunting use, and today this almost always means a hunting scope. To install a scope on a military action may require some conversion of the receiver—grinding the "ears" that act as a protective shield for the rear sight on the 1917 Enfield for example. The receiver must also be drilled and tapped for the scope mount base. Many military actions, like the 1903 Springfield and a number of Mauser models, will need to have the bolt handle altered so that it will not interfere with a low-mounted scope.

The metal finish on many military rifles is very poor, especially on those hastily made during wartime. Such rifles are usually polished and blued along the lines used on commercial and custom rifles.

A new hinged floorplate often replaces the military one, which is usually either solid or difficult to remove. The trigger guard may be replaced also.

Most military triggers are of two-stage design to prevent accidental discharge during the stress of battle and are not ideal for sporting use. These are usually either replaced by a commercial trigger of adjustable design or converted to a single-stage pull that is good for hunting use.

The military stock is not a thing of beauty, nor does its design lend it to fast and comfortable use. It is designed with great strength in mind to withstand the rough handling it will receive. The first thing that is done to the stock to sporterize it is removal of the top handguard, if present. The fore-end is also cut off to the correct length for a sporter. The military sling swivel that is attached to the barrel band may be left on, but both it and the band are better removed and replaced by a narrower and lighter swivel fastened to the fore-end.

The buttstock will be thinned down and a new buttplate or recoil pad added. Many military stocks have been sporterized by building up the comb height—by inletting a piece of matching wood into the original stock—and giving the stock less heel drop. A pistol grip can be attached in the same way. Many military rifles are fully restocked in the sporterizing process.

Sporting Arms and Ammunition Manufacturers Institute, Inc. (SAAMI) SAAMI was formed in 1913 under the name Small Arms and Ammunition Manufacturers' Institute. Its membership was comprised of American suppliers of military materiel, most of it for foreign governments. A prime objective, then as now, was to increase the interchangeability of ammunition in firearms produced by various makers.

Following World War I, membership dwindled and activities were phased out, but with the transition from black powder to smokeless propellants in the ammunition industry, it was apparent there was a need for a revived SAAMI, and it was re-established under its current name in 1926 with membership representing the leading American producers of sporting firearms, ammunition, and smokeless propellants.

SAAMI's programs and activities are controlled by various committees: The Technical Committee has as its major responsibility the review of technical and safety practices and procedures developed by the firearms industry. Until the early 1960s, the Promotional Guidance Committee sponsored a variety of programs to stimulate a greater public awareness in the shooting sports. These activities were merged in 1963 with the National Shooting Sports Foundation. Traffic and transportation topics specific to shippers of sporting firearms and ammunition is the concern of the Traffic Committee. The International Trade Committee maintains surveillance of the international trade area and reports on the actual or potential influence of foreign and domestic government policy and regulations upon imports and exports. The Legislative and Legal Affairs Committee receives and analyzes reports of proposed legislation that may affect industry interests.

Relatively few SAAMI functions are directed to the general public, except as they help to ensure maintenance and improvement of product safety. SAAMI does offer publications that relate to recommended proper storage of smokeless powder, primers, and sporting ammunition. Today SAAMI is located in New York City.

Sporting Clays   A clay target sport that was invented in England in the 1920s to stimulate game shooting in wooded areas and fields is called Sporting Clays or, simply, Sporting. It gradually amassed considerable popularity in the U.K., and has been increasingly followed by shooters in the U.S. since the early 1980s.

In Sporting Clays, a shooter progresses from stand to stand on a rambling course that can vary considerably from club to club, and he is presented with a series of challenges at each stand. The stands, by rule, must emulate the movement of some kind of game, be it bird or hare. Examples of Sporting Clays stands are the springing teal, bounding hare, incoming mallard, high pheasant, crossing grouse, diving chukar, and the duck tower. It is a game that can be enjoyed by everyone from a casual hunter to a sophisticated competitor.

The essential gun for Sporting Clays is a 12 gauge. Rules prohibit shot charges heavier than 1⅛ ounces at the present time, and shot sizes are limited to Nos. 7½, 8, 8½, and 9. Some people shoot Sporting with their smallbore field guns to remain familiar with them for hunting, but in tournaments the 12 gauge dominates because of its dense pattern. Contrary to popular thinking that Sporting Clays start swiftly and a shooter should have a short, light gun; the champions at this sport use barrels of 28 to 30 inches for a forward balance to produce a "forced" follow through. Over/unders dominate the game, but some gas operated autoloaders do well, too. Pump guns do not fare well in Sporting Clays because of the speed of the targets, which is greater than that of American skeet and trap targets, and because of the high number of doubles.

Sporting Clays uses different sizes of clay targets for varying flight and optical effects, including a standard size plus a midi, mini, and a few specialty types like a heavy-rimmed "rabbit." The traps are generally special machines with powerful springs for long, fast target flights, and the targets are made harder than basic American skeet and trap clays.

Sports Afield   Sports Afield is the oldest of the major outdoor publications. The first issue, subtitled *Journal for Gentlemen*, appeared in 1888 and was published in Denver. Founder and first editor Claude King took up the cause of conservation by attacking the commercial slaughter of wildlife. The magazine moved to Chicago in 1894, to Minneapolis in 1930, and to New York in 1953 when it was purchased by the Hearst Corporation. Its present circulation is approximately 450,000.

spot shot   A device that inserts into a shotgun barrel and projects a beam of light when the gun's trigger is pulled. It is supposed to reveal where the gun's pattern would center if live ammunition were fired. It is used for home practice in gun mounting and pointing and also by some gunsmiths and custom gunmakers for fitting a gunstock to an individual shooter.

Also a wingshooting technique in which the hunter quickly shoots at a point ahead of a flying target without a swing or follow-through.

spotting scope   A spotting scope is a single-tube optical device that is used for checking targets and spotting game and is generally of higher power than the more commonly used binocular. Some spotting scopes are of adjustable power, the 15X–60X being an example. Other spotting scopes are fixed in power; the most popular magnification in fixed models is 20X.

The spotting scope may have an eyepiece that is offset from the tube at 45 degrees. This is useful for the target shooter, who can train the scope on the target and then merely move his head either to right or left, remaining in the shooting position, but being able to see through the offset angle of the lens.

spreader load Often called "thicket loads" or "scatter loads," these are shotshells designed to provide extra-large patterns at shorter ranges than standard shells. This is accomplished in American loads with a series of extra wad partitions in the shot column or X-shaped wads; some European spreader loads use square or flattened shot pellets. Most spreader loads pattern less evenly than standard loads, but open to usable patterns at shorter ranges.

spring activated firing pin Any firing pin that does not depend on the blow of a hammer or striker to drive it forward is spring activated. The spring, which is compressed on cocking the gun, is released by the sear when the trigger is pulled, propelling the tip of the firing pin against the primer. (See FIRING PIN.)

Springfield Armory The origin of Springfield Armory can be traced to 1777, when a "laboratory" was founded in what is now downtown Springfield, Massachusetts, through the efforts of Lieutenant Henry Knox, of General George Washington's staff. Originally established for the manufacturer of the paper cartridges used in the military muskets of that time, it also became a depot for military stores from other parts of New England. Largely demobilized after the Revolution, except for the construction of a large powder magazine in 1782, it was later authorized as Springfield Armory by an act of the Third Congress on April 2, 1794. The first weapons produced at Springfield Armory were copies of the French Charleville musket, thousands of which had been supplied by France to the American colonies during the Revolution.

Although best known for the development and manufacturer of shoulder arms, it was a developmental, technical, and scientific center for a range of military weapons, including rifles, pistols, machine guns, and aircraft armament. It was deactivated on April 30, 1968 and, although many of the original buildings remain, only a small museum remains active.

Seven basic kinds of shoulder arms, in about 40 different models, were produced at Springfield Armory in the 174 years of its existence as an active arsenal. These were:

Flintlock smoothbore muskets, starting with the copies of the Charleville Model 1763, in 1795.

Percussion smoothbore muskets, appearing about 1842.

Percussion rifled muskets, the first all-new model appearing in 1845 (though it is referred to as the Model 1842).

Breechloading, single-shot rifles and carbines, starting in 1866.

Bolt-action repeating rifles and carbines, starting with the Krag in 1892 and followed by the famous Springfield Model 1903, for which the armory is probably best known.

Semiautomatic rifles, with work starting shortly after World War I, culminating in the adoption of the Garand rifle in 1937. Springfield produced more than 4,000,000 of these in World War II.

The M-14 rifle, a modification of the Garand, usable for either semi- or full automatic fire, adopted in 1957.

sprue The opening in a bullet or ball casting mold provided for pouring molten metal into the mold. Sprue also refers to the excess metal that hardens in and over this opening and that is sheared off by a sprue cutter. Sprue metal is reusable. (See BULLET MOLD.)

sprue cutter A swinging plate pivoted to a bullet mold having a concentric hole that matches the sprue hole in the mold. It is used to cut excess metal away from the casting. (See SPRUE.)

spud See COLLIMATOR.

spur trigger See SHEATH TRIGGER.

squib load A cartridge characterized by a mild report assembled by a handloader, usually with a cast lead bullet and a reduced powder charge. Since squib loads are intended for practice purposes, an effort is made to produce them inexpensively: In handguns, squib loads may have half-jacketed bullets; in rifles, small charges of fast-burning powders.

squirrels, guns and loads for When the leaves are off the trees so that the hunter can see the squirrels easily, many sportsmen prefer the .22 rimfire rifle with a 3X or 4X scope. The scope aids not only in magnifying the target but also in picking out targets in dim light. The favored .22 cartridge is the Long Rifle with a solid point. The hollow point tears up too much meat if the animal is not hit in the head. Other hunters like the .22 Short; the Long Rifle, they say, is inclined to go right through a squirrel and often leaves him on top of a branch or hung up in a crotch so that the tree must be climbed to make the retrieve. The Short expends its energy inside the squirrel and therefore often knocks him out of the tree. Many hunters shoot only for the head in order to spoil no meat, but a .22 through the lungs destroys little that is edible.

When there is considerable foliage, a shotgun is often used, anything from a .410 to a 12 gauge. No. 6 is a good shot size, and in 12 gauge most hunters use 1¼-ounce loads. If, however, you have trouble making clean kills, use No. 5 shot. Modified choke is best in the big gauges, but in the smaller gauges full choke puts more shot on the squirrel. A compromise is an over/under combination gun. Use the .22 on sitting squirrels and the shotgun tube when they are running.

SR powder An abbreviation for Du Pont Co. Sporting Rifle Powder, a series of smokeless propellants introduced in 1913. The first, SR 80, was made from 1913 to 1939. It was replaced by SR 4759, which is still manufactured. This series of powders is fast-burning and is suited for loads in small-capacity rifle cases such as the .25/20, or for reduced loads in larger cases.

stabilizer In target handguns, a stabilizer is a weight or weights that is attached to the barrel near the muzzle. The purpose of the stabilizer is to minimize muzzle jump and perceived recoil, thereby reducing the amount of time required for the shooter to regain the correct sight picture. The added muzzle weight also facilitates steady holding.

stadia wire In a telescopic rifle sight, a part of a reticle system in which a secondary horizontal crosswire is so placed that it encompasses a specific amount of space at a specific distance. At 300 yards, for example, the two horizontal wires might subtend 15 inches. By knowing the size of a distant object and determining how much of that object is occupied between the two horizontal wires, an estimation of the distance of the object from the shooter may be made. If an object has a breadth of 15 inches, for example, and the two wires encompass that breadth perfectly, then the object is 300 yards from the shooter. The shooter can then adjust his hold to compensate for trajectory. (See RANGEFINDER RETICLE.)

standing breech In a break-action gun, the solid, vertical side of the action that contains the firing pin(s) and supports the base of the cartridge when the action is closed is referred to as the standing breech.

star crimp See SHOTSHELL CRIMP.

star gauge A metallic device, which when inserted into the barrel of a rifle, can measure tiny variations in the interior dimensions of the bore, to determine the quality, smoothness, and consistency of the boring and rifling. Stargauged 1903 Springfields were once considered highly desirable. The star gauge has been replaced by the air gauge. (See BORE GAUGE.)

Star handguns See SPANISH GUNMAKERS.

starter A short rod or peg used to start a ball down the barrel of a muzzleloading arm. Most starters—brass, aluminum, plastic, or wood—are simply handle affairs with a 1- to 2-inch peg on one side and a 4- to 6-inch peg on the other; the ends of the pegs are cupped to fit the balls used. The short peg is used to seat a patched ball just below the muzzle, where the patch can be cut; the longer peg is used to push a ball far enough into the barrel so that it can then be seated on the powder with a ramrod.

steady pin In a sidelock gun, the steady pin is a small projection that extends from the end of a mainspring and fits into a depression in the sideplate to anchor the spring in place.

steel bedding In order to ensure a more precise fit of an action into its stock and to prevent the action from shifting under repeated firing, a gunsmith will sometimes inlet steel plates into the stock, thereby achieving a metal-to-metal contact. This procedure is difficult and is rarely done.

A more common method of steel bedding is the use of steel-base epoxy cements such as Devcon. Used chiefly by benchrest shooters, this kind of bedding is relatively simple—like any other glass-bedding method—and provides good results. (See BEDDING; GLASS BEDDING.)

steel jacketed bullet In some highly specialized forms of sporting ammunition, such as large-caliber cartridges for African game, penetration is of more importance than expansion. To construct bullets that will not expand on impact, a steel jacket is used; the bullet is also covered with a copper coating to prevent erosion and excessive wear on the rifling. (See SOLID BULLET.)

steel shot Nontoxic shotshell pellets made from annealed steel wire were originally designed to reduce losses of wild waterfowl that ingest common toxic lead pellets and may, as a result, develop lead poisoning. These pellets, in any size, are only about 70 percent as heavy as the comparable lead pellets, but to some extent compensate for this lack of density by retaining excellent roundness, or form factor, which provides higher retained energy and penetration capability than their weight would otherwise indicate. (Soft lead pellets lose some of their efficiency because of deformation within the shell at the time of firing [setback deformation] and deformation in passage through the choke even when protected by shortcup wads.)

Because of a diamond point hardness (DPH) of around 90, which is considerably harder than the best hardened lead pellets, steel shot retains its roundness well, but can cause abrasion of shotgun barrels if not protected by extra-thick, tough plastic shotcup wads. In some guns with very soft or thin barrels, or extremely sharp and tight choke angles, steel shot has been found to create barrel rings. These bulges are most likely to occur in old doubles or over/unders with a great deal of choke constriction, or in AL-5 Browning autoloaders made in Belgium and choked full. Although a few barrels have burst with steel shot, there is no conclusive data indicating that the bursts were directly related to steel shot rather than barrel obstruction. Most modern pumps, autoloaders, and single-barrels show no obvious change after using steel shot, and some manufacturers, Winchester and Remington among them, have stated that the use of steel shot in their guns of this kind will not result in a shortening of the useful life of the gun. Barrels made by the hammer-forging process (the one most commonly used in Japan) seem to have additional resistance to steel shot. Recent Browning autoloaders, doubles, and over/unders made in Japan have less acute choke angles than Belgian Brownings and are much less susceptible to barrel ring bulges. Ithaca pumpguns and autoloaders carry a special steel shot warranty guaranteeing that the barrels will handle either steel or lead shot. Most doubles and over/unders of modern manufacture are not damaged by steel shot provided the choke is no tighter than modified.

Steel shot does not react the same to choking as many soft lead loads, tending to pattern tighter and having shorter, more efficient shot strings than easily deformed lead pellets. Most modified barrels will throw full choke patterns with steel loads, and with most guns steel shot patterns at least one choke designation tighter than common nonbuffered lead loads.

At this time steel loads are available only in 12 gauge, but experiments indicate that 20-gauge loads can be produced with range and killing capability comparable to most standard nonbuffered 20-gauge lead loads.

Reloading of steel pellets has been strongly dis-

couraged by the Sporting Arms and Ammunition Manufacturers Institute because of the lack of special heavy duty shotcup wads, special primers, powders, etc. required to obtain maximum performance and safety from steel pellets. However, there are indications that such components may be available to reloaders in the future.

Field hunting tests in which shooters were unaware of the kind of pellets they were shooting have indicated that there is little or no difference in effective range, bagging, or crippling between the best modern steel shot loads and common lead loads, although the finest plastic buffered lead loads show a slight advantage in killing range. In one test, conducted by the Illinois Department of Natural Resources, steel BB-sized pellets in 3-inch magnum loads outperformed, in bagging and with less crippling, No. 2 3-inch magnum loads in lead.

Despite these tests, opposition to use of steel shot remains strong among waterfowlers, many of whom are convinced steel shot may lose more birds by crippling than would be saved from lead poisoning by its use.

Early steel shot loads, some of which were ballistically inferior to those now available, convinced many hunters that steel shot is no good. Another great source of resistance to steel shot has been the high price for factory loaded shells; some Magnums have sold for more than $13 per box. Prices range widely in various areas, and for various brands, and a Congressional inquiry was launched in 1978 into steel shot pricing and also into the lack of loading components released by the industry for individual reloading.

The controversy has perhaps been a dangerous one for the future of waterfowl hunting, since it has caused a split between conservation organizations, such as the National Wildlife Federation, and some hunting organizations that oppose steel shot. In general, environmentalist groups support steel shot as necessary to reducing lead-ingestion poisoning; many hunters oppose it on the basis of crippling, high cost, and the lack of proven data on numbers of birds lost to lead poisoning. The issue may ultimately be decided in court. Steel shot is presently required only in special "steel only" zones designated by the Fish and Wildlife Service, but these zones include some of the finest waterfowl hunting in America. (See NILO SHOTSHELL EFFECTIVENESS TEST; PATUXENT TEST; RINGED BARREL; SHOT.)

stereoscopic vision   A shooter who aims with both eyes open receives two images, which combine to produce a single image of greater depth and more accurate perspective—stereoscopic vision—than the image seen by a shooter who closes one eye while aiming.

Stevens, J. C. (company) The origins of this gun manufacturing firm can be traced to the Stevens Arm & Tool Co., which was active in the early 1850s in Chicopee Falls, Massachusetts. In 1864, the name was changed to J. C. Stevens & Co., and in 1886 the firm was incorporated as J. C. Stevens Arms & Tool Co. In 1915, Stevens was acquired by Westinghouse, and after World War I by Savage, which retains the name in its product line.

Stevens was best known for its series of single-shot .22 rifles, based on an exposed-hammer falling block design. This mechanism was used as the basis for a wide range of guns, varying from inexpensive boys' rifles to sophisticated and expensive target arms. Stevens also made an extensive line of .22 bolt-action rifles.

Steyr-Daimler-Puch (company) This company was founded in the town of Steyr, Austria, in 1903, as the Österrechische Waffenfabrik Gesellschaft (Austrian Arms Manufacturing Company). The company is familiarly referred to as Steyr-Mannlicher (because of its long association with Count von Mannlicher, the arms designer), or simply as Steyr. The founder, Josef Werndl, began by converting military muzzleloaders to breechloaders, but soon thereafter began original manufacture. At the close of World War I, the company was renamed Steyrwerke AG (Steyr Works Corporation). The company absorbed the Austro-Daimler and the Puch organizations to become Steyr-Daimler-Puch, the present name, after World War II. This conglomerate produces automobiles, automotive equipment, and agricultural machinery. In the 1950s, Steyr resumed the manufacture of arms.

In its early days, Steyr produced several innova-

tive pistols designed by Karel Krnka, Roth, and Mannlicher, including the remarkable blow-forward Mannlicher pistol. Perhaps its most widely used handgun was the famous Steyr Model 1911, a locked breech semiautomatic chambered for a special 9mm cartridge. The pistol was top loaded through the open action with a clip. Many of these pistols are found today rechambered for the German 9mm Parabellum.

To the sportsman, Steyr is known primarily for the Mannlicher rifle, one of the most successful rifles ever made that is not of the Mauser type. Military versions of the Mannlicher rifle were adopted by many countries. (See MANNLICHER RIFLE.)

stippling To point, draw, or engrave with a series of dots, resulting in a shading effect, the image merging as a unit. Stippling, in the shooting world, means creating dots on either a metallic or wooden surface, such as the frame or grips of a handgun. The small raised "craters" provide a better grip on the firearm with less slippage and a nonglare surface. Stippling is done by hand with a punch.

stirrup A D- or stirrup-shaped piece of steel used to connect a spring plunger to another part. For example, in Colt double-action revolvers a stirrup connects the hammer to the plunger that rides in the mainspring.

stock The part or parts of a firearm that enable it to be grasped. In long arms, the stock consists of the butt, fore-end, and grip. Stocks are usually made of wood, although fiberglass, metal, and plastics are also used. (See GRIP; RIFLE STOCK; SHOTGUN STOCK.)

stock, handgun See HANDGUN STOCKS.

stock, rifle See RIFLE STOCK.

The Stevens Favorite was a highly popular single-shot .22. This is a commemorative model made by Savage-Stevens.

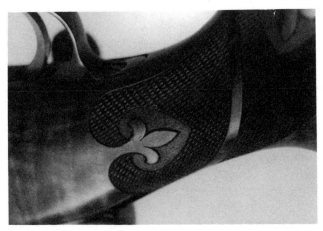

Stippling is a mottled, or matte, pattern that is impressed on wood or metal with a punch. Here, the area surrounding the fleur-de-lis is stippled as a contrast to the checkering.

Stock crawling can result from an ill-fitting stock, poor shooting position, or an improperly mounted scope. This shooter's eye is too close to the ocular lens for safety.

stock, shotgun See SHOTGUN STOCK.

stock crawler A shooter who pushes his head far forward on the stock so that the cheek rests near the forward end of the comb. This places a rifle shooter's brow close to the ocular lens of a scope, and if the gun is one with substantial recoil, a cut eyebrow may result.

stock decoration The art of decorating weapons is an ancient one, and gunstocks have been the object of artistic expression since the inception of the firearm. As practiced in modern times, the most common form of stock decoration is elaborate checkering, which goes beyond a simple pattern of coarse diamonds. Highly elaborate patterns may be laid out, employing fleurs-de-lis, ribbons, special borders, stippling, multipoint patterns, and special insets of super-fine diamonds. As a rule, any checkering pattern that employs diamonds cut finer than 26 lines per inch can be said to be more decorative than functional.

Some stocks employ carved patterns in place of checkering. Basketweave, leaf, and scale patterns are among the most popular. Many higher grade rifles made in Germany and Austria surround the checkering with carved borders, and some have game motifs carved in deep relief on the broad surface of the buttstock.

Rifles of the California school design are made

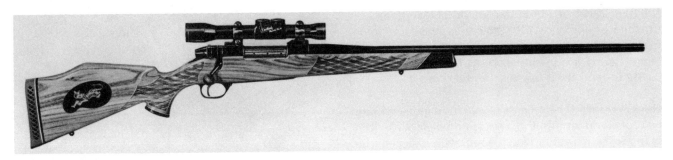

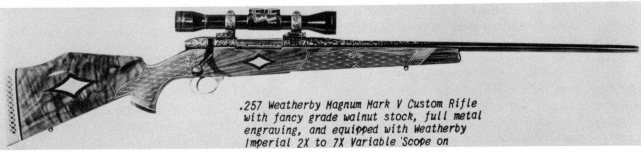

.257 Weatherby Magnum Mark V Custom Rifle with fancy grade walnut stock, full metal engraving, and equipped with Weatherby Imperial 2X to 7X Variable Scope on

These custom Weatherby rifles employ not only fancy checkering patterns, but geometric and animal-figure inlays in contrasting woods.

more elaborate by means of contrasting wood inlays in the buttstock, and occasionally in the fore-end. These may take the form of geometric designs or may depict game animals. Some are quite elaborate and make use of many small pieces of different colored tropical hardwoods.

Best grade British guns frequently have the owner's initials engraved on a small gold oval set into the underside, or belly, of the stock, and this practice is followed by many of the more conservative American craftsmen. (See CALIFORNIA STOCK; CHECKERING.)

stock finish The final stage of creating a gunstock consists of applying a coating to the wood that will enhance its appearance and prevent it from absorbing moisture. This coating is known as the stock finish. For many years, the best stocks were finished with a combination of spar varnish and linseed oil. The varnish was applied, allowed to dry, and then rubbed down to the bare wood. This sealed the pores of the wood. Then the oil was applied in thin coats, allowed to dry, and rubbed down with each coat. The process was laborious, and the raw linseed oil took a great deal of time to dry.

Today, most gunsmiths have turned to synthetics. Many of them use epoxy, either as a sealer coat, in combination with improved, quick-drying linseed oil, or by itself. Others use plastic wood finishes. The advantages of these over the older materials are the rapidity of their drying, superior water-sealing qualities, and the ability to create a thin eggshell-like finish. Most commercial manufacturers use these same materials, but apply them to many stocks at a time, without the hand labor a gunsmith gives to his product. Most of the better grade factory guns are finished in epoxy, while the less expensive models use plastic. Today, only a very few highly priced factory arms are oil finished, as the process is too costly to lend itself to mass production.

stockmaking The process of making a gunstock can be broken down into three separate phases. The first is inletting, in which wood is removed to accept the action and barrel to the proper depth. In mass production, this is accomplished by highly sophisticated cutting machines that work on many stocks at one time and that are, in many cases, computer controlled. The result is an acceptable, if rather imprecise, fit between wood and metal. Custom gunsmiths either inlet entirely by hand, using a highly specialized series of chisels, scrapers, and gouges, or else have a stock rough-inletted by machine and then do the final work by hand.

The second phase, shaping, is also performed by machine in mass production. A metal or plastic form

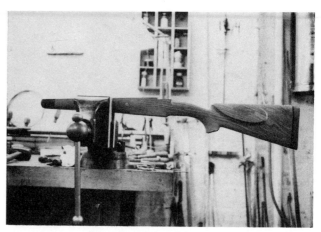

This Griffin & Howe stock has gone through its final sanding. Next, the finish will be applied.

Although much custom stockwork is done strictly by hand, power tools are often used. Here, a Griffin & Howe craftsman inlets a rifle stock with an electric router.

of a finished stock is used as a model by a duplicating machine that can translate its contours to a series of stock blanks. The most precise of these machines are known as pantographs and are capable of great precision and consistency. As with inletting, custom gunsmiths can either work from a rough blank, shaping entire by hand, or, as an increasing number are doing, rely on a pantograph for the rough shaping and do the final work by hand.

Checkering and finishing, the third phase, is now almost entirely automatic. Checkering can either be impressed by rolling a heated mandrel over the wood, or can actually be cut into the wood by computer operated cutters. Finishes are usually sprayed on and dried under heat. Only in this third phase do custom gunsmiths do their work entirely by hand, since the checkering patterns they employ and the quality of the finish that they require cannot be achieved by machine. (See CHECKERING; CUSTOM GUNS; INLETTING; STOCK DECORATION; STOCK FINISH.)

stock panel The stock panel is a slightly raised portion of the stock, usually found on German bolt-action rifles and on some German bolt-action shotguns.

It usually extends the full length of the action and acts as decoration as well as a stock reenforcement.

stock woods The majority of gunstocks are made from hardwoods of different varieties. Wood qualities deemed desirable in gunstocks limit the kinds of tree woods that are suitable for stocks, however. Lightness is prized, but it must be coupled with a density that will give the wood durability and the hardness to hold checkering and carving designs, as well as the ability to take inletting without splintering. For shotguns and high-powered rifles, stock wood must be extremely strong to withstand the repeated battering of recoil. Density contributes to strength and reduces the absorption of moisture, which can lead to warping of the fore-end. And since nearly every stock aspires to a degree of visual attractiveness, the color and grain pattern in a piece of wood have often been regarded as the prime criteria of stock wood desirability. Attractive stocks possess rich, contrasting color tones and an intricate grainwork, or "figure." Burl (swirling) designs,

feathery grain that changes shades with the play of light, and vertical striping patterns called "tigertail stripes," occur with some high-quality woods.

A relatively few tree species have been used for stock woods. Historically, the walnut family has provided more stock wood than any other. English walnut, which originally grew in Persia (now Iran) is considered to make the very best of walnut gunstocks. It grows now over much of Europe, and France has produced so much of it that the tree is often called French walnut. Another variety of the same tree, called Circassian walnut, grows in a region of the USSR north of Turkey and is highly prized for its rich, beautiful color tones and grain. Because of export restrictions, wood actually grown in Circassia is almost impossible to obtain. All European walnut picks up its attractiveness from the minerals and the arid, rocky conditions under which the best of it grows. English walnut grown in irrigated orchards in California will not produce wood with the stock potential of the same species grown on a mountain slope in France. In the United States, American black walnut, much of which comes from the Ozark Mountains, is extensively used to stock commercial sporting arms and was used for military small arms until the advent of the plastic-stocked M-16. Exceptional black walnut stocks approach good European stocks in color and grain. Claro walnut, another American species, is used on many custom firearms around the world, as well as being a prized furniture wood.

Many trees other than walnuts are used for stock woods. In Colonial North America, sugar maple and silver maple—heavy, dense woods—were highly regarded for their workability, strength, and striped grain. Although most mahogany is used for furniture, some has been used for gunstocks. It is lighter and more stable than walnut, but both grain and color tend to be monotonous. Woods from certain apple, cherry, and pear trees have made very fine and beautiful gunstocks; they are hard and dense

The finest of all woods for gunstocks is Juglans regia, usually called French or Circassian walnut. It combines light weight, strength, beauty, and good working properties. Because of steadily increasing demand, it is growing scarce, and a first-rate blank such as this one commands the same price that a first-rate finished rifle would have not too many years ago.

woods, but their use is not widespread. Some early Kentucky rifles were, however, made with such stocks, particularly from cherry. Birch, although light in color, is used for stocks to some extent in Europe, particularly on sporters made by Sako. Since the 1940s, a distinctive yellow/brown streaked stock has been made in the United States from screw-bean mesquite wood. Sycamore and birch have come into increasing use as stock wood since walnut supplies have become harder to find. Both woods are softer, lighter in color, and straighter in grain than walnut; some contemporary manufacturers use them on their less expensive models and usually finish them with walnut stains. Stocks have also been made from such woods as rosewood, yama, monkeypod, koa, madrone, sassafras, persimmon, and others, usually for novelty effect.

During World War II, the Germans experimented with making gunstocks by using strips of wood laminated with glue. These laminated stocks offer creative possibilities and seem to resist warping somewhat. An increasing percentage of stocks are made of nonwood products, such as Kevlar or fiberglass. Although these offer manufacturing and stability advantages, they lack the character, warmth, and beauty of wood stocks.

Sadly, the demand by furniture makers and stockers has had the effect of seriously depleting certain species of trees. For this reason, the trend toward stock woods other than walnut, and the use of nonwood materials for stocks, is likely to increase.

stop, optical The diaphragm in a lens system; or, a single marking in a series of stops, as on a camera lens. (See DIAPHRAGM.)

storage, optical instruments Modern optical instruments made for shooting use are extremely rugged and require only a few precautions in storage. The most important is protection for the lenses, which are the most delicate parts of these instruments. Binoculars and spotting scopes should be stored in their cases with lens caps (if included in the design of the instrument) screwed on. Riflescopes should have lens caps attached to prevent dust from collecting on the lenses. Excess humidity should be avoided, as should places of storage where the instruments can be damaged though careless handling.

straight In trap and skeet shooting, when a shooter hits every target thrown, he is said to have shot a straight or straight run.

straight grip stock A firearm stock in which the line from trigger guard to buttplate is straight, with no hint of a pistol grip curve. Originally, it was felt that this kind of stock allowed for smoother lines, ease of entry and exit from a scabbard, and quick trigger switching on a double shotgun. Today, the straight grip stock is found on many English double-barreled shotguns, as well as some of American manufacture. One of the most popular rifles ever made, the Model 94 Winchester carbine, employs the straight grip stock. (See SHOTGUN STOCK.)

straight-pull action In this kind of action, the bolt is pulled directly to the rear and pushed forward by the shooter's hand. Rifle designs of this kind have not been entirely successful, as the straight-pull action lacks the powerful primary extraction stroke of a conventional bolt, which is first lifted upward. In recent years, the only straight-pull action to be introduced was the Browning T-Bolt .22 rimfire rifle. It was a satisfactory action because of the low pressures of .22 ammunition, but it did not meet with wide commercial acceptance, and has been discontinued.

strain gauge This device, which may contain a piezoelectric crystal, attaches to the outside of a rifle chamber and measures the pressure within the chamber by means of cathode-ray oscilloscope analysis of molecular changes within the chamber upon firing. Unlike the crusher gauge measurement system, the rifle chamber does not have to be altered. (See CHAMBER PRESSURE; CRUSHER GAUGE.)

strain screw Some leaf-type mainsprings are equipped with strain screws that bear against them. These can be turned in or out to provide greater or lesser tension on the spring.

striker A rod, housed within a bolt, powered by a spring, and released by a trigger, that either acts upon a separate firing pin or that contains a firing pin in its forward end. (See FIRING PIN.)

string A consecutive series of shots fired in competition. A string usually consists of five or 10 rounds.

The term is also applied to a charge of shot pellets in flight.

stringing This term has two different applications pertaining to firearms. The first refers to the progression, either horizontally or vertically, of a series of bullets striking a target. For example, a rifle with excessive fore-end tension would tend to string its shots progressively higher from the desired point of impact with each pull of the trigger.

In shotgun shooting, the term refers to the phenomenon of a shot charge forming an elongated "string" on its path to the target, with some pellets arriving considerably in advance of others. (See SHOT STRING.)

stripping This term has three nonrelated meanings. Stripping, as it applies to bullets, is the process of a soft bullet being driven though the bore without following the rifling, caused by too-great velocity, and tearing pieces off of itself in the process.

Field stripping is the emergency disassembly of a firearm in the field, usually without tools.

Stripper clips are, in extremely rare instances, used to charge the magazines of sporting arms and transferring the cartridges from clip to magazine is called stripping.

stub twist A particular pattern of Damascus steel used in shotgun barrels. A stub twist barrel is therefore a Damascus barrel. (See DAMASCUS BARREL.)

Sturm, Ruger & Company, Inc. William B. Ruger, whose fascination with firearms began in his childhood in Brooklyn, New York, is still president and chairman of the board of the arms company he helped start in 1949. Sturm, Ruger & Company, Inc. was organized with the financial assistance of partner Alex Sturm, in a small barn in Southport, Connecticut. The company was originally created to manufacture and market a .22 automatic pistol that Ruger had designed.

Sturm died in 1951, leaving Ruger to run the company alone. Ruger began manufacturing several other pistols that he and Sturm had been considering and designing. As production was stepped up, the manufacturing and marketing facilities of the company were greatly enlarged.

In 1960, Sturm, Ruger introduced its first rifle, the Ruger .44 Magnum Carbine. The company continued its growth in the production of rifles by adding such models as the .22 caliber semiautomatic rifle with 10-shot rotary magazine, the Number One single-shot rifle for big game, the bolt-action M-77, and the Mini-14 centerfire autoloader. In 1969, the company introduced a double-action .38 and .357 Magnum revolver series. And in 1977, Sturm, Ruger introduced its first shotgun, an over/under.

styphnate See LEAD STYPHNATE.

subcaliber An imprecise term used to denote a cartridge of extremely small bullet diameter. In America, it refers to .20-, .17-, and .14-caliber cartridges.

subcaliber gauge In skeet shooting, the 28 and .410 are commonly referred to as subcaliber gauges. The latter has also been known as the sub-smallbore event.

suigi finish When fashioning a rifle or shotgun stock out of maple, it is possible to create a more dramatic effect in the wood by employing a suigi finish. When the stock is in its final sanded state, just prior to application of the finish, the wood is lightly scorched with a blowtorch. This accentuates the pattern in the maple (it is most commonly done with stocks of the fiddleback or tiger-stripe variety), but must be performed with great care to avoid damaging the wood. Some stockmakers prefer to use stains to bring out the pattern, claiming that the suigi finish can warp a stock or affect the inletting. (See STOCK FINISH.)

summit velocity The speed of a projectile at the highest point along its trajectory is its summit velocity.

superposed gun See OVER/UNDER GUN.

Super Vel (company) See JURRAS BULLETS.

sustained lead Also called maintained lead, this is a method of leading a moving target with a shotgun. With sustained lead, the shooter starts the shotgun's muzzle moving ahead of the target as it crosses or angles past and maintains that lead for a time to make sure the needed forward allowance has been obtained. During that time, he may make fine adjustments, shorter or longer, as required. When the lead looks right, he pulls the trigger.

This kind of lead works best with birds passing at nearly right angles at long range. For instance, a waterfowl shooter often uses it when geese are circling the blind. Sustained lead does not work well in close-range shooting at birds that are heading for heavy cover, as it takes too much time.

swaged choke Any shotgun choke created by forcing the muzzle into a metal die. It is the cheapest method of choking, but works well.

swaged rifling Swaged rifling is cold formed; that is, pressed into the steel of the barrel under pressure. Commonly, a mandrel bearing a negative impression of the rifling is inserted into a barrel blank that has been drilled to the correct diameter for a given caliber and is somewhat shorter than the finished barrel will be. The barrel blank and mandrel are inserted into a forging press that employs a series of hammers, operating at high speed and with great force, to hammer the blank around the mandrel. This process impresses the rifling on the interior of the blank, and lengthens the barrel as well.

Manufacturers who advocate swaged rifling claim that it results in a smoother bore, and one that resists erosion by powder gases, since the absence of tool marks left by cut rifling gives the gases no "foothold" in the steel. (See BARREL, RIFLED.)

swaging, bullet   See BULLET SWAGING.

swamped rib   A kind of top rib put on a side-by-side double. It swoops away from the line of sight and leaves a visual gap between the breech area and the muzzles, thus allowing the shooter's eye to jump from the breech to the muzzles quickly without any rib or middle bead cluttering up the viewing area. It is one of the fastest-pointing ribs ever made for the side-by-side because it eliminates the shooter's temptation to aim with the rib.

swan shot   Large shotgun intended for hunting swans. They are no longer made because the shooting of swans is now almost universally prohibited. The round pellets were about .268-inch in diameter or 240 to the pound, a little smaller than American No. 4 buckshot. They were also called "swan drops."

SWC bullet   See SEMIWADCUTTER BULLET.

swing-out cylinder   Most revolvers employ a cylinder that is supported in a crane and swings out to the side of the frame for loading and unloading. Exceptions to this are single-action revolvers, which load through a port, and a few double actions of breaktop design, most notably the British Webley or early Smith & Wessons. (See CYLINDER.)

swing-through   A fast method of attaining the needed amount of forward allowance, or lead, to hit a moving target. When the shooter swings through at a crossing or angling target, he comes from behind and swings through the target. When the needed length of lead looks right, he pulls the trigger, being careful to keep the gun moving.

swivel-breech muzzleloader   Early in the 17th century, gunsmiths attempted to solve the problem of increasing a gun's rate of fire by designing arms with barrels that swiveled into position, offering a second shot without reloading. The earliest swivels were handguns, but rifles used the principle as well. A gun would be equipped with two or more barrels—as many as six were used—that could be unlocked and rotated into position for the next shot. Some designs used one lock for all barrels, while others had a separate lock for each barrel. The most popular arrangement was two barrels in an over/under configuration. Swivel-breech guns were in fairly common use until the 1860s. (See PEPPERBOX PISTOL.)

takedown This term applies to a kind of gun that can be shortened in length, generally by breaking into two main sections, for ease of transport. Many rifles have this feature, especially in the .22-caliber class, as well as some shotguns such as the Savage Model 99. Takedown is often accomplished by the removal of only one screw, thus distinguishing a takedown model from an arm that can be broken down, but only with the removal of many bolts. Field stripping, or disassembly of the firearm into its major component parts, is also referred to as takedown.

tang That portion of the firearm's receiver that extends to the rear and is inletted into the stock itself at the wrist section. Normally the tang is quite narrow in dimensions, and is often used to attach the action to the stock via bolts.

tang sight This kind of peep sight was popular during the heyday of the single shot and lever action, roughly, 1870–1920. Tang sights were mounted on the tangs of rifles and usually were hinged to fold forward out of the way. They were often used in combination with an open iron sight, such as a buckhorn, mounted on the barrel. Tang sights used for competition shooting were usually equipped with Vernier scales and were capable of very fine adjustment. (See METALLIC SIGHTS.)

tape primer See MAYNARD TAPE PRIMER.

taper choke Also known as American choke and cone choke, this particular kind of constriction differs from other choking systems in that the bore size decreases gradually toward the muzzle of the gun in a tapering configuration. All degrees of choke from improved cylinder to full can be cut with the same reamer. The deeper the reamer is run, the more open the pattern of the gun will be, since more metal has been removed. (See CHOKE.)

tapered barrel See CONTOURED BARREL.

Tarage tables These mathematical tables have two common uses in shooting. The first is the interpretation of chamber pressures when used in conjunction with a crusher gauge. The second is to convert velocities expressed as time of flight in milliseconds

into velocities in feet per second. (See CRUSHER GAUGE; VELOCITY.)

target Targets for conventional rifle and pistol matches usually consist of a bulls-eye and scoring rings, the dimensions of which are prescribed by the organization governing the particular kind of match. Such targets are made of a special heavyweight paper that permits precise scoring because the bullets cut a clean hole rather than tearing the target sheet. Metallic silhouette matches are fired at metal profiles of chickens, javelinas, turkeys, and sheep. So-called practical matches for rifle, pistol, and shotgun simulate combat and are fired against the clock. Targets in these games are unconventional, and may include steel discs or squares of varying sizes, bowling pins, or pictures of humans.

target backing Target backing is the surface to which paper targets are attached. Also, in some organized match shooting, target backing is an additional sheet of blank paper set at a prescribed distance behind the scoring target. The purpose of this backing is to ensure that each contestant fires the prescribed number of shots at his target. Because of the separation between the scoring target and the backing, bullet holes will be slightly wider apart and thus easier to count. Some benchrest matches require the use of a moving backer, since it is not uncommon for contestants to place all bullets into one tiny hole with actual group diameters being smaller than that of the bullets being used. These moving backing strips may travel either vertically or horizontally. On some benchrest ranges, one long backing strip may move across the rear of the entire line of targets.

target backstop The backstop is an important part of any rifle or pistol range. Its purpose is to stop all bullets from traveling beyond the limits of the range, where they might then become dangerous to life and property. The backstop may be any natural feature of the terrain that will efficiently perform the function of stopping bullets, or it may be constructed for this purpose. Care must be taken that the backstop is either far enough from the firing line to eliminate the possibility of ricochets coming back to the firing line, or constructed of materials that will eliminate all possibility of ricochets.

On outdoor ranges, the backstop must be more

than high enough to stop all bullets fired at normal elevations. Indoor ranges for smallbore rifle or pistol shooting usually have backstops consisting of steel plates set at such an angle that bullets are deflected downward into a deep bed of sand.

target butt The word "butt" itself is a carryover from archery into the firearms field. The target butt on rifle and pistol ranges is the area and equipment immediately adjacent to the targets. On military ranges and other ranges for large-bore rifle shooting, the target butts may include pits or trenches to protect the scorers.

The target butts on many permanent ranges are constructed of thick concrete and steel and may include facilities for the comfort of target pullers and scorers. Telephone or radio communication is maintained between the person in charge of the butts and the range officer on the firing line.

target frame Target frames are constructed of metal or wood to fit the particular target being used. Backing, to which the targets are fastened, is stretched across the openings in the frames.

target grips Grips suitable for serious competitive shooting. Some manufacturers of handguns provide special target grips that are large enough to completely fill the shooter's hand. This kind of grip allows the shooter to better control his gun. These grips are also supplied by makers of custom grips. Target grips usually cover both the front and backstraps or revolver frames and incorporate a filler

Target grips are oversized grips that are designed to fill the hand and give better control over the pistol.

between the back of the trigger guard and the front strap.

target hammer Special target hammers with low, wide spurs that provide for easy and rapid cocking of revolvers intended for target shooting. These hammers are standard equipment on some revolvers and are offered as options on others. They are especially useful in the timed and rapid-fire stages of pistol matches. In recent years, the revolver has been almost entirely replaced by the autoloading pistol except in police matches, and the target hammer does not enjoy its former popularity. (See HAMMER; REVOLVER.)

target paster Paper squares, coated with adhesive on one side, used to cover the holes made by previous shots after the target has been scored. The target may then be reused.

target pit This term is sometimes used interchangeably with target butt, but specifically applies to the trench or pit into which the scorers in large bore matches lower the targets for scoring. The pit must be deep enough to protect scoring personnel from bullets. It must also be far enough from the backstop so that the possibility of bullets ricocheting and entering the pit is minimized.

target trigger Any special trigger designed to aid in smooth firing in competition shooting. On rifles, these are often triggers that are fully adjustable for engagement, weight of pull, and overtravel. Such triggers are supplied as standard equipment on some rifles and as after-market equipment by various custom makers. Target triggers with these features are also standard equipment on some handguns made specifically for target shooting. Some target triggers for revolvers are merely wider than normal triggers. A special target trigger for shotguns used in trapshooting is the release trigger. (See ADJUSTABLE TRIGGER; RELEASE TRIGGER.)

Taylor, John See KNOCKDOWN EFFECT.

teatfire cartridge Invented by D. Williamson in 1864, supposedly to circumvent Smith & Wesson patents, teatfire cartridges were made with the priming contained in either a round or a flat teat. Only two calibers are known to have been made, .32 and .45. They are now collector's items.

Teflon A nonstick substance originally developed as a permanent coating for cooking utensils, but also adopted in liquid form as a lubricant for firearms and for lead bullets that are used in muzzleloaders.

Also, most recently as Teflon tape for covering the bearing section of lead bullets.

telescopic sights The telescope was invented late in 1608 by a Dutch optician named Johannes Lippershey, who, in the course of making spectacle lenses, happened to put two lenses in line in such a way as to discover that the combination made distant objects appear nearer. Lippershey seems to have thought little of the matter and considered the arrangement only an ingenious toy, but half a year later news of the discovery reached Galileo Galilei at the University of Padua in Italy.

One long night of concentrated thought was enough for this genius. The next morning he took a piece of organ pipe, put a convex lens in the forward end and a concave lens in the rear, adjusted them in relationship with each other, and produced the world's first true telescope. It was a 3 power scope full of faults and aberrations, but it was destined to revolutionize astronomy and other fields. In subsequent efforts, Galileo finally produced a 32X telescope of sufficient clarity to study the surface of the moon, discover the moons of Jupiter, and see spots on the face of the sun.

Today, such an arrangement of a positive and a negative lens is still called a Galilean telescope, and a pair of them forms an opera glass. The objective lens is convex and the ocular lens is concave, having a focal length approximately the same as that of the human eye. In effect, the ocular lens neutralizes the eye lens, so that the objective lens may be considered to form its image directly on the retina of the eye. Such an arrangement produces a virtual image, and it is thus impossible to introduce a reticle so that it may be used for aiming.

The German astronomer and mathematician, John Kepler, a contemporary and correspondent of Galileo, theorized the astronomical telescope, consisting of two convex lenses, forming a real image at the focus and thus permitting the use of a reticle, mounted at the focus. Kepler did not produce such an instrument, but he outlined its principles during his studies of the refraction of light. The manufacture of the first such telescope is credited by some to Gascoigne of England and by others to Father Scheiner of Germany. In an astronomical telescope the image is inverted and reversed, right to left. The addition of a third lens, the erector lens, inverts and reverts the image from the ocular lens, making the image seen by the user appear oriented as it would to the unaided eye. Thus, by the early 1600s, everything required to build a sighting telescope for a gun was known to science. This application, however, was to wait for nearly 200 years, while the science of

firearms proceeded to the point where a telescope sight was a useful adjunct to a rifle.

In modern sighting telescopes, the three lenses are each compounds made up of several elements and different kinds of glass to correct for the different wave lengths of the daylight spectrum and other aberrations, and the lenses are coated with an anti-reflection coating of magnesium fluoride. The standard telescope consists of an objective lens, the focal length of which is always less than half the distance to the object to be viewed and that produces a small but exceedingly bright image; an erector lens to invert and revert the image; and an ocular, or eyepiece, lens that is actually a microscope to magnify the image. A reticle may be placed at any focal point where a real image is produced, most often at the focus of the ocular lens.

Early telescopic sights. One of the publications of Bausch & Lomb credits one Charles Newton with being the first to attach a sighting telescope to a gun, in the early 1700s, but reference to the works of several authorities places the date of the general introduction in the 1830s or 1840s. In America, John Chapman, civil engineer and an expert rifleman, introduced the first *practical* rifle telescope and mount, which is described in detail in his 1844 book, *The Improved American Rifle.* Riflescopes of Chapman's design were made by Morgan James of Utica, New York. These had ⅝-inch diameter tubes, ran the full length of the barrel, were made in 10 to 20 power, were fixed focus for one range (usually 40 rods), and did not contain any adjustment for focusing for the eye of the individual shooter. They were adjusted for windage by driving the front mount crosswise in a dovetail in the barrel, and for elevation by a threaded adjustment in the rear mount, on the tang of the breechplug. Riflescopes of this kind had low relative brightness and a very small field of view, but they were generally satisfactory for target shooting. Scopes of this kind, with improvements in mounts and for focusing, were used on sniping rifles in the Civil War and were manufactured and used for target shooting into the early 1900s.

Riflescopes of this general type, with tubes 10 to 18 inches long, were also made during 1860–1890 for use on hunting rifles. The first telescope made in America with internal adjustments for windage and elevation was placed on the market in 1887 by Lawson Cummins of Montpelier, Vermont. Cummins also produced long eye-relief scopes, allowing a full field of view when the scope was mounted with the eyepiece ahead of the receiver on rifles, such as the lever-action Winchester repeaters. An optics designer named Davidson, in England, produced somewhat similar telescopes with short tubes, which were generally mounted on top of the barrel, but which for long range, as in the case of the Whitworth sniper rifles, were mounted on the side of the barrel to permit extreme angles of elevation without interference with the barrel.

The greatest disadvantage of the early rifle telescopes was their delicacy and fragility, and the same was true of most of the early mounts. Both were easily knocked out of adjustment and required great care in handling and in use. Modern riflescopes and mounts are marvels of engineering, combining strength, ruggedness, and accurate adjustments with light weight and optical performance that would astonish a rifleman of the last century.

Pros and cons. The advantages of scope sights are:

1. Better sighting. The view of target or game is magnified. Game almost indistinguishable against a background with the naked eye often stands out clear and sharp through a scope. The reticle or sighting point is optically in the same plane as the target or game, and no eye accommodation is necessary. With iron sights, the eye must line up the object, the front sight, and the back sight. This rapid change of focus is called accommodation and is easy for most people in their youth, but the ability of the eye to accommodate declines with age, and while the older shooter may still see the game or target clearly, he often finds the sights a blur, particularly in dull light.

2. The optical qualities of a good riflescope permit aiming in the early morning or late evening when iron sights would be useless. This lengthens the hunter's day and even that of the target shooter.

3. Greater safety. The apparent brighter image of the telescope in dull light, its magnification, and the ability it gives the user to perceive detail reduce the likelihood of an incautious hunter mistaking a human or a domestic animal for game.

4. For most hunting, except that of game at short range in the brush or jungle, a quality riflescope of low magnification, properly mounted, on a properly stocked rifle, is faster to sight with than any iron sights.

5. Although probably of minor importance, the use of the scope makes it easier to sight without canting the rifle and, because of being mounted higher above the bore of the rifle, makes it possible to sight the rifle for a longer distance, with the bullet trajectory passing closer to the line of sight, at all reasonable ranges, than with iron sights.

The disadvantages of scope sights are:

1. The scope adds weight and bulk to the rifle. When shooting in the wind, the scope adds surface for the wind to act upon, particularly with large target telescopes.

2. The change in eye position caused by the higher line of sight requires a higher comb than with iron sights for most efficient use of the scope. If a detachable scope is used, with iron sights as an auxiliary for bad weather, some compromise in sights or stock must be made.

3. Rain, snow, and fog make problems for the scope user. Water or snow on the lenses seriously impairs vision, and the water or snow in the air between rifleman and target is also magnified, so that the target may appear more indistinct through the scope than it does to the naked eye.

4. Scopes, even those of very low power, are not well adapted for fast short-range shooting, particularly in brushy country.

5. Magnification of the the target also increases the wobble of the shooter's hold.

Riflescopes for hunting. Scopes commonly used for big-game hunting today are from 2 to 10 power, generally with 1-inch diameter tubes and with objective lenses of sizes that, related to power, give a minimum exit pupil of 5mm to provide relative brightness sufficient for dull light. Eye relief must be sufficient so that the ocular assembly will not strike the shooter when the rifle is fired in the less secure positions when mounted on a rifle with heavy recoil. A wide field of view is important, particularly for a scope used in hunting in the woods at relatively short range. Magnifying power, objective size, relative brightness, and field of view are all interrelated. Scopes of higher power must have larger objective lenses to give good brightness and field. (Field, for practical purposes, is inversely proportional to power.) It follows, of course, that scopes of higher power must be bulkier and heavier to give adequate optical performance.

All of today's hunting scopes have internal adjustments for windage and elevation. In the past, a few scopes were made that required adjustments in the mounts, largely to reduce the problems in sealing the scope tube and lenses against the entry of moisture under rain and damp conditions. Improvements in design and manufacture have reduced this problem.

Low power scopes are fixed focus; that is, the focus is adjusted at the factory for a distance of 100 to 150 yards. Scopes above 10X usually have a focusing adjustment for different ranges, and all quality scopes have focus adjustments for the individual eye. It should be understood that a riflescope, like any optical instrument, is in exact focus for only one distance at any one setting. With low powers, the amount of parallax and out-of-focus is acceptable for ranges shorter than that at which the scope is focused and is not noticeable at longer ranges. With the higher powers, it is necessary to focus for range in order to obtain the clarity of view and the precision of aim that is the purpose of using the higher power scope.

Target riflescopes. Generally, in target shooting, relatively high magnification is desirable for greatest accuracy of aim and, in some cases, to enable the shooter to spot bullet holes through the riflescope. The exceptions are situations involving poor light or weather conditions where mirage becomes objectionable at high power, or, as in metallic silhouette shooting, where unsteadiness of position introduces problems with apparent wobble at high power and the shooter tends to snatch at the trigger at the instant when his aim appears correct. Because of high magnification, target scopes have small fields of view, exit pupils are small, and relative brightness is low; but target shooting is primarily a daytime sport, with good light and contrast on the aiming point of the target, so these factors are acceptable.

Early target scopes, as already described, had small tubes extending the full length of the barrel, with mounts providing external adjustments for elevation and windage. The first changes in these were the shortening of the tubes and provision for tubes to slide in the mounts under recoil. Sliding reduced the recoil shock on scope parts and allowed the scope to move away from the eye of the shooter, a definite advantage, as high magnification results in shorter eye relief (in the absence of optical design compromises).

Except for enlargement of the objective lenses, some enlargement of ocular lenses, refinement of design and optics, and more reliable adjustment in the mounts, target riflescope design remained little changed into the 1960s and '70s, and target scopes of traditional design continue to be made and sold. In many ways it is still an excellent design, offering advantages in easy mounting and in the use of one scope on several rifles by the simple expedient of recording the settings of the micrometer thimbles for elevation and windage for different rifles, different ranges, and different ammunition. However, the sliding tube, spring loaded mounts, and the recoil forces involved with the front mount on the barrel and the rear mount on the receiver ring, introduce very tiny errors in the location of the scope tube when the scope is returned to battery after recoil. The benchrest shooters were the first to discover this, because of their requirements for extreme ac-

curacy of aim. Custom work on existing hunting-type scopes of high magnification and with internal adjustments produced better results from the standpoint of accuracy. This was soon followed by factory production of both short and long tube, fixed-mount, internal adjustment scopes of 10 to 30 power. By 1990, the internally-adjusted scope completely eclipsed the older type.

Varmint scopes. Hunting of woodchucks, gophers, crows, etc. is usually done in open country at moderate to long ranges, where there is time to assume a rest or steady position and to take deliberate aim. Under these conditions and with the small targets involved, scopes of 6 to 20 power are commonly chosen for this kind of hunting. In years past, target telescopes of the traditional long tube, external-adjustment type were frequently used, but the knowledgeable buyer today will usually choose a short tube, internal adjustment scope to be mounted on the receiver of the rifle. The scopes developed for benchrest shooting are excellent. Good field of view and relative brightness are important and must be balanced against power.

Scopes of this general description are also useful for plains hunting for game such as antelope and for metallic silhouette shooting. For the latter sport, many scopes are now available with attachable knurled knobs for windage and elevation adjustments to permit quick and definite changes for range.

Variable-power riflescopes. The ability to vary the magnifying power of a riflescope has an appeal for many users, as a low power setting provides a wider field, greater relative brightness, and more universal focus for short-range woods hunting, while a high power setting gives higher magnification for varmint shooting, target shooting, or open plains hunting, although with less field and brightness.

The appeal of the variable-power scope is its apparent versatility, the ability to have a low power, medium power, and high power scope, all rolled into one, for a price of only 20 to 30 percent more than a fixed-power scope of the high magnification of the variable would cost. As always, however, multiple-use requirements result in design compromises.

Variable-power scopes:

1. Are heavier and bulkier than fixed-power scopes of comparable performance.
2. Restrict the choice of mounts, and mounting on some rifles may be a problem because of the space occupied on the tube by the power change ring. Optimum location of the scope for proper eye relief is more difficult, and optimum eye

relief is not the same at both high and low power settings.

3. Generally have a smaller field of view and a smaller exit pupil than a fixed-power scope at the same magnification.

The variable-power scope is not new, though it has only become very popular in the last 20 years. As early as World War I, and perhaps earlier, variable-power scopes were on the market. These early models, made into the 1950s, have only two power settings. The change in magnification is made by changing the position of the erector lenses in the scope tube. The basic function of the erector lenses is to invert and revert the image. However, if they are moved as a unit, there are two positions where the image will be in focus, giving a high and a low magnification. If the power shift mechanism is made with a double cam, so that it not only shifts the position of the erector system but also shifts the relationship of the erectors with each other, the image is always in focus, making the scope usable at any setting from low to high. Obviously, this results in weaknesses. If the mechanical axis of the lens movement system does not remain in line with the optical axes of the total lens system, the point of impact will change with power change. In a quality variable, this change is seldom less than ½-minute of angle, and with a scope tube that is strained out of alignment by misaligned mounting rings, it may easily be 1 minute of angle. Cheap variable scopes often move the point of impact several minutes with full-power change. Since the lenses are mounted so that they can be moved axially, it is evident that there is greater potential for radial movement of the lenses, shot to shot, at any setting, than is possible in fixed-power scopes where the lenses are firmly fixed. Any such movement will result in a change in sighting and, consequently, in bullet impact.

The popularity of variable-power scopes indicates that these compromises and shortcomings are either not noticeable to the average user or that they are not considered significant. Many users of variables "glass" a hunting area with the scope set at high power and feel that it eliminates carrying binoculars. This is a practice to be condemned, as it often results in pointing a loaded rifle at another hunter. Good binoculars are far more efficient than a riflescope for "glassing," and their use involves less movement that may disturb game.

Shotgun scopes. Scopes, nominally of 1 power (no magnification), have been used on shotguns, although they have never attained great popularity. With a very wide field and long eye relief, they are at their best for duck shooting, open shooting at doves, prairie chickens, etc. In areas where shotguns are mandatory for deer hunting, they offer an excellent sight for slug shooting at short range. For the latter purpose, in brushy country, they have also been used on rifles.

Handgun scopes. The last 10 to 15 years have seen the development of several makes and models of pistol scopes, with long eye relief, in fixed powers of 1.3 to 7 and variables as flexible as the 2.5–7X. These have increased the popularity of hunting with handguns. In some areas of the country, benchrest matches are held with the competitors using scope-sighted single-shot pistols, usually of bolt-action type.

Scope reticles. The earliest scopes were provided with crosshair-type reticles, undoubtedly copied from surveying instruments, and these are probably still the best choice for most kinds of target shooting, varmint hunting, and plains hunting. They are available in a variety of diameters, to suit the use, scope magnification, and whims of the user. Low power hunting scopes need a reticle of a size and shape that will stand out against brush and foliage, large enough to be seen distinctly in any light in which game can be seen through the scope and of a shape to provide accuracy of aim under all conditions. Square-ended posts and dots of appropriate sizes are good choices. The crosshair is satisfactory if large enough in diameter to be seen well under minimum sighting conditions. Reticles of the Duplex type have become popular and are offered by many scope manufacturers. These are basically of the crosshair type, with a heavy section extending nearly to the center of the field, then reduced in diameter, giving a medium-to-coarse cross hair for aiming. If a shot has to be taken under poor light conditions, reasonable aim could be taken by judging the location of the reticle center from the ends of the four heavy sections. The heavy sections and the distance between them, if the dimensions subtended are known, can be of help in range estimation and for judging holdover on long shots. Dot reticles offer some similar advantages. Some reticles incorporate stadia wires as a means of rangefinding. (See ABERRATION; EXIT PUPIL; EYE RELIEF; MAGNIFICATION; MICROMETER; MIRAGE; PARALLAX; POWER; RELATIVE BRIGHTNESS; RIFLE SIGHTS; SHOTGUN SIGHT.)

temperature effect The pressure generated by a powder charge can be affected by the temperature of the components at the time of ignition. Thus, a rifle cartridge that normally generates a pressure of 50,000 pounds per square inch at a temperature of 50 degrees Fahrenheit can generate considerably less than that at temperatures below zero, and more at temperatures above 100 degrees.

temperature of ignition That temperature at which a substance can be ignited. As it applies to shooting, it is important in obtaining uniform ignition of powders with various burning rates. For example, a slow-burning powder heavily coated with a burning retardant will perform better with a magnum primer that generates more heat than a standard primer.

tenon See BARREL TENON.

terminal ballistics See IMPACT BEHAVIOR BALLISTICS.

thicket load See SPREADER LOAD.

thimble See RAMROD THIMBLES.

Thomas, Gough (1899–1989) Gough Thomas Garwood was the full name of the English writer whose articles appeared for years in *Shooting Times & Country Magazine*. He was generally accepted as the most knowledgeable authority on shotguns and shotgunning in the British Isles. Thomas was the author of *Shotgun Shooting Facts* (Winchester Press, 1978), and *Shotguns and Cartridges for Game and Clays* (A&C Black, Ltd., Cambs 1989).

threaded hood In America, a threaded hood is the part of a target-type front sight that retains and secures the interchangeable sight inserts or a removable sunshade attached to such a sight. In Britain, the receiver ring is called a threaded hood.

threads See BARREL THREADS.

three-pull system A mechanism employed on double-barreled shotguns with single triggers. When a shooter fires the first and second barrels, there is often an involuntary and unconscious pull in between. With a three-pull system, the first pull fires the first barrel, the second is the involuntary pull, and the third pull fires the second barrel. Some variants of the three-pull system employ the second pull to cock the trigger for the second shot; others employ a delay action so that the trigger is still in the process of being cocked for the second shot when the second pull occurs. Without a three-pull trigger, the second barrel could be fired involuntarily. (See SINGLE SELECTIVE TRIGGER.)

throat In a rifled barrel, that smooth-bored section of the barrel that tapers from chamber diameter to bore diameter is called the throat. It serves to center the bullet in the barrel.

throat diameter The diameter of the forward part of the chamber of a rifle into which a bullet fits prior to firing. It is unrifled and measures the same in a given rifle as its barrel's groove-to-groove diameter.

throat protector When cleaning a rifle from the breech, it is possible to damage the throat of the chamber by abrading it with the cleaning rod. To prevent this, a throat protector is used; it consists of a hollow metal or plastic tube that is inserted in the chamber. The cleaning rod passes through the tube and is held centered in the throat. (See CLEANING ROD.)

through bolt A steel rod, threaded at both ends, that extends through a hole drilled lengthwise in a shotgun or rifle buttstock. The rod attaches to the rear of the receiver and has a washer and nut at its rearward end under the buttplate or recoil pad. Its purpose is to securely attach the buttstock to the receiver.

through lump In the manufacture of a double-barrel shotgun, the barrels are sometimes shaped first and the lump is brazed to them afterward. A lump attached in this manner is known as a through lump. It is considered inferior to the chopper lump, which is forged integrally with the barrel. (See LUMPS.)

thumb cut-out The Model 98 Mauser military rifle, which was loaded by means of a stripper clip, was equipped with a machined cut-out in the top of the left receiver wall, and with a corresponding cut in the stock, to facilitate loading by this means. Commercially made Mauser actions, which do not employ this loading method, are made without the cut-out. (See STRIPPING.)

thumbhole stock A style of buttstock, usually on custom sporting and target rifles and trap guns, in which the line of the comb extends forward to the tang and that incorporates a hole behind the pistol grip to accommodate the shooter's thumb. The high, straight comb line is said to reduce recoil sensation and the design to offer better control in offhand shooting.

thumb rest In order to provide a more secure grip for the shooting hand, some pistol grips are equipped with thumb rests. These can vary from depressions, carved in the wood, into which the thumb fits, to shelves on which it actually lies, as in the case of target grips. (See TARGET GRIPS.)

thumb trigger A trigger activated by the thumb. Thumb triggers consist of a plunger or button, usually on the tang of the gun, that is depressed to fire. The only commercial arm that used the system was

A thumbhole stock is designed to provide the most relaxed position for the hand and the greatest degree of trigger control. Here, it is used on an Anschutz Model 1413 match rifle.

the Winchester Model 1904 Thumb Trigger Rifle, a low-priced .22 bolt-action made until 1923. Thumb triggers have also been adapted to cane-guns and other disguised weapons.

timed fire A semirapid-fire stage of handgun target shooting, normally with a 20-second time allowance for firing five shots at a target. The timing is usually done by an automatic mechanism.

Tikka (company) Tikkakosi Oy, Sakara, Finland, is a manufacturer of military arms, over/under shotguns, combination guns, and centerfire rifles. The rifles are of the Mauser bolt-action type and are noted for sturdiness and reliability. The best-known Tikka gun is perhaps the break-action over/under combination gun with a 20-gauge barrel on top and a .222 centerfire or other small-caliber barrel underneath. This gun is suited for use by a pothunter who takes only sure shots and does not often need a quick second shot. It has proved popular in Finland and Canada, where survival arms are needed. All Tikka firearms are now manufactured by Sako.

tip-off mount Not as rigid as most telescopic sight mounts, the tip-off is found primarily on arms of .22 caliber where the top of the receiver has dovetail cuts to accept the mount. The scope rings are attached directly to these dovetails without any bases at all, a perfectly acceptable situation with low-recoil arms. The tip-off mount may be removed quickly by loosening two screws that usually have very wide heads slotted for a coin. (See SCOPE MOUNTS.)

tipping See BULLET TIPPING.

toe The toe of a rifle or shotgun stock is the intersection of the lower side of the stock and the bottom of the buttplate.

toe plate On a muzzleloader, a metal piece that fits on the bottom of the butt next to the buttplate. These were primarily used to protect the wood and are still used in replica muzzleloaders. Some are highly ornamented, and in some cases it is possible to identify the maker by the toe plate design. They may be made of iron, brass, or German silver.

toggle joint The so-called kneejoint linkage of two bars joined by the ends, but not in direct line with one another. The most notable use of the toggle joint is on the Luger pistol. (See LUGER [PARABELLUM] PISTOL.)

tolerance The difference between the largest and smallest allowable dimensions in parts fitting and/or functioning together, listed as + and − (plus and minus) with the designated measurement. Tolerance is necessary, as parts must have some clearance to move and function properly, but the range must not be too great or too little.

The most dramatic example of tolerance occurs in the fitting of high-quality break-open shotgun actions. These guns will function perfectly without obstruction, but a single thickness of tissue paper or a grain of gunpowder inserted between the rear of the barrels and the standing breech will prevent them from closing.

tong tool Commonly known as the "nutcra.ker," this 19th-century reloading tool remains in use today because of its portability. Used by hand, the device is a miniature loading press that functions by a squeezing action of the handles to size cases, reprime, and seat bullets. It consists of a set of handles on a hinge pin with various chambers that can be screwed in and out. The chambers are similar to dies, one for decapping, another for sizing, and others for expanding case mouths, priming, and seating. (See LOADING DIE; LOADING PRESS.)

top-breaking See HINGED FRAME.

top lever A lever on the top of a break-action firearm that opens the gun and allows the barrel or

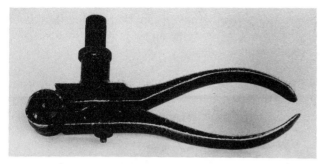

The tong tool (or nutcracker) is actually a miniature reloading press. It can perform both sizing and reloading operations, but lacks the power of a bench-mounted press.

barrels to fall forward into the open breech position for loading and unloading. Found most often on shotguns, the top lever is also a feature on some rifles. (See BREAK-ACTION.)

Topperwein, Adolf (1870–1962) One of the best known and best of the professional exhibition shooters during the early decades of the 20th century, Ad Topperwein, together with his wife, "Plinky," amazed millions with their feats with rifles, shotguns, and pistols. Perhaps the most famous of their stunts was that of "drawing" pictures with bullet holes delivered at rapid fire into cardboard or metal targets.

In 1907, Topperwein, representing Winchester Arms Co., set a new endurance accuracy record by breaking all but 9 out of 72,500 wooden blocks (2¼-inch cubes) tossed 30 feet into the air from a point 30 feet in front of the shooter. The feat required 10 days of shooting. It far exceeded Doc Carver's long-standing record (60,000 out of 60,674 blocks), but in place of Carver's hard-kicking .38-caliber rifles, Topperwein used Winchester Model 1903 (later called Model 63) .22-caliber guns. Topperwein continued as an exhibition shooter for Winchester for more than 50 years.

top wad See OVER-SHOT WAD.

torpedo sling See SLING.

torque The twisting force set up in rifled barrels as the bullet passes through the bore. Torque affects barrel vibration, which in turn affects accuracy. The term is also applied to the amount of screw pressure applied to stock bedding screws.

touch hole See FIRE HOLE.

trajectory The trajectory of a projectile is its path of flight from the point of emergence from the muzzle of the arm to a final destination. This path is determined by the initial velocity of the projectile(s), along with its ballistic characteristics, in conjunction with the atmospheric conditions and the action of gravity.

The trajectory of the missile is initially gauged by its line of departure, which in essence is that path described by theoretical flight in a perfect vacuum without the presence of gravity. This line would be straight if nothing affected the projectile. In other words, if a muzzle were held perfectly parallel to the surface of the ground, the missile would stay the same height above the ground throughout its journey, which would be nonending without an atmosphere or gravity.

In actual practice, the trajectory becomes a curved line and the theoretical trajectory is termed the "line of sight." This line of sight rests along the same path that the eye in the act of sighting would describe, directly from eye to target. The projectile, however, is normally aimed so that it rises upward in its initial journey so that it will later fall back to cross the line of sight. In effect, the missile cuts the line of sight twice, once as it begins its flight and a second time when it falls back down from its upward arch. The "flatter" an arm fires, the less will be this line of departure from the line of sight over normal ranges.

Estimation of trajectory is important to sighting an arm, for the shooter should know how many inches the missile will rise above the line of sight, exactly where that missile will cut the line of sight, and then how far below that line it will fall as it progresses on its journey. An example of employing

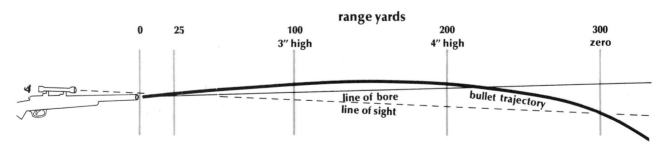

A knowledge of bullet trajectory is essential for effective shooting at long ranges. The most practical arrangement for a high-velocity big-game rifle is to zero in 3 inches high of the bull at 100 yards. This puts the point of impact at dead center at 25 yards, 3 inches high at 100, 4 inches high at 200, and at dead center again at 300.

trajectory knowledge is the case of a flat-shooting bullet that begins its flight underneath the line of sight, crosses that line of sight first at 25 yards, is about 3 inches above the line of sight at 100 yards, 4 inches above the line of sight at 200 yards, again cuts the line of sight on its downward curve at about 300 yards, and then falls to 10 inches below the line of sight at 400 yards and 26 inches below the line of sight at 500 yards.

A knowledge of trajectory such as this would be of use to a big-game hunter who would have to shoot at fairly large targets over estimated ranges. Knowing the exact path that his bullet would follow, and knowing that the vital area of a deer's chest is 12 inches in size, a hunter would know that his rifle had a point-blank range of 25 to 300 yards; that is, he could aim at the center of the deer's chest from any distance between those points and be assured of a hit in the vital zone. At 400 yards, he would have to aim approximately 6 inches high to compensate for the drop of the bullet. A shot at 500 yards would be impractical because of the extreme amount of holdover required. (See BALLISTICS; IN-GALLS TABLES.)

transducer system   A means of recording pounds of pressure per square inch (absolute) by means of a strain gauge and cathode-ray oscilloscope. (See CHAMBER PRESSURE.)

trap   A mechanical catapult used to launch clay pigeons in the shotgun sports, as well as in everyday practice. Traps range from simple hand-held types to sophisticated models that automatically release targets in specific directions under a certain timed element and at preset speeds. Adjustable models will allow for many variations of speed, direction, and timing. (See SKEET SHOOTING; TRAPSHOOTING.)

trap buttplate   A buttplate with a hinged or sliding cover, so arranged that the cover will open to reveal a chamber recessed into the gunstock itself. The chamber is normally lined with a soft material, such as felt, and serves to hold extra cartridges, a miniaturized cleaning kit, spare parts for the arm, or hunting permits and game tags. The plate is some-

times hinged on a spring so that when the cover closes, the trap compartment is very secure. (See BUTTPLATE.)

Trapdoor Springfield   At the end of the Civil War, the Springfield Armory was given the task of converting the Union Army's .58-caliber Springfield percussion muskets to cartridge use. This was done by lining the barrels to reduce the caliber to .50 and by cutting into the breech so that a pivoting breech-block (trapdoor) could be installed. Fitting a new hammer completed the operation. The Model 1865 was the first of the Trapdoor Springfields; it fired a .50-caliber rimfire cartridge.

In 1873, the guns were converted to take the .45/70 cartridge, which offered higher velocity and greater range. Trapdoor Springfields in both calibers were made in rifle and carbine versions and were the main arm of the U.S. Army during the Indian Wars. The guns were accurate, powerful, and, for the most part, reliable. Their main drawback was a tendency to jam when fired rapidly. This defect was most evident at the Battle of the Little Bighorn, where the Trapdoor became something of a scapegoat for the Custer defeat. However, the arm remained the standard service rifle until the Spanish-American War in 1898, when it was replaced by the Krag-Jorgensen.

trap gun   A shotgun, often specially designed or custom built, for use in trapshooting. Twelve gauge is universal, because trap is a long-range game and the smaller gauges do not throw enough shot to break targets consistently. Trap guns usually have long barrels to aid in pointing accurately—30 inches or more—and they usually have rather long, straight stocks for the same reason. Since the gun is mounted before calling for a bird, there is no need for a stock that would permit quick shouldering, and it is virtually impossible to mount a specialized trap gun with any degree of speed.

All trap guns have a ventilated rib because barrels heat up quickly during the rapid shooting, and heat waves in the air can obscure the sights and the target. The holes in the raised ventilated rib keep barrels cool. The sights are mounted on top of the rib. Since the shooter tries to break the target while it is still

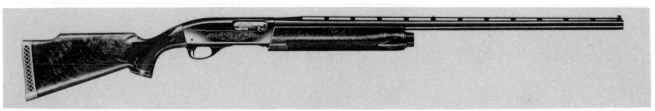

The Remington 1100 autoloader is a highly popular trap model, since its soft recoil makes long strings of shooting less punishing.

rising, these ribs are often higher at the rear than at the muzzle to provide a built-in vertical lead. But specialized trap guns with "humpbacked" ribs to provide built-in vertical lead have disadvantages. If a shooter uses them a great deal, he forgets to lead vertically on a rising live bird when hunting. On the other hand, if he uses such a gun in the field, he will miss many live birds that fly horizontally or even at a downward angle.

Modified choke is good for 16-yard shooting; improved-modified and full chokes are used if the shooter is handicapped by being placed farther from the trap.

Americans use semiautomatics, pumps, over/unders, and single-shot break-action guns for trap. The side-by-side double is seldom seen on an American trap field.

Single-shot specialized trap guns are a delight to shoot, but they cannot be used for doubles. Many shooters never use the single-shot because they shoot doubles and cannot afford to get used to the single gun, no matter how advantageous it is in singles shooting. (See TRAPSHOOTING.)

trap house A wooden, masonry, or concrete structure built to house the traps used in skeet or trapshooting. In trapshooting, there is only one low trap house per field. In skeet, there are two trap houses for each field, one low and one high. On some skeet ranges, however, all trap houses are of the same height, but each one has a low trap opening for one field and a high trap opening for the adjoining field. These are often called combination trap houses. All trap houses should be sturdy enough to protect the person loading birds into the trap magazine if an accidental shot is fired. (See HIGH HOUSE; LOW HOUSE.)

trapshooting A clay target shotgun sport. In the most common form of American trap, shooting posts are arranged in a shallow arc facing a trap house, which contains a spring activated catapult—the trap—that throws clay "birds" into the air at a slightly rising angle. The shooter attempts to shatter the clay birds. The trap is 16 yards from the shooting posts. The posts are numbered one to five from left to right and are a few feet apart. A shooting squad for a round of trap consists of five persons with 12-gauge shotguns, though a lesser number may shoot if too few are present. With one man on each post, each shooter fires in rotation, one through five, until all have fired five shots. Then the first four shooters move one post to the right. The man on No. 5 walks behind the other shooters to post No. 1. This continues until all have fired five shots from all five posts, or 25 shells.

In trapshooting, the gunner places his gun on his shoulder and aligns eye and sight(s), then calls for the bird by saying "Pull!" in a loud, clear voice so that he is easily heard by the trap operator, or puller. This kind of shooting is good practice for much field shooting, and it is a competitive sport in itself. It is unnatural, however, in that the gun is mounted and precisely pointed before the bird appears, something that would never happen in the field.

In regular American singles trap, the catapult swivels back and forth on a horizontal plane so that a bird may angle away to left or right or may fly straightaway. In handicap trap, the more proficient gunners are "put back" from the 16-yard line, depending on their degrees of skill. A very capable shooter may be handicapped all the way back to 27 yards, the maximum.

In trap doubles, the trap catapults two targets simultaneously. The shooter loads two shells and tries to break both birds in flight. In doubles, the trap does not swivel back and forth. It is fixed in position, and the birds are always launched about 35 degrees left and right of straightaway. The most common practice is to break the straighter bird first and then take the angle shot, depending on which of the five posts one is shooting from.

In International trap, a much more difficult form than the American game, 15 fixed traps are used. This gives the shooters birds that may fly almost straight up or almost at the horizontal. At the same time, the birds may be angling very sharply left or right. In addition, the birds fly faster and they are harder in composition, making them harder to break. There are 15 traps in a shallow trench, and the shooter never knows which one will fire when he calls for a target. However, the shooter is permitted to fire twice at each bird. If he breaks it with the second shot, it counts a full point. When those who have shot American trap first try International, they usually score very low indeed.

Modified Clay Pigeon is another form of trap shooting. It is the same as the International form, but there is only one trap, instead of 15, and that trap oscillates vertically and horizontally. The setup is therefore less expensive to build. The game is intended to provide Americans with a way of practicing for the International form of shooting. (See AMATEUR TRAPSHOOTING ASSOCIATION [ATA]; INTERNATIONAL TRAPSHOOTING; MODIFIED CLAY PIGEON; TRAP GUN.)

travel See BOLT TRAVEL.

trickler See POWDER TRICKLER.

trigger Essentially, the mechanical or electrical device that activates a firearm when moved—usually by one finger. There are many variations, such as ring trigger, release trigger, and other modifications.

trigger, adjustable   See ADJUSTABLE TRIGGER.

trigger backlash   See BACKLASH.

trigger control   Proper control of the trigger pull means careful and deliberate squeezing of the trigger so that the arm is moved the least possible amount while the trigger is being squeezed.

trigger creep   Creep is the length a trigger travels freely from its position of rest to its firing point, where a determined pull is necessary to release the sear and fire the gun. In some military rifles this condition is a built-in feature, hence the term "military creep." Such a rifle is fired in two stages. First, all of the slack or creep is taken up by the trigger finger pulling back until it meets with a definite change in required force or exertion. The first stage is very smooth with little resistance. The second stage is pulling the trigger its remaining distance, which will be under tension now, until the arm fires.

Excessive creep in the single-stage trigger of a sporting arm is undesirable, as it can cause jerky firing. (See ADJUSTABLE TRIGGER.)

trigger guard   A protective shield around the trigger that guards against accidental discharge. The guard may be composed of an integral loop of metal that is a part of the gun's undersurface, or it may be attached to the underside by means of screws. Trigger guards are also composed of plastic and many other materials, and they are found on virtually every firearm today, pistol, rifle, or shotgun. (See SHEATH TRIGGER.)

trigger plate   A metal bar extending to the rear of a boxlock or sidelock action to carry the triggers. It is used in some actions to hold the locks as well. (See TRIGGER-PLATE ACTION.)

trigger-plate action   In some double-barrel and over/under shotgun actions (most notably the British Dickson and European Blitz), the trigger and lock mechanisms are carried on a steel bar projecting rearward from the action. In the Dickson, the lock is contained by a vertical plate that is integral with the trigger plate, or bar. The advantage of this system is that it places the trigger in a mechanically advantageous position in regard to the sear, resulting in a smooth trigger pull.

trigger pull   The amount of pressure required to fully release a trigger to fire a gun. Since a heavy trigger pull is detrimental to accurate shooting, the goal of setting the trigger pull is to acquire a very light but totally safe firing point. Ideally, the trigger pull should be crisp, which means an absolute minimum of creep, or the superfluous movement of the trigger from its point of rest to the point of firing. Pull on some firearms is controlled through the use of set triggers, either double or single.

Pull weights (meaning the actual amount of weight required to move the trigger) vary according to individual taste, but as a rule, the following are generally accepted: hunting rifles, 2½ to 4 pounds; target rifles, 2 to 3 pounds; shotguns, 3 to 5 pounds; hunting handguns, 3 pounds. Set triggers can be set to fractions of an ounce. Some are so sensitive that the weight of the trigger itself, when the gun is pointed skyward, is enough to fire the arm.

trigger pull scale   A small spring scale with a finger loop on one end and a long, jointed L-shaped hook on the other. The scale face is calibrated in increments of ounces and grams, up to about 6 pounds on most models. With the gun butt on a solid surface, the hook on the trigger and the finger in the loop, the scale is pulled until trigger releases. The scale pointer shows the weight of pull when trigger release occurs. (See TRIGGER PULL.)

trigger shoe   Curved to fit over the original trigger itself, the shoe is a metal piece that aids in trigger control. It affords a wider contact area for the finger and most shoes are grooved with longitudinal cuts for nonslippage. The shoe is normally secured by small set screws.

trigger stop   As excessive overtravel is undesirable in a trigger's operation, some firearms are fitted with trigger stops. These usually take the form of screws that abut against the trigger, stopping its movement as soon as the sear is released. (See OVERTRAVEL.)

true up   An expression used to denote the reshaping of wood or metal gun parts to "true" shapes, i.e., making flat surfaces truly flat, radii perfectly curved, etc. Truing up is usually performed by custom gunsmiths on firearms prior to final polishing and bluing, or prior to engraving.

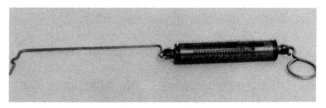

A trigger pull scale is a necessity for the accurate adjustment of any trigger.

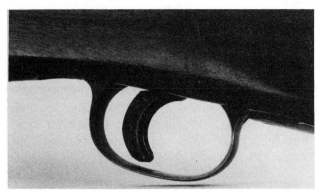

Trigger shoes fit over a standard trigger and are held in place by small setscrews. They provide a broader surface for the trigger finger to work against and, supposedly, better trigger control.

truncated bullet The term "truncated bullet" was once used to describe any flat nosed bullet.

try gun Probably of British development, but used in America also, the try gun is an adjustable gunstock dummy used to measure the fit of a handmade stock to an individual shooter. The wrist of the try gun will move from left to right, as well as up and down, the comb section will rise upward, as well as collapsing flat, and the buttstock will lengthen and shorten. By adjusting the try gun's fully changeable stock until it fits the shooter, the right dimensions of stock length, pitch of stock, and drop can be determined.

tube wash The gradual erosion of the mouths of paper shotshells caused by repeated firing and reloading. Tube wash occurs less rapidly in plastic shotshells.

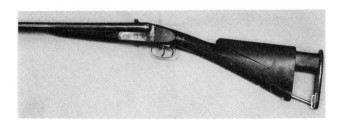

The stock of a try gun is almost infinitely adjustable and enables a skilled fitter to determine the exact stock dimensions for any shooter. The side-by-side was built by Boss; the over/under by Browning.

tubular magazine Cartridges or shells are held end to end in this cylindrical magazine, with the front portion of one shotshell or cartridge up against the rear portion of the one in front of it. Rounds are loaded through a port or gate into the cylinder and are fed into the chamber by spring action and a follower. Since the nose of one projectile butts up against the primer of the round in front of it, making accidental detonation possible, only flat nosed bullets should be loaded into the tube type of magazine. (See MAGAZINE.)

tumbler The central piece of the conventional blackpowder firearm lock; it is activated by pulling back the hammer and contains the full-cock notch, the half-cock notch, and the detent (fly) if there is one. Pulling the trigger causes the tumbler to relinquish its hold on the sear, thereby rotating slightly, allowing the hammer to fall.

Also, a device used in the cleaning and polishing of cartridge cases. (See TUMBLING.)

tumbling The process of agitating empty cartridge cases in a mildly abrasive substance, either liquid or solid, for the purpose of cleaning the cases and polishing them. It is used both in home handloading and by ammunition factories.

Also, the action of a bullet that has failed to retain its rotational axis and has entered into an end-over-end rotation through the air. A bullet can tumble because of a fault in itself, such as an off-center core, or through an improper twist rate in the rifling. (See KEYHOLE.)

tungsten-carbide die Tungsten-carbide resizing dies for handloading metallic cartridges are made in two forms: pistol dies with tungsten-carbide insert rings that resize straight-sided cases full length, and full-length resizing dies that have a carbide insert layer that acts as the resizing medium for bottleneck rifle cases. The very hard, extremely smooth surface of tungsten-carbide steel makes the resizing operation easier and requires no lubricant. (See CASE RESIZING.)

turkey, guns and loads for Although some jurisdictions allow the use of rifles for wild turkey hunting, most specify the use of shotguns only. The circumstances surrounding the hunting of wild turkeys, the largest American upland game birds, make the shotgun the logical choice anyway, unless exceptional conditions are encountered.

The almost universal method of hunting these birds in both spring and fall seasons is to lure the birds close to the gun by the use of various calling devices. Consequently, shots are usually taken at from 30 to 40 yards. Turkeys will often circle the source of the calls and come in from the side or rear of the hunter. They will take advantage of cover and terrain to stay out of sight, and the hunter's view of them will likely be fleeting and momentary. These conditions call for fast gun handling because the hunter must often rise, turn, and shoot in one motion. A rifle would be an inappropriate arm under these circumstances.

The hunter of turkeys need not be overly concerned with stock dimensions. Standard drop at comb and heel, thickness of comb, pitch, and length of pull as furnished by almost all manufacturers are satisfactory for this work. Some hunters reduce stock length slightly to make it easier to swing the gun to the right—for a right-handed shooter—under the sometimes cramped hunting conditions.

The shotgun used for hunting turkeys will most often be aimed like a rifle. The point of aim is the bird's head and upper neck. A well-placed shot into this area will usually anchor the bird. This is *aiming*, pure and simple, and has nothing in common with the use of the shotgun on flying game. (Turkeys are weak fliers.) For this reason, a full choke is desirable in a turkey gun.

Pumps, autoloaders, and side-by-side or over/under double guns are all suitable for turkey hunting. The 12 gauge chambered for either 2¾-inch or 3-inch shells is almost the standard turkey gun. The 2¾-inch 12-gauge magnum loaded with 1½ ounces of No. 6 or No. 9 shot or the 3-inch 12 gauge with 1⅝, 1⅞, or 2 ounces are the best loads for this game. A few hunters use guns chambering 3½ inch 10-gauge magnum shells, but most consider them too heavy. Hunters wishing to use guns chambered for 16-gauge or 3-inch 20-gauge shells should use 1¼-ounce loads of No. 6 shot. In all gauges, a dense pattern of fairly small shot will deliver a clean kill.

In areas where rifles are permitted, any centerfire cartridge up to about .32 caliber will make a good turkey round provided its velocity is not too high. The Marlin Model 94 in .25/20 or .32/20 is ideal. Most factory cartridges are too powerful and will mangle turkeys badly. The exception is the .22 Hornet, probably the ideal turkey cartridge. The .222 Remington when loaded down to Hornet velocities also makes a fine turkey cartridge. No rimfires can be recommended, as none will kill turkeys consistently.

turn-off barrel   At the beginning of the 18th century, a popular kind of pocket pistol employed a barrel that could be unscrewed at the breech for loading. This eliminated the need for a fore-end and ramrod, and resulted in a more compact design. The barrels were often rifled, since the ball did not have to be rammed down the bore. Queen Anne pistols, as guns of this pattern were called, achieved their greatest popularity from 1700 to 1750 or so.

twist   The sequence of rifling turns in a firearm barrels. (See RATE OF TWIST.)

twist-steel barrel   See DAMASCUS BARREL.

two-stage trigger   See DOUBLE-STAGE TRIGGER.

Ugartecha, Ignacio (company) See SPANISH GUN-MAKERS.

ultrarifling See DOUGLAS BARRELS, INC. (COMPANY).

Unceta (company) See SPANISH GUNMAKERS.

under-ignition Under-ignition occurs when a primer fails to properly ignite the powder in a cartridge or shell. Under-ignition may be caused by a faulty primer, a firing pin blow that is too light, or by some foreign substance like water, oil or solvent contaminating the primer mixture. (See IGNITION.)

underlever action An under-lever action is any lever action that has the activating lever on the bottom. (See LEVER ACTION.)

Unertl, John, Optical Co. John Unertl was a German-born optical engineer who immigrated to America shortly after World War I and worked for some years for J. W. Fecker. In the early 1930s, he went into business for himself in Pittsburgh, Pennsylvania, initially manufacturing a recoil absorber for sliding tube, target-type telescopes and making repairs to telescopic rifle sights and other optical equipment. By the mid-1930s, Unertl was manufacturing target telescopes and mounts very similar to those made by Fecker, except that focusing was accomplished by moving the objective lens instead of the erector lens. These were 1¼-inch objective scopes of 8, 10, 12, and 14 power. The line also included small-game and target telescopes with smaller objectives in 3, 4, and 6 power, and 2½X and 3X big-game scopes with internal adjustments.

The company is still in business in Pittsburgh and offers a variety of the traditional sliding tube target telescopes with adjustments in the mounts. These include one model with a 2-inch objective and a tube that is 1 inch in diameter, instead of the ¾-inch that is standard. Unertl also makes conventional hunting telescopes with internal adjustments, as well as spotting scopes. Included among the latter is a team spotting scope with 100mm objective, interchangeable eyepieces of 16X, 24X, and 32X, and a large tripod. (See FECKER SCOPE; TELESCOPIC SIGHTS.)

United States Sporting Clays Association The American organization that regulates the rules and shooter classifications and national championships of stateside Sporting Clays. It is recognized by other international Sporting Clays groups. The address is 50 Briar Hollow, Suite 490 East, Houston, Texas 77027.

universal receiver A massive single-shot receiver designed for the firing of cartridges under laboratory conditions for the determination of pressure and/or velocity. The receiver is fitted with a breechblock, firing mechanism, and often a crusher fixture. It is designed to be used in conjunction with a pressure gun. (See CHAMBER PRESSURE; PRESSURE GUN.)

unrestricted gun The rules for many forms of target-shooting sports restrict the kind, caliber or gauge, weight, sights or configuration of the guns used. However, there are some shooting contests that have no restrictions regarding the gun. Nevertheless, the rules generally give match officials the right to disqualify guns that they consider to be unsafe.

uphill shooting Uphill shooting at game animals poses special problems not always considered by the hunter. As in downhill shooting, bullet drop is the same as it would be from rifle muzzle to game on a horizontal line from the rifle position to directly under the animal; not on a surface line on the slope. As the bullet actually drops less, it will land higher, often over the animal's back. The tendency is to aim lower on the animal because you see both the side and belly, which partially compensates for less bullet drop. (See BULLET DROP.)

upset See BULLET UPSET.

upset forging A method used in forming the steel rod from which a rifle barrel is made. Upset forging shortens the original rod, enlarges the diameter, and adds strength. (See BARREL MAKING.)

U.S. Army Marksmanship Unit See ARMY MARKSMANSHIP UNIT.

variable-power scope A telescopic rifle sight that has the capability of altering the magnification range by mechanically changing the distance between some of the internal optical elements, usually by means of turning a ring on the scope that bears the numbers of the powers available. The range of magnification change varies widely, with 1X–4X, 1½X–4X, 2X–7X, 2X–8X, 3X–9X, 6X–12X, and many other combinations available. (See TELESCOPIC SIGHTS.)

varmints, guns and loads for A varmint is any pest animal or bird usually not under the protection of bag limits or closed seasons. The variety of varmint species is extensive and ranges from the prairie dog to the mountain lion—although varying game laws protect the larger predators in some states.

The most commonly taken varmints, and the ones usually thought of in terms of varmint hunting, are the eastern and western groundhog (woodchuck) and the prairie dog. Both of these rodents, if left unchecked, can be highly destructive to farm and grazing land. Hunting these species involves the use of highly accurate centerfire rifles, powerful telescopic sights, and small, highly frangible bullets propelled at extreme velocity. The sport is not so much a test of hunting skill as of shooting ability.

Varmint shooting was not widely popular until the 1920s. In 1932, the first of the true varmint loads was introduced; this was the .22 Hornet, a cartridge that met all the requirements of the eastern varmint hunter. It was accurate, had a mild report, negligible recoil, and employed a light, fragile bullet that was unlikely to ricochet and create a hazard in settled areas. The Hornet is still a popular cartridge today.

In 1935, a second cartridge was introduced that had a profound effect on the sport. This was the .220 Swift, the first of the ultra-high-velocity varmint loads. Propelling a 48-grain bullet in excess of 4,100

This diagram shows the basic parts of a modern variable-power scope sight. They are: A—objective lens; B—objective lens mount; C—objective lens bell; D—elevation adjustment turret; E—erecting lenses, F—power selection ring; G—reticle; H—ocular lenses.

A varmint is any nongame species that may be legally hunted and can range from prairie dogs to coyotes. Eastern varmint hunting is typically directed at woodchucks and takes place in wooded pastures and meadows, with shots at moderate to long ranges. Western hunting takes place at long range. These two coyotes were killed at over 400 yards. The typical varmint rifle will be heavy-barreled and equipped with a powerful, target-type scope. Varmint cartridges are usually .22 to .24 caliber and employ highly frangible bullets at extreme velocity. This collection is, from left: .22 Hornet, .17 Remington, .222, .223, .222 Remington Magnum, .224 Weatherby, .225 Winchester, .22/250 and .220 Swift.

feet per second, the Swift greatly lengthened the range at which a shooter could deliver accurate fire. Whereas the Hornet's muzzle velocity of 2,700 fps limited a shooter to ranges of 250 yards or less, the Swift added 150 yards to that distance. Its handicap was a loud, sharp report.

Two other cartridges have had a major impact on varmint shooting. The first, the .222 Remington, appeared in 1950. Firing a 50-grain bullet at 3,200 fps, it combined the virtues of the Hornet and the Swift. Capable of excellent accuracy, it offered an effective range of 350 yards, mild report, and minimal recoil. The second was the .243 Winchester (and, to a lesser extent, the .244 Remington), which was brought out in 1955. This cartridge enabled hunters to use one rifle for both varmint and big-game hunting. As loaded by the factory, it fired an 80-grain bullet at 3,500 fps and a 100-grain bullet at

3,070 fps. While the report was sharp, recoil was still very mild, and the heavier bullets offered greater wind-bucking ability at long range than any of the .22 centerfires.

In the more than half-century since varmint shooting became a popular pastime, a certain amount of standardization has taken place in the equipment used. A typical varmint rifle is almost invariably a bolt action, equipped with a target-weight barrel, mounted with a scope of 8X to 20X, and chambered for a cartridge such as the .222, .223, .22/250, .220, .243, or .25/06. There is some variation. Cartridges as small as .14 caliber have been used, as have some .30 calibers. Some shooters prefer single-shot rifles, though it is rare that these can equal the accuracy of the bolt actions.

Extreme accuracy is an absolute necessity. A woodchuck or a prairie dog offers a target of less than a square foot, and at a range of hundreds of yards, the margin for error is minimal. Today, the accepted standard of accuracy for a varmint rifle is ½-minute-of-angle groups at 100 yards. This is half the group size of a highly accurate big-game rifle and requires both a precise rifle and a highly skilled shooter.

Unlike big-game scopes, which can utilize a maximum magnification of 8X or 9X, varmint scopes are considerably more powerful, with the minimum being 8X, and magnifications of 10X and 12X are common. Reticles are considerably finer than those used in hunting scopes. For many years, varmint rifles were equipped with target-type scopes that employed external adjustments. These instruments, while precise, were heavy, bulky, and fragile. They have been superseded in large part by smaller, more compact, internally adjusted sights patterned on hunting scopes.

Because high magnification exaggerates "wobble" in aiming, a light trigger pull is necessary so that the rifle can be fired at the precise instant the cross hairs are aligned on the target. A big-game rifle is well served with a trigger pull of 3 to 4 pounds; a varmint rifle can employ a pull weight of less than half that. Special triggers that can be set to release under the pressure of only a few ounces are sometimes used, but it takes considerable practice to use these effectively.

Although they universally employ scope sights, most varmint hunters also use either binoculars or spotting scopes in order to locate their targets. The higher magnifications are best: in binoculars, 10X, in spotting scopes, 30X or above. When taking shots at extreme long range, where some guesswork is inevitably involved, an effective technique is for one hunter to shoot, and another to spot with binoculars, observing the bullet strikes and helping the rifleman correct for windage and elevation.

Almost without exception, varmint hunters hand-load their ammunition. Originally, this was because bullets far superior to those loaded by the factories were being produced by small manufacturers, and handloading was the only means of obtaining superior projectiles. However, by the late 1960s the major ammunition companies were producing their own varmint-grade bullets, and quite often today's factory loaded ammunition is of as high quality as that which can be assembled by hand. The advantage to handloading, therefore, is the considerable saving in cost, plus the fact that loads can be tailored to individual rifles.

velocity The speed of a projectile, usually expressed in feet per second (fps).

vent A vent is any hole in a firearm or loading die through which air or gas is allowed to pass. Two examples are the hole in a percussion cap nipple and the holes drilled in the receivers of bolt-action rifles to drain off excess gas in the event of a case rupture. The fire hole in a flintlock arm is sometimes also called a vent.

vent, barrel See BARREL VENT.

ventilated rib Employed primarily on target shotguns, the ventilated rib is a strip of metal that is attached to the top barrel (or to the center rib on a double gun) by a series of metal posts. The advantage of the ventilated rib is that it allows the shooter a sighting plane that remains undistorted by heat waves from the barrel. To enhance this effect, some ventilated ribs are placed more than an inch above the barrel.

Some competition handguns are also fitted with ventilated ribs, but it is doubtful if the ribs have any real advantage in this case. (See SHOTGUN SIGHT.)

Venturi shoulder The Venturi cartridge case shoulder was named for the Venturi method of gas-flow measurement, and was originated by Ralph Waldo Miller and E. Baden Powell for the PMVF (Powell-Miller-Venturi-Freebore) line of wildcat cartridges. The shoulder starts at the case body and forms a concave single radius to the neck. The shoulder radius breaks sharply from the case body but flows more gradually into the neck. (See PMVF MAGNUMS.)

Vernier caliper A measuring device that is equipped with a Vernier scale that permits readings as precise as .0001-inch. It can measure length, width, thickness, and depth. Vernier calipers are made in two styles: those that are read directly from the scale, and those that employ a dial for easier reading.

Vernier calipers are widely used by handloaders for measuring case dimensions and by gunsmiths for measuring firearms' parts.

Vernier sight A kind of sight, either front or rear, that is finely adjustable by means of a fine-thread screw system and incorporates a Vernier scale for reference. Rear Vernier sights are invariably of the peep type and, in older guns, are mounted on the tang. These are adjustable for elevation only and must be used with a front sight that is adjustable for windage. Front Vernier sights may have any of several configurations and are adjustable for windage only. (See METALLIC SIGHTS; MUZZLELOADERS, SIGHTS FOR.)

vertex The vertex is the highest point in the trajectory of a projectile, measured in the vertical plane from a straight line between the gun muzzle and the point of impact. For modern rifles and ammunition, at ranges up to the longest distance now fired in target shooting (1,000 to 1,200 yards), the vertex will be located about two-thirds the distance from gun muzzle to target, assuming gun and target are in the same horizontal plane. (See TRAJECTORY.)

"very good" (condition) See GUN CONDITION.

Vetterli, Frederic See S.I.G. (COMPANY).

Vierling A European combination gun with four barrels. They are break-action (top-break) guns. In the most common arrangement, two shotgun barrels are placed side by side on top, with a big bore rifle barrel underneath, though this may be reversed in some rare examples. In the triangular space between the other three barrels, there is a fourth barrel. Because of the small diameter possible, this fourth barrel is usually chambered for a small bore centerfire cartridge, but it may be chambered for the .22 rimfire if the customer so desires.

European combination guns are almost always specially built custom arms; very few Vierlings are built today. (See COMBINATION GUN.)

Vierlingspatrone A cartridge suitable for the fourth, or center, barrel of a European four-barreled combination gun (Vierling). Most often, it is a small bore centerfire cartridge suitable for small-game and pest shooting. Very popular for this purpose is the European form of the .22 Winchester Centerfire (the 5.6x35R), but other small centerfires are also used. The .22 WCF is no longer loaded in America, but European loads, more powerful than the American original, are still manufactured. (See VIERLING.)

vignetting In wide-angle optical systems, such as cameras and scope sights, some rays of light at the edge of the field of view may be wide of the lens. This results in an observed decrease of illumination at the edge of the field, which is known as vignetting.

virtual image A virtual image is one that is formed by light that does not pass through the image point; an example of a virtual image would be the reflection formed in a mirror.

Volcanic rifle The Volcanic Repeating Arms Company of New Haven, Connecticut, was originally organized by Horace Smith and Daniel B. Wesson at Norwich, Connecticut, to manufacture repeating arms. Their first repeater, from a design by B. Tyler Henry, was patented in 1855 and is today called the Volcanic rifle.

Volcanic became insolvent in March 1857, a year after Smith & Wesson moved to Massachusetts to found the company that bears their names. About 3,000 Volcanics were made. The Volcanic assets were acquired by Oliver Winchester, and the new company was named New Haven Arms Co. In 1866 it became the Winchester Repeating Arms Company.

V-ring In big bore target shooting, the inner circle within the 8-inch black bull's-eye of the Military A target, where this bull's-eye has a value of five points. The V-ring is a tiebreaker when two or more shooters have struck the same number of hits into the black; it corresponds to the X-ring on smallbore and pistol targets. (See X-RING.)

wadcutter bullet A flat nosed cylindrical bullet that is essentially all shank. It is a ballistically inferior shape in terms of retained velocity and energy, but it has great accuracy at short range, and cuts a very precise and clean round hole in paper targets. The wadcutter may be solid lead, lead alloy, or full metal jacket, usually with a solid nose section, sometimes with a conical cupped base. Because of its high stability at low velocity, this kind of bullet is often found on the pistol target range.

wad pressure A specific amount of wad pressure, or compression, required in loading shotshells in order to gain maximum efficiency from the powder charge. (See OVER-POWDER WAD.)

walking barrel If a rifle barrel is not perfectly straight and relieved of all internal stresses, it will warp under the heat of repeated firing, shifting its point of impact. Such a barrel is said to be "walking."

Walther (company) This German arms manufacturer has been producing high-quality handguns, rifles, and air guns since 1886, first in Zella-Mehlis, Germany, and presently in Ulm-Donau in West Germany. During World War II, Walther manufactured the 9 mm P-38 double-action automatic pistol for the German armed forces, as well as the PP series of highly compact double-action automatic pistols.

Today, Walther is noted for its target arms: ISU .22 bolt-action rifles, competition air rifles and pistols, and ISU .22 handguns. The firm also exports the P-38 and PP series automatic pistols. The Walther line is imported by Interarms of Alexandria, Virginia.

water table A British term referring to the action bar flats of a side-by-side or over/under shotgun. (See ACTION BAR FLAT.)

wave theory Reduced loads of slow-burning powder, on very rare occasions, are thought by some to produce extremely high breech pressure in rifles, sometimes sufficient to wreck the action. Reproducing this phenomenon under laboratory conditions to analyze just what happens has proved difficult. The H. P. White Laboratory was unable to reproduce it. It is believed to be the result of a resonant wave action, and that it tends to occur under the following conditions:

1. The cartridges used are large capacity and smaller bore—from the .25/06 through the 7mm magnums.
2. The case is filled to considerably less than full capacity with a slow-burning powder whose characteristics are such that a normal full charge would fill or nearly fill the case.
3. Ignition of the powder is marginal, due either to the primers used or to mechanical conditions giving poor ignition. Powder position at the instant of firing may be involved.
4. The firearm used has a worn and roughened throat.

It is theorized that under these conditions only a part of the powder charge starts to burn, producing pressure sufficient to move the bullet into the throat. This movement is accompanied by a break in the rise of the pressure curve because of the additional space created by bullet movement and the inability of the powder to burn fast enough to produce the normal pressure curve. The bullet lodges in the throat, causing the powder gas to rebound between the bullet base and the case head at an extremely high cyclic rate, with the waves of gas in resonance. Movement of gas molecules under these conditions develops tremendous energy, raises the powder burning rate, and probably shatters the powder gran-

Designed for handgun target shooting, the wadcutter is so called because its flat point punches clean holes in the target, making scoring easier.

ules, with these shattered pieces then burning at a rate approaching detonation. The resulting pressure rise is so rapid that the pressure exceeds the strength of the brass cartridge case before the bullet has time to move. The case head ruptures, the brass becomes practically fluid under extreme heat and pressure, and the powder gases are released inside the receiver. Working on this larger area, the high gas pressure simply shatters the receiver, sometimes shearing off bolt lugs, and usually blowing out the magazine box and splintering the stock.

The condition of the powder is probably a factor. The phenomenon was first noticed with 4831 powder, a surplus powder from World War II that had been in long storage. It is not known to occur with powders of fast- and medium-burning rates. Solvents and moisture tend to evaporate under long storage, particularly in hot, dry surroundings, tending to speed up burning rates and causing powder granules to become more brittle. Many handloaders keep powders for long periods under poor storage conditions. It is best to use magnum primers with slow-burning powders, as recommended in the loading manuals, and to load slow-burning powders only in full loads.

Ball powders are heavily coated with a deterrent to slow the initial combustion rate and to produce a more progressive burning rate. These coatings make ignition more difficult, and ball powders have sometimes produced unusual burning characteristics when used in loads leaving considerable airspace in the case. An example of this involved certain lots of .30/06 M2 military ammunition when fired under conditions where the powder charge—positioned at the head of the case—produced peening of the chamber neck at the location of the base of the bullet, apparently as the result of wave action. The firing of a comparatively few rounds would produce an annular ring, starting on the bottom side, and then extending with continued firing to a full ring of a depth that could cause extraction problems. The loading data furnished by some manufacturers of ball powders warn that loads should be used with powder charges exactly as listed, neither using greater nor smaller charges of powder, and with the same components listed. The latter refers particularly to the characteristics of the primers used.

wax bullet   Handgun cartridges can be loaded with wax bullets for indoor target practice. The case mouths are dipped in a paraffin-base wax, which forms a wadcutter "bullet." These projectiles are powered by the force of the primer only; there is no powder loaded into the shell. It helps the performance of wax bullets if the shells' primer holes are enlarged somewhat.

Weatherby (company)   The late Roy E. Weatherby, a native Kansan, had a profound effect on the American firearms industry, both through the development of his magnum cartridges and the popularization of the California-style stock. An amateur ballistician, Weatherby experimented with high-velocity cartridges during the 1940s and, in 1945, opened a small gun shop in South Gate, California. His early rifles were all custom made, built around existing bolt actions.

His business grew and Weatherby acquired a modern counter chronograph, barrel-making machines, and pressure-testing equipment; he also purchased additional land in 1951 and added another building for use as a retail facility and for additional manufacturing.

To complement the line of bolt-action rifles, Weatherby imported the commercial Fabrique Nationale action, manufactured in Belgium. In 1957 he designed and built his own bolt action, known as the Mark V.

Weatherby's original cartridges consisted of the .220 Rocket, .257, .270, .300, and .375 Weatherby Magnums. He later abandoned the .375 in favor of the .378 WM, and added the .224, .240, .340, .416, and .460, all new case designs.

In addition to rifles and ammunition, the firm also sells its own line of shotguns, riflescopes, binoculars, spotting scopes, and gun cases.

Roy Weatherby has exerted a profound influence on the design of sporting rifles and cartridges.

Weaver, W.R., Company The W.R. Weaver Co. has had a great influence upon American shooters, as it popularized the telescopic rifle sight more than any other firm. Founded by William Weaver in 1933 in El Paso, Texas, the company introduced in that year the Model 330, a 2¾X scope that was optically good, reliable, and, most important, affordable. Prior to William Weaver's invention, scopes such as the Noske, Zeiss, and Hensoldt were available, but were priced far out of the reach of the average shooter.

Weaver followed the Model 330 with a 4X scope known as the Model 440. It too was a success, and set the company pattern for manufacturing good-quality telescopic sights at moderate prices.

In 1967, William Weaver retired, and his company was purchased by the Winchester Repeating Arms Co. Weaver scopes are now made in Japan and distributed in the U.S. by Outer's.

web That portion of the cartridge that separates the main part of the primer from the powder charge. Also, the thickness between the hole in a single kernel of smokeless powder and the outside wall of that kernel.

Webley & Scott, Ltd. Founded in 1790 in Birmingham, England, Webley & Scott has become noted for its double-barrel shotguns, air rifles, and the Webley service revolver, which was used, with modifications, from 1887 to 1947 by the British army. (The Webley-Fosbery automatic revolver, which was carried by some British officers during World War I, was never an issue sidearm.)

Webley's side-by-side shotguns have traditionally been available in a wide range of chokes, gauges, and grades. While of good quality, they are not equal to the best London guns and are not well known in the United States. Webley & Scott shotguns were imported by Harrington & Richardson during the mid-1970s.

Weirauch (company) Hermann Weirauch Waffenfabrik (Hermann Weirauch Arms Manufactory, Melrichstadt, Germany) made military small arms before and during World War II. Revived in West Germany after the war, it now makes three revolvers of undistinguished but serviceable design. All have swing-out cylinders. One model is available in .32 Smith & Wesson Long (seven shots) or .22 Long Rifle (eight-shot cylinder). Another is a six-shot target revolver in .22 Long Rifle. The Model HW-7, .22 Long Rifle, was sold by Herter's in the United States under the name Herter's Guide Model. Weirauch also makes an extremely accurate spring operated .177 air rifle for target shooting; it has adjustable sights of the globe type with four differing inserts.

The company uses the "Arminius" trade name and trademark (helmeted warrior), as well as other trade names.

Wesson, Daniel B. See SMITH & WESSON, INC.

Wesson, Edwin (1811–1848) Edwin Wesson, the oldest of three brothers—Daniel Baird and Franklin were the others—was born in Northboro, Massachusetts. All three men were prominent gunmakers in their day, and Daniel B. Wesson went on to found the Smith & Wesson Company.

During his short period of productivity, Edwin Wesson made about 600 rifles of all kinds. He is famous for his target rifles, which were handsome examples of the gunmakers' art. Fairly plain types were made, as were many that were engraved, embellished with sterling silver or gold, and stocked in fancy figured walnuts.

Edwin Wesson's rifles, the only target rifles then available with the invaluable false muzzle, rapidly became great favorites among the early benchrest shooters. They are collectors' items today.

Westley Richards (company) This famous firm of English gunmakers was formed in 1812 in Birmingham by William Westley Richards. His son Westley succeeded the father in 1855. The company made important contributions to the design of the fledgling breechloaders in the 1860–1870 period, including the "doll's-head" extension of the shotgun's top rib and its bolting, actuated by the firm's "snap lever" opening. Then, in 1875, came the world-renowned Anson and Deeley action design, still the basic break-action shotgun design. (Anson was a Westley Richards shop foreman, Deeley the firm's managing officer.)

The Westley Richards hand-detachable lock system was a radical innovation for boxlock shotguns. The bottom of the action, hinged or fully removable, was opened to let the separate locks (two on a double gun) fall into the hand. The company's falling block single-shot sporting rifles were highly popular, as were a variety of rifle cartridges. In the 1960s, Westley Richards introduced a method for salvaging old shotguns, those with damaged or Damascus barrels. The old barrels are cut off some 6 to 8 inches ahead of the breech, the remaining portions are then bored out, and new steel barrels are inserted and worked up. In many cases the top and bottom ribs of side-by-side guns can be restored with the new assembly, preserving the original marks or stampings.

The London operation of Westley Richards was sold to Holland & Holland in 1965, but the firm continues in business in Birmingham.

wheel lock A flintlock variation invented in 1521 and popular with the nobility of the time, the wheel lock was an extremely fast ignition system. The lock had a rotating wheel with notches like saw teeth that rotated rapidly against pyrites and caused sparks to ignite the powder. The wheel was spring driven, the spring being wound before each shot by a key. This gave the wheel great momentum, and ignition was practically instantaneous.

While fast, the wheel lock was expensive and prone to breakage. The snaphaunce superseded the wheel lock in 1580; although not as fast, it was of simple design and the general public could afford it. (See FLINTLOCK; SNAPHAUNCE.)

Whelen sling See SLING.

Whelen, Townsend (1877–1961) Colonel Townsend Whelen was often called "the dean of American outdoor writers" by his contemporaries. For nearly 50 years his writings on guns, hunting, shooting, and the outdoors were read with pleasure by millions.

As a shooter and outdoorsman, Whelen was largely self-educated, learning by studying and analyzing his own experiences. Mustered into the Pennsylvania Volunteers during the Spanish-American War, he decided on a career in the military and was commissioned in 1902. He fired in his first National Matches in 1903. Later that year he was among those selected to test the new Model 1903 Springfield on the rifle range. There followed a distinguished shooting career in which he won the Army Rifle Competitions in 1903, became a Distinguished Marksman in 1905, and won the Adjutant General's Match at Camp Perry in 1909 and the Infantry Rifle Competitions in 1907 and 1909. His 40-year military career included being in command of Frankford Arsenal in the early 1920s, during the period of development of the famous "tin can" .30-caliber National Match ammunition. Whelen was instrumental in the great advances in ammunition accuracy during this pe-

riod, including the M-1 boattail bullet. Later, he was director of research and development at Springfield Armory. His career as a rifleman spanned the period from the black powder .45/70 Springfield to the super-accurate benchrest rifles of the late 1950s.

Author of more than a dozen books on guns and hunting, Whelen also wrote for many magazines, including *The American Rifleman, Field & Stream, Sports Afield,* and *Outdoor Life.*

whirling traps See CRAZY QUAIL.

whitetail deer, guns and loads for The whitetail deer is a highly adaptable creature that is able to exist in close proximity to man and has become our most widely hunted big-game animal. A browsing ungulate, it is now found throughout most of America, and is able to subsist on a wide variety of wild forage and cultivated crops as well. Whitetails tend to be smaller than mule deer; an average buck will weigh 130 to 150 pounds, and it is an exceptional one that is heavier than 200 pounds.

Whitetails rely on stealth and concealment and prefer heavy cover. It has been reliably estimated that an average whitetail lives out its lifetime in a single square mile, assuming there are no major disruptions to its habitat. For this reason, whitetails are almost never taken in the open.

The hunter who is selecting a rifle for this species should bear in mind that whitetails are not large, or tenacious of life, taken at long distances. Traditionally, the rifle selected has been a lever-action carbine chambered for a low-powered cartridge such as the .30/30, .32 Special, or .35 Remington. These loads propel flat pointed bullets of 150 to 200 grains at velocities of 2,100 to 2,500 feet per second. Advocates of these guns point out their fast-handling qualities, rapid repeat fire, and the fact that their cartridges kill effectively with little meat spoilage. Iron sights are not infrequently used on such guns.

Another kind of rifle that has achieved wide popularity is the semiautomatic. These are often cham-

The invention of Colonel Townsend Whelen, the sling that bears his name is a simplification of the U.S. Army rifle sling that was in use during World Wars I and II. It provides a permanently laced loop for the shooter's upper arm and can be adjusted for length by a brass frog. The rifle is a Griffin & Howe custom sporter.

bered in more modern, flat-shooting cartridges such as the .308, .270, and .30/06 (one notable exception is the Ruger Deerstalker, which is chambered for the .44 Magnum), but they are intended for close-range shooting, and their owners place a premium on their ability to deliver a rapid second and third shot. These guns are usually equipped with scope sights.

Increasingly, hunters are turning to bolt actions, which are not fast-firing but offer a degree of precision unobtainable in other rifles. These arms are chambered for the .243, 6mm, .270, .30/06, and .308 for the greatest part, and offer flat trajectory, great accuracy, and greater killing power than lower velocity cartridges. The .243 and 6mm, especially, have gained a wide following because of their very mild recoil.

Since few whitetails are large or heavily muscled, a bullet should be selected that offers rapid expansion rather than great penetration. For the .243 and

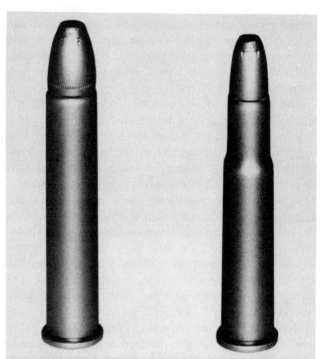

These photographs, taken in Vermont, show typical eastern whitetail cover. The deer can be hunted either by sitting and waiting, or by still hunting—walking slowly and looking hard. There are two schools of thought regarding whitetail cartridges. One holds that light, quick-expanding bullets kill best. A 95-grain 6mm bullet accounted for this Idaho buck. The other claims that heavy slugs of large caliber are better. These are two prime examples: at left, the .375 Winchester Magnum; at right, the .348 Winchester.

6mm, the 100-grain bullet is best; in the .270, the 130 grain; and in the .30/06 or .308, the 150 grain is preferred.

Little magnification is required in a scope for a whitetail rifle. In a fixed-power model, a 4X is preferable, and in a variable model, a 1x4 or 2x7 is satisfactory. The advantages a scope offers are the ability to gather light at dawn and dusk, when most deer are taken, and the ability to look into brush and cover rather than at it, in order to discern the shape of a deer's head and body. The only circumstance under which magnification in a high range might be helpful is in shooting from a stand next to a power line right-of-way.

In choosing a deer rifle, it is important to stress the speed of the first shot. Repeat firepower is not important, because the whitetail's elusiveness makes an aimed second or third shot almost impossible in most circumstances.

wide angle optics Optical systems that make it possible to obtain a wide field of view. Adding magnification to an optical system, such as in a variable-power scope, automatically reduces the field of view, and achieving an extra-wide field of view for a given magnification may result in a heavy lens system. (See TELESCOPIC SIGHTS.)

Wigger, Lones, Jr. (1937–) Lieutenant Colonel Lones Wigger, born in Great Falls, Montana, first gained national attention as a rifleman in the early 1960s after joining the Army and being posted to the Army Marksmanship Unit in Fort Benning, Georgia.

He has since been preeminent in position rifle shooting in International, Olympic, and NRA competitions, has been a strong competitor in other kinds of rifle competitions, both smallbore and high power, and has competed in pistol matches.

Wigger's major shooting accomplishments include the following:

Holds, co-holds, or has held 29 world records, 13 individual and 16 team.

Has won 65 gold, 38 silver, and 8 bronze medals in International competitions, and 20 gold, 10 silver, and 4 bronze medals in Council International Sport du Militaire (CISM) competitions, for a total of 145, which includes three medals at the Olympic Games.

Has won 85 national open rifle championships in the United States in the following categories: smallbore position; smallbore prone; indoor gallery; indoor international; 300-meter free rifle; International air rifle; International standard rifle; and metallic silhouette.

Wigger holds Distinguished Marksman Badges in service rifle, International, smallbore rifle position, and smallbore rifle prone. Probably no one else in the shooting sports has stayed so consistently at the top of national or world competition for so long. (See ARMY MARKSMANSHIP UNIT.)

During his long career in International competition, Lones Wigger has established an incomparable record of victories.

wildcat cartridge The wildcat cartridge—a custom-designed load that is not commercially available—became prominent in the 1920s. Since the brass cartridge case was malleable, it was possible for shooters who wanted to experiment to alter its shape and caliber to create a new round. Major aims of these wildcat cartridge makers were improvement in performance, reloading ease, and better case/powder balance.

All of the wildcats were originally based on commercial rounds; they were factory cartridges being necked up or down and possibly "blown out"—that is, fired in the new chamber so that the brass would swell out and take on new dimensions. However, in time, straight cases were available from the manufacturers, and these cases could then be cut off and sized in reloading dies to the dimensions of the wildcat round.

Some of the wildcats were no better than the original cartridges from which they were formed, and in some cases the wildcat was even less efficient than the original, burning more powder but producing insignificant ballistic increases. Other wildcats, such as the .25/06 Neidner, for example, and the .22/250 Varminter by J. E. Gebby, were so popular and useful that the industry eventually accepted them and in effect turned them into standard commercial cartridges.

Often, a wildcat round was introduced to fill a gap in the standard rounds available. An example of this was the .35 Whelen, a .30/06 case necked up to caliber .35. This wildcat at one time was a filler between the .30/06 size and the .375, and was effective on moose and elk. However, in time the industry produced commercial calibers to fill the gap occupied by the .35 Whelen, and the .338 Winchester, .350 Remington, or the .358 Winchester could be chosen instead of wildcatting to the .35 Whelen.

The major problem with wildcat cartridges is the lack of availability in stores, since they are produced only by hand. However, the wildcat cartridge continues to prosper because of curious shooters who are willing to form cases into new dimensions to see if any gains can be realized. Some wildcats still fill gaps that have never been occupied by commercial rounds, such as the 6mm/222 and 6mm/222 Magnum. These wildcats produce ballistics quite similar to the original .250 Savage loads and are effective on deer-sized game out to 200 yards in the hands of a good shot. The rounds allow for fine accuracy with extremely light recoil.

A few commercial cartridges that began life as wildcats but were later adopted by ammunition makers are the .22/250, .243 Winchester, 6mm Remington, .257 Roberts, .25/06, 7mm/08 Remington, 7mm Remington Magnum, and the .35 Whelen.

Winchester (company)　Oliver F. Winchester was born in 1810, in Boston, Massachusetts. His first association with the firearms business came in 1855 when he became a stockholder in the Volcanic Repeating Arms Company of New Haven, Connecticut. Volcanic had been formed to produce the Volitional Repeater, a rifle designed to utilize rimfire ammunition.

In 1857, the company was declared insolvent, and Winchester invested his funds to assume control of Volcanic. He then hired a skilled gunsmith, Benjamin Tyler Henry, as plant manager. This proved to be a fortunate choice. Henry developed an improved cartridge for Winchester and a repeating rifle to use the ammunition. In 1866, the company charter and name were changed to Winchester Repeating Arms Company. Winchester acquired the assets of the Spencer Repeating Arms Company in 1868. With the growth of production, the manufacturing facilities of Spencer were moved from Bridgeport to New Haven, Connecticut, in 1870. In 1888, the Whitney Arms Company was also purchased.

With the advent of World War I, Winchester received a contract from the British to supply Enfield rifles. In 1915, the company received a contract to produce cartridges for Russia.

Winchester acquired the U.S. Cartridge Company in 1926. But the 1929 stock market crash was financially disastrous for Winchester. The company was saved from bankruptcy in 1931 when it was purchased by the Western Cartridge Company division of the Olin Mathieson Chemical Corporation, later called the Olin Corporation. Franklin W. Olin assumed presidency of Winchester-Western.

During World War II, Winchester supplied Garand rifles to the American government. It also developed the M1 Carbine for the armed forces. The company's growth continued after the war, and in 1956, all commercial ammunition operations were consolidated at East Alton, Illinois. In 1961, Winchester purchased the H. W. Cooey Machine and Arms Company, Ltd. of Canada. Foreign speculation continued, and in 1965, the first overseas plant was opened in Anagni, Italy. Plans were also made to construct a plant in Geelong, Australia.

During late 1979, the Olin Corporation (parent company of Winchester) decided to leave the firearms manufacturing business. As a result, the use of the Winchester name and all manufacturing rights to Winchester centerfire and rimfire rifles and repeating shotguns were sold to a newly formed company made up mostly of former Winchester employees. From that point on, all Winchester rifles have been manufactured by U.S. Repeating Arms Co. (commonly abbreviated as USRAC). Olin still manufactures Winchester ammunition and various powders for use by handloaders.

Over/under double shotguns previously imported from Japan by Winchester are now called the Classic 101 and imported by Classic Doubles.

windage　The horizontal adjustment of the sights on a firearm to bring the missile either to the right or the left of the target.

In black-powder terminology, windage is the distance, measured in thousandths of an inch, between the round ball and the interior of the barrel, with the ball in theoretical dead center of the bore. The windage figure is used in determining the proper thickness of patch to be used with the ball.

Also in black-powder terminology, the escape of gas past the ball in the firing process is the windage. (See KENTUCKY WINDAGE.)

wind drift　See DRIFT.

wind flag　At the target range, small flags normally located between the shooter and the target to indicate the direction of the wind and provide a crude estimation of wind velocity. Studying the wind flag results in a process called "doping the wind," which attempts to determine how far a bullet will drift off of the line of sight from the muzzle to the target.

At some benchrest matches, it is difficult to see the targets for all the flags. Some competitors use three or four flags at various distances between them and their target.

wind gauge A graduated attachment on the rear sight of a rifle by which allowance may be made for the effect of wind on the bullet and for drift caused by gyroscopic action.

wiper See SLOTTED JAG.

witness mark When a rifle barrel is threaded into the receiver, a small line is engraved at the juncture of the two. Thus, if the barrel is removed and replaced, the gunsmith has only to align the witness marks to ensure that the headspace is correct and the sights will align properly. This line is also called an index mark.

wobble trap See INTERNATIONAL TRAPSHOOTING.

woodcock, guns and loads for A migratory bird, the woodcock inhabits dense, low-lying areas where the vegetation is thick and the ground is spongy. Because of its unvarying habitat, the conditions under which the birds are hunted never vary and selecting a suitable shotgun and load for the species presents no problem.

Because of the short ranges at which the birds are taken—rarely more than 30 yards—an open-choked gun is best. Cylinder bore, skeet, and improved constrictions are the most effective. Modified is too tight in most cases.

Advocates of the 12 gauge prefer this bore size because it throws a denser, more effective pattern. However, many woodcock hunters prefer 20- and 28-gauge guns, claiming that the faster handling qualities of these smaller arms more than compensate for the lesser quantity of shot they can propel. Most woodcock flushes are singles, unless a flight of the birds is encountered, and a repeating shotgun offers little advantage with its third shot.

Because the woodcock is a small, frail-bodied bird, a small shot size such as No. 9 is most suitable. In no case is a high-velocity load necessary, and skeet shells perform excellently.

Woodward trigger An exceptionally strong and reliable single trigger design that utilizes the three-pull system; that is, the involuntary pull after the first barrel is fired allows the swinging blade mechanism that engages the sears to switch to the unfired barrel and permit its discharge. The Woodward is a nonselective trigger. (See NONSELECTIVE TRIGGER.)

Woodworth cradle A mechanical rest designed to hold a rifle during accuracy tests. The Woodworth cradle was used by arms and ammunition companies in the 1930s and 1940s, but has since been superseded by other designs.

Wootters, John (1928–) A prolific and highly influential writer, John Wootters was born and educated in Texas, where he still lives. He is a lifelong

The woodcock is not a fast flyer, but is a highly elusive one. It is partial to thick alders and other heavy cover.

Executive Editor, Petersen's Hunting Magazine.

hunter and competitive shooter who has been writing professionally since 1949, with an interruption for service in the U.S. Army during the Korean War.

Wootters has contributed to all major outdoor and shooting magazines and served on the board of directors of the National Rifle Association from 1979 to 1985. He has also been president or director of numerous other hunting and shooting associations. Wootters has hunted throughout North, South, and Central America, and in England, Scotland, and Africa. Since 1977, he has been executive editor of *Petersen's Hunting* magazine.

Wootters' books include *Hunting Trophy Deer* (Winchester Press, New York, 1977) and *The Complete Book of Practical Handloading* (Winchester Press, New York, 1976).

work hardening The flexing of metal results in a hardening action, known as work hardening. The most common instance of this is in the resizing of brass cartridge cases that, after repeated loadings, become too brittle for use and must be annealed to restore their elasticity. (See ANNEALING; CASE RESIZING.)

World Shooting Championships In general, the World Shooting Championships include all the varieties of shooting competition included in the Olympics, but the courses for any particular year are decided by the International Shooting Union and the host country. It is customary that they be held every two years, midway between successive Olympic Games, but this is, of course, subject to world economic and political conditions. Depending on the location, time of year, and the facilities of the host nation, the competitions may include only one phase of shooting, such as the moving target championships, fired with the shotgun, or may include many. One country may hold part of the championships and another hold other parts in the same or successive years. (See OLYMPIC GAMES SHOOTING EVENTS.)

worm If it is desirable to unload a muzzleloading rifle or musket without firing it, a device called a worm can be employed. The worm, which looks like an enlarged corkscrew, is attached to the end of the ramrod and twisted into the barrel so that its coils surround the projectile and patch. When this is done, the charge can be withdrawn.

wrist That part of the stock beginning after the action of the arm and ending at the start of the comb, the wrist may continue straight in line for a straight grip stock, or it may curve to any number of styles from semipistol grip to full pistol grip. It is usually quite narrow to permit the hand to encircle it.

Wundhammer swell Invented by the German-trained custom rifle maker Louis Wundhammer, this is a small bulge of the pistol grip portion of the stock. The bulge is on the right-hand side for right-handed shooters, left side for left-handed shooters, the object being to better fill the palm of the hand with a portion of the stock to increase grip control. It is helpful in offhand shooting, as the hand will return to the same position on the grip each time if the swell does indeed fill the palm.

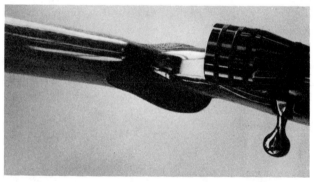

Named for gunsmith Louis Wundhammer, the swell is actually a bulge in the pistol grip that fits into the hollow of the palm and provides a better fit. This stock has Wundhammer swells on either side of the grip for right- or left-handed shooters.

X A symbol used to denote the degree of magnification, or power, in optical instruments. For example, 8X binoculars magnify objects eight times. (See MAGNIFICATION; POWER.)

X-ring On a National Rifle Association smallbore target, the X-ring is the 1-inch-diameter circle that lies inside the 2-inch black bull's-eye. (There are other sizes of bull's-eyes and X-rings on other targets; however, the size relationship remains the same.) The X-ring is used as a tiebreaker to determine a winner when two or more shooters have struck the same number of bull's-eyes. The X-ring corresponds to the V-ring in big-bore target shooting. (See V-RING.)

Y

yager   See JAEGER RIFLE.

yaw   See BULLET YAW.

yoke   Another term for a revolver's cylinder crane. (See CYLINDER CRANE.)

Zeiss, Carl, Inc. In 1866, Carl Zeiss, who was producing microscopes for the University of Jena in Germany, paired up with Ernst Abbe, a mathematical physicist. Abbe was working on the physical laws governing the path of light rays through optical lenses and had established the formula upon which many modern microscopes are built. Together, Zeiss and Abbe produced microscopes, riflescopes, and other optical instruments. After the death of Zeiss in 1889, Abbe and the employees of Zeiss continued to develop and expand the optical line.

After World War II, 126 employees of Zeiss were sent from Soviet-occupied Germany to Oberkochen, West Germany. Here they established a new home office and lens manufacturing plant, which is now the main facility of the Carl Zeiss corporation.

Zeiss has continued to produce such optical instruments as microscopes, binoculars, riflescopes, and telescopes.

zero The condition in which a rifle's sights are adjusted to the proper point of impact. For example, a detachable scope mount that allows exact return to zero is one that can be removed from the gun and replaced while retaining its adjustment for point of impact. (See SIGHTING IN.)

Zimmerstutzen The *Zimmerstutzen*, or "parlor rifle," may be described as a small bore lightweight arm for informal, short-range target shooting, often indoors. Such rifles were used for gallery shooting, a highly popular pastime, especially in Central Europe, in the 19th century and in the early decades of the 20th.

The Zimmerstutzen appeared in Europe as early as 1840. By the 1860s, it had evolved into what became a quite common type, though variations did appear in design and methods of firing. This style used a false barrel except for the front 6 to 8 inches. That short section held the true barrel, about .17 caliber, which was usually an inserted section that could be removed for more convenient cleaning. This short tube, often holding multigroove (12 or more) sharp rifling, was closed at the rear except for a central nipple or tube. On the tube was placed a percussion cap, ordinarily the only propellant force.

The false barrel held a steel rod, bridging the long gap between hammer and percussion cap. To fire, the hammer was brought to full cock, often bringing the other end of the striker rod back with it. Pulling the trigger drove the rod forward to strike the cap, and the round lead ball was propelled to the target. Such rifles gave good results if kept clean and free of leading. At 10 meters, five-shot groups of a half-inch or so could easily be shot.

In later years, these muzzleloading Zimmerstutzen were improved—if complicated—by becoming breechloaders. Hinged or pivoting devices, attached to the rear of the short barrel, could be swung aside for loading; sometimes with the round ball, as before, inserted from the rear, or with special cartridges of very low power, these holding a round or conical bullet. The caliber remained the same, about .17 or 4mm.

Zimmerstutzen may describe a handgun, too. These were most often single-shot caplock pistols in earlier years, of quite small caliber, .17 to .22, and usually firing a round ball propelled by the cap alone or by a tiny amount of black powder.

The modern successor to the Zimmerstutzen is the air rifle.

zinc fouling Zinc, being harder than tin, antimony, or other agents used in combination with lead to form an alloy, will leave traces in a gun barrel when firing undersized bullets of zinc alloy composition. Hence such a projectile should be .001-inch or .002-inch larger than bore diameter—no more—to prevent this residue from forming.

zoom spotting scope The zoom spotting scope usually has a ring that rotates, thereby offering a continuous power change over its entire range of magnification, including magnifications in between whole number settings. A 15X-60X zoom spotting scope, for example, can be used from 15 power in a continuous range up to 60 power, to include settings such as 22, 35, or 55 power. (See SPOTTING SCOPE.)

Zulu shotgun A very long single-barreled flintlock shotgun in various gauges, usually of utility-grade manufacture for heavy field use.

BIBLIOGRAPHY

The Accurate Rifle, Warren Page, Winchester Press, New York, 1973.

The Age of Firearms, Robert Held, The Gun Digest Co., Northfield, Ill., 1970.

American Antique Rifles, Martin Rywell, Pioneer Press, Union City, Tenn., 1956.

American Arms and Arms Makers, Robert E. Gardner, College Book Co., Columbus, Ohio, 1944.

American Firearms and the Changing Frontier, Waldo E. Rosebush, Eastern Washington Historical Society, Spokane, Wash., 1962.

The American Rifle, Major Townsend Whelen, The Century Co., New York, 1918.

American Rifle Design and Performance, Larry R. Wallack, Winchester Press, New York, 1977.

The American Rifleman, Vols. 88 to 138, The National Rifle Association, Washington, D.C., 1940–1990.

The American Shotgun, David F. Butler, Winchester Press, New York, 1973.

American Shotgun Design and Performance, Larry R. Wallack, Winchester Press, New York, 1977.

Americans and Their Guns, James E. Trefethen, and James E. Serven, Stackpole Books, Harrisburg, Pa., 1967.

The Anatomy of Firearms, Larry R. Wallack, Simon and Schuster, New York, 1965.

The Arco Gun Book, ed. Larry Koller, Arco Publishing Co., New York, 1962.

The Art of the Gunmaker, 2 volumes, J. F. Hayward, St. Martin's Press, New York, 1963.

Automatic Arms, Their History, Development and Use, Melvin M. Johnson Jr., and Charles T. Haven, William Morrow & Co., New York, 1941.

"A Better Look at Binoculars," James Samberg, *Field & Stream*, vol. LXXXII, p. 20, August 1977.

Big Game Rifles and Cartridges, Elmer Keith, Samworth, Plantersville, S.C., 1936.

Binoculars and How to Choose Them, Bausch & Lomb Optical Co., Rochester, N.Y.

Black Powder Handbook, Lyman, Middlefield, Conn., 1975.

The Bolt Action: A Design Analysis, Stuart Otteson, Winchester Press, New York, 1976.

Book of Pistols and Revolvers, W. H. B. Smith, Stackpole Books, Harrisburg, Pa., 1968.

The Book of the Rifle, T. F. Fremantle, Longman's, Green & Co., London, 1901.

The Book of Rifles, W. H. B. Smith, and Joseph Smith, Stackpole Books, Harrisburg, Pa., 1963.

The Book of the .22, Richard Arnold, A. S. Barnes & Co., New York, 1962.

The Breech Loading Single Shot Match Rifle, Ned Roberts, and Ken Waters, D. Van Nostrand, Princeton, 1967.

The British Textbook of Small Arms, His Majesty's Stationery Office, London, 1929.

The Bullet's Flight, F. W. Mann, Standard Printing and Publishing Co., Huntington, W. Va., 1942.

The Cadillac Modern Encyclopedia, Max S. Shapiro, and William Jaber, Cadillac Publishing Co., New York, 1973.

Cartridges, Herschel C. Logan, Standard Publications, Huntington, W. Va., 1948.

Cartridges of the World, Frank C. Barnes, Gun Digest Co., Chicago, 1965, revised edition, 1989.

Cartridges of the World, Frank C. Barnes, DBI Books, Inc., Northfield, Ill., 1976.

Clay Target Games, Edward C. Migdalski, Winchester Press, New York, 1978.

Collier's Encyclopedia, Macmillan, New York, 1978.

Complete Book of Pistols and Revolvers, W. H. B. Smith, and Kent Bellah, Stackpole Books, Harrisburg, Pa., 1963.

Complete Book of Rifles and Shotguns, Jack O'Connor, Harper & Row, New York, 1965.

Complete Guide to Handloading, Philip B. Sharpe, Funk & Wagnalls Co., New York, 1937, 1941, 1949, 1953.

Custom Built Rifles, Dick Simmons, Stackpole Books, Harrisburg, Pa., 1949, 1955.

Encyclopedia Americana, Americana Corporation, New York, 1976.

The Encyclopedia Britannica, Encyclopedia Britannica, Inc., 15th ed., 1974.

Encyclopedia of Firearms, Harold L. Peterson, E. P. Dutton, New York, 1964.

Everyday Ballistics, Charles S. Cummings, Stackpole & Heck, Inc., New York, 1950.

The Experts' Book of the Shooting Sports, ed. David E. Petzal, Simon & Schuster, New York, 1972.

Exterior Ballistics, Capt. James M. Ingalls, D. Van Nostrand, New York, 1886.

Exterior Ballistics, Edward J. McShane, John L. Kelley, and Franklin V. Reno, University of Denver Press, Denver, 1953.

Exterior Ballistics of Small Arms Projectiles, E. D. Lowry, Winchester-Western, New Haven, Conn., 1965.

Facts About Hunting Sights, Bausch & Lomb Optical Co., Rochester, N.Y., 1954.

Firearms & Ammunition Fact Book, National Rifle Association, Washington, D.C., 1964.

The Firearms Dictionary, R. A. Steindler, Stackpole Books, Harrisburg, Pa., 1970.

Firearms Encyclopedia, George C. Nonte Jr., Harper & Row, New York, 1973.

The Fireside Book of Guns, Larry Koller, Simon & Schuster, New York, 1959.

Fundamentals of Optics, Francis A. Jenkins, and Harvey E. White, McGraw Hill, New York, 1957.

Gough Thomas' Gun Book, G. T. Garwood, Winchester Press, New York, 1970.

The Gun and Its Development, W. W. Greener, Chartwell Books, Inc. Secaucus, N.J., 1988.

The Gun Collector's Handbook of Values, Charles Edward Chapel, Coward-McCann, Inc., New York, 1966.

Gun Control, Robert J. Kukla, Stackpole Books, Harrisburg, Pa., 1973.

The Gun Digest, DBI Books, Inc. Edited by John T. Amber and Ken Warner, Northfield, Ill. 6th through 45th Edition, espec.: "The Deadly Dependable Double," by Elmer Keith, 21st Edition, p. 166; "The Double Rifle—Are We Missing a Bet?," by Peyton Autry, 10th Edition, p. 119; "Sharpshooters in the Civil War," by Dan Flores, 31st Edition, p. 6.

Gun Owner's Book of Care, Repair and Improvement, Roy Dunlap, Harper & Row, New York, 1974.

Guns and How They Work, Ian V. Hogg, Everest House, New York, 1979.

Guns and Rifles of the World, Howard L. Blackmore, Viking Press, New York, 1965.

Guns and Shooting, Maj. Sir Gerald Burrard, A. S. Barnes & Co., New York, 1962.

Guns, From the Invention of Gunpowder to the 20th Century, Guns-General, U.S. Army Materiel Command, Washington, 1964.

Gunsmithing: A Manual of Firearms Design, Construction, Alteration and Remodeling. For Amateur and Professional Gunsmiths and Users of Modern Firearms, Roy F. Dunlap, Stackpole Books, Harrisburg, 1963.

Guns on the Early Frontiers, Carl P. Russell, University of California Press, Los Angeles, 1962.

Handbook for Shooters and Reloaders, Vol. II, P. O. Ackley, Salt Lake City, 1970.

Handbook of Chemistry and Physics, Charles D. Hodgman, Chemical Rubber Publishing Co., Cleveland, Ohio, 1951.

The Handgun, Geoffrey Boothroyd, Crown Publishers, Inc., New York, 1970.

Handloader's Digest, ed. John T. Amber, Digest Books, Inc., Northfield, Ill., 1975.

Hatcher's Notebook, Maj. Gen. Julian S. Hatcher, The Telegraph Press, Harrisburg, Pa., 1952.

Hatcher's Notebook, Maj. Gen. Julian S. Hatcher, The Stackpole Co., Harrisburg, Pa., 1962, 1966.

A History of Firearms, W. Y. Carman, Routlege & Kegan Paul Ltd., London, 1956.

Hornady Handbook of Cartridge Reloading, Hornady Manufacturing Co., Grand Island, Neb., 1967, 1973.

The Hunter's Counselor, Hofmann & Co., Wuerzburg, West Germany, 1964.

Improved American Rifle, John R. Chapman, D. Appleton & Co., New York, 1848.

Interior Ballistics: How a Gun Converts Chemical Energy into Projectile Motion, E. D. Lowry, Doubleday, New York, 1968.

Interior Ballistics of Guns, U.S. Army Materiel Command, Washington, 1965.

International Shooting Sport, Union Internationale de Tir, D-62, Weisbaden-Klarenthal, Germany, n.d.

The International Shooting Union Official History 1907–1977, A. J. Palmer, International Shooting Union, Weisbaden, Germany, 1978.

Jim Carmichel's Book of the Rifle, Jim Carmichel, Outdoor Life Books, 1985.

The Kentucky Rifle in Its Golden Age, Joe Kindig Jr., George Shumway, York, Pa., 1960.

The Lee-Enfield Rifle, Jamor E. G. B. Reynolds, Arco Publishing Co., New York, 1960.

Machinery's Handbook, 17th ed., Industrial Press, New York, 1966.

Mathematics for Exterior Ballistics, G. A. Bliss, John Wiley & Sons, New York, 1944.

Mauser Bolt Rifles, 3rd ed., Ludwig Olson, F. Brownell & Son, Montezuma, Iowa, 1976.

The Miracle of Vision, Arthur S. Freese, Harper & Row, New York, 1970.

Modern American Rifles, A. C. Gould, Bradlee Whidden, Boston, 1892.

The Modern Rifle, Jim Carmichel, Winchester Press, New York, 1975.

The Modern Shotgun, Maj. Sir Gerald Burrard, Ashford Press, Southampton, 1986.

The Modern Sportsman's Gun & Rifle, J. H. Walsh, Horace Cox, London, 1882.

The Muzzle Loading Cap Lock Rifle, Ned H. Roberts, Granite State Press, Manchester, N. H., 1940.

Nosler Reloading Manual Number One, Nosler Bullets, Inc., Bend, Ore., 1976.

Notes on Sporting Rifles, Maj. Sir Gerald Burrard, Edward Arnold & Co., London, 1929.

NRA . . . Illustrated Reloading Handbook, Walter J. Howe, National Rifle Association of America, Washington, D.C., 1961.

One Hundred Great Guns, Merrill Lindsay, Walker & Co., New York, 1967.

Outdoor Life Gun Data Book, F. Philip Rice, Harper & Row, New York, 1975.

Pageant of the Gun, Harold L. Peterson, Doubleday, Garden City, N.Y., 1967.

The Plains Rifle, Charles E. Hanson Jr., Stackpole Books, Harrisburg, Pa., 1960.

Principles and Practice of Loading Ammunition, Earl Naramore, Stackpole Books, Harrisburg, Pa., 1962.

Remington Arms in American History, A. C. Gould, Bradlee Whidden, Boston, 1892.

The Rifle Book, Jack O'Connor, Alfred A. Knopf, New York, 1964, 1978.

The Rifle in America, Philip B. Sharpe, William Morrow and Co., New York, 1938.

The Rifle in America, Philip B. Sharpe, Funk & Wagnalls, New York, 1953.

Rifles: A Modern Encyclopedia, Henry M. Stebbins, Stackpole Books, Harrisburg, Pa., 1958.

Rifles and Ammunition, H. Ommundsen, and E. H. Robinson, The Waverly Book Co., Ltd., London 1915.

"Running Boar Is a Ball," C. E. Harris, p. 31, Vol. 124, no. 4, *The American Rifleman,* April 1976.

Shooter's Bible Small Arms Lexicon and Concise Encyclopedia, Chester Mueller, and John Olson, Shooter's Bible, Inc., South Hackensack, N.J., 1968.

The Shotgunner's Book: A Modern Encyclopedia, Col. Charles Askins, Stackpole Books, Harrisburg, Pa., 1958.

Shotguns, Elmer Keith, Wolfe Publishing Company, Prescott, 1988.

Shotgun Sighting Equipment, Larry Sterett, The American Shotgunner, Reno, Nev., 1975.

Sierra Bullets Reloading Manual, Sierra Bullets, Santa Fe Springs, Cal., Published by Sierra Bullets, 1989.

Small Arms & Ammunition in the United States Service, B. R. Lewis, Smithsonian Institute, Washington, D.C., 1956.

Small Arms Design & Ballistics, Townsend Whelen, Small Arms Technical Publishing Co., Georgetown, S.C., 1946.

Small Arms Lexicon and Concise Encyclopedia, Chester Mueller, and John Olson, Shooter's Bible, Inc., South Hackensack, N.J., Ryerson Press, Toronto, 1968.

Speer Manual for Reloading Ammunition, no. 6, Laston Printing Co., Spokane, Wash., 1964.

Speer Reloading Manual, no. 9, Speer, Lewiston, Idaho, 1974.

The '03 Springfield, Clark S. Campbell, Fadco Publishing Co., Beverly Hills, Calif., 1957.

The Springfield Armory, Pamphlet, Deactivation Ceremony, Springfield Armory, April 30, 1968.

Theory of the Interior Ballistics of Guns, J. Corner, John Wiley & Sons, New York, 1950.

The Treasury of the Gun, Harold L. Peterson, Ridge Press, New York, and Golden Press, New York, 1962.

United States Firearms: The First Century 1776–1875, David F. Butler, Winchester Press, New York, 1971.

Van Nostrand's Scientific Encyclopedia, D. Van Nostrand Co., Princeton, N.J., 1968.

Weapons of the American Revolution, Warren Moore, Promontory Press, New York, 1967.

Webster's Third New International Dictionary, G. C. Merriam Co., Springfield, Mass., 1962, 1971.

The Winchester-Western Ammunition Handbook, Pocket Books, New York, 1964.

INDEX